Web publishing, like nostalgia, ain't what it used to b … digital equivalent of stone tools to get their pages up and ru… port to allow "non-geeks" to design, write, and publish the … ML. The industrial revolution appears to have hit the Web publishing world.

FrontPage is one of these tools and, based on the number of apparent "non-geeks" using it and the quality of work they're producing, it's one of the best. FrontPage can take you from your very first steps in creating individual Web pages, all the way through creating and managing fairly complex sites … and beyond.

Beyond is where this book comes in. Denise Tyler's *Laura Lemay's Web Workshop: Microsoft FrontPage 97* was highly regarded as THE book to buy to get started in Web publishing with FrontPage. This book, also by Denise Tyler, explores more advanced topics in Web publishing with FrontPage, including working with tables for layout, frames, forms, and stylesheets; integrating your Web site with Microsoft's Office 97 applications or with databases; and working extensively with images, including buttons, icons, backgrounds, banners, animations, and other special effects.

If you're a Web designer (full-time, part-time, for fun, for business, for any reason) and you use FrontPage, this book will help you expand your skills, deepen the quality and usefulness of your pages, and build Web sites that will make even the professionals jealous. And because it's part of the popular *Laura Lemay's Web Workshop* series, you can be certain it'll be friendly, easy to read, and will give you the meat and potatoes topics first—the tricks real-life Web designers are using—without a lot of fluff and background.

Good luck and enjoy!

Laura Lemay
Series Editor

`http://www.lne.com/lemay/`

LAURA LEMAY'S
WEB WORKSHOP

ADVANCED FRONTPAGE™ 97

LAURA LEMAY'S WEB WORKSHOP

ADVANCED FRONTPAGE™ 97

Denise Tyler

Series Editor: Laura Lemay

201 West 103rd Street
Indianapolis, Indiana 46290

FIRST EDITION

International Standard Book Number: 1-57521-308-7

Library of Congress Catalog Card Number: 97-65736

2000 99 98 97 4 3 2 1

Interpretation of the printing code: the rightmost double-digit number is the year of the book's printing; the rightmost single-digit, the number of the book's printing. For example, a printing code of 97-1 shows that the first printing of the book occurred in 1997.

Composed in Frutiger and MCPdigital by Macmillan Computer Publishing

Printed in the United States of America

Publisher and President: Richard K. Swadley
Publishing Manager: Greg Wiegand
Managing Editor: Jodi Jensen
Indexing Manager: Johnna L. VanHoose
Director of Marketing: Kelli S. Spencer
Product Marketing Managers: Wendy Gilbride, Kim Margolius
Associate Product Marketing Manager: Jennifer Pock
Marketing Coordinator: Linda Beckwith

Acquisitions Editor
Christopher Denny

Development Editor
Fran Hatton

Software Development Specialist
Brad Myers

Copy Editors
Tonya Simpson
Marilyn Stone

Indexer
Kelly Talbot

Technical Reviewers
Sue Charlesworth
Robert Reinsch
Christopher Stone
Stephen Tallon

Editorial Coordinators
Mandie Rowell
Katie Wise

Technical Edit Coordinator
Lynette Quinn

Resource Coordinator
Deborah Frisby

Editorial Assistants
Carol Ackerman
Andi Richter
Rhonda Tinch-Mize
Karen Williams

Cover Designer
Alyssa Yesh

Cover Illustrator
Eric Lindley

Book Designer
Alyssa Yesh

Copy Writer
David Reichwein

Production Team Supervisors
Brad Chinn
Charlotte Clapp

Production
Carol Bowers
Georgiana Briggs
Deirdre Smith
Mary Ellen Stephenson

Dedication

To the many who helped me face up to challenges and learn how to cross the finish line.

Overview

Contents

Acknowledgments

There are a lot of very talented people who work behind the scenes to put together a publication such as this. Their efforts are equally as important as those whose names grace the cover. Behind this book is a team of great people who I've come to know as an extended family of sorts. Thanks to Chris Denny, Fran Hatton, and Jodi Jensen for heading up this great team, and for giving me lots of encouragement, advice, and support throughout this project.

I again acknowledge and thank Laura Lemay, the inspiration and force behind this book—truly one of the most dynamic people I've had the pleasure to meet and work with. Thanks, Laura!

About the Author

Denise Tyler is a computer graphics artist/animator and author. After a 15-year career as an engineer with technical writing and customer training experience, she left the corporate world and started her own business in 1991. She combined her technical knowledge with a lifelong interest in art and music, and developed her skills in computer art and animation. She began by specializing in the development of graphics for multimedia presentations and computer games. As the World Wide Web grew, so did Denise's interest in developing and authoring Web pages.

Using her background in technical writing and customer training, Denise began writing tutorials for creating computer graphics. She is coauthor of the best-selling *Tricks of the Game Programming Gurus* and is author of *Fractal Design Painter 3.1 Unleashed*, both published by Sams Publishing. Using the same hands-on style of writing, she is now directing her attention to the World Wide Web, having written *Laura Lemay's Web Workshop: Microsoft FrontPage* and *Laura Lemay's Web Workshop: Microsoft FrontPage 97*, both national best-sellers published by Sams.net.

Tell Us What You Think!

As a reader, you are the most important critic and commentator of our books. We value your opinion and want to know what we're doing right, what we could do better, what areas you'd like to see us publish in, and any other words of wisdom you're willing to pass our way. You can help us make strong books that meet your needs and give you the computer guidance you require.

Do you have access to CompuServe or the World Wide Web? Then check out our CompuServe forum by typing **GO SAMS** at any prompt. If you prefer the World Wide Web, check out our site at `http://www.mcp.com`.

NOTE: If you have a technical question about this book, call the technical support line at 317-581-3833 or send e-mail to `support@mcp.com`.

As the team leader of the group that created this book, I welcome your comments. You can fax, e-mail, or write me directly to let me know what you did or didn't like about this book—as well as what we can do to make our books stronger. Here's the information:

Fax: 317-581-4669

E-mail: `programming_mgr@sams.mcp.com`

Mail: Greg Wiegand
Comments Department
Sams Publishing
201 W. 103rd Street
Indianapolis, IN 46290

Introduction

It has been nearly a year since I finished my first FrontPage book, and it seems like ages ago. Since that first book was published, FrontPage has become a major Web development tool for aspiring and seasoned Web developers. The success of FrontPage and my previous books has kept me in a whirlwind of busy-ness.

Now, with my third FrontPage book, I've endeavored to go beyond what was covered in the first two. This book assumes that you know how to complete basic tasks in FrontPage 97, and that you want to develop pages that go beyond the features supported in the FrontPage Editor. *Laura Lemay's Web Workshop: Advanced FrontPage 97* introduces you to additional techniques. It also shows you how to use FrontPage 97 in conjunction with Office 97 applications to create Web documents for an intranet or a World Wide Web site. You learn how to design documents that utilize some of the custom features in Internet Explorer 3.0 (or later), how to activate your Web sites with forms, database connection, and Active Server Pages, and how to create graphics using Microsoft Image Composer.

- In Part I, "Which Server to Use," you learn how to install and administer the Web servers that are furnished on the FrontPage 97 with Bonus Pack CD-ROM. This section discusses the FrontPage Personal Web Server and the Microsoft Personal Web Server, comparing the features included with each.
- In Part II, "Integrating with Microsoft Office 97," you learn how to create and save Web documents from Word 97, PowerPoint 97, Excel 97, and Access 97. The chapters in this section assume that you are familiar enough with these applications to develop word processing documents, presentations, worksheets and databases, but want to examine the new features that allow you to publish these documents to your Web or intranet.
- In Part III, "Designing for Internet Explorer," you learn how to design and incorporate features that are particular to Internet Explorer 3.0 and later. You learn how to apply advanced table and cell backgrounds, how to design floating frames, and how to implement cascading style sheet properties using FrontPage 97.
- In Part IV, "Activating Your Webs," you learn how to configure forms using the FrontPage Web Bots as form handlers. Then you learn how you can export Access 97 databases into two different Web formats that allow you to interface with your database dynamically. The final chapter in the section shows how Active Server Pages integrate with Access 97 to create Web pages that change content based on a user's selections. Note that

these chapters assume that you have familiarity with advanced Web technologies, such as ActiveX controls and VBScript as well.

- In Part V, "Creating Graphics with Microsoft Image Composer," you learn how to create buttons, banners, montages, and more, using Microsoft Image Composer, a component furnished on the FrontPage 97 with Bonus Pack CD-ROM. You learn how much fun it is to create your own Web graphics in this section!
- Because this book mentions many Web technologies that go beyond its scope, the appendixes contain many references that direct you to additional helpful information. Appendix A contains a sizeable list of online resources, including links to many Knowledge Base articles that will prove useful. Appendix B lists many other books that contain additional references and material about the topics and applications mentioned in this book. Appendix C lists additional files and shareware utilities that are furnished on the CD-ROM that accompanies this book.

Features Used in This Book

The following examples show how this book's tips, sidebars, notes, and cautions help guide you through information you will need to know. CD-ROM icons are placed next to text that shows what you can find on the CD-ROM that comes with this book.

TIP: Tips offer important (or at least interesting) hints and suggestions related to the topic at hand.

General Sidebar

Sidebars give you general information about a topic related to the discussion at hand.

NOTE: Notes provide you with interesting, added information about the subject at hand.

CAUTION: Cautions prompt you with gentle warnings, to help you stay out of trouble.

The CD-ROM icon alerts you to programs and files on the CD-ROM at the back of this book that help with the topic at hand.

Margin notes tell you more about the current topic, as well as provide cross-references to further information.

My support site at `http://www.fpworkshop.com` is in a state of transition and updating to include more information, tips, tricks, and other features that should better serve the readers of my books. The site is being moved to a server that uses the Microsoft Commercial Internet System (formerly known as Normandy), and will include a general newsgroup and chat room where readers can share their FrontPage knowledge with each other. Hope to see you there!

PART I

Which Server to Use

CHAPTER

ONE

Using the FrontPage Personal Web Server

FrontPage 97 enables you to create and manage webs with or without the use of a Web server. However, if your pages contain any features that need the FrontPage Server Extensions (for example, any WebBots that are used at browse time), you need to have a FrontPage-compatible Web server running to test or operate them.

By installing a FrontPage-compatible Web server on your local or network computer, you can take full advantage of all the features that FrontPage has to offer. FrontPage 97 is furnished with two personal Web servers, each with different capabilities. For many users, the FrontPage Personal Web Server, discussed in this chapter, is more than adequate in its capabilities. Most people who use FrontPage to design their personal Web sites will find it so. This chapter examines the capabilities and the shortcomings of the FrontPage Personal Web Server. You'll also learn when you will need to use a more robust server to fulfill your needs.

In this chapter, you

- ❑ Learn whether the FrontPage Personal Web Server can meet your needs
- ❑ Learn where you can install the FrontPage Personal Web Server when you install FrontPage 97
- ❑ Review some things to be aware of when you use the FrontPage 97 version of the FrontPage Personal Web Server with previous versions of FrontPage
- ❑ Learn where the FrontPage Personal Web Server files are installed
- ❑ Learn how to add administrators, authors, and end users to your webs when using the FrontPage Personal Web Server
- ❑ Determine how your file directories relate to your Web server

Tasks in this chapter:

- ❑ Changing the Default Home Page Name
- ❑ Adding Users to Your Web
- ❑ Restricting IP Addresses
- ❑ Changing Passwords
- ❑ Finding the Name of Your Web Server

Knowing Whether This Server Is Right for You

The FrontPage Personal Web Server is exactly that—a *personal* Web server. It enables you to create, manage, and test Web sites that incorporate the majority of features found in FrontPage. You can use this server to navigate through and test the pages in your webs, but there are many limitations to using this server in an online situation. This server is not capable of medium-to-heavy traffic. It is designed to provide a platform on which you can design and test your pages before they are published to your intranet or World Wide Web site. Table 1.1 shows at a glance the capabilities of the FrontPage Personal Web Server.

Table 1.1. FrontPage Personal Web Server capabilities.

Feature	*Supported?*
Number of webs	18, including root web
Active Server Pages	No
Custom CGI scripts	No
FTP services	No
Gopher services	No
High-traffic sites	No
IDC database files/scripts	No
ISAPI interface	No
Multi-homing	No
NSAPI interface	No
NTLM authentication	No
Secure Socket Layer (SSL) communications	No

Table 1.1 is not really as bleak as it appears. For the average home user, the FrontPage Personal Web Server is more than sufficient to develop and test Web pages. This server enables you to create and manage 18 webs—the root web and 17 child webs beneath it. Using this server, you can create and test Web sites that use all the FrontPage WebBot components, Java applets, Netscape plug-ins, ActiveX controls, and scripting languages, such as VBScript or JavaScript. You can develop Active Server Pages, specify custom CGI scripts as form handlers, and provide links to FTP and Gopher sites, but these features cannot be fully tested while running the FrontPage Personal Web Server.

You learn more about working with IDC files in **Chapter 13**.

The FrontPage Personal Web Server is designed for very light traffic. If you want to test features such as custom CGI scripts or Internet Database Connector (IDC) files and scripts, you'll need to move up to the Microsoft Personal Web Server or another more robust server platform such as Microsoft Internet Information Server running on Windows NT Server 4.0. This latter server also enables you to employ or test advanced features such as multi-homing, Secure Socket Layer communications, NTLM authentication, and Active Server Pages.

The Microsoft Personal Web Server, discussed in **Chapter 2** supports FTP, multi-homing, NTLM authentication, custom CGI scripts, and IDC files and scripts.

Installing FrontPage 97 with the FrontPage Personal Web Server

To install the FrontPage Personal Web Server, choose the **C**ustom installation option when you run FrontPage 97 Setup. Figure 1.1 shows the setup screen in which this choice is presented. After you select the **C**ustom installation option, select the **M**icrosoft FrontPage Personal Web Server check box, as shown in Figure 1.2. To install the Server Extensions in addition to the Personal Web Server, select the Server **E**xtensions check box.

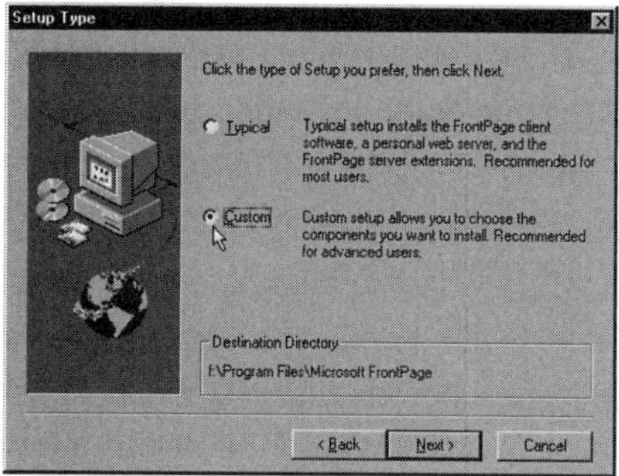

Figure 1.1.
To install the FrontPage 97 Personal Web Server, select Custom installation during setup.

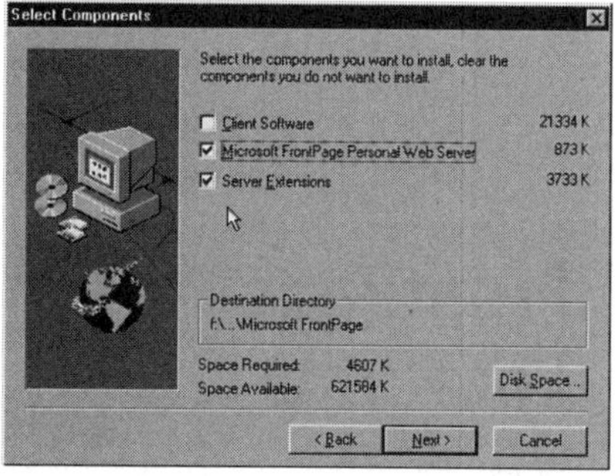

Figure 1.2.
Custom installation options enable you to install the FrontPage 97 Personal Web Server and the FrontPage 97 Server Extensions.

NOTE: The FrontPage Personal Web Server and FrontPage Server Extensions are automatically updated to the FrontPage 97 version when you upgrade from a previous version of FrontPage.

You can install both personal Web servers on your system. If the Microsoft Personal Web Server has already been installed to Port 80, the FrontPage Personal Web Server will be installed to Port 8080. To run the FrontPage Personal Web Server in this case, specify a server name such as `http://myservername:8080` when you browse the webs created with the FrontPage Personal Web Server.

Using FrontPage 97 with Previous Versions of FrontPage

The FrontPage 97 Server Extensions are backward compatible and will work with webs created with FrontPage 1.1. All the features found in FrontPage 1.1 function properly when you use the FrontPage 97 Server Extensions.

The FrontPage 1.1 Server Extensions do not support folder management tasks such as adding and deleting folders and moving or copying files between them. If you attempt to use the FrontPage 97 Explorer to delete a folder that is located on a FrontPage 1.1 server, you might encounter an error message that says the pages cannot be removed. Microsoft suggests trying one of two methods to remedy this situation:

- Upgrade the FrontPage 1.1 Server to the FrontPage 97 Server Extensions, and then use the Delete command in the FrontPage 97 Explorer to delete the folder from the upgraded server.
- Access the Web content on the FrontPage 1.1 Server using telnet, FTP, or the operating system's file management software to delete the folder. Then use the **T**ools | **R**ecalculate Hyperlinks command in the FrontPage Explorer to update the links in the Web.

FrontPage Personal Web Server File Locations

When you install the FrontPage Personal Web Server on a system running the Windows 95 or Windows NT 4.0 operating system, the default directories are as follows:

- The default installation directory for the FrontPage Personal Web Server executable file is `c:\FrontPage Webs\Server`. The file is named `vhttpd32.exe`.
- The default installation directory for the configuration files is `c:\FrontPage Webs\Server\conf`. Files with a `.cnf` extension are the configuration files used by the server extensions. The original configuration file uses an `.org` extension, and the most recent backup copy of the configuration file uses a `.bak` extension. Here, you find access configuration files (`access.cnf`, `access.org`, and `access.bak`), Web server configuration files (`httpd.cnf`, `httpd.org`, and `httpd.bak`), and server resource files (`srm.cnf`, `srm.org`, and `srm.bak`). You'll also find a configuration file for the mime types used on your server (`mime.typ`).
- The `c:\FrontPage Webs\Server\icons` directory contains icon files that you can use for several different file types.
- The default installation directory for your server log files is `c:\FrontPage Webs\Server\logs`.

Running the FrontPage Server Administrator

You use the FrontPage Server Administrator to install, uninstall, and maintain the FrontPage Server Extensions. When you are upgrading from previous versions of FrontPage, the FrontPage 97 Server Administrator will feel very familiar. Server administration is accomplished through the dialog box shown in Figure 1.3. If you prefer to administer your webs from a remote location, consider using the Microsoft Personal Web Server instead.

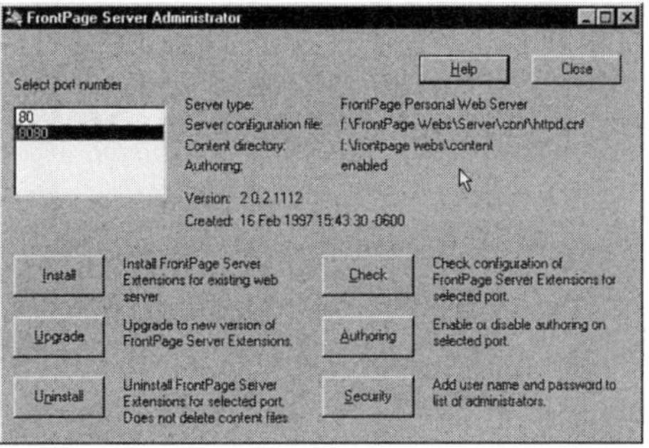

Figure 1.3.
The FrontPage Server Administrator (Windows version) administers your server through a dialog box.

In addition to the Windows version of the FrontPage Server Administrator, there is also a DOS command-line version. Both of these versions are located in the `c:\Program Files\Microsoft FrontPage\bin` directory (Windows 95 and Windows NT 4.0).

- The Windows version of the FrontPage Server Administrator is named `fpsrvwin.exe`.
- You can use the DOS command-line version for batch administration. The file is named `fpsrvadm.exe`.

You can find shortcuts and startup icons for the Windows version of the FrontPage Server Administrator in the following default installation directories:

- Windows 95 and Windows NT 4.0: A shortcut to the Windows version of the FrontPage Server Administrator is placed in your `c:\Program Files\Microsoft FrontPage` directory by default. You can move or copy this shortcut to your Windows desktop for quick access to the FrontPage Server Administrator.
- Windows NT 3.51: A program item for the Windows version of the FrontPage Server Administrator is located in the Microsoft FrontPage group in Program Manager. Double-click the program item to start the server administrator.

CAUTION: Be careful if you have older versions of the FrontPage Server Administrator on your hard disk in addition to the FrontPage 97 Server Administrator. For example, if you attempt to manage the FrontPage 97 Server Extensions with the FrontPage 1.1 Server Administrator, you might receive page fault errors. To remedy this situation, use the FrontPage 97 Server Administrator to manage both FrontPage 1.1 and FrontPage 97 Server Extensions.

What Is Unique About the FrontPage Personal Web Server?

To determine whether you are using the FrontPage Personal Web Server, look on the bottom of your screen at the taskbar. If you see a button that displays the Web Server status, such as the "Web Server Idle" status message shown in Figure 1.4, you are running the FrontPage Personal Web Server. For the most part, the majority of the FrontPage features function the same from one server to the next. However, there are some tasks that are unique to the FrontPage Personal Web Server. The following sections cover these tasks.

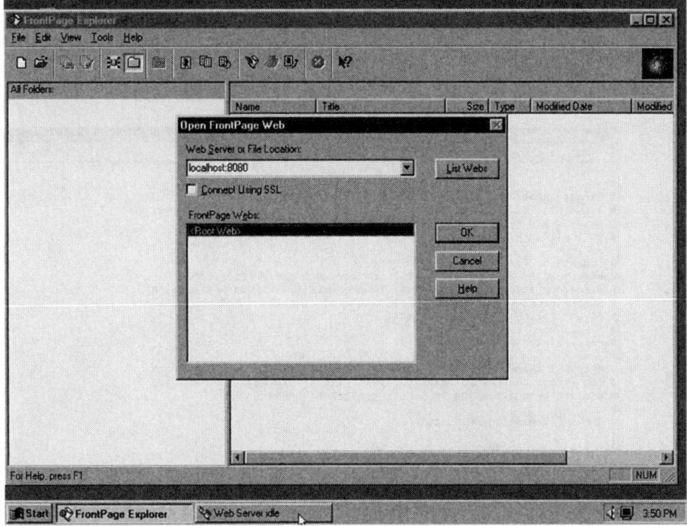

Figure 1.4.
When you run the FrontPage Personal Web Server, a Web Server status button is located in your Windows 95 taskbar.

Changing the Default Home Page Name

If you browse to the home page of your web by entering the web name followed by a backslash (for example: `http://myweb/`), you might see a list of files rather than your home page. This situation is caused when you name your home page other than that which FrontPage expects to see. By default, the FrontPage Personal Web Server uses a home page (or welcome page) name of `index.htm`. Your remote server might require that you use a home page with a different filename, such as `index.html`, `welcome.htm`, or `default.htm`. You can configure FrontPage to use a different home page name if you want. The name you configure for a default home page name is used for all webs.

If you installed FrontPage with its default settings, you can find the configuration file in which you change your default home page name in the following directory:

```
c:\FrontPage Webs\server\conf\srm.cnf
```

Within this file is a section in which you specify your directory index (or home page name), as you can see in Figure 1.5. To specify a directory index file other than `index.htm`, remove the pound sign before the line that reads `DirectoryIndex index.htm`, and revise the filename to reflect the home page designation that you want to use. It should look similar to the last line shown here:

```
# DirectoryIndex: Name of the file to use as a pre-written HTML
# directory index. This document, if present, will be opened when the
```

```
# server receives a request containing a URL for the directory, instead
# of generating a directory index.
#
DirectoryIndex default.htm
```

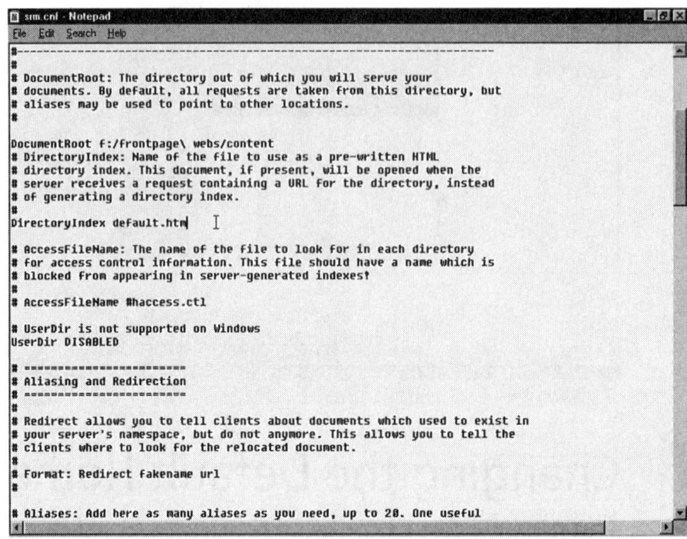

Figure 1.5.
Change the default directory index (home page) name by editing the `srm.cnf` *configuration file in Notepad or WordPad.*

Administering Your FrontPage Personal Web Server Webs

When you use the FrontPage Personal Web Server, you use standard dialog boxes to administer your FrontPage webs. This includes adding, changing, or removing users. You must have administrator status to authorize another end user, author, or administrator. To add users to your web, follow the steps in the next section.

Adding Users to Your Web

When you use the FrontPage Personal Web Server, you add users to your web through the Permissions dialog box. To add administrators, authors, or end users to your web, follow these steps:

For corporate intranet development, you can configure the FrontPage Personal Web Server to allow multiple web administrators and authors. This enables you to assign teams of individuals to develop portions of your intranet webs.

1. From the FrontPage Explorer, choose **T**ools | **P**ermissions. The Permissions dialog box appears, open to the Settings tab as shown in Figure 1.6.
2. Select one of the following options for your Web permissions:
   - ❑ Select the Use **s**ame permissions as root web radio button to configure the child web to inherit the same settings as those used for the root web.

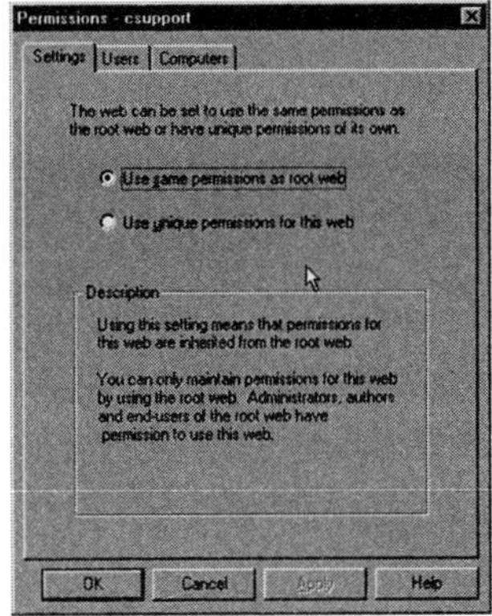

Figure 1.6.
Use the Settings tab in the Permissions dialog box to assign unique permissions for a child web.

- Select the Use **u**nique permissions for this web radio button if you need to configure unique administrators, authors, or end users for a child web. You should also select this option to create a child web that allows only registered users to gain access to the web.

3. Click **A**pply.
4. Click the Users tab, shown in Figure 1.7. From the Users tab, you can add, modify, or remove users as follows:
   - To add a user, click the A**d**d button. The Add Users dialog box shown in Figure 1.8 appears. Enter the new user's name in the **N**ame field and his or her password in the **P**assword field. Spaces are not allowed. Enter the password again in the **C**onfirm Password field. Then, proceed to step 5.
   - To edit access permissions for an existing user, highlight the user you want to edit and click the **E**dit button. The Edit Users dialog box shown in Figure 1.9 appears. Proceed to step 5.

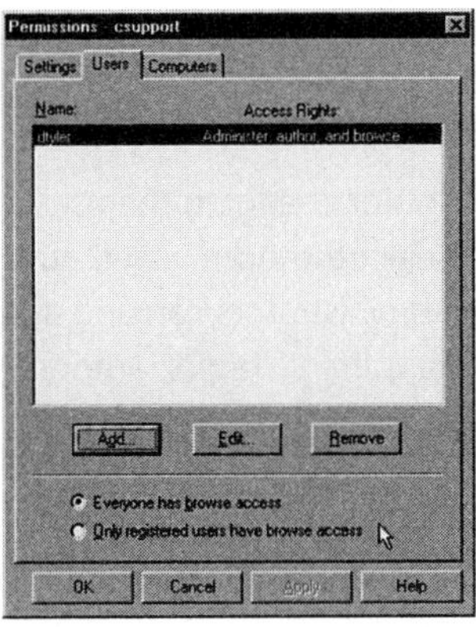

Figure 1.7.
The Users tab in the Permissions dialog box enables you to configure users for a web.

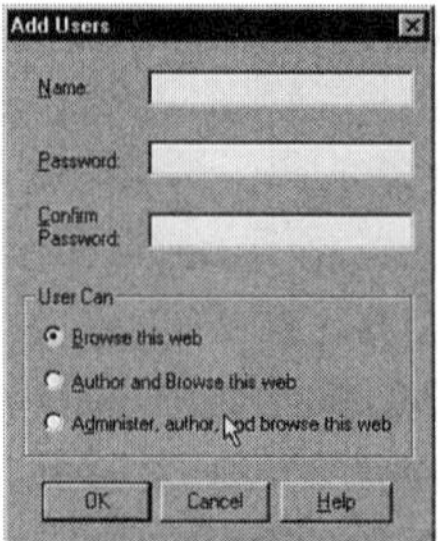

Figure 1.8.
Add a user to your web with the Add Users dialog box.

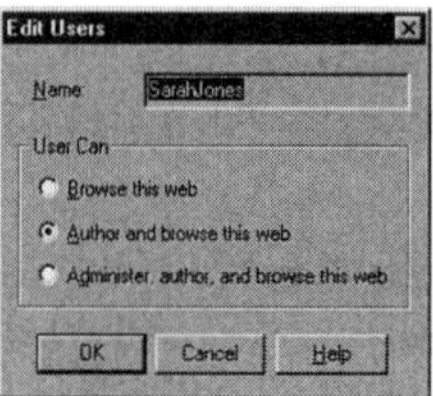

Figure 1.9.
Edit existing user information with the Edit Users dialog box.

- To remove a user, highlight the user you want to remove and click the **R**emove button. The user is removed from the user list. You cannot remove the original administrator whose name was configured during installation of FrontPage.

5. Select the user's level of access as follows:
   - If you are adding or editing an end user to the current registered (protected) web, select the **B**rowse this web radio button. End users are only allowed to browse the web. By default, all end users have access to a Web site. To allow only registered users to gain access to your web, select the Use **u**nique permissions for this web option in step 2. You will also need to design a registration page and locate it in the root web of your server.
   - If you are adding or changing the user to an author for the current web, select the **A**uthor and browse this web radio button. Authors are allowed to create and delete pages.
   - If you are adding or changing the user to an administrator for the current web, select the A**d**minister, author, and browse this web radio button. Web administrators can add and delete webs and pages, designate other administrators, authors, and end users, and restrict end users from accessing certain portions of the Web site.

For more information about user registration forms, refer to **Chapter 12**.

6. Click OK to return to the Users tab in the Permissions dialog box.

7. From the Users tab in the Permissions dialog box (see Figure 1.7), select the type of web you are configuring:
    - If the current web is one that allows access to all end users, choose the Everyone has **b**rowse access radio button.
    - If the current web is a protected web to which only registered users can gain access, choose the **O**nly registered users have browse access radio button.
8. Click OK. The user is added to your web.

Restricting IP Addresses

With the FrontPage Personal Web Server, you can also specify access to your web by IP address. This enables an individual or a group of people sharing IP addresses to gain access to your web at different levels. This option is not available if you are using the Microsoft Personal Web Server.

1. From the FrontPage Explorer, choose **T**ools | **P**ermissions. The Permissions dialog box appears, open to the Settings tab.
2. Choose one of the following options for your web permissions:
    - Select the Use **s**ame permissions as root web radio button to configure the child web to inherit the same settings as those used for the root web.
    - Select the Use **u**nique permissions for this web radio button if you need to configure different administrators, authors, or end users for a child web.
3. Click **A**pply.
4. Click the Computers tab, shown in Figure 1.10. Add, modify, or remove an IP address as follows:

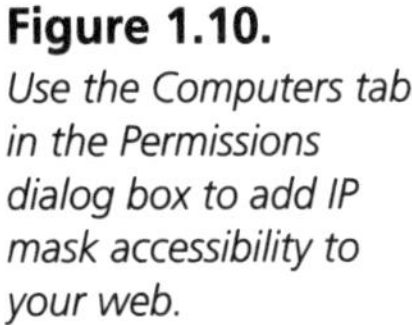

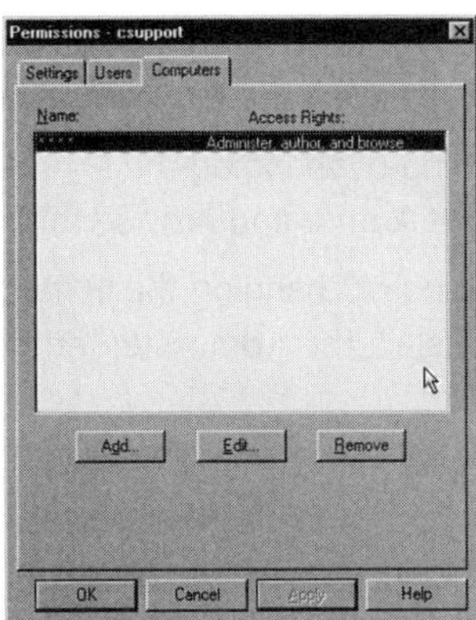

Figure 1.10.
Use the Computers tab in the Permissions dialog box to add IP mask accessibility to your web.

- To add an IP address, click the A**d**d button. The Add Computer dialog box shown in Figure 1.11 appears. Enter the IP address in the IP **M**ask fields. To add a group of computers, enter a wildcard (asterisk) character in place of a specific group. Some sample entries are `127.0.0.1` or `127.*.*.*`, with each number entered in a separate field in the dialog box.

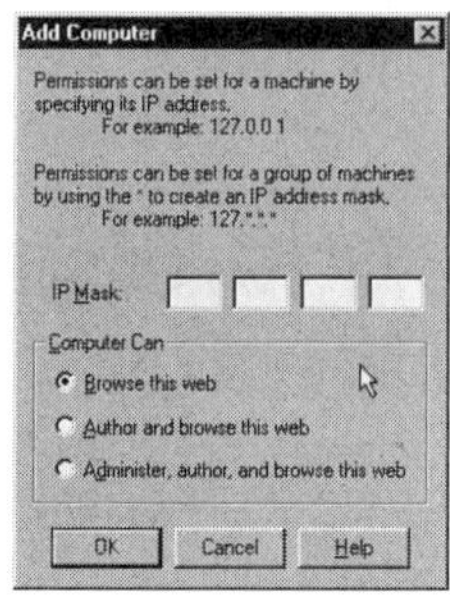

Figure 1.11.
Use the Add Computer dialog box to add an IP mask setting to your web.

- To edit an existing IP mask, highlight the IP mask you want to edit and click the **E**dit button. The Edit Computer dialog box shown in Figure 1.12 appears. Proceed to step 5.

Figure 1.12.
Use the Edit Computer dialog box to edit an existing IP mask configuration.

- To remove an IP mask, highlight the IP mask you want to remove and click the **R**emove button. The IP mask is removed from the user list.

5. Select the level of access for the IP mask as follows:
   - If you are adding or editing an IP mask for the current registered (protected) web, select the **B**rowse this web radio button.
   - If you are adding or changing the IP mask for an author of the current web, select the **A**uthor and browse this web radio button.
   - If you are adding or changing the IP mask for an administrator of the current web, select the A**d**minister, author, and browse this web radio button.
6. Click OK to return to the Computers tab in the Permissions dialog box.
7. Click OK. The computer is added to your web.

Changing Passwords

When you use the FrontPage Personal Web Server, an administrator or author can change his or her password through the Change Password dialog box. This option is disabled when you use the Microsoft Personal Web Server (discussed in Chapter 2). In order for the password to be changed, the existing password must be known.

To change the password for a web user, follow these steps:

1. From the FrontPage Explorer, choose **T**ools | **C**hange Password. The Change Password for *(name)* dialog box, shown in Figure 1.13, appears.

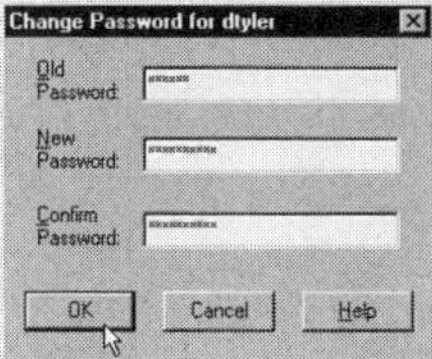

Figure 1.13.
Change the password for a user in your web in the Change Password for (name) *dialog box.*

2. Enter the old password in the **O**ld Password field.
3. Enter the new password in the **N**ew Password field and confirm it again in the **C**onfirm Password field. Spaces are not allowed.
4. Click OK. The password is updated for the user.

How Your File Directories Relate to the Web Server

When you install the FrontPage Personal Web Server on your local computer, the content files for your root web are located, by default, in the following directory on your local hard drive:

```
c:\FrontPage Webs\Content
```

When you create child webs with the FrontPage Explorer, a directory for each child web is placed beneath the root web. For example, if you create a web named personalweb, its home page might have a name as follows:

```
c:\FrontPage Webs\Content\personalweb\index.htm
```

In many cases, you can easily browse your Web content by entering this filename into your browser's URL field. However, when you browse a file on your hard drive, the FrontPage Server Extensions will not function. If your pages contain features that require the FrontPage Server Extensions, you won't be able to test them fully. Therefore, you need to enter the URL of the file as it should be when it is running on your local server. First, you need to determine your server name.

Finding the Name of Your Web Server

When you install the FrontPage Server Extensions on your local computer and start the FrontPage Explorer the first time, the program searches for the name of your server. Normally, the name returned is the name of your local computer as configured in Network Properties. You can use other names to identify your server. To determine the names or IP address you can use, run the TCP/IP Test Utility that is furnished with FrontPage. To run this utility, follow these steps:

1. From the FrontPage Explorer, choose **H**elp | **A**bout Microsoft FrontPage Explorer. The About FrontPage Explorer dialog box shown in Figure 1.14 appears.

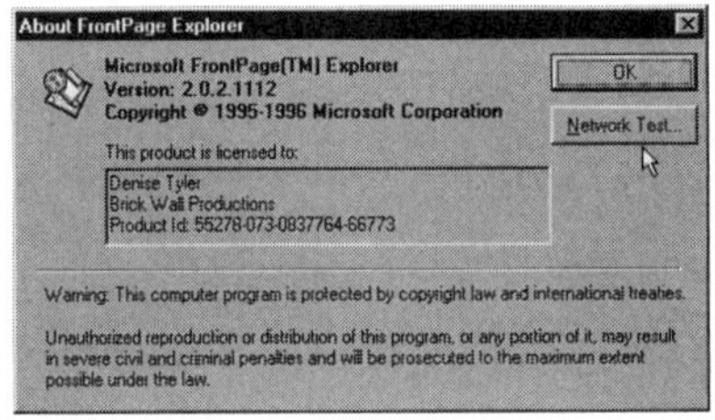

Figure 1.14.
The About FrontPage Explorer dialog box provides a button that enables you to test your network connections.

2. In the About FrontPage Explorer dialog box, click **N**etwork Test. The FrontPage TCP/IP Test dialog box shown in Figure 1.15 appears.

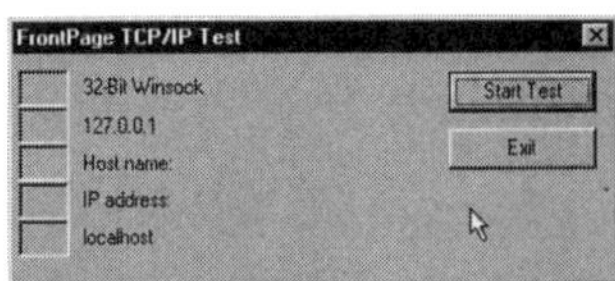

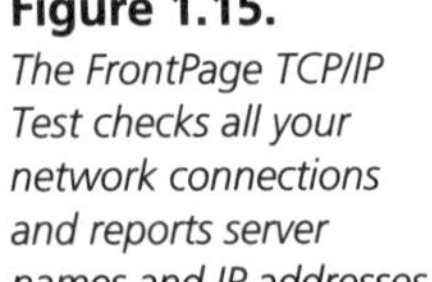

Figure 1.15.
The FrontPage TCP/IP Test checks all your network connections and reports server names and IP addresses you can use.

3. If you normally connect to a remote server while online, dial in to your Internet Service Provider. If you do not, some values will not be reported during the test.
4. Click the Start Test button. Up to four values that you can use for your server name may be returned as follows:

   `127.0.0.1`, which is the IP address for `localhost` (the server on your local computer).

Host name (for example, `myserver`), where the name is that which is configured in Network Properties for your local computer or your Internet Service Provider.

IP address (for example, `255.255.1.1`), where the numbers are the IP address that you have configured in Network Properties (configured from Windows 95 or Windows NT Control Panel) for your local computer or your Internet Service Provider.

`localhost`, which runs the FrontPage Server Extensions on your local computer.

5. Click Exit to return to the About FrontPage Explorer dialog box.
6. Click OK to return to the FrontPage Explorer.

You should be able to use any of the reported addresses as part of the URL when you browse your webs with the FrontPage Server Extensions running in the background. Typically, `localhost` and `127.0.0.1` are used to run the server extensions on your local computer. Use these values when you are not connected to an Internet Service Provider or network server. Use the host name and IP address values to connect to a network server or Internet Service Provider.

When you want to browse on your local computer with the FrontPage Server Extensions running, replace the `c:\FrontPage Webs\Content` portion of the filename with `http:` followed by your server name. Use forward slashes as you normally do when entering Web URLs. The URL to the `c:\FrontPage Webs\personalweb\index.htm` file instead becomes a URL that looks something like this:

```
http://servername/personalweb/index.htm
```

Workshop Wrap-Up

In this chapter, you learned some of the features and limitations of the FrontPage Personal Web Server. The FrontPage Personal Web Server enables you to test pages that feature all of the FrontPage features, with some exceptions. For most who use FrontPage 97 to develop personal Web sites, the FrontPage Personal Web Server might be sufficient for most of their needs. However, to test more advanced features such as custom CGI scripts, Active Server Pages, and database connections, a more robust server might be necessary.

You learned how to install the FrontPage Personal Web Server and where you can find the files after installation. You also learned some of the differences in how you change the home page name, add users, and administer this server with the FrontPage Server Administrator.

Next Steps

In the next chapter, you'll learn some of the features and functions of the Microsoft Personal Web Server, which is a more robust server that enables you to create and test database connectivity and more.

The following articles in the Microsoft Knowledge Base offer additional information about using the FrontPage Personal Web Server and the FrontPage Server Administrator with FrontPage 97. You can view these articles at Microsoft's Web site by entering the URL following each article title.

- Don't Need Web Server to Use FrontPage 97 (Q161154)

  `http://www.microsoft.com/kb/articles/q161/1/54.htm`

- Err Msg: No Server on Port <Port Number> at <Server Name> (Q150684)

  `http://www.microsoft.com/kb/articles/q161/1/54.htm`

- Err Msg: Timed Out While Trying to Connect to a Server (Q150680)

  `http://www.microsoft.com/kb/articles/q150/6/80.htm`

- Files and Folders Created by FrontPage 97 Setup (article Q161780)

  `http://www.microsoft.com/kb/articles/q161/7/80.htm`

- FrontPage: Basic Troubleshooting Utilities (Q143093)

  `http://www.microsoft.com/kb/articles/q143/0/93.htm`

- FrontPage: Browsing Web Returns List of Files (Q143104)

  `http://www.microsoft.com/kb/articles/q143/1/04.htm`

- FrontPage: Error "Unable to open ..." and "404 Not Found" (Q143089)

  `http://www.microsoft.com/kb/articles/q143/0/89.htm`

- FrontPage 97: How to Install the FrontPage Personal Web Server (Q161413)

  `http://www.microsoft.com/kb/articles/q161/4/13.htm`

- FrontPage 97: Start Menu Includes a Single Icon for FrontPage (Q161424)

  `http://www.microsoft.com/kb/articles/q161/4/24.htm`

- FrontPage Personal Web Server Supports Standard CGI Only (Q151042)

  `http://www.microsoft.com/kb/articles/q151/0/42.htm`

- How to Assign a Document Other Than index.htm as Default Page (Q150681)

  `http://www.microsoft.com/kb/articles/q150/6/81.htm`

- How to Create an Alias for FrontPage Personal Web Server (Q151541)

  `http://www.microsoft.com/kb/articles/q151/5/41.htm`

- How to Delete a Disk-Based Web (Q162240)

  `http://www.microsoft.com/kb/articles/q162/2/40.htm`

- How to Start the FrontPage Server Administrator (Q161421)

  `http://www.microsoft.com/kb/articles/q161/4/21.htm`

- How to Upgrade the FrontPage Server Extensions (Q161845)

  `http://www.microsoft.com/kb/articles/q161/8/45.htm`

- New Features in FrontPage 97 (Q161415)

  `http://www.microsoft.com/kb/articles/q161/4/15.htm`

- Personal Web Server Can't Bind to Port 80 (Q149843)

  `http://www.microsoft.com/kb/articles/q149/8/43.htm`

- Switching from FrontPage Personal Web Server to Microsoft PWS (Q161418)

  `http://www.microsoft.com/kb/articles/q161/4/18.htm`

- Using NCSA or CERN Image Maps with Personal Web Server Upgrade (Q151567)

  `http://www.microsoft.com/kb/articles/q151/5/67.htm`

- WebBot Browse-Time Components Don't Function on a Disk-Based Web (Q160227)

  `http://www.microsoft.com/kb/articles/q160/2/27.htm`

- Web Servers Supported by FrontPage 97 (Q161158)

  `http://www.microsoft.com/kb/articles/q161/1/58.htm`

- When to Use FrontPage Personal Web Server Versus Microsoft PWS (Q161417)

  `http://www.microsoft.com/kb/articles/q161/4/17.htm`

- Why Are There Two Versions of the Personal Web Server? (Q161150)

  `http://www.microsoft.com/kb/articles/q161/1/50.htm`

Q&A

Q: Can I develop pages that use custom scripts, Active Server Pages, or database connectivity when I use the FrontPage Personal Web Server?

A: Yes, you can design pages that incorporate these features. However, you will not be able to test them fully before you publish them to the server on which they will reside. If you prefer to test your pages before doing so, the Microsoft Personal Web Server might be a better choice for you.

Q: Are there any limitations as to how many pages I can place in my web when I use the FrontPage Personal Web Server?

A: I tested the FrontPage Personal Web Server with a web that contained over 1000 pages. Although it took quite some time for the web to open, all the pages were listed in the FrontPage Explorer. Tasks such as moving files and folders, using the Verify Links commands, and automatically changing page URLs did not perform quite up to the norm. If you expect to create a large site and want to use the FrontPage Personal Web Server, consider placing general content in the root web and add child webs for topic-specific content. Remember that you can design only 17 child webs while using the FrontPage Personal Web Server.

CHAPTER

TWO

Using the Microsoft Personal Web Server

The FrontPage Personal Web Server enables you to create and test pages that use most of FrontPage 97's built-in features. However, you might find it beneficial to use the Microsoft Personal Web Server instead of or in addition to the FrontPage Personal Web Server. The Microsoft Personal Web Server operates under Windows 95 only. It offers additional capabilities over the FrontPage Personal Web Server, enabling you to test extended features such as custom CGI scripts, FTP services, ISAPI features, and pages that use Internet Database Connector files. You can also install Microsoft Active Server Pages, a component of Internet Information Server 3.0. The server speed is much improved over the FrontPage Personal Web Server, and the limitation of 18 webs per server is gone.

In this chapter, you

- ❑ Review the capabilities of the Microsoft Personal Web Server
- ❑ Learn where the files are located when you install the Microsoft Personal Web Server
- ❑ Learn how to configure and administer the Microsoft Personal Web Server through web-based administration pages
- ❑ Start and stop the Microsoft Personal Web Server automatically or manually
- ❑ Learn how to start, stop, and configure the WWW and FTP servers
- ❑ Administer the WWW and FTP servers
- ❑ Learn where you can go for additional help on the Microsoft Personal Web Server

Tasks in this chapter:

- ❑ Installing the Microsoft Personal Web Server
- ❑ Displaying Your Web Home Page
- ❑ Starting and Stopping the Microsoft Personal Web Server
- ❑ Starting and Stopping the WWW or FTP Servers
- ❑ Administering the Microsoft Personal Web Server
- ❑ Administering the WWW Server
- ❑ Administering the FTP Server
- ❑ Configuring Your Users
- ❑ Viewing Online Documentation

Learning Whether the Microsoft Personal Web Server Is Right for You

The Microsoft Personal Web Server is furnished as part of the FrontPage Bonus Pack. It offers several enhancements over the FrontPage Personal Web Server, one of which is increased speed in performing server tasks. In addition to faster processing, you don't have the limitation of being able to create only 18 webs like you do with the FrontPage Personal Web Server.

The Microsoft Personal Web Server is designed to run under Windows 95 only. It will not run on systems running Windows NT Workstation or Windows NT Server. It includes many of the capabilities that are found in Microsoft Internet Information Server, which is furnished with Windows NT 4.0 Server. Among these capabilities are support of custom CGI scripts, FTP services, Internet Database Connector (IDC) files, multi-homing, ISAPI interface, and increased user access security through NTLM authentication.

NTLM is an authentication scheme used by Windows NT, the Microsoft Internet Information Server, Microsoft Peer Web Services for NT Workstation 4.0, and the Microsoft Personal Web Server for Windows 95.

Additionally, this personal web server also offers the capability of remote administration through the use of web-based administration pages. Table 2.1 summarizes the capabilities of the Microsoft Personal Web Server.

Table 2.1. Microsoft Personal Web Server capabilities.

Feature	*Supported?*
Active Server Pages	Yes (with Active Server Pages installed)
Custom CGI scripts	Yes
FTP services	Yes
Gopher services	No
High traffic sites	No
IDC Database files/scripts	Yes
ISAPI interface	Yes
Multi-homing	Yes
NSAPI interface	No
NTLM authentication	Yes
Secure Socket Layer (SSL) communications	No

Installing the Microsoft Personal Web Server

When you insert the FrontPage 97 CD-ROM into your CD-ROM drive, the FrontPage 97 setup program initially checks to see whether a Web server exists on your system. If you do not yet have a server, setup asks if you would like to install the Microsoft Personal Web Server. Choose Yes to install it.

NOTE: The Microsoft Personal Web Server is compatible with Windows 95 only. Do not install this server if you are developing your webs with Windows NT Workstation or Windows NT Server.

You also can install the Microsoft Personal Web Server by following these steps:

1. Insert the FrontPage 97 CD-ROM into your CD-ROM drive. The FrontPage 97 setup screen shown in Figure 2.1 appears.

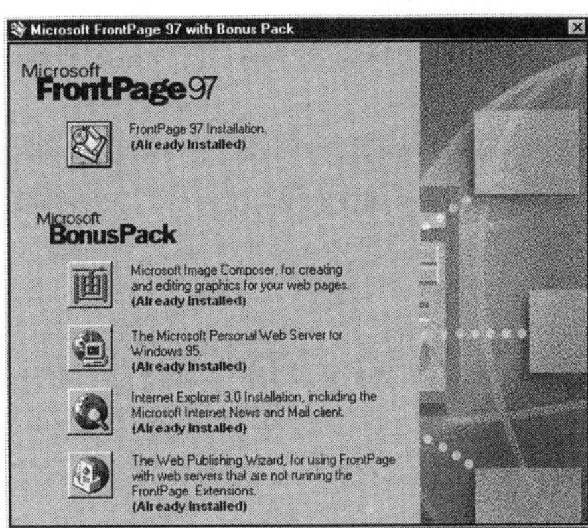

Figure 2.1.
To install the Microsoft Personal Web Server, select the Microsoft Personal Web Server for Windows 95 option in the setup screen.

2. Select the Microsoft Personal Web Server for Windows 95 option. A license agreement screen appears. To continue installation, select I **A**gree.
3. Setup installs several files onto your system, after which a Personal Web Server dialog box appears. You are asked if you want to restart your computer. Answer **Y**es.

If the Microsoft Personal Web Server is the only server on your system, it is installed to port 80. You can browse webs on this server by specifying server addresses similar to the following:

```
http://yourserver/
http://yourserver/childweb/
http://yourserver/childweb/webpage.htm
```

If the FrontPage Personal Web Server has been previously installed on your system, the Microsoft Personal Web Server is installed to port 8080. You can browse webs on the Microsoft Personal Web Server by specifying a server address as follows:

```
http://yourserver:8080/
http://yourserver:8080/childweb/
http://yourserver:8080/childweb/webpage.htm
```

Microsoft Personal Web Server File Locations

When you install the Microsoft Personal Web Server on your computer, the files and images associated with the server are installed to the following default directories:

- The `c:\Program Files\docs` subdirectory contains documentation and help files.
- The `c:\Program Files\htmla` subdirectory contains web administration files.
- The `c:\Program Files\htmlascr` subdirectory contains scripts for the Microsoft Personal Web Server.
- The `c:\Program Files\system` subdirectory contains executable and administration files.
- Web content is saved to the `c:\Webshare\wwwroot` directory by default.
- The FTP server files are located in the `c:\Webshare\ftproot` directory.
- Custom scripts are placed in the `c:\Webshare\scripts` subdirectory.

Setting Microsoft Personal Web Server Properties

You configure the Microsoft Personal Web Server through the Personal Web Server Properties dialog box. From the Windows 95 Start menu, choose Settings and then Control Panel. From the Control Panel group, click Personal Web Server. The Personal Web Server Properties dialog box appears. What follows is a brief overview of the screens that you use to administer and configure your Microsoft Personal Web Server.

Displaying Your Web Home Page

When you first open the Personal Web Server Properties dialog box, it displays the General tab, shown in Figure 2.2. This dialog box displays the Internet address of the Microsoft Personal Web Server (for example, `http://`*`servername`*). Each child web you create resides in subfolders of this server. To browse a child web in your Internet browser, enter a URL similar to `http://`*`servername/childwebname`*.

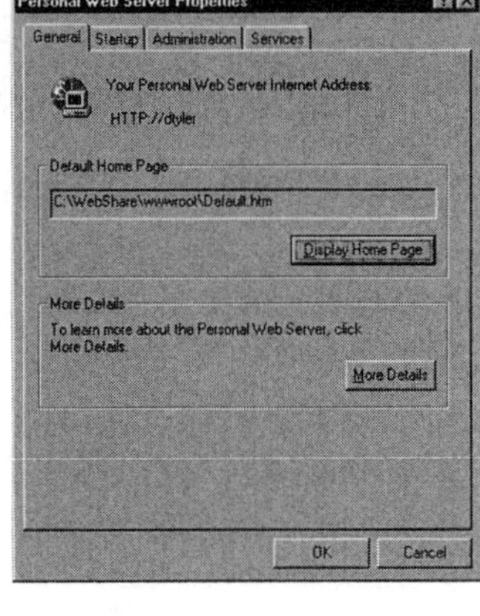

Figure 2.2.
Use the Personal Web Server Properties dialog box to access and configure the Microsoft Personal Web Server.

To edit the contents of the default home page, choose **F**ile | **O**pen FrontPage Web from the FrontPage Explorer. From the list of webs on your server, select the root web. After the root web appears in the FrontPage Explorer, double-click `default.htm` to open the page in the FrontPage Editor.

The URL of your default home page (that is, the home page in your server's root web) is shown beneath the Web server address. To view the default home page in your web browser, follow these steps:

1. From the Windows 95 Start menu, choose Settings, then Control Panel. The Control Panel group dialog box appears.
2. From the Control Panel group, select Personal Web Server. The Personal Web Server Properties dialog box appears, opened to the General tab.
3. In the Default Home Page section, select the **D**isplay Home Page button. The home page that exists in your root web opens in your browser.

Starting and Stopping the Microsoft Personal Web Server

The Startup tab in the Personal Web Server Properties dialog box enables you to start and stop the Microsoft Personal Web Server. You also can configure the Personal Web Server to start automatically whenever Windows 95 starts up. The Startup tab also provides an option to include an icon for the Personal Web Server on your Windows 95 taskbar. To access these features, follow these steps:

1. From the Windows 95 Start menu, choose Settings, then Control Panel. The Control Panel group dialog box appears.
2. From the Control Panel group, select Personal Web Server. The Personal Web Server Properties dialog box appears.
3. Select the Startup tab, shown in Figure 2.3.

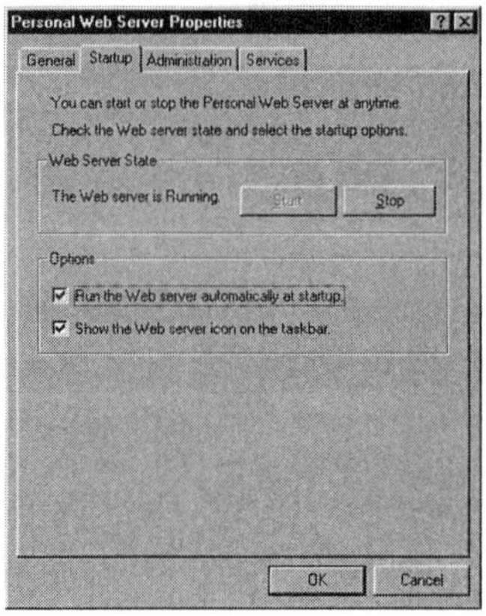

Figure 2.3.
Use the Startup tab in the Personal Web Server Properties dialog box to start and stop the Microsoft Personal Web Server.

4. In the Web Server State section, a status message that displays the current state of the Personal Web Server appears. You are informed if the Web server is running, or if it is stopped.
   - If the Web server is not running, choose **S**tart to start the World Wide Web server.
   - If the Web server is running, choose **S**top to stop the World Wide Web server.
5. The Options section of the Startup tab enables you to start the Microsoft Personal Web Server automatically when Windows 95 starts up. To enable this option, check the Run the Web server automatically at startup check box. If this option is disabled, you will need to start the server manually as outlined in steps 1–4.
6. You also can choose to locate an icon for the Microsoft Personal Web Server in your Windows 95 taskbar. To enable this option, check the Show the Web server icon on the taskbar check box. With the icon in your taskbar, you can perform the following:
   - Double-click the icon to open the Personal Web Server Properties dialog box. You can also open this dialog box if you right-click the icon and choose P**r**operties from the pop-up menu.
   - Right-click and choose **A**dminister to open the Internet Services Administrator Web-Based Server Administration page in your browser.
   - Right-click and choose **H**ome Page to open the home page in the root web of your server.
7. Select another tab in the Personal Web Server Properties dialog box, or choose OK to apply your settings.

Starting and Stopping the WWW or FTP Servers

By default, the WWW server is configured to start automatically when Windows 95 starts. The FTP server does not run by default. You can customize these settings using the Services tab in the Personal Web Server Properties dialog box, shown in Figure 2.4. The display at the bottom of the page tells you the current status of each server. You can tell whether the server is stopped or running and whether the server is started manually or automatically.

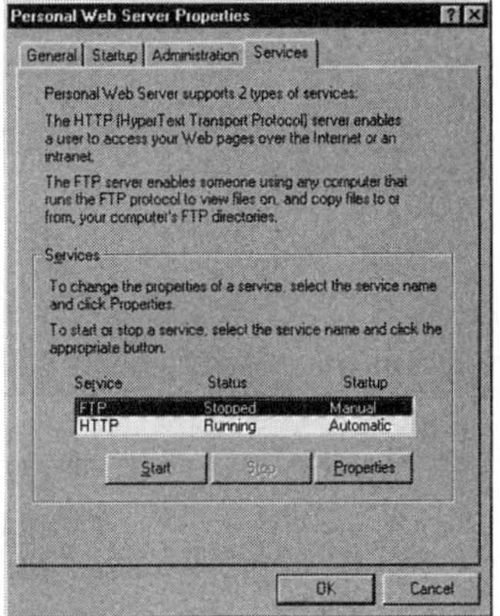

Figure 2.4.
Use the Services tab in the Personal Web Server Properties dialog box to start, stop, or configure your WWW or FTP server.

To start and stop the WWW or FTP services through the Services tab, follow these steps:

1. From the Windows 95 Start menu, choose Settings, then Control Panel. The Control Panel group dialog box appears.
2. From the Control Panel group, select Personal Web Server. The Personal Web Server Properties dialog box appears.
3. Select the Services tab.
4. In the Services section, highlight the server for which you want to start, stop, or change properties.
    - ❑ To start a server that is not running, click the **S**tart button.
    - ❑ To stop a server that is running, click the **S**top button.
    - ❑ To change the configuration of the WWW server, highlight HTTP from the list and click **P**roperties. The HTTP Properties dialog box appears. To start the HTTP server automatically when Windows 95 starts, select the **A**utomatic (HTTP service starts up automatically) radio button. To start the HTTP server manually, select the **M**anual radio button.

Selecting the Change Home Root button or the Change Home Page button opens the WWW Administrator—Directory page, discussed in "Administering the Microsoft Personal Web Server," later in this chapter.

- To change the configuration of the FTP server, highlight FTP from the list and click **P**roperties. The FTP Properties dialog box appears. To start the FTP service automatically, choose the **A**utomatic (FTP Service Starts Up Automatically) radio button. To start the FTP service manually, select the **M**anual button. To change the FTP server's home root directory, select the Change FTP Home **R**oot button.

Administering the Microsoft Personal Web Server

You use the Administration tab of the Personal Web Server Properties dialog box, shown in Figure 2.5, to administer your Microsoft Personal Web Server. From this tab, you gain access to administration tasks for the WWW and FTP servers, as well as the ability to add users and groups to your server.

Figure 2.5.
You use the Administration tab of the Personal Web Server Properties dialog box to gain access to administrator tasks.

1. From the Windows 95 Start menu, choose Settings, then Control Panel. The Control Panel group dialog box appears.
2. From the Control Panel group, select Personal Web Server. The Personal Web Server Properties dialog box appears.
3. Select the Administration tab.
4. Click the Administration button. The Internet Services Administrator Web-based Server Administration page, shown in Figure 2.6, opens in your browser. From this page, you can administer your WWW and FTP servers and add users and groups to your webs.

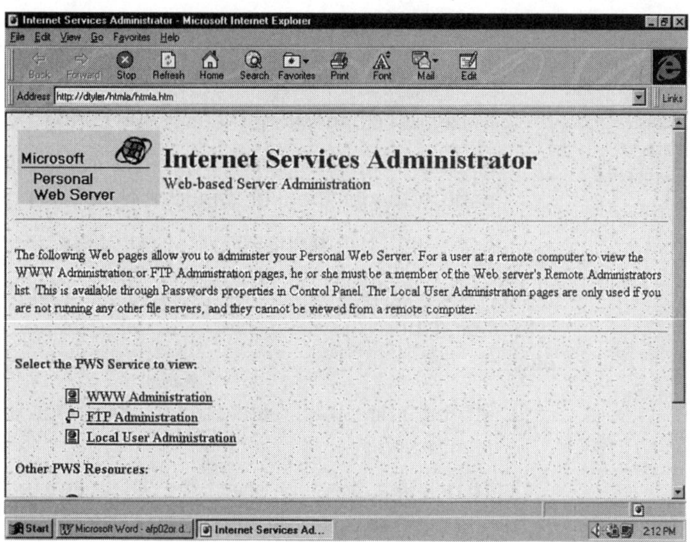

Figure 2.6.
The Internet Services Administrator Web-based Server Administration page enables you to configure your servers and its users.

Administering the WWW Server

When you choose to administer your HTTP (or World Wide Web) server, the Administration page shown in Figure 2.7 opens in your browser. This page contains three tabs: Service, Directories, and Logging.

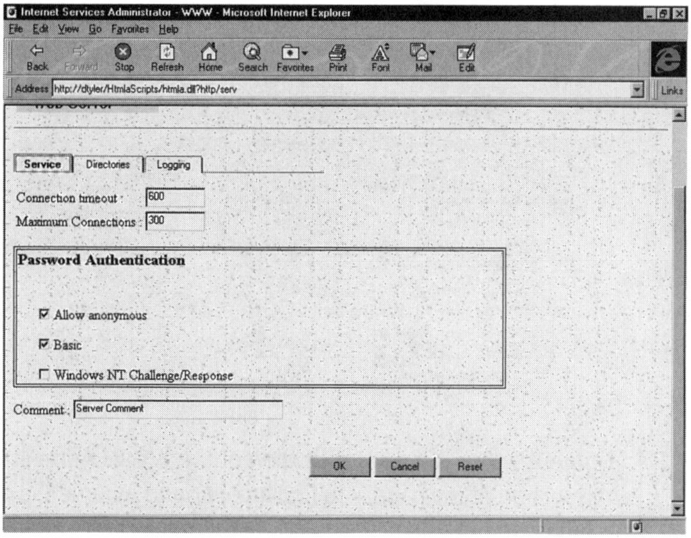

Figure 2.7.
The Service tab on the WWW Administration page.

You can administer the Microsoft Personal Web Server remotely from Web-based administration pages that are located on the server.

The Service tab enables you to configure the following items:

Connection Timeout (default 600 seconds)

Maximum Connections (default 300 connections)

Password Authentication, which lets you enable anonymous connections, basic authentication, or Windows NT Challenge/Response authentication

Comment, which enables you to configure a server comment message

The WWW Administrator—Directory page, the top of which is shown in Figure 2.8, lists all directories on your server. You can edit, add, or delete directories from this page.

- To edit a directory, select the Edit link that is adjacent to the directory you want to edit.
- To delete a directory, select the Delete link that is adjacent to the directory you want to delete.
- To add a directory, click the Add link at the bottom-right side of the directory list.

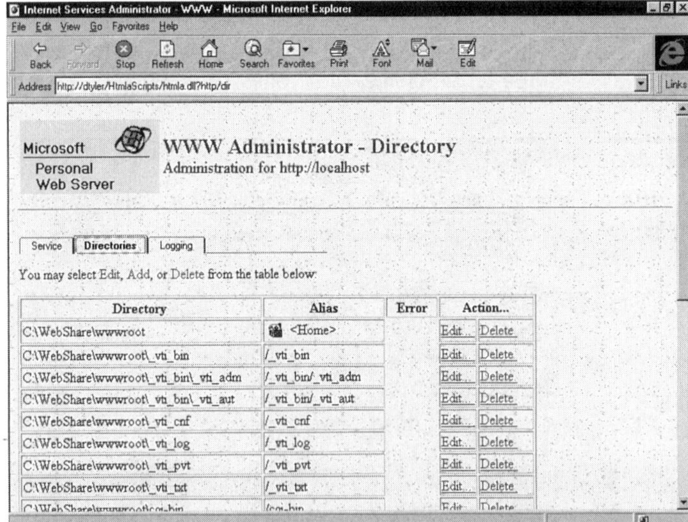

Figure 2.8.
The upper portion of the WWW Administrator—Directory page contains a list of all the directories on your server. You can edit, delete, or add directories on this page.

Figure 2.9 shows the lower portion of the WWW Administrator—Directory page. In this section of the page, you find an option to rename the default home page, which is (appropriately) named `Default.htm`. Enter another name in the Default Document field if you need to.

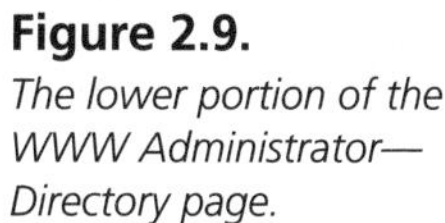

Figure 2.9.
The lower portion of the WWW Administrator—Directory page.

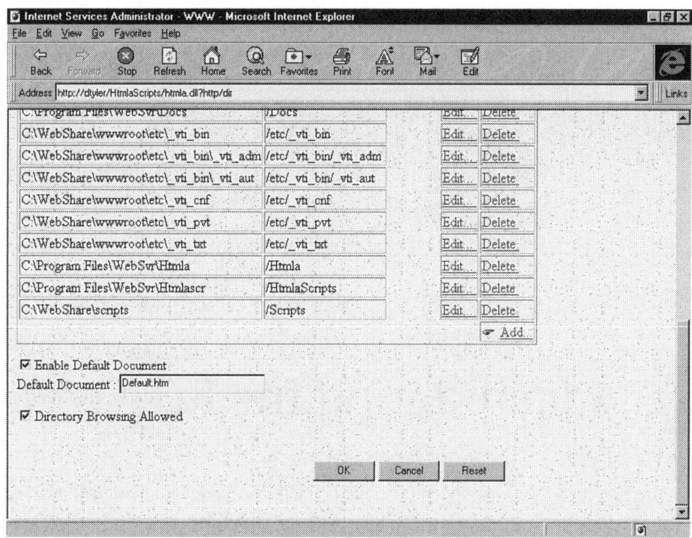

You also have the following options in this portion of the page:

Enable Default Document

Directory Browsing Allowed

The Logging tab, shown in Figure 2.10, lets you enable and disable logging and specify how often you want a log file to be generated. To specify the settings for your logging file, follow these steps:

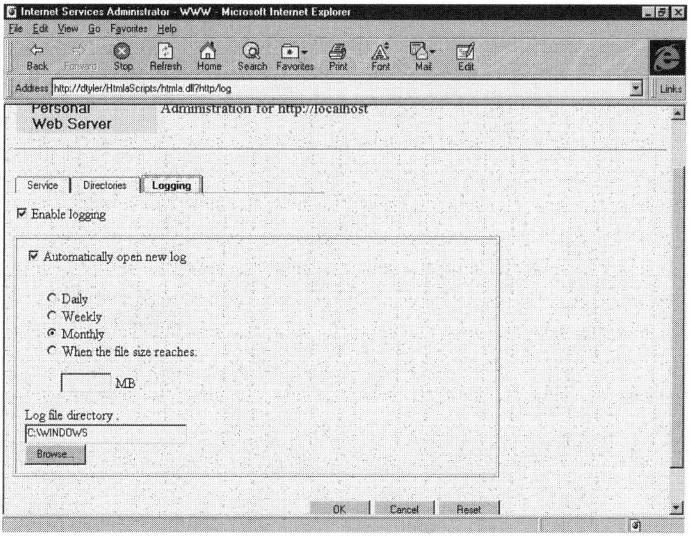

Figure 2.10.
The Logging tab of the WWW Administration page.

1. To enable logging, check the Enable logging check box, which is checked by default. If you disable the check box, no logging file is generated.
2. To automatically open a new log at a specified interval, check the Automatically open new log check box. Then, select how you want a new log file to be generated. The options are Daily, Weekly, Monthly, or when the file size reaches a specified number of megabytes.
3. In the Log file directory field, enter the directory in which you want to store your log file, or click the Browse button to locate a directory on your local or network hard drive.

Administering the FTP Server

The FTP server included in the Microsoft Personal Web Server enables users to download files from your Web site. You can specify a maximum number of people that are allowed to connect to your download area at a given time, generate activity logs, and configure messages and directories for your FTP server. When you choose to configure your FTP server, the Internet Services Administrator—FTP page appears in your browser. This page contains four tabs: Service, Messages, Directories, and Logging. The Service tab is shown in Figure 2.11.

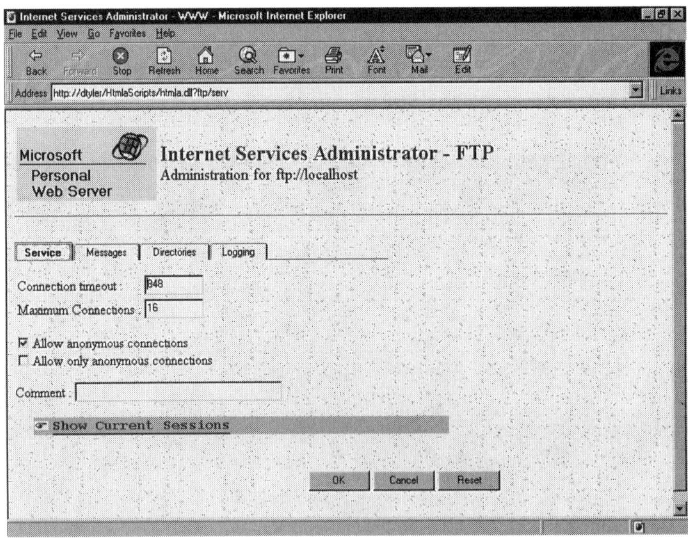

Figure 2.11.
The Service tab of the FTP Administration page.

The Service tab enables you to configure the following items:

Connection Timeout

Maximum Connections

Allow anonymous connections

Allow only anonymous connections

Comment

Show Current Sessions—if you select this link, the Current FTP Sessions page, shown in Figure 2.12, appears. It displays the users who are currently connected to your FTP site and enables you to disconnect the users and close the FTP service.

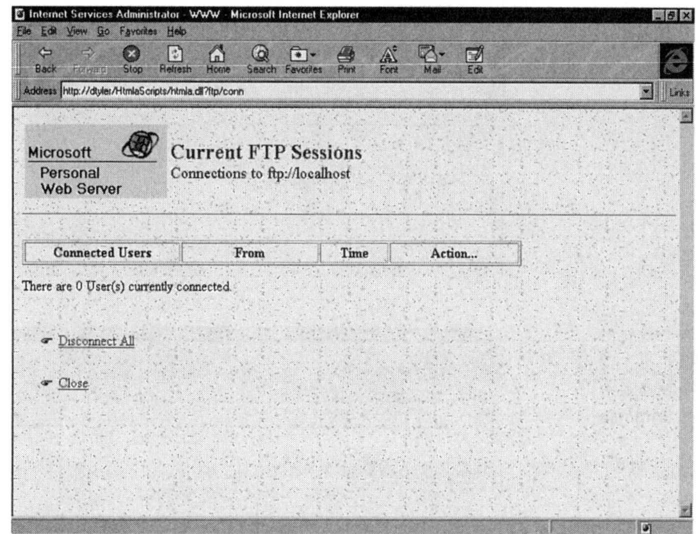

Figure 2.12.
The Current FTP Sessions page displays the users who are connected to your FTP service.

The FTP Administrator—Messages page, shown in Figure 2.13, enables you to configure default messages for your FTP server. You can configure a welcome message, an exit message, and a maximum connections message.

The FTP Administrator—Directory page, shown in Figure 2.14, lists the directories on your FTP server. You can edit, add, or delete directories from this page.

- To edit a directory, select the Edit link that is adjacent to the directory you want to edit.
- To delete a directory, select the Delete link that is adjacent to the directory you want to delete.
- To add a directory, click the Add link at the bottom-right side of the directory list.
- To select a directory listing style, choose either the Unix radio button or the MS-DOS radio button.

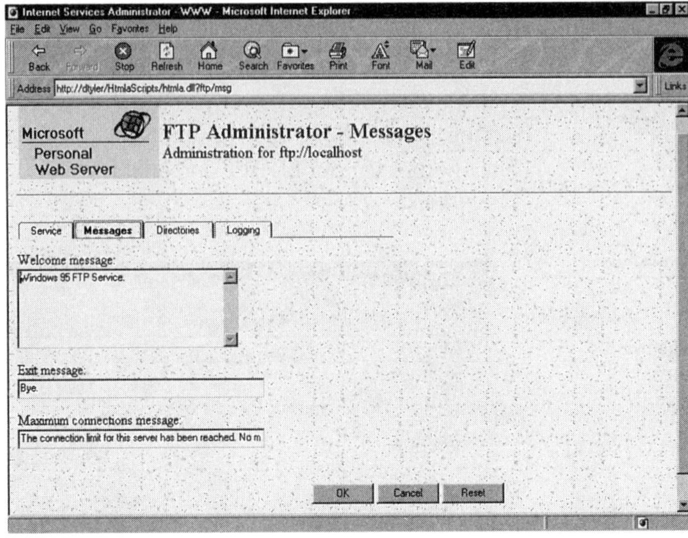

Figure 2.13.
You can configure FTP messages in the FTP Administrator—Messages page.

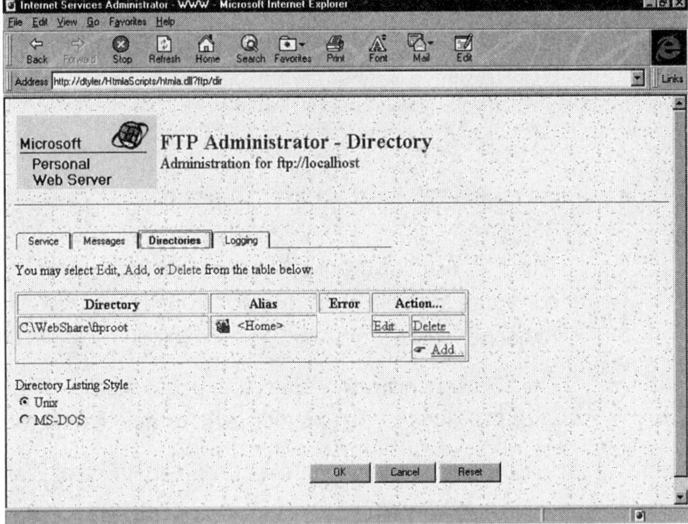

Figure 2.14.
The FTP Administrator—Directory page contains a list of all the directories on your FTP server.

The Logging tab, shown in Figure 2.15, lets you enable and disable logging and specify how often you want a log file to be generated. To specify the settings for your logging file, follow these steps:

1. To enable logging, check the Enable Logging check box, which is checked by default. If you disable the check box, no logging file is generated.
2. To automatically open a new log at a specified interval, check the Automatically Open New Log check box. Then, select how you want a new log file to be generated. The options are Daily, Weekly, Monthly, or when the file size reaches a specified number of megabytes.

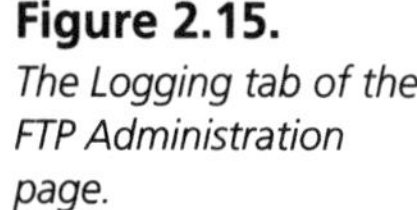

Figure 2.15.
The Logging tab of the FTP Administration page.

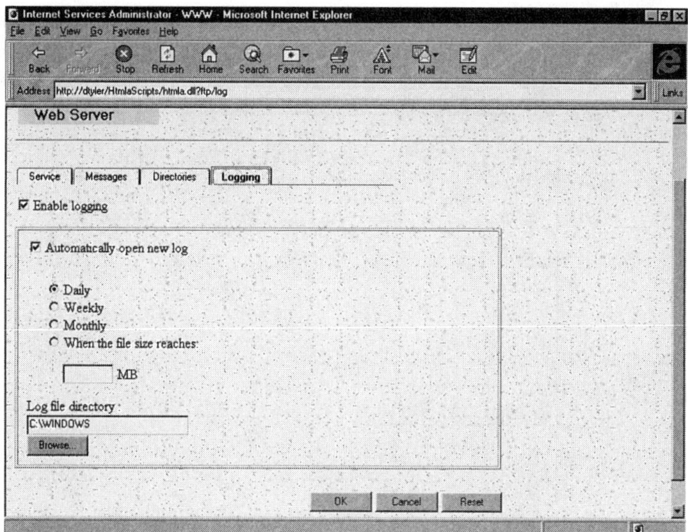

3. In the Log File Directory field, enter the directory in which you want to store your log file, or click the Browse button to locate a directory on your local or network hard drive.

When you use the Microsoft Personal Web Server, you configure users and user groups with Web-based administration pages.

Configuring Your Users

When you choose Local User Administration from the Internet Services Administrator Web-based Server Administration page, the Internet Local User Administrator page opens. This page consists of three tabs: Users (shown in Figure 2.16), Groups, and User/Group.

In the Users tab, you edit, add, and remove users from your server:

- To add a new user, click the New User button. The page shown in Figure 2.17 appears. Enter the user's name and password in the User Name and User Password fields, and then confirm the password in the Confirm Password field. Click the Add button to add the new user.
- To edit the properties of an existing user, click the Properties button.
- To remove a user, select the user you want to remove and click the Remove button.

The Groups tab, shown in Figure 2.18, enables you to add, remove, or change properties of user groups. From the Groups tab, click the New Group button. This takes you to the Add New Group to Web Server Database page shown in Figure 2.19. Enter a group name in the Group Name field and click Add.

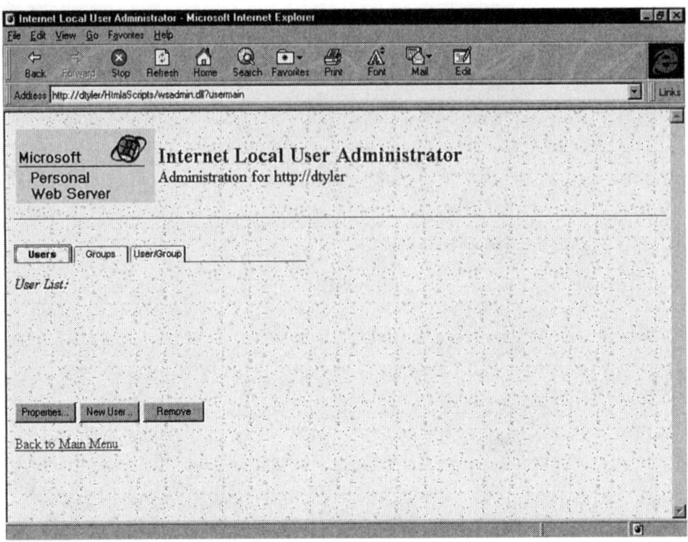

Figure 2.16.
The Users tab of the Internet Local User Administrator page.

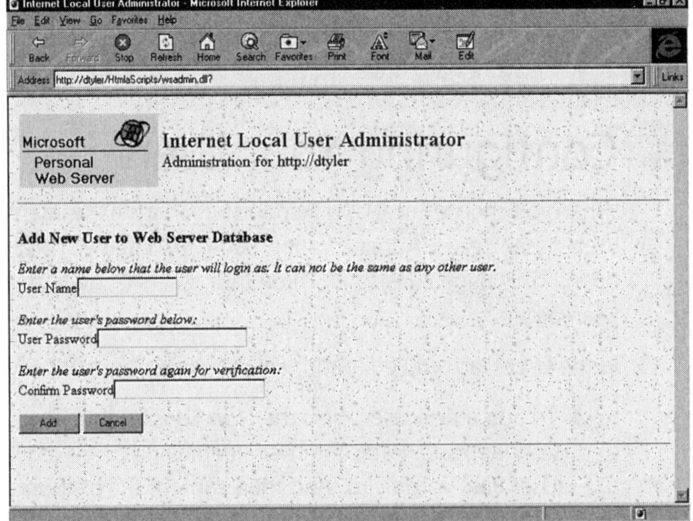

Figure 2.17.
Enter the user's name and password on this page.

NOTE: You also can configure groups and assign users to them by choosing **T**ools|**P**ermissions from the FrontPage Explorer and then selecting the Groups tab in the Permissions dialog box. This tab is not available when you use the FrontPage Personal Web Server.

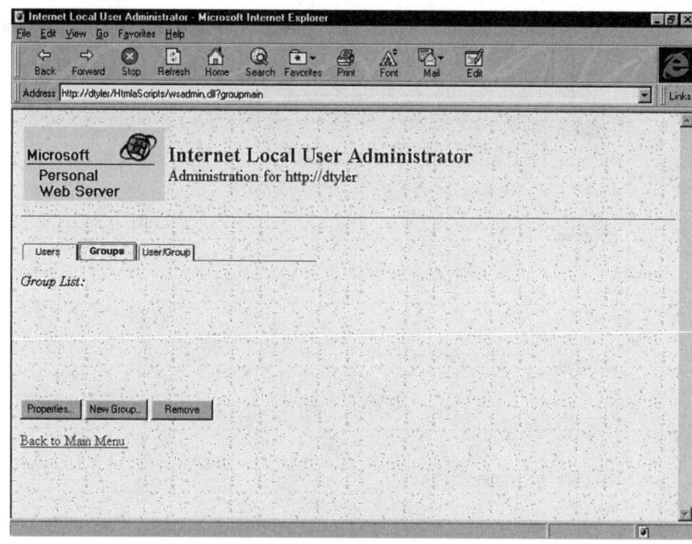

Figure 2.18.
The Groups tab enables you to add, remove, or change properties of user groups.

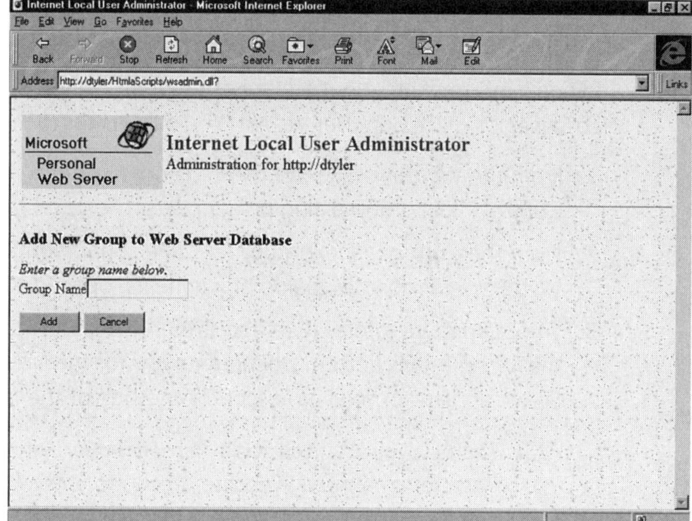

Figure 2.19.
Add user group names on this page.

The User/Group tab lets you assign users to any groups you have configured in your web. This tab takes you to the page shown in Figure 2.20. Highlight a user from the user list, select the group to which you want to add the user, and click the Add User to Group button.

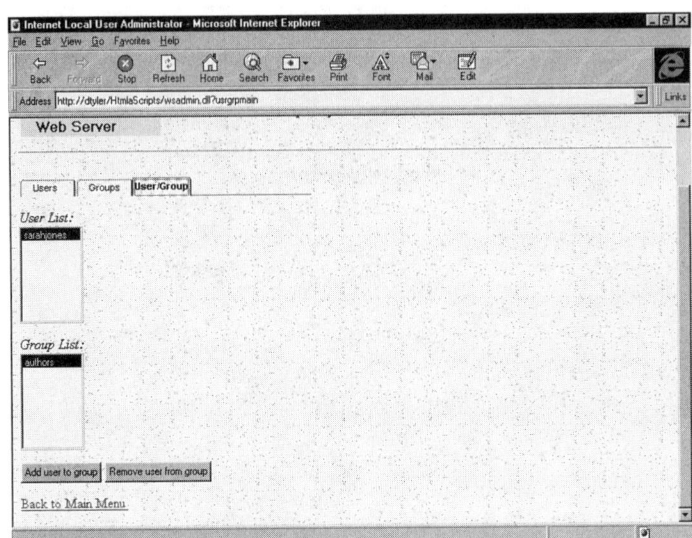

Figure 2.20.
You assign users to groups in the User/Group page.

Viewing Online Documentation

Additional information about administering and configuring the Microsoft Personal Web Server is installed on your system. You gain access to this information as follows:

1. From the Windows 95 Start menu, choose Settings, then Control Panel. The Control Panel group dialog box appears.
2. From the Control Panel group, select Personal Web Server. The Personal Web Server Properties dialog box appears, opened to the General tab.
3. To obtain more information about the Microsoft Personal Web Server, select the More Details button. Documentation for the Microsoft Personal Web Server appears in your browser. Choose one of the following three links:
   - The `Getting Started with Personal Web Server` link provides instructions for creating a Web site on your computer, how to start the Personal Web Server, and how to test servers connected to the Internet and your intranet.
   - The `Personal Web Server Administration` link provides instructions for restricting access to your site, information about basic authentication and Windows NT Challenge/Response authentication, and how to configure user lists and logging.
   - The `FTP Server Administration` link provides instructions for creating an FTP site, configuring its home directory, and restricting access to the FTP site.

Workshop Wrap-Up

In this chapter, you learned the capabilities of the Microsoft Personal Web Server, a Windows 95 server that offers many of the capabilities available in Windows NT's Internet Information Server. When using FrontPage on a system that runs Windows 95, the Microsoft Personal Web Server offers many advantages over the FrontPage Personal Web Server. In addition to the increase in speed and the number of webs that can reside on the server, you can create and test pages that utilize advanced web capabilities. You can develop and test pages that incorporate features such as custom CGI scripts, FTP file transfers, and IDC database connection. Those who require compatibility with ISAPI extensions, used with Internet Information Server, will be pleased to know that this server supports those functions as well. As you learned in this chapter, you can configure and administer this server locally or remotely through the use of web-based server administration pages. You also learned how to locate additional documentation that is installed on your local computer along with the Microsoft Personal Web Server.

Next Steps

In the next chapter, you learn about the new Internet features in Microsoft Word 97, and how you can use this application in conjunction with FrontPage 97. You'll compare the features and capabilities of using either application as a Web page editor.

For additional information about the Microsoft Personal Web Server, check the following articles in the Microsoft Knowledge Base. You can find these articles by navigating to the URLs that follow each document title.

- FrontPage: Error "Unable to open ..." and "404 Not Found" (Q143089)

  `http://www.microsoft.com/kb/articles/q143/0/89.htm`
- FrontPage Explorer Doesn't Accept Blank Password (Q163587)

  `http://www.microsoft.com/kb/articles/q163/5/87.htm`
- How to Make a Web Page that Displays Data from a Database (Q161155)

  `http://www.microsoft.com/kb/articles/q161/1/55.htm`
- IDC Queries to Access Fail from IIS 2.0 or MSPWS 1.0 Servers (Q162245)

  `http://www.microsoft.com/kb/articles/q162/2/45.htm`
- Internet Database Connector Wizard Runs on Non-IDC Server (Q160810)

  `http://www.microsoft.com/kb/articles/q160/8/10.htm`
- Memory Leak in FrontPage Extensions on MS Personal Web Server (Q160225)

  `http://www.microsoft.com/kb/articles/q160/2/25.htm`

- New Features in FrontPage 97 (Q161415)

  `http://www.microsoft.com/kb/articles/q161/4/15.htm`

- Permission Settings Changed After Reinstalling Extensions (Q161847)

  `http://www.microsoft.com/kb/articles/q161/8/47.htm`

- Permissions Not Retained when Web is Renamed (Q161964)

  `http://www.microsoft.com/kb/articles/q161/9/64.htm`

- Personal Web Server Doesn't Support Multiple Queries in IDC File (Q160809)

  `http://www.microsoft.com/kb/articles/q160/8/09.htm`

- Switching from FrontPage Personal Web Server to Microsoft PWS (Q161418)

  `http://www.microsoft.com/kb/articles/q161/4/18.htm`

- Unable to Complete Transaction on Server with NTLM (Q160618)

  `http://www.microsoft.com/kb/articles/q160/6/18.htm`

- WebBot Browse-Time Components Don't Function on a Disk-Based Web (Q160227)

  `http://www.microsoft.com/kb/articles/q160/2/27.htm`

- Web Servers Supported by FrontPage 97 (Q161158)

  `http://www.microsoft.com/kb/articles/q161/1/58.htm`

- When to Use FrontPage Personal Web Server Versus Microsoft PWS (Q161417)

  `http://www.microsoft.com/kb/articles/q161/4/17.htm`

- Why Are There Two Versions of the Personal Web Server? (Q161150)

  `http://www.microsoft.com/kb/articles/q161/1/50.htm`

Q&A

Q: Is there any advantage to using the FrontPage Personal Web Server instead of the Microsoft Personal Web Server?

A: If you are upgrading from previous versions of FrontPage 97, you might feel more at home using the FrontPage Personal Web Server. However, if you're using FrontPage with Windows 95, the Microsoft Personal Web Server does offer many improvements over the FrontPage Personal Web Server. Even if you do not need the additional features that the Microsoft Personal Web Server offers, it is faster, more secure, and more capable in the number of webs you can create.

PART II

Integrating with Microsoft Office 97

CHAPTER

THREE

Word Isn't Just for the Office Anymore

In this chapter, you

- Learn the differences between FrontPage and Word for Web authoring
- Compare the FrontPage 97 commands with those available in Word 97 during Web authoring mode
- Learn how to create Web pages using Word 97's Web templates and Web Page Wizard
- Create hyperlinks to Web pages and other files from FrontPage 97 and Word 97

Tasks in this chapter:

- Creating Web Pages with Word 97
- Designing HTML Forms in Word 97
- Importing your Form to FrontPage and Assigning a Form Handler
- Creating Web Pages from Word 97 Templates and Wizards
- Creating Hyperlinks from FrontPage 97
- Creating Hyperlinks from Word 97

With the recent release of Office 97, incredibly exciting changes are bringing Word to the Web. Not only do Office 97 applications have built-in capability to generate Web documents, but they also integrate seamlessly with Internet Explorer. You can create Office documents that link with each other, Office documents that link to Web pages, and Web pages that link to Office documents. Then you can use Internet Explorer to browse the Web or your intranet with one seamlessly integrated interface that changes when Internet Explorer comes across an Office 97 document. You no longer have to resort to remembering directories and filenames where documents are stored. By organizing your content, you effectively have everything available through your browser.

This chapter focuses on how you can integrate Word 97 with FrontPage to create documents for a Web site or an intranet. You will learn that Word 97 now goes far beyond creating word-processing documents for internal and hard copy use. Word has grown up and found its way to the Web.

Word 97 and FrontPage 97 Comparison

See "Using Word 97 to Create Web Documents" later in this chapter to learn how to create a Web page with the Word 97 Web Page templates and wizards.

With previous versions of Word, you needed to use the Internet Assistant for Word add-in to create Web pages. This add-in furnished alternative Microsoft Word commands that allowed you to build Web pages using HTML commands. Word 97 now has similar HTML capabilities built directly into its menus.

To create a Web page document in Word 97, select one of the templates from the Web Pages tab in the New dialog box. When you do so, the menu commands and toolbars change to display only those commands that the HTML language supports. Figure 3.1 shows an example of the commands available in the Insert menu when you use Word 97 to design word-processing documents. The HTML language does not support several of these commands. Compare the menu choices shown in Figure 3.2, where Word 97 displays a Web page template. You will notice that the commands change to reflect features normally found in Web pages.

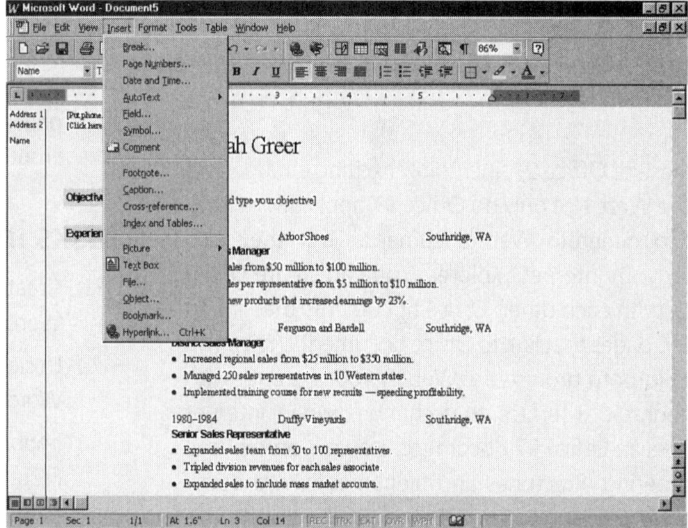

Figure 3.1.
When you use Word 97 to create a word-processing document, the menus display commands that are not supported by the HTML language.

If you are accustomed to using FrontPage 97 for your Web page authoring, you will find that authoring Web pages in Word 97 uses many similar commands. Table 3.1 compares the menu commands from the FrontPage Editor to those available when working in Web page authoring mode in Word 97. As you can see, the commands are quite similar, and Word 97 can implement many of the same HTML tag commands used by FrontPage 97. In some cases, though the commands are identical, the hotkeys are slightly different, as indicated by the boldface in the table.

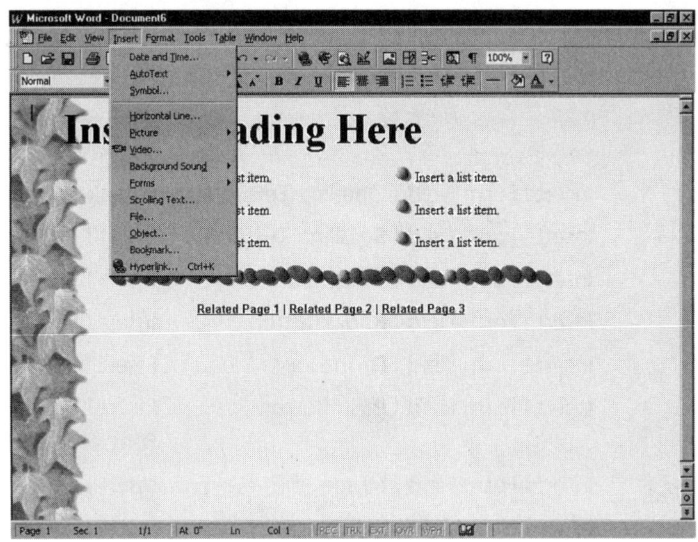

Figure 3.2.
When you select one of the Web page templates provided with Word 97, the menu displays commands that the HTML language supports.

Table 3.1. A comparison of FrontPage 97 and Word 97 Web authoring commands.

<table>
<tr><th>Command in FrontPage 97</th><th>Equivalent Command in Word 97</th></tr>
<tr><td>File | Preview in Browser</td><td>File | Web Page Preview</td></tr>
<tr><td>File | Page Properties</td><td>File | Properties</td></tr>
<tr><td>Edit | Bookmark</td><td>Insert | Bookmark</td></tr>
<tr><td>Edit | Database</td><td>No equivalent</td></tr>
<tr><td>Edit | Hyperlink</td><td>Insert | Hyperlink</td></tr>
<tr><td>Insert | Break</td><td>No equivalent</td></tr>
<tr><td>Insert | Horizontal Line</td><td>Insert | Horizontal Line</td></tr>
<tr><td>Insert | Symbol</td><td>Same</td></tr>
<tr><td>Insert | Comment</td><td>No equivalent</td></tr>
<tr><td>Insert | Image</td><td>Insert | Picture | From File</td></tr>
<tr><td>Insert | Video</td><td>Same</td></tr>
<tr><td>Insert | Background Sound</td><td>Insert | Background Sound | Properties</td></tr>
<tr><td>Insert | File</td><td>Same</td></tr>
<tr><td>Insert | WebBot Component</td><td>No equivalent</td></tr>
<tr><td>Insert | Other Components</td><td>Form fields are inserted as ActiveX controls in your Word 97 document. Macros are in Visual Basic for Applications. Insert PowerPoint animations with</td></tr>
</table>

conti

Table 3.1. continued

Command in FrontPage 97	*Equivalent Command in Word 97*
	the Insert | File command. There is no equivalent for Java applets and plug-ins.
Insert | Form Field | One-line Text Box	Insert | Forms | Text Box
Insert | Form Field | Scrolling Text Box	Insert | Forms | Text Area
Insert | Form Field | Check Box	Insert | Forms | Check Box
Insert | Form Field | Radio Button	Insert | Forms | Option Button
Insert | Form Field | Drop-Down Menu	Insert | Forms | Dropdown Box
Insert | Form Field | Push Button	Insert | Forms | Submit or Insert | Forms | Reset
Insert | Form Field | Image	Insert | Forms | Image Submit
Insert | Marquee	Insert | Scrolling Text
Insert | HTML Markup	No equivalent
Insert | Script	No equivalent
Insert | Hyperlink	Insert | Hyperlink
Format | Font	Same
Format | Paragraph	No equivalent
Format | Bullets and Numbering	Same
Format | Background	Same
Table | Insert Table	Same
Table | Insert Rows or Columns	Table | Insert Rows or Table | Insert Columns
Table | Insert Cell	Table | Insert Cells
Table | Insert Caption	No equivalent
Table | Merge Cells	Same
Table | Split Cells	Table | Split Cells
Table | Select Cell	No menu equivalent. Click in the cells you want to select.
Table | Select Row	Same
Table | Select Column	Table | Select Column
Table | Select Table	Table | Select Table
Table | Caption Properties	No equivalent
Table | Cell Properties	Table | Cell Properties
Table | Table Properties	Table | Table Properties

I am guessing at this point that you are thinking, "Then why do I need the FrontPage Editor if Word 97 can do many of the same things?"

Although Word 97 is a very capable Web page authoring program, FrontPage 97 offers several features that you will not find in Word 97. For example, many Web designers use nested tables to create advanced layouts in their Web pages. Word 97 does not support nested tables. One of the main things that you forfeit when using Word 97 to create Web pages is the use of FrontPage 97's WebBot components. Those components save you a lot of time in the end, because they take the drudgery out of Web page design. The WebBot components allow you to insert time stamps, include the content of one page on another, generate tables of contents automatically, perform a site-wide search of your pages, and more. By far, the nicest application for WebBot components is their use in form handling.

If you use Word 97 to open a Web page that contains nested tables, the page will not appear as originally designed. Use FrontPage 97 to open and edit pages that contain nested tables. You learn more about nested tables and advanced table properties in **Chapter 8**.

In FrontPage 97, you can use the Save Results Bot, Discussion Bot, and Registration Bot as form handlers for the forms you design. This saves a lot of time in writing custom form handlers in Visual Basic, JavaScript, VBScript, or other scripting languages—especially if you aren't really familiar with any of them. Of course, you can author pages that process forms with VBScript in either application if you prefer.

Using Word 97 to Create Web Documents

Take a look now at how you can generate Web documents in Word 97. You can take three different approaches: You can use Word 97 to create an HTML page; create a document in Word format and convert it to HTML format; or create a document in Word format and post it to your Web or intranet in its native format. Each approach has its benefits and limitations.

The FrontPage WebBot components used for form handling are discussed in **Chapter 12**.

NOTE: It is beyond the scope of this chapter and of this book to explain how to add content to your Web pages in Word 97. In this chapter, however, you will learn how to save your Word documents in HTML format and the ways that you can use Word 97 documents in their native formats.

TASK

Creating Web Pages with Word 97

The Web Pages tab in the New dialog box presents two choices to create Web pages: Select either the Blank Web Page or the Web Page Wizard. When you use Word 97 to create an HTML page, the menu commands listed in Table 3.1 become available; those that are not compatible with the HTML format are not present in the menus. In addition, the commands in the Style drop-down menu in the Format toolbar display the styles that are compatible with HTML format.

To create a Web page using the Blank Web Page template, follow these steps:

1. From Word 97, choose **F**ile | **N**ew (Ctrl+N). The New dialog box is displayed.
2. Click the Web Pages tab, shown in Figure 3.3. Then double-click the Blank Web Page icon. A blank page is displayed and places you in Online Layout view.

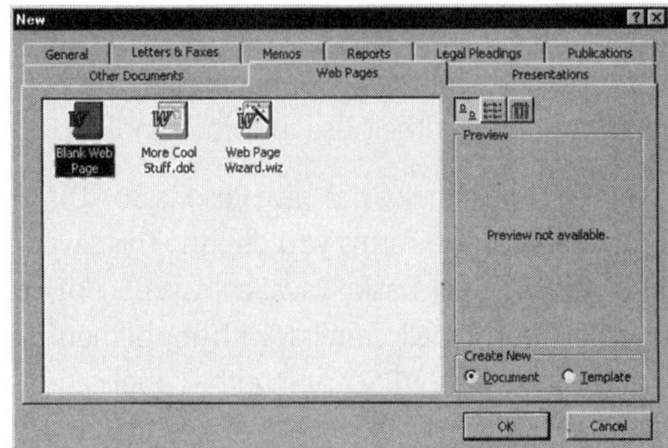

Figure 3.3.
Select the Blank Web Page icon from the Web Pages tab to create a blank Web page.

3. Edit the content on the page as necessary.
4. Save the Web page in HTML format by choosing **F**ile | **S**ave (Ctrl+S) or clicking the Save button in the Standard toolbar. The Save As dialog box shown in Figure 3.4 is displayed.

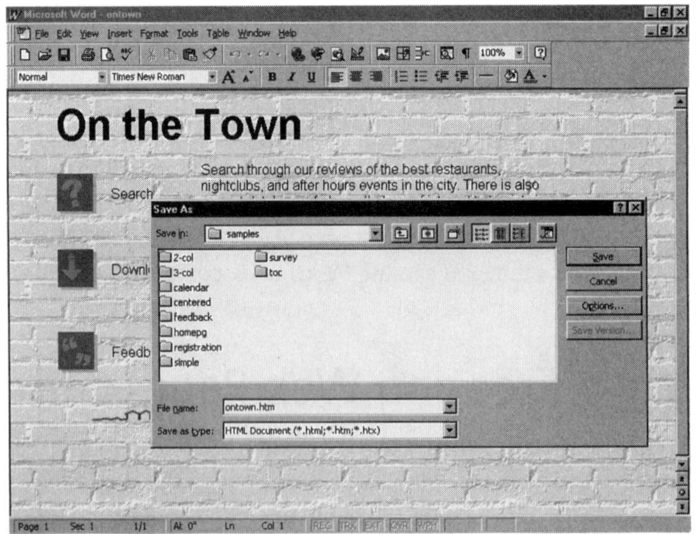

Figure 3.4.
Use the Save As dialog box to assign a filename to your Web page.

5. From the Save **i**n area, choose the drive and directory to which you want to save the file.
6. From the Save as **t**ype field, choose HTML document (`*.html`; `*.htm`; `*.htx`).
7. In the File **n**ame field, enter a name for the Web page. If you do not specify an extension, the page is saved with the `.html` extension. Append the filename with an `.htx` extension if the page contains IDC connector file information.
8. Click S**a**ve. Word 97 saves the Web page and its associated images to the location you specify.

If you do not want to design a Web page from scratch, you can use the Web Page Wizard. Each page created with the Web Page Wizard includes placeholder text, background image, bullet icons, placeholder links, and horizontal rules. The forms that Web Page Wizard creates also contain ActiveX form fields. Just as with FrontPage 97, you will need to create scripts to process the forms. You will find that the pages you create with the Word 97 Web Wizard are even more basic than those generated by the FrontPage templates and wizards. When it comes to Web templates and wizards, FrontPage wins the race. To create a Web page using the Word 97 Web Wizard, follow these steps:

1. From Word 97, choose **F**ile | **N**ew (Ctrl+N). The New dialog box appears.
2. Click the Web Pages tab; then double-click the Web Page Wizard icon. The Web Page Wizard dialog box appears, asking what type of Web page you want to create, as shown in Figure 3.5.

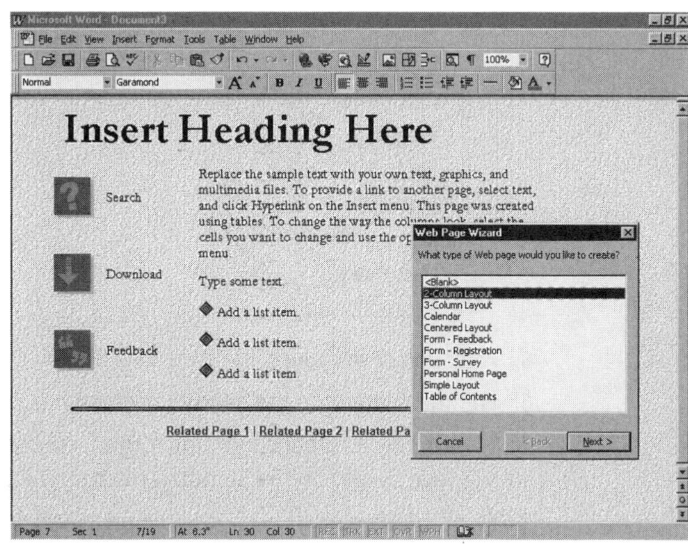

Figure 3.5.
The first screen of the Word 97 Web Page Wizard asks what type of Web page you want to create.

3. Select one of the following page types (you may have more than those shown in the following list if you installed the items from the Office 97 ValuPack):

 <blank>
 2-Column Layout
 3-Column Layout
 Calendar
 Centered Layout
 Form—Feedback
 Form—Registration
 Form—Survey
 Personal Home Page
 Simple Layout
 Table of Contents

NOTE: The CD furnished with this book includes examples of Web pages created with the Word 97 Web Page Wizard. Each page type and style is represented in the examples.

4. After you make your selection, Word 97 displays the page template in its edit window. Click **N**ext to continue with the Web Page Wizard. Word 97 asks what visual style you want on the screen, as shown in Figure 3.6. Select one of the following styles (you may have more if you installed the items from the Office 97 ValuPack):

 Community
 Contemporary
 Elegant
 Festive
 Harvest
 Jazzy
 Outdoors
 Professional

5. After you select your page style, click **F**inish. The page opens in Word 97.
6. Edit the content on the page as necessary.
7. To save the Web page in HTML format, choose **F**ile | **S**ave (Ctrl+S), or click the Save button on the Standard toolbar. The Save As dialog box appears.
8. From the Save **i**n area, choose the drive and directory to which you want to save the file.

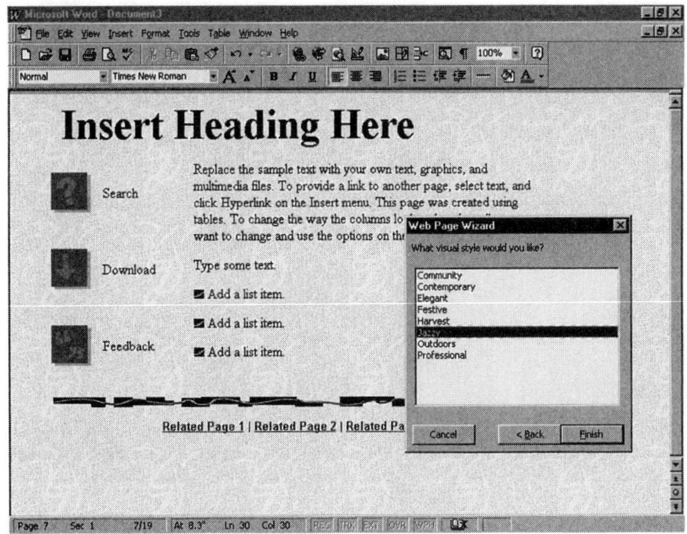

Figure 3.6.
The second screen of the Word 97 Web Page Wizard asks what type of style you want for your Web page.

9. From the Save as **t**ype field, choose HTML document (`*.html`; `*.htm`; `*.htx`).
10. In the File **n**ame field, enter a name for the Web page. If you do not specify an extension, the page is saved with the `.html` extension. Append the filename with an `.htx` extension if the page contains IDC connector file information.
11. Click S**a**ve. Word 97 saves the Web page and all associated graphics to the location you specify.

Designing HTML Forms in Word 97

When you design a form in Word 97, you insert ActiveX form element controls into your Web page. Word 97 inserts boundaries above and below the form fields to designate the top and bottom of the form. All the controls you place on your page should appear within these boundaries, as shown in Figure 3.7.

You can learn more about working with IDC connector files in **Chapter 13**.

To add form fields to your Word 97 Web page, follow these steps:

1. Position the insertion point where you want to insert the form field.
2. Choose **I**nsert | **F**orms, and select one of the form fields from the list of available choices. When you insert a form field on your page, Word 97 automatically places you in Form Design mode. In addition, the Control Toolbox appears, from which you can easily add more form fields to your Web page.

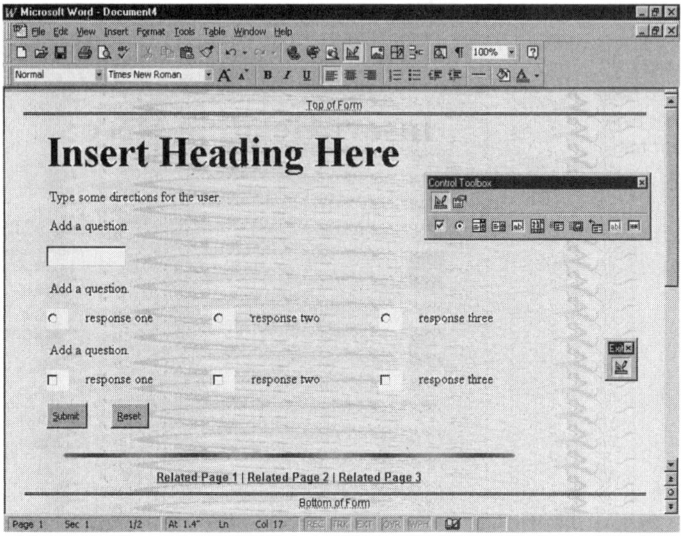

Figure 3.7.
Place all your form fields between the Top of Form and Bottom of Form boundaries in the Word document.

Table 3.1 displays a list of the form field choices available with the **I**nsert | **F**orms command.

3. To edit the properties of the form field, double-click the control to display the properties for the form field. The Properties dialog box appears.
4. Select the Alphabetic tab, shown in Figure 3.8, to list the form field properties alphabetically or the Categorized tab, shown in Figure 3.9, to list the properties by category. Then enter the values for the form fields in the property table.

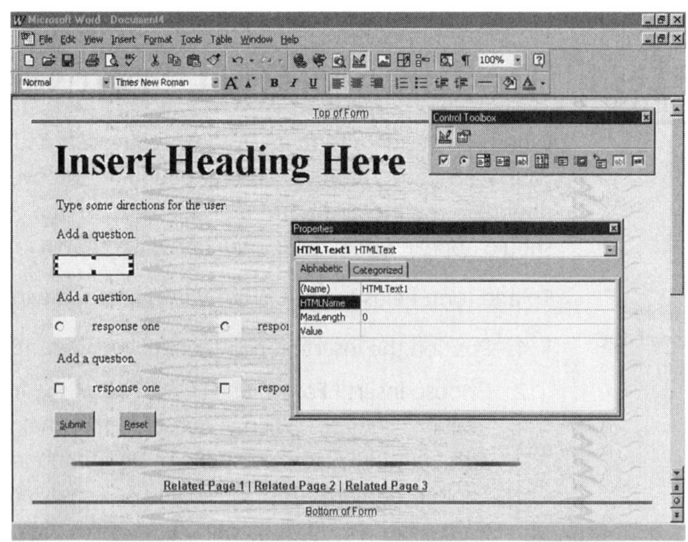

Figure 3.8.
The Alphabetic tab lists all form field properties alphabetically.

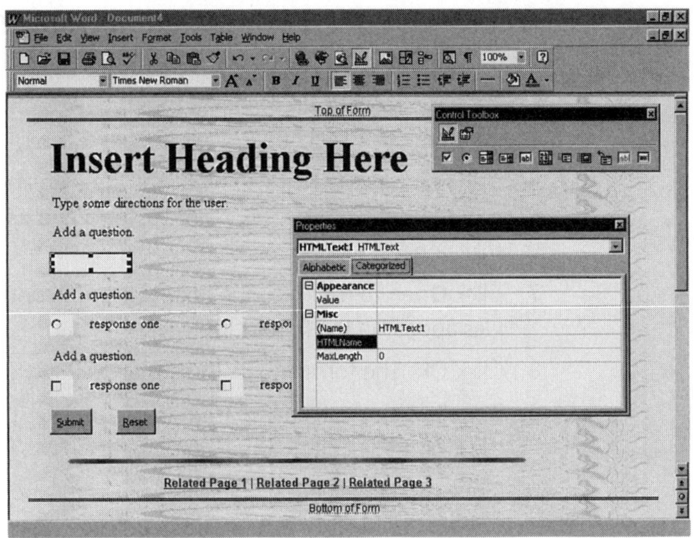

Figure 3.9.
The Categorized tab lists all form field properties by category.

5. Add other controls to your form as outlined in the previous steps. Make sure that you include a Submit or Image Submit button on your form to submit the data entries to the server.
6. When you complete the design of your form, select the Exit Design Mode button in the control toolbox. (This is the first icon in the row above the form fields toolbar.)

Importing Your Form to FrontPage and Assigning a Form Handler

If you want the form to process the data entered by the user, you must write a custom script to process the form. If you are familiar with scripting languages such as VBScript or JavaScript, this should be no problem for you. If you are not familiar with scripting languages, you can import the Web page into a FrontPage web and use a WebBot component to process the form for you.

Any way you decide to process the form, you may find it easier to import your form into a FrontPage web and assign the form handler from there. You can also use FrontPage 97 to generate a VBScript or JavaScript to process the form. To import the form into a FrontPage web, follow these steps:

1. From the FrontPage Explorer, create or open a web in which to import the form.
2. From Folder view in the FrontPage Explorer, select the folder to which you want to import the form and its images.

3. Choose **F**ile | **I**mport. The Import File to FrontPage Web dialog box appears.
4. Click the **A**dd File button. The Add File to Import List dialog box appears.
5. Use the Look **i**n field to locate the drive and directory in which the Word 97 form and its associated images appear.
6. Shift+click or Ctrl+click to highlight the filenames you want to import. Make sure that you include the Word 97 form and its associated images in the selection.
7. Click **O**pen to return to the Import File to FrontPage Web dialog box. The files appear in the Import list.
8. Click OK. The form and its images appear in your web.
9. Double-click the filename from the FrontPage Explorer to open the form in the FrontPage Editor. The page appears in the FrontPage Editor window.
10. Right-click anywhere within the form and choose Form Properties from the pop-up menu. The Form Properties dialog box shown in Figure 3.10 is displayed.

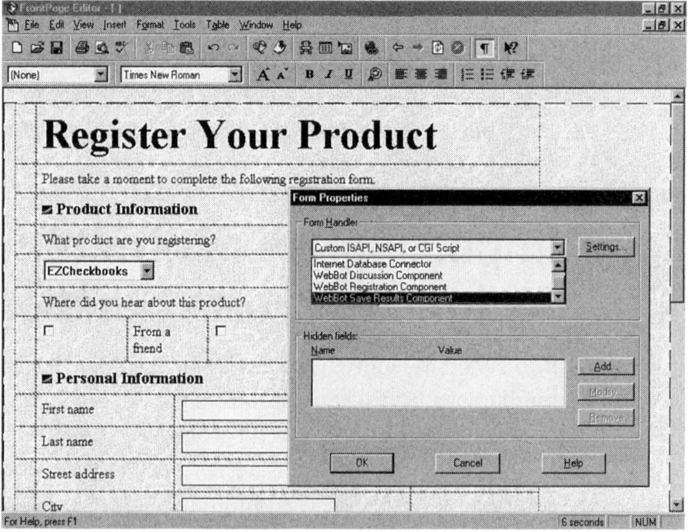

Figure 3.10.
Use the Form Properties dialog box in the FrontPage 97 Editor to assign a form handler to your form.

For more information about forms and form handlers, refer to **Chapter 12**.

11. From the Form **H**andler drop-down menu, select the type of form handler you want to use and then click the Settings button to configure the form handler.

Converting Word Documents to HTML Pages

The second option you have in generating Web documents in Word 97 is to begin your document as a Word document, and then save it to HTML format. Word 97 furnishes several document templates and wizards. However, many of these document templates do not convert to HTML format well.

If your Word document is destined to be an HTML Web page, you should take some precautions while designing it. Remember there are items that will not convert or display well after they convert to HTML. If your documents contain any of the items shown in Table 3.2, they will not appear in your Web page after conversion. Shown in Table 3.3 is a list of items that convert into HTML with some changes in formatting.

For a more detailed explanation of the items shown in Tables 3.2 and 3.3, see the Word 97 Help topic "Learn what happens when you save a Word 97 document as a Web page."

Table 3.2. Items that do not convert into HTML.

Category	*Items that Do Not Convert*
Text Effects	Drop caps, text effects, text boxes, drop shadows, highlighting
Graphic Elements	AutoShapes, text effects, text boxes, drop shadows
Special Formatting	Comments, revision marks, page numbering, borders around paragraphs or words
Page Formatting	Margins, borders, headers, footers, footnotes, endnotes, multiple columns

Table 3.3. Items that convert into HTML with changes.

Original Formatting in Word 97	*Final HTML Result*
Font effects (Emboss, Engrave, All Caps, Small Caps, Double Strike-through, Shadow, and Outline text); animated text; text inserted by fields; tables of contents; tables of authorities; indexes	Normal HTML text[1]
Special underlines, such as dotted underlines	Underlined text
Word picture objects inserted during Web page authoring format; pictures and clip art	GIF images

continues

Table 3.3. continued

Original Formatting in Word 97	*Final HTML Result*
other than JPG images; equations, charts, and other OLE objects	
Lines	Horizontal lines
Tabs	HTML Tab character[2]
Page numbers generated by tables of contents and indexes	Asterisks as hyperlinks
All tables	Fixed-width tables[3]

Notes for Table 3.3:

1. Font sizes convert to the closest HTML size available.
2. Some browsers do not support the HTML Tab character.
3. Tables convert to fixed width tables by default. You can override this by entering `PercentageTableWidth=1` in the `HKEY_LOCAL_MACHINE\Software\Microsoft\Shared Tools\Text Converters\Export\HTML\Options` directory of the Windows 95 Registry.

Creating Web Pages from Word 97 Templates and Wizards

If you are reasonably certain that your Word document will convert to HTML format without too many formatting changes, you can open the document and save it in HTML format.

To create a Word 97 Web page using templates and wizards, follow these steps:

1. From Word 97, choose **F**ile | **N**ew (Ctrl+N). The New dialog box is displayed.
2. Choose the tab that contains the type of document you want to create. The available tabs are General (for blank documents), Letters and Faxes, Memos, Reports, Legal Pleadings, Publications, and Other Documents. To create a blank document, select the Blank Document template shown in Figure 3.11.
3. Verify in the lower-right section of the New dialog box that the Create New **D**ocument radio button is selected (it is selected by default). If you want to create a document template instead, select the Create New **T**emplate radio button.
4. Double-click the template you want to use to create your new document. The page opens in Word 97.
5. Develop your Word document using the precautions described in the "Converting Word Documents to HTML Pages" section earlier in this chapter.

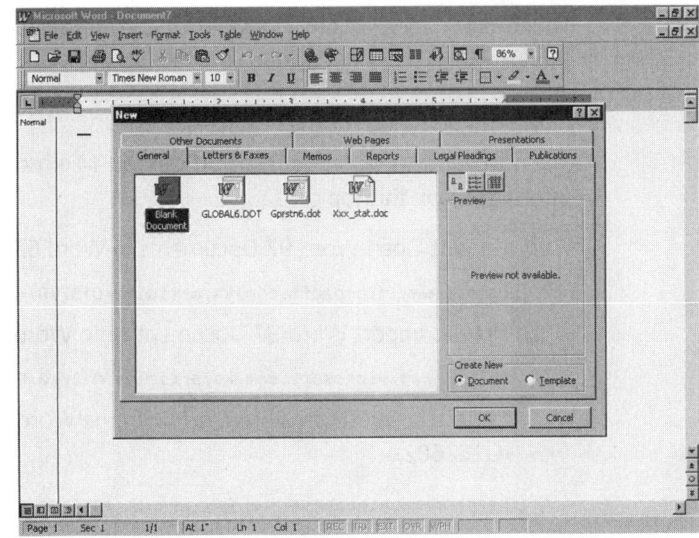

Figure 3.11.
Select a template from the New dialog box. The Blank Document template creates a blank Word document.

6. To save the Web page in HTML format, choose **F**ile | **S**ave (Ctrl+S), or click the Save button on the Standard toolbar. The Save As dialog box appears.
7. From the Save **i**n area, choose the drive and directory to which you want to save the file.
8. From the Save as **t**ype field, choose HTML document (`*.html`; `*.htm`; `*.htx`).
9. In the File **n**ame field, enter a name for the Web page. If you do not specify an extension, the page is saved with an `.html` extension.
10. Click **S**ave to save the page to your hard disk.

Using Native Word 97 Documents in Your Web

There is one important advantage to using your Word 97 documents on the Web or an intranet in their native format: You do not need to be concerned about the features you use in your Word documents, because they appear the same whether you view them in hard print or through a Web browser. There is a downside, however. If you publish your Word document to the Web or an intranet, users will not be able to view the document online unless they have a Word viewer or Word 97.

This also brings up another issue: Is it best to save the document in Word 97 format or in an older file format? Generally, it is best to provide a file format that the majority of users can view. A file converter for Word 6 and Word 95 enables users of these versions to view Word 97 documents. You can download it from the following URL, which gives an excellent overview of the differences between Word 97 and its predecessors:

`http://www.microsoft.com/word/freestuff/converters/wrd97cnv.htm`

The following Knowledge Base articles on Microsoft's Web site offer additional information on this topic:

- Cannot Open Word 97 Documents in Word 6.0 or 7.0 (Q157666):

  `http://www.microsoft.com/kb/articles/Q157/6/66.htm`
- How to Import Word 97 Documents into Word 2.x, 6.x, 7.x (Q157091):

  `http://www.microsoft.com/kb/articles/Q157/0/91.htm`
- Word 97: Questions About Saving in the Word 6.0/95 File Format (Q162602):

  `http://www.microsoft.com/kb/articles/Q162/6/02.htm`

The Microsoft Word Viewer for Windows 95, version 7.1, allows users to view documents created in Word 1.0 and later. This viewer is freeware, and you can download it from the following URL:

`http://www.microsoft.com/word/internet/viewer/viewer95/default.htm`

Linking Between Word 97 and FrontPage 97 Documents

You'll learn more about arranging and integrating Web pages and Office 97 content in **Chapter 7**.

Now you know three ways you can use Word to help you develop content for your Web or intranet site. You can also create hyperlinks between Word 97 and your Web pages, or you can create hyperlinks from your Web pages to your Word 97 documents. Depending on how you arrange your content, you'll need to create links to documents that reside in your current FrontPage web, on your intranet server, or on your local or network hard drive. Fortunately, it is easy to create hyperlinks in Word 97 and FrontPage 97.

Creating Hyperlinks from FrontPage 97

There are several ways you can organize your content after it is developed. One approach is to import all content into webs that exist on your Web server. You can use the FrontPage Explorer to import and manage all the content on the server and the FrontPage Editor to create links to and from all the Web content.

To create a link to a document in your current web, follow these steps:

1. From the FrontPage Explorer, use the **F**ile | **I**mport command to import the content into your current FrontPage web. The steps to complete this are similar to those outlined in "Importing Your Form to FrontPage and Assigning a Form Handler" earlier in this chapter.
2. Choose **T**ools | Show Fr**o**ntPage Editor or click the Show FrontPage Editor button on the toolbar. The FrontPage Editor opens.
3. From the FrontPage Editor, create or open a page on which to place the link.
4. Enter or select the text on which the user will click to navigate to the target document.
5. Choose **E**dit | Hyperlin**k** (Ctrl+K), or click the Create or Edit Hyperlink button on the Standard Toolbar. The Create Hyperlink dialog box appears.
6. Select the Current FrontPage Web tab, shown in Figure 3.12, if it is not already selected.

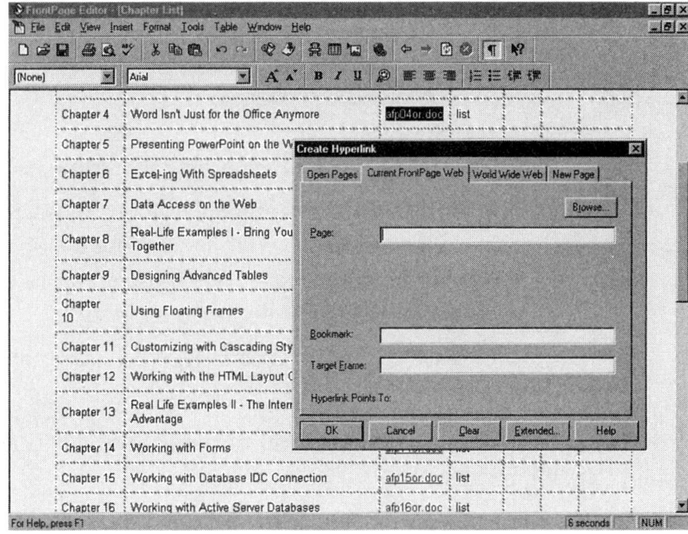

Figure 3.12.
Use the Current FrontPage Web tab to create links to documents that reside in your currently opened FrontPage web.

7. In the **P**age field, enter the relative URL of the page or document to which you want to link. Alternatively, choose the B**r**owse button. The Current Web dialog box appears. Locate the file in your current web, and click OK to return to the Current FrontPage Web tab.
8. Click OK to exit the Create Hyperlink dialog box. The link appears on your page.

Sometimes you need to create links to documents that reside on the same server, but not in the currently opened web. For this situation, use the World Wide Web tab of the Create Hyperlink dialog box, and select the Other protocol.

To create a link to a document in another web on your server, follow these steps:

1. From the FrontPage Editor, create or open a page on which to place the link.
2. Enter or select the text on which the user will click to navigate to the target document.
3. Choose **E**dit | Hyperlin**k** (Ctrl+K), or click the Create or Edit Hyperlink button on the Standard toolbar. The Create Hyperlink dialog box appears.
4. Select the World Wide Web tab shown in Figure 3.13.

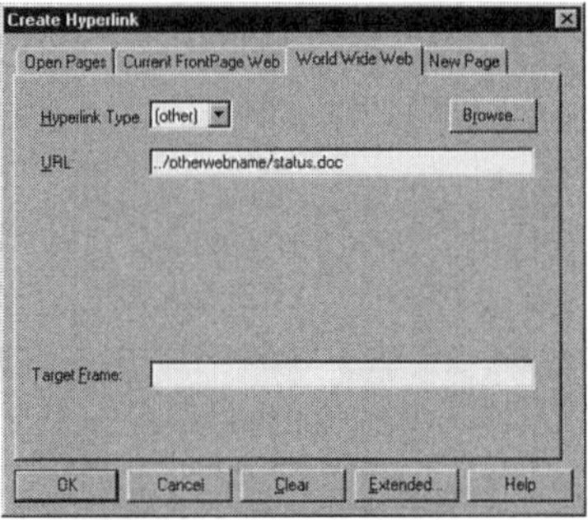

Figure 3.13.
Use the `Other` protocol in the World Wide Web tab to enter relative URLs to files that reside in other webs on your server.

5. From the **H**yperlink Type drop-down menu, select the `Other` protocol.
6. In the URL field, enter the relative URL of the page or document to which you want to link. Alternatively, choose the B**r**owse button to navigate to the page with your browser. When you return to the World Wide Web tab, verify that the **U**RL is displayed correctly.
7. Click OK to exit the Create Hyperlink dialog box. The link is displayed on your page.

To create a link to a Word 97 document on your local or network hard drive, follow these steps:

1. From the FrontPage Editor, create or open a page on which to place the link.
2. Enter or select the text on which the user will click to navigate to the target document.
3. Choose **E**dit | Hyperlin**k** (Ctrl+K), or click the Create or Edit Hyperlink button on the Standard toolbar. The Create Hyperlink dialog box appears.
4. Select the World Wide Web tab.
5. From the **H**yperlink Type drop-down menu, select the `file:` protocol.
6. In the URL field, enter the absolute URL of the page or document to which you want to link. (An example is shown in Figure 3.14.) Alternatively, choose the B**r**owse button to navigate to the document with your browser. When

you return to the World Wide Web tab, verify that the **U**RL appears correctly.

7. Click OK to exit the Create Hyperlink dialog box. The link appears on your page.

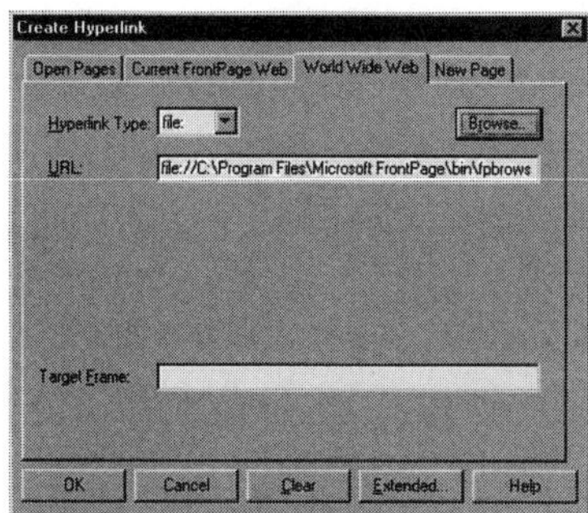

Figure 3.14.
Choose the `file:` *protocol in the Create Hyperlink dialog box to create a link to a file on your local or network hard drive.*

Linking to and from Office 97 Documents in File Directories

The steps to create hyperlinks in Word 97 differ slightly from those in FrontPage 97. You can create hyperlinks to Web pages, documents on your local hard drive, or documents on a network hard drive from a single dialog box. You also can create links to bookmarks from the same dialog box.

Creating Hyperlinks from Word 97

Use the Insert Hyperlink dialog box to create hyperlinks to Web or Office documents. To create a hyperlink from Word 97, follow these steps:

1. Enter or select the text that the user will click to navigate to the Web page or Office 97 document.
2. Choose **I**nsert | Hyper**l**ink (Ctrl+K), or click the Insert Hyperlink button on the Standard toolbar. You may be prompted to save your document before the Insert Hyperlink dialog box shown in Figure 3.15 appears.
3. In the **L**ink to file or URL field, enter the path to the file that you want to link to, or use the B**r**owse button to locate the file on your local or network hard drive. After you select the file, choose OK from the Link to File dialog box to return to the Insert Hyperlink dialog box.
4. To link to a bookmark on the page, enter the name of the bookmark in the **N**amed location in file (optional) field, or use the Bro**w**se button to select the bookmark from those available on the page.

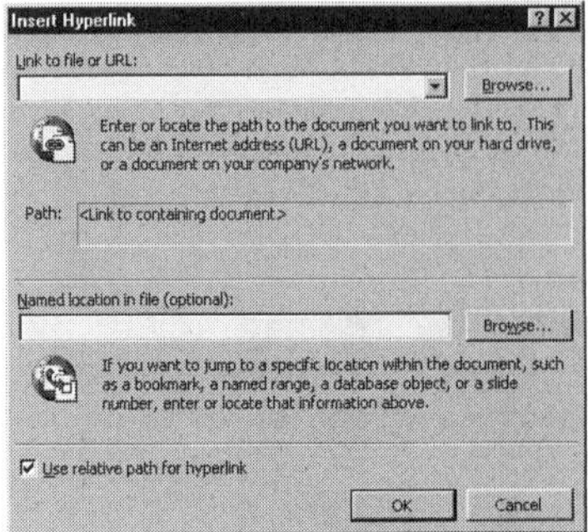

Figure 3.15.
The Insert Hyperlink dialog box in Word 97 allows you to create links to Web pages and other documents.

5. To create a relative URL, select the **U**se relative path for hyperlink check box. Deselect this option to create an absolute URL to the file.
6. Choose OK to create the hyperlink. The hyperlink appears in your Word document.

Workshop Wrap-Up

In this chapter, you got a quick overview of some of the key elements in creating Web pages with Word 97. You compared the commands that Word 97 uses for Web authoring with those found in FrontPage. You learned how to generate Web pages with Word 97's Web Page Wizard. You learned how to place form fields into a Word document, and where you can edit the properties of the form fields. Finally, you compared how to create hyperlinks in FrontPage 97 with how to create hyperlinks in Word 97.

Admittedly, this chapter only scratches the surface of how you can use Word 97 to develop Web pages. However, because you have FrontPage 97, you can leave Word 97 to accomplish what it really does best—creating word-processing documents that you can use in your Web site or your intranet. Although Word 97 is a very capable Web page authoring tool, it shines best in its capability to create word-processing documents. And as you will learn in Chapter 7, you can link to native Word 97 documents in your web or intranet.

Next Steps

In Chapter 4, "Presenting PowerPoint on the Web," you will examine how to use PowerPoint 97 to create presentations and animated banners for your Web site or intranet. To learn more about how Office 97 documents can integrate with your FrontPage Web site, refer to the following chapters:

- In Chapter 5, "Excel-ing with Spreadsheets," you learn how to use Microsoft Excel 97 to generate Web page content.

- Chapter 6, "Data Access on the Web," teaches you how to generate database files that create dynamic interactive content for your Web or intranet.
- Chapter 7, "Real-Life Examples: Bringing Your Intranet Together," provides examples of how FrontPage 97 and Office 97 can be used in concert to pull all content on an intranet together.
- To learn how to communicate with Access databases through Internet Database Connector files, see Chapter 13, "Working with IDC Database Connection."
- In Chapter 14, "Using Active Server Databases," you learn how to use Access to generate databases that work with Internet Information Server's Active Server Pages.

Q&A

Q: When I try to follow a hyperlink to a Word document from a page in the FrontPage Editor, I get a message that reads "*filename*. This file is already in use. Select a new name or close the file in use by another application." I don't have the file open anywhere. What's wrong?

A: Verify that the hyperlink to your file is correct. One of the things you should verify is the number of slashes after the `file:` protocol and before the path to the file.

Q: When I try to follow a hyperlink to a Word document from a page in the FrontPage Editor, I get an Open File As dialog box. It asks me if I want to open the file as an HTML, RTF, or Text document. How do I open it in Word format from FrontPage?

A: If you are following a hyperlink to a Word document from the FrontPage Editor, FrontPage opens the Word document as an HTML page in the FrontPage Editor. If it is your intention to convert the document to a Web page and save it to your web, choose to open the file in RTF format.

However, if you want to open the document from FrontPage in the native Word 97 format, you must open the document from the FrontPage Explorer. First, configure Word as an editor in FrontPage. To do this, open the FrontPage Explorer. Choose Tools | Options and select the Configure Editors tab in the Options dialog box. To add Word as your `.doc` file editor, click the Add button. In the File Type field, enter `doc`. In the Editor Name field, enter `Word 97`. In the Command field, enter the path to the Word 97 executable file, or use the Browse button to locate the file on your hard drive. The default installation location for the executable file is `c:\Program Files\Microsoft Office\Office\winword.exe`.

To view the document in native Word format, right-click the name of the Word document you want to see from Hyperlink view or Folder view in the FrontPage Explorer. Then choose Open With from the pop-up menu, and select Microsoft Word as your editor.

CHAPTER

FOUR

Presenting PowerPoint on the Web

In this chapter, you

- ❑ Learn to add hyperlinks between your PowerPoint presentation and other documents in your web
- ❑ Learn to create hyperlinks that link to other Office documents and to Web pages
- ❑ Create hyperlinks from text, images, and action buttons in your presentation
- ❑ Save your presentations in HTML format
- ❑ Learn how to create a banner, insert clip art and text, and save it as a PowerPoint animation file

Tasks in this chapter:

- ❑ Creating a PowerPoint Presentation for the Web
- ❑ Creating Text Hyperlinks to Other Slides in PowerPoint 97
- ❑ Creating Image Hyperlinks to Web Pages
- ❑ Using Action Buttons for Hyperlinks
- ❑ Saving Your Presentations to HTML Format
- ❑ Creating and Saving Banners with PowerPoint
- ❑ Inserting and Animating Clip Art

Many office professionals use presentation software to introduce ideas, facilitate meetings, and assist in sales and marketing. Now, with PowerPoint 97, you can do all this and more on the Web or your intranet. As with other Office 97 applications, you can create links between PowerPoint 97 applications and Web pages to create seamless interfaces that blend the needs of the office with the power of the Web. PowerPoint contains built-in features that bring animated presentations to your Web pages. You can also use PowerPoint to create animated banners and graphics. This chapter introduces you to some of the basic commands you need to create PowerPoint Presentations for the Web or your intranet. It also addresses how to import this content into your FrontPage web and incorporate it into your Web pages.

Creating Web-Based Presentations

You can use PowerPoint to create a presentation for the Web or your intranet using all the commands that are available when developing

Learn about other ways you can economize images in **Chapter 18**.

presentations for computer displays or hard copy. If you are developing presentations for a closed internal intranet (a site connected through network adapters only, for example), bandwidth consideration is usually not an issue. However, when you place your presentation on a public access site, you must consider modem speeds and bandwidth. To do so, you can keep the presentation neat and trim by limiting the use of large bitmapped graphics and using clip art or small bitmaps instead, for example. Also, you can avoid using large movie clips, as animation files can get quite large; use animated text effects in your presentations instead.

Creating a PowerPoint Presentation for the Web

There are several ways to begin creating your presentation in PowerPoint. You can access different templates and styles from the New dialog box, which is displayed after you choose the **F**ile | **N**ew command, or choose the New button on the standard toolbar. In brief, the various tabs in the New dialog box perform the following functions:

- ❑ The Blank Presentation template in the General tab allows you to begin a new presentation from scratch. Each slide in the presentation has a white background with placeholders for text and other content, depending on the slide template you choose.
- ❑ The selections in the Presentation Design tab allow you to create a single slide based on a presentation style and slide template.
- ❑ The selections in the Presentations tab allow you to create a series of slides based on a presentation style. The Auto Content Wizard is also in this tab. (You will use this wizard in the Corporate Home Page task described next.)
- ❑ The selections in the Web Pages tab provide two templates for Web page banners.

In the following task, you use the Auto Content Wizard to create a presentation. PowerPoint 97 comes with many presentation styles for business or personal use, which are ideal for use in office intranets and Web sites. The Auto Content Wizard allows you to create several different styles, as listed in Table 4.1.

Table 4.1. Presentation styles available in the Auto Content Wizard.

Category	*Style*
General	Recommending a Strategy
	Reporting Progress
	Generic

Category	*Style*
Corporate	Company Meeting
	Corporate Home Page
	Financial Overview
Projects	Status
	Project Overview
Operations/HR	Information Kiosk
	Organization Overview
Sales/Marketing	Marketing Plan
	Business Plan
	Products/Services Overview
Personal	Announcement Flyer
	Personal Home Page
Carnegie Coach	Facilitating a Meeting
	Introducing a Speaker
	Managing HR's Changing Role
	Motivating a Team
	Presentation Guidelines
	Presenting a Technical Report
	Selling Your Ideas
	Thanking a Speaker

Complete the following task to create a Corporate Home Page presentation. I used this template to create the example used in this chapter. Begin with the following steps:

1. Choose **F**ile | **N**ew (Ctrl+N). The New Presentation dialog box is displayed.
2. Click the Presentations tab, shown in Figure 4.1. Several presentation templates appear. A preview of the presentation style is displayed on the right side of the New Presentation dialog box.
3. Double-click the Auto Content Wizard. The Auto Content Wizard screen shown in Figure 4.2 is displayed.
4. Click **N**ext to select your presentation type from the screen shown in Figure 4.3. You can select from one of the presentation styles listed in Table 4.1. For this example, choose the Corporate button and select the Corporate Home Page template.

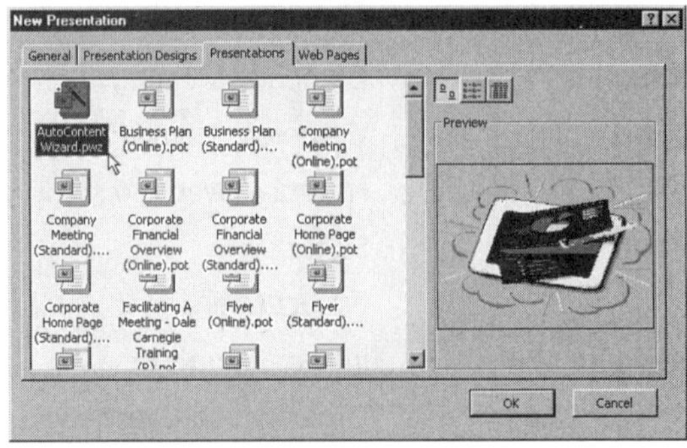

Figure 4.1.
Choose the Auto Content Wizard from the Presentations tab in the New Presentation dialog box.

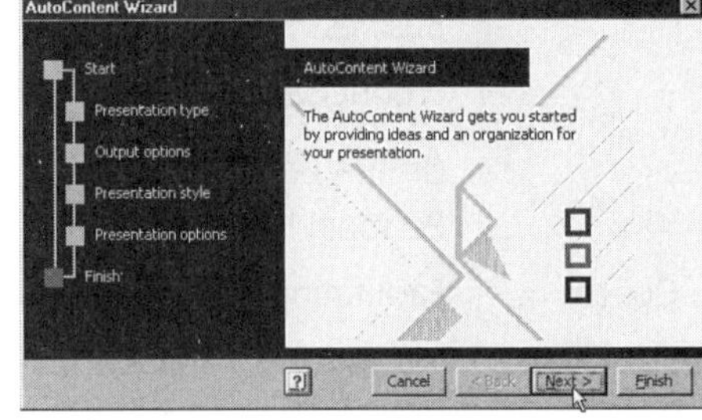

Figure 4.2.
The first screen of the Auto Content Wizard.

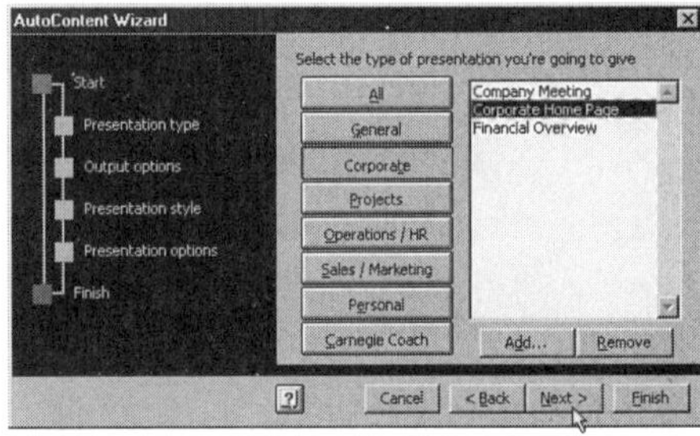

Figure 4.3.
Click the Corporate button and select the Corporate Home Page template.

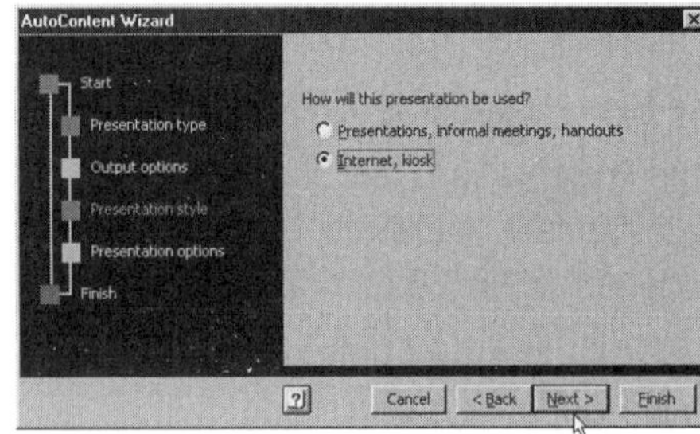

Figure 4.4.
Choose Internet, kiosk to create a presentation for the Web.

5. Click **N**ext to choose how you will use the presentation. The screen in Figure 4.4 is displayed. Select **I**nternet, kiosk.
6. Click **N**ext to choose additional information you want in your presentation. The screen in Figure 4.5 is displayed. Select any of the following additional items:

- To include a copyright notice on each page of the presentation, check the **C**opyright notice on each page check box, and enter your name or company name in the box beneath the check box.
- To include the date that the presentation was last updated, check the **D**ate last updated check box.
- To include your e-mail address, check the E-Mail address check box, and add your e-mail address in the box beneath the check box.

7. Click **N**ext, and then click **F**inish to generate the presentation slides. PowerPoint creates several sample slides to which you can add additional text, images or animation, and hyperlinks.

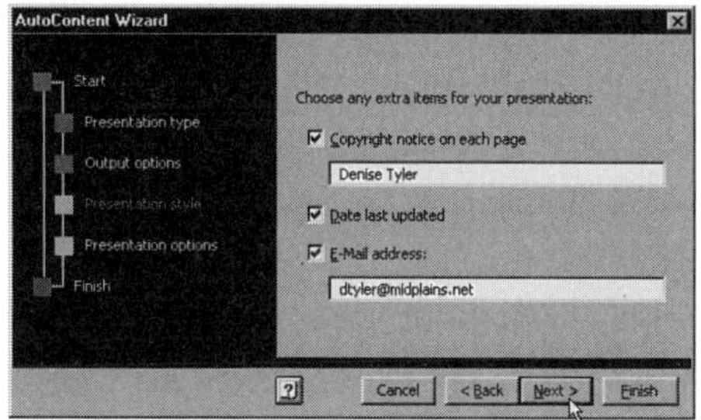

Figure 4.5.
Choose additional items that you want to appear on each slide in your presentation.

For a more thorough discussion of the features in PowerPoint 97, refer to *Microsoft Office 97 Unleashed* by Paul McFedries, et al., by Sams Publishing. This comprehensive desktop reference book covers many features found in all Office 97 applications.

Now that you have a series of slides, you can edit the content to suit the needs of your presentation. When the presentation opens in PowerPoint, you will see the slides listed in Outline view. From this view, you can easily change the titles of each slide in the presentation. To add another blank slide in the presentation, position the insertion point at the beginning or end of a slide title in the outline and press the Enter key. To edit the content of the slides, choose **V**iew | **S**lide. This places you in Slide view, from which you can edit and add content to your pages.

Preparing the Project Files for This Chapter

Sample files are included on the CD that accompanies this book. To complete the following tasks, you need to create a web in FrontPage 97. After you create the web, import the sample files into the home directory in your web. Then double-click the presentation file to open it in PowerPoint 97.

To create the web and open the presentation file, follow these steps:

1. From the FrontPage Explorer, choose **F**ile | **N**ew | FrontPage **W**eb (Ctrl+N). The New FrontPage Web dialog box is displayed.

2. From the **T**emplate or Wizard field, select Empty Web and choose OK. The Empty Web Template dialog box is displayed.
3. In the **W**eb Server or File Location field, choose the server on which you want to create the web from the drop-down list box.
4. In the **N**ame of New FrontPage Web field, enter `Chapter4`.
5. Choose OK. FrontPage creates the web. It does not include a home page.
6. To import the project files that are located on the CD, choose **F**ile | **I**mport from the FrontPage Explorer. The Import File to FrontPage Web dialog box is displayed.
7. Click the **A**dd File button. The Add File to Import List dialog box is displayed.
8. Locate the directory on the CD that contains the sample files for this chapter. Highlight the following files:

    ```
    Chapter4.ppt
    default.htm
    worddoc.doc
    ```

9. Click **O**pen. When you return to the Import File to FrontPage Web dialog box, the files appear in the Import list.
10. Choose OK to import the files. They appear in the root directory of your web.
11. From the root directory, double-click the `Chapter4.ppt` presentation file to open it. PowerPoint opens, and the first screen of the presentation is displayed.

Adding Hyperlinks

With the presentation now open in PowerPoint 97, you can create hyperlinks to other content in your web. The first way you can add interactivity to your presentations is to create hyperlinks that navigate through the presentation slides and to other Office 97 and web documents. Just as you can create hyperlinks from text and images in a web page, you can also do so with your presentations.

Creating Text Hyperlinks to Other Slides in PowerPoint 97

It is important to save any changes you make to your presentation before you create a hyperlink. Office 97 applications base relative URLs on the present location of the file. In the case of our example, the presentation file is located in the home directory of your FrontPage web. By importing your presentation into your FrontPage web, you can maintain the proper relationship between your presentation and the other content in your web. PowerPoint 97 creates both absolute and relative URLs. In most cases, you should create relative URLs to other content within your web.

When you open your PowerPoint presentation, the first slide in the presentation is displayed. To create some hyperlinks, use the Page Down key to navigate to the second slide in the presentation, titled "Adding Hyperlinks." You will create links from text and images on this slide.

To create the links on this slide, follow these steps:

1. From the first presentation slide in PowerPoint 97, use the Page Down key to navigate to the "Adding Hyperlinks" slide.
2. Click and drag the mouse to highlight the text that reads "Using PowerPoint for the Web," as shown in Figure 4.6.

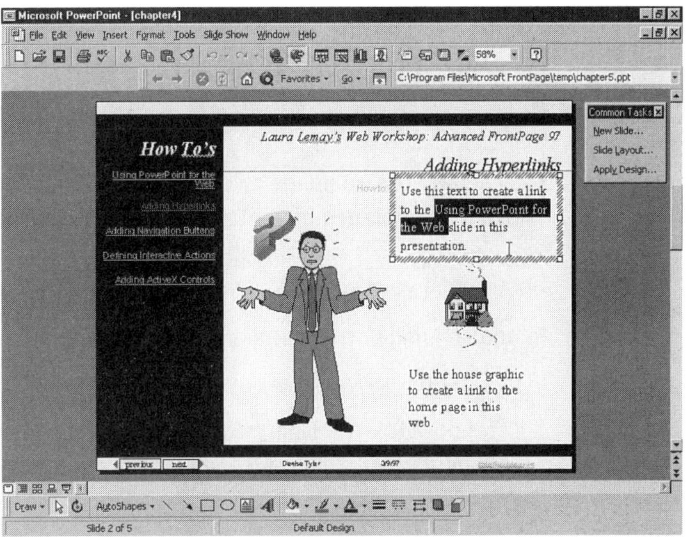

Figure 4.6.
Select the text that reads "Using PowerPoint for the Web" to create the hyperlink in your presentation.

3. Choose **I**nsert | Hyper**l**ink, or click the Insert Hyperlink button on the Standard toolbar. The Insert Hyperlink dialog box shown in Figure 4.7 is displayed.
4. Select the Bro**w**se button in the **N**amed location in file (optional) section. The Hyperlink to Slide dialog box is displayed.
5. Select the slide to which you are linking from the **S**lide Title field. For this example, choose the "Using PowerPoint for the Web" slide.
6. Click OK to exit the Hyperlink to Slide dialog box.

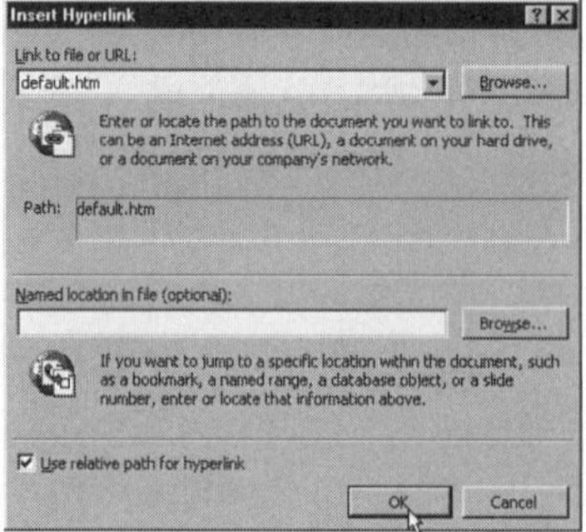

Figure 4.7.
Use the Insert Hyperlink dialog box to create the hyperlinks in your presentation.

7. If you want to create a relative URL for the link, verify that the **U**se relative path for hyperlink check box is checked. (It is checked by default.)
8. Click OK to exit the Insert Hyperlink dialog box. PowerPoint 97 creates a link to the slide.

Creating Image Hyperlinks to Web Pages

You can also use an image to create a hyperlink in a PowerPoint presentation. The following example demonstrates two features: creating image hyperlinks and creating hyperlinks to pages in your web. The "Adding Hyperlinks" slide contains an image of a house that you can use to create a hyperlink to the home page in your web.

To add an image hyperlink to your home page, follow these steps:

1. Click the picture of the house displayed on the "Adding Hyperlink" slide.
2. Choose **I**nsert | Hyperl**i**nk, or click the Insert Hyperlink button on the Standard toolbar. The Insert Hyperlink dialog box is displayed.
3. In the **L**ink to File or URL field, enter `default.htm`.

TIP: You can also use the **L**ink to File or URL field to create a link to another Office 97 document in your web.

4. To create a relative URL for the link, verify that the **U**se relative path for hyperlink check box is checked. (It is checked by default.)
5. Click OK to exit the Insert Hyperlink dialog box. PowerPoint 97 creates a link to the home page.

Using Action Buttons for Hyperlinks

PowerPoint 97 also includes action buttons that you can place on your presentation. They feature commonly used symbols that are easily recognizable. The first action button is a Custom button on which you can place text or an image. There are also buttons for creating links to Home, Help, Information, Back or Previous, Forward or Next, Beginning, End, Return, Document, Sound, and Movie.

You will use the next slide to create some action buttons. Use the Page Down key to navigate to the slide titled "Adding Navigation Buttons." Then create an action button to the next slide in the presentation as follows:

1. Use the Page Down key to navigate to the "Adding Navigation Buttons" slide.
2. Choose Sli**d**e Show | **A**ction Buttons. A flyout menu is displayed on which there are 12 action button previews, as shown in Figure 4.8.

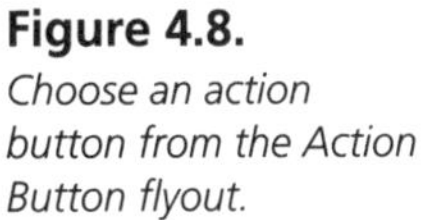

Figure 4.8.
Choose an action button from the Action Button flyout.

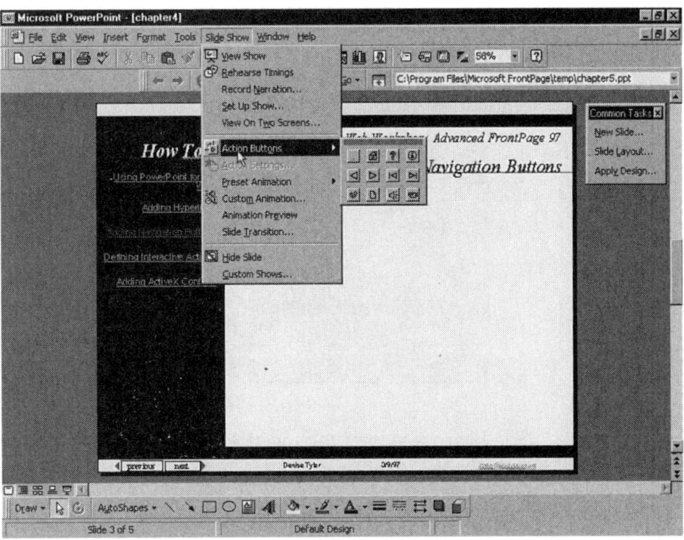

3. Choose the Forward or Next action button (the second button in the second row). The mouse cursor changes into a crosshair pointer and waits for you to place the action button on the slide.
4. Beginning at the top left corner of the button, click and drag to place the button on your page, as shown in Figure 4.9. You will see an outline of the image on the button as you create it. To complete the button, release the mouse button. The Action Settings dialog box shown in Figure 4.10 is displayed.

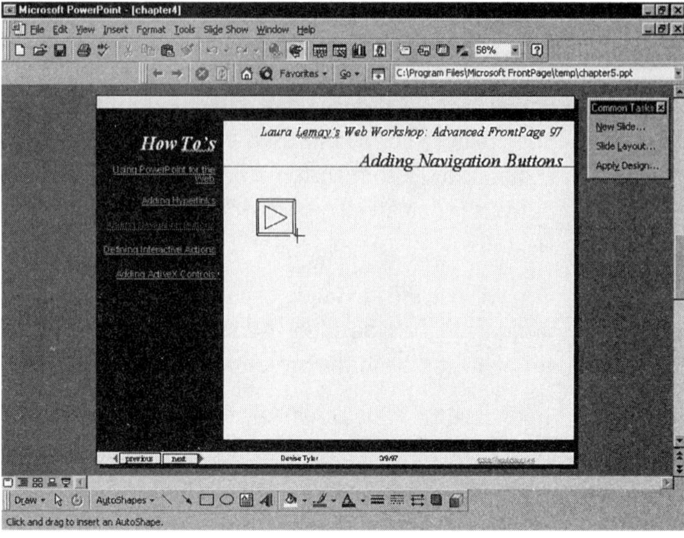

Figure 4.9.
Click and drag to place the action button on your slide.

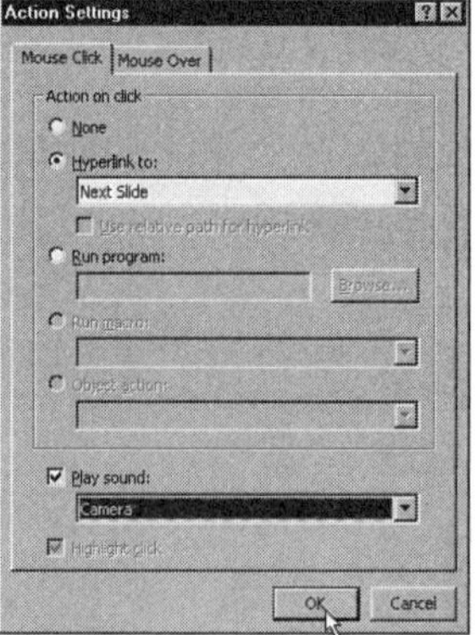

Figure 4.10.
When you complete the action button, the Action Settings dialog box is displayed.

5. There are two tabs in the Action Settings dialog box: The Mouse Click tab creates a hyperlink when the user clicks the button (this is the option to choose for your action button now), and the Mouse Over tab creates a hyperlink when the user moves the mouse over the button. You can also combine both actions:
    - ❑ Select the Mouse Click tab to create a hyperlink that navigates to the destination page when the user clicks the hyperlink area. Choose this option for the action button on your slide.
    - ❑ Select the Mouse Over tab to create a hyperlink that navigates to the destination page when the user moves the mouse over the hyperlink area.

- ❑ To assign more than one action to the same object, you can enter properties in both the Mouse Click and the Mouse Over tabs. A good application for this configuration is to use the Mouse Click tab to set up the hyperlink and the Mouse Over tab to play a sound.

6. In either or both the Mouse Click and Mouse Over tabs, select **H**yperlink to and choose Next Slide. Other available choices are as follows:

   Previous Slide
   First Slide
   Last Slide
   Last Slide Viewed
   End Show
   Custom Show…
   Slide…
   URL…
   Other PowerPoint Presentation…
   Other File…

7. To play a sound when the user selects the link, check the **P**lay sound check box. A good complement to a button-click sound is the Camera sound, which you can choose from the drop-down menu.
8. Choose OK. PowerPoint adds the hyperlink to your presentation. You can preview the operation of the hyperlink by clicking the Slide Show icon that is displayed at the lower-left corner of the PowerPoint window.

Now you'll create another example of an action button. This time, you'll use the Home action button to create a link to the home page in your web. To create this action button, follow these steps:

1. Choose Sli**d**e Show | **A**ction Buttons.
2. Choose the Home action button from the flyout menu.
3. Beginning at the top-left corner of the button, click and drag to place the button on your slide. The Action Settings dialog box is displayed.
4. Select the Mouse Click tab.
5. Select **H**yperlink to and choose URL…. The Hyperlink To URL dialog box shown in Figure 4.11 is displayed.
6. Enter the relative path to the home page in the URL field. In this case, the home page is located in the same directory as the presentation file. Enter `default.htm`.

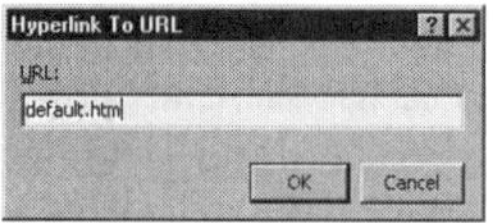

Figure 4.11.
Use the Hyperlink To URL dialog box to create a hyperlink to a page in your web.

7. Check the **P**lay sound check box, and select the Camera sound from the drop-down menu.
8. Choose OK. PowerPoint adds the hyperlink to your presentation.

The last action button you will add on your pages is to a Word document located in your web. To complete this button, follow these steps:

1. Choose Sli**d**e Show | **A**ction Buttons.
2. Choose the Document action button from the flyout menu.
3. Beginning at the top-left corner of the button, click and drag to place the button on your slide. The Action Settings dialog box is displayed.
4. Select the Mouse Click tab.
5. Select **H**yperlink to and choose Other File.... The Hyperlink to Other File dialog box shown in Figure 4.12 is displayed.

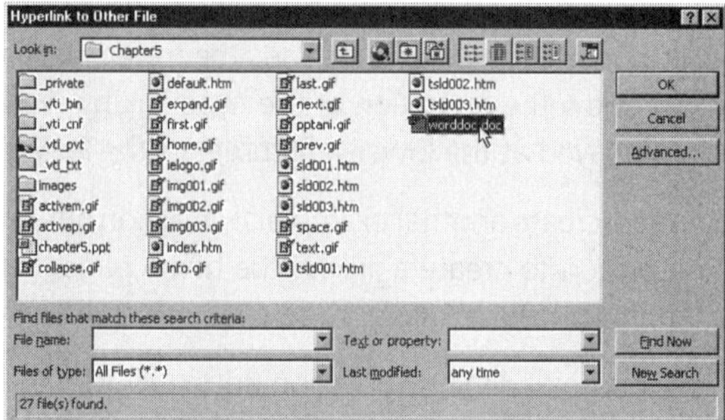

Figure 4.12.
Use the Hyperlink to Other File dialog box to create a hyperlink to an Office 97 document in your web or on your local or network hard disk.

6. When you create a link to a file, you must navigate to the directory in which the file is located and select the file from those in the directory. If you are using the FrontPage Personal Web Server, the file will be located in the following directory by default:

   ```
   c:\FrontPage Webs\Content\Chapter4\worddoc.doc
   ```

   If you are using the Microsoft Personal Web Server, the file is located in the following directory:

   ```
   c:\Webshare\Chapter4\worddoc.doc
   ```

   If your web is located on an Internet Information Server web on your intranet server, you must connect to the network drive to create the link. By

For additional information on these Web servers, refer to **Chapter 1** and **Chapter 2**.

default, Internet Information Server places content in the `c:\InetPub\wwwroot` directory, but yours might differ. The path looks similar to this:

```
c:\InetPub\wwwroot\Chapter4\worddoc.doc
```

After you locate the file, double-click the filename to create the hyperlink.

7. Check the **U**se relative path for hyperlink checkbox beneath the Hyperlink to field. Notice that the directory path is removed from the Hyperlink to field and now reads `worddoc.doc`.
8. Check the **P**lay sound checkbox, and select the Camera sound from the drop-down menu.
9. Choose OK. PowerPoint adds the hyperlink to your presentation.

Saving Your Presentations for the Web

PowerPoint 97 includes a built-in Internet Assistant that allows you to save your presentations in Web page format. In the following example, you will save your presentation as individual Web pages. You can also save your presentations as Web pages in a frameset or as PowerPoint animations.

Saving Your Presentations to HTML Format

Before you save your Web pages, it's a good idea to run the slide show while you are in PowerPoint 97. This will ensure that all the hyperlinks you created in your presentation go to the correct places. To view your slide show, choose **V**iew | Slide Sho**w**, or click the Slide Show button on the toolbar in the lower-left corner of your PowerPoint screen. Then test each of the links in the presentation to make sure that they navigate to the proper places.

After you verify all your hyperlinks, follow these steps to save your presentation to individual HTML Web pages:

1. Before you save your pages in HTML format, it is a good idea to save it in PowerPoint format first. From PowerPoint, choose **F**ile | **S**ave. This saves the presentation to your web again. Switch to the FrontPage Explorer to remove the presentation file from the Import File to FrontPage Web list. FrontPage will do this for you automatically when you switch to the FrontPage Explorer.
2. From PowerPoint 97, choose **F**ile | Save as **H**TML. The Save as HTML Wizard screen shown in Figure 4.13 is displayed.

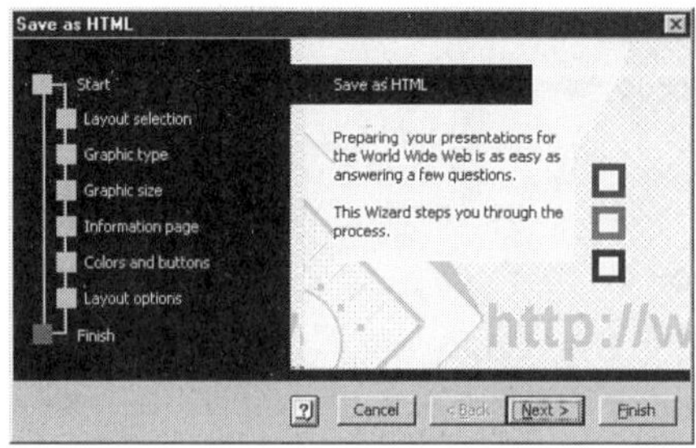

Figure 4.13.
The Save as HTML Wizard guides you through the process of saving your presentation as HTML pages.

3. Click **N**ext. On the screen shown in Figure 4.14, you are asked to choose a new or existing layout. If there are no existing layouts, the **L**oad existing layout option is disabled. Select **N**ew layout to create a new Web page layout for your presentation.

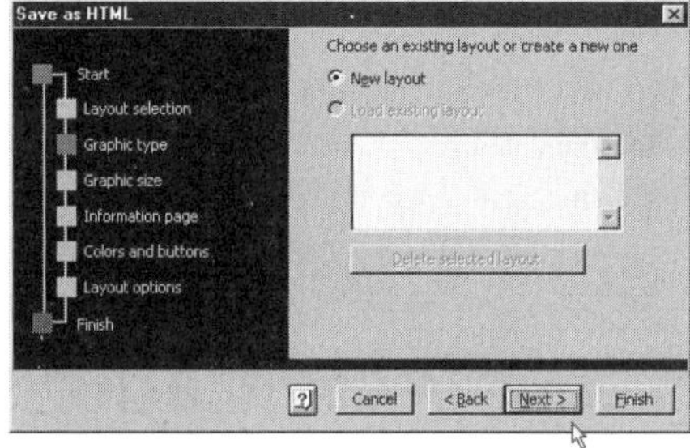

Figure 4.14.
Create a new HTML layout or select an existing layout.

4. Click **N**ext to select a page style from the screen shown in Figure 4.15. Choose **S**tandard to create pages that are not displayed in frames or **B**rowser frames to create slides that display in a frameset. For this example, choose **S**tandard.

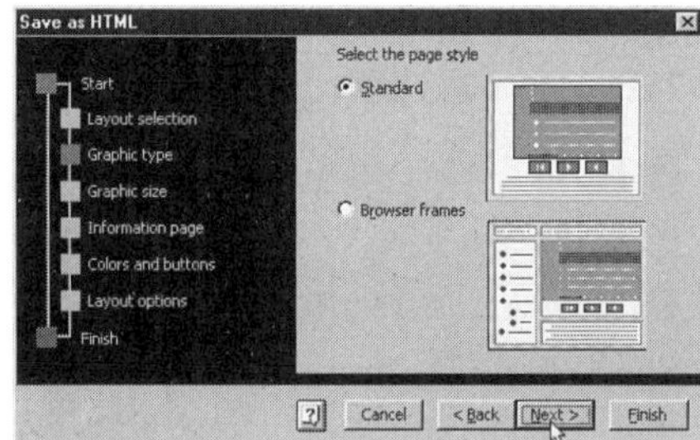

Figure 4.15.
Choose to place your slides on standard Web pages or pages that display in a frameset.

5. Click **N**ext to choose a graphic type for your presentation Web pages from the screen shown in Figure 4.16. Select one of the following options:
   - ❑ Choose **G**IF—Graphics Interchange Format to save your presentation slides as GIF images. This is a good choice if your presentation contains

For additional information on the GIF and JPEG file formats, refer to **Chapter 18**.

clip art images or other graphics that do not contain more than 256 colors. Choose this option for the example in this chapter.

- ❑ Choose **J**PEG—Compressed File Format if your presentation contains photographs or other images that contain more than 256 colors. Enter the amount of compression you want to use for the images in the **C**ompression value field. Generally, ranges between 60% and 85% work best, with 100% being best quality. Lower values create smaller files, but can cause deterioration in appearance.
- ❑ Choose **P**owerPoint animation to convert your presentation into a PowerPoint animation file. You will use this option in the "Creating Banners with PowerPoint" section when you create animated banners for your Web pages.

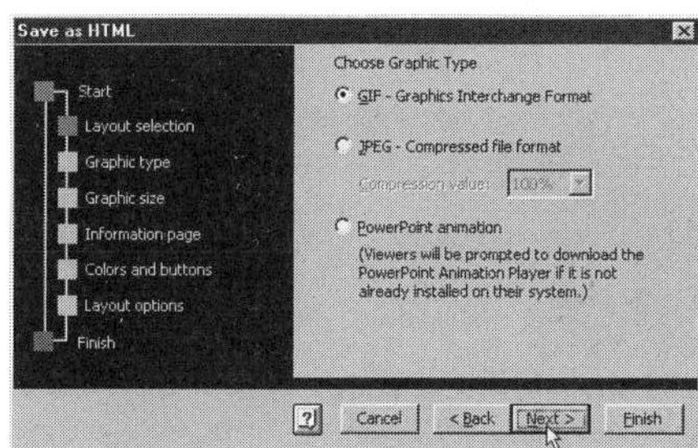

Figure 4.16.
Select the graphic format in which your presentation is saved.

6. Choose **N**ext. On the screen shown in Figure 4.17, the wizard asks what screen resolution in which to save the graphics and how large your presentation slides should appear. For this example, select **6**40×480, which creates Web pages that look best when viewed in that resolution. Then, from the **W**idth of graphics drop-down menu, choose 3/4 width of screen.

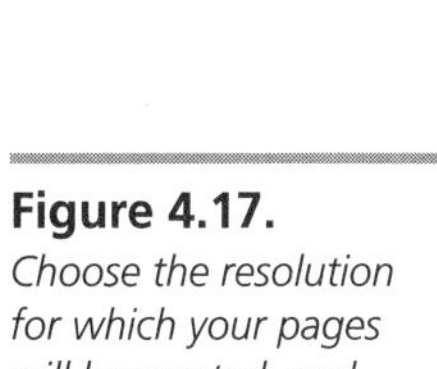

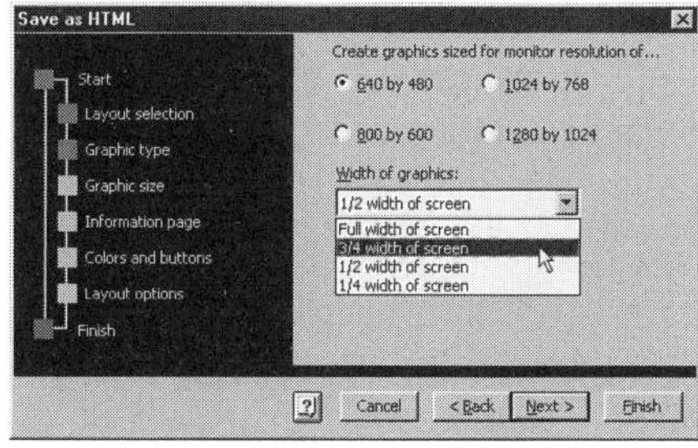

Figure 4.17.
Choose the resolution for which your pages will be created, and select the percentage of screen resolution in which the presentation slides appear.

7. Choose **N**ext. On the screen shown in Figure 4.18, choose the additional information that you want to display in your Web pages. Choose one or more of the following options, and enter your information in the spaces provided:

- E-mail address: Choose this option if you want your e-mail address to appear on each Web page that the wizard generates.
- Your home page: Choose this option if you want your home page URL to appear on each Web page that the wizard generates.
- Other information: Enter additional information, such as company address or contact information, in this field.
- Download original presentation: Choose this option if you want the wizard to place a link on each page that allows the user to download the original PowerPoint presentation file.
- Internet Explorer download button: Choose this option if you want the wizard to place a link on each page that allows the user to download Internet Explorer. This is recommended if you save your presentation as a PowerPoint animation.

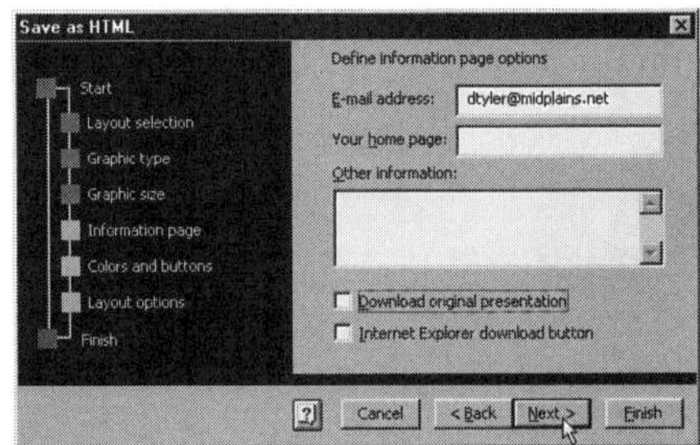

Figure 4.18.
Choose the additional information that should appear on the Web pages.

8. Choose **N**ext. On the screen shown in Figure 4.19, select the color scheme for your Web pages. If you select the **U**se browser colors option, your Web pages use a gray background and standard text and link colors. To create a color scheme that works well with the colors in your presentation, choose the **C**ustom colors option and select the following options:
   - Click the Change **B**ackground button and select black (the first color in the last row) for a background color. Click OK to return to the wizard screen.
   - Click the Change **T**ext button, and then click **D**efine Custom Colors. Enter color values as follows: `Red 255`, `Green 255`, `Blue 204`. This creates a light yellow color. Click OK to return to the wizard screen.
   - Click the Change **L**ink button, and then click **D**efine Custom Colors. Enter color values as follows: `Red 204`, `Green 0`, `Blue 0`. This creates a medium-red color. Click OK to return to the wizard screen.
   - Click the Change **V**isited button and select silver (the sixth color in the last row) for a visited link color. Click OK to return to the wizard screen.

- ☐ Click the Transparent buttons check box if you want to create buttons that show the background color of the Web page. Leave this option unchecked for this example.

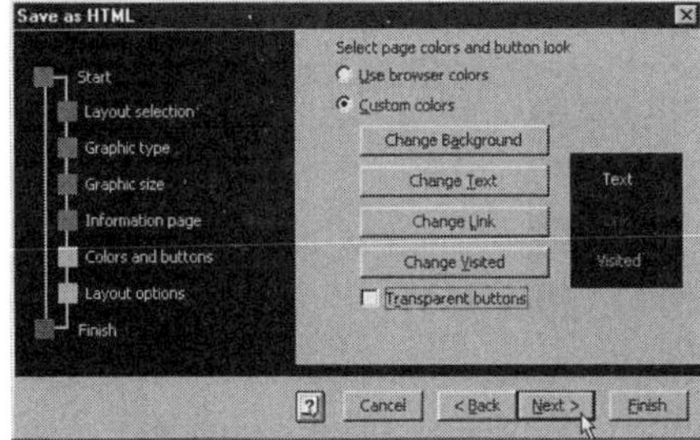

Figure 4.19.
Create the color scheme for the Web pages on which the presentation slides appear.

9. Choose **N**ext. On the screen shown in Figure 4.20, select the navigation button style. For this example, select the rectangular button; other choices are square buttons, circular buttons, or text navigation.

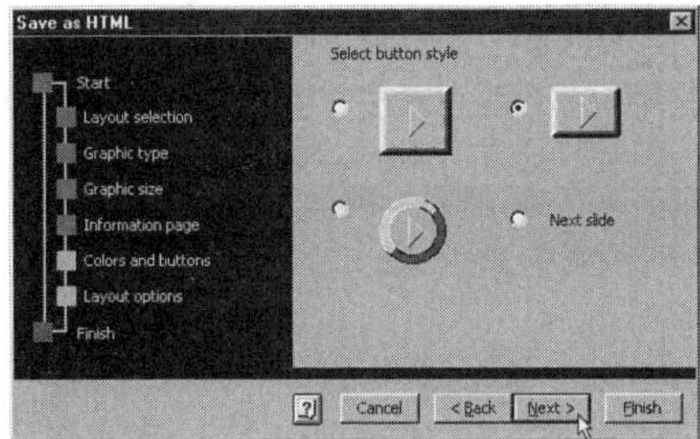

Figure 4.20.
Choose the navigation button style you want for your Web pages on this screen.

10. Choose **N**ext. On the screen shown in Figure 4.21, select where you want your navigation buttons to appear on your Web pages. For this example, choose to locate the buttons on the right side of each Web page; other choices are top, bottom, or left side of the page.

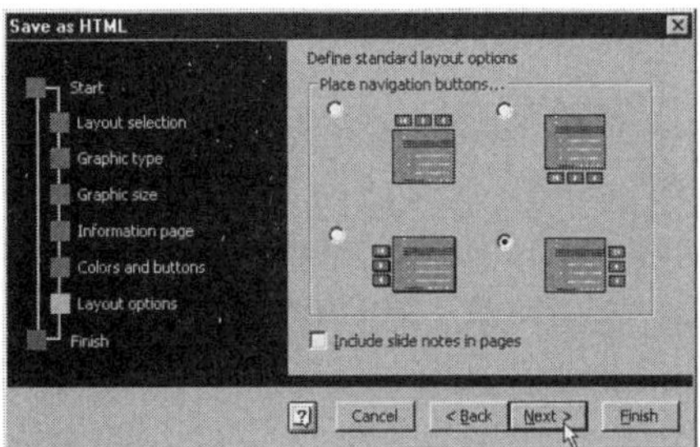

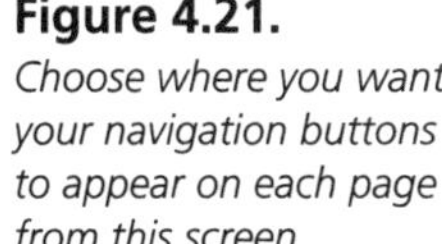

Figure 4.21.
Choose where you want your navigation buttons to appear on each page from this screen.

11. Choose **N**ext. On the screen shown in Figure 4.22, the wizard asks you to define the directory in which you want the presentation files to be created. Use the **B**rowse button to select any directory on your local hard drive (`c:\temp`, for example).

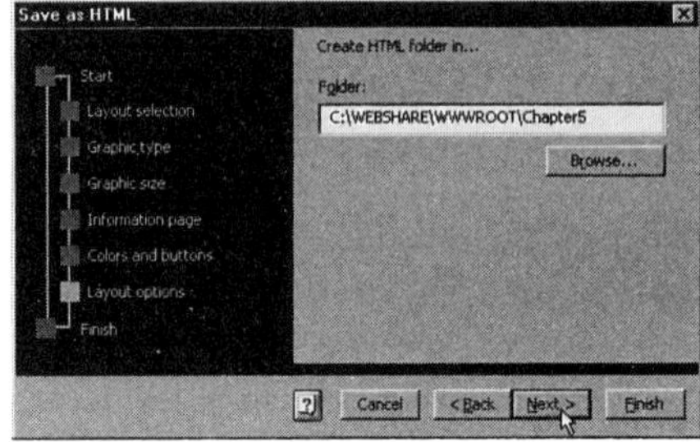

Figure 4.22.
Save the presentation file to a directory on your local hard drive.

12. Choose **N**ext; then click **F**inish. The Save as HTML dialog box shown in Figure 4.23 is displayed. The wizard asks for a name for the folder in which to place your HTML file conversions. Enter **`Chapter4`**, and click **S**ave. PowerPoint saves the pages to a subdirectory within the folder you selected in the previous step (for example, `c:\temp\Chapter4`).

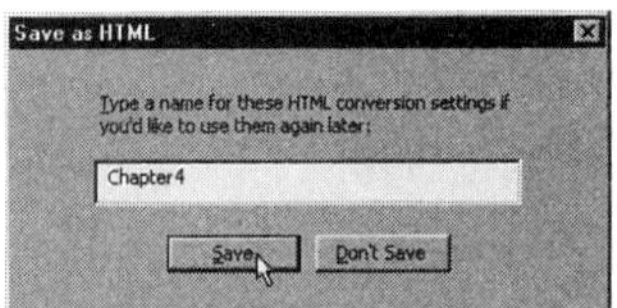

Figure 4.23.
Use the Save as HTML dialog box to define a folder name for your presentation content.

13. To import the new content into your FrontPage web, return to the FrontPage Explorer and choose **F**ile | **I**mport. Select **A**dd File from the Import File to FrontPage Web dialog box, and select all of the content displayed in the folder to which you saved your presentation. Choose OK to import the content into your web.

NOTE: PowerPoint saves the home page of a presentation with the filename `index.htm`. If your FrontPage web already has a home page filename of `index.htm`, rename the presentation home page before you import the presentation pages into your web.

Creating Banners with PowerPoint

You can also use PowerPoint to create animated banners for your Web pages. To see a few examples of this, choose one of the samples from the Web Pages tab in the New dialog box.

The trick to making animated banners is to make each slide different. You can create the illusion of movement if you move graphics from one slide to the next or change colors. You will learn some of these techniques in the following example.

Learn other ways that you can create animated GIF files in **Chapter 22**.

To create an animated banner from PowerPoint, start with a blank presentation. You will need to change the page setup for the presentation to create slides that are sized for a banner.

To create a new presentation for a banner, follow these steps:

1. From PowerPoint, choose **F**ile | **N**ew (Ctrl+N) or click the New button on the Standard toolbar. The New Presentation dialog box is displayed.
2. Click the General tab, and double-click the Blank Presentation icon. The New Slide dialog box is displayed.
3. Double-click the blank slide (the last slide in the bottom row) to create a blank slide.
4. To resize the slide for a banner, choose **F**ile | Page Set**u**p. The Page Setup dialog box shown in Figure 4.24 is displayed.
5. From the **S**lides sized for drop-down menu, select Banner, and choose OK. The slide size in your presentation changes.

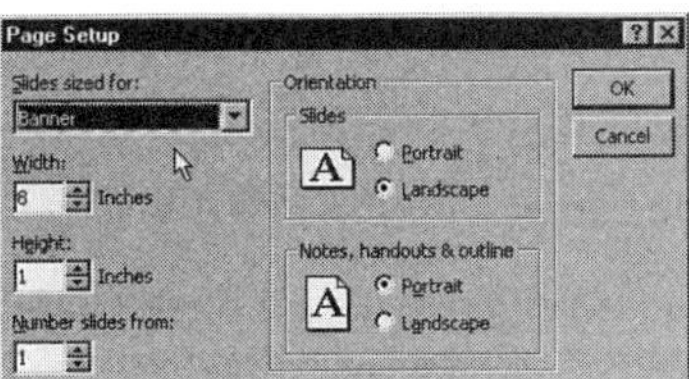

Figure 4.24.
Use the Page Setup dialog box to change the size of your presentation slides.

Inserting and Animating Clip Art

There are many ways you can approach each slide in your banner; this example gives you one idea to get you started. In the next task, you will add some clip art text to your banner using some of the clip art furnished with Office 97.

NOTE: If you do not have the clip art installed, you'll need to run Office 97 Setup again. Save your work in PowerPoint and close the application. Insert your Office 97 CD and choose **A**dd/Remove from the setup screen. Scroll down the list of options and select Office Tools. Then select the Chan**g**e Option button. Check the Popular Clipart and Clip Gallery options, and choose OK. Click Continue to complete the remaining steps for the installation.

To create each slide in the banner, follow these steps:

1. Choose **I**nsert | **P**icture | **C**lip Art. The Microsoft Clip Gallery screen is displayed.
2. Choose the Animals category, and scroll down about five-sixths of the way through the selections until you see the spider web shown in Figure 4.25. Double-click to place the spider on your page, and move it to the left side of the banner.

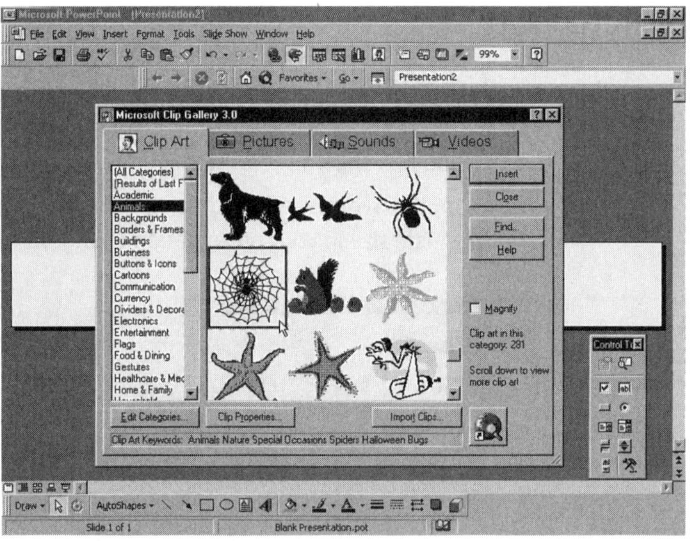

Figure 4.25.
Select the spider web from the Animals clip art category.

3. Choose **I**nsert | **P**icture | **C**lip Art again, and select the spider from the Animals category. You'll find the spider just before the web image you inserted in the previous step. Double-click to select the spider, and move it to the right side of your page.
4. Right-click the spider and choose Show Picture Toolba**r** from the pop-up menu. The picture toolbar is displayed.

You can use Microsoft Image Composer to create your own clip art and graphics. Many of the features of this program are covered in Part V, "Creating Graphics with Microsoft Image Composer."

5. Select the Recolor Picture button shown in Figure 4.26. Click the black color square and select **M**ore Colors from the drop-down menu. The Colors dialog box is displayed.

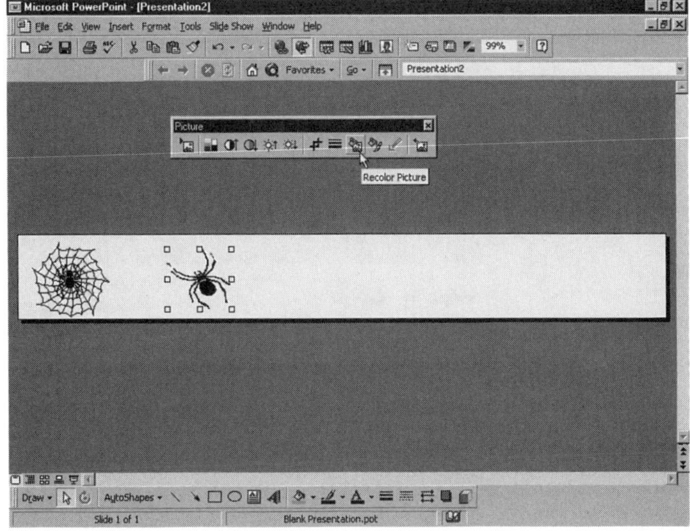

Figure 4.26.
Select the Recolor Picture option to change the color of the spider.

6. Select the last color in the bottom row of the color hexagon (a brown color). Choose OK twice to return to the slide. The spider turns brown.
7. Choose the Rectangle from the toolbar on the bottom of your screen (shown in Figure 4.27). Draw a rectangle on the banner that takes up the space between the web and the spider.

Figure 4.27.
Select the Rectangle button to draw a rectangle between the web and the spider.

8. Click the rectangle to select it. Next, click the arrow next to the Fill color icon at the bottom of your screen (shown in Figure 4.28). Select a banner color of your preference, but keep the color in the light to medium range. I selected a light blue for my banner.

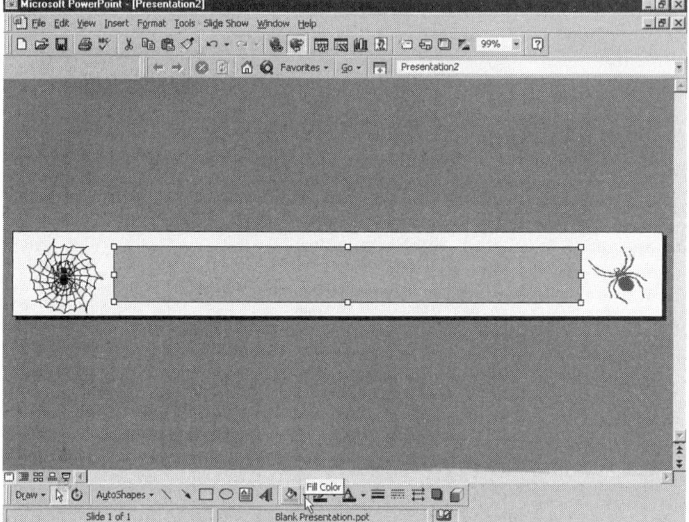

Figure 4.28.
Select the arrow next to the Fill color icon at the bottom of your screen to change the color of the rectangle.

9. Choose **I**nsert | Te**x**t Box, and draw a text box rectangle slightly within the boundaries of the colored rectangle you just placed on your page. Enter `Banners for the Web are Easy!!!` as shown in Figure 4.29.

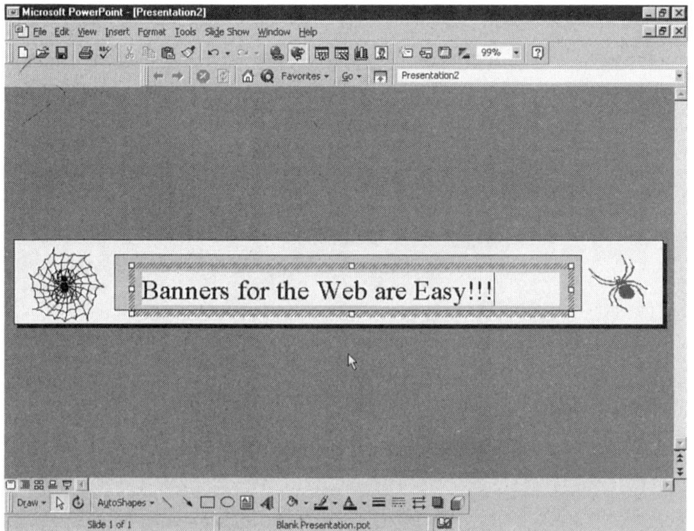

Figure 4.29.
Size a text box almost as large as the colored rectangle, and enter the banner text.

10. Choose **E**dit | Select A**l**l (Ctrl+A). Then choose **E**dit | **C**opy (Ctrl+C) to copy the contents of the page into your clipboard.
11. Choose **I**nsert | **N**ew Slide (Ctrl+M). Select the blank slide and choose OK. Insert the clipboard contents into the new slide using **E**dit | **P**aste (Ctrl+V).
12. Click to select the spider. Then right-click and choose O**r**der | Bring to Fron**t** from the pop-up menu shown in Figure 4.30. Use the Left arrow key to nudge the spider 10 nudges toward the left.

Figure 4.30.
Move the spider to the front of the banner with the Bring to Front command.

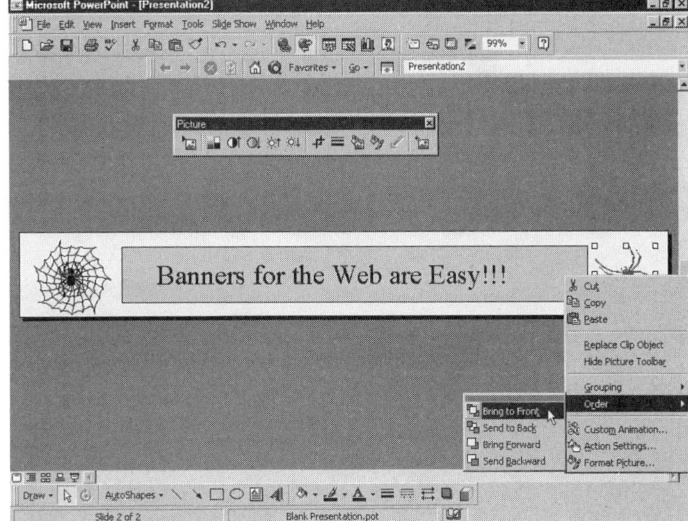

13. Click three times in the text box to select all the text. Change the text in the new banner to read `Use PowerPoint to create them!!!`
14. Repeat steps 10 through 12 to create a new slide and move the spider 10 more spaces to the left.
15. Click three times in the text box to select all the text. Change the text in the new banner to read `Even if you hate spiders…`
16. Repeat steps 10 through 12 to create a new slide and move the spider 10 more spaces to the left.
17. Click three times in the text box to select all the text. Change the text in the new banner to read `You'll love the Web!` Figure 4.31 shows all four slides completed, with slide 1 at the top and slide 4 at the bottom.
18. Now you need to add some timing and transition so that the banner changes by itself. Choose Sli**d**e Show | Slide **T**ransition. The Slide Transition dialog box shown in Figure 4.32 is displayed.

Figure 4.31.
All four slides after they are complete.

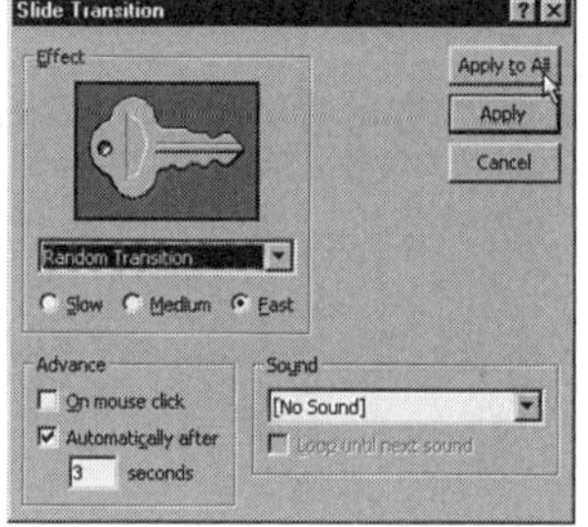

Figure 4.32.
Add timing and transition effects to your slides with the Slide Transition dialog box.

19. From the **E**ffect drop-down menu, select Random Transition. Select the **F**ast radio button.
20. From the Advance area, check Automati**c**ally after, and enter 3 seconds.
21. Click Apply **t**o All. This applies the transition effect settings to all slides in the presentation.
22. Choose **F**ile | **S**ave to save the presentation to your disk in its original format. Save the presentation file as `banner.ppt`. You will save the banner as a PowerPoint Animation in the next task.

Saving Your Banner

Use the Save as HTML Wizard to save your banner as a PowerPoint Animation. This time, however, you can take a few shortcuts. The only file you are interested in from the many that the wizard generates is the PowerPoint Animation file.

To save your banner as a PowerPoint animation, follow these steps:

1. Choose **F**ile | Save as **H**TML. The Save as HTML wizard screen is displayed.
2. From the left side of the Save as HTML screen, click the square next to Graphic Type. Advance to the graphic type selection screen in the wizard.
3. Select the **P**owerPoint animation radio button, as shown in Figure 4.33.

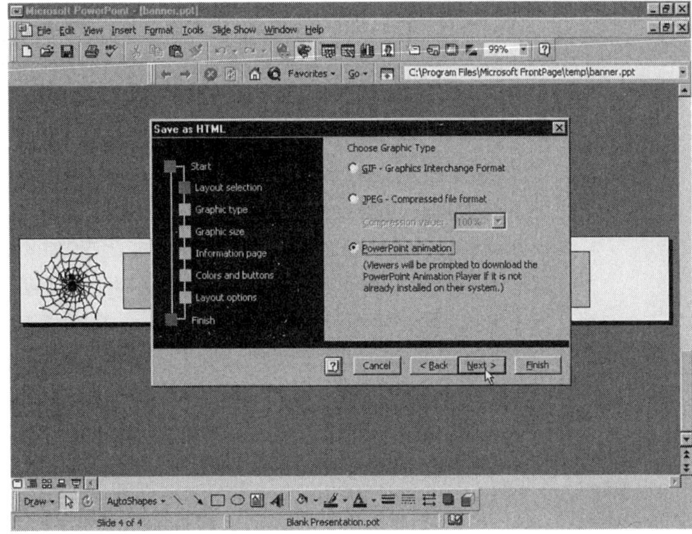

Figure 4.33.
Choose to save your banner as a PowerPoint animation.

4. From the left side of the Save as HTML screen, click the square next to Finish. Advance to the screen in which you name a directory to save the presentation files.
5. Enter the directory to which you want to save the file (example: `c:\temp`). Then click the **F**inish button on the lower-right corner of the screen. PowerPoint creates several files in the `c:\temp\banner` folder. The PowerPoint animation file that you want to import into your FrontPage Web has a `.ppz` extension.

In **Chapter 7** you will learn how to import the PowerPoint animation file into your FrontPage web and how to insert it into your Web page.

Workshop Wrap-Up

In this chapter, you learned some basic techniques to create PowerPoint presentations for the Web, and how to use the Auto Content Wizard to create presentations for the Web. You completed hands-on examples to create hyperlinks with text, images, and action buttons. You learned how to save your presentation in HTML format and how to import the content into your FrontPage web. You also learned how to create animated banners with PowerPoint 97, using clip art and text and saving the banner as a PowerPoint animation. Now you have an idea of some of the ways that you can use PowerPoint to bring your Web content together. Using the techniques you learned in this chapter, you can create presentations that interface with word processing files, spreadsheets, databases, and Web pages. You'll learn more about how you bring all of your Office 97 applications together in Chapter 7.

Next Steps

In Chapter 5, "Excel-ing with Spreadsheets," you will learn how you can integrate Excel 97 spreadsheets with your Web content. You can find additional information about working with PowerPoint and other Office 97 applications in the following related chapters:

- ❑ Refer to Chapter 3, "Word Isn't Just for the Office Anymore," to learn the comparisons between FrontPage and Word 97 for Web authoring and how you can use Word documents in your Web or intranet.
- ❑ Refer to Chapter 6, "Data Access on the Web," for information on how you can integrate databases in your FrontPage webs.
- ❑ See Chapter 7, "Real-Life Examples: Bringing Your Intranet Together," for more examples of using Office 97 and FrontPage 97 content together in an intranet environment.
- ❑ Refer to all the chapters in Part V, "Creating Graphics with Microsoft Image Composer," to learn how to create custom graphics that you can use in your PowerPoint Web presentations and banners.

Q&A

Q: I notice that you can put ActiveX controls in PowerPoint presentations. Do they work the same as the ActiveX controls that I can put on my Web pages?

A: That is what ActiveX controls are designed to do. When you insert ActiveX controls in any Office 97 document, you program them with Visual Basic for Applications. I didn't cover ActiveX controls in this chapter, but you will find additional information about using ActiveX controls with Access 97 in Chapter 6, "Data Access on the Web," and in Chapter 14, "Using Active Server Databases." The principles are the same for each application.

Q: Are there any other special applications that may be necessary when using PowerPoint presentations on the Web?

A: There are a few PowerPoint viewers and players that will be necessary for you to use with some browsers. Office 97 comes with the PowerPoint Viewer, which you can find in the `\Valupak\ppt4view` directory on your

Office 97 CD-ROM. Office 97 also comes with the Microsoft PowerPoint Animation Player for Windows 95, which allows you to view the PowerPoint animations you place on your Web pages as ActiveX controls or Netscape Plug-Ins. You can use this viewer with Internet Explorer 3.0 or higher. You can also use this player with Netscape Navigator 3.0 if you insert the animation on your Web page as a Netscape plug-in.

CHAPTER

FIVE

Excel-ing with Spreadsheets

In this chapter, you

- Learn about three add-in programs furnished with Excel 97 that allow you to work with data on your intranet or the Internet
- Learn how to install and configure Excel add-ins
- Save Excel data and charts to HTML format using the Internet Assistant Wizard
- Use the Template Wizard with Data Tracking to save a worksheet created from one of the Excel templates to a format that adds information to a database
- Review the steps of the Web Form Wizard, which saves an Excel form to your Internet Database Connector or CGI Web server

Tasks in this chapter:

- Installing the Excel Add-Ins
- Configuring the Add-Ins
- Using the Internet Assistant Wizard
- Using the Template Wizard with Data Tracking
- Using the Excel Web Form Wizard

Excel 97 adds many new features that allow you to integrate with spreadsheet data on an intranet or Internet site. Several different add-ins and wizards provide you with many ways that you can use Excel to link with other worksheets or database files. This chapter discusses three of the possibilities: the Internet Assistant for Excel 97, the Template Wizard with Data Tracking, and the Excel Web Form Wizard.

Add-In Programs for Excel

This chapter presumes that you are familiar with the features of Microsoft Excel 97 and how to develop and design worksheets, charts, macros, and queries. After you develop your worksheets in Excel, you can use them in several different ways on your intranet or the Internet. There are three add-ins that will be of interest to Web developers:

- The Internet Assistant Wizard is used to save worksheet cells and charts to static HTML format. You can use this wizard to save your cells and charts to stand-alone Web pages, or you can save them directly to your FrontPage Web.

- The Template Wizard with Data Tracking add-in helps you create a template that links worksheet cells with database fields. You can use the templates to create a new workbook into which data is entered in linked cells. The data from the cells is copied into the corresponding data fields in the database. The files are used on a local or network hard drive.
- The Excel Web Form Wizard is an add-in program that allows you to set up a form on a Web server. The data entered in this form is added to a database.

Installing the Excel Add-Ins

There are several different add-ins available for Microsoft Excel 97, and you can install them from the Excel 97 or Office 97 Setup program. To install the add-ins, follow these steps:

1. Close all programs.
2. From the Windows Start menu, choose **S**ettings; then select **C**ontrol Panel. The Control Panel dialog box is displayed.
3. Double-click Add/Remove Programs. The Add/Remove Programs Properties dialog box is displayed.
4. From the Install/Uninstall tab, choose Microsoft Office or Microsoft Excel; then click Add/**R**emove. You are prompted to insert your Office 97 or Excel 97 CD.
5. Insert the CD and choose OK. Setup searches for installed components and then displays the screen shown in Figure 5.1. Select **A**dd/Remove. The Maintenance screen is displayed.

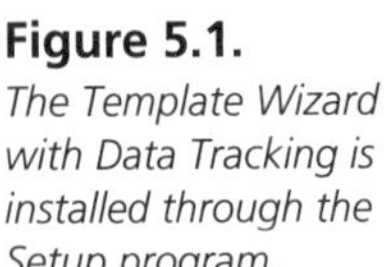

Figure 5.1.
The Template Wizard with Data Tracking is installed through the Setup program.

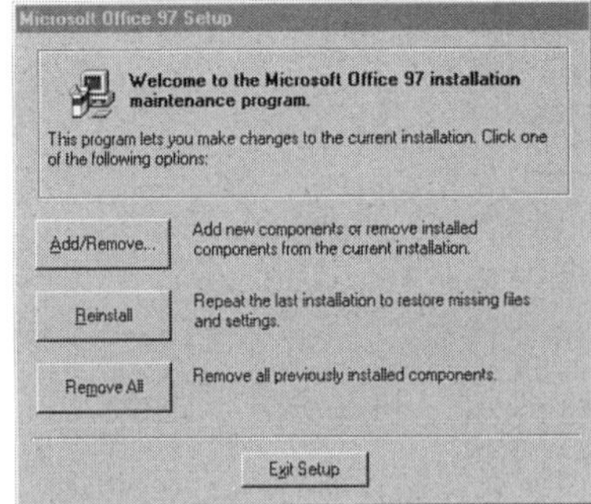

6. Install the add-in of your choice as follows:
   - To install the Internet Assistant for Microsoft Excel and the Web Form Wizard, select Web Page Authoring (HTML) from the **O**ptions list, and choose **C**ontinue. Follow the remaining instructions in the Setup program.

- ❏ To install the Template Wizard for Data Tracking from the Microsoft Office CD, select Microsoft Excel from the **O**ptions list, and click the Chan**g**e Option button. The Microsoft Excel screen shown in Figure 5.2 is displayed. Skip this step if you are installing the Template Wizard for Data Tracking from the Excel 97 CD.

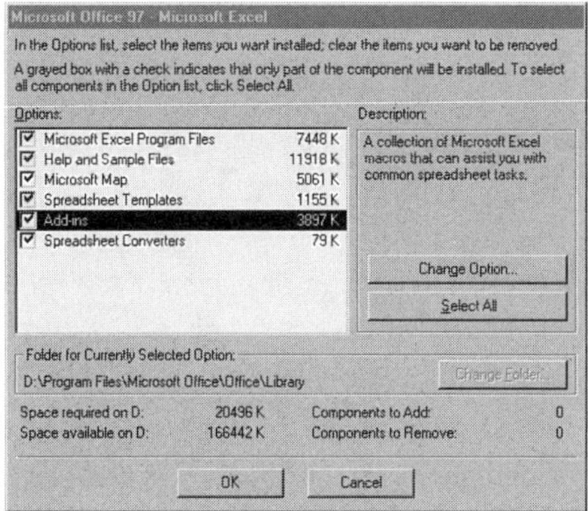

Figure 5.2.
From Office 97 Setup, select Microsoft Excel from the Options list, and select Change Option.

7. Select Add-ins, and click Chan**g**e Option. A list of add-ins available for Microsoft Excel is displayed, as shown in Figure 5.3. Select Template Wizard with Data Tracking and choose OK for all subsequent screens until you return to the Maintenance screen. Then choose Continue to install the wizard. Follow the remaining instructions in the Setup program.

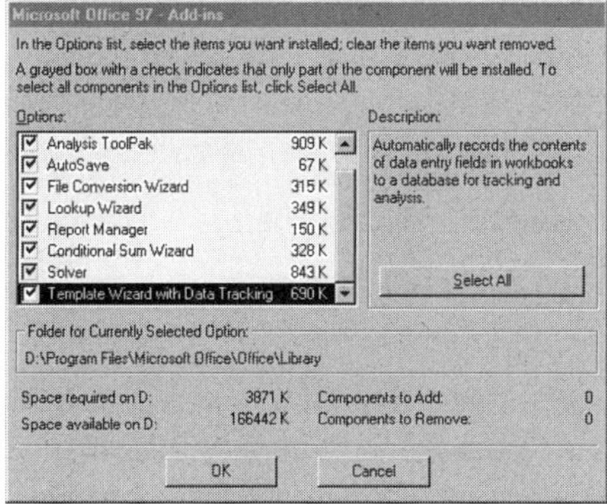

Figure 5.3.
Select the Template Wizard with Data Tracking from the list of available add-ins.

Configuring the Add-Ins

You enable the use of Excel add-ins through the **T**ools | Add-**I**ns command in Microsoft Excel. When you choose this command, a list of all available add-ins is displayed. Then follow these steps to configure the add-ins:

1. From Microsoft Excel, choose **T**ools | Add-**I**ns. The Add-Ins dialog box shown in Figure 5.4 is displayed.

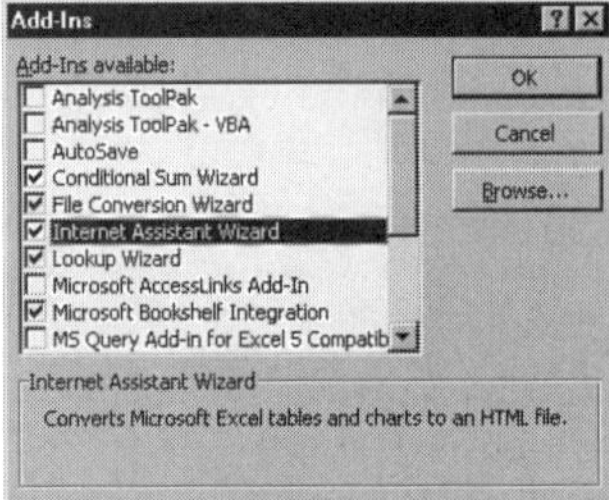

Figure 5.4.
Enable the Internet Assistant Wizard, Template Wizard with Data Tracking, and Web Form Wizard add-ins through the Add-Ins dialog box.

2. If your add-in is not displayed in the list of available add-ins, click **B**rowse. The Browse dialog box is displayed. Use the Look in box to locate the folder in which the add-in is displayed. (They are located in the Addins or Library folder beneath your Office 97 or Excel 97 directory by default.) The file will have an `.xla` or `.xll` extension. Double-click the filename to open it.
3. From the Add-Ins available list, check the box beside the add-in you want to enable, such as Internet Assistant Wizard, Template Wizard with Data Tracking, or Web Form Wizard.
4. Choose OK. The add-ins are configured.

Using the Internet Assistant Wizard

Of the three add-ins that are associated with Web pages, the Internet Assistant Wizard is the easiest to use. You can use the Internet Assistant Add-In to save your worksheet data to a static HTML Web page. This Web page can be saved to your local or network hard drive or directly to your currently opened FrontPage web.

To save your worksheet data or chart as a Web page, follow these steps:

1. Click a cell or range of cells in the data that you want to convert to a Web page.
2. Choose **F**ile | Save as **H**TML. The first screen in the Internet Assistant Wizard, shown in Figure 5.5, is displayed. The cell or range of cells that you selected is displayed in the **R**anges and charts to convert list.
3. To add more cell ranges or charts, click the **A**dd button. The Internet Assistant Wizard dialog box shown in Figure 5.6 is displayed. Click and drag to select a range of cells in your worksheet, or click to select a chart. Then choose OK. You return to the Internet Assistant Wizard.
4. After you select all the cell ranges and charts you want to include in your Web page, click Next to continue.

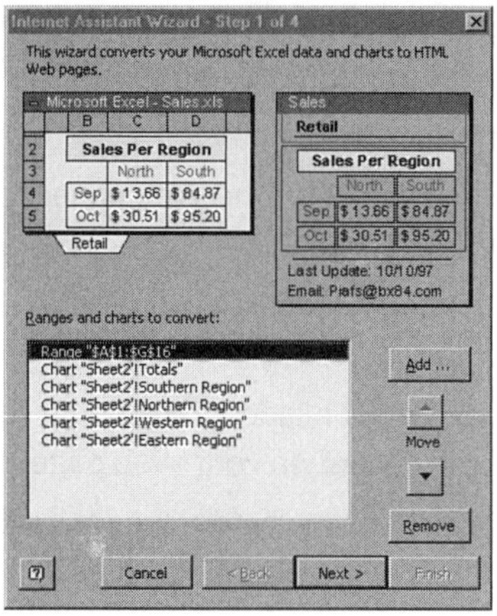

Figure 5.5.
Use the first screen in the Internet Assistant Wizard to select the cells or charts you want to convert to Web pages.

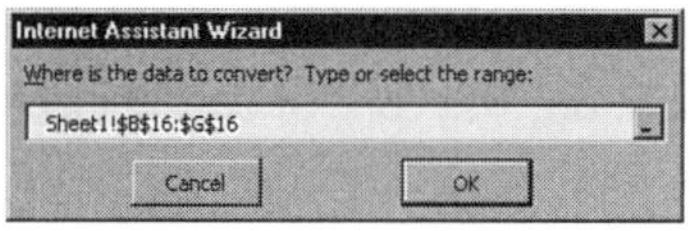

Figure 5.6.
Use the Internet Assistant Wizard dialog box shown here to add more cells or charts to the Web page.

5. On the second screen in the Internet Assistant Wizard, shown in Figure 5.7, you choose whether you want to save the data to a new or existing Web page. Choose one of the following options:

   ❑ Create an independent, ready-to-view HTML document that contains your formatted data (header, table, and footer will be created).

   ❑ Insert the converted data into an existing HTML file (just the table will be created).

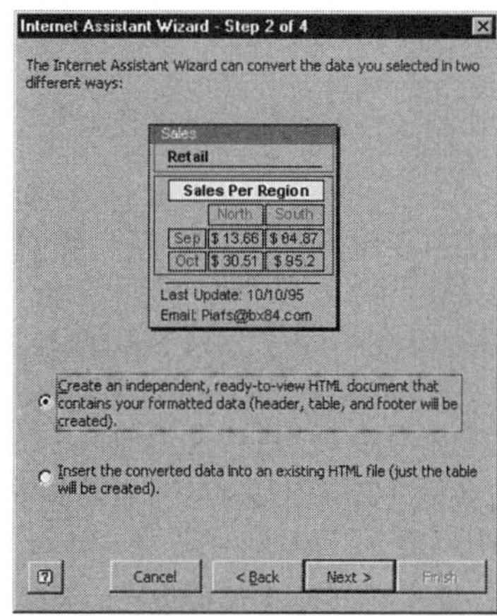

Figure 5.7.
Use this screen to create a new HTML file, or add the Excel data to an existing Web page.

6. Click Next to continue. The third screen of the Internet Assistant Wizard is displayed. You choose formatting options in the screen shown in Figure 5.8.

   Enter the following information:

   Title: Enter the title for the Web page. The default title is the filename of your existing worksheet.

   Header: Enter a header for your Web page. The default header is the sheet number in your existing worksheet.

   Description below header: Enter some introductory text to appear beneath the header on your Web page.

   Insert a horizontal line before the converted data: Check this option to include a horizontal rule before the worksheet data on your Web page.

   Insert a horizontal line after the converted data: Check this option to include a horizontal rule after the worksheet data on your Web page.

   Last Update on: The current date is inserted into this field.

   By: Enter your name.

   Email: Enter your e-mail address.

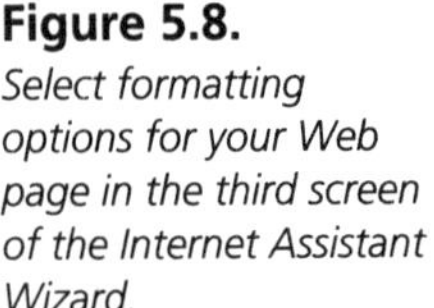

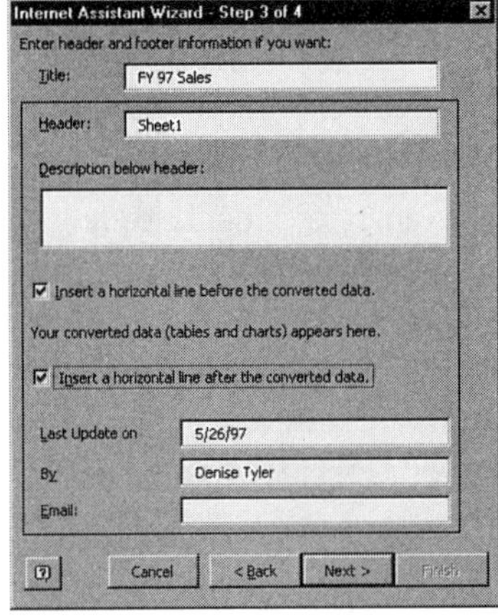

Figure 5.8.
Select formatting options for your Web page in the third screen of the Internet Assistant Wizard.

7. Click Next to continue. The fourth screen of the Internet Assistant Wizard, shown in Figure 5.9, is displayed. Enter the following information:

   Which code page do you want to use for your Web page? Select one of the following from the drop-down menu: US/Western European (default), MS-DOS United States, MS-DOS Multilingual (Latin I), Japanese (EUC), Japanese (JIS), Korean (ISO-2022-KR), or Multilingual (UTF-8)/KSC 5700.

   How do you want to save the finished HTML Web page? Select Save the result as an HTML file to save your Web page to a drive or directory on your local or network hard drive. Select Add the result to my FrontPage Web to save your Web page to the web that you currently have opened in FrontPage.

In the URL address field, enter the path and filename to which you want to save the Web page, or use the Browse button to locate a drive and directory to which to save the Web page.

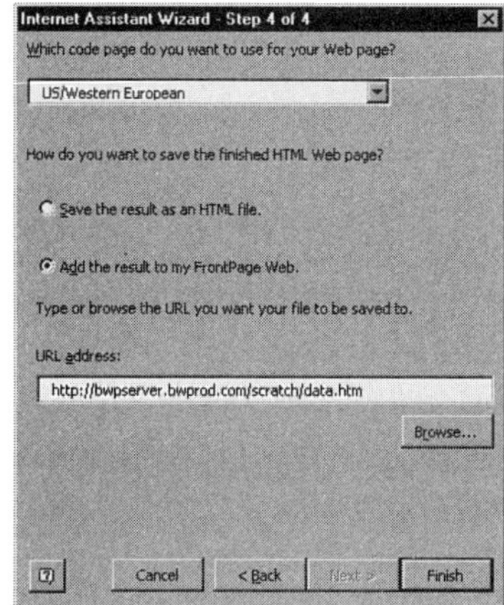

Figure 5.9.
On the final screen in the Internet Assistant Wizard, you choose to save your data to a stand-alone Web page on your local or network hard drive or to a FrontPage web.

8. Click Finish. Microsoft Excel saves your Web page. Figure 5.10 shows the Web page in the FrontPage Editor.

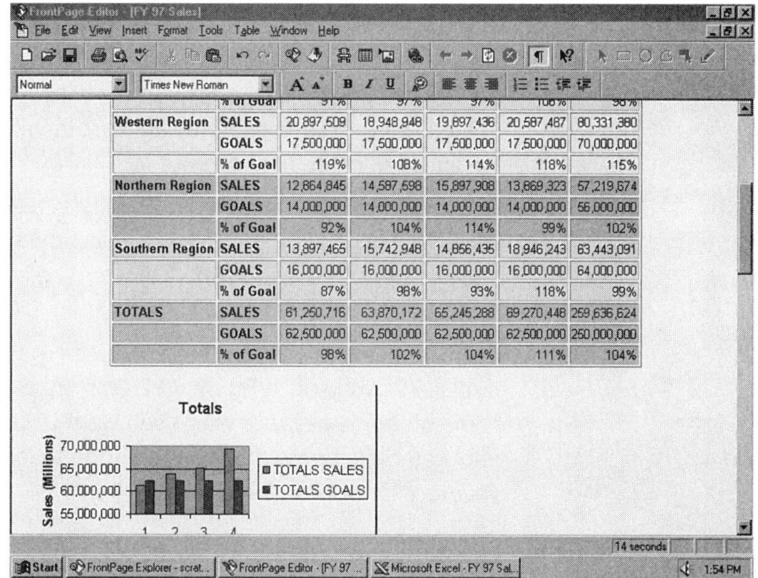

Western Region	SALES	20,897,509	18,948,948	19,897,436	20,587,487	80,331,380
	GOALS	17,500,000	17,500,000	17,500,000	17,500,000	70,000,000
	% of Goal	119%	108%	114%	118%	115%
Northern Region	SALES	12,864,845	14,587,598	15,897,908	13,869,323	57,219,674
	GOALS	14,000,000	14,000,000	14,000,000	14,000,000	56,000,000
	% of Goal	92%	104%	114%	99%	102%
Southern Region	SALES	13,897,465	15,742,948	14,856,435	18,946,243	63,443,091
	GOALS	16,000,000	16,000,000	16,000,000	16,000,000	64,000,000
	% of Goal	87%	98%	93%	118%	99%
TOTALS	SALES	61,250,716	63,870,172	65,245,288	69,270,448	259,636,624
	GOALS	62,500,000	62,500,000	62,500,000	62,500,000	250,000,000
	% of Goal	98%	102%	104%	111%	104%

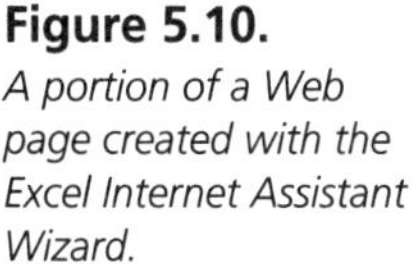

Figure 5.10.
A portion of a Web page created with the Excel Internet Assistant Wizard.

Template Wizard with Data Tracking

The Template Wizard with Data Tracking allows you to use an Excel worksheet in conjunction with a database on your local or network hard drive. You begin by using Excel to create a form that requests information from the user. Then you use the Template Wizard to create a template from the form and link the template to a central database, which can be a Microsoft Excel list or a Microsoft Access, Microsoft FoxPro, dBASE, or Paradox database. The ODBC driver that is compatible with your database should be installed on your system, and the database should be stored in a network location that is accessible by all users of the form.

Using the Template Wizard with Data Tracking

To learn what the Template Wizard with Data Tracking does, in this task you create a new worksheet using the Expense Statement template furnished with Excel 97. This will help you learn how to develop your own forms for use with the Template Wizard with Data Tracking

To use the Template Wizard with Data Tracking, follow these steps:

1. Open the workbook into which you will enter the data that will be copied into the database, or create a new workbook based on a form that you have already saved as a template.
2. Enter labels for the data that you want entered into the worksheet. Each label is used for field names in the database and should be entered in a cell above or to the left of the cell that contains the data. Examples of the labels in the Expense Statement template are Statement Number, Employee Name, Employee Number, and so on.
3. Choose **D**ata | Te**m**plate Wizard. The first screen of the Template Wizard, shown in Figure 5.11, is displayed. Select the name of the workbook that you want to create a template from, and enter a name for the template in the Type a name for the template field.
4. Click Next to continue. The second screen of the Template Wizard is displayed, as shown in Figure 5.12. You are asked to type the location and name of the database to which you want to connect. Enter the path to a new database, or use the Bro**w**se button to locate an existing database on your local or network hard drive.

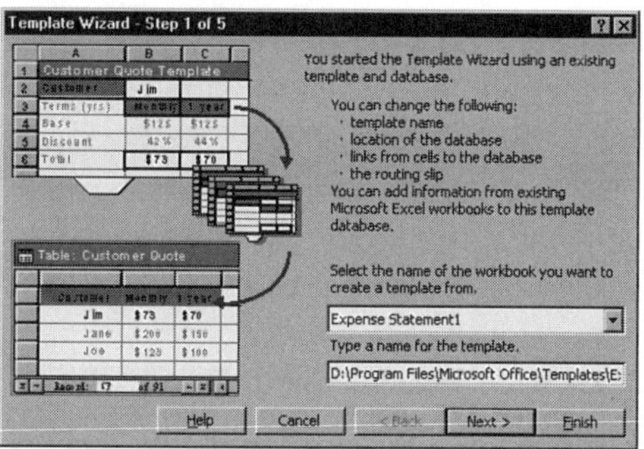

Figure 5.11.
Use the Template Wizard to create a worksheet that is used in conjunction with a database.

NOTE: When you use the Template Wizard to create a new database, it contains only one table or worksheet. If you want to track data in multiple tables or sheets, you must create a database in Access 97 or another database program.

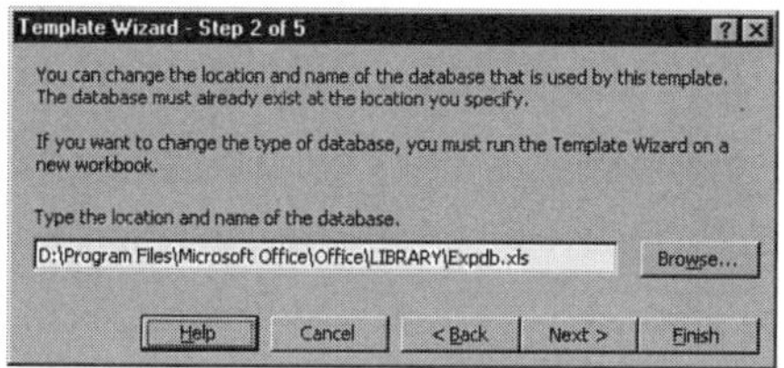

Figure 5.12.
To create a new database, enter a location and name in the second wizard screen, or use the Browse button to locate an existing database.

5. Click Next to continue. You use this screen to change the cells into which the user enters data. To change a cell, click the icon with the small red arrow that appears to the right of the Cell column (shown in Figure 5.13). A dialog box is displayed, after which you click in your worksheet to select a new cell. Again, click the icon with the small red arrow at the right of the cell designation to return to the Template Wizard.

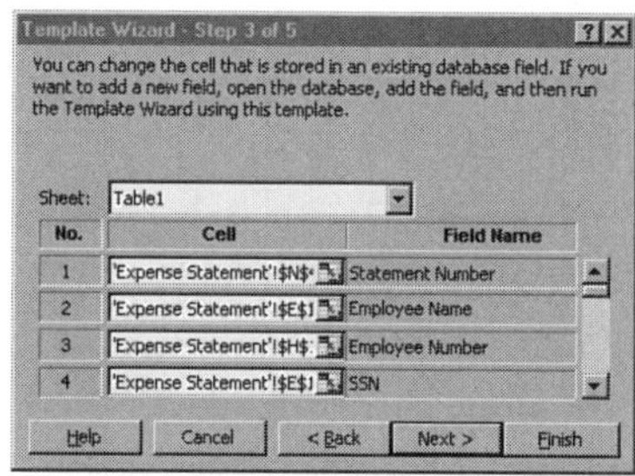

Figure 5.13.
You can change the cells in which users enter data in this wizard screen.

6. Choose Next to continue. You are asked if you would like to add information from existing workbooks into the database. Choose **Y**es, include or **N**o, skip it. Then click Next to continue.
7. On the final wizard screen, shown in Figure 5.14, you are informed that the Wizard has created your template and database, and it lists the location of the files in the dialog box. Click **F**inish to save the changes.

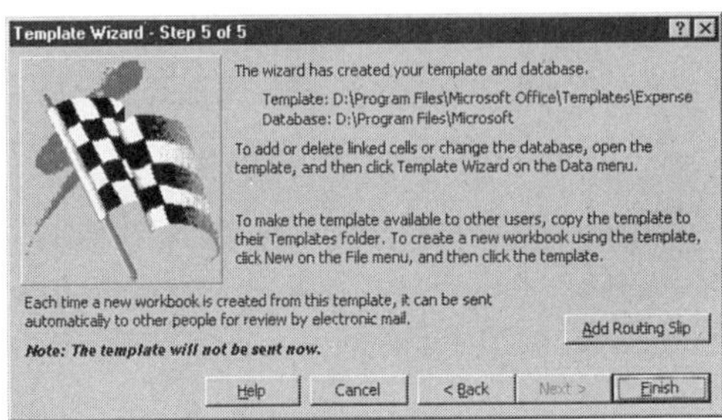

Figure 5.14.
The final screen of the wizard notifies you that the files have been created and identifies their location.

Using the Excel Web Form Wizard

You use the Web Form Wizard to publish Web forms that interface with databases on your Internet or intranet site. When you create forms for use with the Excel Web Form Wizard, you use the controls on the Forms toolbar. Assign or create macros to process the fields in the form.

After you develop your form, run the Web Form Wizard using the following steps:

1. From Microsoft Excel, choose **T**ools | **W**izard | **W**eb Form. The first screen of the Web Form Wizard, shown in Figure 5.15, is displayed.

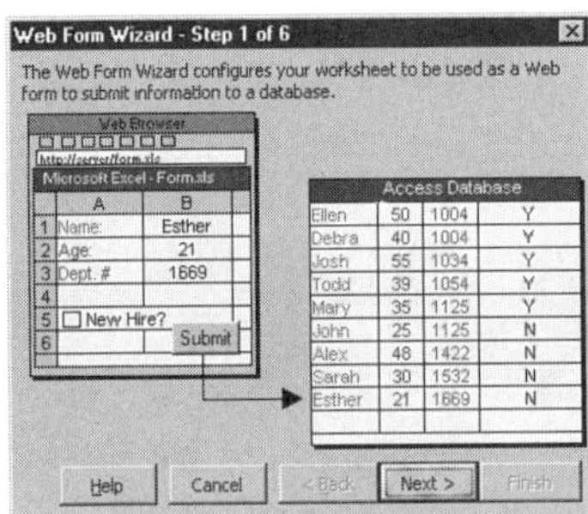

Figure 5.15.
Use the Web Form Wizard to configure your worksheet as a Web form to submit information to a database.

2. Click Next to continue. On the screen shown in Figure 5.16, you are asked to select the controls and cells in your worksheet into which you want users to supply data. Initially, the form fields you added with the Forms toolbar are in the list. There are two columns in the Controls and cells field: The left

column lists the database field name in which the user will enter data, and the right column lists the name of the control.

- ❑ To add a worksheet cell to the list, click **A**dd a cell. Enter a reference to a single cell.
- ❑ To remove a worksheet cell from the list, click the cell you want to remove, and click **R**emove.
- ❑ To change the name of the database field, select a cell from the Controls and cells list. Enter the new name in the **F**ield name of the selected control field. Then click the Change **N**ame button.

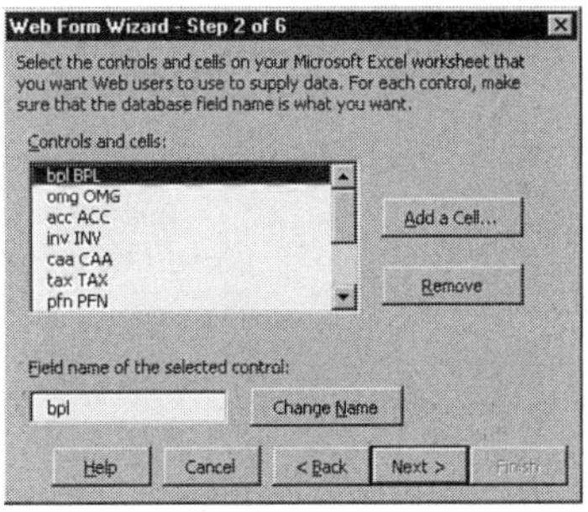

Figure 5.16.
Add the controls and cells in which you want Web users to supply data from the second screen in the Web Form Wizard.

3. Click Next to continue. From the screen shown in Figure 5.17, the wizard asks what interface your Web server uses.
   - ❑ Choose Microsoft Internet Information Server with the Internet Database Connector if you want to generate a page that works with IDC files. Note that your Web must reside on a server that uses the Internet Information Server interface.
   - ❑ Choose Common Gateway Interface (CGI) compliant Web server if your server does not support the IIS interface. Most Web servers support CGI.

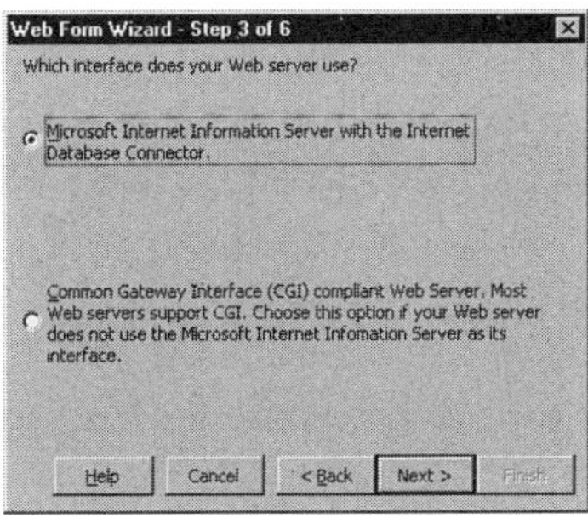

Figure 5.17.
Select Internet Database Connector or CGI Web server interface from the third screen in the Web Form Wizard.

4. Choose Next to continue. In the screen shown in Figure 5.18, you are asked to choose how to save the result.

- ❑ Choose **S**ave the result as a Microsoft Excel file if you do not want to save the file to your FrontPage web.
- ❑ Choose **A**dd the result to your FrontPage Web to save the file into a FrontPage web. Make sure that FrontPage is running and that a server is open before you choose Next.
- ❑ In the File **p**ath field, enter the path to which you want to save the file. If you are saving your worksheet to a local or network hard drive, enter the complete path (`c:\`*`foldername`*`\`*`subfoldername`*`\`*`filename`*`.xls`). If you are adding the file to your FrontPage web, enter the URL (`http://`*`servername`*`/`*`webname`*`/`*`foldername`*`/`*`filename`*`.xls`).

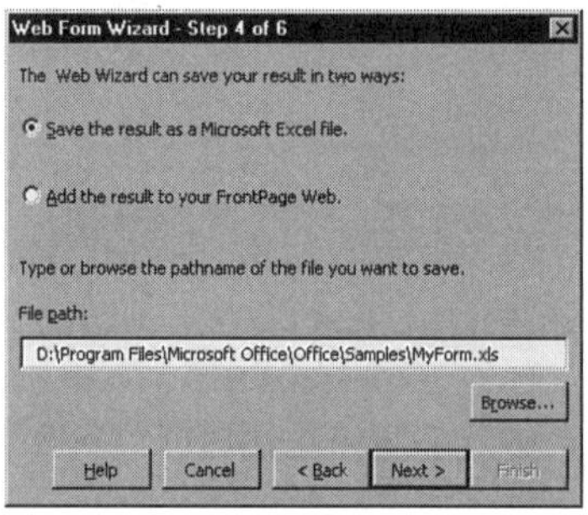

Figure 5.18.
In this screen, you choose to save your results as a Microsoft Excel file or to add the result to your FrontPage web.

5. Click Next to continue. On the screen shown in Figure 5.19, you are asked what message you want to send to users after they register the data on the server. This page serves as a message that confirms that the data has been received by the server. In the **T**itle field, enter the information that you want to be displayed in the title bar of the message window. In the **H**eader field, enter the information that you want to be displayed in the first line of the message window. In the Text field, enter the text of the message.
6. If you elected to save your worksheet to IDC format, you enter the path to the IDC file in the URL path field as follows:

   ```
   http://servername/Scripts/filename.idc
   ```

   If you elected to save your worksheet to CGI (Common Gateway Interface) format, you are prompted to type the URL of the Perl script. Enter an example similar to the following:

   ```
   http://servername/Scripts/filename.pl
   ```

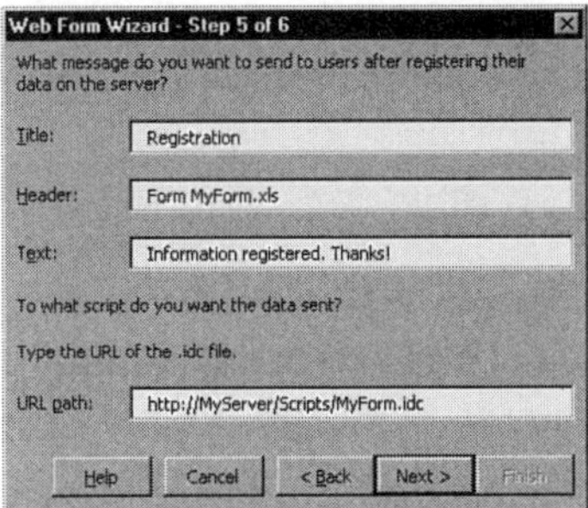

Figure 5.19.
Enter a title, header, return message, and URL for your Internet Database Connector file in the fifth screen of the wizard.

7. Click Next to continue. The Excel Web Wizard creates the files necessary to process your form. If you selected the IDC option, the wizard generates the `.xls`, `.idc`, `.htx`, and `.mdb` files necessary for data collection. The files should be moved into the proper Web subdirectories, and proper permissions should be assigned.
8. Click Finish. The Excel Web Wizard closes.

Workshop Wrap-Up

Excel 97 offers several different methods to use your spreadsheet data on an intranet or the Internet. You can use Internet Explorer to browse through your spreadsheet data in native format. The Internet Assistant for Excel 97 can save your worksheet data and charts to static HTML format, to either a directory on your network or a FrontPage web. The Template Wizard with Data Tracking allows you to interface between Excel worksheets and database files on a network. Finally, the Excel Web Form Wizard allows you to create Excel Web forms that interface with Internet Database Connector files or CGI-based scripts on a server.

Next Steps

In Chapter 7, "Real-Life Examples: Bringing Your Intranet Together," you'll learn how you can combine Office 97 documents and FrontPage webs together. To learn additional information about working with Office 97 documents, refer to the following chapters:

- Chapter 3, "Word Isn't Just for the Office Anymore," to learn the differences between using Word 97 and FrontPage 97 to create Web pages.
- Chapter 4, "Presenting PowerPoint on the Web," to learn how to export PowerPoint presentations to static or animated Web formats.
- Chapter 6, "Data Access on the Web," to learn more about how to install and configure your server for database access on the Web.

- Chapter 7, "Real-Life Examples: Bringing Your Intranet Together," for a simple example of how to integrate Office 97 and Web documents together.

Q&A

Q: Are there other available resources that can help me learn more about using Excel 97 to create Web pages that I can use in Front-Page 97?

A: The following books will provide additional assistance in creating web documents with Excel 97 and the rest of the Office 97 applications:

- *Microsoft Office 97 Unleashed, Second Edition*; Paul McFedries, Sue Charlesworth, et al.; Sams Publishing; December 1996 (0-672-31010-4)
- *Teach Yourself Microsoft Office 97 in 24 hours, Second Edition*; Greg Perry; Sams Publishing; December 1996 (0-672-31009-0)
- *Teach Yourself Web Publishing with Office 97 in a Week*; Michael A. Larson; Sams.net Publishing; February 1997 (1-57521-232-3)

Appendix A, "Online Resources," contains a list of Knowledge Base articles that discuss Excel 97. These articles are located on Microsoft's Web site and contain workarounds or answers to technical questions in using Excel 97 to create Web-related documents.

CHAPTER

SIX

Data Access on the Web

In this chapter, you

- Review database elements
- Learn how to display a Web page in an Access form
- Save a database to HTML format
- Learn how to use the Publish to the Web Wizard in Access 97
- Prepare your server to interface with your database Web application dynamically

Tasks in this chapter:

- Installing the Sample Northwind Database
- Reviewing Database Objects
- Displaying Web Pages in an Access Form
- Exporting Objects to Static HTML Format
- Publishing Your Database to Static HTML Format
- Importing the Database into Your FrontPage Web
- Installing the Microsoft Access Desktop Driver
- Defining Your Database as a Data Source
- Setting Read and Execute Permissions in Windows NT 4.0 Server
- Configuring Your Directory in the Microsoft Personal Web Server

With the release of Office 97 Professional and Access 97, databases have made the official move to the Web. Using tools and features built into the latest version of this popular database software, you can publish your database on the Web or your intranet. You can choose from three HTML formats when you save your databases, two of which dynamically interface with your data. This chapter shows you how to save your databases in Web formats and how to prepare your server to interface with your data dynamically.

Developing Web Applications with Access 97

In this chapter, I assume that you are familiar with the process of developing database applications with Microsoft Access. For additional help with the material in this chapter, look in the `ValuPack\Access` folder furnished on the Microsoft Office 97 Professional or Microsoft Access 97 CD. You can find the following items in the `ValuPack\Access` folder:

- The `readme.txt` file contains information about the "Building Applications in Microsoft Access 97" web furnished on the CD.
- The `openbook.htm` file opens the "Building Applications in Microsoft Access 97" web in your browser.

Refer to **Appendix A** for additional online references pertaining to Microsoft Access 97 and Microsoft Office 97. **Appendix B** lists other books that can help you develop database applications with Microsoft Office 97 and Microsoft Access 97.

- The `\Webhelp` subdirectory includes a help file that provides help with the Microsoft Web Browser Control.
- The `\Bldapps` subdirectory contains the pages and images used in the "Building Applications in Microsoft Access 97" online book.

Reviewing Microsoft Access 97 Database Objects

In the following tasks, you look briefly at the elements contained in the Northwind database, a sample database furnished with Microsoft Access 97 and Microsoft Office 97 Professional. This will help you to become familiar with how databases are built. You will compare the original database files with the HTML pages as they are published to your web.

Refer to **Chapter 13** to see how the Northwind database elements look when exported to HTX/IDC format. Refer to **Chapter 14** to view pages as they are exported to ASP format.

To review the examples in this chapter, open the Northwind database sample application that is furnished on your Office 97 Professional or Access 97 CD. You can open this database as read-only by choosing the `nwind.mbd` file from the Samples directory (`Office\Samples` in Office 97) on your CD-ROM.

If you want to make changes to the database, you can install it from the Microsoft Office 97 Professional CD using steps in the following section. (The steps will be similar if you have the Microsoft Access 97 CD.)

Installing the Sample Northwind Database

To install the sample database after Office 97 Professional (including Access 97) has been installed to your system, follow these steps:

1. Insert your Microsoft Office 97 Professional CD into your CD-ROM drive.
2. From the Start menu, choose **S**ettings | **C**ontrol Panel. The Control Panel dialog box is displayed.
3. Double-click the Add/Remove Programs icon. The Add/Remove Programs Properties dialog box is displayed.
4. Highlight Microsoft Office 97 Professional Edition, and click Add/**R**emove. You are prompted to insert your CD. Choose OK to continue.
5. Setup searches for installed components, and the Setup dialog box is displayed. Click **A**dd/Remove. The Maintenance dialog box is displayed.

6. Select Microsoft Access from the **O**ptions list; then click the Chan**g**e Option button. The Microsoft Access dialog box is displayed.
7. Highlight Sample Databases from the **O**ptions list shown in Figure 6.1, and click Chan**g**e Option. The Sample Databases dialog box is displayed.

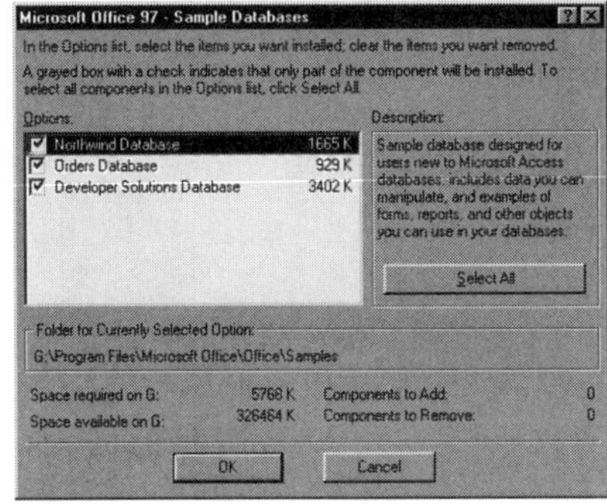

Figure 6.1.
You can find the Sample Databases in the Microsoft Access | Sample Databases dialog box.

8. Select Northwind Database and choose OK.
9. Click **C**ontinue and complete the instructions in the Setup Wizard. Setup installs the file to the `Program Files\Microsoft Office\Office\Samples` directory, using the filename `northwind.mdb`.

Reviewing Database Objects

After you install the sample Northwind database, open it in Microsoft Access. A welcome screen is displayed. After you close the welcome screen, you see the Northwind: Database dialog box, which lists all the tables, queries, forms, reports, macros, and modules in the database. Step through each tab, and examine the items in the following tasks.

Tables

Tables can be saved to HTML, HTX/IDC, or ASP format during export or publishing to Web formats. Refer to **Chapters 13** and **14** to learn how tables export to dynamic formats.

Tables store your database entries in a logical manner. Because Access 97 is a multirelational database, you can program your application so that several different tables work together to respond to queries and data entries.

To quickly review the information and elements that are contained in a table, follow these steps:

1. Open the Northwind database from its installation directory. Click OK to close the introductory screen. The Northwind: Database dialog box is displayed.

2. Click the Tables tab, shown in Figure 6.2. From the list of tables in the database, double-click Categories. The Categories table opens in Datasheet view.

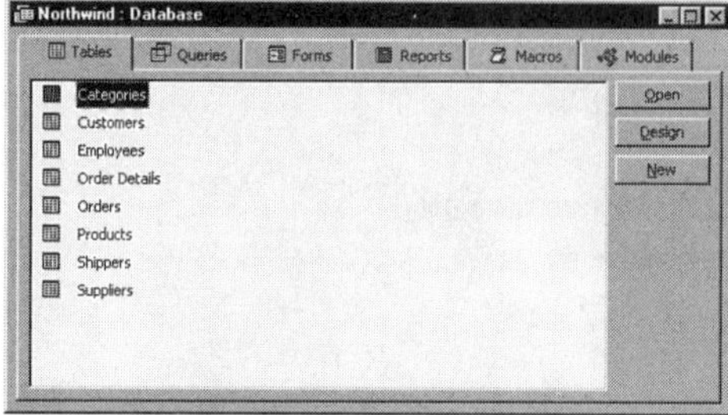

Figure 6.2.
Use the Tables tab to select the table that you want to view or edit.

3. To view the properties of the table columns, click **V**iew | **D**esign View. Your screen now looks like Figure 6.3, where the properties are listed in a table editor.

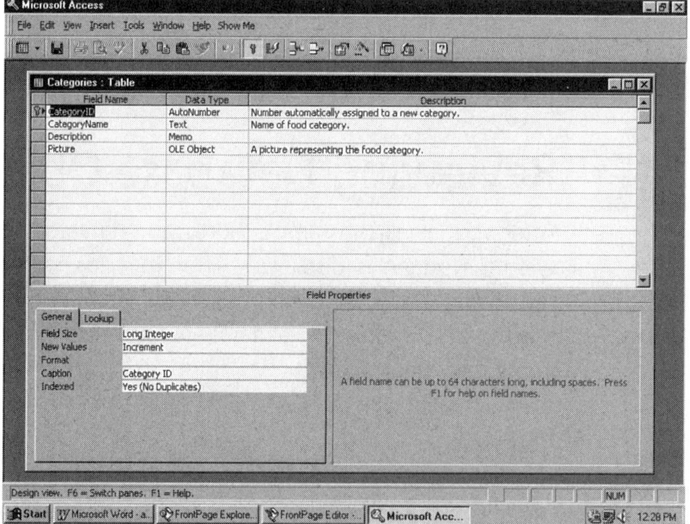

Figure 6.3.
In Design view, you can edit the properties for the columns in the table.

4. Notice that each column in the table has three elements. The Field Name identifies the column table and can contain up to 64 characters. The Data Type defines the type of data stored in the table field. Choices are Text, Memo, Number, Date/Time, Currency, AutoNumber, Yes/No, Hyperlink, and Lookup Wizard. The Description element is optional; it provides a description of the data stored in the table field.

5. Notice the tabs in the lower half of the dialog box. This is where you assign the properties for the column. The General properties you set here are based on the Data Type specified for the column. The Lookup properties appear for only some of these data types.
6. Choose **V**iew | Data**s**heet View. You are asked if you want to save changes to the table. Click **Y**es. You return to Datasheet view.
7. Close the table window using the X button in the upper-right corner of the table window. You return to the Northwind Database dialog box.

Queries

Queries can be saved to HTML, HTX/IDC, or ASP format during export or publishing to Web formats. Refer to **Chapters 13** and **14** to learn how queries export to dynamic formats.

Queries instruct the database driver how to retrieve information that you want to use in reports. Select queries ask questions about the data you store in your database. The result of the query returns without changing data. You can view the data in underlying tables.

To quickly review the information and elements that are contained in a query, follow these steps:

1. With the Northwind database open, click the Queries tab, shown in Figure 6.4. From the list of queries, double-click Category Sales for 1995. The Category Sales for 1995—Select Query dialog box is displayed.

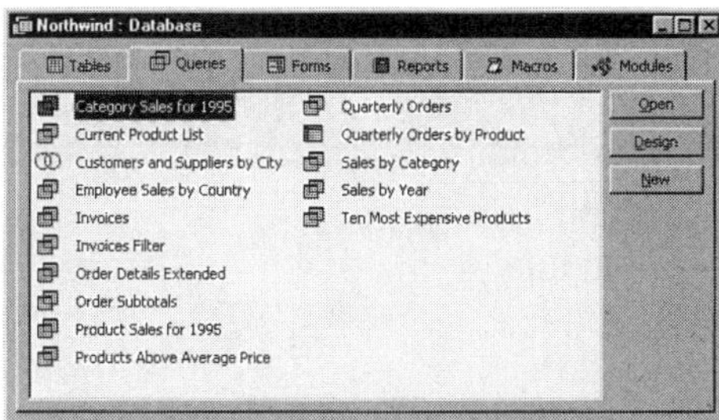

Figure 6.4.
The Queries tab lists all the queries in your database.

2. To view the properties of the query, click **V**iew | **D**esign View. Your screen now looks as shown in Figure 6.5.
3. In Design view, assign properties as follows: Field (the name of the field you want to query), Table (the table in which the field is displayed), Total (how you want the query tabulated), Sort (how you want the results sorted), Show (check to show the results), Criteria (restrictions you place on the query), and a query operator (AND or OR).

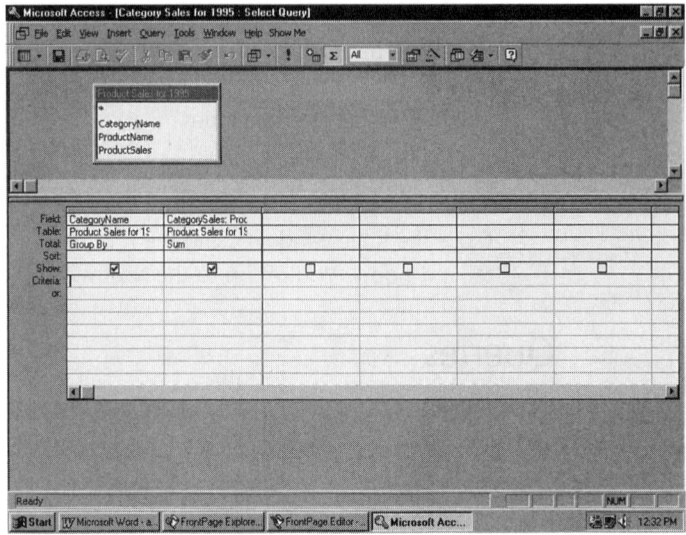

Figure 6.5.
Use Design view to view and edit your queries.

4. To view the query in SQL mode, choose **V**iew | S**Q**L View. The dialog box shown in Figure 6.6 is displayed. You can use this dialog box to enter the query if you are more familiar with the SQL query language.
5. Close the Select Query window using the X button in the upper-right corner of the table window. You return to the Northwind Database dialog box.

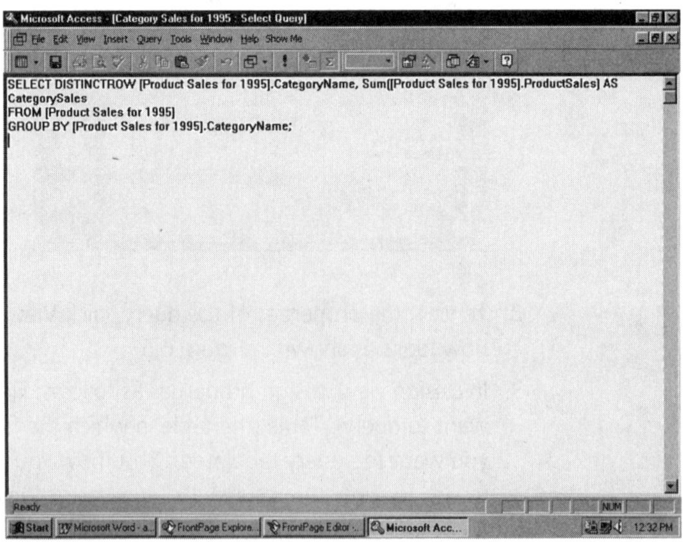

Figure 6.6.
If you are familiar with SQL query language structure, you can enter your query in SQL view.

Forms

Forms can be designed to provide an easy-to-use interface between your database and its users. You insert ActiveX controls into your forms to interface with the data. When you export or publish your database files to HTML format, forms can be saved as HTM, IDC, or ASP files.

Forms can be saved to HTML, HTX/IDC, or ASP format during export or publishing to Web formats. Refer to **Chapters 13** and **14** to learn how forms and associated scripts export to dynamic formats.

To quickly review the information and elements that are contained in forms, follow these steps:

1. With the Northwind database open, click the Forms tab, shown in Figure 6.7. From the list of forms, double-click Categories. The Categories form is displayed.
2. To view the properties of the form fields, click **V**iew | **D**esign View. Your screen now looks like Figure 6.8. An ActiveX Control toolbox is displayed, from which you can add controls to the form. To assign field-specific properties to the form field, right-click and choose Properties from the pop-up window.

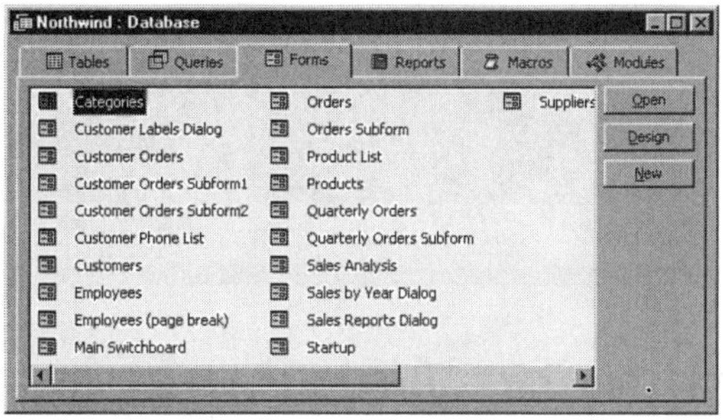

Figure 6.7.
To view or edit one of the forms in your database, select the Forms tab.

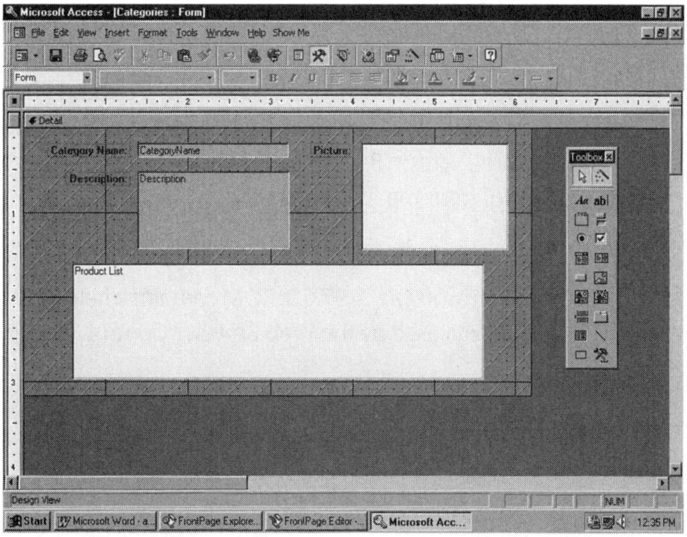

Figure 6.8.
When you are in Design view, you can add ActiveX controls and other properties to your forms.

You can display Web pages in your Access 97 forms by using the Web Browser Control, described in the section titled "Displaying Web Pages in an Access Form."

3. You assign events to the form field by clicking the Event tab in the form field's properties dialog box, shown in Figure 6.9. You can also apply an event to a form field if you right-click on the form field and choose Build **E**vent from the pop-up menu. You use the Expression Builder, Macro Builder, and Code Builder to design the code and procedures that process the data from the forms.
4. To exit Design View, choose **V**iew | **F**orm View.

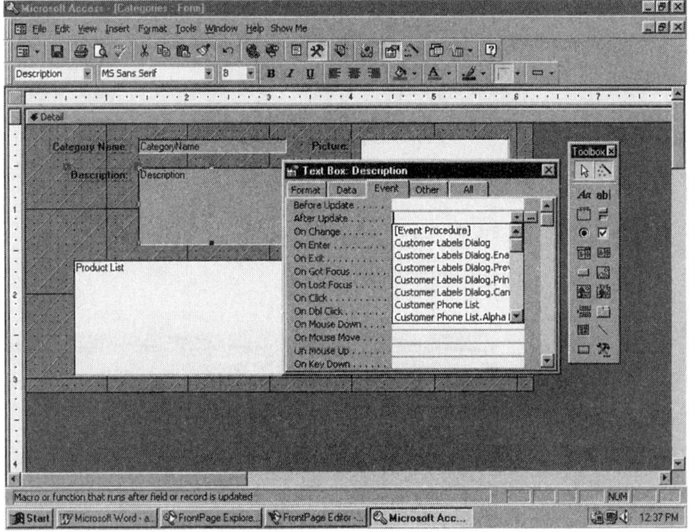

Figure 6.9.
Use the Event tab in the form field's properties dialog box to add an event to the form field.

Displaying Web Pages in an Access Form

To display a Web page in an Access form, you must use the Web Browser Control, an ActiveX control that allows you to view Web pages from a Microsoft Access form. You automatically register this control on your system when you install Microsoft Internet Explorer, version 3.0 (included with Microsoft Office 97). You can also download the control from the following URL:

`http://www.microsoft.com/`

The Microsoft Office 97 CD-ROM contains a help file that lists the methods, properties, and events used by the Web Browser Control. (Find the `\ValuePack\Access\Webhelp` folder and copy the `Iexplore.hlp` and `Iexplore.cnt` files to your hard disk.) You can also find this information at the following URL:

```
http://www.microsoft.com/intdev/sdk/docs/iexplore/
```

To add the Web Browser Control to your form, follow these steps:

1. Open the form in Design view.
2. Click the More Controls tool in the toolbox (the right icon in the bottom row). A menu lists all the ActiveX controls that are registered on your system, as shown in Figure 6.10.

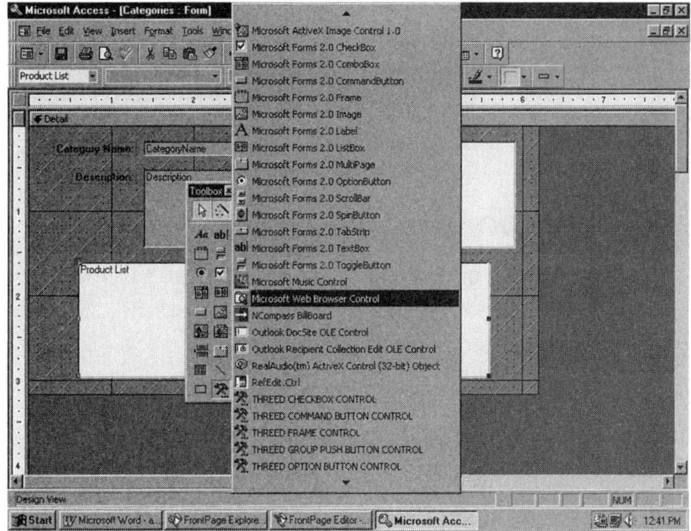

Figure 6.10.
Choose the Web Browser control from the list of ActiveX controls that are registered on your system.

3. Select Microsoft Web Browser Control.
4. Click where you want to place the control in your form, and size the control to the area in which you want to display the Web page. The area displays scrollbars if the page is too wide or long for the display area. You should try to make the control wide enough to display a standard Web page, as shown in Figure 6.11.
5. Use the control's Navigate method to open a Web page within the Web Browser window. For example, the following code loads the home page of Microsoft's Web site:

```
Private Sub Form_Load
   Me!ActiveXCtl0.Navigate "http://www.microsoft.com/"
End Sub
```

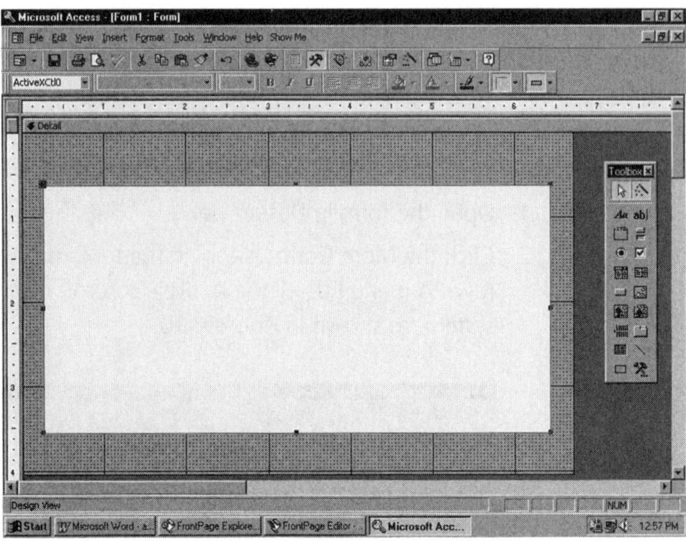

Figure 6.11.
Define an area in your form that is wide enough to display a Web page.

Reports

Reports display the results of a query in a formatted file. When you export reports to HTML format, they are always saved in HTML file format; HTX/IDC or ASP files are not generated for reports.

To view a report file, follow these steps:

1. With the Northwind database open, click the Reports tab, shown in Figure 6.12. From the list of reports, double-click Alphabetical List of Products. The report is displayed in a separate window, as shown in Figure 6.13.

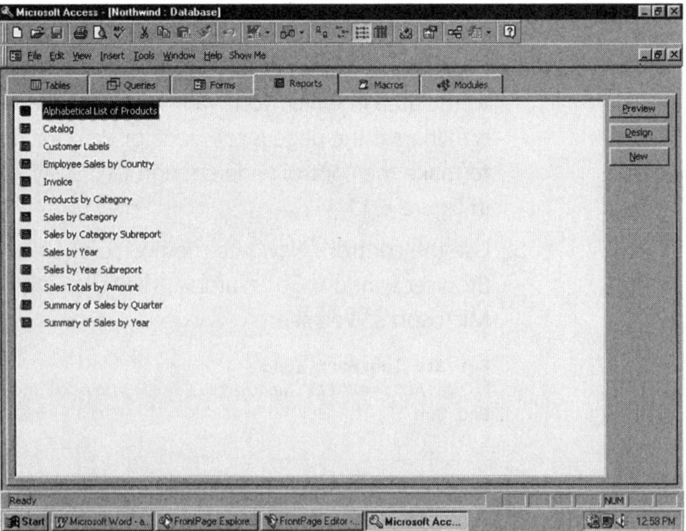

Figure 6.12.
Choose the report that you want to view or edit from the Reports tab.

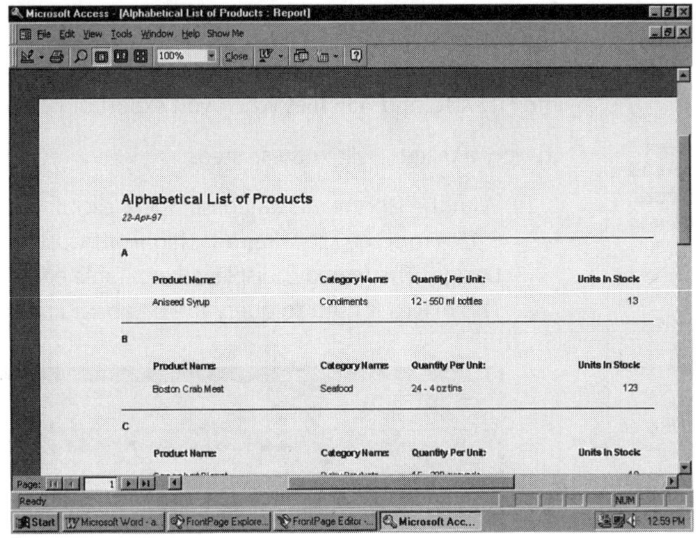

Figure 6.13.
When the report first opens, you see a preview of the report.

2. Choose **V**iew | **D**esign View. The display changes to show design properties of the report, as shown in Figure 6.14. The ActiveX Control Toolbox also is displayed in Design view. If you right-click on a control field, you can view or edit the properties of the form field.

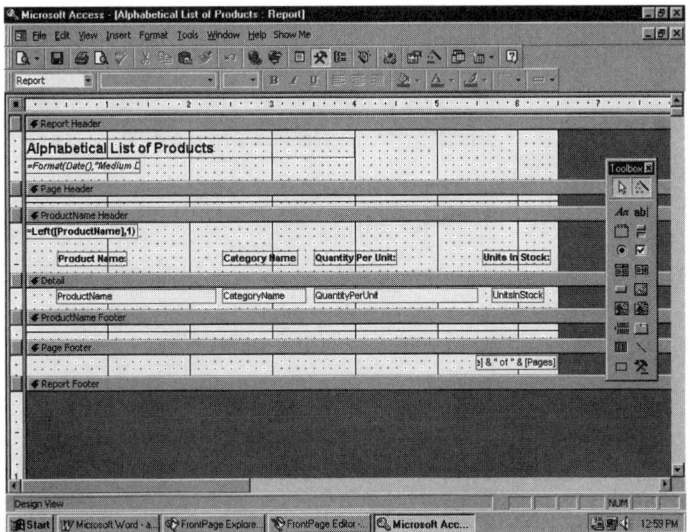

Figure 6.14.
Design your report field areas and assign properties to them in Design view.

3. To exit Design view, choose **V**iew | La**y**out Preview. You return to the preview of your report.
4. Close the report by clicking the X in the upper-right corner of the report preview window.

Macros

Use macros to assign custom actions and code to a form or control. Macros are merged into HTX/IDC and ASP files when you export or publish your databases to the Web.

Refer to **Chapters 13** and **14** to learn how macros incorporate with your Web pages.

To view a macro, follow these steps:

1. With the Northwind database open, click the Macros tab, shown in Figure 6.15. From the list of reports, highlight Customer Labels Dialog, and click **D**esign. The macro is displayed in a table editor, as shown in Figure 6.16. This macro is used to query the database and print mailing labels.

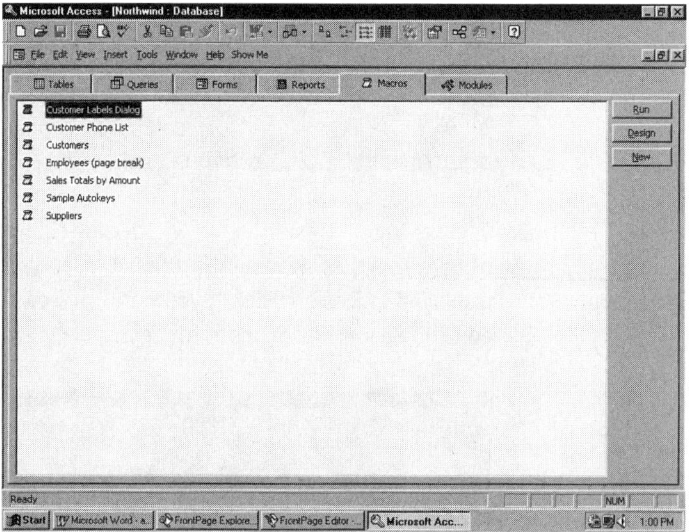

Figure 6.15.
The Macros tab lists all the macros in your database.

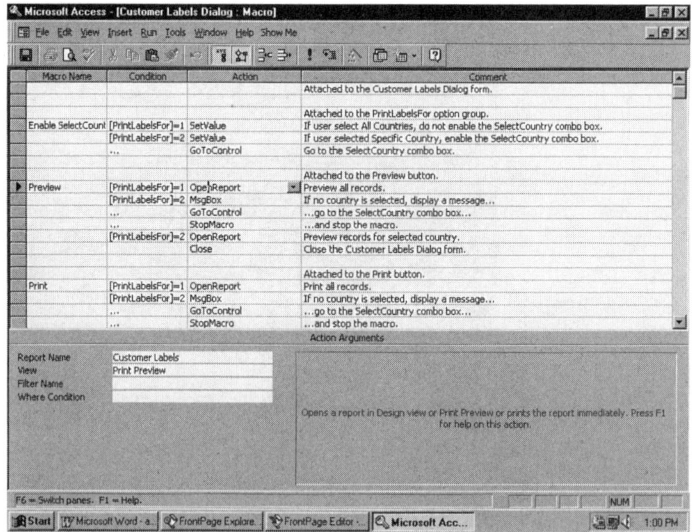

Figure 6.16.
Use the Design table editor to edit your macro.

2. Each statement in a macro contains four parts: Macro Name (a unique name for the macro), Condition (a conditional expression built with the Expression Builder), Action (selected from a drop-down menu when you click the Action field), and an optional Comment that describes the function of the macro.
3. After you select an action in the third column, the Action Arguments display (at the bottom of the screen) changes. The properties you set here are applicable to the type of action you assign in the third column of the table.
4. Close the Macro window by clicking the X in the upper-right corner of the report preview window. Access 97 asks if you want to save changes to the design of the macro. Choose **Y**es to save changes, or **N**o to exit without saving. Choose Cancel to continue designing your macro.

Using HTML Templates and Tokens

When you export your database files to HTML format, you can use an HTML template to create a consistent look and feel and add navigation through your Web pages. The default location for template files is the `\Program Files\Microsoft Office\Templates\Access` folder. You can change the default folder in the Options dialog box. Select the Hyperlinks/HTML tab, and enter your template folder in the HTML Template field.

If you use tags that reference files such as images, assume that the files reside in the same folder that your output files are located in. You can choose the folder when you publish your Access database using the Publish to the Web Wizard or the Save As/Export command on the File menu.

To use your own HTML templates, include some tokens in the HTML file. These tokens are unique to Microsoft Access, and they determine where data should be inserted into the page. When you export your database to an HTML format, the template file is merged with the database output files. When you specify a dynamic HTML format such as IDC files or Active Server Pages, the HTML template is merged with the `.htx` or `.asp` file during output. The tokens are replaced with the information shown in Table 6.1.

Table 6.1. HTML tokens and replacements.

Token	*Replacement*
`<!--AccessTemplate_Body-->`	Replaced with the object output.
`<!--AccessTemplate_FirstPage-->`	Replaced with an anchor tag to the first page.

continues

Table 6.1. continued

Token	*Replacement*
<!--AccessTemplate_LastPage-->	Replaced with an anchor tag to the last page.
<!--AccessTemplate_NextPage-->	Replaced with an anchor tag to the next page.
<!--AccessTemplate_PageNumber-->	Replaced with the current page number.
<!--AccessTemplate_PreviousPage-->	Replaced with an anchor tag to the previous page.
<!--AccessTemplate_Title-->	Replaced with the object name, which is placed in the title bar of the Web browser.

Saving Databases to HTML Format

Microsoft Access can be used to create applications for the World Wide Web. For example, you can use Access to create anything from a simple corporate home page with a form to a complete online catalog. You can export or publish database objects to one of three formats:

- *Static HTML.* Select this format when you do not expect your data to change frequently or do not require forms. This method is compatible with all servers and all browsers, but you will need to republish your data files when they change.
- *Dynamic IDC/HTX.* Use this format when your data changes frequently and you store or retrieve live data from your database using forms. This method is compatible with all browsers and can run on the following servers:

  Microsoft Internet Information Server 1.x and 2.0 using Internet Database Connector on Windows NT Server, version 3.5.1

  Microsoft Internet Information Server, version 2.0 or higher, using Internet Database Connector or ActiveX Server on Windows NT Server, version 4.0 or higher

  Microsoft Personal Web Server on Windows 95 or higher or on Windows NT Workstation, version 4.0 or higher

- *Dynamic ASP (Active Server Pages).* Use this format when your data changes frequently and you store or retrieve live data from your database using forms. This method is compatible with Internet Explorer 3.0 or higher and can run on the following servers:

  Microsoft Internet Information Server, version 2.0 or higher, using Internet Database Connector or ActiveX Server on Windows NT Server, version 4.0 or higher

  Microsoft Personal Web Server on Windows 95 or higher or on Windows NT Workstation version 4.0 or higher

There are two ways to save your Access 97 database objects to Web format: The first method uses the **F**ile | Save **A**s/Export command to save a single database object. The second method uses the Publish to the Web Wizard, which stores all the documents you choose as a complete Web publication. Datasheets and forms can be saved to static or dynamic HTML formats. In addition, the Publish to the Web Wizard creates a home page and copies the files to a single folder in the Web server. You also have the option of saving the Web publication profile to use at a later time.

The Publish to the Web Wizard also works in conjunction with the Web Publishing Wizard to publish your Access database to a server. The Web Publishing Wizard is furnished on the Microsoft Office 97 or Microsoft Access 97 CD. To install it, run the `ValuPack\WebPost\WebPost.exe` file and follow the installation instructions in the Setup wizard.

Exporting Objects to Static HTML Format

Static HTML pages take a snapshot of the data in your database at publication time. You must republish when your data changes. (Reports are always saved in static HTML format.)

To export a datasheet to static HTML format, follow these steps:

1. In the Database window, click the name of the table, query, or form you want to export.
2. Choose **F**ile | Save **A**s/Export. The Save As dialog box is displayed.
3. Click To an **E**xternal File or Database and choose OK. The Save *object name* As dialog box shown in Figure 6.17 is displayed.

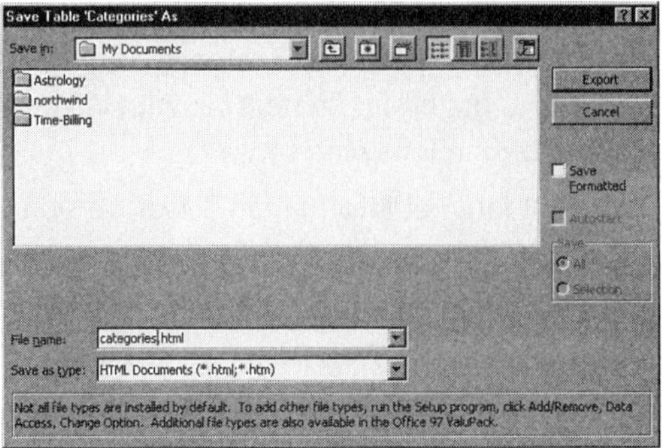

Figure 6.17.
The Save As dialog box saves a single database object to HTML, HTX/IDC, or ASP format.

4. Use the Save **i**n box to locate the drive and directory to which you want to save the database files.
5. From the Save as **t**ype box, select HTML Documents (`*.html`; `*.htm`).
6. In the File **n**ame field, enter the name you want to use for the saved file.
7. If you want to save your datasheet in a format that looks similar to that which you see in Datasheet view in Access 97, select Save **F**ormatted.
8. Select the Aut**o**start check box if you want to display the results of your HTML file in your Web browser after the file exports.
9. Click Export. If you selected Save **F**ormatted in step 7, the HTML Output Options dialog box is displayed. Use the **B**rowse button to specify an HTML template to use for your pages. Click OK twice to continue saving your page.

Publishing Your Database to Static HTML Format

To publish your database to HTML format using the Publish to the Web Wizard, follow these steps:

1. Choose **F**ile | Save as **H**TML. The Publish to the Web Wizard screen shown in Figure 6.18 is displayed.
2. If you have previously created a Web publication profile that you want to reuse, select I want to use a Web publication profile I already created with this wizard. Highlight the profile from the list beneath the prompt.
3. Click **N**ext. In the second screen, shown in Figure 6.19, you select the items you want to publish. Select the items from the Tables, Queries, Forms, or Reports tabs, and click the **S**elect button. To publish the entire database, choose the Select **A**ll button in the All Objects tab.

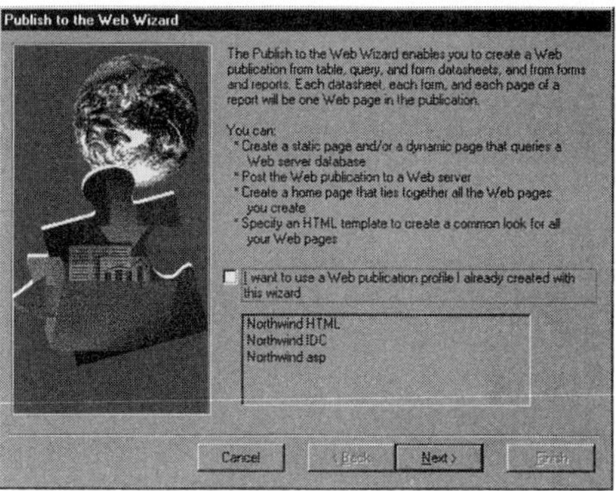

Figure 6.18.
Use the Publish to the Web Wizard to publish part or all of your database to a Web site or file directory.

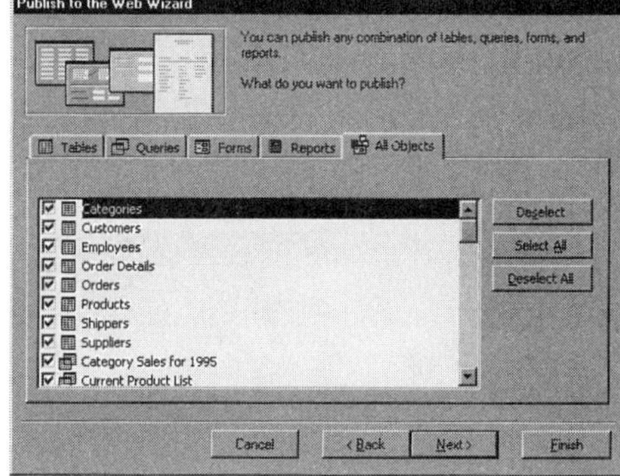

Figure 6.19.
Select the items you want to publish from this screen.

4. Click **N**ext. You are asked to specify an HTML document for a template. Click the **B**rowse button to open the Select an HTML Template dialog box. Use the Look in field to locate the drive and directory in which your template is saved. Double-click the template filename to assign it. You return to the wizard. Click **N**ext and proceed to step 6 if you do not want to choose additional templates; otherwise, follow step 5.
5. To select different templates for some items, check the I want to select different templates for some of the selected objects button. When you click **N**ext, the screen shown in Figure 6.20 is displayed. Select the objects to which you want to assign another template. (Shift-click to select contiguous items, or Ctrl-click to select random multiple objects.) Then click the B**r**owse button to choose another template. After you have selected your templates, click **N**ext to continue.

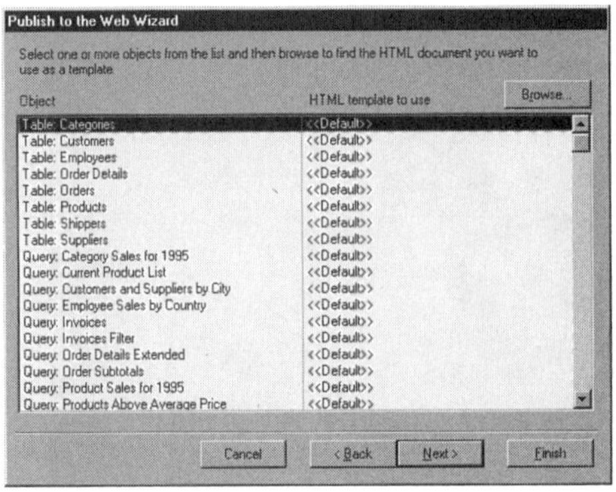

Figure 6.20.
You can choose additional templates for a portion of your Web in this screen.

6. You are asked to select a file format for your Web publication from the screen shown in Figure 6.21. Choose **S**tatic HTML. If you want to publish to multiple formats, click the I want to select different format types for some of the selected objects and proceed to step 7; otherwise, proceed to step 8.

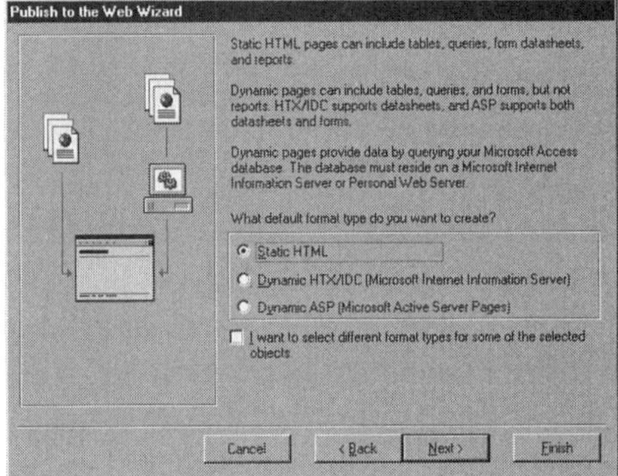

Figure 6.21.
Select the file format to which you want to publish your database in this screen.

7. To select additional file formats, click **N**ext. Highlight the items that you want to publish to another file format, and choose the **H**TML, HTX/ID**C**, or **A**SP radio button to specify the file format.
8. Click **N**ext. On the screen shown in Figure 6.22, you are asked where you want to publish your files. In the I want to put my Web publication in this folder field, click the B**r**owse button. The Choose a directory for the objects you have selected dialog box is displayed.
9. Use the Look in box to choose the drive and directory to which you want to publish your files. Click Select to return to the wizard.

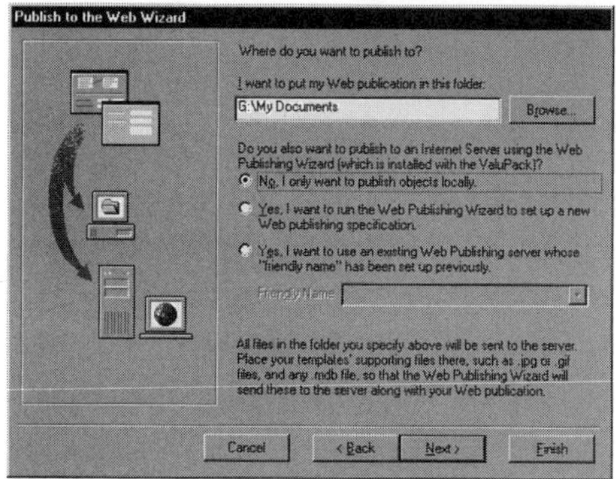

Figure 6.22.
Select the directory or folder to which you want to publish your database from this screen.

10. You are asked if you also want to publish to an Internet Server using the Web Publishing Wizard. You are given the following options:
    - *N**o**, I only want to publish objects locally.* Choose this option if you do not want to connect to a server to publish your pages. If you publish your database in this manner, you can use the FrontPage Explorer's File | Import command or Import Web Wizard to import the database publication into your Web.
    - ***Y**es, I want to run the Web Publishing Wizard.* Choose this option to set up a new Web publishing specification that you can use at a later time and to publish your database to a server.
    - *Y**e**s, I want to use an existing Web Publishing server whose 'friendly name' has been set up previously.* Choose this option to publish your database to a server that has already been configured in the Web Publishing Wizard. Select the profile from the list.

    For this task, choose N**o**, I only want to publish objects locally.
11. Click **N**ext. On the screen shown in Figure 6.23, you are asked if you also want to create a home page that ties all your pages together. *Choose **Y**es, I want to create a home page.* In the *What file name do you want for your home page?* field, enter a name for your home page. The default is `Default`. You do not need to enter an extension.
12. Click **N**ext. On the screen shown in Figure 6.24, you are asked if you want to save your selections to a Web publication profile. If so, choose Yes, I want to save wizard answers to a Web publication profile. Enter `Northwind HTML` in the **P**rofile Name field.

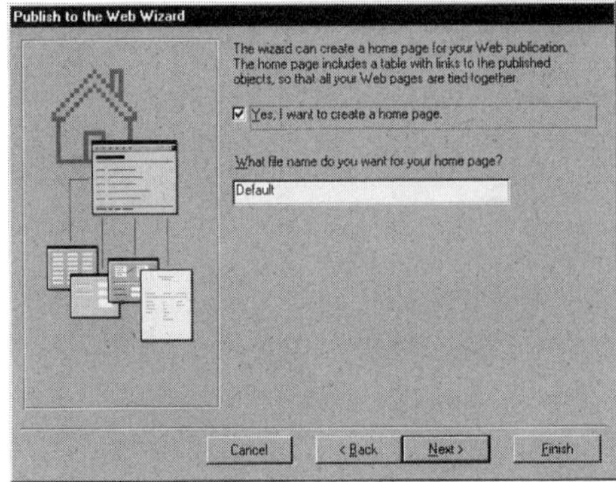

Figure 6.23.
Elect to create a home page and assign a name to it in this screen.

13. Click **F**inish. Access 97 outputs the objects to HTML format. As the Northwind database is saved, you are prompted for some values to use within the publication. When you are prompted for a starting date, enter `1/1/95`. Use `12/31/95` for an ending date. Also, when you are prompted for a starting record number, enter `1`.

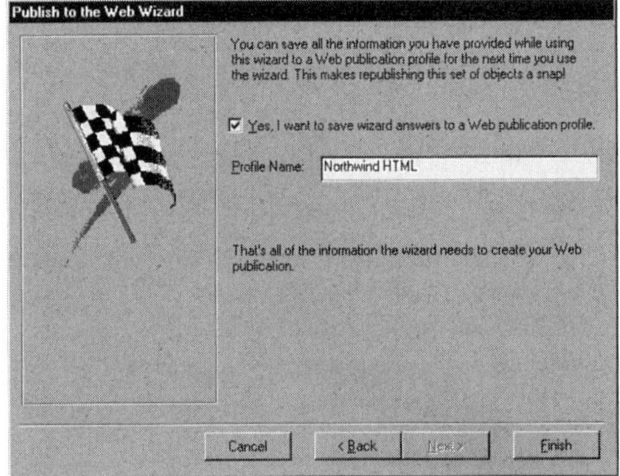

Figure 6.24.
Choose Yes, I want to save wizard answers to a Web publication profile to save your publication settings for later use.

Preparing Your Server for Dynamic Databases

In Chapter 13, you learn how to publish an Access database to Web pages that interact with your database dynamically. For these types of databases to work properly, you must follow some preliminary setup procedures that are common to both types of dynamic pages. Basically, your server must meet the following requirements:

- Copy your Microsoft Access database to the Web server, or note the network location. You will need this information when you define your data source.

- Install the Microsoft Access Desktop Driver on the Web server.
- Define your database as a system data source or file data source on the server.
- Set the necessary logon permissions for the database, and assign sharing properties for the folder in which the `.idc` or `.asp` files reside on the server.
- Configure read and execute permissions for the directory in which the `.idc` files and `.asp` files are published.

NOTE: Note that dynamic HTML files work best when accessed by a limited number of users; the maximum limit is 64 concurrent users. If you expect that your Web will need more capacity, you can use the Microsoft Access Upsizing Tools to convert your Access 97 database to a Microsoft SQL Server database. To obtain more information from Microsoft's Web site, connect to the Internet. From Microsoft Access 97, choose **H**elp | Microsoft On The **W**eb | **F**ree Stuff, or use the following URL:

`http://www.microsoft.com/OfficeFreeStuff/Access/`

You will find many items of interest at this URL. Included are sample databases, utilities, wizards, product updates, trial software, viewable code, and add-ins.

Importing the Database into Your FrontPage Web

To import the database file into your FrontPage web, follow these steps:

1. From the FrontPage Explorer, create or open a web into which the database files will be published.
2. Select the directory into which you want to import the database file.
3. Choose **F**ile | **I**mport. The Import File to FrontPage Web dialog box shown in Figure 6.25 is displayed.
4. Click **A**dd File. The Add File to Import List dialog box is displayed.
5. Use the Look **i**n box to locate the drive and directory in which your database file is saved. Double-click the file to add it to the import list. You return to the Import File to FrontPage Web dialog box.
6. Click OK. FrontPage imports the database file to the directory you selected.

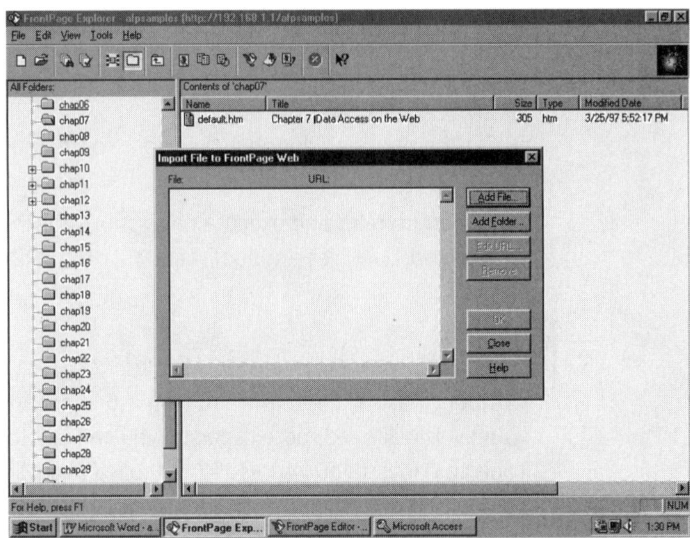

Figure 6.25.
Use the Import File to FrontPage Web dialog box to import database objects that are not yet included in your web.

Installing the Microsoft Access Desktop Driver

To access your Microsoft Access database from your Web server, you will need to install the Microsoft Access Desktop Driver (`odbcjt32.dll`) on the Microsoft Internet Information Server or Microsoft Personal Web Server. In Internet Information Server, you can install this driver by selecting ODBC Drivers and Administration during the Setup process. The Microsoft Personal Web Server does not include this driver.

You can use your Microsoft Office 97 Professional or Microsoft Access 97 CD to install this driver onto either server. If you have not yet installed Access 97 on your hard drive, you can install the Microsoft Access Desktop Driver by performing steps 6–9 from the following task as you select the Access 97 components you want to install.

To install the Microsoft Access Desktop Driver after Access 97 has been installed on your system, follow these steps:

1. Insert your Microsoft Office 97 Professional or Microsoft Access 97 CD into your CD-ROM drive.
2. From the Start menu, choose **S**ettings | **C**ontrol Panel. The Control Panel dialog box is displayed.
3. Double-click the Add/Remove Programs icon. The Add/Remove Programs Properties dialog box is displayed.

4. Highlight Microsoft Office 97 Professional Edition, and click Add/**R**emove. You are prompted to insert your CD. Choose OK to continue.
5. Setup searches for installed components, and the Setup dialog box is displayed. Click **A**dd/Remove. The Maintenance dialog box is displayed.
6. Select Data Access from the **O**bjects list; then click the Chan**g**e Option button. The Data Access dialog box is displayed.
7. Highlight Database Drivers from the **O**ptions list, and click Chan**g**e Option. The Database Drivers dialog box shown in Figure 6.26 is displayed.
8. Select Microsoft Access Driver and choose OK.
9. Click **C**ontinue and complete the instructions in the Setup Wizard.

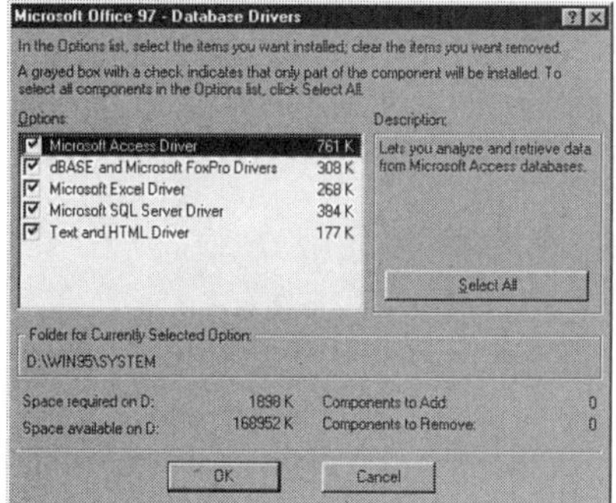

Figure 6.26.
Select the Microsoft Access driver from the Data Access | Database Drivers options screen during setup.

Defining Your Database as a Data Source

Assume, for the following task, that you are going to publish the Northwind database to your Web server. To define the Northwind database as a system data source in Windows NT 4.0 or Windows 95, follow these steps:

1. Click the Windows Start button, and choose **S**ettings | **C**ontrol Panel. The Windows Control Panel opens.
2. Double-click the 32bit ODBC icon (Windows 95) or the ODBC icon (Windows NT). The ODBC Microsoft Access 97 Setup dialog box is displayed.
3. Click the System DSN tab, shown in Figure 6.27.
4. Click A**d**d. The Create New Data Source dialog box shown in Figure 6.28 is displayed.

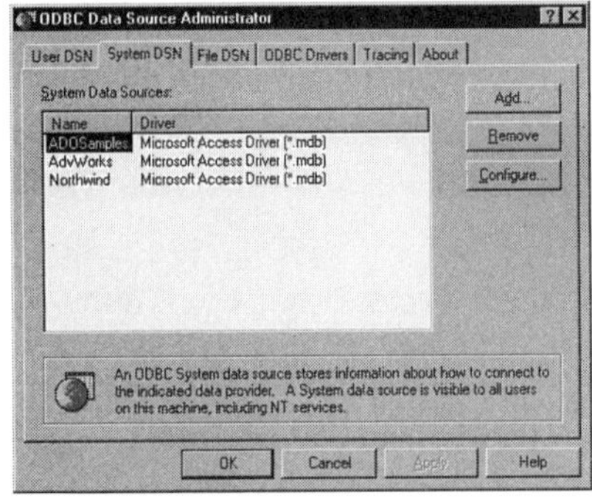

Figure 6.27.
Use the System DSN tab to create a system data source name for your Access 97 database file.

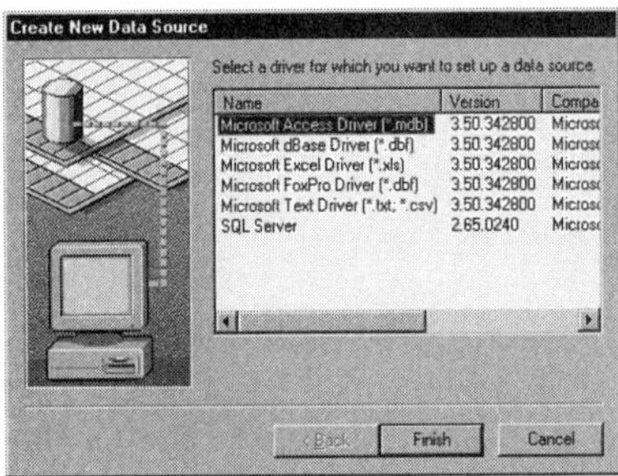

Figure 6.28.
Add the database source in the Create New Data Source dialog box.

5. Highlight Microsoft Access Driver (`*.mdb`), and click Finish. You return to the ODBC Microsoft Access 97 dialog box.
6. In the Data Source **N**ame field, enter `Northwind`.
7. Click **S**elect. Use the Drives and Directories fields to locate the folder in which the Northwind database is saved. If you imported the database file to your Web server, you will need to enter the file path (not the URL) to the database file (for example, `c:\InetPub\wwwroot\`*`webname`*`\`*`folder`*`\northwind.mdb`). After you select the file, choose OK to return to the ODBC Microsoft Access 97 Setup dialog box.
8. Choose OK to exit the dialog boxes. Your database is configured as a system data source.

Setting Read and Execute Permissions in Windows NT 4.0 Server

To set read and execute permissions for Internet Information Server 2.0 running under Windows NT 4.0 Server, follow these steps:

1. From the Start menu, choose **P**rograms | Microsoft Internet Server (Common) | Internet Service Manager. The Microsoft Internet Service Manager is displayed.

2. Expand the tree and double-click WWW (Running). The WWW Service Properties for *servername* dialog box is displayed.
3. Click the Directories tab, shown in Figure 6.29.

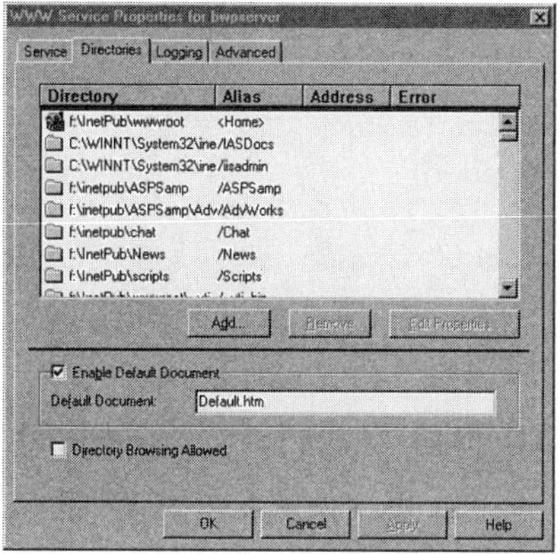

Figure 6.29.
The Directories tab allows you to select the directory into which you want to publish your dynamic database files.

4. To add the folder to which your IDC or ASP files are published, click A**d**d. The Directory Properties dialog box is displayed.
5. Click the **B**rowse button near the **D**irectory field. The Select Directory dialog box shown in Figure 6.30 is displayed.

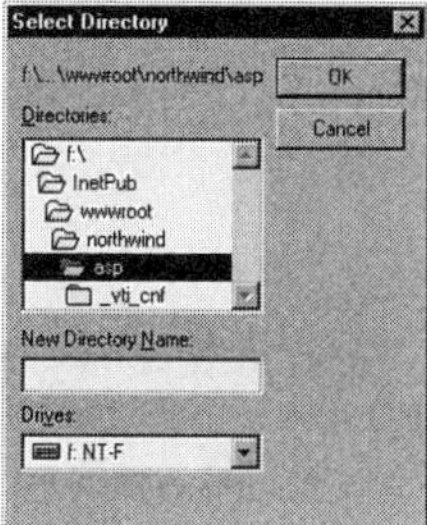

Figure 6.30.
Use the Select Directory dialog box to choose your publishing directory.

6. Use the Dri**v**es and **D**irectories boxes to locate the directory on your server into which you will publish your database (for example, `c:\InetPub\wwwroot\northwind\idc` or `c:\InetPub\wwwroot\northwind\asp`). Click OK to return to the Directory Properties dialog box.
7. Check the **V**irtual Directory radio button, and enter `/northwind/idc` or `/northwind/asp` in the A**l**ias field.
8. In the Access area of the dialog box, select the **R**ead and **E**xecute check boxes, as shown in Figure 6.31.
9. Choose OK to exit the Directory Properties and WWW Service Properties dialog boxes. Close the Microsoft Internet Service Manager. Your directory is configured for Read and Execute permissions.

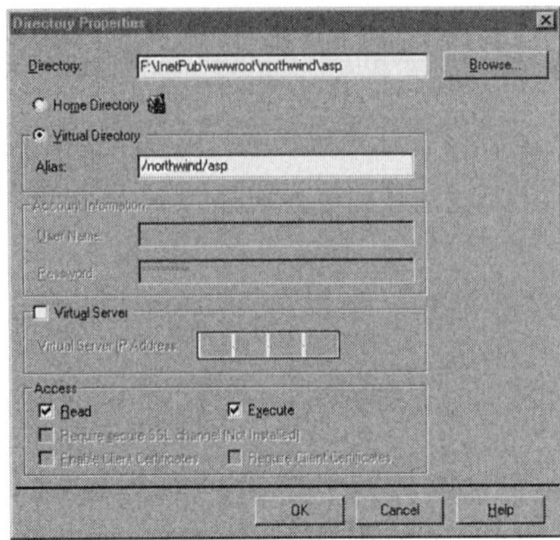

Figure 6.31.
Assign read and execute permissions for the directory.

Configuring Your Directory in the Microsoft Personal Web Server

To set sharing properties for Microsoft Personal Web Server running under Windows 95 or Windows NT Workstation 4.0, follow these steps:

1. From the Start menu, choose **S**ettings | **C**ontrol Panel. The Control Panel dialog box is displayed.
2. Double-click the Personal Web Server icon. The Personal Web Server Properties dialog box is displayed.
3. Click the Administration tab. Then click the **A**dministration button. The Internet Services Administrator page shown in Figure 6.32 opens in your browser.

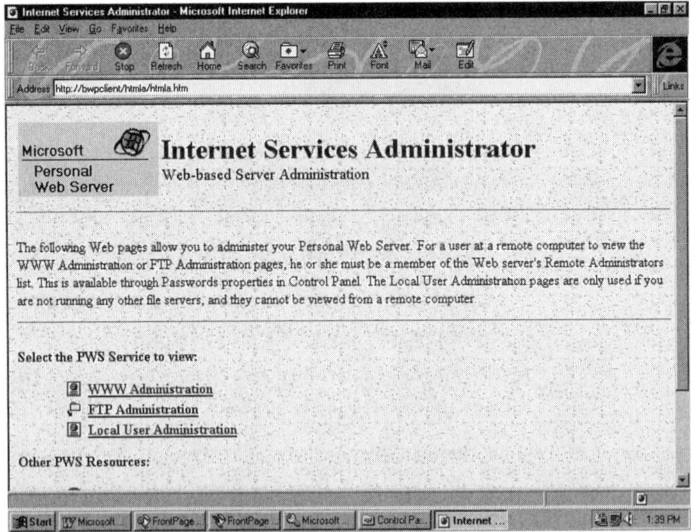

Figure 6.32.
The Internet Services Administrator page allows you to administer the Microsoft Personal Web Server.

4. Click the WWW Administration link. The Internet Services Administrator—WWW page shown in Figure 6.33 is displayed.

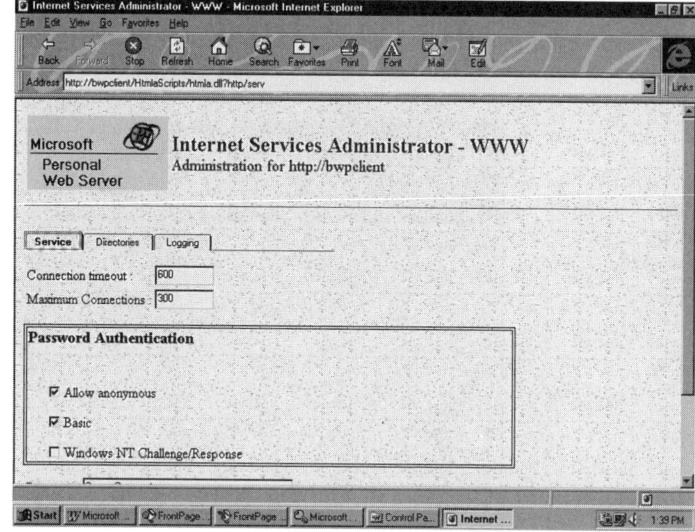

Figure 6.33.
The Internet Services Administrator—WWW page allows you to configure the WWW portion of the Microsoft Personal Web Server.

5. Click the Directories tab. Scroll to the bottom of the table that lists all the directories on your server, and click Add (it appears on the bottom-right side of the table, as shown in Figure 6.34). The WWW Administrator—Directory Add page is displayed. (If you know the path into which you will publish your files, enter it in the Path field (for example, `c:\WEBSHARE\WWWROOT\northwind\idc` or `c:\WEBSHARE\WWWROOT\northwind\asp`), and skip steps 6–9.)

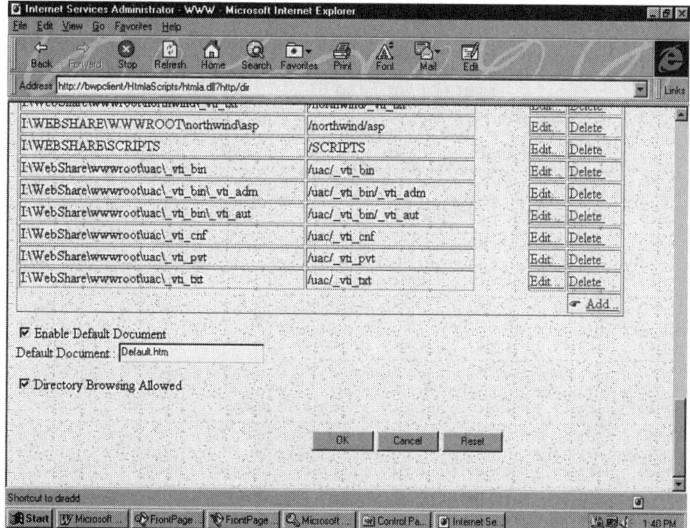

Figure 6.34.
To add your database directory, click the Add button at the bottom-right side of the directories list table.

6. To locate the directory by browsing, click the Browse button. The Select Directory page is displayed.
7. Scroll to the Drives section at the bottom of the page, shown in Figure 6.35. Click the drive on which your WWW server is located. The page refreshes and displays the directories on that drive.

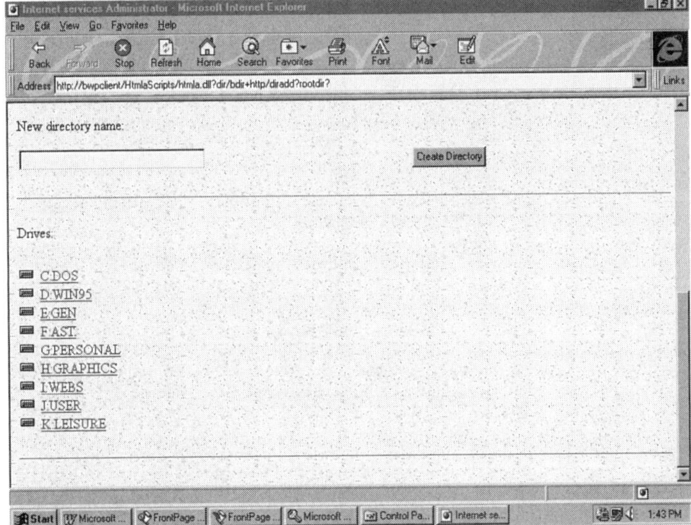

Figure 6.35.
Select the drive to which you are saving your database objects from the Drives section of the Select Directory page.

8. From the Directories list, click each subfolder until you locate the directory into which your files will be published.
9. After the correct path is displayed in the Path field, as shown in Figure 6.36, click OK. You return to the WWW Administrator—Directory Add page.
10. Check the Virtual Directory radio button, and enter `/northwind/idc` or `/northwind/asp` in the Directory Alias field.
11. In the Access area of the page, select the Read and Execute check boxes, as shown in Figure 6.37.
12. Choose OK. You return to the WWW Administrator—Directory page. The directory is displayed in the table.

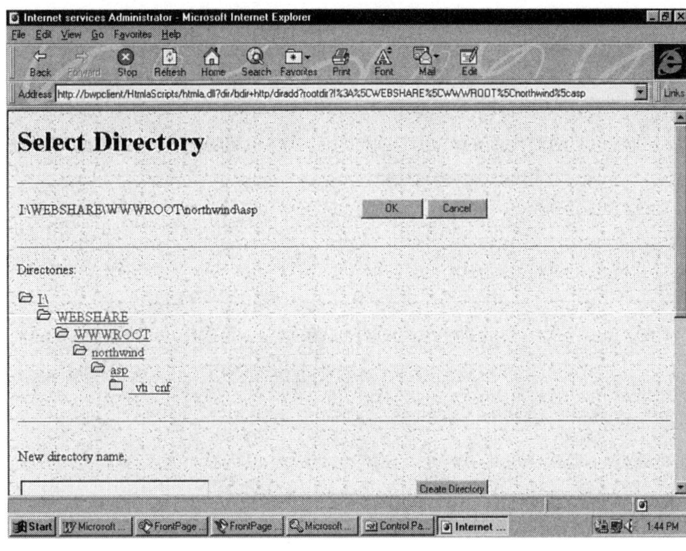

Figure 6.36.
After the correct path is displayed in the Path field, click OK to return to the WWW Administrator—Directory Add page.

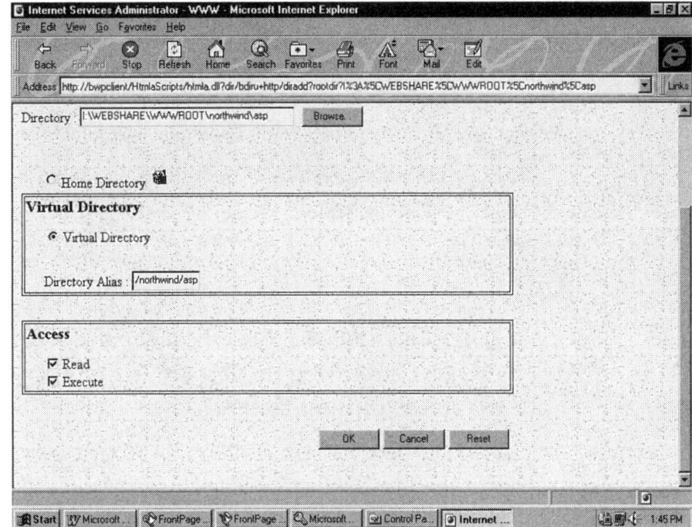

Figure 6.37.
Select the Read and Execute check boxes to assign proper permissions to the directory.

Workshop Wrap-Up

In this chapter, you received a quick review of the elements contained in a Microsoft Access 97 database, and you learned how to export your database to static HTML format. You also learned how to configure permissions and database drivers in Internet Information Server and Microsoft Personal Web Server so that you can communicate with your databases dynamically.

Next Steps

In Chapters 13 and 14, you will learn how to export your Access databases to dynamic formats and what happens to the database files after they get published. You can learn more about using Access 97 databases on your intranet or the World Wide Web in the following chapters:

- In Chapter 7, "Real-Life Examples: Bringing Your Intranet Together," you learn how to combine Office 97 documents together to organize information on your intranet or WWW site.
- In Chapter 13, "Working with IDC Database Connection," you learn how to export your databases to HTX/IDC format and how the pages are constructed.
- In Chapter 14, "Using Active Server Databases," you learn how to export your databases to Active Server Pages (ASP) format and how the pages are constructed.
- In Chapter 16, "Real-Life Examples: Interacting with the Outside World," you learn about some practical applications that dynamically interface with the outside world.
- In Appendix A, "Online Resources," you find a list of online references that can assist you with your database applications.
- In Appendix B, "Additional Books," you find a list of books that you can use for additional help.

Q&A

Q: I notice that the Publish to the Web Wizard saves Web pages with an `.html` extension by default. Is there any way I can change the default extension to `.htm`?

A: Unfortunately not. If you want to save a page with an `.htm` extension, you will need to use the File | Save As/Export method and enter the extension in the File name dialog box.

Q: The HTML template file and images are not saved into the directory to which I exported my database files. Do I need to import those into my FrontPage web?

A: You do not need to import the HTML template file into your web, but you will need to use the File | Import command from the FrontPage Explorer to import any images that appear on the template.

SEVEN

Bringing Your Intranet Together

With all the templates and wizards available at your disposal in Office 97 and FrontPage 97, you are sure to find many ways to get your intranet site off and running quickly. With many document, worksheet, database, and Web page examples to choose from, you can quickly form the basis of your intranet site. Hyperlinks between your Office 97 and FrontPage 97 documents provide seamless integration with all of the documents on your intranet. This chapter gives you some examples of how to tie your documents together.

In this chapter, you

- Review ways that you can use Office 97 and FrontPage 97 together to create your intranet site
- Learn about the many different templates and wizards available with Office 97 and FrontPage 97 and the categories into which they fall
- Create a simple Web site that contains hyperlinks between Office 97 documents and Web pages
- Learn how to add hyperlinks between different types of Office 97 documents and Web pages
- Browse your Web content with the seamless interface of Internet Explorer

Tasks in this chapter:

- Creating a Simple Web for an Intranet
- Creating a New Office Document for Your Intranet Web
- Adding Links Between Office 97 Documents
- Creating Links from Office 97 Documents to Web Pages
- Creating Links from Web Pages to Office 97 Documents
- Moving Your Files to New Directories

Using Office 97 and FrontPage 97 Together

There are clear advantages to using Office 97 and FrontPage 97 together in your intranet. Both applications offer a wealth of templates and wizards that can get you off and running quickly as you develop your intranet. These templates and wizards come in several different business categories, and you can modify them to suit your individual needs. Table 7.1 lists the templates and wizards available in each of the Office 97 and FrontPage 97 applications, arranged by categories that will work well together. You will use some of these templates and wizards in the "Creating Links from Office 97 Documents to Web Pages" task to create a simple intranet site that links Office 97 documents and Web pages together.

Table 7.1. Office 97 and FrontPage templates and wizards.

Category	*Template or Wizard*	*Program*
Corporate	Business Plan	PowerPoint
	Business Planner	Excel
	Company Meeting	PowerPoint
	Corporate Home Page	PowerPoint
	Corporate Presence Wizard	FrontPage Explorer
	Financial Overview	PowerPoint
	Office Directory	FrontPage Editor
	Organizational Overview	PowerPoint
Accounting	Asset Tracking	Access
	Expense Statement	Excel
	Expenses	Access
	Inventory Control	Access
	Invoice	Excel
	Ledger	Access
	Order Entry	Access
	Purchase Order	Excel
	Time and Billing	Access
	Timecard	Excel
Customer Relations	Customer Support Web	FrontPage Explorer
	Feedback Form	FrontPage Editor
	Survey Form	FrontPage Editor
General	Bibliography	FrontPage Editor
	Confirmation Form	FrontPage Editor
	Database Connector Wizard	FrontPage Editor
	Database Results	FrontPage Editor
	Discussion Web Wizard	FrontPage Explorer
	Faxes	Word
	Flyer	PowerPoint
	Form Page Wizard	FrontPage Editor
	Frames Wizard	FrontPage Editor
	Frequently Asked Questions	FrontPage Editor
	Glossary of Terms	FrontPage Editor

Category	*Template or Wizard*	*Program*
	Guest Book	FrontPage Editor
	Hot List	FrontPage Editor
	Hyperdocument Page	FrontPage Editor
	Lecture Abstract	FrontPage Editor
	Letters	Word
	Meeting Agenda	FrontPage Editor
	Memos	Word
	Reports	Word
	Search Page	FrontPage Editor
	Seminar Schedule	FrontPage Editor
	Table of Contents	FrontPage Editor
	User Registration	FrontPage Editor
	What's New	FrontPage Editor
Human Resources	Human Resources Information	PowerPoint
	Employee Directory	FrontPage Editor
	Employment Opportunities	FrontPage Editor
	Resume	Word
Management	Resource Scheduling	Access
	Service Call Management	Access
Personal	Personal Web	FrontPage Explorer
	Personal Home Page Wizard	FrontPage Editor
Products/Services	Product Description	FrontPage Editor
	Product or Event Registration	FrontPage Editor
	Product Overview	PowerPoint
	Software Data Sheet	FrontPage Editor
Projects	Project Overview	PowerPoint
	Project Status	PowerPoint
	Project Web	FrontPage Explorer
	Reporting Progress	PowerPoint
Sales/Marketing	Address Book	Access
	Change Request	Excel
	Contact Management	Access

continues

Table 7.1. continued

Category	*Template or Wizard*	*Program*
	Directory of Press Releases	FrontPage Editor
	Marketing Plan	PowerPoint
	Press Release	FrontPage Editor
	Sales Quote	Excel

There is another advantage to using FrontPage 97 and Office 97 together in your intranet: You can use the Web management tools in the FrontPage Explorer to maintain your links for you, ensuring that as your Web grows and changes, your links are maintained. When you import your Office 97 documents into your FrontPage web, the FrontPage Explorer keeps track of the links between your Office 97 and FrontPage documents and automatically corrects the links if they are moved to different directories in your web.

The key to creating hyperlinks that update automatically is to generate relative URLs in your Office 97 documents. One way to generate relative URLs that will work with Office 97 and FrontPage 97 is to first create a web in the FrontPage Explorer. As you create your Office 97 documents, import them into the FrontPage web before you create your links. To edit your Office 97 documents, open them from the FrontPage Explorer. When you save your edited Office 97 document, the FrontPage Explorer automatically imports the new file into your FrontPage web.

Creating a Simple Web for an Intranet

In the following tasks, you'll create a simple web that contains some Office 97 and Web documents that are interlinked. First, you must create a FrontPage web that will hold all the documents.

To create the web, follow these steps:

1. From the FrontPage Explorer, choose **F**ile | **N**ew | FrontPage **W**eb (Ctrl+N). The New FrontPage Web dialog box shown in Figure 7.1 is displayed.

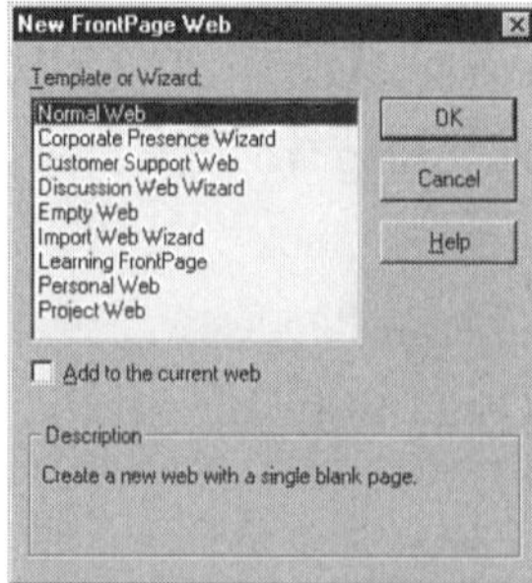

Figure 7.1.
Use the New FrontPage Web dialog box to create a Normal Web in the FrontPage Explorer.

2. In the **T**emplate or Wizard field, highlight Normal Web and choose OK. The Normal Web Template dialog box shown in Figure 7.2 is displayed.

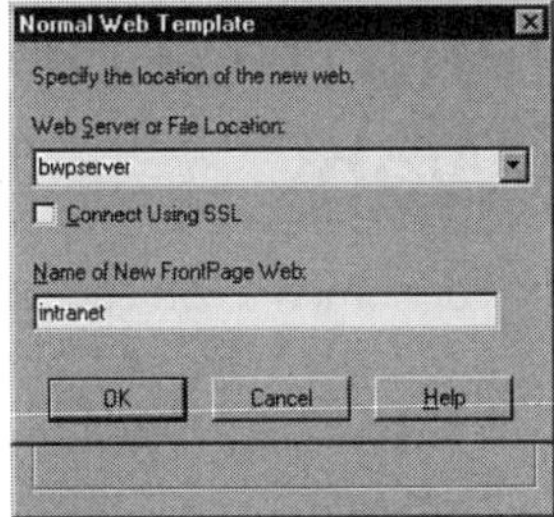

Figure 7.2.
Choose your server and name your FrontPage Web in the Normal Web Template dialog box.

3. In the Web **S**erver or File Location field, enter the URL of your server, or choose from the drop-down list.
4. If you want to connect to your server using Secure Socket Layer communication, select the **C**onnect Using SSL check box.
5. In the **N**ame of New FrontPage Web field, enter `intranet`.
6. Choose OK. FrontPage generates a web with a single home page in it.
7. Included on the CD that accompanies this book are some Office 97 documents that have already been created; import these files into your `intranet` Web by choosing **F**ile|**I**mport. The Import File to FrontPage Web dialog box shown in Figure 7.3 is displayed.

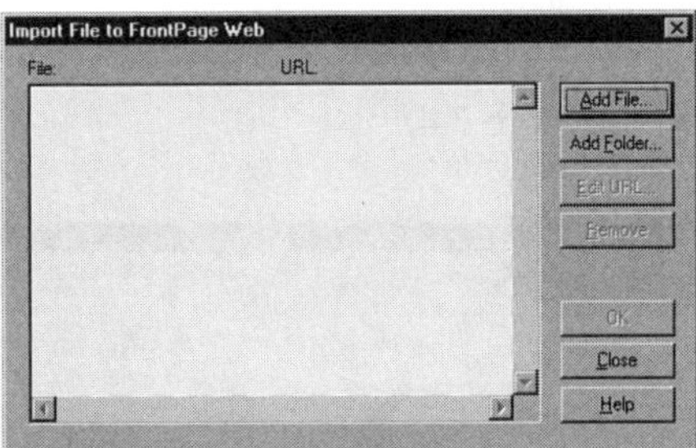

Figure 7.3.
Use the Import File to FrontPage Web dialog box to import files into your new Web.

8. Click **A**dd File. The Add File to Import List dialog box is displayed.
9. Use the Look **i**n box to choose your CD-ROM drive and locate the directory that contains the following files:

```
1996-annual.doc
FY 95 Sales.xls
```

Select the files and click Open. You return to the Import File to FrontPage Web dialog box.

10. Choose OK to import the files to your current web. They are imported into the web's home directory.

Creating a New Office Document for Your Intranet Web

When you create a new Office document, you can save the file in one of two ways. Some Web developers prefer to save new or edited documents directly to the appropriate directory on the Web server. The next time the Web is refreshed, the new documents appear in the list of files available in the Web. However, when you use this approach, the author is listed as "unknown," so your Web administrator might discourage this practice.

What you can do instead is create an Office 97 document and temporarily save it to a directory on your local or network hard drive. Then you can use the **F**ile | **I**mport command in the FrontPage Explorer to import the Office 97 document into your FrontPage Web. When you edit the file, open it from the FrontPage Explorer. When the file is saved, the FrontPage Explorer automatically imports the edited file. The following task illustrates how you can create a new PowerPoint presentation for your `intranet` web.

To create a new office document for your `intranet` web, follow these steps:

1. From PowerPoint 97, choose **F**ile | **N**ew (Ctrl+N). The New Presentation dialog box is displayed.
2. Click the Presentations tab, and choose `Corporate Home Page (Online).pot`, as shown in Figure 7.4.

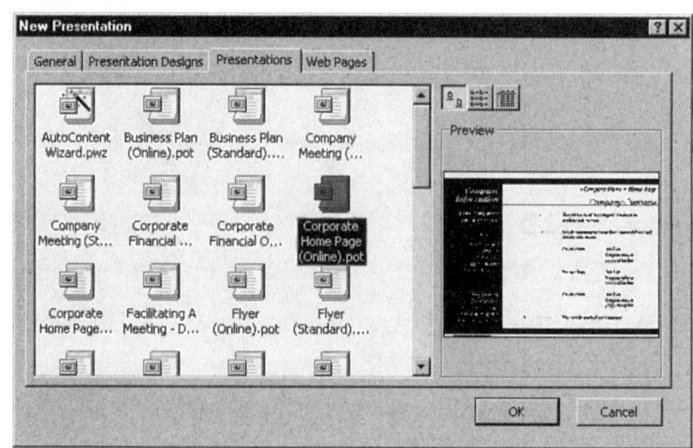

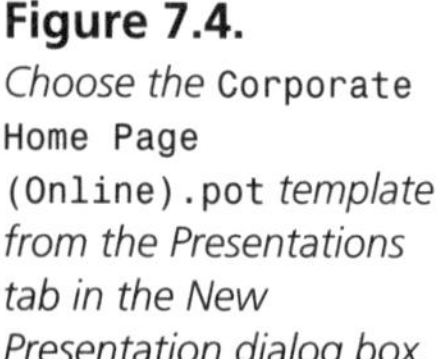

Figure 7.4.
Choose the `Corporate Home Page (Online).pot` *template from the Presentations tab in the New Presentation dialog box.*

3. Click OK. The presentation opens in PowerPoint.

4. Choose **F**ile | **S**ave (Ctrl+S). The Save dialog box is displayed. Save the presentation file to any directory on your local or network hard drive as `corphome.ppt`. Click **S**ave to save the presentation. You return to PowerPoint.
5. Open the `intranet` web in the FrontPage Explorer if it is not still open.
6. From the FrontPage Explorer, choose **F**ile | **I**mport. The Import File to FrontPage Web dialog box is displayed.
7. Click **A**dd File. The Add File to Import List dialog box is displayed.
8. Use the Look **i**n box to locate the presentation file on your local or network hard drive. Highlight the file and click **O**pen.
9. Choose OK to import the file to your current web. It is imported into the web's home directory.
10. Close PowerPoint and use the Windows Explorer to delete the file that you saved to your local or network hard drive. The copy that you imported into your FrontPage web remains.
11. To reopen the PowerPoint presentation from the FrontPage Explorer, choose **V**iew | **F**older View. From the list of files in your home directory, which will look something like Figure 7.5, double-click the `corphome.ppt` presentation file to open it in PowerPoint.

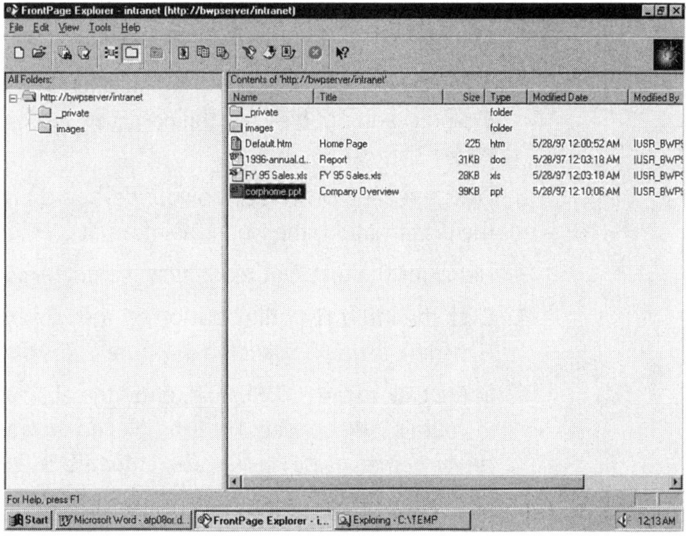

Figure 7.5.
Open the presentation file from the FrontPage Explorer to edit it.

NOTE: If the Office 97 file does not open, you must configure an editor association in the FrontPage Explorer. Choose **T**ools | **O**ptions. The Options dialog box is displayed. Click the Configure Editors tab; then click the **A**dd button. The Add Editor Association dialog box is displayed. To add an association for a PowerPoint presentation, enter `ppt` in the File Type field. In the Editor Name field, enter `PowerPoint 97`. In the Command field, enter the path to the PowerPoint executable file, or use the Browse button to locate it on your local or network hard drive. Then choose OK twice to return to the FrontPage Explorer. You will probably want to add editor associations for each type of Office 97 document (`.doc` for Word 97, `.xls` for Excel 97, `.mdb` for Access 97, and so on) .

Adding Links Between Office 97 Documents

In the following task, you will create links from the PowerPoint presentation file to the Excel spreadsheet and the Word document that you imported into your FrontPage web earlier in this chapter. Though the steps outlined here create hyperlinks in PowerPoint 97, the procedure is fairly similar for all Office 97 applications.

To create the hyperlinks, follow these steps:

1. If you do not have the presentation open in PowerPoint, open the FrontPage Explorer, and double-click the `corphome.ppt` presentation file to open it in PowerPoint 97.
2. Press the Page Down key on your keyboard until you reach the third slide in the presentation (the Financial Information slide, shown in Figure 7.6).
3. Highlight the text that reads `1996 Annual Report`.
4. Click the Insert Hyperlink button on the PowerPoint 97 toolbar. The Insert Hyperlink dialog box shown in Figure 7.7 is displayed.
5. In the Link to file or URL field, enter the absolute URL to the Word document in your FrontPage web. For example, if you created your `intranet` web on a server named `www.myserver.com`, enter a URL as follows:

   ```
   http://www.myserver.com/intranet/1996-annual.doc
   ```
6. Choose OK. A link to the Word document is created in your presentation.
7. Highlight the text that reads `Financial Highlights from 1995`.
8. Click the Insert Hyperlink button on the PowerPoint 97 toolbar. The Insert Hyperlink dialog box is displayed.

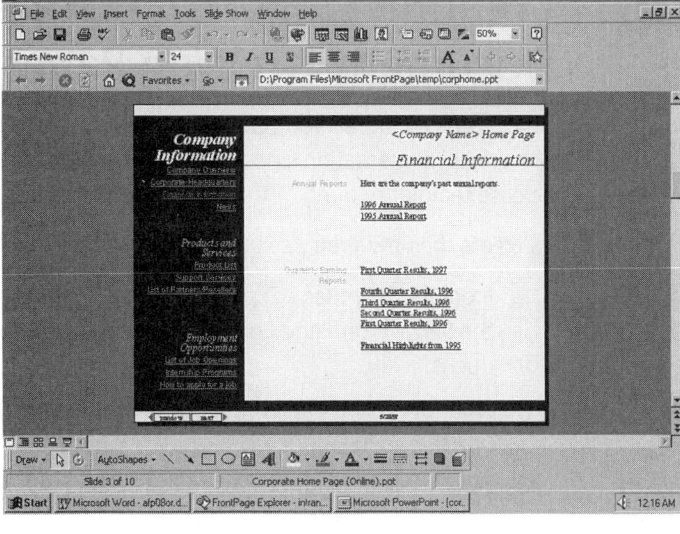

Figure 7.6.
Use the Page Down key to move to the Financial Information slide in the presentation.

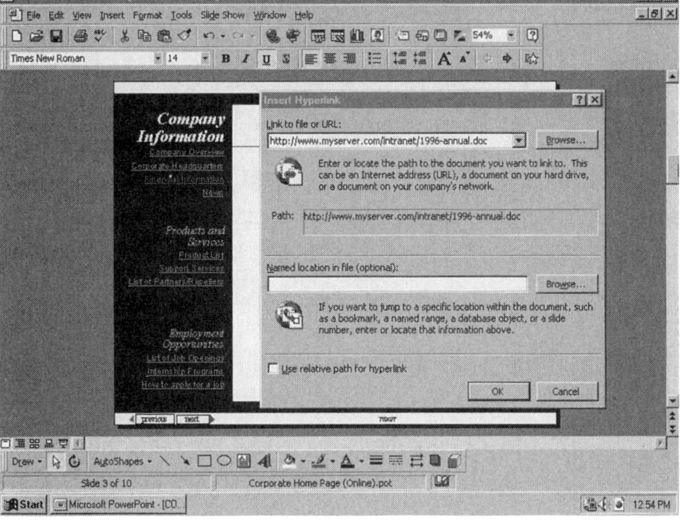

Figure 7.7.
Use the Insert Hyperlink dialog box to create a hyperlink to the Word document.

9. In the Link to file or URL field, enter the absolute URL to the Excel worksheet. For example:

```
http://www.myserver.com/intranet/FY 95 Sales.xls
```

10. Choose OK. A link to the Excel worksheet is created in your presentation. Leave PowerPoint 97 open while you complete the next task.

Creating Links from Office 97 Documents to Web Pages

Next, you'll create a Web page with the FrontPage Editor and create a link in the PowerPoint presentation to the new Web page. For this example, you will use the Press Release template, found in the New Page dialog box in the FrontPage Editor.

To create the new Web page and link from the presentation file, follow these steps:

1. From the FrontPage Explorer, choose **T**ools | Show Fro**n**tPage Editor, or click the Show FrontPage Editor button on the toolbar. The FrontPage Editor opens.
2. From the FrontPage Editor, choose **F**ile | **N**ew (Ctrl+N). The New Page dialog box shown in Figure 7.8 is displayed.
3. From the Template or Wizard list, select Press Release and choose OK. The page opens in the FrontPage Editor.

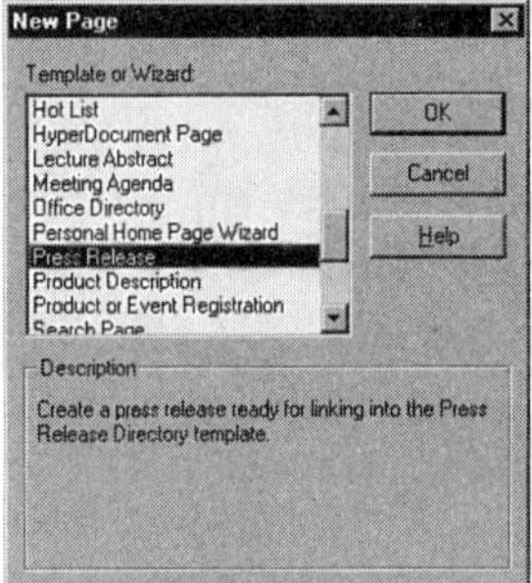

Figure 7.8.
Select the Press Release Template from the New Page dialog box in the FrontPage Editor.

4. Edit the line that reads `Page Title` to read `ACME Corporation Establishes Web Site`.
5. Choose **F**ile | **S**ave (Ctrl+S) or press the Save button on the Standard toolbar. The Save As dialog box shown in Figure 7.9 is displayed.
6. The Page **T**itle field defaults to `ACME Corporation Establishes Web Site`. In the File **p**ath within your FrontPage web field, enter `pressrel01.htm`.
7. Choose OK. The file is saved to your web.
8. Return to PowerPoint 97. Press the Page Down key to move to slide number 4 (the News page).
9. Highlight the first line that reads `Title of press release, date`, and edit it to read `ACME Corporation Establishes Web Site`, followed by today's date.
10. Highlight the line again and select the Insert Hyperlink button on the PowerPoint toolbar. The Insert Hyperlink dialog box is displayed.

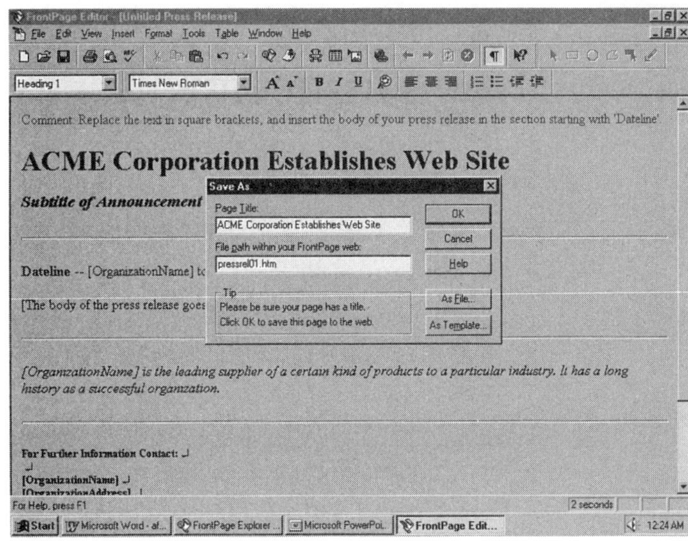

Figure 7.9.
Save the Press Release Template to the home directory in your web.

11. In the **L**ink to file or URL field shown in Figure 7.10, enter the absolute URL of the Press Release web page (for example, `http://www.myserver.com/pressrel01.htm`.

12. Choose **F**ile | **S**ave (Ctrl+S) to update the PowerPoint presentation to your web. When you return to the FrontPage Explorer, the presentation file is automatically imported into your web from the Import File to FrontPage Web dialog box.

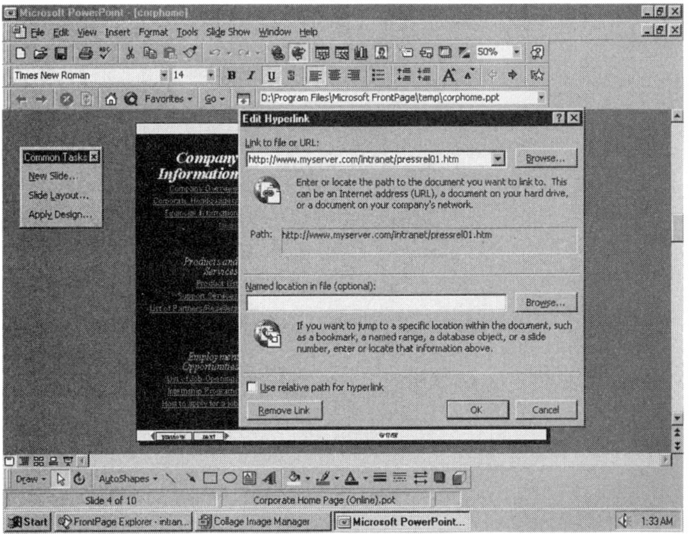

Figure 7.10.
Create a hyperlink with a relative URL to the press release Web page.

Creating Links from Web Pages to Office 97 Documents

In this task you'll open the home page in your web and create hyperlinks to the Office 97 documents that you have imported into your web.

To add the links to the home page, follow these steps:

1. From the FrontPage Editor, choose **F**ile | **O**pen (Ctrl+O) or click the Open button on the Standard toolbar. The Open File dialog box is displayed.
2. From the Current FrontPage Web tab, double-click your home page to open it. It is displayed in the FrontPage Editor.
3. Format the first line to Heading 1, using the Change Style drop-down menu on the Format toolbar. Enter `ACME Corporation Home Page`.
4. Press Enter, and choose Bulleted List from the Change Style drop-down menu on the Format toolbar. The bulleted list will provide links to the other content in the web. Enter the following lines of text on the page:

```
Company Overview
Fiscal Year 1995 Sales
1996 Annual Report
ACME Corporation Establishes Web Site
```

5. Press Enter twice to end the bulleted list. At this point your page should look similar to Figure 7.11.

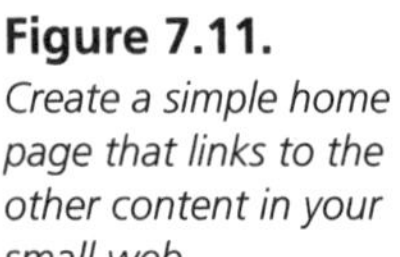

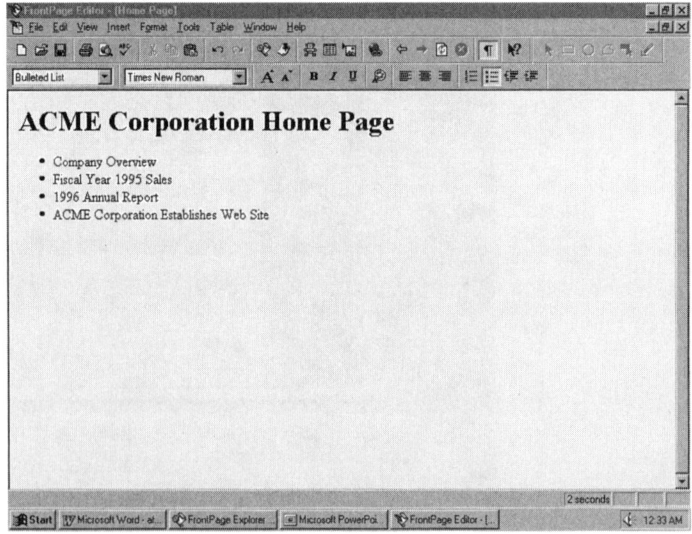

Figure 7.11.
Create a simple home page that links to the other content in your small web.

6. Highlight the first bulleted list item (`Company Overview`), and choose the Create or Edit Hyperlink button on the Standard toolbar. The Create Hyperlink dialog box shown in Figure 7.12 is displayed.

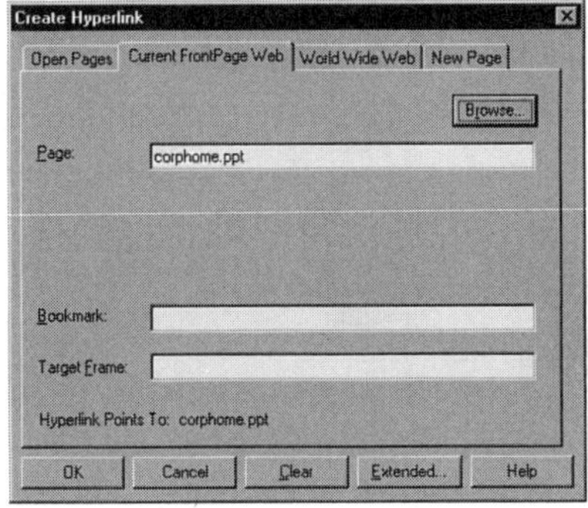

Figure 7.12.
Use the Current FrontPage Web tab in the Create Hyperlink dialog box to create a link to the PowerPoint Presentation file.

7. Choose the Current FrontPage Web tab, and click the B**r**owse button to open the Current Web dialog box.
8. Double-click `corphome.ppt`. The URL is displayed in the Create Hyperlink dialog box.
9. Choose OK to create the link.
10. Repeat steps 6–9 to create a similar link from the `Fiscal Year 1995 Sales` bulleted list item on the Web page to the `FY 95 Sales.xls` Excel Worksheet file in your web.
11. Repeat steps 6–9 to create a similar link from the `1996 Annual Report` bulleted list item on the Web page to the `1996-annual.doc` Word document in your web.
12. Finally, repeat steps 6–9 to create a link from the `ACME Corporation Establishes Web Site` bulleted list item on the Web page to the Web page named `pressrel01.htm`.
13. Choose **F**ile | **S**ave (Ctrl+S) to save the home page to your web.

Moving Your Files to New Directories

Assume now that your Web site has grown quite a lot, and you want to organize your Web content into subfolders. This is where you will find an advantage to using the FrontPage Explorer to manage your Web site. As you move your files, the FrontPage Explorer automatically edits the hyperlinks in your Web, both in your Web pages and in your Office 97 documents. To illustrate this, follow these steps:

1. From the FrontPage Explorer, highlight the home folder in your `intranet` web and choose **F**ile | **N**ew | **F**older. Name the folder `pressrel`, as shown in Figure 7.13.

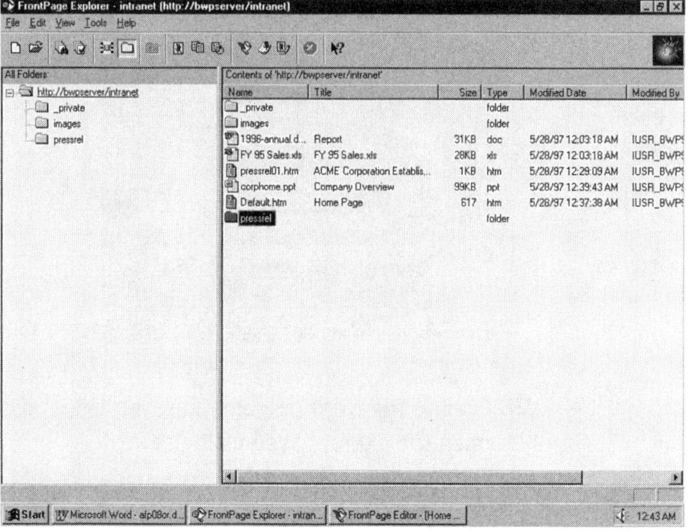

Figure 7.13.
Create a new folder named `pressrel` in your web, and move the `pressrel01.htm` Web page into it.

2. Click and drag the `pressrel01.htm` Web page to move it into the `pressrel` folder. The FrontPage Explorer changes the URL to `pressrel/pressrel01.htm` and updates all links that appear in the Web. If you open the PowerPoint presentation and view the link properties, as shown in Figure 7.14, you see that the relative URL to the press release is also changed in PowerPoint 97.

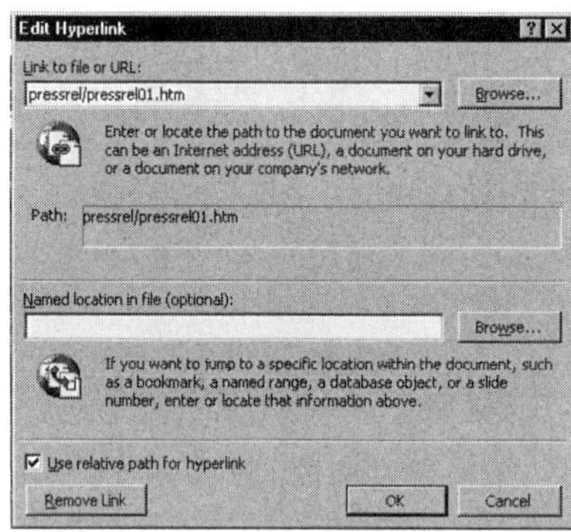

Figure 7.14.
The FrontPage Explorer also updates the hyperlink in the PowerPoint presentation, as shown in the Edit Hyperlink dialog box in PowerPoint 97.

3. Highlight the home folder again, and create a new folder named `sales`.

4. Click and drag the `FY 95 Sales.xls` worksheet file to move it into the sales folder. The FrontPage Explorer changes the URL to `sales/FY 95 Sales.xls` and updates all links that appear in the Web and the PowerPoint presentation.

Browsing Your Content with Internet Explorer 3.01

Internet Explorer 3.01 is furnished on the Office 97 CD for good reason. You will notice some nice features when you use this browser in conjunction with FrontPage 97 and Office 97. For example, begin a browsing session by opening your `intranet` site home page in the FrontPage Editor. Then use the **F**ile | Preview in **B**rowser command to open the page in Internet Explorer. The home page is displayed in the browser, as shown in Figure 7.15.

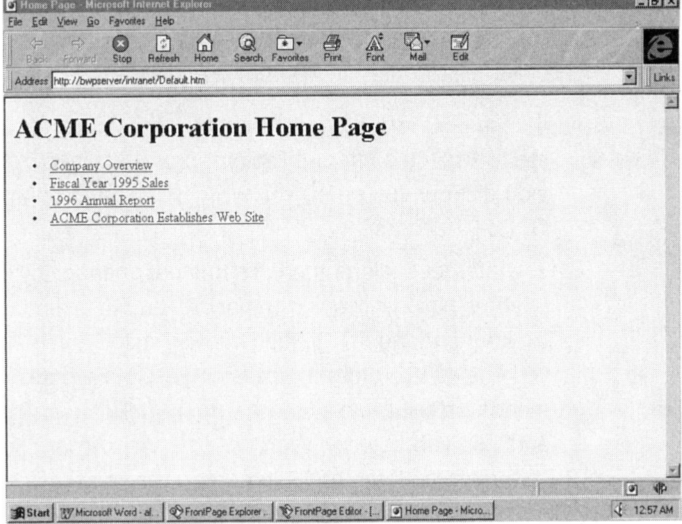

Figure 7.15.
Open the home page of your `intranet` web in Internet Explorer 3.01.

Next, follow the 1996 Annual Report hyperlink to navigate to the `1996-annual.doc` file in your FrontPage web. If you have Office 97 installed on your computer, you remain in what seems to be Internet Explorer. However, you quickly see that it is no longer "just" Internet Explorer. There are additional menu commands, as shown in Figure 7.16. What you see now is a combination of Internet Explorer and Word 97 commands.

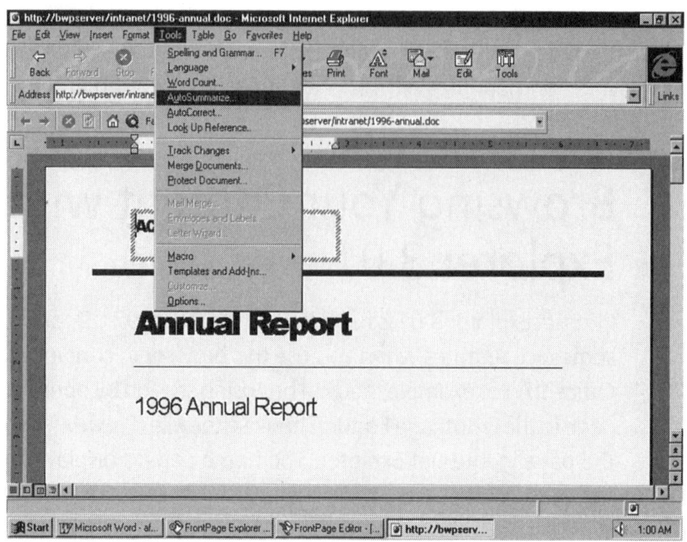

Figure 7.16.
Internet Explorer opens the Office documents and displays Office 97 commands in its menus. You must have Office 97 applications installed on your system for this to be true.

Here is what happens when Internet Explorer navigates to a Word 97 document (such as the `1996-annual.doc` file in your `intranet` web):

- If Office 97 exists on your computer, the Office document opens in what seems to be the Internet Explorer browser window. If Office 97 does not exist on your computer, you will need the appropriate viewer files to view Office 97 documents.
- The Internet Explorer menu commands change. Instead of the normal Internet Explorer menu commands, you see a combination of Internet Explorer and the associated Office 97 menu commands. For example, when you open a Word document, the File, Go, Favorites, and Help menu commands are the same as those you normally find in Internet Explorer. In addition, you now see Word 97 Edit, View, Insert, Format, Tools, and Table commands in Internet Explorer. You can browse *and* edit your Word documents while retaining the majority of commands available when you edit documents directly from Word 97.
- A Tools icon is displayed in the Internet Explorer toolbar. Clicking this Tools icon displays or hides the Word 97 toolbars.

Next, use the Back button in the browser to return to the home page. Follow the link to the Excel worksheet (the bulleted list item that reads `Fiscal Year 1995 Sales`). As you see in Figure 7.17, you again see what looks like Internet Explorer, with a combination of Excel menus and commands. You can edit your worksheet from this interface.

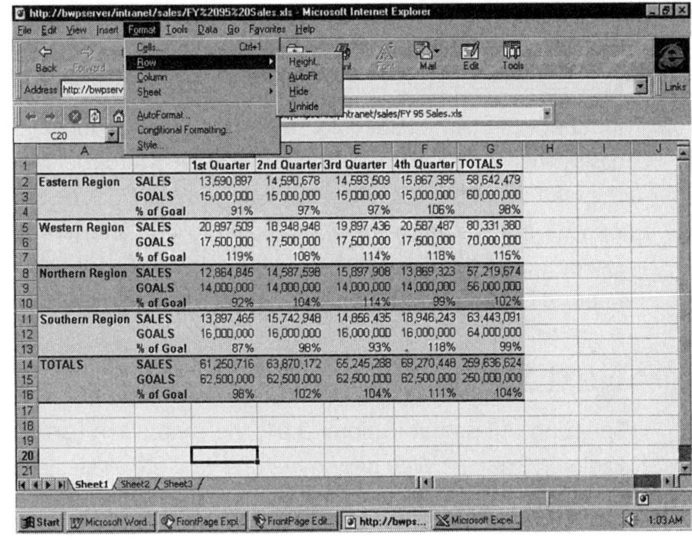

Figure 7.17.
Like the Word 97 commands, Excel commands are found in Internet Explorer when an Excel worksheet opens. You must have Excel 97 installed on your system for this to be true.

Use the Back button in the browser to return to the home page again. This time, follow the link to the PowerPoint presentation (the `Company Overview` bulleted list item). The presentation file opens in Internet Explorer. Again, you can edit the content of the presentation (see Figure 7.18).

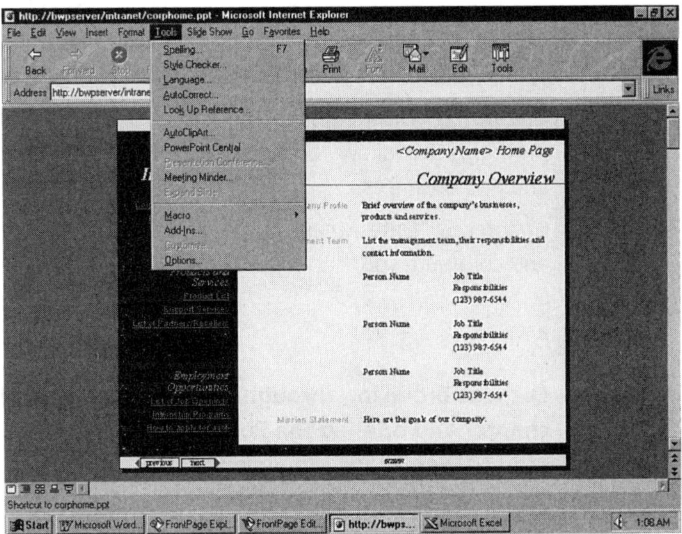

Figure 7.18.
PowerPoint commands also are found in Internet Explorer when a PowerPoint presentation is opened. You must have PowerPoint 97 installed on your system for this to be true.

Workshop Wrap-Up

Now you have a fairly good idea of how FrontPage 97 can help you organize your intranet. You can create links between Office 97 documents and your Web pages easily. Then, by importing Office 97 documents into your FrontPage webs, you can use the features of the FrontPage Explorer to keep track of all the links in your intranet. As your intranet grows and additional folders and files are added, the FrontPage Explorer does the dirty work of keeping track of your links. In addition, you can use Internet Explorer 3.01 to browse through and edit the content in your Web!

Next Steps

Speaking of Internet Explorer 3.01, the chapters in Part III, "Designing for Internet Explorer," discuss Web design features that are available in Internet Explorer 3.0 or higher. Those who browse the Web using this browser can view advanced tables, floating frames, and cascading style sheets, among other features. Read on for an introduction to these Web features and how you can implement them in FrontPage.

To learn more about the subjects discussed in this chapter, refer to the following chapters:

- Chapter 3, "Word Isn't Just for the Office Anymore," to learn how Word 97 and FrontPage 97 compare in creating Web pages.
- Chapter 4, "Presenting PowerPoint on the Web," to learn how you can create Web-based presentations for your Internet or intranet site.
- Chapter 5, "Excel-ing with Spreadsheets," to learn about some of the add-in programs that allow you to integrate Excel worksheets with your Web pages and database files.
- Chapter 6, "Data Access on the Web," to learn more about how to install and configure your server for database access on the Web.

Q&A

Q: I was browsing through the Internet site that I created in this chapter and opened the PowerPoint Presentation in Internet Explorer. Then I chose to view the presentation in slide view while in IE 3.0. In some cases, I could not follow the hyperlinks; I would get an error message that the file could not be located. Other times, I received an error message that the file could not be located, and then when I clicked OK the file opened anyway. When I reviewed the hyperlinks in PowerPoint, the URLs seemed valid, and my FrontPage Web shows no broken hyperlinks. What's wrong?

A: I did some experimenting to see what situations would occur after different types of hyperlinks were created in the PowerPoint presentation, and here is what I found:

- In PowerPoint 97, I created hyperlinks that used relative URLs to the Office 97 documents and Web pages in the FrontPage web. The PowerPoint presentation was opened in PowerPoint and then in Internet Explorer. When I tried to follow links to the Office 97 documents, I received an "Unable to open file" message. When I tried to follow the link to the press release Web page in the FrontPage web, I received a message that read "An unexpected error has occurred."

  Using this approach, FrontPage 97 updated the relative URLs correctly in the FrontPage Explorer and the PowerPoint presentation when documents were moved into new directories in the FrontPage web. In this case, the "Unable to open file" message could have related to the Internet Explorer cache rather than to FrontPage 97 or to PowerPoint 97.

- For the second test, I used the **B**rowse button in PowerPoint 97's Insert Hyperlink dialog box to create a hyperlink to the actual file location of the documents in the FrontPage web. (For example, if the web resides on a system running under Windows NT Server 4.0 using Internet Information Server, the file path to the annual report appears like `c:\InetPub\wwwroot\intranet\1996-annual.doc`). I used the same approach to create the hyperlink to the press release Web page in the FrontPage web. This time, when I followed the hyperlinks in the PowerPoint presentation, the Office 97 documents opened fine. I again received the "An unexpected error has occurred" message when I tried to navigate from the presentation file to the Web page.

  Using this approach, FrontPage 97 did *not* update URLs correctly in the FrontPage Explorer and in the PowerPoint presentation when documents were moved into new directories in the FrontPage Web.

- For the third test, I used the approach discussed in this chapter. When I created hyperlinks, I entered the absolute URL to the files in the FrontPage Web. When I followed the hyperlinks in the PowerPoint presentation, the Office 97 documents opened fine. I received the "An unexpected error has occurred" message when trying to navigate from the presentation file to the press release Web page. FrontPage 97 update the URLs correctly in the FrontPage Explorer and in PowerPoint 97 when documents were moved into new directories in the FrontPage web.

I was not able to determine the cause of the "An unexpected error has occurred" message that was received when I tried to navigate from the PowerPoint presentation to the press release Web page. This appears to be a problem that is related more to PowerPoint 97 or Office 97 than to FrontPage 97.

Q: Can I create navigation bars using FrontPage and then insert them into my Office documents with an Include Bot?

A: No, but one thing that can improve navigation between Web pages and Office 97 documents is a frameset for your Web site. Use smaller frames to provide navigation bars, and place your Office 97 documents and your Web pages into a larger main frame. This serves a similar purpose.

PART III

Designing for Internet Explorer

C H A P T E R

EIGHT

Creating Advanced Tables

In this chapter, you

- Add light and dark background images to a basic table and create text colors that are suitable for both
- Change the border colors and border appearances of a table
- Add background colors, images, and borders to individual cells within a table
- Use additional HTML tags that allow you to display rules, or dividing lines, between designated areas in your tables
- Create nested tables

Tasks in this chapter:

- Starting with a Basic Table
- Assigning Your Page Properties
- Adding Background Images and Colors to Tables
- Changing Table Border Colors
- Adding Background Images to Cells
- Defining Column Groups
- Adding Vertical Rules to the Table
- Creating Nested Tables
- Defining Table Headers, Body, and Footers
- Changing Cell Background and Border Colors
- Adding Horizontal Rules Between Rows

Tables are used for much more than presenting data on Web pages. Many Web designers use tables to design Web page layouts that closely resemble online newsletters, multimedia presentations, and inventive interfaces. Internet Explorer provides several tags that allow you to go beyond using solid colors for table cells and border colors. By using nested tables, background images, additional HTML tags, and extended table attributes, you can create truly striking pages. This chapter introduces you to some of the techniques.

Starting with a Basic Table

Before you start adding all the enhanced elements to your table, note that it more effective to develop your tables as you want them to appear in browsers that do not support these extra features. This includes formatting the basic table elements, adding the content, and choosing the basic colors.

To insert a basic table into your page, follow these steps:

1. From the FrontPage Editor, choose the New button in the Standard toolbar to create a new blank page.
2. Choose T**a**ble | **I**nsert Table. The Insert Table dialog box shown in Figure 8.1 is displayed.

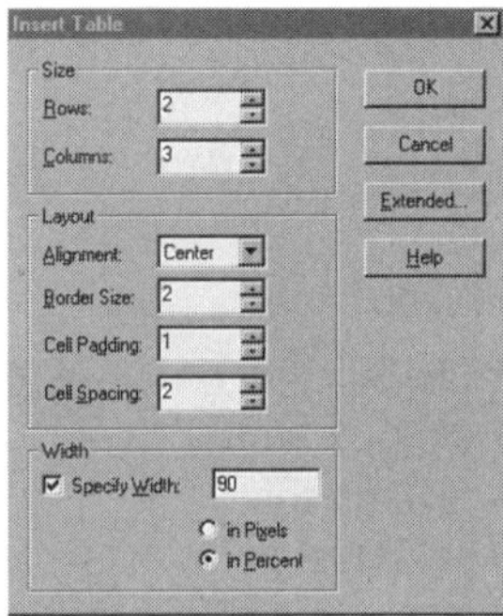

Figure 8.1.
Use the Insert Table dialog box to define a basic table.

3. Enter the following settings in the Insert Table dialog box:

Rows:	`2`
Columns:	`3`
Alignment:	`Center`
Border Size:	`2`
Cell Pa**d**ding:	`1`
Cell **S**pacing:	`2`
Specify **W**idth:	`90, in Percent`

4. Choose OK. The table is displayed on your page.
5. Position the insertion point in the upper-left cell. Press the Bold button on the Format toolbar. Type `Links to Favorite Places`.
6. Press Enter, and click the Bulleted List button on the Format toolbar. A bullet is displayed. Enter some placeholder text for some links on your page, pressing the Enter key after each line. For example:

   `Link 1` (press Enter)
   `Link 2` (press Enter)

`Link 3` (press Enter)
`Link 4` (press Enter)
`Link 5`

7. Position the insertion point in the middle cell of the top row. Choose Heading 2 from the Change Style drop-down menu in the Format toolbar. Enter `Page Title`.
8. Press Enter, and add some placeholder text to represent the first paragraph in the page, such as `Main section of the page`. Copy the text into the clipboard using Ctrl+C or the Copy button on the Standard toolbar. Paste it on the new line, beneath the page title heading, several times using Ctrl+V or the Paste button on the Standard toolbar. Separate each paste with a space.
9. Press Enter to begin a new line after the first paragraph. Choose Heading 3 from the Change Style drop-down menu in the Format toolbar. Enter `Heading`.
10. Press Enter, and paste some additional placeholder text beneath the heading.
11. Position the insertion point in the upper-right cell, and paste a few short paragraphs of placeholder text in that cell.
12. Position the cursor immediately to the left of the first row of cells; it turns into a selection arrow. Click to select the first row of cells.
13. Press Alt+Enter. The Cell Properties dialog box is displayed. Choose Top from the **V**ertical Alignment drop-down menu shown in Figure 8.2.
14. Choose OK to exit the Cell Properties dialog box. Your table should look similar to Figure 8.3.

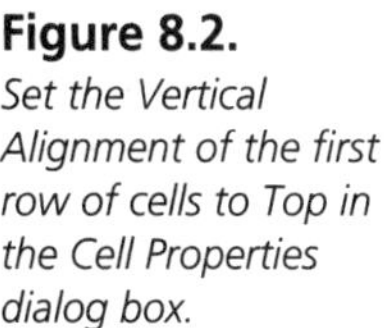

Figure 8.2.
Set the Vertical Alignment of the first row of cells to Top in the Cell Properties dialog box.

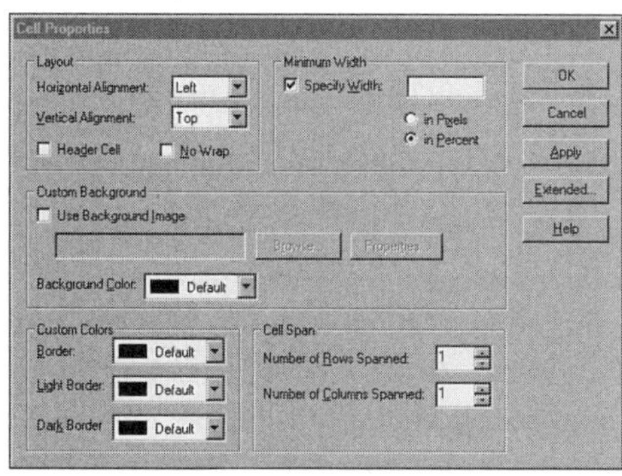

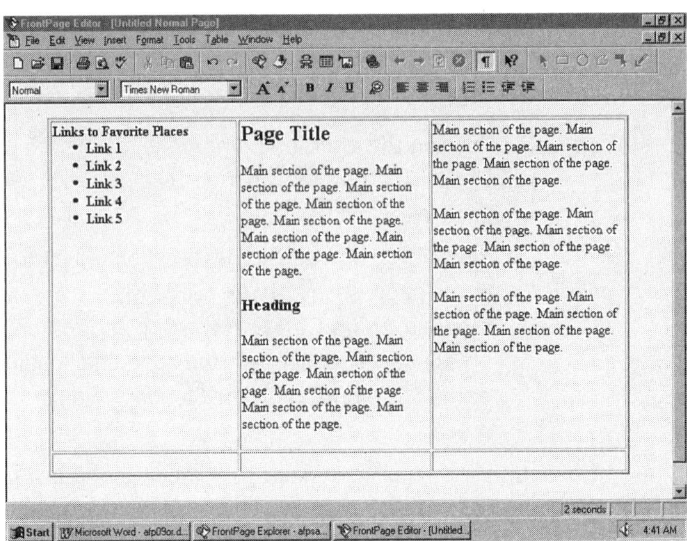

Figure 8.3.
Your table has content in the first row.

Assigning Your Page Properties

The images that you will place in the background of your cells should be either very dark colored or very light colored. Though you can assign custom colors to portions of your page, not all browsers recognize custom text colors. To be safe, choose intermediate text and link colors that will be visible on both light and dark backgrounds. For example, if part of your page has a black background and another part has a white background, use a medium gray text color that is easily read on both backgrounds.

For the page in this example, we will use text and link colors that fall in the middle range of green, blue, gold, and gray. This way, the text and link colors will be legible on both the light and dark backgrounds in the table cells.

To specify the text and link colors for the page, follow these steps:

1. Choose **F**ile | Page Propert**i**es. The Page Properties dialog box is displayed.
2. Click the Background tab, shown in Figure 8.4.
3. From each of the fields in the following list, choose Custom from its respective drop-down list box. Choose or create custom colors for each element, using the **R**ed, **G**reen, and **B**lue fields in the Color dialog box. Each field accepts a value between `0` and `255`. If you use numerical values `0`, `51`, `102`, `153`, `204`, and `255` in your color formula, the colors will not dither in 256-color display mode. Create text and link colors as follows:

Background:	White
Text:	Custom Color: Red 51 Green 153 Blue 51 (Medium Green)
Hyperlink:	Custom Color: Red 204 Green 153 Blue 51 (Medium Gold)
Visited Hyperlink:	Custom Color: Red 153 Green 102 Blue 51 (Darker Gold)
Active Hyperlink:	Custom Color: Red 255 Green 204 Blue 51 (Bright Gold)

4. Choose OK to exit the Page Properties dialog box. The settings are applied to your page.

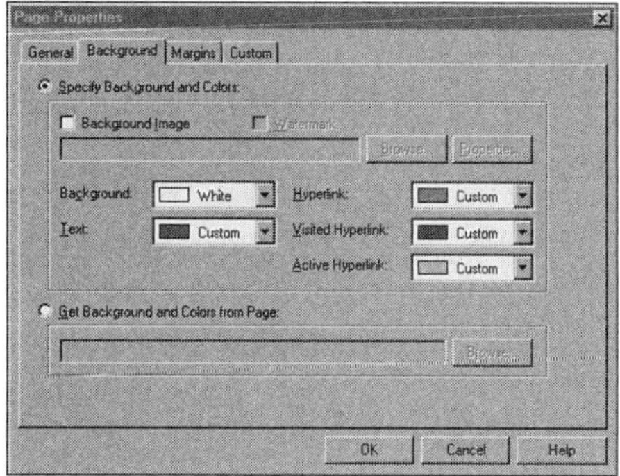

Figure 8.4.
Use the Background tab of the Page Properties dialog box to change your text and link colors.

Adding Background Images and Colors to Tables

When you assign a background image to a table or a cell, you must keep in mind that not all browsers display them. It is wise to choose a background color for the table or cells that closely matches your background image so that you achieve a similar effect in browsers that display table and cell colors but not background images in cells. For example, the background image that is used for the table has very pale green tones. In the following steps, you specify both a background color and a background image for your table.

To assign the table backgrounds, follow these steps:

1. From the FrontPage Editor, right-click anywhere in the table, and choose Table Properties from the pop-up menu. The Table Properties dialog box shown in Figure 8.5 is displayed.
2. From the Custom Background section, select the Use Background Image check box.
3. Click the Browse button. The Select Background Image dialog box is displayed.

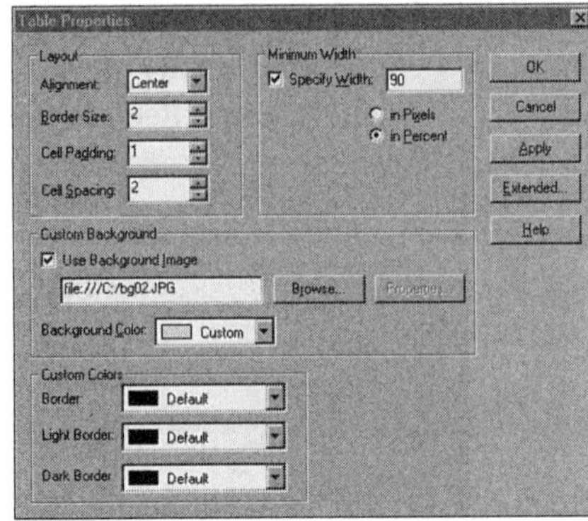

Figure 8.5.
Use the Table Properties dialog box to select your table background image and color.

4. To insert the `bg02.jpg` image from the CD that accompanies this book, select the Other Location tab; then choose the From **F**ile radio button. Click the **B**rowse button to open another Select Background Image dialog box, shown in Figure 8.6. Use the Look **i**n box to locate the directory on your CD in which `bg02.jpg` is saved, and double-click the image filename. You return to the Table Properties dialog box, and the path to the image is displayed in the Use Background **I**mage field.

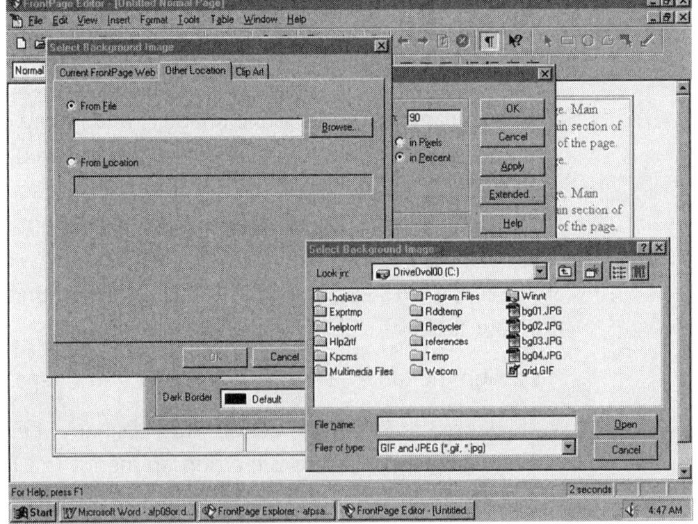

Figure 8.6.
Use the Other Location tab and the Select Background Image dialog box to select a background image for your table.

NOTE: You can also choose a background image using one of the following methods:

- Choose the Current FrontPage Web tab to select an image that already exists in your current web. Double-click the directory in which your image is saved; then double-click the image. You return to the Table Properties dialog box, and the path to the image is displayed in the Use Background **I**mage field.
- To use a background image that exists on the World Wide Web, select the Other Location tab. Choose the From **L**ocation radio button. Enter the URL of the image that you want to use in the From Location field. When you insert an image from the World Wide Web, the image is not imported into your web; instead, the browser inserts the image from its original location on the World Wide Web.

5. To assign a custom color for the background, select Custom from the Background **C**olor drop-down menu in the Custom Background section. The Color dialog box is displayed.

NOTE: The Background Color, Border, Light Border, and Dark Border drop-down list boxes also provide 16 predefined system colors from which you can choose: Black, White, Green, Maroon, Olive, Navy, Purple, Gray, Yellow, Lime, Aqua, Fuchsia, Silver, Red, Blue, or Teal.

6. Enter the following color formula to create a pale green background: **R**ed `204`, **G**reen `255`, **B**lue `204`.
7. Choose OK to return to the Table Properties dialog box.
8. Choose OK again to exit the Table Properties dialog box and update your table colors. The image is displayed in the table background as shown in Figure 8.7.

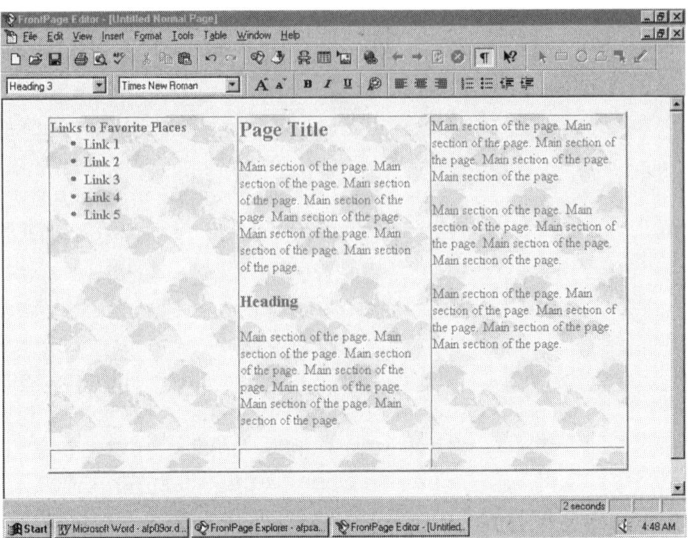

Figure 8.7.
Your table now has a background image.

Changing Table Border Colors

You can also specify a border color or colors for a table using one of two methods. When you specify a color with the Border drop-down list box, it creates a solid border around the table. To create a border that has a three-dimensional appearance, use the Light Border and Dark Border drop-down list boxes. The light border color is displayed at the top and left sides of the table, and the dark border color is displayed at the right and bottom sides of the table. In the following example, you will create a solid border around the table using the Border drop-down list box.

To specify a custom background color for the borders in this table, follow these steps:

1. From the FrontPage Editor, right-click anywhere in the table, and choose Table Properties from the pop-up menu. The Table Properties dialog box is displayed.
2. From the Custom Colors section, select Custom from the Border drop-down list box. The Color dialog box is displayed.
3. Define a custom color using the **R**ed, **G**reen, and **B**lue fields in the lower-right portion of the dialog box. Enter this color formula: **R**ed `51`, **G**reen `153`, **B**lue `51`.

NOTE: You can also create a custom color using one of the following methods:

- ❑ Choose one of 48 predefined colors in the Basic colors section in the upper-left portion of the dialog box.
- ❑ Define a custom color using the Hu**e**, **S**at, and **L**um fields in the lower-right portion of the dialog box. Each field accepts a value between `0` and `255`. As you enter your color formula, a preview of the color is displayed in the Color/Solid square.

4. Choose OK to return to the Table Properties dialog box. Your color is displayed in the Border color swatch as a custom color.
5. Choose OK to exit the Table Properties dialog box and update your table colors. The table now has a dark green border, as shown in Figure 8.8. There is also a dark green border around the contents of each cell.

NOTE: The border color does not appear if you create a table that has a border size of 0. To adjust the width of the border, use the **B**order Size setting in the Table Properties dialog box.

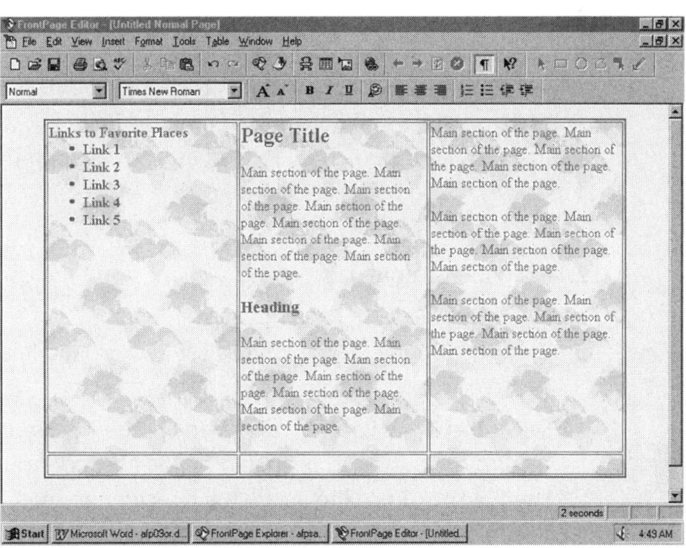

Figure 8.8.
The table has a dark green border around the outside edges. There is also a dark green border around the contents of each cell.

Adding Background Images to Cells

Just as you can apply a background image to an entire table, you can also apply a background image to a single cell or a group of selected cells. When you apply a background image to a cell, the background image tiles to fit the contents of the cell. The image or color used for the entire table is displayed around the cell.

To use a background image in a table cell, follow these steps:

1. Right-click inside the first cell in the table and choose Cell Properties from the pop-up menu. The Cell Properties dialog box shown in Figure 8.9 is displayed.

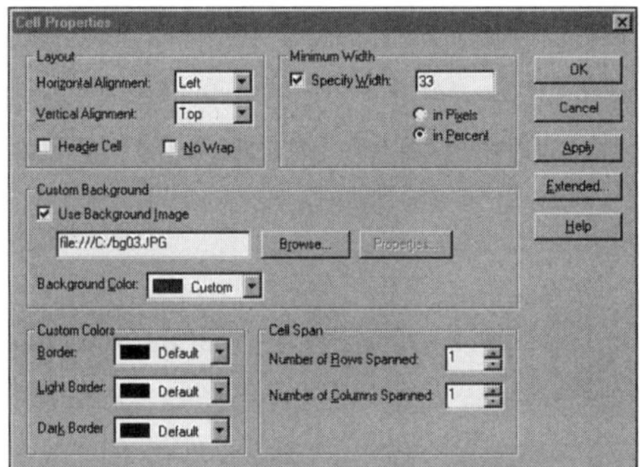

Figure 8.9.
Use the Cell Properties dialog box to select a background image and background color for your cell.

TIP: To select multiple cells, click inside the first cell you want to select. Choose T**a**ble | Select C**e**ll. Then shift-click to select the additional cells. After you select all your cells, press Alt+Enter, or right-click over any of the highlighted cells and choose Cell Properties from the pop-up menu. The Cell Properties dialog box is displayed.

2. From the Custom Background section, select the Use Background **I**mage check box.
3. Click the B**r**owse button. The Select Background Image dialog box is displayed.

4. Select the Other Location tab; then choose the From **F**ile radio button. Click the **B**rowse button to open another Select Background Image dialog box. Use the Look **i**n box to locate the directory on the CD in which `bg03.jpg` is saved, and double-click the image filename. You return to the Cell Properties dialog box, and the path to the image is displayed in the Use Background **I**mage field.

5. Choose Custom from the Background **C**olor drop-down list box, and create a custom color of **R**ed `0`, **G**reen `102`, **B**lue `0`. This closely approximates the background color of the image.
6. Choose OK to return to the Cell Properties dialog box.
7. Choose OK to exit the Cell Properties dialog box and update your cell colors. The image is displayed in the background cell, as shown in Figure 8.10.

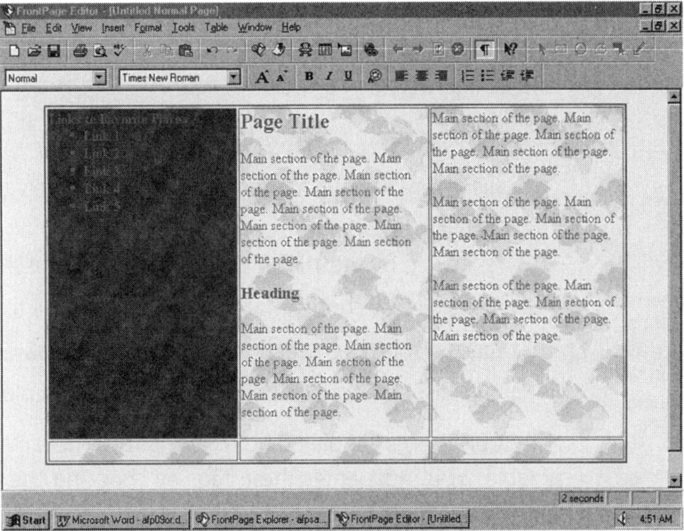

Figure 8.10.
The first cell in the top row of the table has a different background image.

Defining Column Groups

We want to enhance the appearance of the table a little bit, by removing the borders between the first and second rows in the table. It might also enhance the appearance of the page to align the text in the right column to the right side of the cells. One way to accomplish both these features is to define column groups and then use a `RULES` tag to display vertical lines between the columns in the table. The rules between the rows in the table will be removed.

Use the `COLGROUP` and `COL` tags to apply global properties to all cells in a column or in multiple consecutive columns in a table. The `COLGROUP` tag includes several attributes:

- `HALIGN` allows you to specify the horizontal alignment of the contents of the cell, which can be aligned to the `CENTER`, `LEFT`, or `RIGHT` of the cells in the column. The default value is `CENTER`.
- `VALIGN` allows you to specify the vertical alignment of the contents of the cells. The contents can be aligned to the `TOP`, `MIDDLE`, or `BOTTOM` of the cells. The default is `MIDDLE`.

- The SPAN attribute allows you to specify how many consecutive columns are in the column group, and for which columns the properties in the column group are set.
- The WIDTH attribute allows you to specify the width (in pixels) of each cell in the column.

Use the RULES tag to draw dividing lines between the elements in your table. The width of the rule is defined by the **B**order Size setting in the Table Properties dialog box, and its color is defined by the Border color setting in the Custom Colors section of the Table Properties or Cell Properties dialog boxes. You can use different colors for the table and cell borders if you desire.

The RULES attribute uses the following values:

- NONE removes all interior table borders. This is the default.
- GROUPS displays horizontal borders between all table groups. Groups are specified by the THEAD, TBODY, TFOOT, and COLGROUP elements.
- ROWS displays horizontal borders between all table rows.
- COLS displays vertical borders between all table columns.
- ALL displays borders between all rows and columns.

You learn more about the THEAD, TBODY, and TFOOT tags later in this chapter, in "Defining Table Headers, Body, and Footers."

The Table Properties dialog box does not provide a means to apply column groups to a table. You must enter these tags by choosing the **V**iew | **H**TML command in the FrontPage Editor.

To create column groups that display rules between the columns and align the text in the third column to the right, follow these steps:

1. Choose **V**iew | **H**TML. The View or Edit HTML dialog box shown in Figure 8.11 is displayed.
2. Figure 8.11 shows the HTML code that defines the table properties. It should look similar to the following, although the path to the background image will differ in your case:

   ```
   <table border="2" width=90%
     background="file:///pathname/bg02.jpg" bgcolor="#CCFFCC"
     bordercolor="#339933">
   ```
3. Position the insertion point after the last line in this code, and press Enter. The insertion point moves to the next line. The code that follows creates two column groups: The first column group spans two columns and aligns the text within the columns to the left, and the second line of code aligns the text in the third column to the right. Figure 8.12 highlights the placement of the following code:

   ```
   <colgroup span=2 align=left>
   <colgroup align=right>
   ```

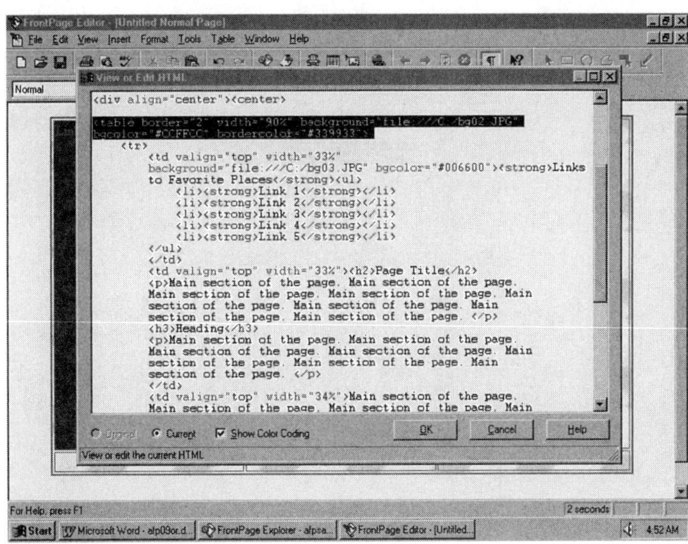

Figure 8.11.
Use the View or Edit HTML window to edit your HTML code.

4. Choose OK. You return to the FrontPage Editor. The contents of the table appear to shift, but this effect does not appear when you view your pages in Internet Explorer, as you will see in the next step.
5. Choose **F**ile | Preview in **B**rowser, and preview your page in Internet Explorer 3.0 or higher. You are prompted to save your page. In the Page **T**itle field, enter `Table Examples`. In the File **p**ath within your FrontPage web field, enter `tables.htm`. When you are asked if you want to save your images to the Web, select Yes to All. When the page opens in Internet Explorer 3.0 or higher, the rules between the first and second rows do not appear, as shown in Figure 8.13.

If the columns within groups require different properties, you can use the `COL` tag to set them. Assume, for example, that you want rules to be displayed between the second and third columns as in the previous example. You also want to align the text in the first column to the left and the text in the second column to the center of the cells. The `COL` tag allows you to individually set properties of one or more columns in a column group. The values you specify with the `COL` tag override those specified in the `COLGROUP` tag.

The attributes that you set with the `COL` tag are as follows:

- `ALIGN` allows you to specify the horizontal alignment of the contents of the cell to the `CENTER`, `LEFT`, or `RIGHT` of the cells in the column. The default is `CENTER`.
- The `SPAN` attribute allows you to specify how many consecutive columns to assign the properties to.

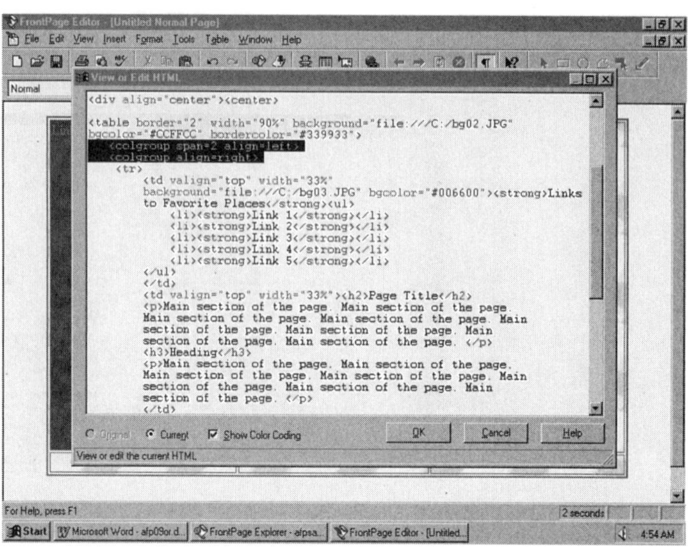

Figure 8.12.
The `COLGROUP` *tags and attributes define where the vertical rules are displayed and how the text in each of the columns should be aligned.*

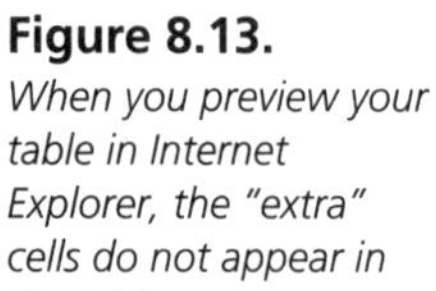

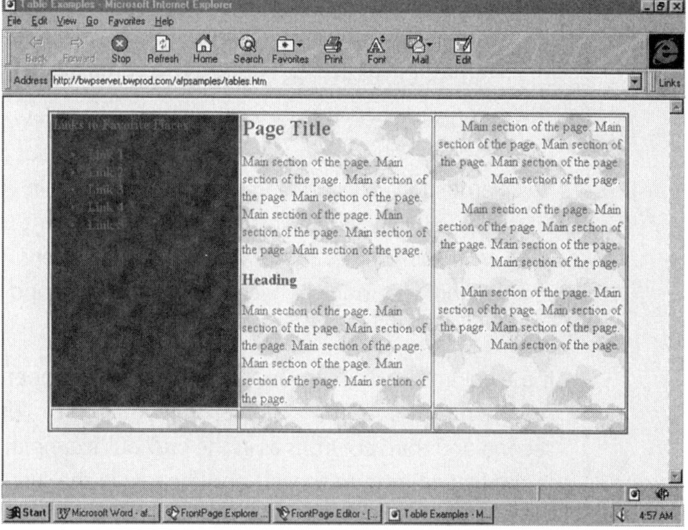

Figure 8.13.
When you preview your table in Internet Explorer, the "extra" cells do not appear in the table.

To align the first column to the left and the second column to the center, you could modify the code from the previous task to read as follows. (The code formats the contents of the table as shown in Figure 8.14.)

```
<table border="2" width=90%
  background="file:///pathname/bg02.jpg" bgcolor="#CCFFCC"
  bordercolor="#339933">
  <colgroup span=2>
    <col align="left">
    <col align="center">
  <colgroup align=right>
```

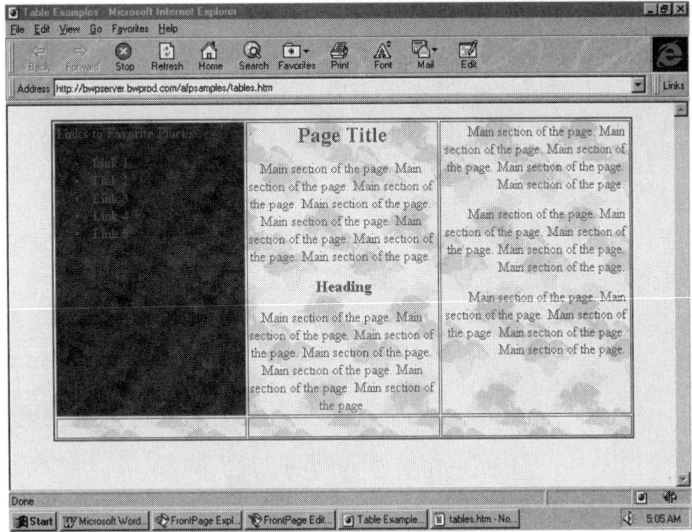

Figure 8.14.
You can format the first and second columns in the first column group differently by using the `COL` *tag.*

Adding Vertical Rules to the Table

In the following task, you will apply an extended attribute that adds vertical rules between the column groups in the table. Follow these steps:

1. Position the insertion point anywhere in the table, and right-click. Choose Table Properties from the pop-up menu to open the Table Properties dialog box.
2. Click the **E**xtended button. The Extended Attributes dialog box is displayed.
3. Click the **A**dd button. The Name/Value Pair dialog box shown in Figure 8.15 is displayed.
4. In the **N**ame field, enter `rules`. In the **V**alue field, enter `groups`.
5. Choose OK to exit the Name/Value Pair, Extended Attributes, and Table Properties dialog boxes. You return to the FrontPage Editor.
6. Choose **F**ile | Preview in **B**rowser to preview your table in Internet Explorer 3.0 or higher. You might need to use the Refresh button to update the page in your browser. Notice now that the rules between the first and second rows in the table no longer appear, as shown in Figure 8.16.

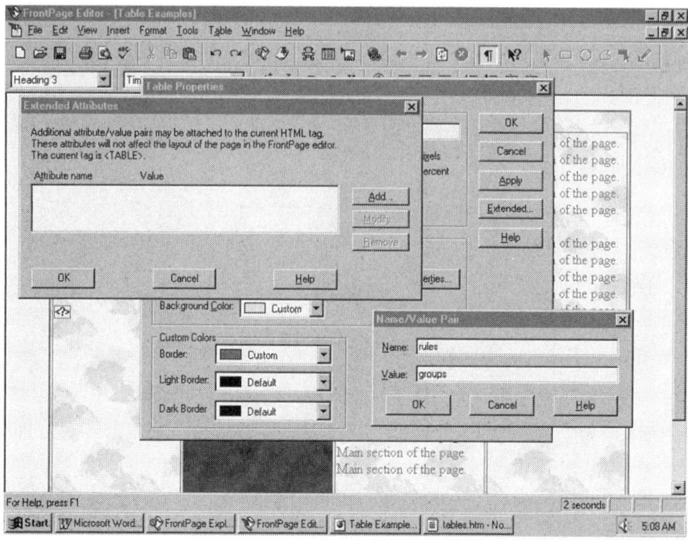

Figure 8.15.
Use the Name/Value Pair dialog box to specify an extended attribute for a table.

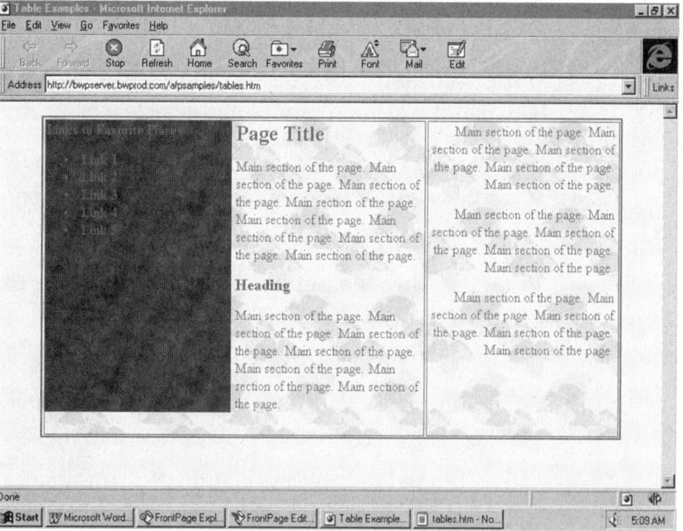

Figure 8.16.
After you apply the `rules` *attribute, the dividers between the first and second rows in the table no longer appear.*

TASK

Creating Nested Tables

You can use nested tables—tables that appear within other tables—to create more complex layouts in your pages. In the following example, you will use a nested table to present a table of data on the page. The Width of the nested table is set to 100%, and its Cell Padding and Cell Spacing settings are set to 0; therefore, the new table will completely fill the cell in which it is inserted.

To create a nested table within an existing table, follow these steps:

1. Click inside the cell into which you want to insert another table. In this case, the FrontPage Editor has displaced the contents of the bottom row in the table. Insert the new table into what appears to be the third cell in the bottom row of the table shown in Figure 8.17.

TIP: You'll notice that the FrontPage Editor has shifted the contents of your table because you added the `COLGROUP` tags in the previous example. When designing your own pages, you may find it easier to add extra HTML tags (`COL`, `COLGROUP`, `RULES`, `THEAD`, `TBODY`, and `TFOOT` tags) after you completely design your table and insert all its contents.

2. Choose T**a**ble | **I**nsert Table. The Insert Table dialog box shown in Figure 8.17 is displayed.

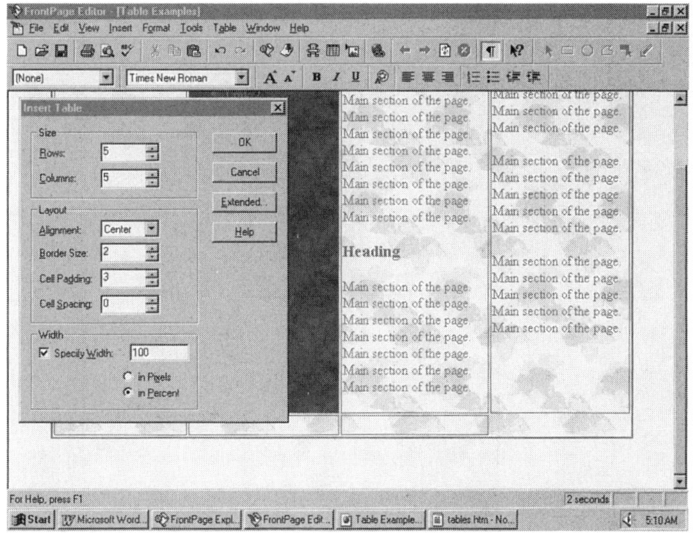

Figure 8.17.
Use the Insert Table dialog box to create a table within your first table.

3. Enter the following settings in the Insert Table dialog box:

Rows:	`5`
Columns:	`5`
Alignment:	`Center`
Border Size:	`2`
Cell Pa**d**ding:	`3`
Cell **S**pacing:	`0`
Specify **W**idth:	`100, in Percent`

4. Choose OK. The table is displayed within the third cell of your first table.
5. Select the first row of cells in the new table by positioning your cursor at the left edge of the table. It becomes a selection pointer. Click to select the first row of cells.
6. With the cells selected, click the Bold button on the Format toolbar.
7. Enter `Header` in all five cells in the first row of the table. The cells in the second through fourth rows should read `Body`, and the last row of cells should read `Footer`. When you have entered your text, the table should look like Figure 8.18.

TIP: You can enter the text in one column of the table. Then copy the contents into the clipboard using Ctrl+C, and paste into the other columns using Ctrl+V.

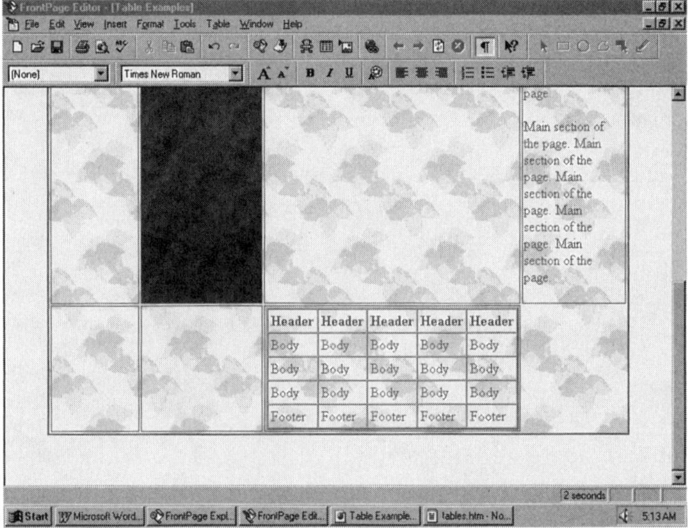

Figure 8.18.
Enter some preliminary text in the table to help you determine where the header, body, and footer of the table are placed.

8. Choose **F**ile | Preview in **B**rowser, and preview your table in Internet Explorer 3.0 or higher. Refresh the display in the browser if necessary. Verify that your new table is in the correct position. It should look similar to the table shown in Figure 8.19.

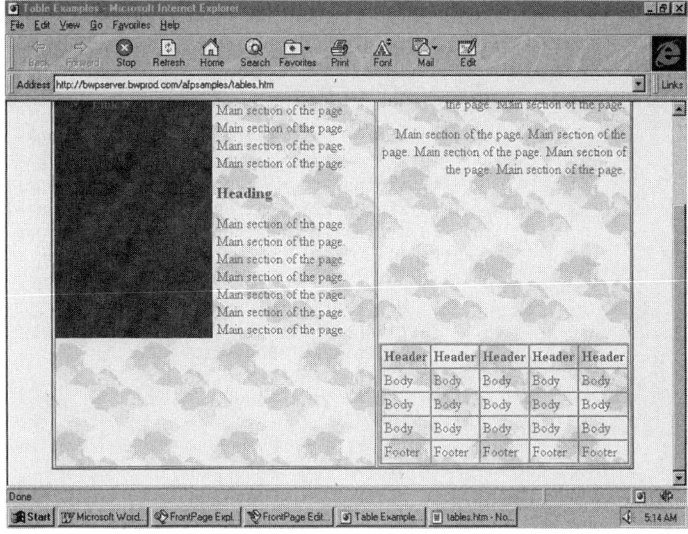

Figure 8.19.
Preview your table in Internet Explorer 3.0 or higher to verify that your new table is displayed in the correct position.

Defining Table Headers, Body, and Footers

You'll notice that your new table doesn't stand out very much from the rest of the page contents. You can enhance the appearance of this new table by adding some text formatting and defining rules that separate the table header and footer from the body of the table.

The THEAD, TBODY, and TFOOT tags, respectively, define the header, body, and footer of a table. You can assign several attributes to each of these tags, such as the following:

- You can assign a cascading style sheet class to table headers, body, and footers using a CLASS attribute. Use the STYLE attribute to apply cascading style sheet properties to these elements.
- You can apply horizontal and vertical alignment properties to the table header with the ALIGN and VALIGN tags, respectively. The table header can be aligned horizontally to the LEFT, CENTER, or RIGHT of the table. You can also use the JUSTIFY tag to span the contents of the header across the entire width of the cell if the contents are long. You can align the header to the MIDDLE, TOP, or BOTTOM of the header cell.

You learn more about cascading style sheets in **Chapter 10**.

To define the header, body, and footer of the new table, follow these steps:

1. Choose **V**iew | **H**TML. The View or Edit HTML dialog box is displayed.

2. Scroll down through the HTML code of your page until you find the code for the second table. The following code is displayed:

```
<table border="0" cellpadding="0" cellspacing="0" width="100%">
  <tr>
    <td width="20%"><strong>Header</strong></td>
    <td width="20%"><strong>Header</strong></td>
    <td width="20%"><strong>Header</strong></td>
    <td width="20%"><strong>Header</strong></td>
    <td width="20%"><strong>Header</strong></td>
  </tr>
  <tr>
    <td width="20%">Body</td>
    <td width="20%">Body</td>
    <td width="20%">Body</td>
    <td width="20%">Body</td>
    <td width="20%">Body</td>
  </tr>
  <tr>
    <td width="20%">Body</td>
    <td width="20%">Body</td>
    <td width="20%">Body</td>
    <td width="20%">Body</td>
    <td width="20%">Body</td>
  </tr>
  <tr>
    <td width="20%">Body</td>
    <td width="20%">Body</td>
    <td width="20%">Body</td>
    <td width="20%">Body</td>
    <td width="20%">Body</td>
  </tr>
  <tr>
    <td width="20%">Footer</td>
    <td width="20%">Footer</td>
    <td width="20%">Footer</td>
    <td width="20%">Footer</td>
    <td width="20%">Footer</td>
  </tr>
</table>
```

3. Position the insertion point after the first line that reads `<tr>` and press Enter. The insertion point moves to the next line.

4. Enter the following code, which defines the first row in the table as a header and aligns its contents to the center and bottom of the cells:

```
<thead align=center valign=bottom>
```

The first section of your table should now read as follows:

```
<table border="0" cellpadding="0" cellspacing="0" width="100%">
  <tr>
  <thead align=center valign=bottom>
    <td width="20%"><strong>Header</strong></td>
    <td width="20%"><strong>Header</strong></td>
    <td width="20%"><strong>Header</strong></td>
    <td width="20%"><strong>Header</strong></td>
    <td width="20%"><strong>Header</strong></td>
  </tr>
```

5. The first row of cells in your table ends with a line that reads </tr> (the last line of code shown in the previous example). The second row of cells begins on the following line with a line that reads <tr>. To define the second through fourth rows of the table as the table body, position the insertion point at the end of the <tr> line and press Enter. Then enter the following line of code:

```
<tbody>
```

6. Because you are including a header and footer in your table, you must end the body of the table with a closing tag. You have three rows of cells that you want to place in the body (the second through fourth rows in the table), and the closing element must come after the closing element in the fourth row of cells. Add a </tbody> tag at the end of the fourth row of cells in your table. Your code for the body of the table should now look like this:

```
<tr>
<tbody>
  <td width="20%">Body;</td>
  <td width="20%">Body;</td>
  <td width="20%">Body;</td>
  <td width="20%">Body;</td>
  <td width="20%">Body;</td>
</tr>
<tr>
  <td width="20%">Body;</td>
  <td width="20%">Body;</td>
  <td width="20%">Body;</td>
  <td width="20%">Body;</td>
  <td width="20%">Body;</td>
</tr>
<tr>
  <td width="20%">Body;</td>
  <td width="20%">Body;</td>
  <td width="20%">Body;</td>
  <td width="20%">Body;</td>
  <td width="20%">Body;</td>
</tr>
</tbody>
```

7. To define the footer of the table, press Enter after the </tbody> tag that you just entered, and enter <tfoot>. A closing tag is not required. Now, the completed code for the footer of the table should appear as follows:

```
  <tfoot>
  <tr>
    <td width="20%">Footer</td>
    <td width="20%">Footer</td>
    <td width="20%">Footer</td>
    <td width="20%">Footer</td>
    <td width="20%">Footer</td>
  </tr>
</table>
```

8. Choose OK to exit the View or Edit HTML dialog box and apply the new code to your page. HTML Markup Bots appear on the page as small yellow

icons with question marks in them. You can double-click these icons to edit the code within them.

Changing Cell Background and Border Colors

To make the header and footer of the new table stand out more, you can change their color. In addition, you can specify a different border color for the cells in the body of the table.

To specify a custom background color for the header and footer cells, follow these steps:

1. Position the cursor immediately to the left of the Header row of cells in the table, as shown in Figure 8.20, and click to select them.

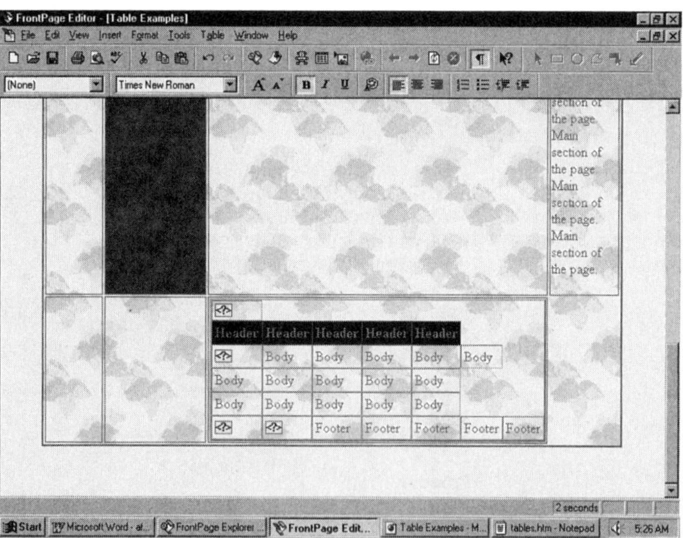

Figure 8.20.
Position the cursor to the left of the first row in the table to select the first row.

2. Shift-click to select all cells in the bottom row of the table as well (those labeled Footer).
3. Press Alt+Enter to open the Cell Properties dialog box.
4. From the Custom Background section, choose Custom from the Background **C**olor drop-down menu. Define a custom color of **R**ed `255`, **G**reen `204`, **B**lue `102`. Choose OK to return to the Cell Properties dialog box.
5. From the Custom Colors section, choose Custom from the **B**order drop-down menu. Define a custom color of **R**ed `255`, **G**reen `204`, **B**lue `102`. Choose OK to return to the Cell Properties dialog box.

6. Choose OK to exit the Cell Properties dialog box and update your cell colors. The header and footer cells are now gold with a gold border color, as shown in Figure 8.21.

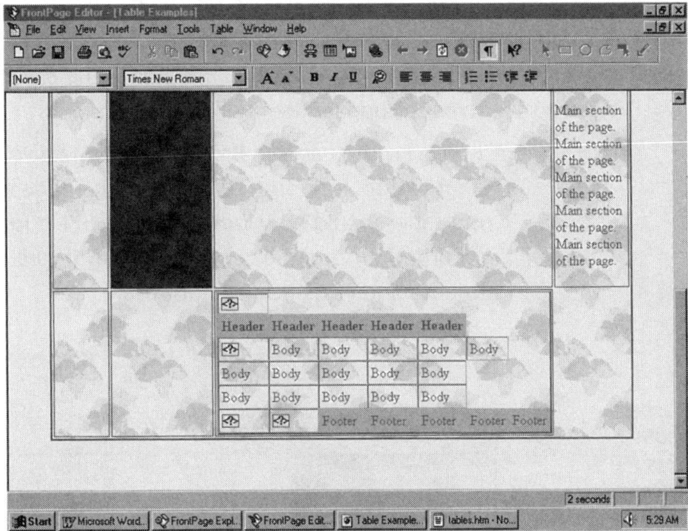

Figure 8.21.
The Header and Footer rows change to gold with a gold border.

7. Position the cursor immediately to the left of the second row of cells; it becomes a selection pointer. Click and drag to select the cells in the second, third, and fourth rows (the Body cells).
8. Press Alt+Enter to open the Cell Properties dialog box.
9. From the Custom Colors section, choose Custom from the **B**order drop-down menu. Define a custom color of **R**ed `255`, **G**reen `204`, **B**lue `102`. Choose OK to return to the Cell Properties dialog box. The borders of the body cells turn to gold.
10. Choose OK to return to the FrontPage Editor.

Adding Horizontal Rules Between Rows

In the following task, you will apply an extended attribute that applies horizontal rules between the table header, table body, and table footer. The rules will not appear around other cells. This creates a table that does not display borders around the body cells. Follow these steps:

1. Position the insertion point anywhere in the nested table, and right-click. Choose Table Properties from the pop-up menu to open the Table Properties dialog box.

2. Click the **E**xtended button. The Extended Attributes dialog box is displayed.
3. Click the **A**dd button. The Name/Value Pair dialog box is displayed.
4. In the **N**ame field, enter `rules`. In the **V**alue field, enter `groups`.
5. Choose OK to exit the Name/Value Pair, Extended Attributes, and Table Properties dialog boxes. You return to the FrontPage Editor.
6. Choose **F**ile | **S**ave (Ctrl+S), or choose the Save button on the Standard toolbar to update the page in your Web.
7. Choose **F**ile | Preview in **B**rowser to preview your table in Internet Explorer 3.0 or higher. Refresh the display of the page in your browser if necessary. Your table should now look as shown in Figure 8.22. Notice that there are no borders around the cells in the body of the table. The `rules=groups` attribute and value achieve this result.

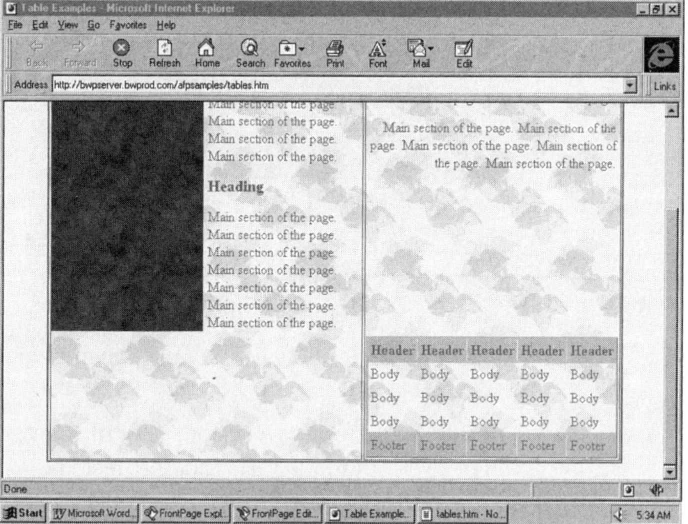

Figure 8.22.
Horizontal rules appear between the header, body, and footer of the nested table, but do not appear around the cells in the body of the table.

Workshop Wrap-Up

By combining background images and colors in your tables, you can create some interesting layouts. Nested tables with different background images and border sizes can be used to create multicolored borders around tables. Horizontal and vertical rules can further enhance the appearance of tables. And as you'll learn in Chapter 9, "Using Floating Frames," you can insert a floating frame to display other Web pages within a table.

In this chapter, you learned how Internet Explorer 3.0 provides additional enhancements to tables and table cells. You learned how to apply background images to tables and cells and how to change border colors. You also learned how to use additional tags that allow you to specify where rules, or dividing lines, appear between the cells in your table. And, by using nested tables, you learned how to accent data in your pages.

Next Steps

In Chapter 9, you will learn another way that Internet Explorer uses frames. Rather than display your pages in fixed frames, Internet Explorer gives you the advantage of placing a frame anywhere on a Web page. This offers some creative alternatives to page layout.

To learn more about the features incorporated in Internet Explorer, refer to the following chapters:

- In Chapter 10, "Using Cascading Style Sheets," you will learn how to go beyond using style sheets that specify background, text, and link colors. Using cascading style sheets, you can define font faces, colors, and sizes that can be used to standardize the appearance of all the pages in your Web.
- In Chapter 11, "Real-Life Examples: The Internet Explorer Advantage," you will learn how to combine all the techniques discussed in Part III, "Designing for Internet Explorer," as well as learning additional tips that allow your pages to be viewed in browsers that do not support Internet Explorer features.

Q&A

Q: In the exercises in this chapter, you used the `COLGROUP` and `COL` tags in one table, and the `THEAD`, `TBODY`, and `TFOOT` tags in another table. Can I use all these tags in the same table?

A: Yes, you can combine these tags into one table if you like. When you apply the `RULES=GROUPS` extended attribute to a table with all these elements, rules appear between the column groups and between the header, body, and footer of the table.

Q: Do these additional tags offer any other advantages besides those you show here?

A: You can also use these tags in concert with cascading style sheets. With cascading style sheet definitions, you can specify the font faces, sizes, and colors to be used in the defined areas within the table.

Q: Can you offer additional tips on designing for multiple browsers?

A: When you design features that are specific to one browser, or a small number of browsers, start as though you are designing a page for all browsers. Add as much "generic" content as you can before you add features that are browser specific. As you add enhanced features, preview the changes in browsers that do not support them. You might discover that you need to "give a little and take a little" to reach a happy medium. When all else fails, you can design an alternate page and provide a link to it for those who find your enhanced features unreadable.

CHAPTER NINE

Using Floating Frames

Framesets allow multiple Web pages to be displayed within the space of a single browser window. FrontPage provides a Frames Wizard, which allows you to generate standard framesets quite easily. This type of frameset can be viewed in any frame-compatible browser such as Netscape 2.0 (or higher), or Internet Explorer 3.0 (or higher).

Internet Explorer 3.0 has some additional tricks in its repertoire: In addition to having the capability to display standard framesets, it also allows you to display *floating frames* anywhere on any web page. Having the ability to place one or more frames anywhere on any web page gives you some very creative layout capabilities.

What Are Floating Frames?

In a standard frameset, as shown in Figure 9.1, your browser window is divided into multiple frames. You specify the settings for these frames in FrontPage's Frames Wizard. The main use for framesets is to provide clean and organized interfaces that allow a user to navigate through a web site more efficiently. Standard framesets have the advantage of being compatible with more browsers, but alas—many people don't like them. Not only are you somewhat limited in how your page can be laid out, but frames can sometimes detract from a Web page's appearance.

In this chapter, you

- Learn what makes up a floating frame and review the attributes supported by the `IFRAME` tag
- Create a web in which to place your floating frame pages
- Create basic floating frames that display the contents of another web page within them
- Align floating frames to the right and center of your page
- Create borderless floating frames that give the page a seamless look
- Add scrolling and white space to a floating frame
- Get an introduction of how to display other pages in floating frames

Tasks in this chapter:

- Creating a Web for Your Floating Frame Tasks
- Adding a Floating Frame to Your Web Page
- Aligning the Floating Frame
- Changing the Borders of a Floating Frame
- Specifying How a Floating Frame Scrolls
- Adding White Space Around Floating Frames
- Linking to Pages in Floating Frames

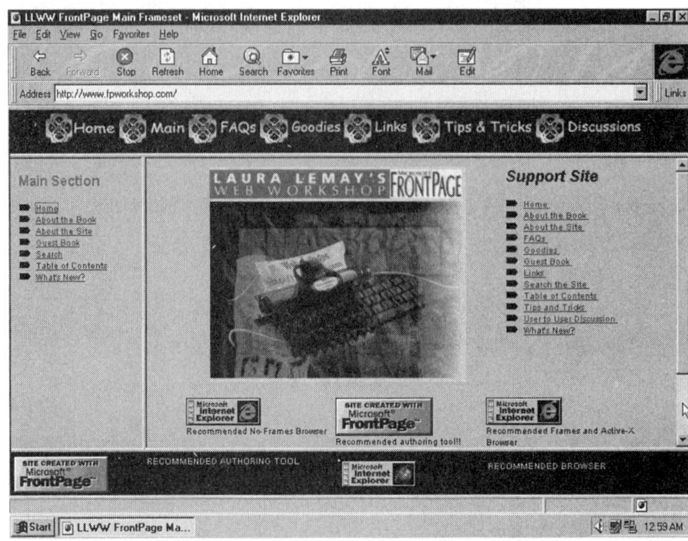

Figure 9.1.
Standard framesets divide the browser window into multiple frames.

Floating frames provide a bridge between a standard Web page and a frameset. They are similar to standard framesets in that they allow the contents of another Web page to be displayed in a defined space; but that is where the similarity ends. A floating frame can appear anywhere within a Web page—even within tables and forms. Figure 9.2 shows a floating frame placed in the right cell of a table. With floating frames, contents of other pages can appear just about anywhere imaginable, much like placing images on your pages. Gone are the boundaries that confine frame placement within a designated portion of your browser window.

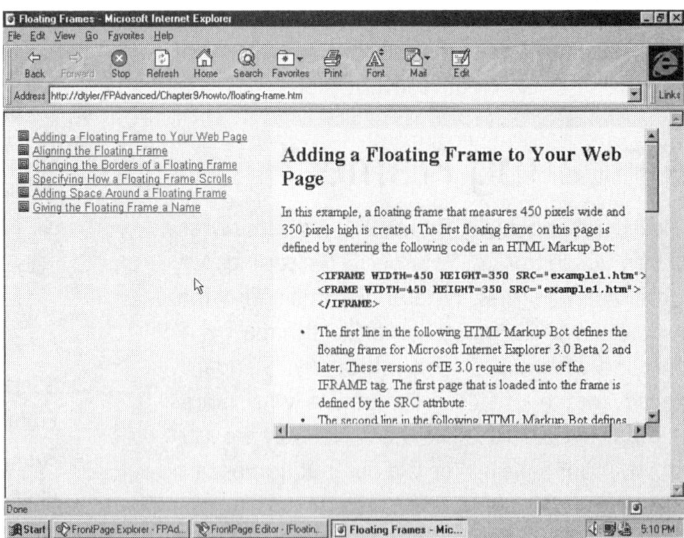

Figure 9.2.
A floating frame can appear anywhere on a Web page. Here, a floating frame is placed in the right cell of a table.

Floating frames differ from standard framesets in the following ways:

- One or more floating frames can be placed anywhere on a Web page. You can place a floating frame anywhere that an image can be placed.
- The browser window is not divided into different frames. Instead, areas within your Web page are defined as frames. This allows more flexibility in page design, especially when used in conjunction with tables.
- Floating frames use the `IFRAME` tag in Microsoft Internet Explorer 3.0 Beta 2 and higher, including the final release. For the Beta 1 release of Internet Explorer 3.0, floating frames are implemented with the `FRAME` tag. If both tags appear in the same page, compatibility with all releases of Microsoft Internet Explorer 3.0 is ensured.
- One drawback to floating frames is that you cannot specify an alternative content source. Normal framesets allow you to designate a page, which displays in lieu of the frameset when a frame-compatible browser is not detected; the `IFRAME` tag does not. When a browser that does not support floating frames comes across a page that includes them, it is as if nothing exists in that portion of the page; no contents appear there at all. So, if you decide to incorporate floating frames into your pages, provide a means to display alternative content for browsers that do not support them.

You learn more about using floating frames and how to design alternative content in **Chapter 11**.

The Anatomy of Floating Frames

The final and Beta 2 releases of Microsoft Internet Explorer 3.0 utilize the `IFRAME` tag to define a floating frame. You can implement this tag in FrontPage using the **I**nsert | **H**TML Markup or **V**iew | **H**TML commands. The `IFRAME` tag uses the attributes and values listed in Table 9.1.

Table 9.1. Attributes for the IFRAME tag.

Attribute	*Value*	*Description*
`ALIGN`	`LEFT`	Aligns the floating frame to the left margin of the page. This is the default value if no alignment is specified.
`ALIGN`	`RIGHT`	Aligns the floating frame to the right margin of the page.
`FRAMEBORDER`	`0`	Creates a borderless floating frame, giving it a seamless look.
`HEIGHT`	*n*	Defines the height of the floating frame in pixels. See also `WIDTH` attribute.

continues

Table 9.1. continued

Attribute	*Value*	*Description*
`HEIGHT`	*n%*	Defines the height of the floating frame in percentage of browser window. See also `WIDTH` attribute.
`HSPACE`	*n*	Defines the size of the margin around the horizontal (top and bottom) sides of the frame in pixels. See also `VSPACE` attribute.
`NAME`	*`framename`*	Assigns a name to the floating frame. This name can be referenced as a target frame when creating links to pages that should appear within the floating frame.
`SCROLLING`	`AUTO`	Creates a floating frame that contains scrollbars as necessary.
`SCROLLING`	`NO`	Creates a floating frame that does not contain scrollbars.
`SCROLLING`	`YES`	Creates a floating frame that contains scrollbars on the right and bottom sides of the frame.
`SRC`	*`url`*	Defines the URL that is loaded into the floating frame when the page first opens. The URL should be relative to the folder in which the floating frame resides.
`VSPACE`	*n*	Defines the size of the margin around the vertical (left and right) sides of the frame in pixels. See also `HSPACE` attribute.
`WIDTH`	*n*	Defines the width of the floating frame in pixels. See also `HEIGHT` attribute.
`WIDTH`	*n%*	Defines the width of the floating frame in percentage of browser window. See also `HEIGHT` attribute.

Creating a Web for Your Floating Frame Tasks

To complete the tasks in this chapter, you'll need to create an empty web in which to save the pages. You will also need to import a sample content page from the CD-ROM that accompanies this book (or you can create your own if you wish). To create the web, follow these steps:

1. From the FrontPage Explorer, choose **F**ile | **N**ew | Front Page **W**eb (Ctrl+N). The New FrontPage Web dialog box is displayed.
2. From the **T**emplate or Wizard field, select Empty Web and choose OK. The Empty Web Template dialog box is displayed.
3. From the Web **S**erver or File Location drop-down menu, select the server on which you want to create the web. If the server supports Secure Socket Layer communications, check the **C**onnect Using SSL check box.
4. In the **N**ame of New FrontPage Web field, enter `floatingframes`.
5. Choose OK. FrontPage creates the web.
6. To import the sample contents page, choose **F**ile | **I**mport. The Import File to FrontPage Web dialog box is displayed.
7. Click **A**dd File. The Add File to Import List dialog box is displayed.

8. Locate the `sample.htm` page in the Chap09 folder on the CD-ROM that accompanies this book. Double-click the file to add it to the import list. You will return to the Import File to FrontPage Web dialog box.
9. Click OK. The file is displayed in the home directory of your `floatingframes` web.

Adding a Floating Frame to Your Web Page

You add a floating frame to your page in an HTML Markup Bot. Although you can enter or edit HTML code directly from FrontPage by using the **V**iew | **H**TML command, FrontPage checks the code you enter for compatibility with the tags supported by the FrontPage Editor. It makes its best attempt at interpreting the code but sometimes alters it before any unsupported code is placed into an HTML Markup Bot for you. By defining your floating frames in an HTML Markup Bot right away, you will avoid any of these alterations.

NOTE: If you enter the HTML code for your floating frame in the View or Edit HTML Window (using the **V**iew | **H**TML command), the code is verified and edited slightly by the FrontPage Editor. Enter your HTML code in the HTML Markup Bot to avoid this situation.

At the most basic level, you specify the size of the floating frame and the relative URL of the page displayed in it when you first open the page. All other attributes are optional.

In the following task, a basic floating frame that measures 450 pixels wide and 350 pixels high is defined on the page. The floating frame displays a page named `sample.htm` when the page first opens. You will create a new page on which to place two basic floating frames. The first floating frame is sized in pixels, and the second is sized in percentage of browser window width and height. After you add the frames to your page, you will save the page to your current web and preview the floating frames in Microsoft Internet Explorer 3.0.

To create and view the page, follow these steps:

1. From the FrontPage Explorer, click the Show FrontPage Editor button on the Explorer toolbar. The FrontPage Editor opens.
2. From the FrontPage Editor, click the New button on the Standard toolbar. A new blank page is displayed in the FrontPage Editor.
3. Choose Heading 3 from the Change Style drop-down menu on the Format toolbar. Enter `Floating Frame Sized in Pixels.`
4. Press Enter. The insertion point moves to the next line.
5. Choose **I**nsert | **B**ot | **H**TML Markup. The HTML Markup dialog box is displayed.
6. To define a basic floating frame that measures 450×350 pixels and displays the `sample.htm` page within it, enter the following code in the HTML Markup dialog box:

```
<IFRAME WIDTH=450 HEIGHT=350 SRC="sample.htm">
<FRAME WIDTH=450 HEIGHT=350 SRC="sample.htm">
</IFRAME>
```

NOTE: The second line of code in Step 6 shows the floating frame definition that is compatible with Internet Explorer 3.0, Beta 1. The first beta release of Internet Explorer 3.0 uses the `FRAME` tag to define a floating frame. This was revised in the Beta 2 release, when the `IFRAME` tag was implemented instead. If you want your floating frame to be compatible with all versions of Microsoft Internet Explorer 3.0, the second frame definition should appear in your code.

7. Choose OK. The HTML Markup Bot is displayed on your page.
8. Press Enter to move to the next line, and select Heading 3 from the Change Style drop-down menu on the Format toolbar. Enter `Floating Frame Sized in Percentages.`
9. Press Enter. The insertion point moves to the next line.
10. Choose **I**nsert | **B**ot | **H**TML Markup. The HTML Markup dialog box is displayed.

11. To define a basic floating frame that measures 75 percent of the browser window's width and height and displays the `sample.htm` page within it, enter the following code into the second HTML Markup dialog box:

```
<IFRAME WIDTH=75% HEIGHT=75% SRC="sample.htm">
<FRAME WIDTH=75% HEIGHT=75% SRC="sample.htm">
</IFRAME>
```

12. Choose OK. The HTML Markup Bot is displayed on your page.
13. Choose **File**|**S**ave (Ctrl+S) or click the Save button on the Standard toolbar. The Save dialog box is displayed.
14. In the Page **T**itle field, enter `Basic Floating Frames`. In the File **p**ath within your FrontPage web field, leave the URL at its default: `basic.htm`.
15. Choose OK. The page is saved to your web.
16. Choose **File**|Preview in **B**rowser. The Preview in Browser dialog box is displayed.
17. From the Browser list, select Microsoft Internet Explorer 3.0. Select the resolution in which you want to preview the page from the **W**indow Size field.
18. Choose OK. The floating frames appear on the page in your browser window. Figure 9.3 displays a floating frame sized in pixels, and Figure 9.4 displays a floating frame sized at 75 percent of the browser window's width and height.

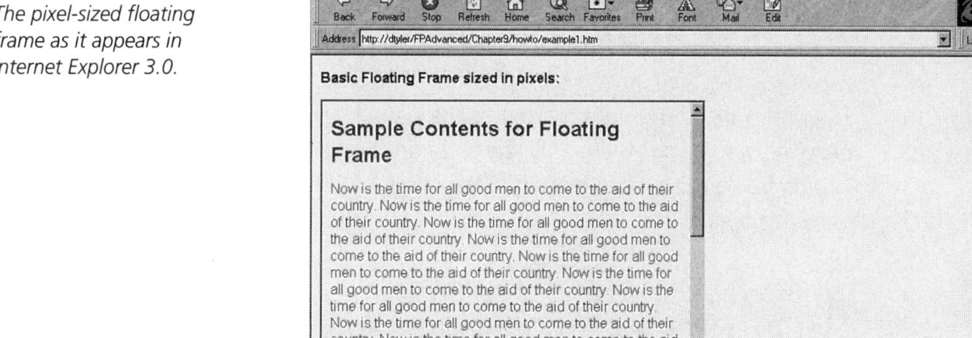

Figure 9.3.
The pixel-sized floating frame as it appears in Internet Explorer 3.0.

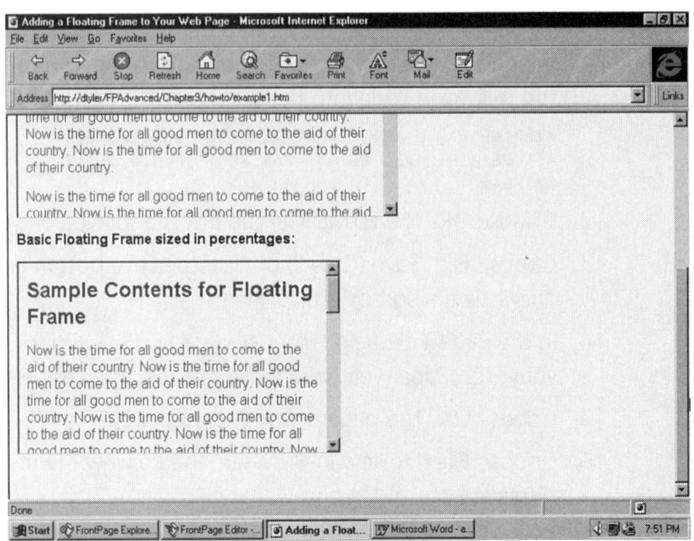

Figure 9.4.
The floating frame sized for 75% of browser window width and height as it appears in Internet Explorer 3.0.

By default, a floating frame appears as though it is recessed into the page, giving it a three-dimensional look. It is aligned to the left margin of the page. Scrollbars appear in the floating frame when the contents of the page within it exceed its size. These default values can be overridden by using the additional attributes described in the remainder of the chapter.

Aligning the Floating Frame to the Right Margin

Just as you can align images to the left or right margin of the page, you can align a floating frame to the right margin of the page by using the `ALIGN` attribute. In the following steps, you will modify the code on the page you just created to align the floating frame to the right margin of the page. Modify the code in the HTML Markup Bot as follows:

NOTE: You are also allowed to align images to the center of the page, but the `IFRAME` tag does not support the `ALIGN=CENTER` attribute and value. To align a floating frame to the center of the page, insert it into a table, as discussed in the "Aligning the Floating Frame to the Center of the Page" section.

1. In the FrontPage Editor, double-click the first HTML Markup Bot on your `basic.htm` page to open it. The HTML Markup dialog box is displayed.
2. To specify right alignment for the floating frame, add the `ALIGN=RIGHT` attribute/value pair to the floating frame definition in the HTML Markup dialog box as follows:

```
<IFRAME WIDTH=450 HEIGHT=350 ALIGN=RIGHT SRC="sample.htm">
<FRAME WIDTH=450 HEIGHT=350 ALIGN=RIGHT SRC="sample.htm">
</IFRAME>
```

3. If your web page will have additional content beneath the floating frame, ensure that the content clears the floating frame by adding a line break in the HTML Markup Bot. To do this, add a line that reads `<BR CLEAR=RIGHT>` or `<BR CLEAR=ALL>` after the closing `IFRAME` tag. The code in your HTML Markup Bot should appear as follows:

```
<IFRAME WIDTH=450 HEIGHT=350 ALIGN=RIGHT SRC="sample.htm">
<FRAME WIDTH=450 HEIGHT=350 ALIGN=RIGHT SRC="sample.htm">
</IFRAME>
<BR CLEAR=ALL>
```

4. Choose OK. You will return to the FrontPage Editor.
5. Optionally, double-click the second HTML Markup Bot to edit the code as follows, and choose OK to return to the FrontPage Editor:

```
<IFRAME WIDTH=75% HEIGHT=75% ALIGN=RIGHT SRC="sample.htm">
<FRAME WIDTH=75% HEIGHT=75% ALIGN=RIGHT SRC="sample.htm">
</IFRAME>
<BR CLEAR=ALL>
```

6. Choose **F**ile | Save **A**s. The Save As dialog box is displayed.
7. In the Page **T**itle field, enter `Aligned Floating Frames`. In the File **p**ath within your FrontPage web field, enter `aligned.htm`.
8. Choose OK. The page is saved to your web.
9. Choose **F**ile | Preview in **B**rowser. The Preview in Browser dialog box is displayed.
10. From the Browser list, select Microsoft Internet Explorer 3.0. Select the resolution in which you want to preview the page from the **W**indow Size field.
11. Choose OK. The floating frames appear on the page in your browser window. They should be aligned to the right margin of the page, as shown in Figure 9.5.

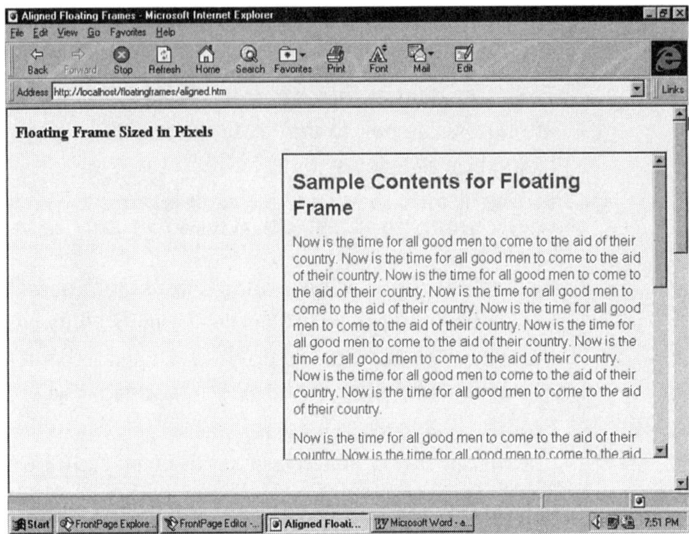

Figure 9.5.
The floating frame aligns to the right of the page by adding the `ALIGN=RIGHT` *attribute and value.*

Aligning the Floating Frame to the Center of the Page

The `ALIGN=CENTER` attribute and value is not supported by the `IFRAME` tag. To align a floating frame to the center of the page, you can create a table that contains one row and one column. Then you can insert an HTML Markup Bot into the table to define your frame. The steps to complete this are as follows:

1. Return to your `aligned.htm` page in the FrontPage Editor. Position the insertion point after the last HTML Markup Bot and press Enter to move to the next line.
2. Choose Heading 3 from the Change Style drop-down menu on the Format toolbar, and enter `Floating Frame Centered in Table.`
3. Press Enter. The insertion point moves to the next line.
4. Choose T**a**ble | **I**nsert Table. The Insert Table dialog box is displayed.
5. Assign the following properties to the table in the Insert Table dialog box:

Rows:	1
Columns:	1
Alignment:	Center
Border Size:	0
Cell Pa**d**ding:	0
Cell **S**pacing:	0
Specify **W**idth:	Unchecked

TIP: When you deselect the Specify **W**idth option in the Insert Table dialog box, the table cell expands to fit the dimensions of the floating frame.

6. Choose OK. The table is displayed on your page.
7. Click inside the single cell of the table, and choose **I**nsert | **H**TML Markup. The HTML Markup dialog box is displayed.
8. Enter the following code into the HTML Markup dialog box. You do not need to add the `ALIGN` attribute, because the table handles the floating frame alignment for you.

```
<IFRAME WIDTH=450 HEIGHT=350 SRC="sample.htm">
<FRAME WIDTH=450 HEIGHT=350 SRC="sample.htm">
</IFRAME>
```

   If you prefer to designate the width and height of the floating frame in percentages of browser window, enter code similar to the following:

```
<IFRAME WIDTH=75% HEIGHT=75% SRC="sample.htm">
<FRAME WIDTH=75% HEIGHT=75% SRC="sample.htm">
</IFRAME>
```

9. Choose OK. The HTML Markup Bot is displayed within the table.
10. Save the page to your web by choosing **F**ile | **S**ave (Ctrl+S). Then choose the **F**ile | Preview in **B**rowser command, and select Internet Explorer 3.0 from your list of available browsers. The floating frame aligns to the center of the page, as shown in Figure 9.6.

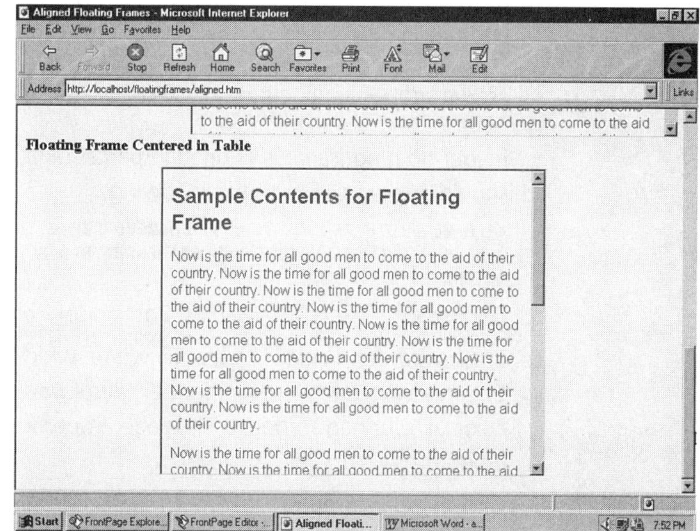

Figure 9.6.
When you center a floating frame with a table, it is displayed in the center of the page.

Changing the Borders of a Floating Frame

You may notice in the preceding examples that a floating frame appears as though it is recessed into the page by default. This gives it a three-dimensional appearance. You can create a more seamless appearance by adding the FRAMEBORDER=0 attribute/value pair to your floating frame code by following these steps:

TIP: The FRAMEBORDER attribute does not allow you to create solid lined borders around a floating frame (Example: FRAMEBORDER=5). To place a colored border around a floating frame, insert it into a table and apply the border to the table instead.

1. From the FrontPage Editor, choose **F**ile | **O**pen (Ctrl+O) or choose the Open button in the Standard toolbar. The Open dialog box is displayed.
2. From the list of pages in your current web, select `basic.htm` and choose OK. The page opens in the FrontPage Editor.
3. Double-click the first HTML Markup Bot. The HTML Markup dialog box is displayed, with code inside.
4. To change the borders of the floating frame, add the FRAMEBORDER=0 attribute and value to your HTML code in the HTML Markup dialog box. The code should be similar to the following:

   ```
   <IFRAME WIDTH=450 HEIGHT=350 FRAMEBORDER=0 SRC="sample.htm">
   <FRAME WIDTH=450 HEIGHT=350 FRAMEBORDER=0 SRC="sample.htm">
   </IFRAME>
   ```

   If your floating frame is defined in percentage width and height, the code should appear similar to the following:

   ```
   <IFRAME WIDTH=75% HEIGHT=75% FRAMEBORDER=0 SRC="sample.htm">
   <FRAME WIDTH=75% HEIGHT=75% FRAMEBORDER=0 SRC="sample.htm">
   </IFRAME>
   ```
5. Choose OK. The HTML Markup Bot is displayed on your page.
6. The background color is currently white, which will make it difficult to see the area where the floating frame is displayed. To change the background color of your page, choose File | Page Properties. The Page Properties dialog box is displayed.
7. Click the Background tab. From the Ba**c**kground drop-down menu, choose a light background color of your preference. (Yellow, aqua, or silver will be suitable for this example.) You can also choose a light-colored background image as an alternative.

8. Choose OK. The background color of your page changes.
9. Choose **F**ile|Save **A**s. The Save As dialog box is displayed.
10. In the Page **T**itle field, enter `Borderless Floating Frames`. In the File **p**ath within your FrontPage web field, enter `borderless.htm`.
11. Choose OK. The page is saved to your web.
12. Choose **F**ile|Preview in **B**rowser. The Preview in Browser dialog box is displayed.
13. From the Browser list, select Microsoft Internet Explorer 3.0. Select the resolution in which you want to preview the page from the **W**indow Size field.
14. Choose OK. The floating frames appear on the page in your browser window. They should now appear borderless, as shown in Figure 9.7.

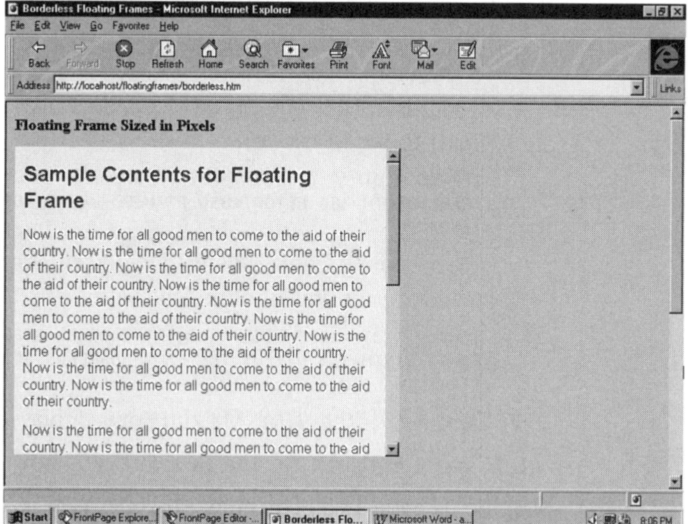

Figure 9.7.
Seamless borders can be created around a floating frame with the `FRAMEBORDER=0` *attribute and value.*

Specifying How a Floating Frame Scrolls

In the previous examples, you may notice that scrollbars have appeared on the right side of the floating frames. If you do not specify a scrolling option for a floating frame, scrollbars are added by default if the contents of the page warrant it. You can override this by using the `SCROLLING` attribute, which has the following three values associated with it:

- `SCROLLING=AUTO` adds scrollbars to the right edge, bottom edge, or both edges of a floating frame if the contents of the source page exceed the dimensions of the frame. It is not necessary to use this attribute, because floating frames use this by default.

- SCROLLING=NO disables scrollbars in the floating frame. Generally, use of this attribute is not advised unless you are certain that the contents of the frame will fit within the floating frame dimensions. If, for example, the source page contains only an image map, you can create a floating frame with the same dimensions and set scrolling to no.
- SCROLLING=YES displays scrollbars along the right and bottom edges of the floating frame regardless of whether the contents of the page require them.

In the following example, you will create a floating frame that includes scrollbars along the right and bottom sides. To complete the example, follow these steps:

1. Return to the borderless.htm page in the FrontPage Editor.
2. Double-click the first HTML Markup Bot to open the HTML Markup dialog box.
3. To create a frame with scrollbars, add the SCROLLING=YES attribute and value to your HTML code in the HTML Markup dialog box. The code should be similar to the following:

   ```
   <IFRAME WIDTH=450 HEIGHT=350 FRAMEBORDER=0 SCROLLING=YES SRC="sample.htm">
   <FRAME WIDTH=450 HEIGHT=350 FRAMEBORDER=0 SCROLLING=YES SRC="sample.htm">
   </IFRAME>
   ```

   If your floating frame is defined in percentage width and height, the code should appear similar to the following:

   ```
   <IFRAME WIDTH=75% HEIGHT=75% FRAMEBORDER=0 SCROLLING=YES SRC="sample.htm">
   <FRAME WIDTH=75% HEIGHT=75% FRAMEBORDER=0 SCROLLING=YES SRC="sample.htm">
   </IFRAME>
   ```

4. Choose **O**K. The HTML Markup Bot is displayed on your page.
5. Choose **F**ile|Save **A**s. The Save As dialog box is displayed.
6. In the Page **T**itle field, enter Floating Frames with Scrollbars. In the File **p**ath within your FrontPage web field, enter scrollbars.htm.
7. Choose OK. The page is saved to your web.
8. Choose **F**ile|Preview in **B**rowser. The Preview in Browser dialog box is displayed.
9. From the Browser list, select Microsoft Internet Explorer 3.0. Select the resolution in which you want to preview the page from the **W**indow Size field.
10. Choose OK. The floating frames appear on the page in your browser window. The floating frames are still borderless, but they now have scrollbars along the right and bottom edges, as shown in Figure 9.8.

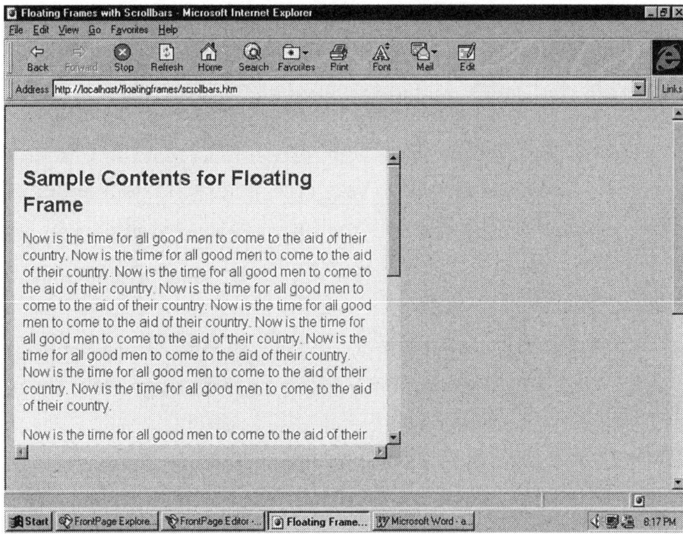

Figure 9.8.
Use the SCROLLING *attribute to enable or disable scrolling in the floating frame.* SCROLLING=YES *provides scrollbars along the right and bottom edges of the floating frame.*

Adding White Space Around Floating Frames

If there is other content on your page before or after the floating frame that you place on your page, you can create additional white space around the floating frame by using the HSPACE and VSPACE attributes. The numerical values you enter following the HSPACE or VSPACE attributes are the number of pixels that you want between the floating frame and surrounding contents.

1. Return to the `scrollbars.htm` page in the FrontPage Editor.
2. Double-click the first HTML Markup Bot to open the HTML Markup dialog box.
3. To add more white space around the floating frame, add the HSPACE and VSPACE attributes and values to your HTML code in the HTML Markup dialog box. The code should be similar to the following:

```
<IFRAME WIDTH=450 HEIGHT=350 FRAMEBORDER=0 HSPACE=15 VSPACE=15
➥SCROLLING=YES SRC="sample.htm">
<FRAME WIDTH=450 HEIGHT=350 FRAMEBORDER=0 HSPACE=15 VSPACE=15
➥SCROLLING=YES SRC="sample.htm">
</IFRAME>
```

If your floating frame is defined in percentage width and height, the code should appear similar to the following:

```
<IFRAME WIDTH=75% HEIGHT=75% FRAMEBORDER=0 HSPACE=15 VSPACE=15
➥SCROLLING=YES SRC="sample.htm">
<FRAME WIDTH=75% HEIGHT=75% FRAMEBORDER=0 HSPACE=15 VSPACE=15
```

```
➥SCROLLING=YES SRC="sample.htm">
</IFRAME>
```

4. Choose OK. The HTML Markup Bot is displayed on your page.
5. Choose **F**ile | Save **A**s. The Save As dialog box is displayed.
6. In the Page **T**itle field, enter `Floating Frames with White Space`. In the File **p**ath within your FrontPage web field, enter `whitespace.htm`.
7. Choose OK. The page is saved to your web.
8. Choose **F**ile | Preview in **B**rowser. The Preview in Browser dialog box is displayed.
9. From the Browser list, select Microsoft Internet Explorer 3.0. Select the resolution in which you want to preview the page from the **W**indow Size field.
10. Choose OK. The floating frames appear on the page in your browser window. The borderless floating frames have scrollbars along the right and bottom edges. Now you'll notice additional white space between the floating frames and the content above and below them. Refer to Figure 9.9 for an example.

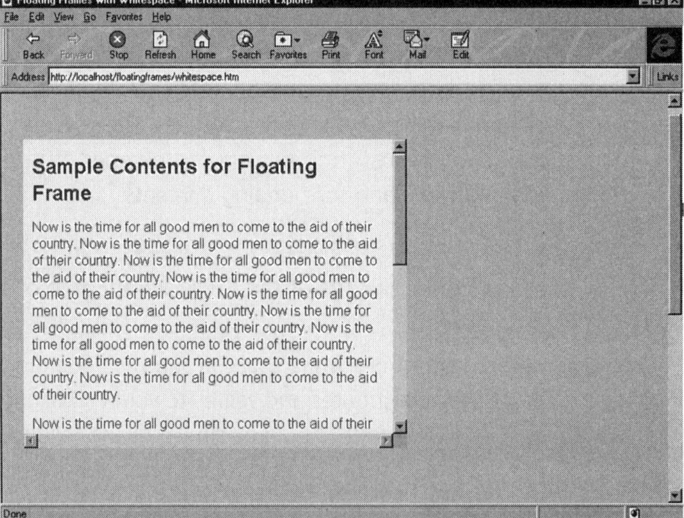

Figure 9.9.
Use the HSPACE *and* VSPACE *attributes to create additional white space to the horizontal and vertical sides of the floating frame.*

Linking to Pages in Floating Frames

Now you know how to construct floating frames and assign different attributes to them. Up until this point, you know how to display only one page in a floating frame. Just as standard framesets can display different contents when the user selects a link, floating frames can do the same. First, you must name your floating frame. This is easily done by adding the NAME attribute to your floating frame definition.

To assign a name to your floating frame, follow these steps:

1. Position the insertion point where you want the floating frame to appear.
2. Choose **I**nsert | **H**TML Markup. The HTML Markup dialog box is displayed.
3. To name your floating frame, add the NAME attribute and a name for the frame to your HTML code in the HTML Markup dialog box. If your floating frame is defined in pixels, the code should be similar to the following:

```
<IFRAME WIDTH=450 HEIGHT=350 FRAMEBORDER=0
➥NAME=mainframe SRC="sample.htm">
<FRAME WIDTH=450 HEIGHT=350 FRAMEBORDER=0
➥NAME=mainframe SRC="sample.htm">
</IFRAME>
```

   If your floating frame is defined in percentage width and height, the code should appear similar to the following:

```
<IFRAME WIDTH=75% HEIGHT=75% FRAMEBORDER=0
➥NAME=mainframe SRC="sample.htm">
<FRAME WIDTH=75% HEIGHT=75% FRAMEBORDER=0
➥NAME=mainframe SRC="sample.htm">
</IFRAME>
```

4. Choose OK. The HTML Markup Bot is displayed on your page.

The basic steps to load a page into a floating frame are similar to those used when you link to pages in a standard frameset. You'll find it easier to create the links if the pages already exist in your current web. The steps to create a link to a page that displays in a floating frame are briefly described here. '

To create a link to a page that displays in a floating frame, follow these steps:

1. On the same page on which the floating frame is displayed, create the text, image, or hotspot on which you want the user to click to load the linked page into the floating frame.
2. Select the text or image, and choose the Create Hyperlink button on the FrontPage Editor's Standard toolbar. The Create Hyperlink dialog box is displayed.
3. Select the Current FrontPage Web tab, and choose the page to which you are linking.
4. In the Target Frame field of the Create Hyperlink dialog box, enter the name of the floating frame (such as `mainframe` in the previous task), as shown in Figure 9.10.

You'll get hands-on experience in creating links to pages that appear in floating frames in **Chapter 11**.

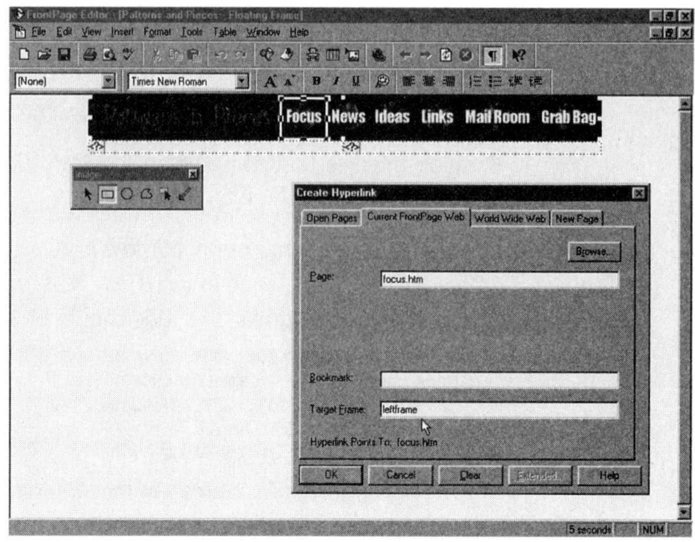

Figure 9.10.
Specify the frame in which linked pages appear in the Target Frame field of the Create Hyperlink (shown) or Edit Hyperlink dialog boxes.

5. Choose OK. The hyperlink to the page that displays in the floating frame is displayed on your page.

Workshop Wrap-Up

Floating frames are a creative alternative to framesets, because you can place them anywhere on your Web page. Because the contents of floating frames are not restricted to defined sections of your browser window, you are free to be as creative as you like in their arrangement. Use them to display lists, forms, and artwork that change content depending on a user's selection.

In this chapter, you learned the basics of creating floating frames, an Internet Explorer 3.0 enhancement. You learned, through example, how floating frames differ from standard framesets. You added several different floating frames to Web pages while learning how various attributes affect the appearance of a floating frame. You also learned how to assign a name to a floating frame so that linked pages could appear within it.

Next Steps

In Chapter 10, "Using Cascading Style Sheets," you will learn about another capability of Internet Explorer 3.0—cascading style sheets. This capability allows you to customize headings, margins, font styles, and more for all or part of your web.

To learn more about the unique features supported by Internet Explorer 3.0, and how to use floating frames in conjunction with them, refer to the following chapters:

- Refer to Chapter 8, "Creating Advanced Tables," to learn how you can assign background images, border effects, and more to your tables.
- See Chapter 10, "Using Cascading Style Sheets," to learn how you can customize the look of your pages with consistent headings, margins, font faces, and colors.
- Learn how to put it all together and examine alternatives for content in Chapter 11, "Real-Life Examples: The Internet Explorer Advantage."

Q&A

Q: I placed a floating frame on my page, but when I viewed it in Internet Explorer, the floating frame displayed an HTTP File Not Found message. What did I do wrong?

A: When you specify a source file for your floating frame, the page that it loads should appear as a relative URL. This URL should be relative to the location of the page on which the floating frame is displayed. If the page that you are loading is in the same directory as the page with the floating frame, you simply enter the filename of the page (for example, `frame-contents.htm`). If the page that you display within the floating frame is in a different directory, you must provide a relative URL. For a simple example, assume that the page that contains the floating frame has the following URL:

```
http://myweb/floating/page1.htm
```

The page that you want to include in the floating frame has the following URL:

```
http://myweb/funstuff.htm
```

When you specify the relative URL to the `funstuff.htm` page in your HTML Markup Bot, enter the following:

```
SRC="../funstuff.htm"
```

If you need additional information on relative URLs, refer to *Teach Yourself HTML 3.2 in 14 Days* by Laura Lemay (published by Sams.net).

Q: Can you create a floating frame that is sized by pixels in width and by percentage in height; or by percentage in width and pixels in height?

A: Yes, you can size them this way if the floating frame is placed directly on a Web page. However, when you insert a floating frame into a table, it behaves much better when its dimensions are specified in pixels.

Q: Can I include a page that contains another floating frame within a floating frame?

A: Sure you can! Just like standard frames, though, you don't want to have so many different frames on your page that your content becomes impossible to read. Too many scrollbars and tiny areas are difficult to browse and can really detract from the appearance of a Web page.

CHAPTER

TEN

Using Cascading Style Sheets

In this chapter, you

- Learn about the elements that make up a style sheet
- Use extended attributes to apply styles to your page content
- Build a style sheet using features supported with Internet Explorer

Tasks in this chapter:

- Creating a Simple CSS
- Adding Font Families and Sizes to Your Classes
- Aligning and Decorating Text
- Applying Page Margins
- Choosing Background and Text Colors
- Using a Single Style Sheet for Multiple Pages

How many times do you find yourself using different fonts, colors, and sizes of text in your Web pages for emphasis and interest? Assume, for example, that you want all of the headings in your pages to be a different color than the normal text. Using standard procedures in FrontPage, you highlight each heading and use the Text Color button in the Format toolbar to change the color of each heading one at a time. Later, if you want to revise the color scheme of your pages, you have to go back to each page and change the colors again. It amounts to tedious work, indeed.

Fortunately, there is a solution to this problem that you can use to standardize the appearance of text, headings, and margins on your pages. By using cascading style sheets (CSSs), you can customize the total appearance of your pages. This chapter shows you some ways that you can implement CSSs as supported by Internet Explorer 3.0 and higher using FrontPage 97.

What Is a Cascading Style Sheet?

A *cascading style sheet* (CSS) uses rules to define the styles you use in your pages. Basically, the syntax of a CSS rule incorporates two elements: a *selector,* which defines the element or class that you want to apply properties to, and a *declaration,* which defines the properties for the element or class. The declaration also consists of two elements: the *property*, or attribute that you want to define, and its *value*. Table 10.1 shows some examples of selectors, properties, and values that you can use in style sheets.

Table 10.1. Examples of CSS selectors, properties, and values.

Selector	*Property*	*Value*	*Description*
`H1`	`font-family`	`Arial`	Renders Heading 1 in Arial font
`P.red`	`color`	`red`	Renders paragraph text assigned to the `red` class in the color red

How Browsers Handle CSSs

The tags used with CSSs are still under discussion and development, and few browsers support them. Browsers that do provide CSS support do so in varying degrees. Therefore, when you design pages that utilize CSS tags, always consider what the page looks like in browsers that do not support CSS at all.

Fortunately, when a browser that does not support CSSs encounters STYLE tags, it ignores them. Because each browser has its own built-in style sheet, the browser formats the page contents as it sees fit, using the background and text color settings you specify in the Page Properties: Background tab instead. The text on the page displays in default HTML fonts (usually Times New Roman or equivalent for proportional-width fonts and Courier or equivalent for fixed-width fonts).

Cascading style sheets offer the capability of creating some incredibly artistic effects using text and background colors. For example, you can create shadowed text by superimposing two separate lines of text in such a manner that they are slightly offset from one another. These types of effects will not translate well in browsers that do not support CSSs, so you should provide other page alternatives for browsers that do not support CSS tags.

If the user's system does not support fonts specified within the style sheet, they can disable the use of style sheets through Internet Explorer with the Advanced tab in the Options dialog box.

To disable CSSs, follow these steps:

1. From Internet Explorer, choose **V**iew | **O**ptions. The Options dialog box is displayed.
2. Click the Advanced tab, shown in Figure 10.1.

3. In the lower portion of the dialog box, deselect the Use style sheets check box.
4. Choose OK. You return to Internet Explorer. The settings take effect immediately.

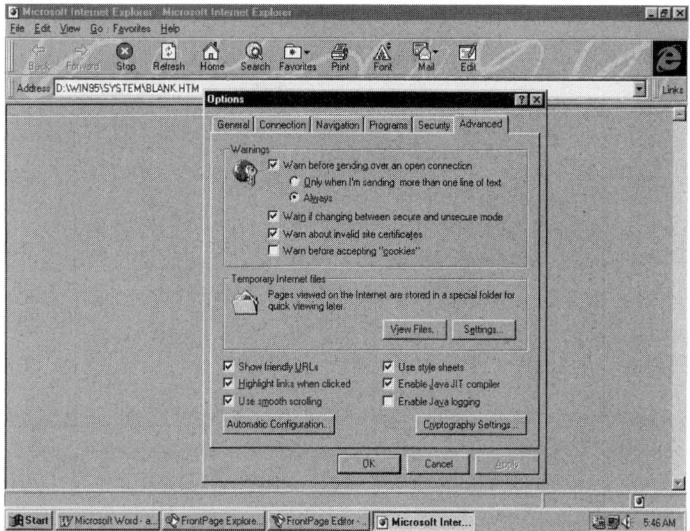

Figure 10.1.
Remember that users can disable the use of style sheets in Internet Explorer. Plan your pages accordingly!

CSS1 Tags Supported by Internet Explorer 3.0

Internet Explorer 3.0 does not support all the properties and values that are defined in the CSS1 style specifications. In some cases, when a property is supported, only some of the values are supported. You will find that Internet Explorer 3.0 does support the most common elements of each property.

You should also take care when you use "shorthand" to define your styles and classes in Internet Explorer 3.0. You have to experiment quite a bit to determine the order in which you place your selectors, properties, and values, because of the manner in which Internet Explorer parses the code. The examples I show in this chapter render correctly in the Windows 95 version of Internet Explorer 3.0, but they have not been tested in other browsers that support CSSs.

Two pages on the Internet provide a thorough overview of all the properties supported by Internet Explorer, as well as some workarounds that you can use to achieve proper rendering. One page covers the Windows version of Internet Explorer, and the other covers the Macintosh version. Each property is examined in great detail.

For a complete treatise on the tags supported by Internet Explorer, refer to the following two pages:

- CSS1 Support in Microsoft Internet Explorer 3.0

  `http://www.shadow.net/~braden/nostyle/ie3.html`

- CSS1 Support in MSIE 3.0 for Macintosh

  `http://www.cwru.edu/lit/homes/eam3/css1/msie-css1.html`

How FrontPage Handles Style Sheet Tags

When you create a style sheet, you embed tags at the beginning of your document, within the HEAD tag. You can't access this area of your code with the HTML Markup Bot, so you must use the View or Edit HTML window, shown in Figure 10.2. You access this window by choosing **V**iew | **H**TML. Before you add your code, I'll explain a bit about the elements that you add in each task.

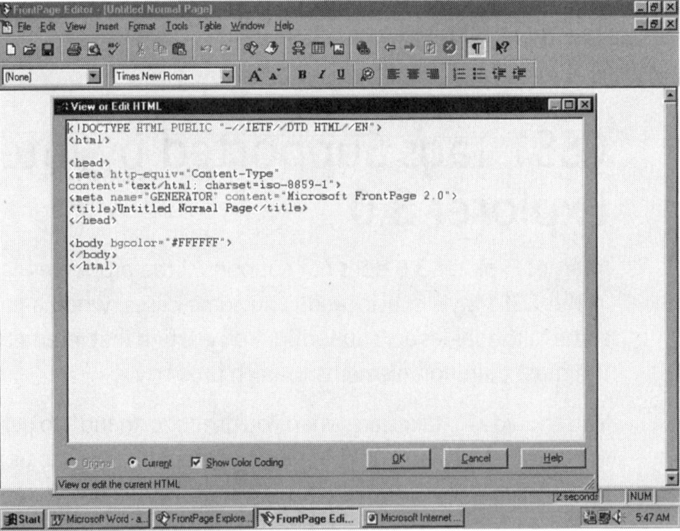

Figure 10.2.
Add style sheet properties and values using the View or Edit HTML window in the FrontPage Editor.

Creating a Simple CSS

To create a simple CSS, add a STYLE block at the top of your Web page. This block should be located between the <HEAD> and </HEAD> tags at the top of your Web page. The STYLE tag has one property named TYPE. You use this property to designate the Internet media type as `text/css`.

In the process of defining your style sheet, you can also assign the font that you want to use for your body text. (You learn more about font tags in the "Defining Fonts" section.) For now, you will assign a sans serif font to your body text.

To assign a particular font to your body text, follow these steps:

1. From the FrontPage Editor, click the New button on the Standard toolbar. A new blank document is displayed in the FrontPage Editor window.
2. From the FrontPage Editor, choose **V**iew | **H**TML. The View or Edit HTML window is displayed. The code at the head of your page should be as follows:

```
<!DOCTYPE HTML PUBLIC "-//IETF//DTD HTML//EN">
<html>
<head>
<meta http-equiv="Content-Type"
content="text/html; charset=iso-8859-1">
<meta name="GENERATOR" content="Microsoft FrontPage 2.0">
<title>Untitled Normal Page</title>
</head>
```

3. Position the insertion point after the line that reads `<title>Untitled Normal Page</title>` (just before the closing `</head>` tag), and press Enter. Type the following code, which defines the page as a style sheet and renders the body text in 12-point Arial, Helvetica, or another sans serif font:

```
<style type="text/css">
<!--
  body {font: 12pt "arial" "helvetica" sans-serif;
    }
-->
</style>
```

4. Choose **O**K to exit the View or Edit HTML window.
5. Enter the following text on your page:

```
The body text will render in Arial, Helvetica, or sans-serif font.
```

6. Choose **F**ile | **S**ave (Ctrl+S) or click the Save button on the Standard toolbar. The Save As dialog box is displayed.
7. In the Page **T**itle field, enter `Cascading Style Sheet Example`. In the File **p**ath within your FrontPage web field, enter `csstasks.htm`.
8. Choose **F**ile | Preview in **B**rowser. Select Microsoft Internet Explorer 3.0 or higher, and click Preview. The text you entered on your page is displayed in Arial font, as shown in Figure 10.3. Continue by defining the styles for your pages as outlined in the following tasks.

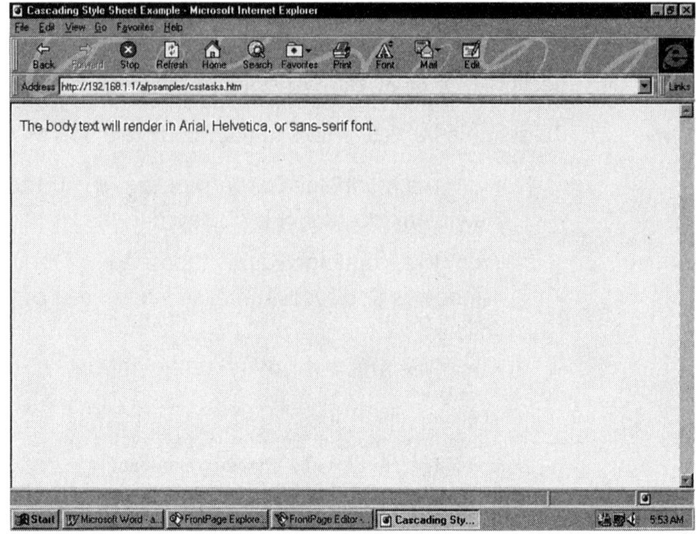

Figure 10.3.
Begin your style sheet by adding STYLE *tags and defining your body text font. When you preview the page, it renders in Arial font.*

Using Style Classes

One solution that simplifies the task of changing pages on a global basis is to develop a style sheet that lists all the styles you use in your entire web or a portion of it. You use *style classes* to define the font faces, sizes, and colors in this global style sheet. You define style classes with code that looks similar to the following:

```
BODY { background: black;
       color: silver}
P {    color: silver;
       font-size: 12px;
       font-family: arial, helvetica, sans-serif }
.quote { color: silver;
         font-size: 10px;
         font-style: italics;
         text-align: center;
         font-family: arial, helvetica, sans-serif }
.quotesource { color: silver;
         font-size: 10px;
         font-style: italics;
         text-align: center;
         text-indent: 30px;
         font-family: arial, helvetica, sans-serif }
A:link { font-size: 12px;
         text-decoration: none;
         color: #AAAAAA;
         font-family: arial, helvetica, sans-serif }
A:visited { font-size: 12px;
            text-decoration: none;
            color: #AAAAAA;
            font-family: arial, helvetica, sans-serif }
```

This code defines styles for body and paragraph text, but it also defines styles for classes named `quote` and `quotesource`. In addition, styles are specified for link and visited link colors. After you define your global styles and classes, you link your individual Web pages to the global style sheet. The styles and classes are applied to the text on your page through extended attributes or HTML Markup Bots. Later, when you want to revise the look of your page, you only need to change the styles in the global style sheet.

Defining Fonts

There are several different font properties that define the fonts you use on your pages. Define your font face with the `font-family` property. Use the `font-size` property to set the size of the text. The `font-style` property defines normal or italic text. Finally, the `font-weight` property defines whether your text is normal or bold.

The `font-family` Property

The CSS1 styles mentioned in this section are those supported only by Internet Explorer 3.0 and higher.

The `font-family` property sets the typeface, or font, used for the text. You can specify a single typeface or alternatives separated by commas. If the browser does not find the first font in the list, it tries the second one; if the browser does not find the second font, it tries the third; and so on.

Some designers make a general rule to end the `font-family` property with a generic family name. This way, if the browser does not find any of the fonts in the style definition, it uses the closest example found on the user's system instead. Internet Explorer 3.0 supports three generic family names: `serif` (which renders proportional fonts similar to Times New Roman or Garamond), `sans-serif` (which renders proportional fonts similar to Arial or Helvetica), and `monospace` (which renders fixed-width fonts similar to Courier or Courier New).

When you specify font names that use whitespace, or multiple words (such as `"Courier New"`, `"Arial Black"`, and `"Times New Roman"`), enclose the font names in quotes. When multiple words appear in a font name, you should also terminate the definition with a semicolon (;). This allows Internet Explorer to parse the styles in the correct manner.

Examples of the `font-family` property are as follow:

```
{font-family: "arial"}
{font-family: "arial" "helvetica" "arial narrow"; }
{font-family: "arial" "helvetica" "arial narrow"; sans-serif }
```

The `font-size` Property

The `font-size` property sets the size of the text in points (pt), inches (in), centimeters (cm), or pixels (px). You can also use a percentage value, based on the default point size of the font.

Examples of the font-size property follow:

```
{font-size: 12pt}
{font-size: 1in}
{font-size: 8cm}
{font-size: 24px}
```

The `font-style` Property

Internet Explorer 3.0 supports two values for the `font-style` property: normal or italics.

The following is an example of the syntax used for the font-style property:

```
{font-style: italic}
{font-style: normal}
```

The `font-weight` Property

The `font-weight` property sets the thickness of the type, varying from `extra-light` to `extra-bold`. The default is `medium`. The values used with this property are dependent on the fonts installed on the user's system. Most fonts support `medium` and `bold` font weights.

The legal values for the `font-weight` property are `extra-light`, `light`, `demi-light`, `medium`, `demi-bold`, `bold`, and `extra-bold`. Of these values, Internet Explorer 3.0 only supports two: the `medium` and `bold` values.

Examples of the syntax are as follows:

```
{font-weight: medium}
{font-weight: bold}
```

Adding Font Families and Sizes to Your Classes

You can combine font tags by shorthand, which simplifies the task of entering your font properties. For example, instead of entering two lines of code to define a font family and font size, you can combine both into a `font` property and enter code similar to the following:

```
{font:24pt "arial" "helvetica"}
```

However, be aware that when you start combining tags, Internet Explorer is very particular about the syntax and the order in which tags are arranged. There seems to be no hard and fast rule, so you might find that you need to experiment to get the pages to render properly.

In the following task, you will add class names to your style sheet and assign fonts to the classes. You might find the code easier to read if you indent these lines by a few spaces.

To add more styles and classes to your page, follow these steps:

1. From the FrontPage Editor, choose **V**iew | **H**TML. The View or Edit HTML window is displayed.
2. Position the insertion point after the code that reads as follows:

   ```
   body {font: 12pt "arial" "helvetica" sans-serif;
       }
   ```

3. Press Enter to begin a new line. Enter the following code to define styles for your Heading 1 and Heading 2 styles:

   ```
   H1 {    font-size: 24pt;
           font-weight: bold;
           font-family: arial, helvetica, sans-serif }
   H2 {    font-size: 16pt;
           font-style: italic;
           font-weight: bold;
           font-family: arial, helvetica, sans-serif }
   ```

4. Choose **O**K to exit the View or Edit HTML window.
5. Position the insertion point at the beginning of your page and press Enter. Return to the first line and choose Heading 1 from the Change Style drop-down menu in the Format toolbar. Enter the following text on your page:

   ```
   Heading 1
   ```

6. Press Enter, and choose Heading 2 from the Change Style drop-down menu in the Format toolbar. Enter the following text on your page:

   ```
   Heading 2
   ```

7. Choose **F**ile | **S**ave (Ctrl+S) or click the Save button on the Standard toolbar. The file is updated to your web.
8. Choose **F**ile | Preview in **B**rowser. Select Microsoft Internet Explorer 3.0 or higher, and click **P**review. Refresh the browser if necessary. Internet Explorer applies the style specifications to the text you formatted as Heading 1 and Heading 2 on your page, as shown in Figure 10.4. You don't need to add more code to assign styles that are identified by "traditional" HTML tags.

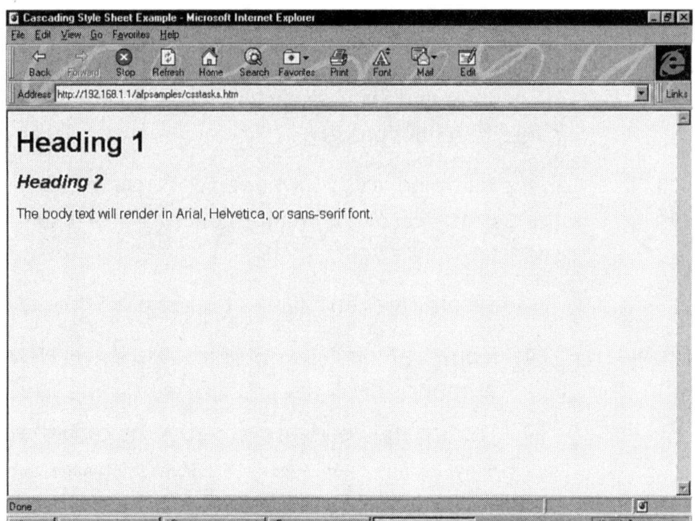

Figure 10.4.
Two heading styles are defined on your page with CSS tags.

To create different classes for your headings, continue with the following steps:

9. From the FrontPage Editor, choose **V**iew | **H**TML. The View or Edit HTML window is displayed.
10. Position the insertion point after the code that reads as follows:

```
H2 {   font-size: 16pt;
       font-style: italic;
       font-weight: bold;
       font-family: arial, helvetica, sans-serif }
```

11. Press Enter to begin a new line. Enter the following code to define styles that display Heading 2 in blue and red:

```
H2.blue {   color: blue;
            font-size: 16pt;
            font-style: italic;
            font-weight: bold;
            font-family: arial, helvetica, sans-serif }
H2.red  {   color: red;
            font-size: 16pt;
            font-style: italic;
            font-weight: bold;
            font-family: arial, helvetica, sans-serif }
```

12. Choose **O**K to exit the View or Edit HTML window.
13. Select the text on your page that reads `Heading 2` and copy it to your clipboard using Ctrl+C. Position the insertion point at the beginning of the first Heading 2, and use Ctrl+V to paste two more copies, pressing the Enter key after each to place them on separate lines.
14. Right-click anywhere within the second Heading 2 line. Choose Paragraph Properties from the pop-up menu. The Paragraph Properties dialog box is displayed.

15. Click the **E**xtended button. The Extended Attributes dialog box is displayed.
16. Click **A**dd. The Name/Value Pair dialog box shown in Figure 10.5 is displayed. Enter the following:

    Name: `class`
    Value: `blue`

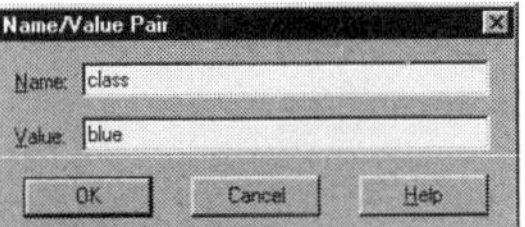

Figure 10.5.
Apply the `CLASS` *property to the second Heading 2 in the* `Name/Value Pair` *dialog box.*

17. Choose OK to exit the Name/Value Pair, Extended Attributes, and Paragraph Properties dialog boxes.
18. In a similar manner, repeat steps 13–17 to assign the following for the third Heading 2:

    Name: `class`
    Value: `red`

19. Choose **F**ile | **S**ave (Ctrl+S) or click the Save button on the Standard toolbar. The file is updated to your web.
20. Choose **F**ile | Preview in **B**rowser. Refresh your browser if necessary. The second heading renders in blue, and the third in red.

As you learned in the "Adding Font Families and Sizes to Your Classes" task, you can use extended attributes to apply styles, classes, and IDs to elements on your page. Though some of the tags listed in Table 10.2 are not suited for style sheets, it is a complete list of tags that use extended attributes. You can apply the `ID`, `STYLE`, and `CLASS` attributes and values to the tags listed in Table 10.2 through the Extended Attributes dialog box.

Table 10.2. HTML tags that support extended attributes.

TAG	*Associated Dialog Box*
`A`	Create Hyperlink or Edit Hyperlink
`ADDRESS`	Paragraph Properties (for Address paragraph)
`APPLET`	Java Applet Properties
`BODY`	Page Properties, General Tab
`BR`	Line Break Properties

continues

Table 10.2. continued

TAG	*Associated Dialog Box*
CAPTION	Caption Properties
DIR	List Properties (for Directory List)
DL	List Properties (for Definition List)
EMBED	Plug-In Properties
FORM	Form Properties
H1	Paragraph Properties (for Heading 1)
H2	Paragraph Properties (for Heading 2)
H3	Paragraph Properties (for Heading 3)
H4	Paragraph Properties (for Heading 4)
H5	Paragraph Properties (for Heading 5)
H6	Paragraph Properties (for Heading 6)
HR	Horizontal Line Properties
IMG	Image Properties
INPUT	Text Box Properties
	Check Box Properties
	Radio Button Properties
	Push Button Properties
	Image Form Field Properties
LI	List Item Properties
MARQUEE	Marquee Properties
MENU	List Properties (for Menu List)
OBJECT	ActiveX Control Properties
OL	List Properties (for Numbered List)
P	Paragraph Properties (for Normal Paragraph)
PRE	Paragraph Properties (for Formatted Paragraph)
SELECT	Drop-Down Menu Properties
TABLE	Table Properties
TEXTAREA	Scrolling Text Box Properties
TD	Cell Properties
UL	List Properties (for Bulleted List)

The `line-height` Property

The `line-height` property sets the leading, or distance between the baselines of the text, in points (pt), inches (in), centimeters (cm), pixels (px), or percentage (%). Internet Explorer adds space before, rather than after, the line. A common use for this property is to create more distance between headers and normal text in your pages. You often see the line-height sized two points (or more) larger than the text size.

You can also use the `line-height` property creatively. For example, if you have a background image that looks like lined notebook paper, you can space your text so that it appears as though it is written on the lines of the paper. (However, you should not use this property on a line that contains different point sizes on the same line.)

Examples of the `line-height` property follow:

```
{line-height: 16pt}
{line-height: .8in}
{line-height: 6cm}
{line-height: 20px}
{line-height: 125%}
```

The `text-align` Property

The `text-align` property determines how the text is justified on the page. Acceptable values are `left`, `center`, and `right`. The `justify` value is not supported by Internet Explorer.

Examples:

```
{text-align: left}
{text-align: center}
{text-align: right}
```

The `text-indent` Property

The `text-indent` property sets the distance from the left margin of the page in points (pt), inches (in), centimeters (cm) or pixels (px).

Some examples follow:

```
{text-indent: 16pt}
{text-indent: .8in}
{text-indent: 6cm}
{text-indent: 20px}
```

The `text-decoration` Property

The `text-decoration` property assigns special formatting or accents to the text. The values supported by Internet Explorer are `none`, `underline`, or `line-through`.

Some examples follow:

```
{text-decoration: none}
{text-decoration: underline}
{text-decoration: line-through}
```

Aligning and Decorating Text

In the following example, you will align all the headings to the center of the page and create link classes that are not underlined. To add these features to your style sheet, follow these steps:

1. From the FrontPage Editor, choose **V**iew | **H**TML. The View or Edit HTML window is displayed.
2. Add the `text-align` property to your headings, so that your code reads as follows:

```
H1 {    font-size: 24pt;
        font-weight: bold;
        text-align: center;
        font-family: arial, helvetica, sans-serif }
H2 {    font-size: 16pt;
        font-style: italic;
        font-weight: bold;
        text-align: center;
        font-family: arial, helvetica, sans-serif }
H2.blue {    color: blue;
             font-size: 16pt;
             font-style: italic;
             font-weight: bold;
             text-align: center;
             font-family: arial, helvetica, sans-serif }
H2.red  {    color: red;
             font-size: 16pt;
             font-style: italic;
             font-weight: bold;
             text-align: center;
             font-family: arial, helvetica, sans-serif }
```

3. Position the insertion point at the end of the last line of code in the previous step, and enter the following link classes (the `A:link` class defines your link color and style, and the `A:visited` class defines your visited link color and style):

```
A:link { color: blue;
         font-size: 12pt;
         text-decoration: none;
         font-family: arial, helvetica, sans-serif }
A:visited { color: purple;
            font-size: 12pt;
            text-decoration: none;
            font-family: arial, helvetica, sans-serif }
```

4. Choose **O**K to exit the View or Edit HTML window.

5. Position the insertion point on the line beneath the normal text on the page. Enter `Link Color`.
6. Choose the Create or Edit Hyperlink button on the Standard toolbar. The Create Hyperlink dialog box is displayed.
7. Click the World Wide Web tab. Enter the following to create a "dummy" link to a fictitious page on the World Wide Web:

   Hyperlink Type: `http:`
   URL: `http://www.server.com/fake.htm`

8. Choose OK to return to the FrontPage Editor.
9. Choose **F**ile | **S**ave (Ctrl+S) or click the Save button on the Standard toolbar. The file is updated to your web.
10. Choose **F**ile | Preview in **B**rowser. Refresh the browser if necessary. The headings should be displayed in the center of the page, and the link should not be underlined, as shown in Figure 10.6.

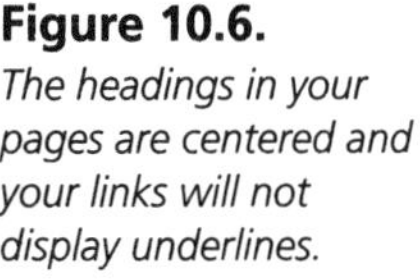

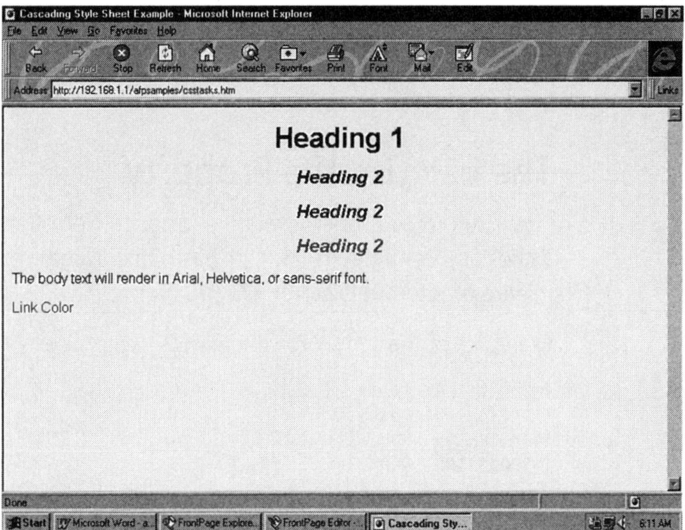

Figure 10.6.
The headings in your pages are centered and your links will not display underlines.

Defining Your Page Margins

The final release of Microsoft Internet Explorer 3.0 provides support for some additional tags that were not supported in the beta release, including the `margin-top` property. In addition, the final release added support for specifying negative values for left margin, right margin, top margin, and text indent, which allows you to outdent text as well as indent.

The `margin-left` Property

The `margin-left` property sets the distance from the left margin of the page in points (pt), inches (in), centimeters (cm), or pixels (px). Negative values outdent text in the final release of Internet Explorer 3.0 and higher.

Examples of the syntax for the `margin-left` property follow:

```
{margin-left: 16pt}
{margin-left: .8in}
{margin-left: 6cm}
{margin-left: 20px}
```

The `margin-right` Property

The `margin-right` property sets the distance from the right margin of the page in points (pt), inches (in), centimeters (cm), or pixels (px). Negative values outdent text in the final release of Internet Explorer 3.0 and higher.

Examples of the syntax for the `margin-right` property follow:

```
{margin-right: 16pt}
{margin-right: .8in}
{margin-right: 6cm}
{margin-right: 20px}
```

The `margin-top` Property

The `margin-top` property sets the distance from the top of the page in points (pt), inches (in), centimeters (cm), or pixels (px). Negative values outdent text in the final release of Internet Explorer 3.0 and higher.

Examples of the syntax for the `margin-top` property follow:

```
{margin-top: 16pt}
{margin-top: .8in}
{margin-top: 6cm}
{margin-top: 20px}
```

Applying Page Margins

1. From the FrontPage Editor, choose View | HTML. The View or Edit HTML window is displayed.
2. Position the insertion point after the code that reads as follows, and press Enter:

   ```
   body {font: 12pt "arial" "helvetica" sans-serif;
   ```

3. Enter the following code:

   ```
   margin-left: 50px;
   margin-right: 50px;
   margin-top: 25px;
   ```

4. Choose **O**K to exit the View or Edit HTML window.
5. Choose **F**ile | **S**ave (Ctrl+S) or click the Save button on the Standard toolbar. The file is updated to your web.
6. Choose **F**ile | Preview in **B**rowser. Refresh your browser if necessary. The page margins are indented 50 pixels from the right and left margins, and the top margin is set to 25 pixels. Your page should look like Figure 10.7. When you compare this to Figure 10.6, notice the extra space between the top margin and the first heading. Likewise, there is more space between the left margin of the page and the text on the page.

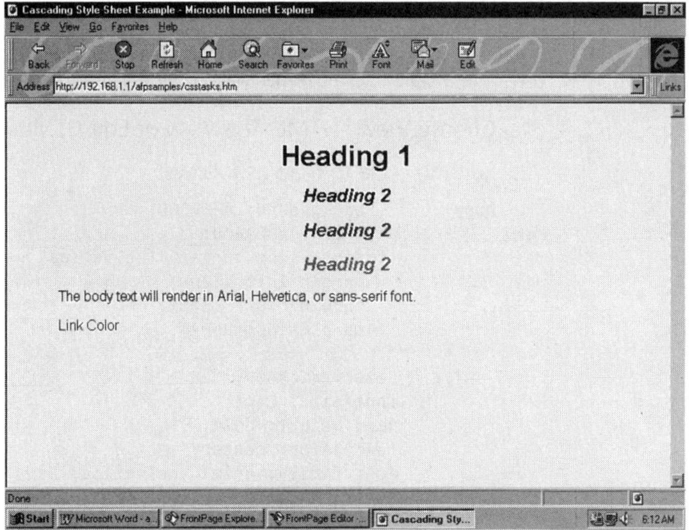

Figure 10.7.
The left and right margins are set to 50 pixels, and the top margin is set to 25 pixels.

Choosing Background and Text Colors

You can use background colors and images on any element in Internet Explorer 3.0. You can repeat, scroll, and position background images precisely.

The `background` Property

Using the `background` property, you can set the URL of a background image or background color. The acceptable color names are `black`, `silver`, `gray`, `white`, `maroon`, `red`, `purple`, `fuschia`, `green`, `lime`, `olive`, `yellow`, `navy`, `blue`, `teal`, and `aqua`. You can also specify colors in the hexadecimal equivalent of a Red/Green/Blue (RGB) color formula.

The following examples show the use of the background property:

```
{background: "http://servername/background.gif"}
{background: "background.gif"}
{background: "../background.gif"}
```

```
{background: red}
{background: white}
{background: #00CC33}
```

The `color` Property

The `color` property sets the color of text either by one of 16 color names or by an RGB triplet. The color names are the same as those listed in "The `background` Property" section.

Examples of the proper syntax for the color property follow:

```
{color: blue}
{color: black}
{color: #003333}
```

To define a color scheme for your CSS, follow these steps:

1. Choose **V**iew | **H**TML. The View or Edit HTML window is displayed.
2. Edit the code to read as follows:

```
body {      background: #FFFFCC;
            color: #CCAA00;
            font: 12pt "arial" "helvetica" sans-serif;
            margin-left: 50px;
            margin-right: 50px;
            margin-top: 25px;
    }
  H1 {   color: #CCAA00;
         font-size: 24pt;
         font-weight: bold;
         text-align: center;
         font-family: arial, helvetica, sans-serif }
  H2 {   color: #CCAA00;
         font-size: 16pt;
         font-style: italic;
         font-weight: bold;
         text-align: center;
         font-family: arial, helvetica, sans-serif }
  H2.blue { color: teal;
            font-size: 16pt;
            font-style: italic;
            font-weight: bold;
            text-align: center;
            font-family: arial, helvetica, sans-serif }
  H2.red { color: maroon;
            font-size: 16pt;
            font-style: italic;
            font-weight: bold;
            text-align: center;
            font-family: arial, helvetica, sans-serif }
  A:link { color: #336666;
           font-size: 12pt;
           text-decoration: none;
           font-family: arial, helvetica, sans-serif }
  A:visited { color: #990099;
              font-size: 12pt;
              text-decoration: none;
              font-family: arial, helvetica, sans-serif }
```

3. Choose **O**K to exit the View or Edit HTML window.
4. Choose **F**ile | **S**ave (Ctrl+S) or click the Save button on the Standard toolbar. The file is updated to your web.
5. Choose **F**ile | Preview in **B**rowser. Refresh the browser if necessary. The background properties of your page should change. The background color is light yellow, normal text and headings are gold, and alternative heading colors and link colors are different. Figure 10.8 shows the layout of the page.

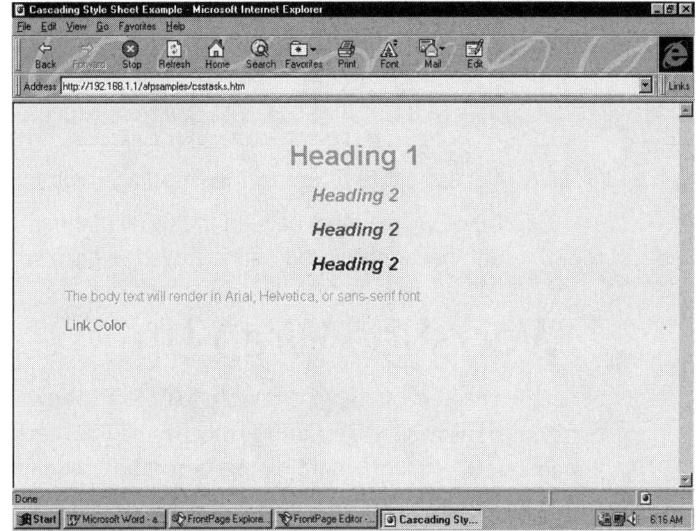

Figure 10.8.
The background is light yellow, the normal text is gold, and the headings and links display in a new color.

TASK

Using a Single Style Sheet for Multiple Pages

At this point, you have a self-contained style sheet. You can save this page with a `.css` extension and link other pages to it so that they all use the same styles and classes. To use a single style sheet for several Web pages, you must add a link to the target page (the page to which you are assigning the style sheet).

The steps to link another page to your style sheet follow:

1. With your current style sheet open, choose **F**ile | **S**ave As (Ctrl+A). The Save As dialog box is displayed.
2. Leave the Page **T**itle field as it is. In the File **p**ath within your FrontPage Web field, enter `csstasks.css`. Choose OK to save the page to your Web. When FrontPage informs you that it is not a valid URL, choose **Y**es to save the page.

3. Choose the New button on the Standard toolbar. A new page is displayed in the FrontPage Editor.
4. From the FrontPage Editor, choose **V**iew | **H**TML. Locate the header for the Web page, which should look like the following:

```
<head>
<meta http-equiv="Content-Type"
content="text/html; charset=iso-8859-1">
<meta name="GENERATOR" content="Microsoft FrontPage 2.0">
<title>Untitled Normal Page</title>
</head>
```

5. Position the insertion point at the end of the title line and press Enter. The URL that you enter with the HREF tag must be relative to the current page. In the following example I assume that the CSS and the current page will be saved in the same directory in the web. Therefore, add the following code:

```
<LINK REL=STYLESHEET HREF="csstasks.css" TYPE="text/css">
```

6. Choose OK to return to the FrontPage Editor.
7. Develop your Web page in the usual manner, using content that is appropriate for the styles you define. Save the page with an `.htm` or `.html` extension.

Workshop Wrap-Up

In this chapter you were introduced to CSSs and how to implement them in FrontPage 97. CSSs allow you to customize much more than background and text colors; you can define custom fonts, margins, text decoration, indentation, and more. With CSSs your pages can be formatted more like those you design in a word processor. In Chapter 11, "Real-Life Examples: The Internet Explorer Advantage," you'll learn how to use CSSs and FrontPage style sheets together.

Next Steps

In Chapter 11, you'll learn how to combine tables, floating frames and cascading style sheets together to create pages that have a consistent appearance. You can learn more about Internet Explorer 3.0 features in the following chapters:

- Refer to Chapter 8, "Creating Advanced Tables," to learn how to apply advanced properties to tables.
- Refer to Chapter 9, "Using Floating Frames," to learn one way you can place frames anywhere on your page.
- Refer to Appendix A, "Online Resources," for additional online references about CSSs.

Q&A

Q: You mentioned that CSSs allow you to create page layouts that look similar to those in word processing programs. Does that mean that I can create classes for items like footnotes, quotations, references, and items of that nature?

A: Yes. A class does not always have to be a subclass of an "official" HTML tag. You can create classes named `.footnotes`, `.quotations`, `.references`, and so on and apply the classes to pertinent text on your page. To apply the text to a single paragraph, use the Extended button in the Paragraph Properties dialog box. If you want to apply a style to a `DIV` tag, use the HTML Markup Bot to assign the style or class.

Q: Are there any additional references for CSSs that provide examples?

A: There are some very creative examples of style sheets on Microsoft's Web site. In these examples, you see how cascading style sheet tags and properties are used to create pages with a more artistic flair. You can find them at the following URL:

`http://www.windows.com/workshop/author/howto/css.htm`

ELEVEN

The Internet Explorer Advantage

In this chapter, you

- Learn how to combine some of the Internet Explorer features discussed in this section and apply them to a Web site
- Apply CSSs to pages created by the FrontPage Corporate Presence Web Wizard
- Add a floating frame that displays the main pages in a Web site

Tasks in this chapter:

- Creating the Style Sheet
- Attaching the Style Sheet to Your Web Pages
- Adding a Floating Frame
- Linking Your Pages to the Floating Frame

As you have learned so far in the chapters in Part III, "Designing for Internet Explorer," Internet Explorer allows you to add some interesting features to your pages. You can combine floating frames, advanced tables, and cascading style sheets (CSSs) to help your pages look unique while maintaining consistency throughout your site.

The Web site in this chapter begins with the Corporate Presence Web Wizard, one of the wizards available in the FrontPage Explorer. As you can see, the pages achieve quite a different appearance when combined with some of Internet Explorer's features.

Using Internet Explorer Features Together

The Web pages in this chapter began in the Corporate Presence Web Wizard, which you can access by choosing **F**ile | **N**ew | FrontPage **W**eb (Ctrl+N) from FrontPage Explorer. Select the Corporate Presence Wizard from the New FrontPage Web dialog box shown in Figure 11.1. If you choose all options available through the wizard, the FrontPage Explorer creates 15 different pages, including a home page, a what's new page, press releases, a site search page, and products and services pages. With some modification, you can make these pages a little more interesting. The examples in this chapter are fairly simplistic, but they give you an idea of how to use Internet Explorer features together.

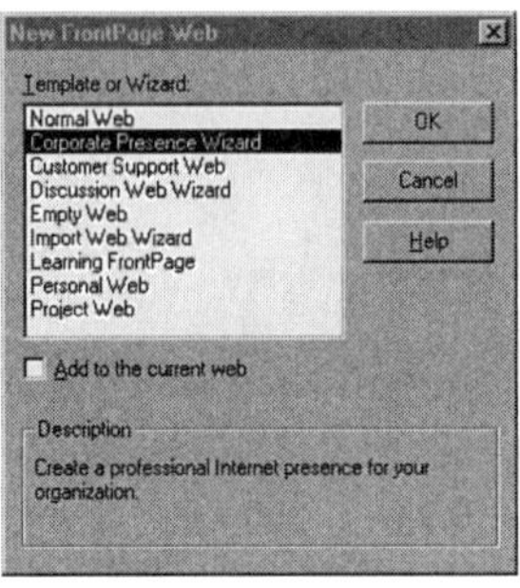

Figure 11.1.
The examples in this chapter are pages that were generated using the Corporate Presence Web Wizard, available from the New FrontPage Web dialog box in the FrontPage Explorer.

Creating the Style Sheet

When you generate pages with the Corporate Presence Web Wizard, the FrontPage Explorer generates a page titled "Web Colors," which applies the same background, text, and link colors to all of the pages in your Web. If you like, you can use this style sheet in combination with your CSS to generate the colors for your Web. This makes your background, text, and link colors consistent from page to page, regardless of whether a browser supports CSSs. The CSS in the following task adds more colors for the headings in the pages and specifies the font styles used on the pages.

The Corporate Presence Web Wizard generates pages that contain three different heading sizes, normal paragraphs, bulleted lists, and definition lists. I felt it would be easiest to define my CSS styles using the standard HTML tag definitions used by the pages (`P`, `DD`, `DT`, `UL`, and so on). By doing so, I eliminated the need to apply individual styles to the pages that already existed. It also allowed me to preview my style definitions on multiple pages as I developed the CSS.

The first thing that you should do is create your CSS and attach it to the pages in your Web. To begin, follow these steps:

1. From the FrontPage Editor, click the New button on the Standard toolbar. A new blank document is displayed in the FrontPage Editor window.
2. From the FrontPage Editor, choose **V**iew | **H**TML. The View or Edit HTML window is displayed. The code at the head of your page is displayed as follows:

```
<!DOCTYPE HTML PUBLIC "-//IETF//DTD HTML//EN">
<html>
<head>
<meta http-equiv="Content-Type"
content="text/html; charset=iso-8859-1">
```

```
<meta name="GENERATOR" content="Microsoft FrontPage 2.0">
<title>Untitled Normal Page</title>
</head>
```

3. Position the insertion point at the end of the line that reads `<title>Untitled Normal Page</title>` (just before the closing `</head>` tag), and press Enter. Type the following code, shown in Figure 11.2, which defines the page as a style sheet:

```
<style type="text/css">
<!--
```

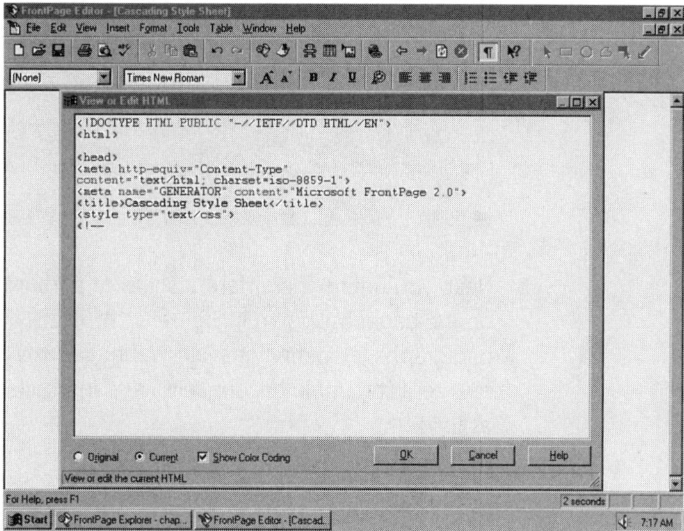

Figure 11.2.
The first line after the page title defines the page as a CSS.

4. Press Enter, and define three heading styles. Headings 1 and 2 are 24 points and 16 points, respectively, and are primarily used as headings and subheadings on the pages. These two headings will be teal and rendered in bold Impact, Arial, Helvetica, or another sans-serif font. Heading 5 is 8 points, rendered in bold Verdana, Arial, Helvetica, or other sans-serif font, and is primarily used in the page footers. It will also be colored teal. Enter code as follows and as shown in Figure 11.3:

```
H1 { color: teal;
     font-size: 24pt;
     font-weight: bold;
     font-family: impact, arial, helvetica, sans-serif }
H2 { color: teal;
     font-size: 16pt;
     font-weight: bold;
     font-family: impact, arial, helvetica, sans-serif }
H5 { color: teal;
     font-size: 8pt;
     font-weight: bold;
     font-family: verdana, arial, helvetica, sans-serif }
```

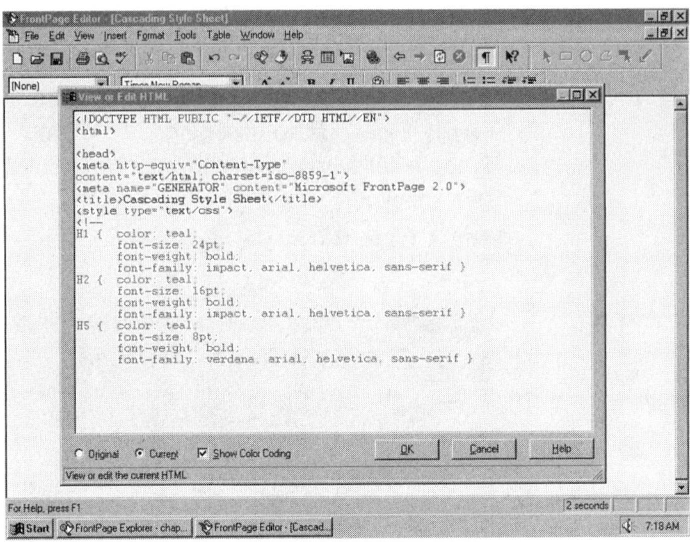

Figure 11.3.
Three different heading styles are used within the pages. The two larger headings are rendered in bold Impact font, and the smaller heading, used in footers, is rendered in bold Verdana.

5. Next, you define the different styles of paragraphs, lists, and table text used on the page, as shown in Figure 11.4. The styles are in this order: normal paragraphs (P), definitions (DD), defined terms (DT), table data cells (TD), table row cells (TR), table header cells (TH), and bulleted lists (UL). The code reads as follows:

```
P {  font-size: 10pt;
     font-family: verdana, arial, helvetica, sans-serif;
DD   font-size: 10pt;
     font-style: italic;
     font-family: verdana, arial, helvetica, sans-serif }
DT   font-size: 10pt;
     font-weight: bold;
     font-family: verdana, arial, helvetica, sans-serif }
TD   font-size: 10pt;
     font-family: verdana, arial, helvetica, sans-serif }
TR   font-size: 10pt;
     font-family: verdana, arial, helvetica, sans-serif }
TH { color: teal;
     font-size: 10pt;
     font-weight: bold;
     font-family: verdana, arial, helvetica, sans-serif }
UL { font-size: 10pt;
     font-family: verdana, arial, helvetica, sans-serif }
```

6. Complete the style definitions with the following two lines of code:

```
-->
</style>
```

7. Choose OK to return to the FrontPage Editor.
8. Choose **F**ile | **S**ave (Ctrl+S) or click the Save button on the Standard toolbar. The Save As dialog box shown in Figure 11.5 is displayed.

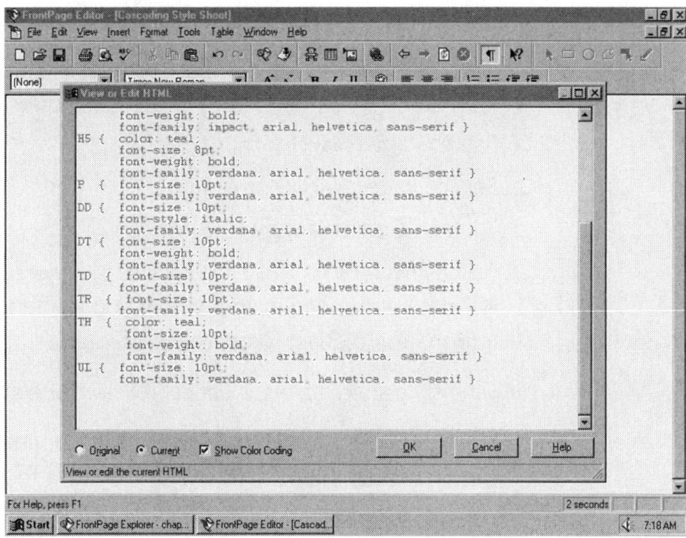

Figure 11.4.
Paragraph and list styles are also defined in the style sheet.

9. In the Page **T**itle field, enter `Cascading Style Sheet`. In the File **p**ath within your FrontPage web field, enter `_private/sitecss.css`. This saves the style sheet to the `_private` directory in your web.

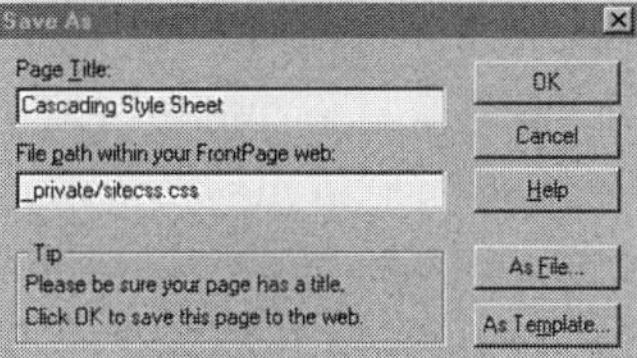

Figure 11.5.
Save the CSS to the `_private` directory in your web using a `.css` extension.

Attaching the Style Sheet to Your Web Pages

The next step is to attach the CSS to the Web pages to which you want to apply the styles. The Corporate Presence Wizard generates several pages. The Included Logo Page (`logo.htm`) and Included Navigation Links page (`navbar.htm`) contain graphics only—no text. The CSSs do not apply for these pages. You do not need to apply the CSS to the Web Colors page (`style.htm`), either.

Apply the style sheet to each of the following pages in the Corporate Presence Web:

- ❑ Home Page (`default.htm`, `index.htm`, `index.html`, or your home page name).
- ❑ Feedback Page (`feedback.htm`).

- ❑ News Page (`news.htm`).
- ❑ Press Release Pages (`pr01.htm`, `pr02.htm`, `pr03.htm`, and so on).
- ❑ Product Pages (`prod01.htm`, `prod02.htm`, and so on).
- ❑ Search Page (`search.htm`).
- ❑ Service Pages (`serv01.htm`, `serv02.htm`, and so on).
- ❑ Table of Contents Page (`toc.htm`).
- ❑ Results from Form 1 of Page `prod01.htm` (`_private/inforeq.htm`). This page will not be included in your web if you elected to save the results of your information request forms to text format.

To link the style sheet to these pages, follow these steps:

1. From the FrontPage Editor, choose **F**ile | **O**pen (Ctrl+O) or click the Open button. Select the page to which you want to attach the CSS.
2. Choose **V**iew | **H**TML. Locate the header for the Web page, which reads much like the following:

```
<head>
<meta http-equiv="Content-Type"
content="text/html; charset=iso-8859-1">
<meta name="GENERATOR" content="Microsoft FrontPage 2.0">
<title>title name</title>
</head>
```

3. Position the insertion point at the end of the title line and press Enter. Add the following code, as shown in Figure 11.6. The URL that you enter with the `HREF` tag must be relative to the current page. For those pages that are in the `_private` directory (the same directory as the CSS), do not include the folder name in the code, as shown in the following example. All the Web pages that are saved in the Web's main directory should include the directory name, like this:

```
<LINK REL=STYLESHEET HREF="_private/sitecss.css" TYPE="text/css">
```

4. Choose OK to return to the FrontPage Editor.
5. Choose **F**ile | **S**ave (Ctrl+S), or click the Save button to update the Web page in your current Web. The style sheet is now attached to the file.

After you assign the style sheets to your Web pages, you should be able to preview and test your style sheets in Internet Explorer. If the fonts reside on your computer (they should all be there if you have Internet Explorer 3.0 or higher installed), you should see the text on your pages rendered in the fonts you specified in your CSS. To preview your pages, choose **F**ile | Preview in **B**rowser, and select Internet Explorer 3.0 or higher. The page is displayed in your browser, as shown in Figure 11.7.

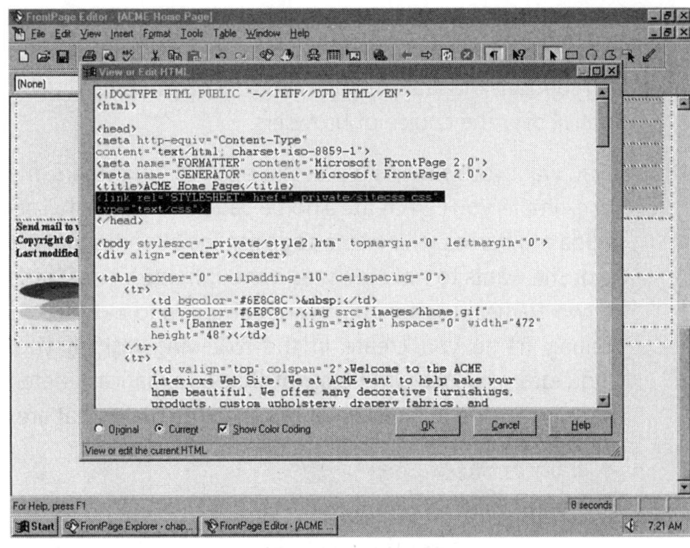

Figure 11.6.
Edit the HTML code of each Web page to which you want to attach the style sheet.

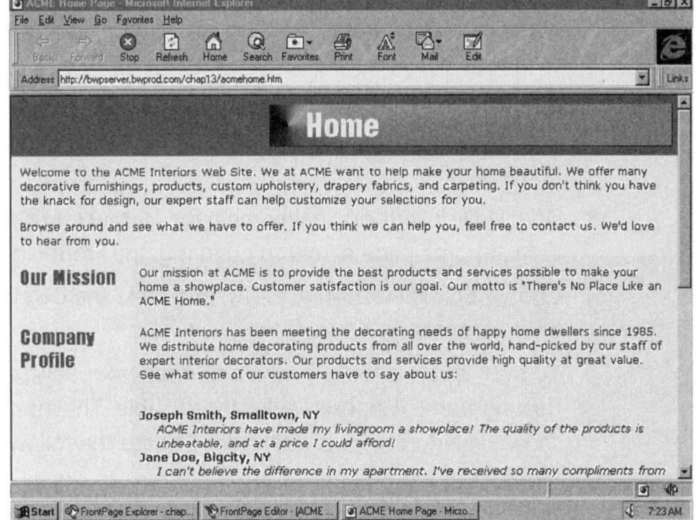

Figure 11.7.
When you preview your pages in Internet Explorer, you will see the fonts you specified in your CSS, if they exist on your computer.

Adding a Floating Frame

In the following task, you modify the home page in the Web to include a floating frame that displays the main pages in the Web. Note, however, that this creates a home page that can be viewed only in browsers that support floating frames (such as Internet Explorer 3.0 or higher). Browsers that do not support floating frames will see a blank screen where the floating frame is supposed to be. Therefore, you should probably use this approach only when you are certain that all who visit your site will use a browser that supports this feature, such as if your page is on an intranet, where you might have control over the choice of browsers.

If you want your site to be accessible by more browsers, there are some alternatives. For example, you can create a home page that loads a full page rather than a frameset or floating frames. This home page can include links that allow the user to select how he or she wants to view the site: without frames, in a standard frameset that consists of two frames (`top` for the navigation bar and `main` for the main pages), or in the floating frame you create in the following task. If you're clever with scripting languages, you can write a script that automatically detects the capabilities of the user's browser and directs him or her to the pages that are most appropriate for the browser in use.

To create a floating frame in your home page, follow these steps:

1. From the FrontPage Explorer, highlight the home page in your Web (`default.htm`, `index.htm`, or the default name you have chosen for your home pages), and use Ctrl+C to copy it into your clipboard. Then, use Ctrl+V to paste a copy into the same directory.
2. Highlight the copy and rename it to `acmehome.htm`. You now have the original home page renamed to a different file, and you can edit the original home page.
3. Double-click your original home page (`default.htm`, `index.htm`, or your default home page name) to open it in the FrontPage Editor.
4. Choose **E**dit | Select A**l**l (Ctrl+A), and press the Delete key to remove all the page contents.
5. You will create a table in which to insert your navigation bar and your floating frame. Choose T**a**ble | **I**nsert Table. The Insert Table dialog box shown in Figure 11.8 is displayed. Choose the following settings for your table:

Rows:	`2`
Columns:	`1`
Alignment:	`Center`
Border Size:	`0`
Cell Pa**d**ding:	`0`
Cell **S**pacing:	`0`
Specify **W**idth:	`Deselected`

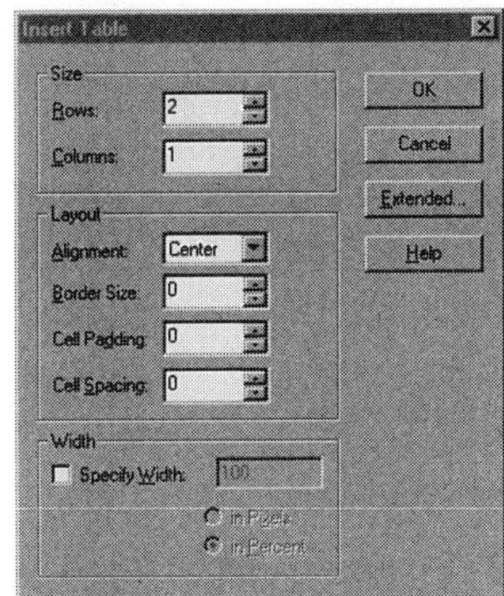

Figure 11.8.
Insert a table with two rows and one column in which you will place your navigation bar and floating frame.

6. Position the insertion point in the upper cell in the table, and choose **I**nsert | **W**ebBot Component. The Insert WebBot Component dialog box is displayed.
7. From the **S**elect a component list, double-click Include. The WebBot Include Component Properties dialog box shown in Figure 11.9 is displayed.
8. In the Page URL to include field, enter `_private/logo.htm`, or use the **B**rowse button to locate the file in the `_private` directory of your current web. (Note: I modified my `_private/logo.htm` page to include both the company logo graphic and the navigation buttons found in the `_private/navbar.htm` page. If you want to keep these files separate, include the `navbar.htm` page here instead.)
9. Choose OK to exit the WebBot Include Component Properties dialog box. You return to the FrontPage Editor, and the included page is displayed in your home page.
10. Click inside the bottom cell in the table, and choose **I**nsert | **H**TML Markup. The HTML Markup dialog box shown in Figure 11.10 is displayed.
11. The following code creates a floating frame that is designed for an 800×600 browser window. It also assigns a frame name of `main` to the floating frame. Enter the following code in the HTML Markup dialog box:

```
<iframe width=750 height=350 src="acmehome.htm" name=main>
<frame width=750 height=350 src="acmehome.htm" name=main>
</iframe>
```

12. Choose **O**K to return to the FrontPage Editor. The HTML Markup Bot is displayed on your page. Your floating frame is created.

If you want to design your floating frame for 640×480 resolution, reduce the width to 600 and the height to 230.

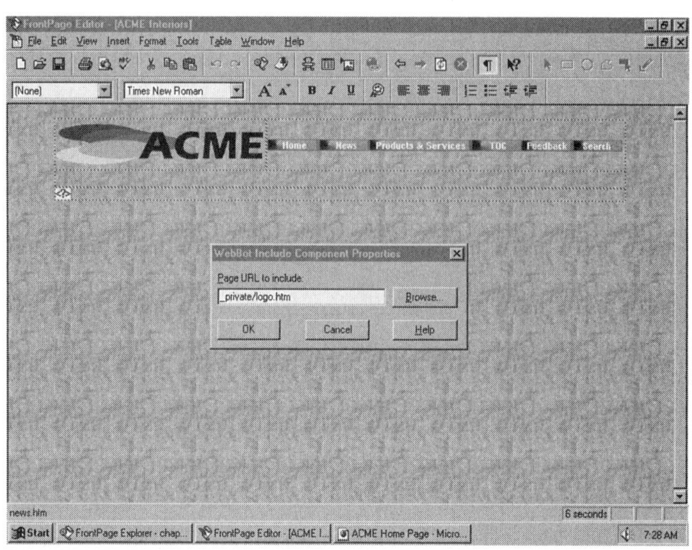

Figure 11.9.
The Include Bot places a combined logo and navigation bar into the top cell in the table.

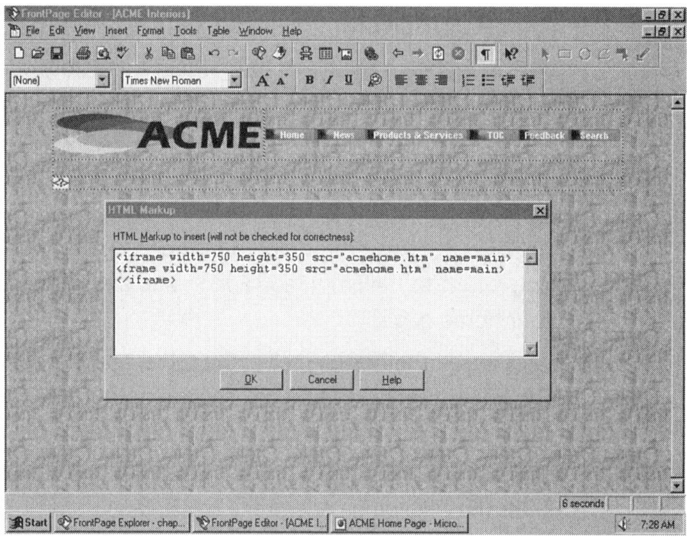

Figure 11.10.
Define your floating frame in the HTML Markup dialog box.

Linking Your Pages to the Floating Frame

You link your pages to your floating frame using the same procedures as you would to link to a standard frame set. As I mentioned in the "Adding a Floating Frame" section, I combined the logo image and the navigation bar into the `logo.htm` page. If you do not want to do this, edit the links on your `navbar.htm` page instead. Both are included in the Web's `_private` directory.

To modify the `logo.htm` page so that it includes a navigation bar, follow these steps:

1. From the FrontPage Editor, click the Open button on the Standard toolbar. Open `_private/logo.htm`.
2. Choose T**a**ble | **I**nsert Table. The Insert Table dialog box is displayed. Choose the following settings for your table:

Rows:	`1`
Columns:	`2`
Alignment:	`Center`
Border Size:	`0`
Cell Pa**d**ding:	`0`
Cell **S**pacing:	`0`
Specify **W**idth:	`100 in Percent`

3. Choose OK. The table is displayed on your page.
4. Cut the existing logo graphic from the page using Ctrl+C, and paste it into the left cell in the table using Ctrl+V. You will no doubt want to modify this graphic at a later time.
5. Position the insertion point in the right cell in the table. Choose **I**nsert | **W**ebBot Component. The Insert WebBot Component dialog box is displayed.
6. Double-click Include to open the WebBot Include Component Properties dialog box. In the Page URL to include field, enter `_private/navbar.htm`, or use the **B**rowse button to locate the file. Choose OK to return to the FrontPage Editor. The navigation bar is displayed in the right cell in the table, as shown in Figure 11.11.
7. Right-click on the Include bot, and choose Open `//pathname/_private/navbar.htm`, where *`pathname`* is the server and Web in which your navigation bar is displayed. The navigation bar opens in the FrontPage Editor.
8. Click on the Home graphic (the first one in the navigation bar); then click on the Create or Edit Hyperlink button in the Standard toolbar. The Edit Hyperlink dialog box is displayed.

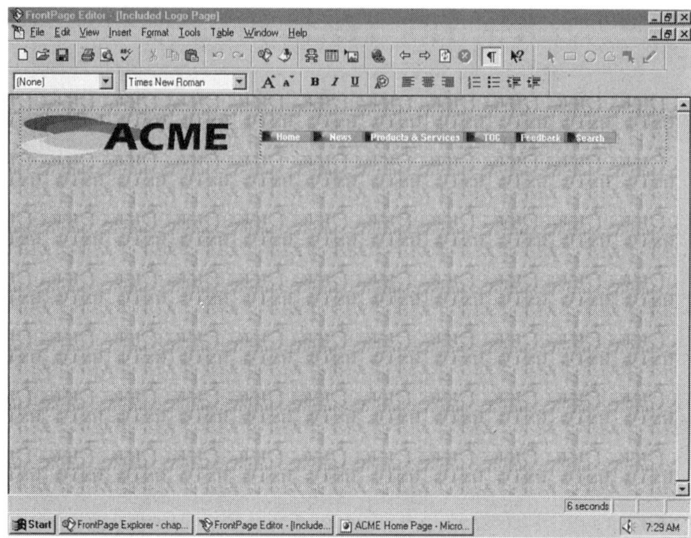

Figure 11.11.
The logo and navigation bar are displayed on the same page.

9. Select the Current FrontPage Web tab. In the **P**age field, you can enter `../acmehome.htm`, or you can use the B**r**owse button to locate the revised ACME Home page.
10. In the Target **F**rame field of the Current FrontPage Web tab, enter `main`. This loads the ACME Home Page in the main (floating) frame.
11. Choose OK. You return to the FrontPage Editor.
12. Assign the target frame of `main` to all remaining link graphics on the page, as shown in Figure 11.12. When you are finished, save the new `logo.htm` file to your web using the **F**ile | **S**ave (Ctrl+S) command or the Save button on the Standard toolbar.

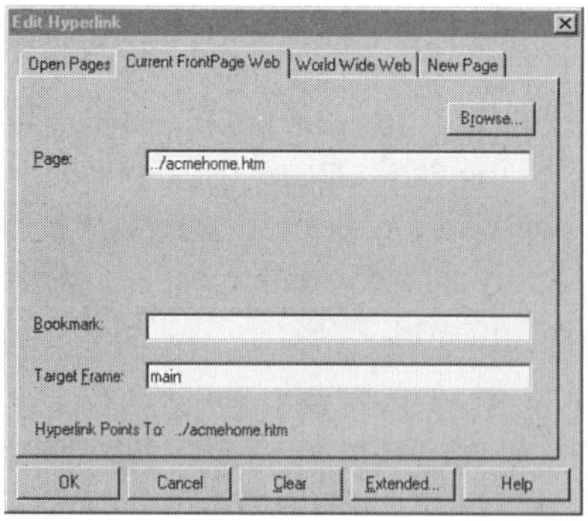

Edit Hyperlink
Open Pages | Current FrontPage Web | World Wide Web | New Page
Browse...
Page: ../acmehome.htm
Bookmark:
Target Frame: main
Hyperlink Points To: ../acmehome.htm
OK | Cancel | Clear | Extended... | Help

Figure 11.12.
Assign a target frame of `main` *to each of the links on the navigation bar.*

Now you should be able to load the home page (`default.htm`, `index.htm`, and so on) into the FrontPage Editor and preview both the frameset and the CSS results in your browser.

Dressing Up the Pages

All that remains now is to dress the pages up a little bit with tables. You can use tables to create a more interesting layout for your pages. To review the colors and table settings used here, see the examples included on the CD that accompanies this book. In brief, review the following:

- A second copy of the logo/navigation bar was placed at the bottom of each main page. Figure 11.13 shows the home page with the navigation bar and logo at the bottom. This was done to provide links on each page in the event that they are not displayed in a floating frame or a frameset.

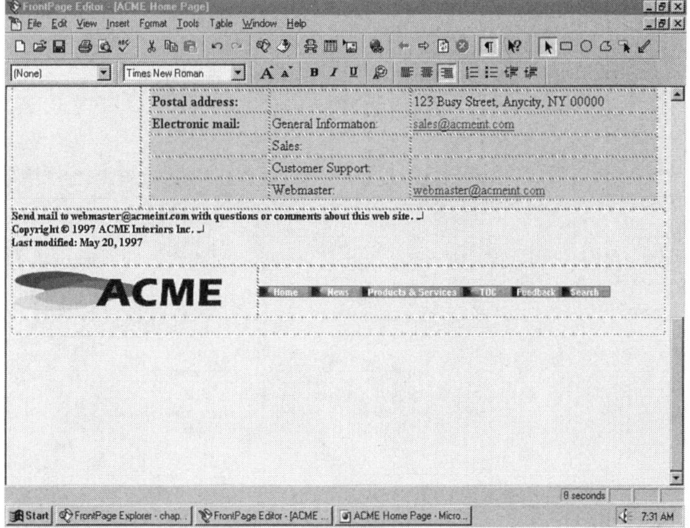

Figure 11.13.
A copy of the logo and navigation bar is displayed at the bottom of each main page.

- You can create more complex color arrangements by using nested tables, as shown in Figure 11.14. For example, a nested table is used to make the contact information at the bottom of the home page (`acmehome.htm`) stand out a little bit more, by using a slightly darker color. Also, descriptive text is placed in the left columns of the tables on the page, and important information is placed in the right side of each page and accented with a different cell background color than the background color. This draws the eye to the important information on each page.

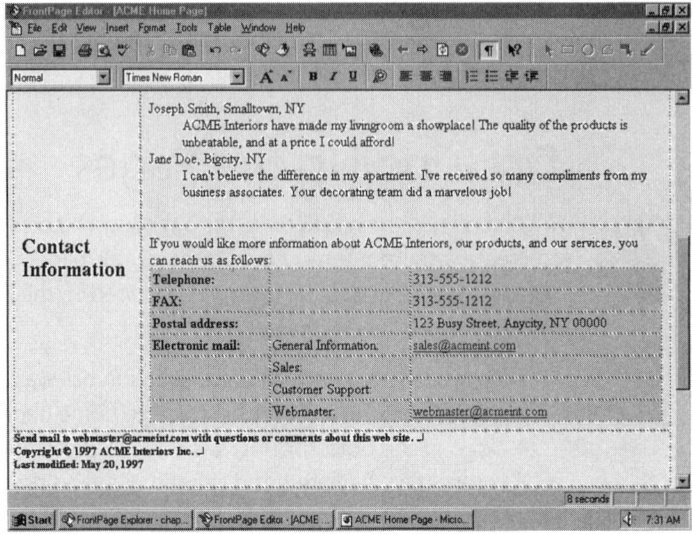

Figure 11.14.
Nested tables and different cell background colors can be used to draw the user's eye to the more important areas on the page.

- You can also use table outlines or cell outlines to make a table stand out even further. An example of this is shown in the Products Page (`products.htm`) in Figure 11.15.

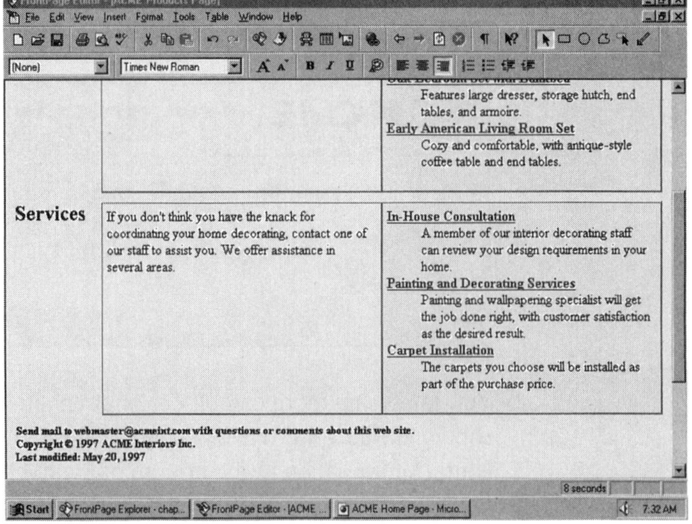

Figure 11.15.
Use borders around table cells to make important information stand out even more.

- You can also create a second style sheet (`_private/style2.htm` in the examples on the CD). You can assign the second style sheet to the main pages and the original style sheet to the `default.htm` home page. This gives the pages that appear within the floating frame a different background.

You can experiment further by using background images in your table cells rather than solid colors as shown here. Background images should not be so bold as to conflict with the text in each cell. As a general rule, use light backgrounds with dark text and dark backgrounds with light text. Try not to use backgrounds that are too bold and busy, as they can detract from the text on the page.

Workshop Wrap-Up

Now you have a general idea of how you can use tables, floating frames, and CSSs together to make your pages more interesting. As you can see from the preceding examples, CSSs and floating frames really enhance the look of your site while providing a consistent appearance. Though the examples in these chapters are simple and clean, they should give you a grasp of the basic techniques used for each of the Internet Explorer features. As you experiment with CSS features, remember that you may need to "tweak" the code and rearrange the order in which style definitions appear to get the code to parse correctly. As you learn more about these topics, you'll develop your own favorite combinations of font styles and effects.

Next Steps

In Part IV, "Activating Your Webs," you'll learn several different ways that you can use forms, newsgroups, and chats to add interactivity and dynamic communication to your Web site. For additional information regarding Internet Explorer features, refer to the following chapters:

- Chapter 8, "Creating Advanced Tables," for more information about the properties that you can apply to your tables.
- Chapter 9, "Using Floating Frames," for more details about using additional floating frame tags.
- Chapter 10, "Using Cascading Style Sheets," for further descriptions of the various properties that Internet Explorer supports for CSSs.
- Appendix A, "Online Resources," for additional online references about these topics.

Q&A

Q: You said that browsers that do not support floating frames see a blank area where a floating frame should be displayed. Is there a way I can specify an alternate page to be displayed instead, like I can with a regular frameset?

A: At the present time, no. Although floating frames offer more freedom in placing your framed content, the lack of support for an ALT attribute in Internet Explorer 3.0 is a drawback. You'll have to keep this in mind when you design your pages and provide alternatives for those who do not use browsers that support floating frames.

Q: Are there other ways to use CSSs besides changing fonts and backgrounds?

A: Actually, CSSs were created to provide a means to emulate features that you could incorporate in a word processor, but you can see some creative examples of using CSS tags on Microsoft's Web site. At the present time, Microsoft Internet Explorer 3.0 offers limited support for CSSs; however, with Internet Explorer 4.0, we will probably see support for more CSS tags. In addition, Internet Explorer 4.0 will support Dynamic HTML (DHTML), which will provide even greater benefits for page layout, multimedia elements, and more.

PART IV

Activating Your Webs

CHAPTER TWELVE

Working with Forms

In this chapter, you

- ❑ Learn how to configure the FrontPage WebBots that process forms
- ❑ Examine forms that use each of the WebBots
- ❑ Learn how to create and save a page that registers users of a private (or protected) Web

Tasks in this chapter:

- ❑ Configuring a Private Web
- ❑ Configuring a WebBot Registration Component
- ❑ Configuring the Results File
- ❑ Saving Your User Registration Page
- ❑ Working with the WebBot Save Results Component
- ❑ Configuring a Confirmation Field Bot
- ❑ Adding a WebBot Search Component
- ❑ Configuring a Form to Use Custom Scripts

The chapters in this section are about reaching out and communicating with the outside world. When you design Web sites, there are lots of different ways that you can accomplish this. One method is to use forms to gather input from your visitors.

FrontPage 97 offers some components that allow you to process forms without writing any code. If you prefer to write your own code, though, you can assign a custom script to process your form instead. This chapter shows you how to do both.

Designing Forms with FrontPage 97

Although I assume you are familiar with the process of designing forms in FrontPage, I will give a brief overview. The quickest way is to start with one of the page templates that include form fields in them already. The page templates are available in the New Page dialog box, which is displayed after you select the **F**ile | **N**ew command in the FrontPage Editor. From the New Page dialog box, shown in Figure 12.1, you can select one of the following page templates to create a form quickly:

> *Confirmation Form:* Creates a page that is returned to the user after he or she submits a form. You will need to edit the WebBot Confirmation Field components on the page to match the form fields on the form that you are confirming.

Feedback Form: Creates a page that contains placeholders for generic questions. You must customize this form to suit your needs and edit all the form field properties accordingly. It uses the WebBot Save Results Component for a form handler.

Guest Book: Creates a page that enables users to sign a guest book on your Web site. This page needs very little editing. It uses the WebBot Save Results Component for a form handler.

Product or Event Registration page: Enables the user to register a software product or sign up for an event. This page uses the WebBot Registration Component for a form handler.

Search Page: Creates a form that enables the user to search through your entire Web site or through the articles contained in a discussion group. This page uses the WebBot Search Component for a form handler.

Survey Form: Creates a page that contains several different questions requiring user response. You will need to edit the questions and form fields on the page to suit your needs. This page uses the WebBot Save Results Component for a form handler.

User Registration page: Creates a page that enables a user to gain access to a private Web site. It uses the WebBot Registration Component for a form handler.

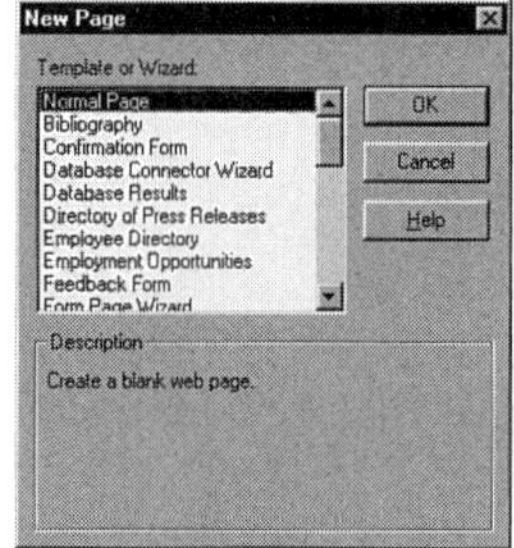

Figure 12.1.
There are several page templates, found in the New Page dialog box, that generate forms very quickly.

The quickest way to design your own custom forms for your Web pages is to use the Forms Wizard, found in the FrontPage Editor. You can invoke the Forms Wizard from the New Page dialog box in the FrontPage Editor as well. The Forms Wizard prompts you to choose one of 14 question types, examples of which are shown in Figure 12.2. You then enter a prompt for the question and configure the properties for the form fields directly in the Forms Wizard. After you complete your form, it is displayed on a Web page with all its form field properties configured for you. You can save the page to the Web or cut and paste the form into another page.

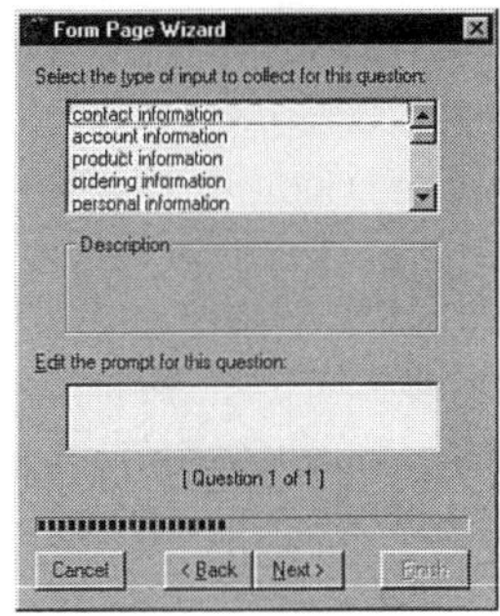

Figure 12.2.
You can use the Forms Wizard to design custom forms. Select from 14 types of prompts or questions, a few of which are shown here, to generate the form fields.

You can also design a form by inserting form fields into a page. Generally, this method is the most time-consuming. You can find the form fields in the **I**nsert | Form Fiel**d** menu of the FrontPage Editor, as shown in Figure 12.3.

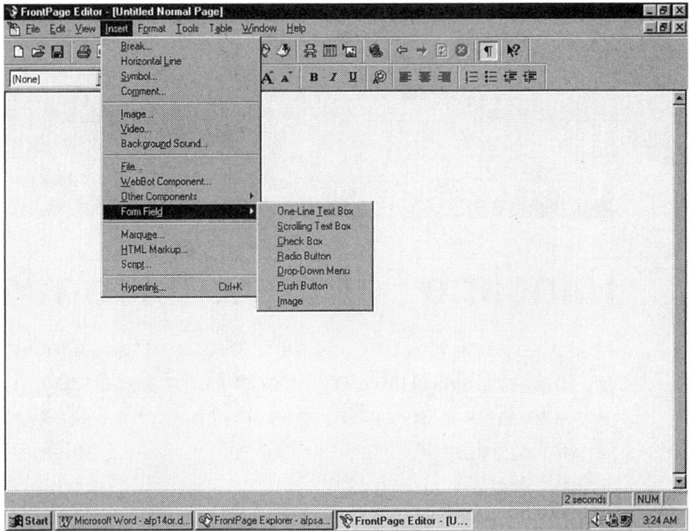

Figure 12.3.
You can also add form fields to a page with the commands available in the Insert | Form Field menu.

You can insert one of the following types of form fields:

One-Line Text Box—Used for single-line text responses

Scrolling Text Box—Used for multi-line text responses

Check Box—Generally used for boolean (yes/no, on/off) type responses or to select one or more items from a group of selections

Radio Button—Generally used to select one or more of a range of responses provided in a group

Drop-Down Menu—Used to select one of several items in a group

Push Button—Used to submit or clear the form

Image—Used to use a custom image as a button.

After you place the form fields on your page, double-click the form field to edit its properties. When you do so, a Properties dialog box that pertains to the form field type is displayed. Figure 12.4 shows values being entered into the Drop-Down Menu Properties dialog box. Each form field type has its own set of properties to configure.

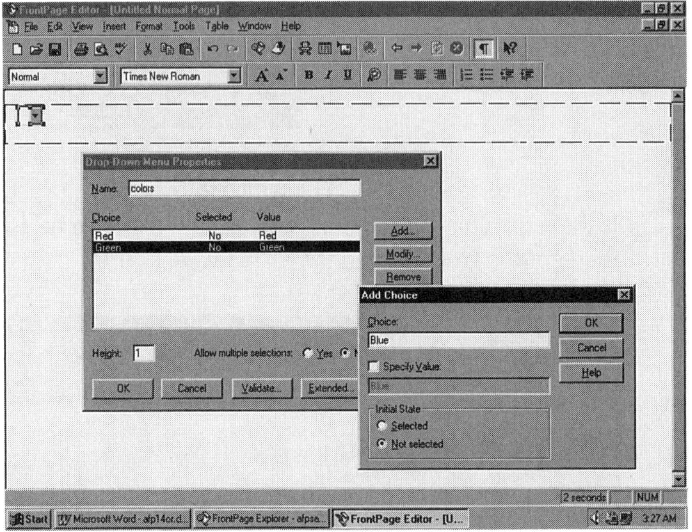

Figure 12.4.
After you insert a form field into your Web page, use its respective Properties dialog box to configure the settings.

Handling Forms with FrontPage 97

After you design your form, it is time to assign a form handler to it. FrontPage 97 allows you to assign several different types of form handlers to your Web pages. The majority of the form handlers discussed in this chapter require that you have the FrontPage Server Extensions installed on your server. The "Configuring a Form to Use Custom Scripts" section, later in this chapter, discusses using custom ISAPI, NSAPI, or CGI scripts to process your forms.

To configure a form handler, go to the Form Properties dialog box. You are presented with five selections for a form handler, shown in Figure 12.5.

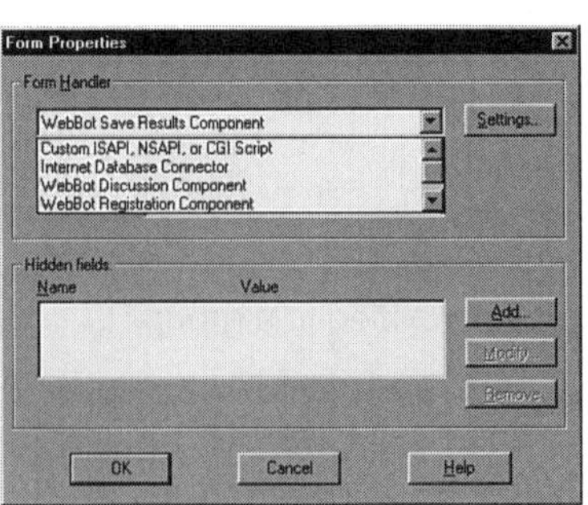

Figure 12.5.
There are five form handlers from which you can choose in the Form Properties dialog box.

You can choose one of the following form handlers from the Form Properties dialog box:

- *Custom ISAPI, NSAPI, or CGI Script.* Select this option if your remote server does not have the FrontPage Server Extensions installed, or if you prefer to use your own custom scripts to process forms.
- *Internet Database Connector.* Select this option if you want your form to integrate with database files that use Internet Database Connector (IDC) files.

See **Chapter 13** to learn more about using IDC files with your forms and databases.

See **Chapter 15** to learn more about discussion groups and other ways to talk with the outside world.

- *WebBot Discussion Component.* This WebBot component is used to process FrontPage 97 discussion groups. In most cases, you can configure discussion groups very quickly using the Discussion Web Wizard in the FrontPage Explorer. It requires that the FrontPage Server Extensions be present on the remote server.
- *WebBot Registration Component.* This WebBot component is typically used on a registration page. The registration page can provide access to a private Web site or register a user for technical support for a product. It requires that the FrontPage Server Extensions be present on the remote server.
- *WebBot Save Results Component.* This WebBot component is used for general-purpose forms that do not fall into any of the previously named categories. It requires that the FrontPage Server Extensions be present on the remote server.

There are two additional items that are not classified as form handlers but that relate to form input or data retrieval: The WebBot Search Component is used to create a search form that allows a user to search through your entire Web, or through all the articles in a discussion group; and the Confirmation Field WebBot is used to design a page that returns form field values to a user. This allows the user to confirm that the server has received the data correctly. You can find both of these items in the **I**nsert | **W**ebBot Component command. This opens the Insert WebBot Component dialog box, shown in Figure 12.6.

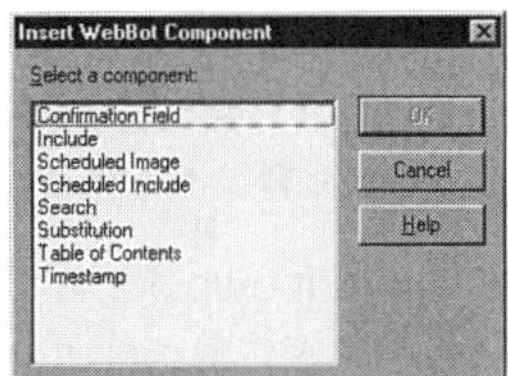

Figure 12.6.
The Confirmation Field WebBot and the Search WebBot are available in the Insert WebBot Component dialog box.

Restricting Access to a Web

The first example in this chapter is a registration page that prompts the user for his or her name and password before gaining access to a Web (see Figure 12.7). Registration pages of this type must be saved in the server's root web. They prevent access to an entire Web site; you cannot configure a portion of a Web site for private access with the FrontPage WebBot Registration Component.

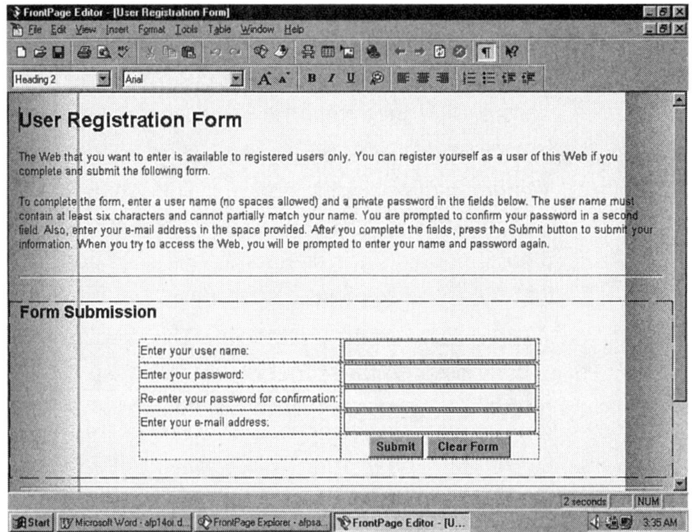

Figure 12.7.
Use the WebBot Registration Component as a form handler for a User Registration Form page.

It is important to note that the most basic level FrontPage-enabled Web sites exist as child webs beneath the remote server's root web. Before you design your private Web site, verify with your Web presence provider that you have permission to locate your user registration page in the root web of their FrontPage server. They may not allow this at all, and if they do, you'll need to assign your registration page a unique name. You don't want to overwrite anyone else's registration pages! If you have permission to design a private Web, keep in mind that your Web is entirely public or entirely private, but not both. If you want to create both public and private pages, you must obtain another FrontPage-enabled account or a domain name for your Web.

If you have your own domain name, or your own server, you basically have your own root web. This is true even if your Web resides on a remote server sponsored by a Web presence provider. Therefore, you can create child webs beneath your own root web and use the **T**ools | **P**ermissions command to assign special permissions for private webs.

Configuring a Private Web

To configure a child web as a private web that allows only registered users to gain access, use the Permissions dialog box in the FrontPage Explorer. Follow these steps:

1. From the FrontPage Explorer, open or create the web that you want to configure as a private web.
2. Choose **T**ools | **P**ermissions. The Permissions dialog box for the current web is displayed, opened to the Settings tab, as shown in Figure 12.8.

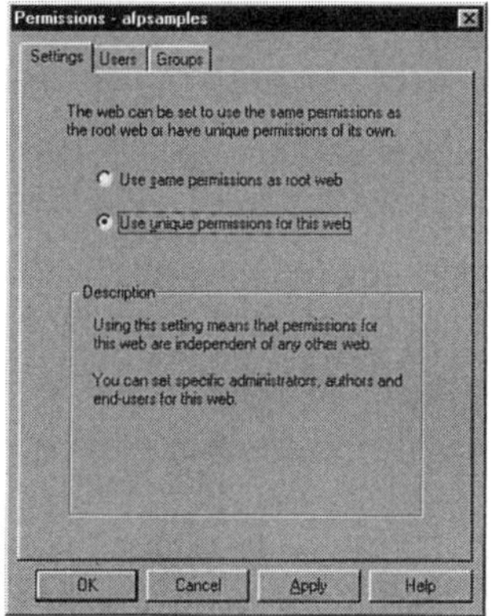

Figure 12.8.
Use the Settings tab in the Permissions dialog box to configure special settings for a private web.

3. Select Use **u**nique permissions for this web and click **A**pply.
4. Click the Users tab.
5. Select **O**nly registered users have browse access, as shown in Figure 12.9.
6. If your web is to be authored and administered by persons other than those who are configured for your root web, use the **A**dd button to add new administrators and authors. Otherwise, click OK to apply the settings to your web.

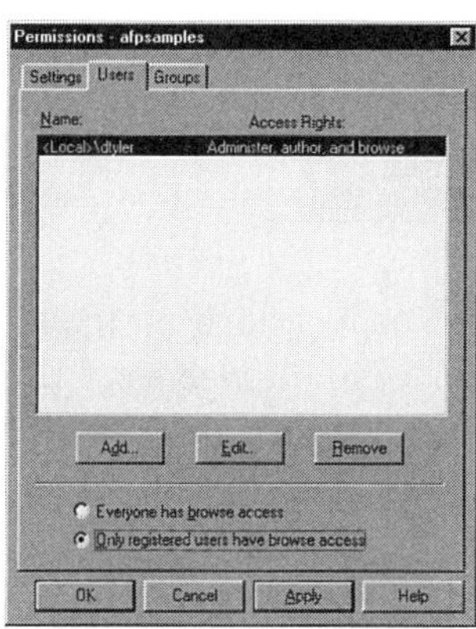

Figure 12.9.
To configure a private web, select ***O****nly registered users have browse access from the Users tab of the Permissions dialog box.*

Configuring a WebBot Registration Component

The next step is to create your registration form. An example of a registration form for a private web is furnished on the CD-ROM that accompanies this book. You can also choose the User Registration template from the New dialog box when you create a new page in the FrontPage Editor.

To examine the registration page furnished on the CD-ROM, follow these steps:

1. From the FrontPage Editor, choose **F**ile | **O**pen (Ctrl+O) or click the Open button on the Standard toolbar. The Open dialog box is displayed.
2. Use the Look **i**n box to locate the CD-ROM drive and directory in which the `userreg.htm` file is saved. Double-click the file to open it.
3. Right-click anywhere in the form (surrounded by dotted lines) and choose Form Properties from the pop-up menu. The Form Properties dialog box is displayed.
4. From the Form **H**andler drop-down menu, choose WebBot Registration Component.
5. Click **S**ettings to configure the WebBot Registration Component. The Settings for Registration Form Handler dialog box shown in Figure 12.10 is displayed. By default, it opens to the Registration tab.

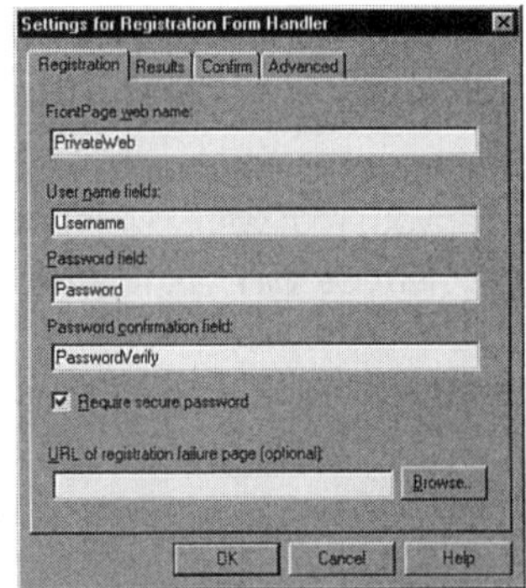

Figure 12.10.
Configure the settings for your WebBot Registration Component in the Registration tab of the Settings for Registration Form Handler dialog box.

6. In the FrontPage **w**eb name field, enter the web name for which you're creating the registration form. The web name URL is relative to the location of the root web. The URL of a child web of the root looks something like this:

```
/RegisteredWeb
```

7. In the User **n**ame fields, enter the names of one or more form fields on the registration form. The WebBot Registration Component constructs the username from these fields. The values you enter here should agree with the field names in which the user enters his or her username in your Registration form, as in the following examples:
   - If the user enters his or her name in a single field, your entry might look like this:

     `Username`

   - If the user enters his or her name in two fields, your entry might look like this:

     `First, Last`

   - If the user enters his or her name in three fields, your entry might look like this:

     `First, Middle, Last`

8. In the **P**assword field section, enter the name of the form field in which the user enters his or her password. In the registration form used in the example, this field is named `Password`.
9. In the Password **c**onfirmation field section, enter the name of the form field in which the user enters his or her password confirmation. In the registration form used in the example, this field is named `VerifyPassword`.
10. If you want the user to enter a secure password, select the **R**equire secure password check box. A secure password must contain at least six characters and cannot partially match the username.
11. In the **U**RL of registration failure page (optional) field, enter a page URL or use the **B**rowse button to select a page from your current Web site. If you do not enter a URL here, a default failure page is generated if the user makes an error in his or her name or password. This page informs the user that he or she must enter a correct password to gain access to the page or Web site.
12. Choose another tab in the Settings for Registration Form Handler dialog box, or click OK to configure the registration form.

Configuring the Results File

A results file is the page on your web that stores the data that the user submitted with the form. It can be saved to your web as a text file or an HTML file. The procedures to identify results files are similar for the WebBot Registration Component and the WebBot Save Results Component (discussed in the "Working with the WebBot Save Results Component" section).

Configure a results file for a WebBot Registration Component or WebBot Save Results Component as follows:

- To configure a results file for a WebBot Registration Component, click the Results tab (the second tab) in the Settings for Registration Form Handler dialog box.
- To configure a results file for a WebBot Save Results Component, click the Results tab (the first tab) in the Settings for Saving Results of Form dialog box.

Both bots offer several choices for how to store the results from forms on your Web site. You have the option to store results in HTML or text format. When you choose an HTML option, the FrontPage Server Extensions generate the HTML page at runtime. Although HTML files are easier to browse, they can make your Web site slower because more results are appended to the page.

Here are the options for HTML results files:

HTML—Stores the results file in an HTML page that uses normal text with line endings.

HTML Definition List—Stores the results file as a definition list in an HTML file. The names of the form fields appear as terms, and the values of the form fields are displayed as the definition.

HTML Bulleted List—Stores your results file as a bulleted list in an HTML file.

Formatted Text Within HTML—Stores your results file in formatted paragraphs with line endings.

If you want to maintain a database of users, you can save your results in formatted text format. The results file can be separated by comma, tab, or space if you intend to import the user registration database into a database or spreadsheet program.

Here are the choices for text results files:

Formatted Text—Saves the results file as formatted text, without separators.

Text Database Using Comma as a Separator—Saves the results file as a text file that uses commas to separate the values.

Text Database Using Tab as a Separator—Saves the results file as a text file that uses tabs to separate the values.

Text Database Using Space as a Separator—Saves the results file as a text file that uses spaces to separate the values. If you expect that you will have multiple-word responses in your form fields, do not select this option.

To configure the settings for the results file, follow these steps:

1. In the Settings for Registration Form Handler dialog box, click the Results tab, shown in Figure 12.11.

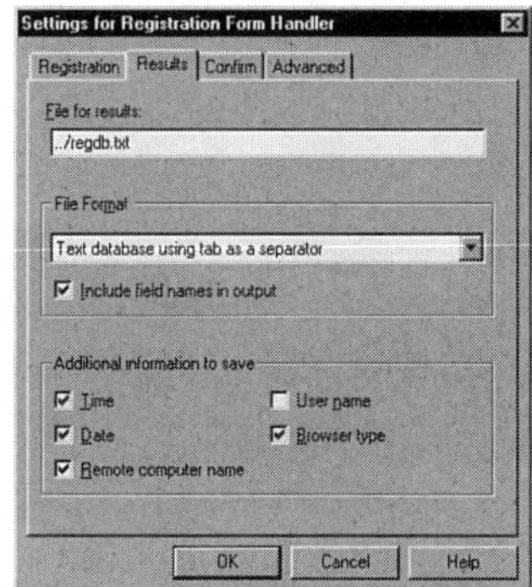

Figure 12.11.
Use the Results tab to configure the file format to which you want to save the user's responses.

2. Enter a filename for the results file in the **F**ile for results field. Enter a page URL with relative path if the results file exists in your current web or an absolute path to a filename that exists in a location outside your current web. If you want to save your results file in text format, be sure to enter a `.txt` extension when you specify the filename. If you do not create this file yourself, FrontPage creates one for you automatically the first time the form is submitted.
3. From the File For**m**at drop-down menu, select the format in which you want to store the results file. (The formats are mentioned earlier in this section.)
4. Select the **I**nclude field names in output check box to save both the name and value of each form field. If you deselect this option, only the responses from the user are written to the file, which can sometimes make it difficult to determine which questions the responses apply to.
5. You can save additional information with your form, besides that which is displayed on the form, from the Additional information to save section. Available options are **T**ime, **D**ate, **R**emote computer name, User **n**ame, and **B**rowser type.
6. Click the Confirm tab to configure a confirmation page (discussed in the "Configuring a Confirmation Field Bot" section).
7. Click the Advanced tab to configure a second results file and additional form fields.

NOTE: You can configure a second results file to save the form results in a different file format. Use the Advanced Tab in the Settings for Saving Results of Form or Settings for Registration Form Handler dialog box. The file types from which you can select are the same as those listed previously in the "Configuring the Results File" section. You can also use the Advanced tab to specify additional fields that are returned in the results file.

8. Click OK to exit the Settings for Registration Form Handler and Form Properties dialog boxes. You are returned to the FrontPage Editor, and the form is complete.

Saving Your User Registration Page

When you complete your registration page for your private web, you must save it to your server's root web. If the root web is common to sites created by others (such as on a server sponsored by a Web presence provider) you must coordinate this with the system administrator. If you have your own root web, no problem!

To save your registration page to the root web, follow these steps:

1. With the registration page still opened in the FrontPage Editor, choose **T**ools | Show Fro**n**tPage Explorer, or click the Show FrontPage Explorer button on the Standard toolbar.
2. From the FrontPage Explorer, choose **F**ile | **O**pen FrontPage Web, or click the Open FrontPage Web button on the toolbar. The Open FrontPage Web dialog box shown in Figure 12.12 is displayed.

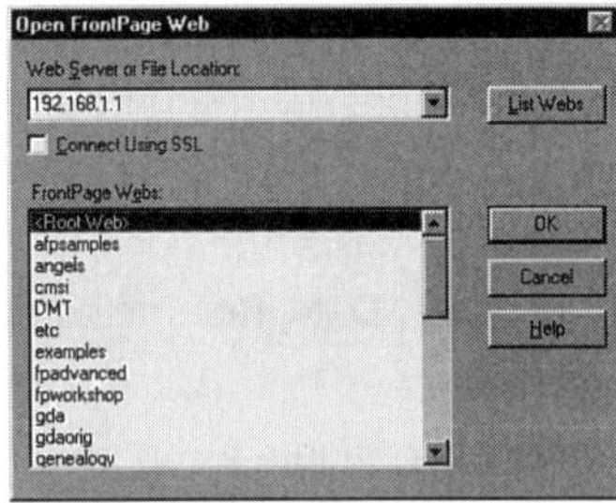

Figure 12.12.
Use the Open FrontPage Web dialog box to select the root web from your local or remote server.

3. From the Web **S**erver or File Location field, enter or choose the server in which the root web is located. Click the **L**ist Webs button if the list of webs on the server does not automatically appear.
4. Select the **C**onnect using SSL check box if the Web resides on a server that uses Secure Socket Layer communication.

5. From the list of webs in the FrontPage Webs list, select `<RootWeb>` and choose OK. The root web opens in the FrontPage Explorer.
6. Return to the FrontPage Editor by clicking the FrontPage Editor button on your taskbar.
7. From the FrontPage Editor, choose **F**ile | **S**ave (Ctrl+S), or click the Save button on the Standard toolbar. The Save As dialog box is displayed.
8. In the Page **T**itle field, enter a title for the page, such as `webname User Registration Page`, where *webname* is the name of the private web.
9. In the File **p**ath within your FrontPage web field, enter a filename for the web page. Make sure you do not assign a name that is already in use in the root web.
10. Click OK. FrontPage saves the registration page to your root web.
11. To test the page, make sure that the FrontPage Server Extensions are running on your server. Then choose **F**ile | Preview in **B**rowser from the FrontPage Editor. Your registration page should appear, and you can enter a name and password to test the form.

Working with the WebBot Save Results Component

You use the WebBot Save Results Component as a form handler for general forms. The quickest way to generate a form is to use the Form Page Wizard in the FrontPage Editor. After your form is designed, you assign the WebBot Save Results Component as a form handler.

Another example of a general form is on the CD-ROM furnished with this book and is shown in Figure 12.13. This general form prompts the user for what he or she wants in his or her "Dream Home." To configure a form handler for a general form such as this form, proceed as follows:

1. From the FrontPage Editor, choose **F**ile | **O**pen (Ctrl+O) or click the Open button on the Standard toolbar. The Open dialog box is displayed.
2. Use the Look **i**n box to locate the CD-ROM drive and directory in which the `dreamhome.htm` file is saved. Double-click the file to open it.
3. Right-click anywhere in the form (surrounded by dotted lines) and choose Form Properties from the pop-up menu. The Form Properties dialog box is displayed.
4. From the Form **H**andler drop-down menu, choose WebBot Save Results Component.

5. Click **S**ettings to configure the WebBot Save Results Component. The Settings for Saving Results of Form dialog box is displayed. By default, it opens to the Results tab, as shown in Figure 12.14.

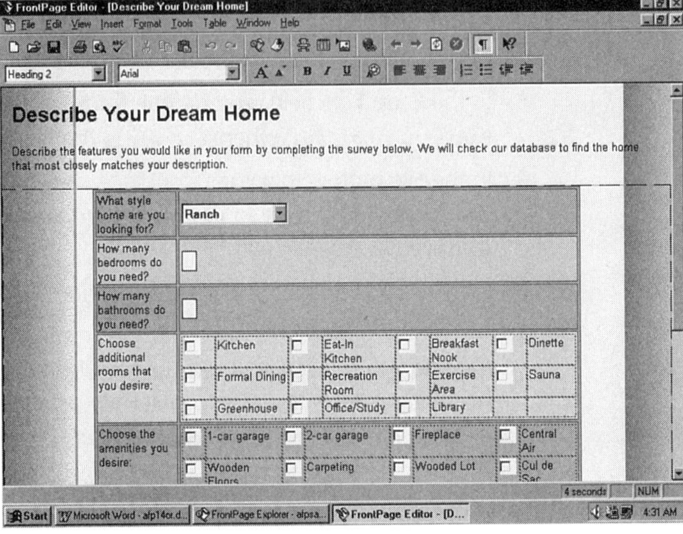

Figure 12.13.
The WebBot Save Results Component is used as a form handler for general-purpose forms.

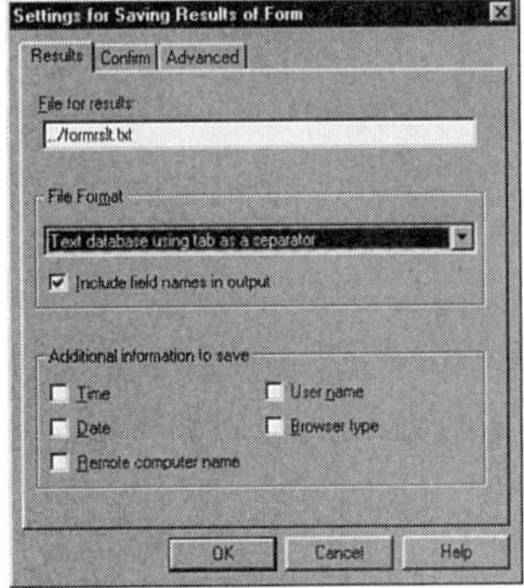

Figure 12.14.
Configure your WebBot Save Results Component in the Settings for Saving Results of Form dialog box.

6. Use the steps outlined in the "Configuring the Results File" section to complete the settings in the Results tab.

7. To configure a confirmation page for the form, click the Confirm tab, shown in Figure 12.15. Enter a relative path to the page that you want to use as a confirmation page. A confirmation page returns the responses to the user so that he or she can review the choices. If you leave this field blank, FrontPage generates a default confirmation page. In the example shown, the filename `dreamconf.htm` is entered here. This form is discussed in more detail in the "Configuring a Confirmation Field Bot" section.

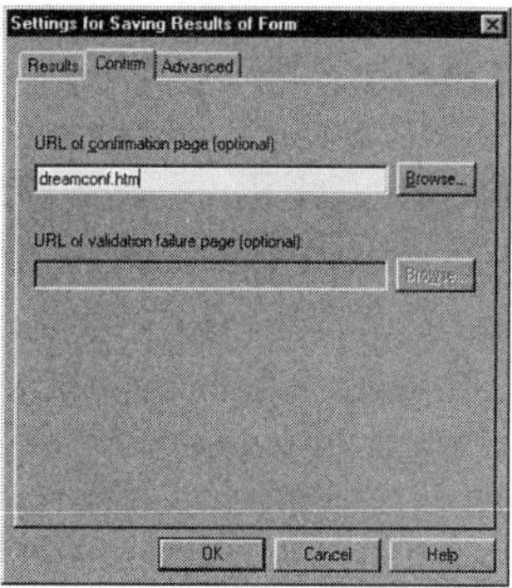

Figure 12.15.
Enter the path to your confirmation page in the Confirm tab of the Settings for Saving Results of Form dialog box.

8. Use the Advanced tab to configure a second results file, if desired.
9. Click OK to return to the FrontPage Editor. The form handler is configured.
10. To test the page, make sure that the FrontPage Server Extensions are running on your server. Then choose **F**ile | Preview in **B**rowser from the FrontPage Editor. Enter some values in the form field and submit the form. You should see a confirmation page return the values that you entered in the form.

Configuring a Confirmation Field Bot

In the previous task, you entered a URL that returns the results of the "Dream Home" page. The URL referenced a page named `dreamconf.htm`, which is included on the CD-ROM that accompanies this book. This confirmation page contains several confirmation field bots that return the user's entries.

When you design your own confirmation page, you must name the confirmation field bots the same as those used in the page that you are confirming. Typically, this is the name as it is entered in the **N**ame field of each form field's properties dialog box.

Follow these steps to configure a confirmation field bot:

1. Position the insertion point where you want the confirmation field bot to appear.
2. Choose **I**nsert | **W**ebBot Component. The Insert WebBot Component dialog box is displayed.
3. From the Select a component field, double-click Confirmation Field. The WebBot Confirmation Field Component Properties dialog box shown in Figure 12.16 is displayed.

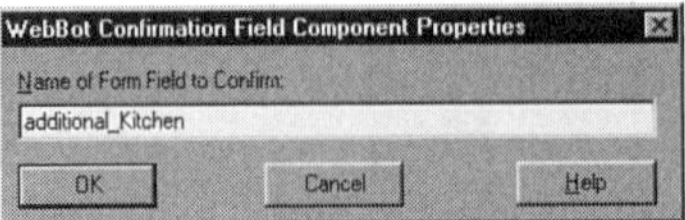

Figure 12.16.
Enter the name of the form field you want to confirm.

4. In the Name of Form Field to Confirm field, enter the exact name of the form field that you are confirming. To find the name, double-click the form field on the original form to open its dialog box. The entry listed in the **N**ame field is the value you enter in the WebBot Confirmation Field Component Properties dialog box.
5. Choose OK. The confirmation bot is displayed on your page, containing the name of the confirmed form field and surrounded by brackets.

The Dream Home Confirmation Form page (shown in Figure 12.17 and furnished on the CD-ROM that accompanies this book) contains many confirmation field bots. Open this page in the FrontPage Editor to compare it with the Dream Home form page (`dreamhome.htm`) to see how the confirmation field bots relate to the form.

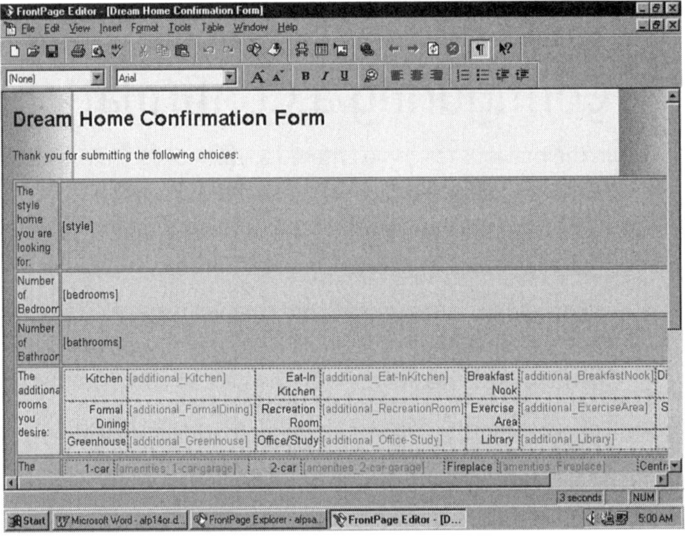

Figure 12.17.
Compare the Dream Home Confirmation Form page with the Dream Home form to learn more about how you can use confirmation field bots.

Adding a WebBot Search Component

The WebBot Search Component allows you to create a text search page for your webs. This WebBot component is not really classified as a form handler; rather, it is a handy component that includes a text field and submit and clear buttons, along with commands that instruct the server to search your web for the terms entered by the user. You can configure the WebBot Search Component to search your entire web or to search articles in discussion groups. The CD-ROM that accompanies this book includes a search page, shown in Figure 12.18.

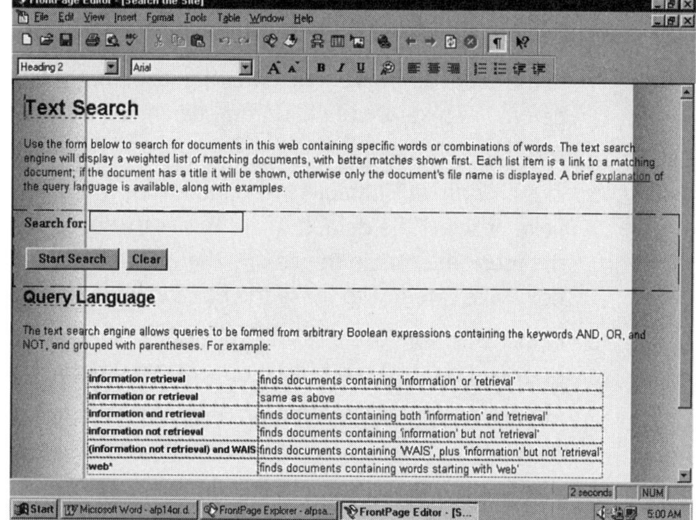

Figure 12.18.
Use the WebBot Search Component to design a page that searches your entire site or articles in a discussion group.

Follow these steps to insert the WebBot Search Component onto your page:

1. Position the insertion point where you want to place the search form.
2. Choose **I**nsert | **W**ebBot Component, and choose Search from the Insert WebBot Component dialog box. The WebBot Search Component Properties dialog box shown in Figure 12.19 is displayed.
3. Configure the WebBot search component as outlined in the next steps.

To review the search page that is included on the CD-ROM, follow these steps:

1. From the FrontPage Editor, choose **F**ile | **O**pen (Ctrl+O) or click the Open button on the Standard toolbar. The Open dialog box is displayed.
2. Use the Look **i**n box to locate the CD-ROM drive and directory in which the `search.htm` file is saved. Double-click the file to open it.

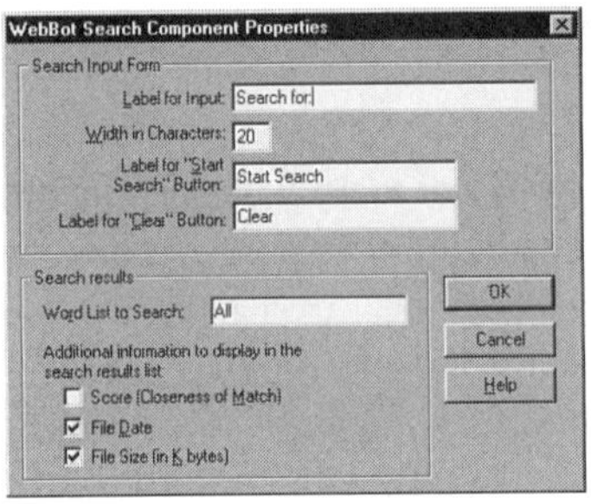

Figure 12.19.
The WebBot Search Component Properties dialog box allows you to configure a search page for your entire Web site or for articles in a discussion group.

3. Double-click the WebBot Search Component (surrounded by dotted lines). The WebBot Search Component Properties dialog box is displayed.
4. In the Label for Input field, enter the label that you want to be displayed before the text input field on the search form. The default text is `Search for:`.
5. In the Width in Characters field, enter the width in characters of the input field, or select the default of `20`. This entry does not limit the length of text the user can enter in the field; rather, it limits the width of the text entry box. Take care not to make the box too wide for the page.
6. In the Label for "Start Search" Button field, enter the text you want to be displayed on the Start button or accept the default of `Start Search`.
7. In the Label for "Clear" Button field, enter the text you want to appear on the Clear button or accept the default of `Clear`.
8. In the Word List to Search field, enter one of the following values:
   - To create a search page that searches your entire Web site (except discussion group articles), enter `All`.
   - To create a search page that searches all the articles in a discussion group, enter the name of the discussion group directory that contains your discussion group articles. Discussion group articles are usually located in directories that are preceded by an underscore (_).
9. You can configure the WebBot Search Component to return the file date, file size, and closeness of match to his or her search terms. From the Additional information to display in the search results list field, choose any of the following additional items.
   - Score (Closeness of **M**atch). Indicates the quality of the match to the text the user enters.
   - File **D**ate. Reports the date and time of the document that matches the user's search entry. The date reported is the date the document was last modified.

- ❑ File Size (in **K** bytes). Reports the size of the matching document in kilobytes.

10. Choose OK to accept your selections and return to the FrontPage Editor.

Using Custom Scripts

You might prefer to use a custom ISAPI, NSAPI, or CGI script to process your forms. If your Internet service provider does not have the FrontPage Server Extensions installed on the server, this might be one of the few alternatives you have to process your forms.

There are three types of custom scripts that you can configure for form handlers. Common Gateway Interface (CGI) scripts are platform dependent, and they reside on your service provider's server. You must coordinate use of CGI scripts with them. Internet Server Application Programming Interface (ISAPI) is an interface developed by Process Software and Microsoft Corporation and can be used with Microsoft Internet Information Server and Microsoft Personal Web Server for Windows 95. Netscape Server Application Programming Interface (NSAPI) is an interface developed by Netscape Communications Corporation and runs only on Netscape servers, such as Netscape Commerce.

If your web resides on a remote server, check with your service provider to see whether you can use custom CGI scripts on your site and to coordinate the requirements. You must enter the appropriate path and extension when you configure your form handler. Sometimes, CGI scripts must be assigned a `.cgi` extension to be recognized on the server; other times, they must be placed in a specific directory to function properly.

Configuring a Form to Use Custom Scripts

You assign an ISAPI, NSAPI, or CGI script to your FrontPage form in much the same way as you assign any of the other form-handling bots—with the Form Properties command. Follow these steps:

1. Right-click anywhere inside the form; then choose Form Properties from the pop-up menu to open the Form Properties dialog box.
2. From the Form **H**andler field, choose Custom ISAPI, NSAPI, or CGI Script.
3. Click **S**ettings to configure the form handler. The Settings for Custom Form Handler dialog box shown in Figure 12.20 is displayed.

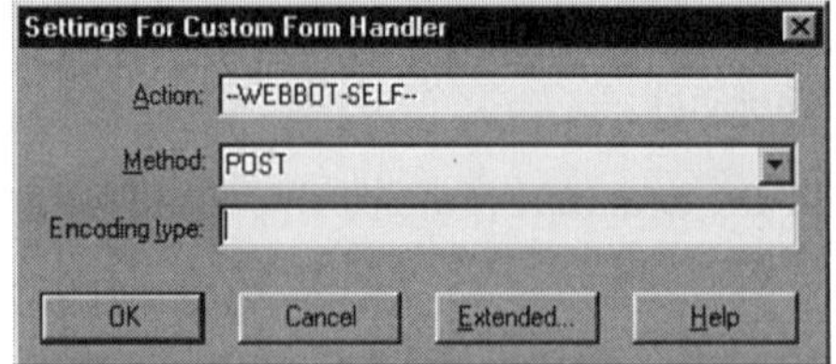

Figure 12.20. *Configure a custom form handler in the Settings for Custom Form Handler dialog box.*

4. In the **A**ction field, enter the absolute URL of the form handler. For example, if your form handler is named `guestbk.cgi` and it resides in the `/cgi-bin` subdirectory of your Web site, the absolute URL might look something like this:

   `http://www.yourserver.com/~yourdirectory/cgi-bin/guestbk.cgi`

5. In the **M**ethod field, enter the method the form handler needs to process the form. If you're using one of the examples from either of the sites mentioned earlier, you can see which method was used by examining the HTML page example provided with the CGI script. You typically have one of the following options:

   `POST` (default). This method passes the name/value pairs to the form handler as input.

   `GET`. This method encodes the name/value pairs of the form and assigns the information to a server variable called `QUERY_STRING`.

6. In the Encoding **t**ype field, enter the default encoding method to be used for the form. If you leave this field blank, the following encoding method is used by default:

   `application/x-www-form-urlencoded`

7. Click OK to close each of the Settings for Custom Form Handler and Form Properties dialog boxes.

Workshop Wrap-Up

FrontPage 97 contains some built-in form handlers that make it quite easy to design forms. In addition, you can easily configure custom scripts to process your forms. These features help activate your Web site and gather information from the outside world. By using the FrontPage 97 WebBot components, you can design forms without programming at all. For those who need form handlers that go beyond the basics, custom ISAPI, NSAPI, or CGI scripts can be used as form handlers.

In this chapter, you learned how to configure several different types of form handlers. For those who don't know how to program custom scripts, the FrontPage WebBot Components can fill the need. These form handlers require that the FrontPage Server

Extensions reside on the server. You learned how to configure three of these WebBot components, creating registration pages, general forms, and Web site search pages. You also learned how to add confirmation fields to your own custom confirmation pages and how to assign custom scripts as form handlers.

Next Steps

In Chapter 13, "Working with IDC Database Connection," you'll learn how to integrate forms and databases together using IDC files. You can create forms that input data to ODBC-compliant (Open Database Connectivity) databases on your server.

To learn additional information about integrating with the outside world, refer to the following chapters:

- In Chapter 6, "Data Access on the Web," you learn how to use Microsoft Access to design forms that integrate with database files.
- In Chapter 14, "Using Active Server Databases," you learn how to use Microsoft Access in conjunction with Active Server Pages.
- In Chapter 15, "Adding Discussions, Chats, and Newsgroups," you learn how to communicate with the outside world through message boards and live chats.
- In Chapter 16, "Real-Life Examples: Interacting with the Outside World," you put all these features together into one Web site.

Q&A

Q: When I preview my form, I receive an error message that says my browser is unable to open the page because a connection with the server cannot be established. What's wrong?

A: The Web server may not be running. Check with your system administrator to see if this is the case. If you are using the Microsoft Personal Web Server on your own local computer, you can restart the server from the Personal Web Server icon in the Windows 95 Control Panel.

Q: The Web server is running, but I'm having problems with my forms. When I submit the form I receive a message that states that there is an executable file that cannot be found. What's wrong in this case?

A: Your server may not have the FrontPage Server Extensions installed. If you use any of the WebBot components mentioned in this chapter to process your forms, you must locate your pages on a FrontPage-enabled server.

CHAPTER

THIRTEEN

Working with IDC Database Connection

In this chapter, you

- ❑ Learn how to use Access 97 databases with HTX/IDC files
- ❑ Review IDC connection with the Microsoft Personal Web Server
- ❑ Review IDC connection with Internet Information Server

Tasks in this chapter:

- ❑ Exporting Database Objects to Dynamic HTX/IDC Files
- ❑ Publishing Your Database to HTX/IDC Format
- ❑ Creating a Database Results File from FrontPage 97
- ❑ Adding a Detail Section
- ❑ Adding Database Column Values
- ❑ Adding an IDC Parameter Value
- ❑ Adding an If-Then Conditional Section
- ❑ Adding an Else Conditional Section
- ❑ Removing Database Directives
- ❑ Using the Internet Database Connector Wizard

In Chapter 6, "Data Access on the Web," you learned about some of the new features in Access 97 and how you can export your database files to different formats. This chapter examines one of the dynamic formats that you can use with your database applications. Using dynamic HTX/IDC files, you can interface dynamically with your database using any Web browser. When you export your Access 97 databases, two types of files are created: One file serves as a template for the data returned by the query, and the other contains the query and database connection information.

Using Access 97 Databases with HTX/IDC Files

In Chapter 6, you learned how to save your Access 97 databases to static HTML format. The disadvantage of saving your databases to a static format is that your data does not update dynamically; you must republish your pages when they change.

Access 97 allows you to publish your database to dynamic HTX/IDC format, which is compatible with most browsers. These files are compatible with the Microsoft operating systems and servers listed in Table 13.1.

Table 13.1. Operating systems and servers compatible with HTX/IDC files.

Operating System	*Server/Add-Ons*
Windows NT Server 3.51	Internet Information Server 1.x or 2.0, using Internet Database Connector
Windows NT Server 4.0	Internet Information Server 2.0 or higher, using Internet Database Connector or ActiveX Server
Windows NT Workstation 4.0	Microsoft Personal Web Server
Windows 95	Microsoft Personal Web Server (will not run on FrontPage Personal Web Server)

When you choose to export or publish your database objects in Dynamic HTX/IDC format, Access 97 automatically creates the HTX and IDC files for you. Access 97 tables, queries, forms, and macros are converted into HTX pages that contain tables. Within the tables are detail sections that insert contents from a database column. An associated IDC file contains the query and the database to which the query connects. Reports are always published to `.html` format.

Exporting Database Objects to Dynamic HTX/IDC Files

There are two ways that you can publish your Access 97 database forms and objects to dynamic HTX/IDC format. The first method saves a single table, query, form, or other object. In the following example, you will learn how to save a table from the sample Northwind database to a directory on the hard disk.

Refer to **Chapter 6** to learn how to configure your server to interface with a dynamic database.

To save your database to dynamic HTX/IDC files, follow these steps:

1. From Access 97, select the table, query, or form you want to export from the database window.
2. Choose **F**ile | Save **A**s/Export. The Save As dialog box is displayed.
3. Select To An **E**xternal File or Database and choose OK. The Save *database object* As dialog box shown in Figure 13.1 is displayed.
4. Use the Save **i**n box to locate the drive and directory to which you want to save the file or files.
5. From the Save as **t**ype drop-down menu, select Microsoft IIS 1-2 (`*.htx`, `*.idc`).
6. In the File **n**ame field, enter the name with which you want to save the page.
7. Click Export. The HTX/IDC Output Options dialog box shown in Figure 13.2 is displayed.

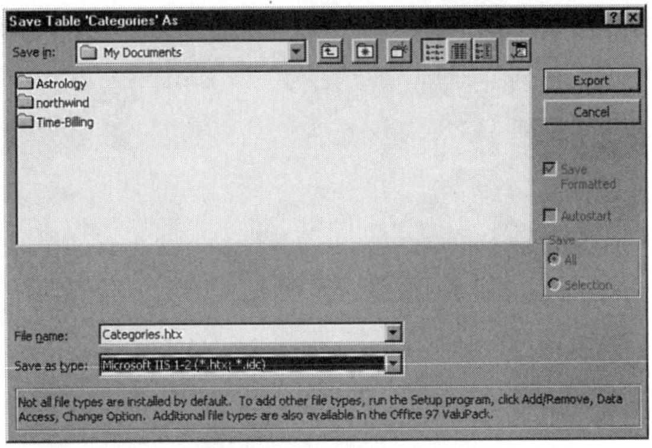

Figure 13.1.
Use the Save As dialog box to select a file format for the object you are exporting.

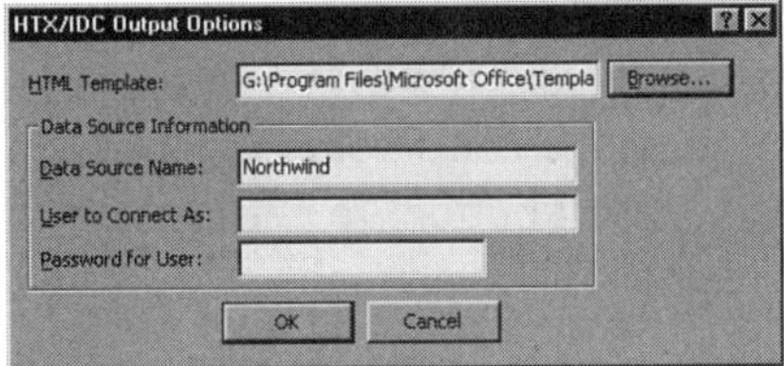

Figure 13.2.
Select an HTML template and identify the database to which you want to connect in the HTX/IDC Output Options dialog box.

8. Use the **B**rowse button in the **H**TML Template field to select an HTML template for your page. The database information is merged with the HTML template to create your Web page.
9. In the **D**ata Source Name field, specify the machine or file data source name that you will use on the WWW server. For this example, enter `Northwind`.
10. Enter a username and password to open the database (if required).
11. Choose OK. The HTX and IDC files are saved to the directory you selected.

Refer to **Chapter 6** to learn about tokens that you should place in your HTML template.

Publishing Your Database to HTX/IDC Format

Access 97 also allows you to publish all or part of your database to HTX/IDC format using the Publish to the Web Wizard. You can use this method to export several pages at once.

To use the Publish to the Web Wizard, follow these steps:

1. With your database open in Access 97, choose **F**ile|Save as **H**TML. The first screen of the Publish to the Web Wizard is displayed (see Figure 13.3).
2. If you have previously created a Web publication profile that you want to reuse, select **I** want to use a Web publication profile I already created with this wizard. Highlight the profile from the list beneath the prompt.

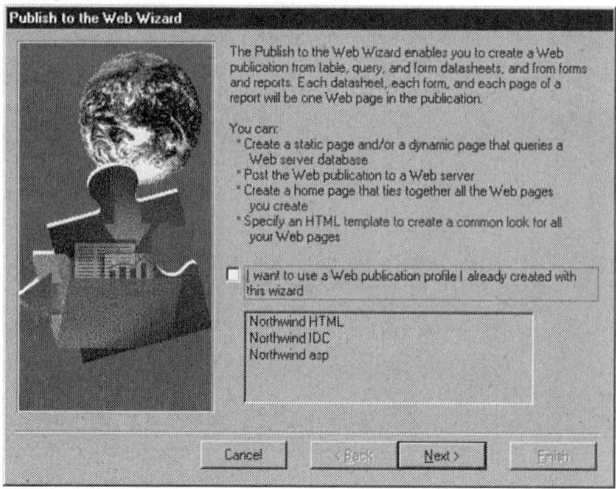

Figure 13.3.
Use the first screen in the Publish to the Web Wizard to publish a Microsoft Access 97 database to HTX/IDC format.

3. Click **N**ext. In the screen shown in Figure 13.4, select the items you want to publish. Choose the items from the Tables, Queries, Forms, or Reports tabs and click the **S**elect button. To publish the entire database, choose the Select **A**ll button in the All Objects tab.

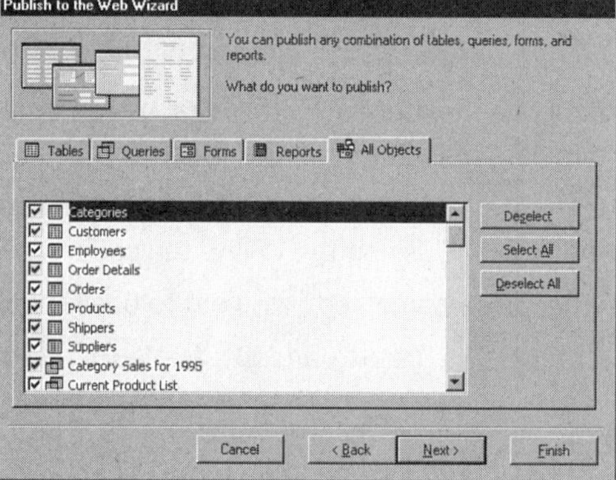

Figure 13.4.
Select the database objects that you want to publish with the wizard.

4. Click **N**ext. In the screen shown in Figure 13.5, you are asked to specify an HTML document for a template. Click the B**r**owse button to open the Select an HTML Template dialog box. Use the Look **i**n field to locate the drive and directory in which your template is saved. Double-click the template filename to assign it. You return to the wizard. Click **N**ext and proceed to step 6 if you do not want to choose additional templates as mentioned in step 5.
5. To select different templates for some items, check the **I** want to select different templates for some of the selected objects button. When you click **N**ext, the screen shown in Figure 13.6 is displayed. Select the objects to which you want to assign another template. Shift-click to select contiguous

items, or Ctrl-Click to select random multiple objects. Then, click the B**r**owse button to choose another template. After you select your templates, click **N**ext to continue.

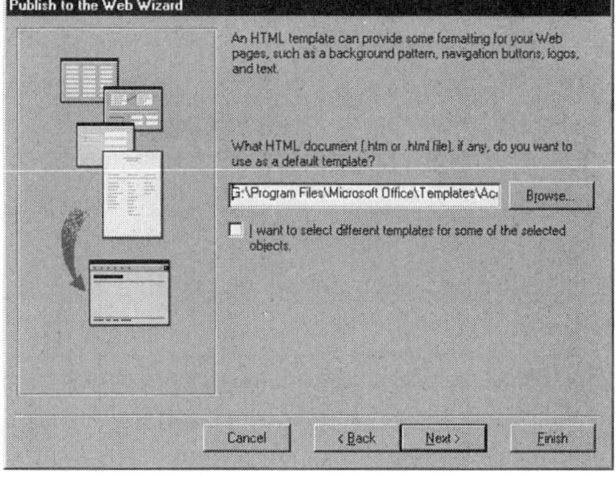

Figure 13.5.
Specify the HTML template that you want to use. This creates pages that are consistent in appearance.

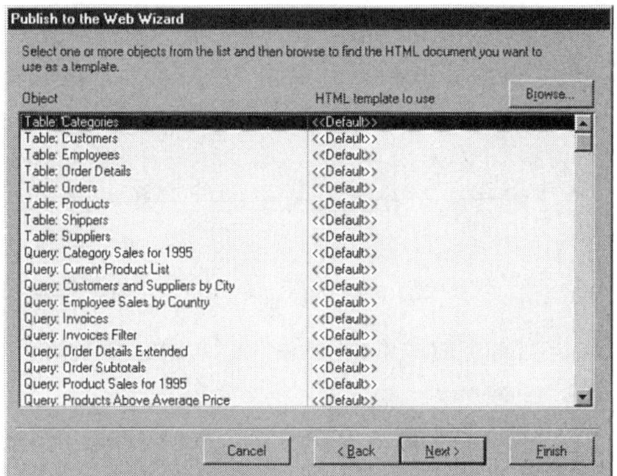

Figure 13.6.
You can select different HTML templates for portions of your database in this screen.

6. On the screen shown in Figure 13.7, you are asked to select a file format for your Web publication. Choose **D**ynamic HTX/IDC (Microsoft Internet Information Server). If you want to publish to multiple formats, click the **I** want to select different format types for some of the selected objects, and proceed to step 7; otherwise, proceed to step 8.
7. To select additional file formats, click **N**ext. A dialog box similar to that shown in Figure 13.6 is displayed. Highlight the items that you want to publish to another file format, and choose the **H**TML, HTX/ID**C**, or **A**SP radio button to specify the file format.

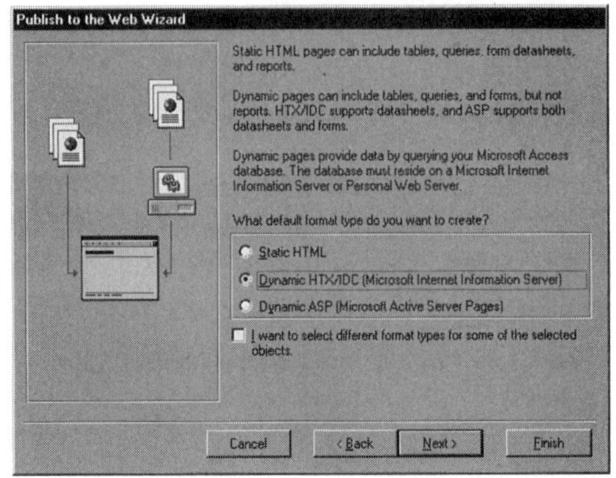

Figure 13.7.
Choose to publish your database to Dynamic HTX/IDC format in this screen.

8. Click **N**ext. On the screen shown in Figure 13.8, you are asked what the settings are for your Internet database. Using the Northwind database sample application for an example, enter or choose the following in the Data Source Information area:

Data Source Name:	`Northwind IDC`
User Name (optional):	If your database requires a secure connection, enter your username in this field. Leave blank for this exercise.
Password (optional):	If your database requires a secure connection, enter your password in this field. Leave blank for this exercise.

In the Microsoft Active Pages Output Options area, enter or Server choose the following:

Server URL:	Enter the name of your server (such as `http://servername/webname/foldername`).
Session **T**imeout (min):	Enter the number of minutes after which a timeout should occur, or accept the default of `10`.

You must configure the Data Source Name on your server. Refer to **Chapter 6** for more information on how to configure data sources in Internet Information Server and the Microsoft Personal Web Server.

9. Click **N**ext. On the screen shown in Figure 13.9, you are asked if you also want to publish to an Internet Server using the Web Publishing Wizard. Select the first of the following options:

   - ❑ Select N**o**, I only want to publish objects locally if you do not want to connect to a server to publish your pages. If you publish your database in this manner, you can use the FrontPage Explorer's **F**ile | **I**mport command or Import Web Wizard to import the database publication into your Web.

- ❑ Choose **Y**es, I want to run the Web Publishing Wizard to set up a new Web publishing specification to set up a "friendly name" for your server connection and publish the database to that server.
- ❑ Choose Y**e**s, I want to use an existing Web Publishing server whose "friendly name" has been set up previously to publish your database to a server that already has a Web Publishing profile set up in the Publish to the Web Wizard. Select the profile you want to use from the list.

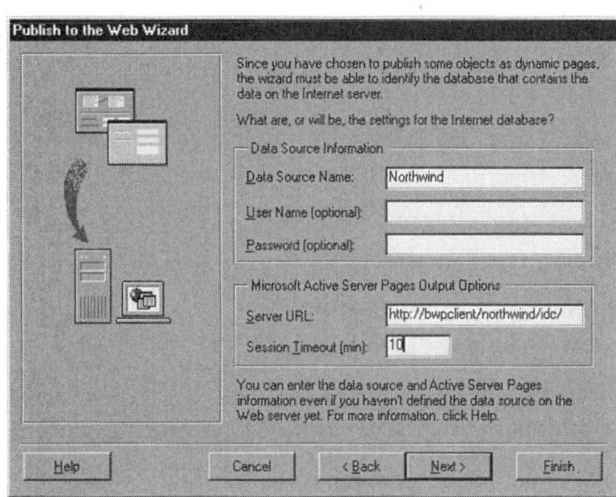

Figure 13.8.
Define your data source, username and password, server URL, and session timeout in this screen.

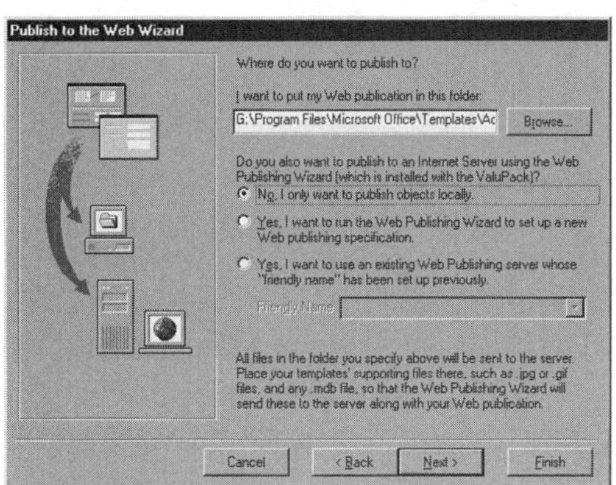

Figure 13.9.
Choose whether you want to publish your database locally or to another server in this dialog box.

10. Click **N**ext. On the screen shown in Figure 13.10, you are asked if you also want to create a home page that ties all your pages together. Choose **Y**es, I want to create a home page. In the What file name do you want for your home page? field, enter a name for your home page. The default is `Default`. If you do not enter an extension, the default is `.html`.

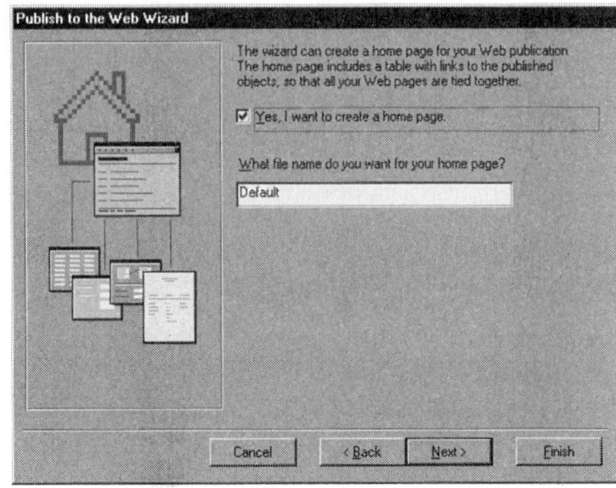

Figure 13.10.
In this screen, you elect to create a home page and assign a home page name.

11. Click **N**ext. You are asked if you want to save your selections to a Web publication profile from the screen shown in Figure 13.11. If so, choose Yes, I want to save wizard answers to a Web publication profile. Enter `Northwind IDC` in the **P**rofile Name field.

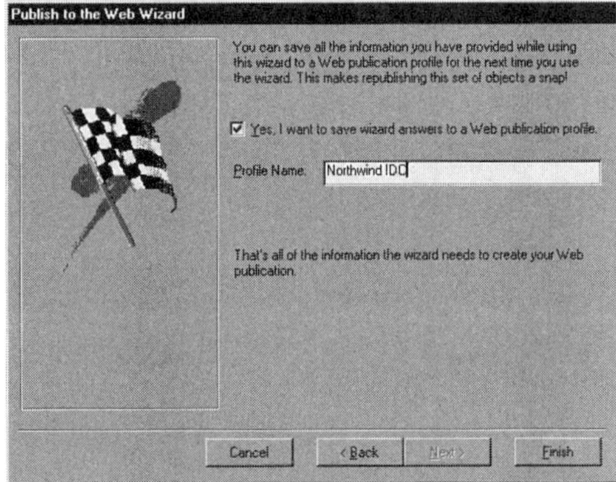

Figure 13.11.
Use this screen to save your settings to a Web publication profile that you can use at a later date.

12. Click **F**inish. Access 97 outputs the objects to HTX/IDC format. During the export procedure, you are prompted for some values to use within the publication. As you export the Northwind database, you are prompted for starting and ending dates and a database record number. For a starting date, enter `1/1/95`. Use `12/31/95` for an ending date. Also, when you are prompted for a starting record number, enter `1`.

Creating a Database Results File from FrontPage 97

Pages that use HTX/IDC for dynamic database connections require two different types of files. One file, which is saved with an `.htx` extension, is used for the results file. Basically, a database results file is nothing more than an HTML file with some special directives placed inside. You also enter query data into the page with commands found in the **E**dit | **D**atabase menu of the FrontPage Editor.

Figure 13.12 shows one of the results files created from the Northwind database. This file, created from the Categories table in the database, is named `Categories_1.htx`. It contains the following items:

- HTML markup bots define the header (THEAD tags), body (TBODY tags), and footer (TFOOT tags) of the table. To see the contents in the markup bots, double-click the yellow symbols with the question marks inside.
- Starting and ending detail section markers define the area where results from the database query are entered into the table. (The detail section markers are the icons that look like bent arrows.)
- Three database column values define the columns from the original database file from which to extract the information in the table. The database column values are those items enclosed in brackets and percentage signs (for example, `<%CategoryID%>`).

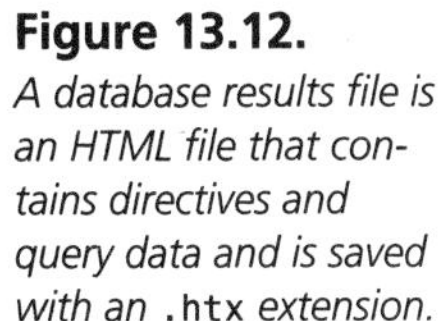

Figure 13.12.
A database results file is an HTML file that contains directives and query data and is saved with an `.htx` *extension.*

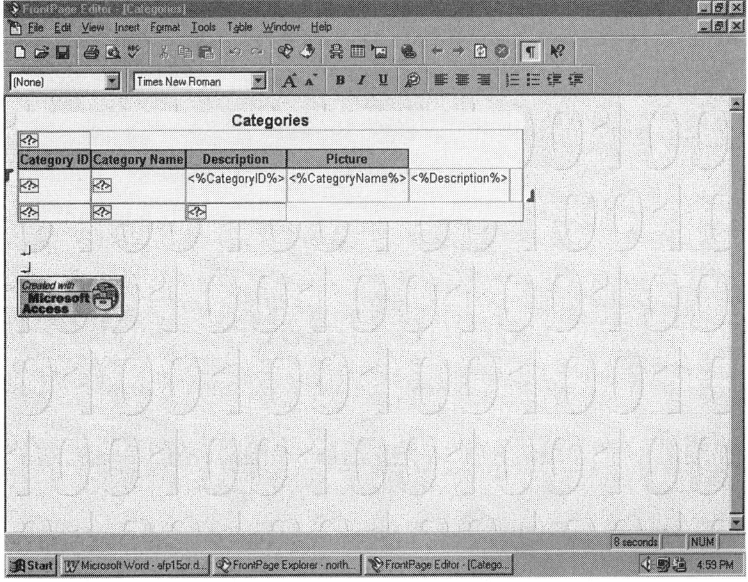

You begin to create a database results file as follows:

1. From the FrontPage Editor, choose **F**ile | **N**ew (Ctrl+N). The New Page dialog box is displayed.
2. From the **T**emplate or Wizard field, select Database Results and click OK. A new database results page is displayed.
3. Add Detail Sections, Database Column Values, IDC Parameter Values, and If-Then-Else statements as outlined in the "Adding a Detail Section" task.
4. Save the file with an `.htx` extension. You will enter this filename in the Query Results Template field in the first panel of the Internet Database Connector Wizard.

Adding a Detail Section

A detail section defines an area in the results file that returns HTML information once for each record that the query returns. It can contain database column values, IDC parameters, and If-Then-Else statements. As mentioned in the "Creating a Database Results File from FrontPage 97" section, detail section markers are shown within the table in Figure 13.12.

To create a detail section, follow these steps:

1. Create or open your database results file. This file should have an `.htx` extension.
2. Select the region on your Web page that you want to define as a detail section. For example, if you want the detail section to appear within a row in a table, select the table row by positioning your mouse to the immediate left of the row that you want to select. When the cursor becomes a selection pointer, click to select the row.
3. Choose **E**dit | **D**atabase | De**t**ail Section.
4. Click OK. Detail section markers are displayed on your page. Insert your other database objects between the detail section markers.

Adding Database Column Values

To return the values from a database column in your results file, insert a Database Column Value into your HTX page. The column names must agree with the column names set in your ODBC database table. In addition, they must be contained within the detail section that you inserted on your page. Database column values are surrounded by brackets and percentage signs when they are displayed on your page (for example, `<%CategoryID%>`).

To add a database column value to your HTX file, follow these steps:

1. Create or open your database results file. This file should have an `.htx` extension.
2. Position the insertion point where you want the database column value to be displayed.
3. Choose **E**dit | **D**atabase | **D**atabase Column Value. The Database Column Name dialog box shown in Figure 13.13 is displayed.
4. In the **D**atabase column name field, enter the name of a column in the database record associated with the current database results file. You don't need to enter the brackets and percentage signs. A sample entry is `CategoryID`.
5. Click OK. The database column name is displayed on your page, surrounded by brackets and percentage signs.

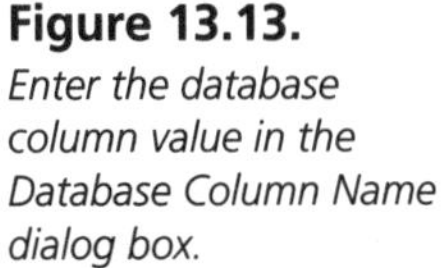

Figure 13.13.
Enter the database column value in the Database Column Name dialog box.

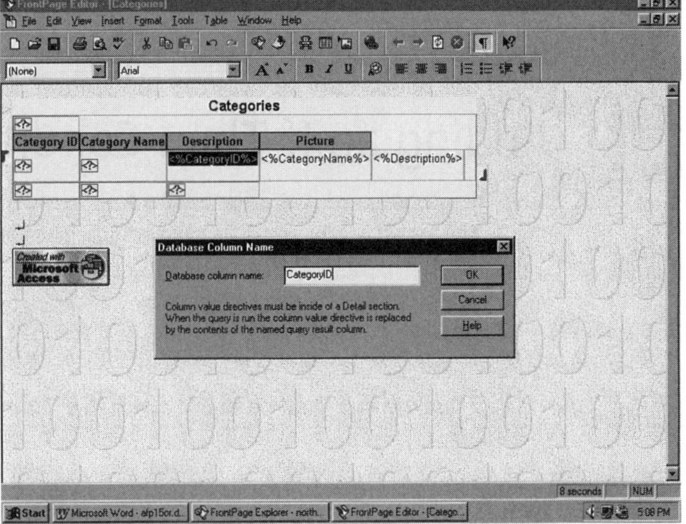

Adding an IDC Parameter Value

When you need to extract information from a specific field in a database, use an IDC parameter value. An IDC parameter value can be the name of one of the form fields used to compose a database query or a default parameter specified in an IDC file. For example, you might configure the results file to return the first and last names of a single entry in a guest book.

To display an IDC parameter, follow these steps:

1. Create or open your database results file. This file should have an `.htx` extension.
2. Position the insertion point where you want the IDC parameter value to be displayed.
3. Choose **E**dit | **D**atabase | IDC **P**arameter value. The IDC Parameter Value dialog box shown in Figure 13.14 is displayed.
4. In the **P**arameter name field, enter the name of the IDC parameter to display (for example, `FirstName`).
5. Click OK. The IDC parameter name is displayed on your page, surrounded by brackets and preceded by `idc` (for example, `<%idc.FirstName%>`).

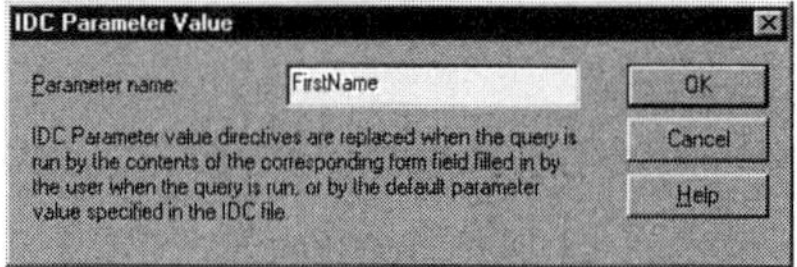

Figure 13.14.
IDC parameters are added to the page in the IDC Parameter Value dialog box.

Adding an If-Then Conditional Section

An If-Then conditional section displays a portion of an `.htx` file if a boolean expression is true. The FrontPage Editor marks the beginning of an If-Then conditional statement with an If-Then condition marker and its end with an End condition marker. You can add any content within the section after it is defined.

To create an If-Then conditional section, follow these steps:

1. Create or open your database results file. This file should have an `.htx` extension.
2. Enter and select the contents on your page that you want to display when the boolean expression evaluates as true.
3. Choose **E**dit | **D**atabase | **I**f-Then conditional section.
4. Click OK. The If-Then Conditional Section dialog box shown in Figure 13.15 is displayed.
5. The purpose here is to define a boolean statement that says, "If the First item relates to the Second item in the condition I select, then display the text I just highlighted." In the First item section, select the type of data you are using to define the first part of the boolean expression from the **T**ype drop-down menu. Available choices are the following:

Database Column Value specifies the value of a database column.

IDC Parameter Value specifies the value of an IDC parameter. This is usually a value used by the query.

Constant Value specifies a constant value, which can be a number or a string.

CurrentRecord always equals the number of records returned by the current database query. If no matching sections are found, the value is 0. No value is required.

MaxRecords is the maximum number of records that can be returned from a database query. No value is required.

HTTP Variable specifies the value of an HTTP variable.

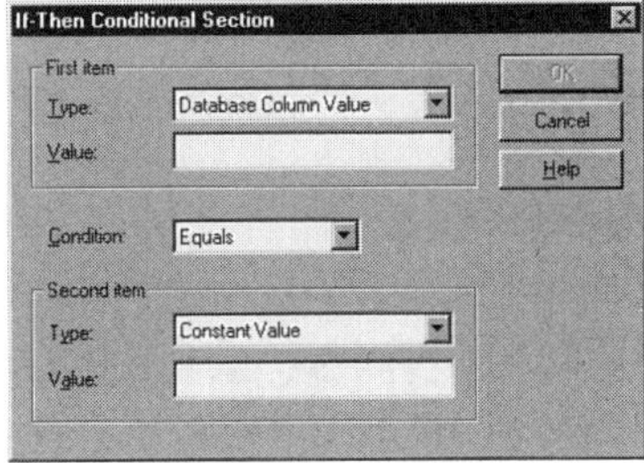

Figure 13.15.
Define your If-Then statement in the If-Then Conditional Section dialog box.

6. If the First item type is anything other than CurrentRecord or MaxRecords, enter a value for the first item in the First item's **V**alue field.
7. Select a comparison operator from the **C**ondition drop-down menu. Available choices follow:

    Equals. The value of the first item should equal the value of the second item to equate as true.

    Less Than. The value of the first item should be less than the value of the second item to equate as true.

    Greater Than. The value of the first item should be greater than the value of the second item to equate as true.

    Contains. Any part of the value of the first item should be contained within the value of the second item to equate as true.

8. To define the second item in the boolean expression, select the type of data from the Second item's T**y**pe drop-down menu. The available choices are the same as those listed in step 5 for the first item.
9. If the Second item type is anything other than CurrentRecord or MaxRecords, enter a value for the second item in the Second item's V**a**lue field.

10. Click OK. The If-Then markers are displayed on your page, surrounding the data that you selected.

Adding an Else Conditional Section

You add an Else conditional section to display a section of the page when your If-Then Conditional Section (described in the previous task) equates to false. All content between the Else marker and the End Condition marker is displayed when the condition is false.

You can only add an Else conditional section inside an If-Then conditional section. To add an Else conditional section, follow these steps:

1. Position the insertion point inside an If-Then conditional section in an HTX file.
2. Choose **E**dit | **D**atabase | **E**lse Conditional Section. An Else Conditional Statement marker is displayed on your page. Enter the data that you want to display before the marker.

Removing Database Directives

When you delete database directives, all IDC parameter values, database column values, beginning and ending markers for detail sections, and beginning and ending markers for conditional statements are removed.

To remove database directives from a database results file, follow these steps:

1. Select the region that contains one or more database directives.
2. Choose **E**dit | **D**atabase | **R**emove Database Directive.
3. Click OK. The directives are removed from the selected area.

Using the Internet Database Connector Wizard

Before you use the Database Connector Wizard, your server administrator will need to set up and configure the ODBC data source file on your server. Setup will vary depending on the ODBC driver that you use. To use the Database Connector Wizard, you'll need to know the name of the ODBC data source, a username and password required to log on to the data source (optional), and the name of a query results template that will be used to handle the data received from the query.

Refer to **Chapter 6** to learn how to install and configure the Microsoft Access 97 driver on your server.

Creating an IDC File

An Internet Database Connector (IDC) file works with any Open Database Connectivity (ODBC) compliant database. ODBC is a standard used to access different database systems. Structured Query Language (SQL) queries are used to communicate with any ODBC compliant database that is accessible from the Web server. Using these queries, you can extract information from the database. The connection information is specified in the IDC file. The IDC file includes the name of the data source, the name of the results file (`.htx` extension), SQL queries and additional instructions, and a username and password if one is required to log on to the database.

In Microsoft FrontPage 97, you use the Internet Database Connector Wizard to create an IDC file. The Database Connector Wizard automatically is displayed when you open an existing IDC file from the FrontPage Explorer or the FrontPage Editor. When you open an IDC file that was created from Microsoft Access, the items in the Database Connector Wizard are already entered for you, including the queries that you configured in Access 97. You can use the Database Connector Wizard to edit the IDC files after they appear in your Web.

The steps to create a new IDC file are as follows:

1. To create a new IDC file from the FrontPage Editor, choose **F**ile | **N**ew (Ctrl+N). Select Database Connector Wizard from the Template or Wizard field in the New Page dialog box and choose OK.
2. From the Template or Wizard field, select Database Connector Wizard.
3. Choose OK. The Database Connector Wizard opens.

NOTE: You can also start the Database Connector Wizard by clicking the Database Connector Wizard button on the Advanced toolbar.

Specifying Your ODBC Data Source

The first step in creating an IDC file is to identify your ODBC data source, results filename, and connection options in the screen shown in Figure 13.16. To complete the screen, follow these steps:

1. In the **O**DBC data source field, enter the data source to which you want to connect, as configured by the ODBC or Web system administrator.
2. If your database system requires a username and password for access, check the **U**sername box, and enter the name of the user. If a password is required, check the **P**assword field, and enter the password.

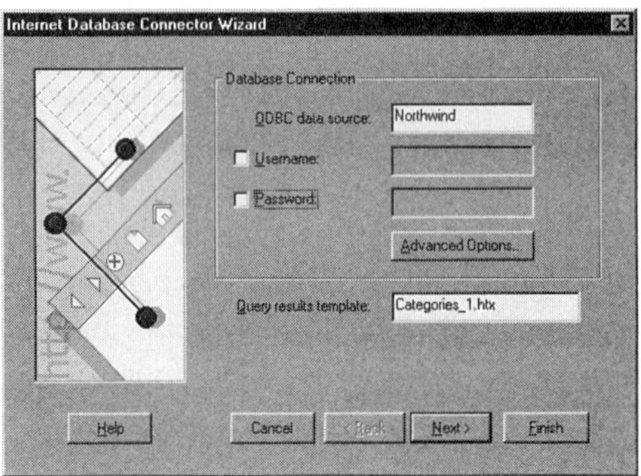

Figure 13.16.
In the first screen of the Internet Database Connector Wizard, you specify your ODBC data source, results filename, and connection options.

3. To set optional advanced options, click the **A**dvanced Options button. For more information, see the "Specifying Advanced Options" section.
4. In the **Q**uery results template field, enter the name of your `.htx` results file (`Category_1.htx`, as shown in the example), or click the B**r**owse button to locate the folder and file in your current web. The URL you enter here should be relative to the location of the IDC file. After you select your file from the Current Web dialog box, click OK to return to the Database Connector Wizard.
5. Click **N**ext to continue with the FrontPage Internet Database Connector Wizard.

Inserting SQL Queries

When you design your databases in Access 97, you enter queries that extract data from your database. These queries appear when you edit the IDC file in the Database Connector Wizard. You enter or edit your SQL queries in the screen shown in Figure 13.17. The query is entered into the data field provided in the dialog box. Where a database parameter name is required, insert the parameter name with the **I**nsert Parameter button.

To insert queries, follow these steps:

1. Enter the text for your query in the query field. Consult your ODBC driver documentation for additional information on the parameters that the ODBC driver can accept.
2. To insert a database parameter name into the query, click the **I**nsert Parameter button. The Insert Parameter dialog box shown in Figure 13.18 is displayed.
3. In the **F**orm field name field, enter the name of the form field that will be used to retrieve the information for the parameter.

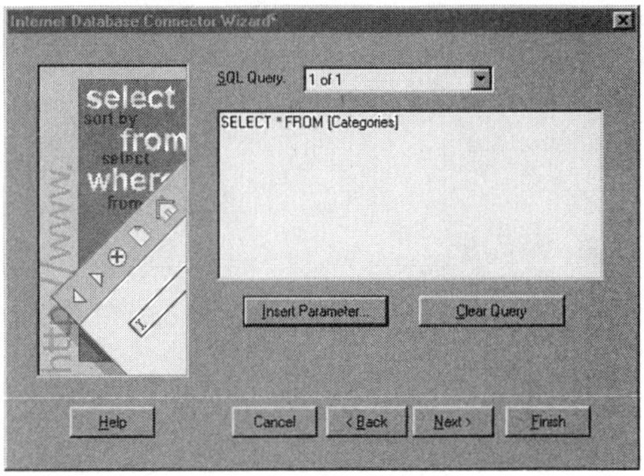

Figure 13.17.
Add query information in the second screen of the Internet Database Connector Wizard.

Figure 13.18.
Enter the parameter name and value in the Insert Parameter dialog box.

4. Choose OK. You return to the wizard screen, and the form field name is displayed in the SQL query list, surrounded by percentage signs.
5. Add additional parameters as necessary. If you click the Clear Query button, all queries are removed from the query list.
6. To add another query to the same IDC file, click the arrow on the **S**QL Query drop-down menu, and select Create Additional Query. Repeat steps 1–5 as necessary.
7. When your queries are complete, click **N**ext to continue.

Specifying Default Parameter Values

In the third screen of the Internet Database Connector Wizard, shown in Figure 13.19, you specify default parameter values. These are parameter values that will always be used whenever the SQL query is run. These parameters are combined with those entered by the user and passed to the form handler. If a user follows a link to the IDC file, only these parameters are used.

To specify default parameter values, follow these steps:

1. Click the **A**dd button. The Add Parameter dialog box is displayed.
2. In the **P**arameter name field, enter the name of the parameter.
3. In the **D**efault value field, enter the default value for the parameter.
4. Click OK to return to the wizard screen.
5. Add other default parameters as required.
6. Click **F**inish to generate the IDC parameter file.

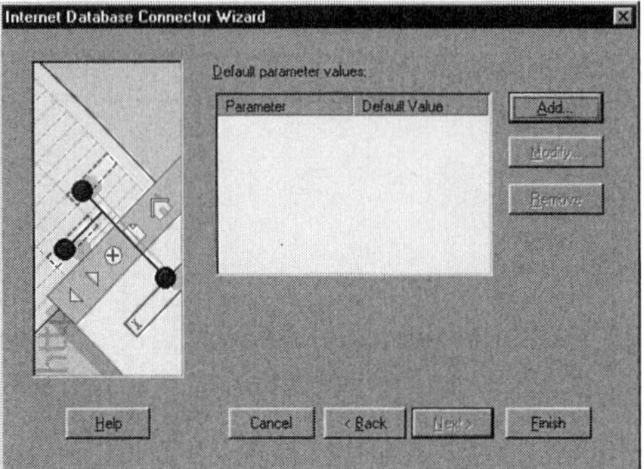

Figure 13.19.
Add default parameter values, if required, in the third screen of the Internet Database Connector Wizard.

NOTE: To modify a default parameter value, highlight the parameter you want to modify, and click the **M**odify button. The Modify Parameter dialog box is displayed. Edit the Parameter name or Default value and choose OK. You return to the Internet Database Connector Wizard.

To remove a default parameter value, highlight the default parameter name you want to remove, and click the **R**emove button. The parameter is removed from the list.

Saving Your HTX File

Before you exit the Internet Database Connector Wizard, the Current Web dialog box shown in Figure 13.20 is displayed. You are prompted to save your IDC file into the current web. You must save the page into a directory in which executable scripts can be stored.

NOTE: To determine if a folder can hold executable scripts, open the FrontPage Explorer. Select Folder View. Highlight a folder and choose **E**dit | Propert**i**es. If the Allow Scripts or Programs to be Run checkbox is selected, the directory can hold executable scripts.

Refer to **Chapter 6** to learn how to assign read and execute properties to Internet Information Server 2.0 and Microsoft Personal Web Server directories.

To save your HTX file, follow these steps:

1. In the Current Web dialog box, use the Look **i**n box to locate a directory in your current web that can contain executable files.

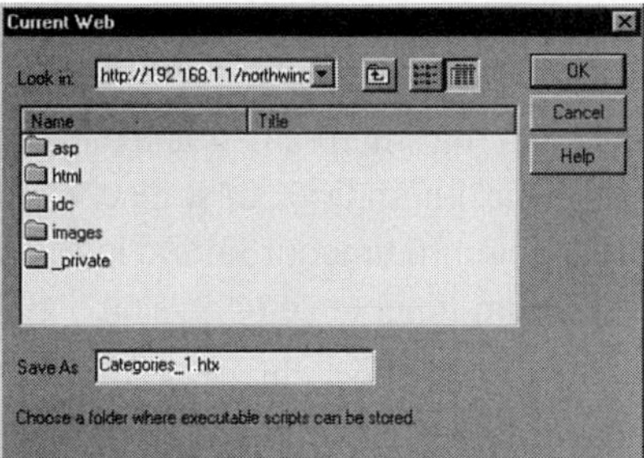

Figure 13.20. *Use the Current Web dialog box to save your Internet Database Connector File to a directory in your web that allows executable scripts to be run.*

2. In the Save As field, enter the name of the IDC file, or select a file from the current web. IDC files must have an `.idc` extension. If no extension is supplied, the Internet Database Connector Wizard adds one.
3. Click OK. The Database Connector Wizard closes, and you return to the FrontPage Editor.

Specifying Advanced Options

Advanced options in the Internet Database Connector Wizard require familiarity with ODBC system administration procedures. Consult your ODBC driver documentation for further recommendations on settings to be used here. You can access the Advanced Options settings from the first screen in the Database Connector Wizard by clicking the **A**dvanced Options button.

Specifying Query Options

Query options allow you to specify settings for SQL escape sequence scanning, cached results expiration times, query timeouts, transaction isolations, and content type. If your ODBC content also requires foreign character translations, you can specify the translation files here.

To specify advanced query options, select the Query tab in the Advanced Options dialog box, shown in Figure 13.21. Check one or more of the following options, and enter values in the respective data entry fields:

> ***D**o not scan for SQL escape sequences.* Select this option to prevent the ODBC driver from scanning SQL strings for escape clauses. The statements will be sent directly to the data source instead. If your SQL statement does not contain any ODBC escape clauses (enclosed by curly braces), you will see a small performance gain if you check this option.
>
> ***C**ached results expiration time (sec).* Enter the number of seconds to wait before refreshing a cached output page. Use this when you want to force another query of the database after a certain period of time. IDC only caches pages when this field is used.

Query Timeout (sec). Check this option to set the number of seconds to wait for an SQL statement to execute before the query is canceled. If the timeout value exceeds the maximum timeout setting in the data source, the driver substitutes the maximum timeout setting value. If the query timeout value is less than the minimum timeout setting in the data source, the driver substitutes the minimum timeout setting value.

Transaction isolation. Check this option to set the transaction isolation level. This setting allows you to retrieve data that has not been committed to the database by other transactions.

Content type. Check this option to specify the type of content that will be contained in the `POST` request. The default is `text/html`.

HTML Translation File. Check this option if your database is in a language other than English. A translation file maps each special character in the following format: *`value=string`*`<CR>`, where *`value`* is an international character, and *`string`* is the HTML translation code. Enter the full path to the file that maps non-English characters so that Web browsers can display them properly in HTML format.

ODBC Translation DLL. Check this option to enter the name of a DLL that contains the functions `SQLDriverToDataSource` and `SQLDataSourceToDriver`. These functions are used to perform tasks such as character set translation.

ODBC Translation Option. Check this option to specify a value that controls translation functionality, specific to the translation DLL being used. Consult the documentation for the ODBC driver and translation DLL for details.

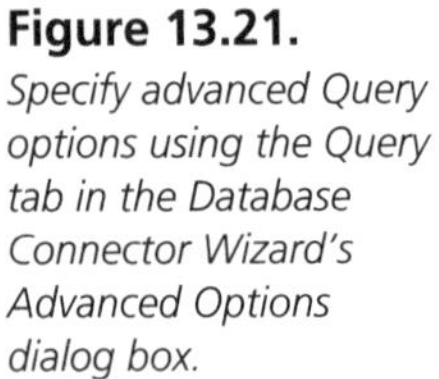

Figure 13.21.
Specify advanced Query options using the Query tab in the Database Connector Wizard's Advanced Options dialog box.

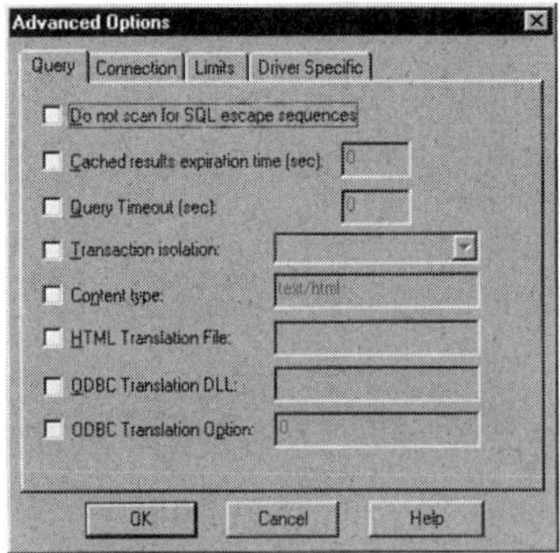

Specifying Connection Options

Connection options allow you to enable read-only access, specify a logging file of ODBC calls, turn ODBC connection pooling on or off, specify an SQL logon timeout value, and specify a network packet size.

To specify advanced connection options, select the Connection tab (shown in Figure 13.22) in the Database Connector Wizard's Advanced Options dialog box. Choose one or more of the following options, and enter values in their respective data entry fields:

Read-only access. Checking this option will prevent the IDC connection from changing the data in the data source that it connects to.

Enable logging of ODBC calls. Select this option to log each function call made by the ODBC driver. To use a logging file other than a default name of `sql.log`, enter a name in the **L**og File field.

ODBC connection pooling. Select this option and choose **O**n to keep the connection to the data source open in between data requests.

SQL logon timeout (sec). Check this option to specify the number of seconds to wait for a logon request before disconnecting, and enter a value in seconds in the timeout field. If you enter a value of zero, the timeout is disabled and waits indefinitely.

Network packet size (bytes). Check this option to specify the network packet size. This option is not supported by some data sources.

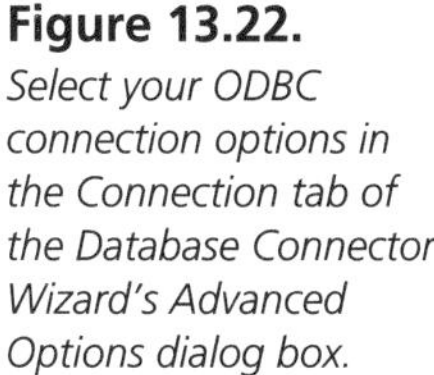

Figure 13.22.
Select your ODBC connection options in the Connection tab of the Database Connector Wizard's Advanced Options dialog box.

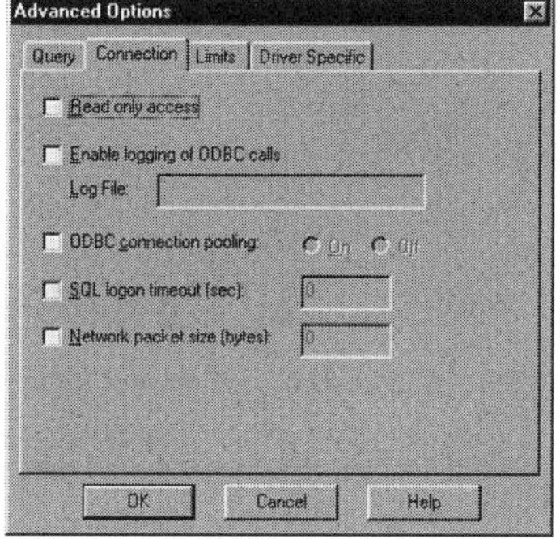

Specifying Limits Options

Use the Limits tab in the Advanced Options dialog box, shown in Figure 13.23, to specify advanced settings for ODBC driver limits and IDC limits.

To specify ODBC driver limits options, use the ODBC Driver Limits section in the Limits tab.

Maximum field length (bytes). Check this option to specify the maximum amount of data returned from a character or binary column. This should only be used when the data source in a multiple-tier driver can implement it.

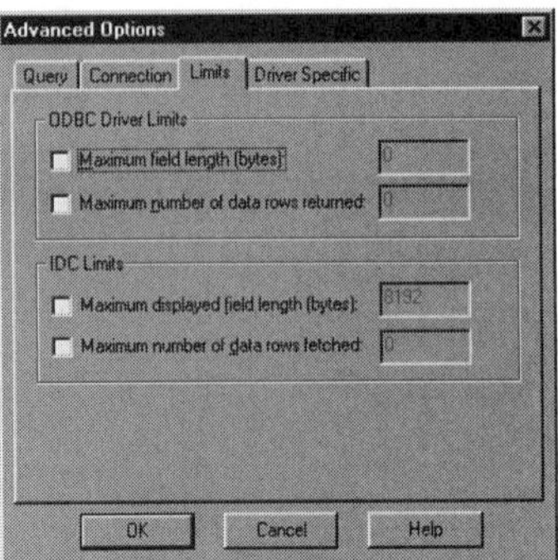

Figure 13.23.
Specify ODBC driver and IDC limits in the Limits tab of the Advanced Options dialog box.

*Maximum **n**umber of data rows returned.* Check this option to specify the maximum number of rows returned for a SELECT statement. All rows are returned by default.

Use the IDC Limits section in the Limits tab to specify the following Internet Database Connector options:

*Maximum displayed **f**ield length.* Check this option to specify the maximum buffer space allocated per field by the IDC file. Any characters beyond this space are truncated. The default value is 8,192 bytes.

*Maximum number of **d**ata rows fetched.* Check this option to limit the number of records returned from one query. No value is specified by default, so a query can return up to 4 billion records.

Specifying Driver-Specific Options

To specify driver-specific options, use the Driver Specific tab (shown in Figure 13.24) in the Advanced Options dialog box of the Database Connector Wizard. Refer to your ODBC driver documentation for descriptions of available options.

To specify driver-specific options, follow these steps:

1. Click the Add button. The Add Option dialog box is displayed.
2. Specify the option number and value, and click OK to return to the Driver Specific tab. The option and value is displayed in the ODBC driver-specific options field.
3. To modify an existing value, click the Modify button. The Modify Option dialog box is displayed. Specify a new option number or value, and click OK to return to the Driver Specific tab.
4. To remove an existing value, highlight an option and click Remove. The option is removed from the list.

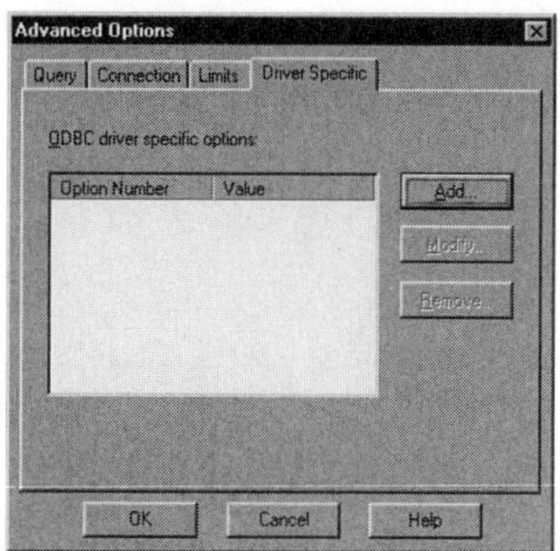

Figure 13.24.
Use the Driver Specific tab in the Advanced Options dialog box to specify driver-specific options.

Designing Web Forms for Dynamic HTX/IDC Databases

So far in this chapter, you have learned how to export an Access 97 database to HTX/IDC format and how to design HTX and IDC files from scratch. There is still one piece of the puzzle missing—how the user interfaces with these files.

In most cases, Access 97 exports its forms as tables. If queries contain search criteria that involve user input, Access 97 creates form fields in an HTML file. Here, the user can enter the search criteria and run the query. This is the case with the `Employee Sales by Country_1.html` page, exported from the Northwind database (shown in Figure 13.25). The page contains a form with two form fields in which the user inputs the beginning and ending dates. The form field names agree with those identified in the original database. After the user inputs the dates, he or she submits the form with the Run Query button, and all sales that occurred between those two dates are returned in the results file.

If you right-click within the form on the page, the Form Properties dialog box is displayed. As shown in Figure 13.26, the Form **H**andler field specifies Internet Database Connector as a form handler. When you click the Settings button, the Settings for Database Connector dialog box shown in Figure 13.27 is displayed. Use this dialog box to specify the name of the IDC file that contains the query for the form and the database connection information.

If you choose the Edit button from this dialog box, the Database Connector Wizard opens, and you can edit your IDC file. The second screen of the Database Connector Wizard displays the query originally generated in Access 97. It reads as follows:

```
SELECT DISTINCTROW Employees.Country, Employees.LastName, Employees.FirstName,
  Orders.ShippedDate, Orders.OrderID, [Order Subtotals].Subtotal AS SaleAmount
FROM Employees INNER JOIN (Orders INNER JOIN [Order Subtotals] ON
Orders.OrderID =
  [Order Subtotals].OrderID) ON Employees.EmployeeID = Orders.EmployeeID
WHERE (((Orders.ShippedDate) Between #%Beginning Date%# And #%Ending Date%#));
```

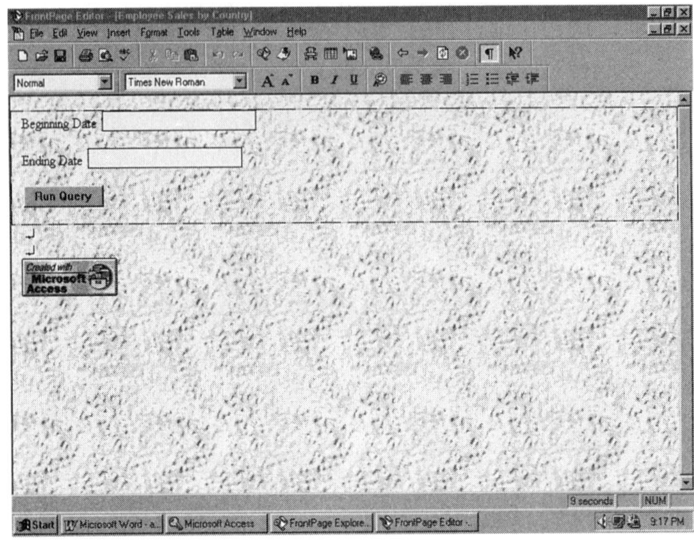

Figure 13.25.
The Employee Sales by Country page contains some form fields that query the database for sales between a starting and ending date.

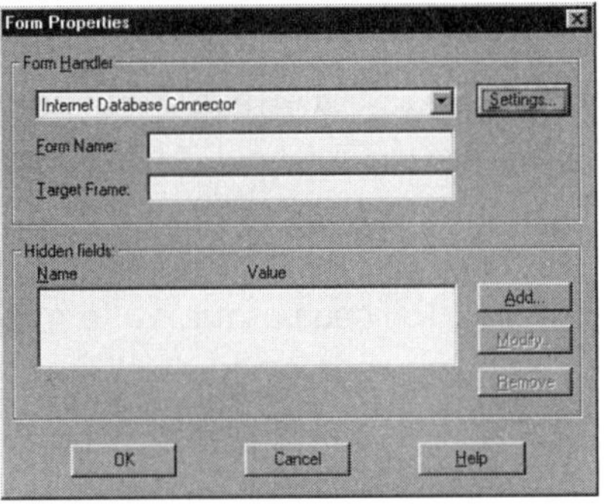

Figure 13.26.
From the Form Properties dialog box, choose the Internet Database Connector for a form handler.

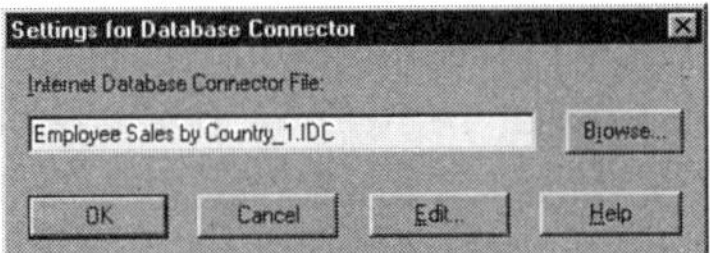

Figure 13.27.
Use the Settings for Database Connector dialog box to specify the IDC file that contains the query and database information.

The two fields that are present on the form (Beginning Date and Ending Date) are surrounded by pound signs and percentage signs in the query and appear in the last line of the code.

Workshop Wrap-Up

In this chapter you reviewed the elements used to create dynamic databases that communicate through IDC files. Using Access 97 and FrontPage 97 together, you can develop pages that query your databases through forms. You export your database objects from Access 97, which creates the IDC and results files (HTX) for you. The forms you create can use the Internet Database Connector files as a form handler and extract data from the databases through queries.

Next Steps

In the next chapter, you will learn about another way to dynamically interface with your databases. Using Active Server Pages on Internet Information Server 3.0 or the Microsoft Personal Web Server with Active Server extensions, you can create forms that query your databases through VBScript. You can use Internet Explorer 3.0 to browse these types of databases.

Unfortunately, the topic of designing databases goes far beyond the scope of this book. There are many resources available that can help in this regard. For additional help on creating and using Internet Database Connector files, refer to the following:

- Chapter 6, "Data Access on the Web," to learn how to configure your server to interface with the database.
- Appendix A, "Online Resources," for a list of online resources that discuss IDC files and Access 97.
- Appendix B, "Additional Books," for a list of other books that discuss Access 97 and Office 97.

Q&A

Q: I first published my database on one Web site or server, but I am changing my server location. Will FrontPage's Publish FrontPage Web command transfer the HTX/IDC pages from my original site without error, or should I republish my database from Access 97 to the new server?

A: In some cases, Access 97 generates absolute URLs when it saves files to Web formats. This is most noticeable in the VBScript it generates (which mainly applies to Active Server Pages, covered in Chapter 14, "Using Active Server Databases") but is not as common when you publish to HTX/IDC format. You can first try FrontPage's Publish FrontPage Web command to transfer your web to the new server and do a complete test of the transferred pages. If you assign the same Data Source Name on your new server (for example, Northwind IDC, as used in this chapter), the transfer should go fairly smoothly, providing there aren't many absolute URLs referencing your old site. You can use Access 97's File | Save As/Export command to republish the pages that no longer work.

Q: Are there any other ways to provide dynamic content on a Web site?

A: As you will learn in the next chapter, "Using Active Server Databases," you can also save your Access databases so that they work in conjunction with Active Server Pages. In addition, there are some exciting developments in store for Internet Explorer 4.0. Using new Dynamic HTML (DHTML) technology, you can build dynamic content right into your Web pages. Refer to Chapter 11, "Real-Life Examples: The Internet Explorer Advantage," for more information about this hot, upcoming technology.

CHAPTER

FOURTEEN

Using Active Server Databases

In this chapter, you

- ❑ Learn about dynamic ASPs and how to save your database forms to ASP format
- ❑ Learn how to publish one or more database objects to ASP format
- ❑ Compare how ActiveX Control Properties are configured in Access 97 and FrontPage 97
- ❑ Examine some of the HTML code and VBScript code that is generated with ASPs

Tasks in this chapter:

- ❑ Saving an Access 97 Form to ASP Format
- ❑ Publishing Your Access Database to ASP Format
- ❑ Adding ActiveX Controls
- ❑ Assigning ActiveX Control Properties

Of the three Web formats to which you can export Access 97 databases, the most advanced is to publish your database in the Active Server Pages (ASP) format. ASPs work through the ActiveX server, a component found in Microsoft Internet Information Server 3.0 or higher. Though the server and browser requirements are more stringent, ASPs allow you to integrate with your database in much the same way you do from within Access 97 itself. Your Access 97 forms are exported to ASP pages that contain form fields and VBScript that connect to an ODBC data source through ActiveX controls and VBScript. You can truly customize your online database using this method of Web publication.

Designing Databases for ASP Output

Although this chapter focuses on generating Active Server Pages with Access 97, you can also use Visual FoxPro, SQL, and other ODBC-compliant databases, providing that the correct ODBC drivers are installed on your server. The FrontPage Editor is also included with Microsoft Visual Interdev, a Web development product geared more toward working with Active Server Pages and advanced Web technologies. If you plan to work with databases and Active Server Pages, this product is highly recommended, as Visual Interdev can do even more than Access 97 and FrontPage 97 do.

Before you begin designing databases and ASPs, you must install the proper server and configure your data source name. ASPs run on the operating systems and servers listed in Table 14.1 can be browsed with Internet Explorer 3.0 or higher. (Refer to Chapter 6, "Data Access on the Web," to learn how to configure the server for use with ASPs.)

Table 14.1. Operating systems and servers compatible with ASP files.

Operating System	*Server/Add-Ons*
Windows NT Server 4.0	Internet Information Server 2.0 or higher, using Active Server Pages Extensions; or Internet Information Server 3.0
Windows NT Workstation 4.0	Microsoft Personal Web Server with Active Server Pages
Windows 95	Microsoft Personal Web Server with Active Server Pages

If you want to design your database for use with ASPs, you will find it necessary to study the sections that pertain to ActiveX controls, queries, and custom macros and scripts. ASPs use these features to a great extent, to interface between your database and your Web pages. The subject of Access 97 database programming is quite involved and beyond the scope of this book. Added to that is the challenge of learning about the ActiveX controls you can use in your pages and the VBScript used to process the data.

Fortunately, free help is readily available. I've always found it helpful to study working examples to learn how things fit together, and you'll do a bit of that in this chapter. The sample databases furnished with Microsoft Office 97 Professional and Microsoft Access 97 contain many pages that utilize ASP features. In addition, excellent ASP documentation and help furnished with Internet Information Server 3.0 exist. These files will serve you well to get you started. You can also refer to the additional references listed in Appendix A, "Online Resources."

Dynamic ASP Format

When you choose to export or publish a Microsoft Access database object to ASP format, Access 97 generates ASP files instead of HTM files. These files contain HTML tags and one or more SQL queries, along with VBScript code that processes the form fields on the pages. ODBC connection information in the ASP file includes the data source name and a username and password if security is required. This is another option that you can choose for your Access datasheets and forms.

Saving an Access 97 Form to ASP Format

Refer to **Chapter 6** for instructions on how to install the Northwind database. It is furnished on your Office 97 Professional or Access 97 CD-ROM.

If your database contains forms, you can export them to ASPs. View forms display records in the database. Switchboard forms act as a home page to your database or navigate to related pages. Data entry forms allow users to dynamically add, update, and delete records from the database.

To save your database forms to ASP format, follow these steps:

1. Open the Northwind database. From the Database window shown in Figure 14.1, select the form you want to export.

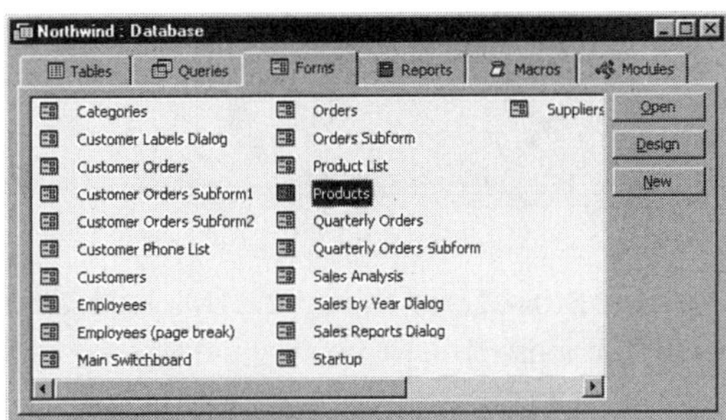

Figure 14.1.
Select the form or other database object that you want to export from the Database window.

2. Choose **F**ile | Save **A**s/Export. The Save As dialog box is displayed.
3. Select To an **E**xternal File or Database and choose OK. The Save *database item* As dialog box shown in Figure 14.2 is displayed.

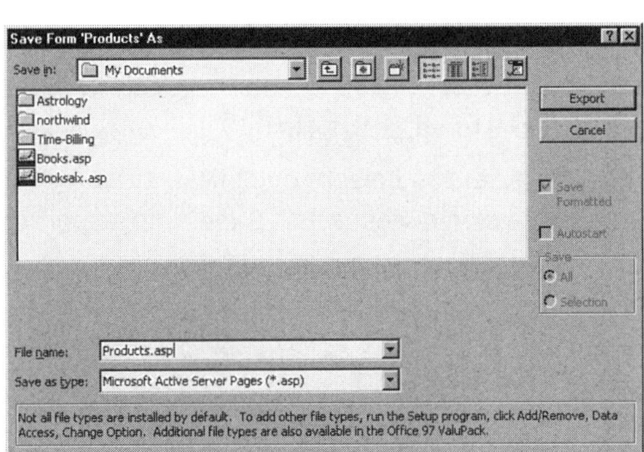

Figure 14.2.
Use the Save As dialog box to choose the drive and directory to which you want to save your database form or other object.

4. Use the Save **i**n box to locate the drive and directory to which you want to save the file or files.
5. From the Save as **t**ype drop-down menu, select Microsoft ActiveX Server Pages (`*.asp`).
6. In the File **n**ame field, enter the name to which you want to save the page, such as `products.asp`. You do not need to enter the extension.
7. Click Export. The Microsoft Active Server Pages Output Options dialog box shown in Figure 14.3 is displayed.

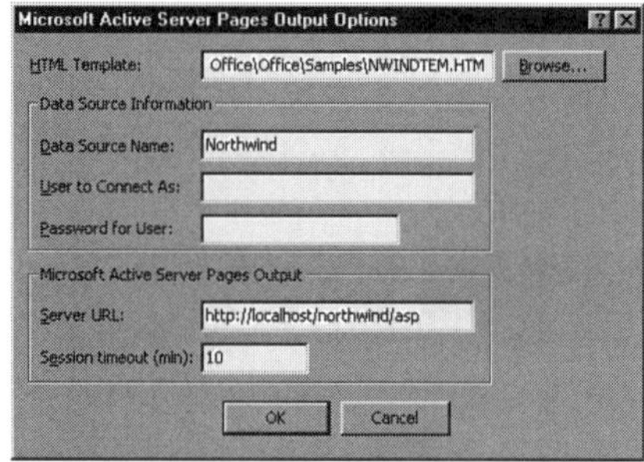

Figure 14.3.
Use the Microsoft Active Server Pages Output Options dialog box to specify your data source name and server connections.

8. Use the **B**rowse button in the HTML template area to select a template for your database. The Northwind database uses the template installed as `\Program Files\Microsoft Office\Office\Samples\Nwindtem.htm` by default.
9. Use the **D**ata Source Name field to specify the machine or file data source name that you will use on the WWW server (for example, `Northwind`). It must agree with the data source name that is configured on your server.

Refer to **Chapter 6** to learn how to configure the data source name on your server.

10. In the **U**ser to Connect As field, enter the username that is used to log on to the server, if required. Enter the password in the **P**assword for User field.
11. In the **S**erver URL field, enter the path to the server on which the ASP files will be stored, such as `http://`*`servername`*`/`*`webname`*`/`*`foldername`*`/`.
12. In the S**e**ssion timeout (min) field, enter the number of minutes after which the session disconnects if there is no response from the user.
13. Choose OK. The file is saved to the location you specify.

Publishing Your Access Database to ASP Format

To publish your database to HTX/IDC format using the Publish to the Web Wizard, follow these steps:

1. Open the Northwind database. Choose **F**ile | Save as **H**TML. The first screen of the Publish to the Web Wizard is displayed, as shown in Figure 14.4.

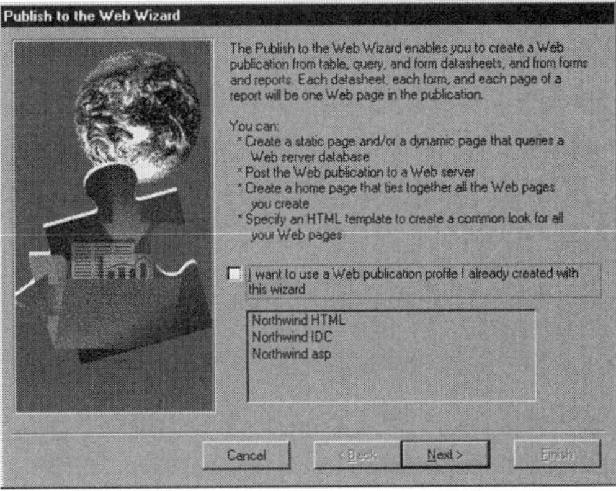

Figure 14.4.
The Publish to the Web Wizard allows you to save all or part of your database to ASP format.

2. If you have previously created a Web publication profile that you want to reuse, select **I** want to use a Web publication profile I already created with this wizard. Highlight the profile from the list beneath the prompt.
3. Click **N**ext. From the screen shown in Figure 14.5, select the items you want to publish. Select items from the Tables, Queries, Forms, or Reports tab and click the **S**elect or Select **A**ll button. To publish the entire database, choose the Select **A**ll button on the All Objects tab. To deselect an item, highlight the item you want to remove from the list and choose the De**s**elect button.

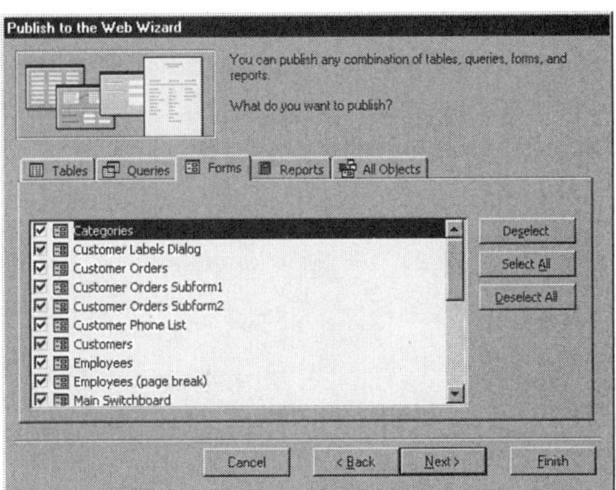

Figure 14.5.
Use this wizard screen to select the forms and other database objects that you want to save.

4. Click **N**ext. You are asked to specify an HTML document for a template. Click the **B**rowse button to open the Select an HTML Template dialog box. Use the Look in field to locate the `\Program Files\Microsoft Office\Office\Samples\Nwindtem.htm` template. Double-click the template

filename to assign it. You return to the wizard. Click **N**ext and proceed to step 6 if you do not want to choose additional templates as mentioned in step 5.

5. To select different templates for some items, check the **I** want to select different templates for some of the selected objects button. When you click **N**ext, the screen shown in Figure 14.6 is displayed. Select the objects you want to assign another template to. Shift-click to select contiguous items, or Ctrl-Click to select random multiple objects. Then, click the B**r**owse button to choose another template. After you select your templates, click **N**ext to continue.

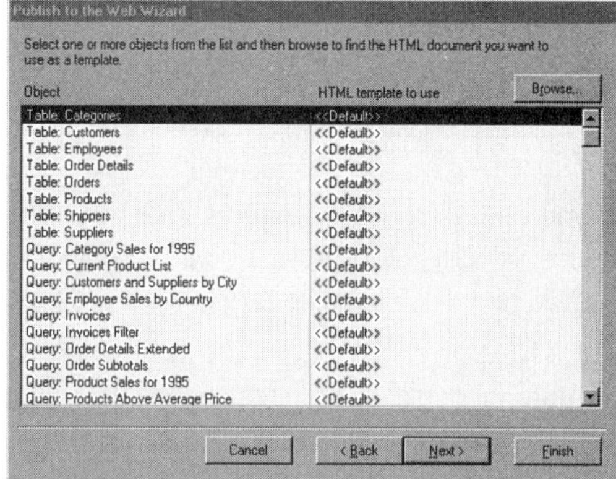

Figure 14.6.
Use this screen to choose pages to which you want to assign another template.

6. From the screen shown in Figure 14.7, you are asked to select a file format for your Web publication. Choose Dynamic ASP (Microsoft Active Server Pages). If you want to publish to multiple formats, select **I** want to select different format types for some of the selected objects and proceed to step 7; otherwise, proceed to step 8.

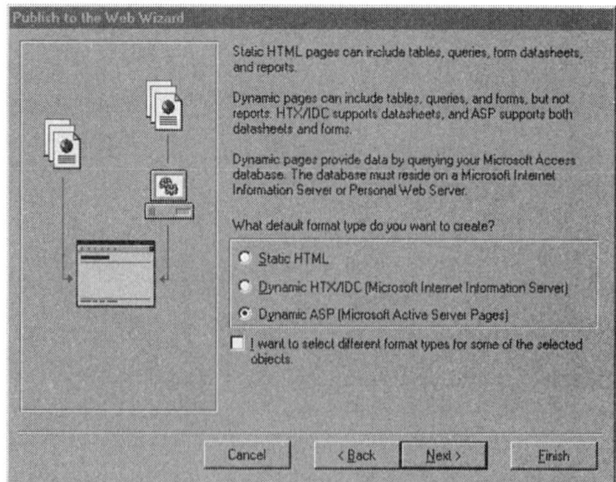

Figure 14.7.
Choose to publish your database objects as Dynamic ASP (Microsoft Active Server Pages) from this screen.

7. To select additional file formats, click **N**ext. A dialog box similar to that shown in Figure 14.6 is displayed. Highlight the items that you want to publish to another file format, and choose the **H**TML, HTX/ID**C**, or **A**SP radio button to specify the file format.

8. Click **N**ext. In the screen shown in Figure 14.8, you are asked what the settings are for your Internet database. In the Data Source Information area, enter or choose the following:

Data Source Name:	`Northwind ASP`
User Name (optional):	If your database requires a secure connection, enter your username in this field. Leave blank for this exercise.
Password (optional):	If your database requires a secure connection, enter your password in this field. Leave blank for this exercise.

In the Microsoft Active Server Pages Output Options area, enter or choose the following:

Server URL:	Enter the name of your server (such as `http://`*`servername`*`/`*`webname`*`/`*`folder`*`/`)
Session **T**imeout (min):	Enter the number of minutes after which a timeout should occur, or accept the default of `10`.

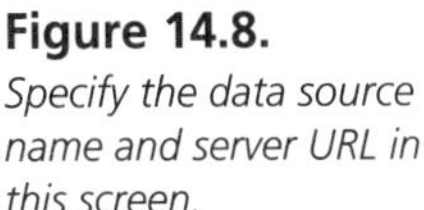

Figure 14.8.
Specify the data source name and server URL in this screen.

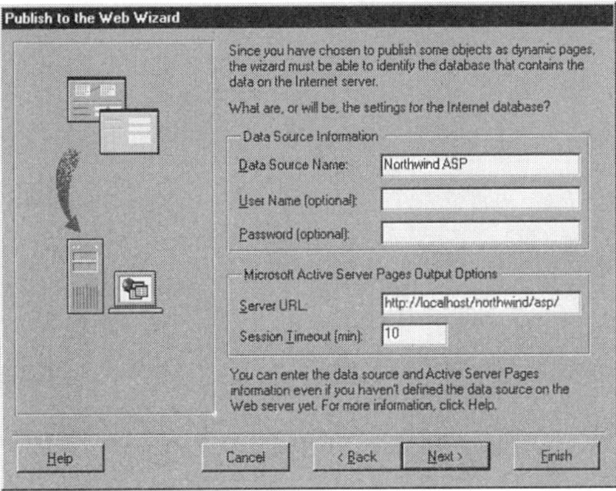

9. Click **N**ext. From the screen shown in Figure 14.9, you are asked if you also want to publish to an Internet Server using the Web Publishing Wizard. Select the first of the following options:

- Select *No, I only want to publish objects locally* if you do not want to connect to a server to publish your pages. If you publish your database in this manner, you can use the FrontPage Explorer's File | Import command or Import Web Wizard to import the database publication into your Web.
- Choose *Yes, I want to run the Web Publishing Wizard to set up a new Web publishing specification* to configure a "friendly name" for your server connection and publish the database to that server.
- Choose *Yes, I want to use an existing Web Publishing server whose "friendly name" has been set up previously* to publish your database to a server that already has a Web Publishing profile set up in the Publish to the Web Wizard. Select the profile you want to use from the list.

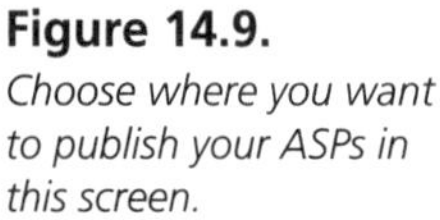

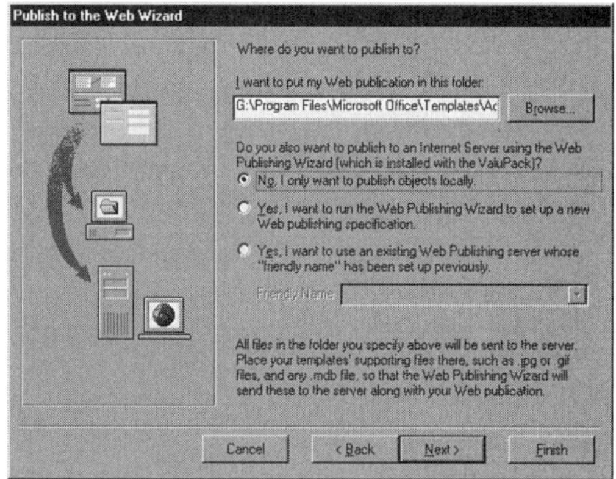

Figure 14.9.
Choose where you want to publish your ASPs in this screen.

10. Click **N**ext. From the screen shown in Figure 14.10, you are asked if you also want to create a home page that ties all your pages together. Choose **Y**es, I want to create a home page. In the What file name do you want for your home page? field, enter a name for your home page. The default is `Default`. You do not need to enter an extension.

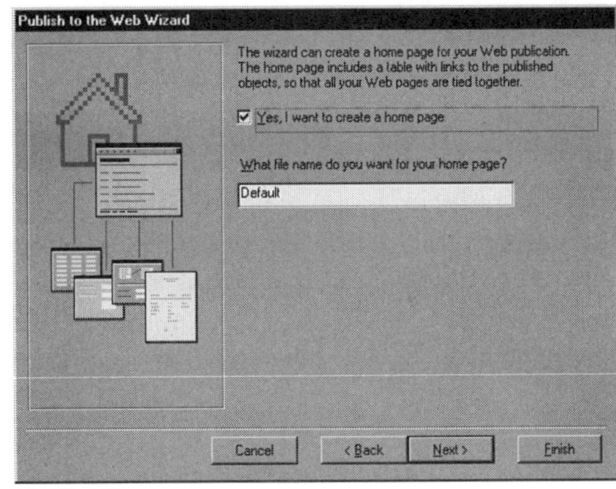

Figure 14.10.
If you want to create a home page for your publication, specify its name in this screen.

11. Click **N**ext. From the screen shown in Figure 14.11, you are asked if you want to save your selections to a Web publication profile. If so, choose **Y**es, I want to save wizard answers to a Web publication profile. Enter `Northwind ASP` in the **P**rofile Name field.

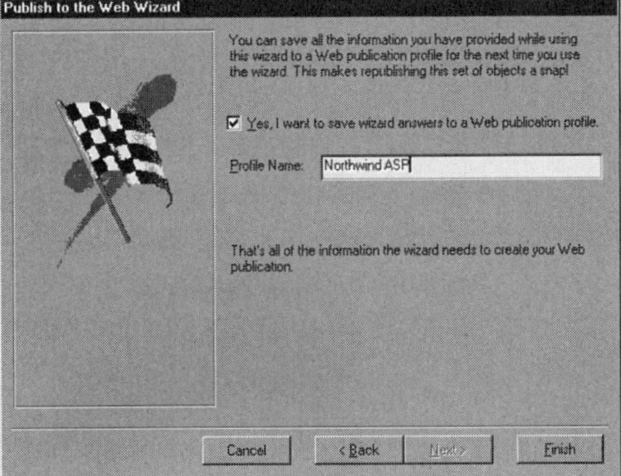

Figure 14.11.
You can save your settings to a Web publication profile to use at a later time.

12. Click **F**inish. Access 97 outputs the objects to ASP format. Reports are always saved in HTML format. During the export procedure, you are prompted for some values to use within the publication. When you are prompted for a starting date, enter `1/1/95`. Use `12/31/95` for an ending date. Also, when you are prompted for a starting record number, enter `1`.

After the Conversion

After you export your database to ASPs, you will find a number of files in the directory that use an `.asp` extension; in the case of forms, you will find two `.asp` pages. For example, when you export the sample Northwind database to ASPs, the Products form creates one page named `Products_2alx.asp`, which defines the layout of the form and sends queries to the server in the form of VBScripts. The other related page is named `Products_2.asp`, which processes the results file. These are your ASPs. The next few tasks compare the Products form as seen before and after its conversion to ASP format.

FrontPage 97 recognizes the `.asp` extension and opens it in the FrontPage Editor. However, some concerns and cautions are provided here to help you when you open existing Active Server Pages using the FrontPage Editor.

When you open an `.asp` file, you find HTML Markup Bots and VBScript icons that are displayed within the pages. The HTML Markup Bots contain HTML commands that are not directly supported by the FrontPage Editor and are represented by small yellow rectangles with question marks inside. If you double-click the HTML Markup Bot icon, you can enter code or edit existing code within it.

The FrontPage Editor may not always interpret the original code correctly before it inserts it into the HTML Markup Bot or Script icon, and may even rewrite it slightly. Thus, when you save your Active Server Page, it may no longer work correctly.

Before you save your imported Active Server Page, you can use the **V**iew | **H**TML command to compare the code as it appeared in the original file to the code as it was interpreted by the FrontPage Editor. Compare the areas within the Markup Bots and the Script icons to the related areas in the original HTML code.

When the View or Edit HTML dialog box appears:

- ❑ Select the "O**r**iginal" radio button at the bottom of the View or Edit HTML window to view the original HTML code.
- ❑ Select the "Curre**n**t" radio button to review the code as modified by the FrontPage Editor.

Adding ActiveX Controls

To add an ActiveX control to a form in Access 97, you must view the form in Design View. You add ActiveX controls through the toolbox, following these steps:

1. From the Database window, click the Forms tab, shown in Figure 14.12. Highlight the Products form, and click **D**esign (or click **N**ew to create a new form). The form opens in Design view, as shown in Figure 14.13.

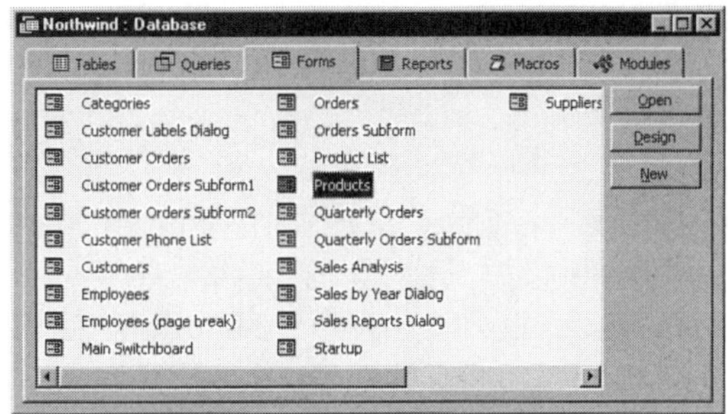

Figure 14.12.
Choose the Products form from the Northwind database window, and click Design.

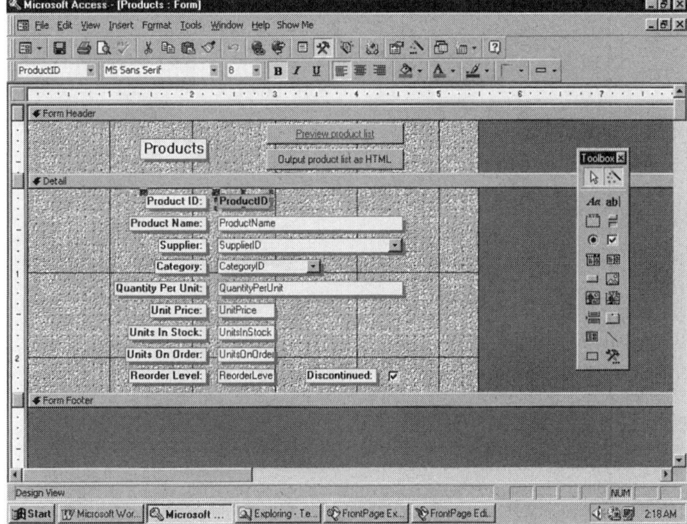

Figure 14.13.
Use Design view to add and edit form fields.

2. From the Toolbox, shown in the right side of Figure 14.13, select a control to add to your form. Choices are Label, Text Box, Option Group, Toggle Button, Combo Box, List Box, Command Button, Image, Unbound Object Frame, Bound Object Frame, Page Break, Tab Control, Subform/Subreport, Line, Rectangle, and More Controls (which allows you to select from other controls installed on your system).
3. Position your mouse in the form design window, and click at the upper-left corner of the area where you want the control to appear. Drag to the lower-right corner and release the mouse button.

4. Double-click the form field to assign the properties that apply to the form field.

NOTE: Depending on the control you add, one of two things displays on your page: the control or a control wizard. For example, when you insert a command button, the Command Button Wizard is displayed, and you can define the action that occurs when the user clicks the command button.

To add an ActiveX control to a form in FrontPage 97, you add the control to your Web page. Follow these steps:

1. From the FrontPage Editor, create or open a page on which you will design your form.
2. Choose **I**nsert | **O**ther Components | **A**ctiveX Control. The ActiveX Control Properties dialog box shown in Figure 14.14 is displayed.

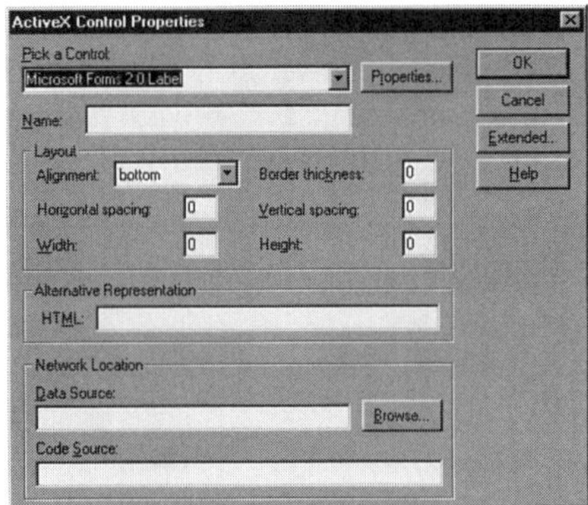

Figure 14.14.
Use the ActiveX Control Properties dialog box to select an ActiveX Control to insert into your Web page.

3. From the **P**ick a Control field, choose the control that you want to insert into your page. For example, select the Microsoft Forms 2.0 Label control.
4. Click the P**r**operties button to assign the form properties that apply to your form field.

Assigning ActiveX Control Properties

When you add an ActiveX control form field to your form in Access 97, the properties that apply to the form field are written in an ActiveX Layout page that is associated with the form. In the case of the Products form from the Northwind database, the form field properties are located in the `Products_2alx.asp` page.

To assign form field properties in Access 97, follow these steps:

1. From Form Design view, double-click the control to which you want to apply properties. For example, click the Supplier label in the form.
2. Click the Format tab, shown in Figure 14.15. You see several properties listed in this tab. For example, the Supplier label has properties that read as follows:

Caption	Supplier:
Visible	`Yes`
Display When	`Always`
Left	`1.5729"` (based on position in the form)
Top	`0.5833"` (based on position in the form)
Width	`0.6146"` (based on position in the form)
Height	`0.1979"` (based on position in the form)
BackStyle	`Normal`
Back Color	`13434879`
Special Effect	`Shadowed`
Border Style	`Solid`
Border Color	`8421504`
Border Width	`3pt`
Fore Color	`8388608`
Font Name	`MS Sans Serif`
Font Size	`8`
Font Weight	`Bold`
Font Italic	`No`
Font Underline	`No`
Text Align	`General`

3. Click the Other tab, shown in Figure 14.16. The Supplier label lists the following properties:

Name	`Supplier Label`
ControlTip Text	blank
Help Context ID	`0`
Shortcut Menu Bar	blank
Tag	blank

FrontPage 97 also lists ActiveX control properties in a table editor, but in some cases the names for the properties differ from those used in Access 97. Also, where the coordinates are listed in inches in Access 97, they are listed in points in the FrontPage Editor (one point being 1/72 of an inch).

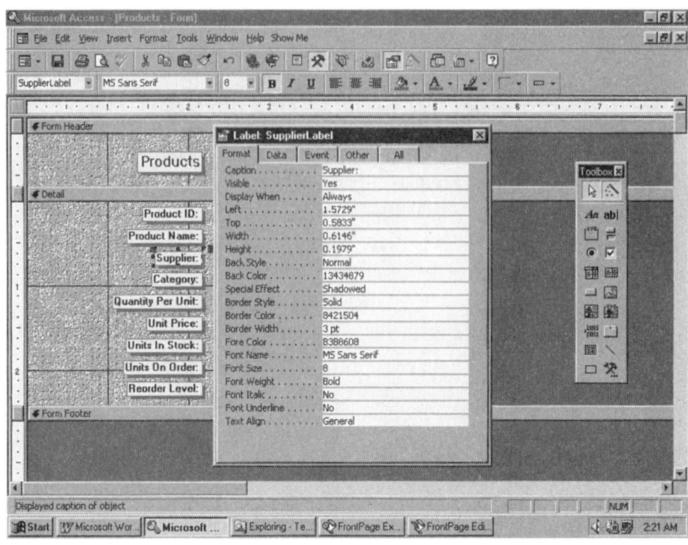

Figure 14.15.
The Format tab allows you to specify formatting for the Supplier label in the form.

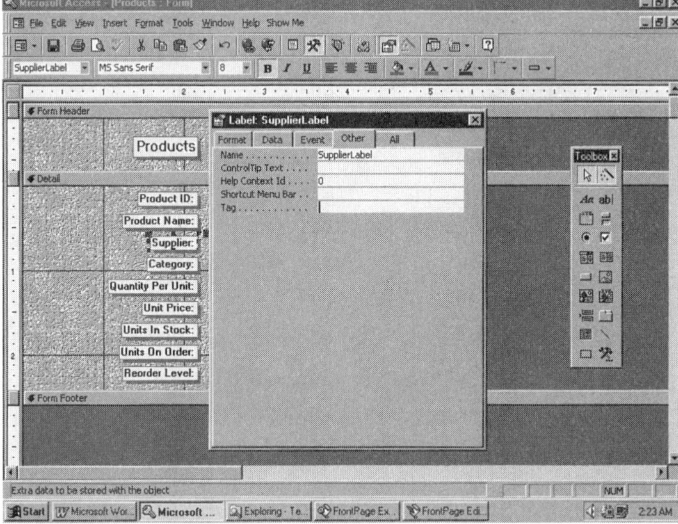

Figure 14.16.
The Other tab allows you to assign a name and other properties for the Supplier label.

To assign properties to an ActiveX control in FrontPage 97, follow these steps:

1. From the FrontPage Editor, open the ActiveX Layout page associated with your database form. In the case of the Products form from the Northwind database, open `Products_2alx.asp`. The page opens in the FrontPage Editor.
2. Double-click the Supplier label. The ActiveX Control Properties dialog box is displayed.

3. The following items are displayed in the ActiveX Control Properties dialog box, as shown in Figure 14.17:

Pick a Control:	`Microsoft Forms 2.0 Label`
Name:	`SupplierLabel`
Alignment:	`Baseline`
Width	`86`
Height	`23`

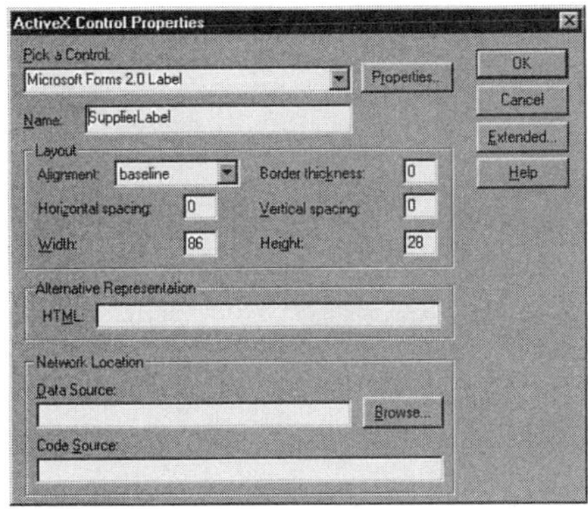

Figure 14.17.
Assign a control name, alignment, width, and height in the ActiveX Control Properties dialog box.

4. Click the **Pr**operties button. The Properties dialog box for the Supplier label is displayed, as shown in Figure 14.18. You will notice some differences in property names compared with those used in Access 97; there are additional properties listed here that do not appear in Access 97. The following properties appear for the Supplier label:

AutoSize	`0—False`
BackColor	`00ccff—Unknown`
BackStyle	`1—Opaque`
BorderColor	`00808080—Unknown`
BorderStyle	`1—Single`
Caption	`Supplier:`
Codebase	blank
Enabled	`-1—True`
Font	`8 pt MS Sans Serif, Bold`
ForeColor	`00800000—Unknown`
Height	`21`
ID	`SupplierLabel`
Left	`4.65`
MouseIcon	(none)
MousePointer	`0—Default`
Picture	(none)

PicturePosition	`7—Above Center`
SpecialEffect	`0—Flat`
TabIndex	`0`
TabStop	`0—False`
TextAlign	`1—Left`
Top	`4.65`
Visible	`-1—True`
Width	`66`
WordWrap	`-1—True`

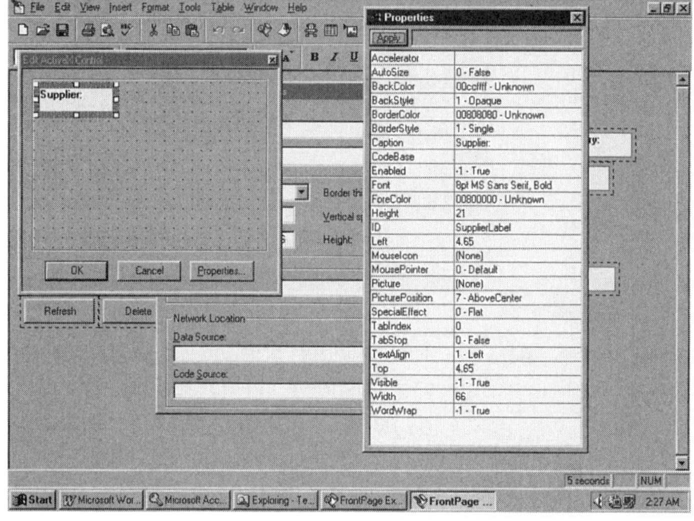

Figure 14.18.
The property names in FrontPage 97 differ slightly from those available in Access 97. In addition, more properties can be set here.

5. Choose OK from the layout window (the layout window that displays the control within it) to exit the Properties dialog box. You return to the ActiveX Control Properties dialog box.
6. Click the **E**xtended button. The Extended Attributes dialog box shown in Figure 14.19 is displayed.
7. To add a new attribute, click **N**ew. To review or change an existing attribute, click **M**odify. The Name/Value Pair dialog box shown in Figure 14.20 is displayed. The following values appear in the dialog box:

   Name: `style`

   Value: `TOP:175;LEFT:226;WIDTH:88;HEIGHT:28;ZINDEX:1;`

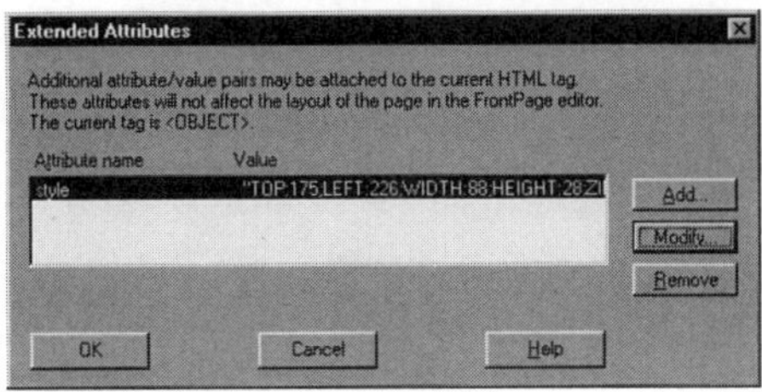

Figure 14.19.
Use the Extended Attributes dialog box to add other features required for the ActiveX control.

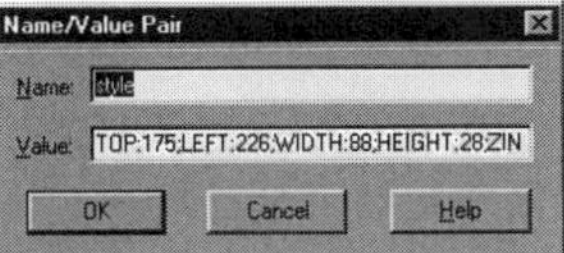

Figure 14.20.
Add or modify an extended attribute in the Name/Value Pair dialog box.

8. Choose OK to exit the Name/Value Pair, Extended Attributes, and ActiveX Control Properties dialog boxes. You return to the FrontPage Editor.

To view the HTML code that is generated for the ActiveX Control Properties dialog box, choose **V**iew | **H**TML from the FrontPage Editor. The View or Edit HTML window shown in Figure 14.21 is displayed. The HTML code for the Supplier label reads as follows (edited for clarity):

```
<object
  id="SupplierLabel"
  classid="CLSID:978C9E23-D4B0-11CE-BF2D-00AA003F40D0"
  align="baseline"
  border="0"
  width="86"
  height="28"
  style="TOP:175;LEFT:226;WIDTH:88;HEIGHT:28;ZINDEX:1;">
  <param name="BackStyle" value="1">
  <param name="BackColor" value="13434879">
  <param name="BorderStyle" value="1">
  <param name="BorderColor" value="8421504">
  <param name="Caption" value="Supplier:">
  <param name="ForeColor" value="8388608">
  <param name="FontHeight" value="160">
  <param name="FontWeight" value="700">
  <param name="Font" value="MS Sans Serif">
  <param name="FontName" value="MS Sans Serif">
  <param name="Size" value="2288;728">
  <param name="VariousPropertyBits" value="8388635">
  <param name="FontEffects" value="1">
</object>
```

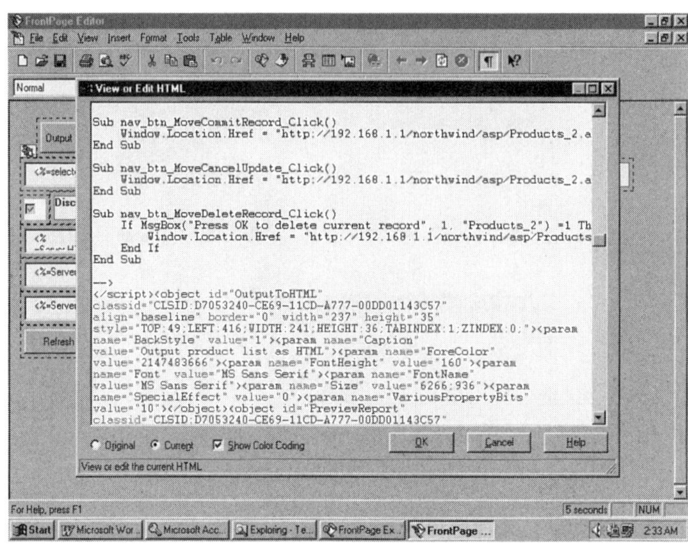

Figure 14.21.
You can view the code generated by Access 97 using the View or Edit HTML window.

Reviewing the VBScript

When you develop forms in Access 97, scripts are automatically generated in VBScript language and are based on the parameters you choose during your database design. The label control you examined in the previous tasks does not have a script associated with it, because it is just a text label that is displayed on the form.

The field associated with the Supplier label on the Northwind database Products form is the Supplier drop-down menu. Rather than show all the properties as they appear in Access 97 and FrontPage 97, I will just show the HTML code that is displayed for this control in the `Products_2alx.asp` page. The code reads as follows (edited for clarity):

```
<object id="SupplierID"
  classid="CLSID:8BD21D30-EC42-11CE-9E0D-00AA006002F3"
  align="baseline"
  border="0"
  width="322"
  height="28"
  style="TOP:175;LEFT:330;WIDTH:328;HEIGHT:28;TABINDEX:2;ZINDEX:0;">
  <param name="Value" value=" <%=selectedVarSupplierID%>">
  <param name="BackStyle" value="1">
  <param name="BackColor" value="13434879">
  <param name="BorderStyle" value="1">
  <param name="BorderColor" value="8421504">
  <param name="DisplayStyle" value="3">
  <param name="ForeColor" value="0">
  <param name="FontHeight" value="160">
  <param name="Font" value="MS Sans Serif">
  <param name="ShowDropButtonWhen" value="2">
```

```
  <param name="FontName" value="MS Sans Serif">
  <param name="Size" value="8528;728">
  <param name="MatchRequired" value="1">
  <param name="ListRows" value="8">
  <param name="BoundColumn" value="1">
  <param name="ColumnCount" value="2">
  <param name="Width" value="0;328;">
  <param name="cColumnInfo" value="2">
  <param name="TextColumn" value="2">
  <param name="VariousPropertyBits" value="746604571">
</object>
```

Of particular note in this code is the entry in the `Value` parameter (the first line of code preceded by the `<param name` tag). Notice that the value is surrounded with brackets and percentage signs and reads as follows:

```
<%=selectedVarSupplierID%>
```

This property value extracts the Supplier ID from the database and inserts it into the form field.

The `Products_2alx.asp` page also contains another section of code that pertains to the Supplier ID field:

```
Sub SupplierID_AfterUpdate()
    call AddCtrlToList("SupplierID", "SupplierID")
    call UpdateRefreshBtn()
End Sub
```

This code is automatically generated by Access 97 during the export process. Similar code is generated for each form field in your page that requires user input or inserts data from a table or query.

The `Products_2.asp` page (the page that returns the results from the form) includes the following code for the Supplier ID field in the form (again, the code is automatically generated when Access 97 exports the form):

```
If cstr(Request.QueryString("SupplierID")) <> "" Then
    rs.Fields("SupplierID").Value = Request.QueryString("SupplierID")
End If
```

Workshop Wrap-Up

By far, the most sophisticated way to interface with your Access 97 databases is to use ASPs. The forms you create in Access 97 appear almost exactly the same in your Web pages as they do in Access 97. You can add, edit, or delete items in the database from your Web pages using this method of publication. Keep in mind, however, that your Web pages should reside on a server that supports ASPs (Microsoft Internet Information Server 3.0 or the Microsoft Personal Web Server with Active Server Pages) and that Internet Explorer 3.0 or higher should be used to browse the Active Server Web.

Next Steps

In Chapter 16, "Real-Life Examples: Interacting with the Outside World," you'll tour an example of how Active Server Pages are used in conjunction with databases to design a Web site that updates its content dynamically. For further information about dynamic content, refer to the following chapters:

- In Chapter 6, "Data Access on the Web," you learn how to configure your server for use with dynamic HTML content.
- In Chapter 12, "Working with Forms," you learn other ways that you can develop forms in FrontPage 97.
- In Chapter 13, "Working with IDC Database Connection," you learn how to use IDC files in conjunction with your forms.

Q&A

Q: There is a lot of other VBScript code in the `Products_2.asp` and `Products_2alx.asp` pages besides that which defines the form fields on the page. Where did it all come from?

A: When you export a form from Access 97, a lot of the code that connects to the data source name and interfaces with the server is automatically generated for you by Access 97. This greatly simplifies the process of creating ASPs. A portion of the code is generated by values that you define in the Publish to the Web Wizard, and the rest of it is generated by queries that you define during the database design process.

Q: Can I generate a form with the Forms Wizard in FrontPage 97 and use that with ASPs?

A: The Forms Wizard uses standard HTML form fields, which are quite different and limited in comparison with the ActiveX control form fields. You'll find the easiest way to generate your forms is to develop them as you develop your database in Access 97—especially in light of the fact that Access 97 generates a sizable amount of VBScript code for you automatically!

CHAPTER FIFTEEN

Adding Discussions, Chats, and Newsgroups

In this chapter, you

- Learn how to create a discussion group with the Discussion Web Wizard
- Learn how to view the discussion group articles in your web
- Review the WebBot Discussion Component on the discussion group's Submission Form
- Learn how to create links to newsgroups on public and private servers
- Review commercial-grade alternatives for newsgroups and chats

Tasks in this chapter:

- Using the Discussion Web Wizard
- Starting the Discussion Web Wizard
- Choosing Your Pages
- Naming Your Discussion
- Selecting Article Headings
- Choosing Open or Registered Discussions
- Sorting the Articles
- Choosing Your Home Page
- Deciding What the Search Form Reports
- Choosing Your Page Colors
- Choosing Frame Options
- Completing the Discussion Web
- Viewing Your Discussion Group Articles
- Configuring the Submission Form
- Creating a Link to a Newsgroup

Though forms and databases provide ways that you can use your Web site to obtain data from your users, there will be times when your users need information from you. If you want your Web site to reach out to your visitors on a more personal level, you can add discussion groups, newsgroups, and chats to your Web site. Use discussion groups or newsgroups to answer questions about a product or service, provide technical support, field prospective customers, or just shoot the breeze on a casual level. Use real-time chats for urgent technical support, online training, corporate meetings, and such. This chapter shows some ways that you can provide two-way communication with your visitors.

Creating a Discussion Group

One way to add communications to your Web site is to create a discussion group. This is much like adding a Web-based bulletin board system to your Web site. Discussion articles, or posts, are stored on your site in individual HTML pages.

Using the Discussion Web Wizard

The Discussion Web Wizard allows you to create a discussion group in your web with a minimal amount of effort. These discussion groups post each article in consecutively numbered Web pages. The first article in the discussion is named `00000001.htm`, the second `00000002.htm`, and so on. The discussion groups utilize the WebBot Discussion Component, which requires that the FrontPage Server Extensions reside on your server.

The Discussion Web Wizard enables you to customize your discussion web before the pages are created. You can link a style sheet to your discussion pages, which enables you to use colors other than the standard World Wide Web gray, for example. You can also place the discussion articles in frames or create a discussion on a protected web.

To create a discussion web with the Discussion Web Wizard, follow these steps:

1. To add your discussion to an existing Web, choose **F**ile | **O**pen FrontPage Web, or use the Open Front Page Web button. Open the Web to which you want to add the discussion.
2. To add or create a discussion group using the Discussion Web Wizard, choose **F**ile | **N**ew | FrontPage **W**eb (Ctrl+N) or use the New FrontPage Web button on the toolbar. The New FrontPage Web dialog box shown in Figure 15.1 is displayed.

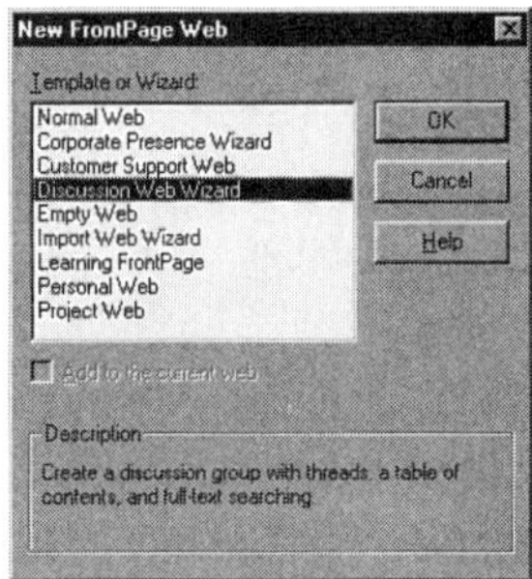

Figure 15.1.
Use the New FrontPage Web dialog box to create a discussion group with the Discussion Web Wizard.

3. In the **T**emplate or Wizard field, highlight Discussion Web Wizard.
4. Select the **A**dd to the current web check box if you want to add the discussion web to the web you currently have opened in the FrontPage Explorer.
5. Choose OK to continue. If you are creating a new web for the discussion, the Discussion Web Wizard dialog box shown in Figure 15.2 is displayed. If you are adding your discussion to an existing web, proceed to the "Starting the Discussion Web Wizard" section.

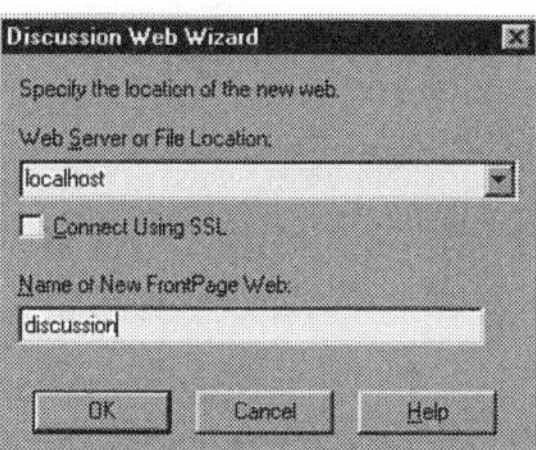

Figure 15.2.
Select your Web server and name your web in the Discussion Web Wizard dialog box.

6. From the Web **S**erver or File Location drop-down menu, select the server in which you want to create a new web, or enter the name of an existing server or directory on your local hard drive.
7. Select the **C**onnect Using SSL check box if you want to connect to a server that supports Secure Socket Layer (SSL) communications.
8. In the **N**ame of New FrontPage Web field, enter a name for the new web. Web names must use the character restrictions on your server. Typically, no spaces are allowed.
9. Choose OK or press Enter. Enter your administrator name and password, if prompted, using the name and password you entered in the FrontPage Server Administrator when you installed FrontPage. The first screen of the Discussion Web Wizard is displayed.

As you step through the Discussion Web Wizard, it guides you through the process of creating a discussion web. After you complete the initial steps outlined in the previous task, the Discussion Web Wizard's introductory screen is displayed.

Starting the Discussion Web Wizard

The introductory screen of the Discussion Web Wizard describes what the wizard will do. A progress bar is displayed beneath the picture on the left side of the dialog box, showing you how far along you are in the process.

You can use the navigation buttons at the bottom of each screen in the wizard to step through the wizard and review your selections at any time:

- Click the Cancel button to exit the wizard without creating the web. The FrontPage Explorer asks whether you want to remove the empty web that was created when you began the process.
- Click the **B**ack button to review or change choices that you made in previous steps.
- Click the **F**inish button to create the web with the pages you have selected so far.

Click **N**ext to continue setting up the discussion web.

Choosing Your Pages

The second screen of the Discussion Web Wizard asks what types of pages you want to include in the discussion web. From the screen shown in Figure 15.3, follow these steps:

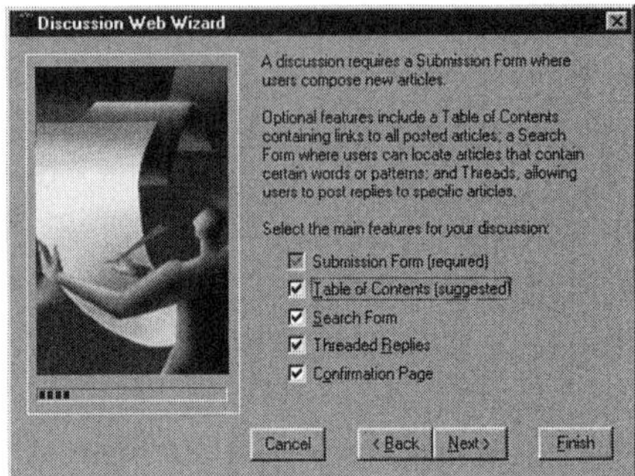

Figure 15.3.
Select the pages that you want to include in your discussion from this screen.

1. Check the pages you want to include in your web from the following options:
   - *Submission Form (required).* Users enter their articles into your discussion group with the submission form. This page is a required form and is automatically included when you create the discussion group. When the page is created, it is named `xxxxpost.htm`, where `xxxx` is a designation assigned to your files based on the name that you give to the discussion web.
   - ***T**able of Contents (suggested).* The Table of Contents page lists all the articles in the discussion group. As articles are submitted to the discussion group, the title of the article is automatically entered in the table of contents page. It is an optional page, but it is recommended that you include it in your discussion group. When the wizard creates the page, it is named `xxxxtoc.htm`.
   - ***S**earch Form.* If you choose to add a search page to your discussion group, the user can search through all the discussion group articles for a word or phrase. This option creates a page named `xxxxsrch.htm`.
   - *Threaded **R**eplies.* When you choose threaded replies, the discussion group articles are arranged by subject. All the replies to an article follow the original posting.
   - *C**o**nfirmation Page.* When you generate a confirmation page, users receive a confirmation message when they submit articles to the discussion. This file is named `xxxxcfrm.htm`.
2. Click **N**ext to continue to the next screen.

Naming Your Discussion

In the third screen of the Discussion Web Wizard, shown in Figure 15.4, you give the discussion a descriptive title. This title is displayed on all the pages in the discussion group.

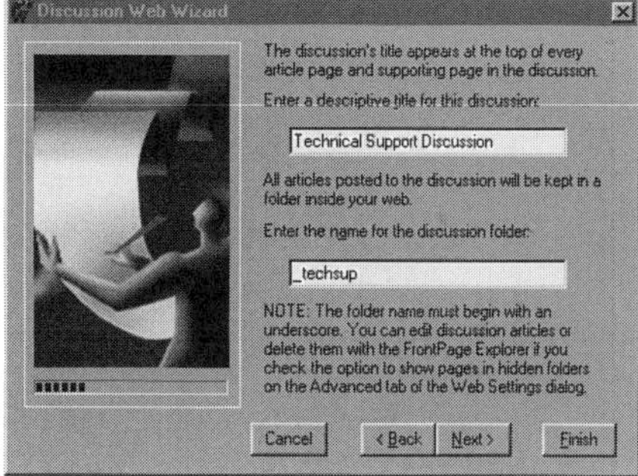

Figure 15.4.
Assign a name and folder name for your discussion in this screen.

To name your discussion, perform the following steps in the screen:

1. Enter a descriptive **t**itle for this discussion. For example, enter `Technical Support Discussion`.
2. Enter the n**a**me for the discussion folder. The name must be preceded by an underscore, as in `_techsup`.
3. Click **N**ext to continue to the next screen.

Selecting Article Headings

The fourth screen of the Discussion Web Wizard, shown in Figure 15.5, asks you to choose a set of input fields for the submission form. The input fields you select here are included as form fields on the page in which the user enters his or her article.

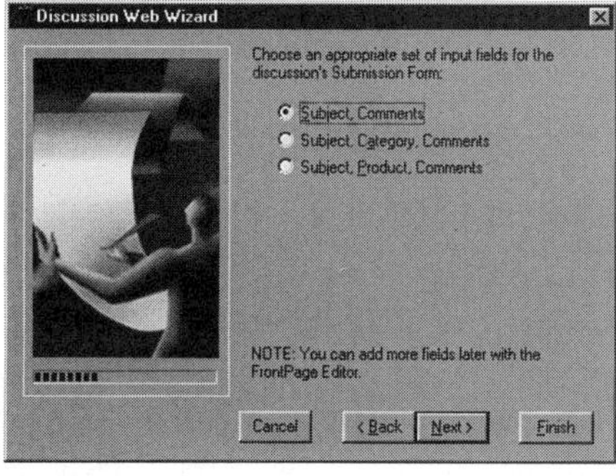

Figure 15.5.
Select the input fields you want to include in your submission form from this screen.

To choose the input fields you want to include on your submission form, follow these steps:

1. Choose from the following options:
   - *Subject, Comments.* If you choose this option, the user enters the subject of the article in a text box. The body of the article is entered into a scrolling text box.
   - *Subject, Category, Comments.* In addition to the subject and comments, the user chooses a category for the article from a drop-down menu.
   - *Subject, Product, Comments.* In addition to the subject and comments, a drop-down menu displays a list of products from which the user can choose as a topic of discussion.
2. Click **N**ext to continue to the next screen.

Choosing Open or Registered Discussions

The fifth screen of the Discussion Web Wizard, shown in Figure 15.6, asks whether the discussion will take place on a protected web.

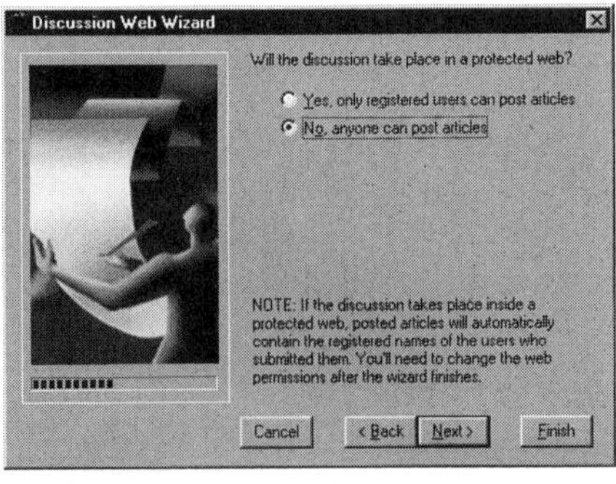

Figure 15.6.
In this screen, you choose whether you want a private or public discussion group.

Protected webs are closed to the general public and require a username and password to access them. If you choose to create a private discussion, the Discussion Web Wizard generates a user registration form that you place in the root web of the server. You learn how to create and save registration pages in **Chapter 12**.

Choose your response as follows:

1. Choose the type of Web you want to create from the following options:
   - ***Y**es, only registered users can post articles.* Choose this option if you want to create a protected web in which only registered users can post articles. A web self-registration form is displayed after the discussion web is generated in your current web. You then save this registration form into the root web of your server. A user must enter his or her

name and password into this registration form before gaining access to the protected web.

- *No, anyone can post articles.* This option creates a public web in which anyone can post articles.

2. Click **N**ext to continue to the next screen.

NOTE: You cannot mix protected areas and public areas in the same FrontPage web. If you want to create a protected discussion, you cannot include it in a site that is public. You must create a separate web for the private discussion. Refer to Chapter 12, "Working with Forms," for complete instructions.

Sorting the Articles

The sixth screen of the Discussion Web Wizard is shown in Figure 15.7.

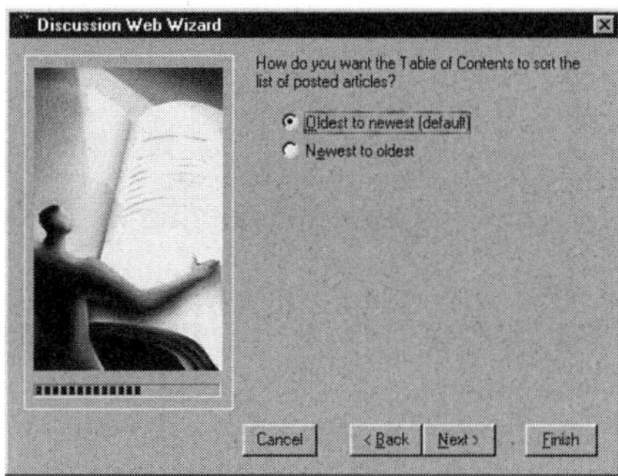

Figure 15.7.
This screen provides the choice to sort the discussion articles from oldest to newest, or newest to oldest.

This screen asks how the table of contents should sort the list of posted articles.

1. Choose a method of sorting for your articles:
   - ***O**ldest to newest (default).* Choose this option if you want to list the articles in chronological order.
   - *N**e**west to oldest.* Choose this option if you want the most recent postings to appear at the top of the table of contents.
2. Click **N**ext to continue to the next screen.

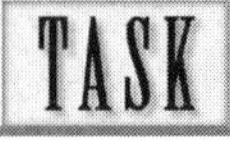

Choosing Your Home Page

The seventh screen of the Discussion Web Wizard, shown in Figure 15.8, asks whether you want the Table of Contents page for the discussion to be the home page of the Web.

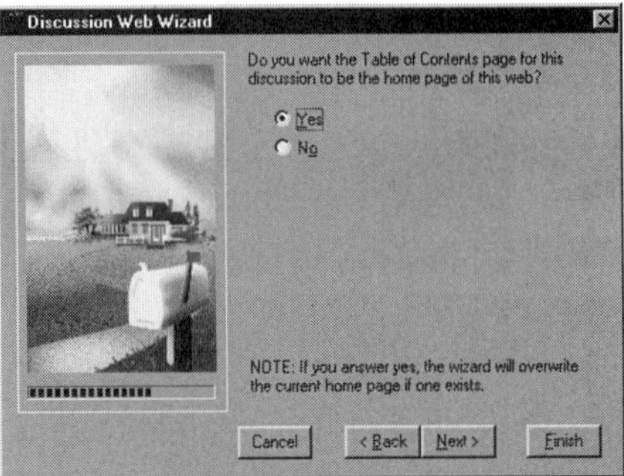

Figure 15.8.
This screen allows you to make the table of contents page the home page in your Web. Choose No if you have an existing home page.

1. Select one of the following options:
   - ❑ ***Y**es.* Choose this if you do not already have or intend to add any other home page in your web. If you choose this option, the Table of Contents page is named `index.htm` (or the filename you set as default for your Web server) and will be the home page in the Web. The wizard reminds you that if you choose Yes, any existing home page is overwritten.
   - ❑ *N**o**.* Choose this if you are adding this web to an existing web or if there is another home page in your web. The Table of Contents page is named `xxxxtoc.htm`.
2. Click **N**ext to continue to the next screen.

Deciding What the Search Form Reports

The eighth screen of the Discussion Web Wizard is shown in Figure 15.9. It asks what information the Search form should report if it finds pages that match the user's search requirements. To complete this screen, follow these steps:

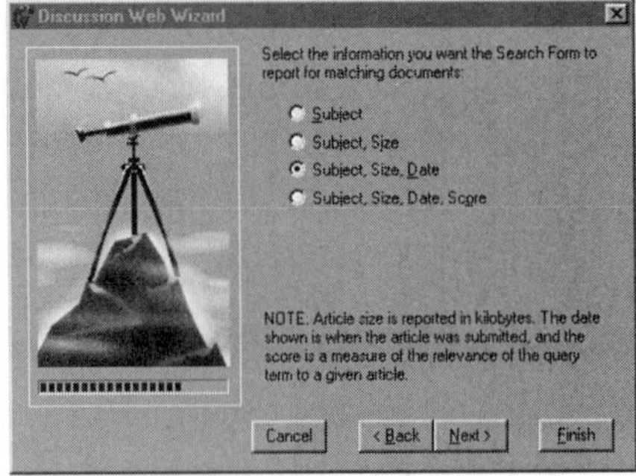

Figure 15.9.
Use this screen to select information to be reported when the Search page finds documents that match the user's search terms.

1. Choose one of the following reporting methods:
   - ❑ ***S**ubject.* The results report only the subject of the article.
   - ❑ *Subject, S**i**ze.* The results report the subject of the article and its size in kilobytes.
   - ❑ *Subject, Size, **D**ate.* The results report the subject of the article, its size in kilobytes, and the date the article was submitted.
   - ❑ *Subject, Size, Date, Sc**o**re.* In addition to the article's subject, size, and date of posting, the results report the degree of relevance to the term or terms used in the Search form.
2. Click **N**ext to continue to the next screen.

Choosing Your Page Colors

In the ninth screen of the Discussion Web Wizard, you choose the color scheme for your pages from the screen shown in Figure 15.10. Your selections are used to create a Web Colors page in your Web. Each of the pages in the discussion group uses the Web Colors page as a style sheet, creating a consistent appearance for all the pages in the discussion group.

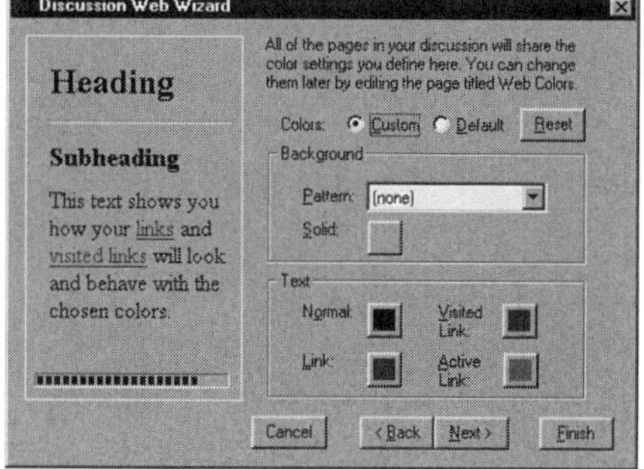

Figure 15.10.
Use this screen to create a style sheet for all the pages in the discussion.

To create your discussion group style sheet, proceed as follows:

1. To use the standard World Wide Web background and text and link colors, choose the **D**efault radio button. Click **N**ext to skip the remaining steps and return to the wizard.
2. To assign custom colors, choose the **C**ustom radio button.
3. To change the background texture, click the arrow in the **P**attern drop-down menu box. A list of several choices is displayed. A preview of the texture is displayed in the preview window as you highlight each selection.

4. If you want a solid background, choose None from the **P**attern drop-down menu. To change the background color, click the **S**olid color square. The Windows Color dialog box is displayed. After you select the background color, click OK to return to the wizard.
5. To change the N**o**rmal, **V**isited Link, **L**ink, and **A**ctive Link text colors, follow the same procedure that you did for choosing the background color. As you select your colors, they update in the preview screen. To view the active link color that you select, click and hold either link in the preview window. Release the mouse button when you are done.
6. Click **N**ext to continue to the next screen.

Choosing Frame Options

In the tenth screen of the Discussion Web Wizard, you choose the frame options for the discussion from one of four options in the screen shown in Figure 15.11.

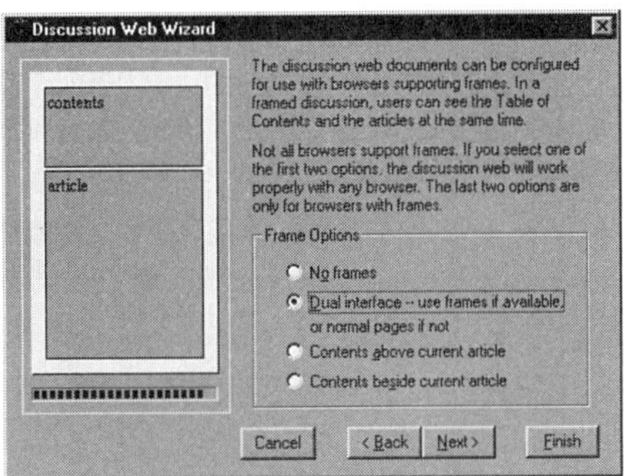

Figure 15.11.
Choose whether you would like your discussion group displayed in a frameset from this screen.

TIP: Keep in mind that older browsers do not support framesets. You may find that the default option **D**ual interface—use frames if available or normal pages if not is the best choice.

To choose a frameset option, perform the following steps:

1. Select a method of using frames from the following options:
   - ❑ ***N**o frames.* Choose this option if you do not want your discussion articles to be displayed in frames.
   - ❑ ***D**ual interface—use frames if available or normal pages if not.* This default choice is the best one to select if you want to take advantage of frames. Your articles are displayed in frames if the browser is frame compatible; alternate pages appear if the browser is not.

- *Contents **a**bove current article.* This option places the table of contents for the discussion above the articles. When the user selects an article from the table of contents, it is displayed in the frame below the contents. No alternate pages are generated with this option.
- *Contents be**s**ide current article.* This option places the table of contents for the discussion on the left side of the page. When the user selects an article from the table of contents, it is displayed in the right portion of the screen. No alternate pages are generated with this option.

2. Click **N**ext to continue to the next screen.

Completing the Discussion Web

The final screen of the Discussion Web Wizard notifies you that you have answered all the questions. This screen, shown in Figure 15.12, also tells you the titles of the main pages in your discussion.

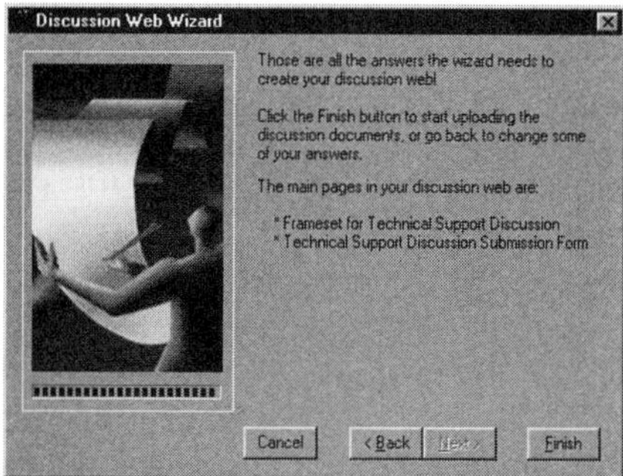

Figure 15.12.
The final screen in the Discussion Web Wizard tells you the titles of the main pages in your discussion.

Click the **F**inish button to create the web and upload the files that you selected when you stepped through the Discussion Web Wizard. If you installed FrontPage using the default settings, the files are copied from the `Program Files\Microsoft FrontPage\Webs\Vtidisc.wiz` directory on your hard drive. The discussion web is saved in the FrontPage Explorer.

Pages Generated by the Discussion Web Wizard

Table 15.1 lists all the pages that the Discussion Web Wizard places in the home directory in your web if you select a full-featured discussion. Figure 15.13 shows these pages listed in Folder view. In the examples shown in the table, the discussion group is named Technical Support Discussion, and its prefix is techsup. The home page in the discussion is named `index.htm`. The pages you choose in your discussion group will vary according to the options you select.

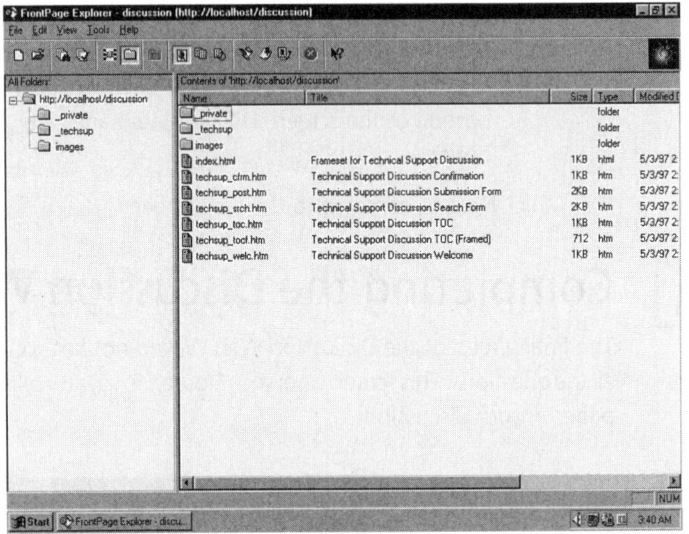

Figure 15.13. *The main pages in your discussion group are saved into the home directory in your web.*

Table 15.1. Discussion group pages in the home directory of your web.

URL	*Title and Comments*
`index.htm`	If you elected to make the table of contents the home page for your web, the home page is the Frameset for Technical Support Discussion. If you open this file, the Frames Wizard allows you to edit the settings for the frameset.
`techsup_frm.htm`	The name of the frameset if you elected not to make the table of contents the home page in your discussion group.
`techsup_cfrm.htm`	Technical Support Discussion Confirmation. This page displays after the user submits an article into the discussion group.
`techsup_post.htm`	Technical Support Discussion Submission Form. This is the form into which the user types his or her article. You can modify the settings of the WebBot Discussion Component if you view the properties of the form on this page.

URL	Title and Comments
`techsup_srch.htm`	Technical Support Discussion Search Form. This page contains a WebBot Search component, configured to search through all articles contained in the `_techsup` directory.
`techsup_toc.htm`	Technical Support Discussion TOC. This table of contents displays when the user does not have a frame-compatible browser. The table of contents is generated automatically as articles are submitted to the discussion.
`techsup_tocf. htm`	Technical Support Discussion TOC (Framed). This table of contents displays when the user has a frame-compatible browser. Like the previous page, the table of contents is generated automatically as articles are submitted to the discussion.
`techsup_welc.htm`	Technical Support Discussion Welcome. This page contains a welcome message that displays when the user enters the discussion group.

The Discussion Web Wizard also generates some pages that are placed into your web's `_private` directory, shown in Folder view in Figure 15.14. If you change any of the pages listed in Table 15.2, the changes are applied to many or all pages in the discussion group. Among the pages that are saved to the `_private` directory are headers and footers that appear on the main pages in your Web, and in all discussion group articles. In addition, the style sheet that you created in the Discussion Web Wizard is placed here. You can change the appearance of all pages in the discussion group if you modify this style sheet.

Table 15.2. Discussion group pages in the `_private` directory.

URL	Title and Comments
`techsup_aftr.htm`	Included Article Footer for Technical Support Discussion. This footer is displayed on all articles in the discussion group.
`techsup_ahdr.htm`	Included Article Header for Technical Support Discussion. This header is displayed on all articles in the discussion group.
`techsup_foot.htm`	Included Footer for Technical Support Discussion. This footer is displayed on all the main pages in the discussion group.

continues

Table 15.2. continued

URL	*Title and Comments*
`techsup_head.htm`	Included Header for Technical Support Discussion. This header is displayed on all the main pages in the discussion group.
`techsup_styl.htm`	Web Colors. This page is the style sheet on which all the pages in the discussion group are based. If you change the colors of this page, all the main pages and articles in the discussion group will change to use the new colors.

Finally, you will notice a directory in which the discussion group articles are placed. Based on the settings in the example, this folder is named `_techsup`. When you first create the discussion group, there are no contents in this folder. As articles are submitted to the discussion, they are saved as consecutively numbered Web pages (`00000001.htm`, `00000002.htm`, and so on) .

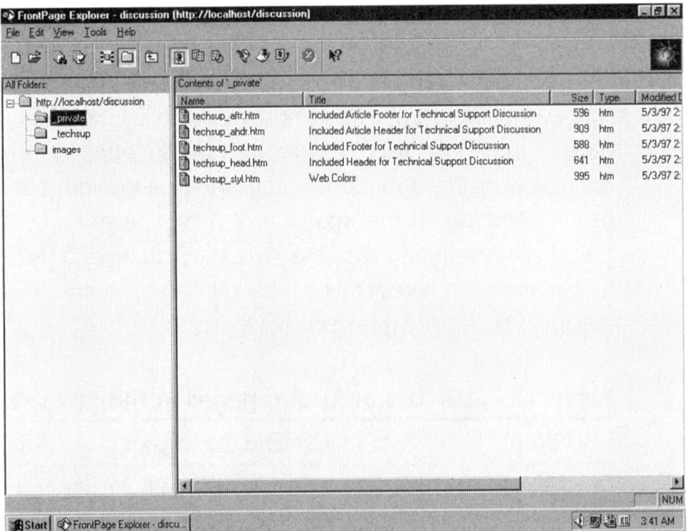

Figure 15.14.
The `_private` directory contains headers, footers, and the style sheet used for the discussion group.

Viewing Your Discussion Group Articles

There is one Web setting that you should apply to your web when you have a discussion group: If you want to use the FrontPage Explorer to view the contents of the discussion group article directory, you must configure the Web settings to show documents in hidden directories. To do this, follow these steps:

1. From the FrontPage Explorer, choose **T**ools | **W**eb Settings. The FrontPage Web Settings dialog box is displayed.
2. Click the Advanced tab, shown in Figure 15.15.
3. From the Options section, select the Show documents in **h**idden directories check box.
4. Click OK to exit the dialog box and apply the new settings to your web. FrontPage informs you that the changes will take effect after the web is refreshed from the server and asks if you want to refresh the web now. Choose **Y**es to refresh the web. You will now be able to view the contents of the discussion group directory from the FrontPage Explorer.

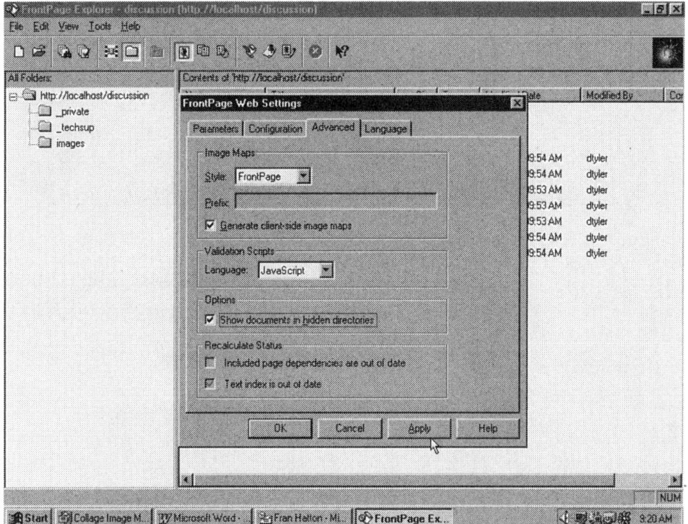

Figure 15.15.
Use the Advanced tab to configure FrontPage to display documents that reside in hidden directories in your web.

Configuring the Submission Form

The next thing to do after the Discussion Web Wizard generates your discussion group pages is customize the submission form. If you added a Category or Product field in your submission form, you must define them there. While you're at it, review what makes the discussion group tick: The WebBot Discussion Component also is displayed in this page.

To customize your submission form, follow these steps:

1. With the FrontPage Explorer open to the home directory in your web, double-click the Discussion Submission Form to open it in the FrontPage Editor. In the case of the example given in this chapter, the filename is

`techsup_post.htm`, and its title is Technical Support Discussion Submission Form. The page opens in the FrontPage Editor, as shown in Figure 15.16.

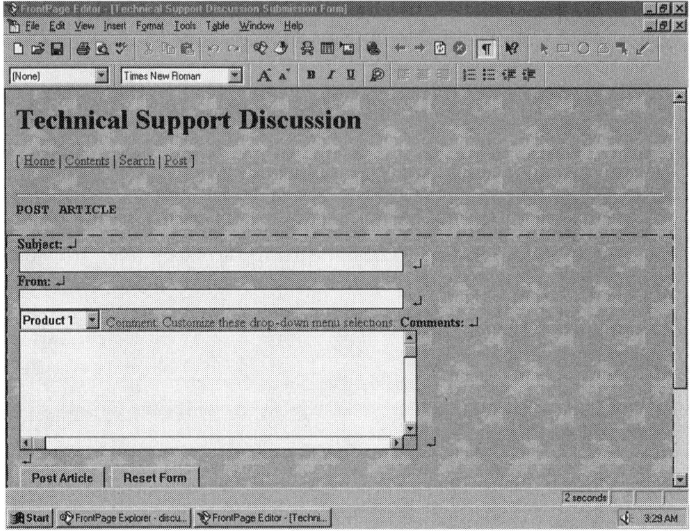

Figure 15.16.
The discussion submission form opens in the FrontPage Editor.

2. The Product drop-down menu is displayed beneath the Subject and From text boxes on the page. Click the drop-down menu and press Alt+Enter to open the Drop-Down Menu Properties dialog box shown in Figure 15.17.

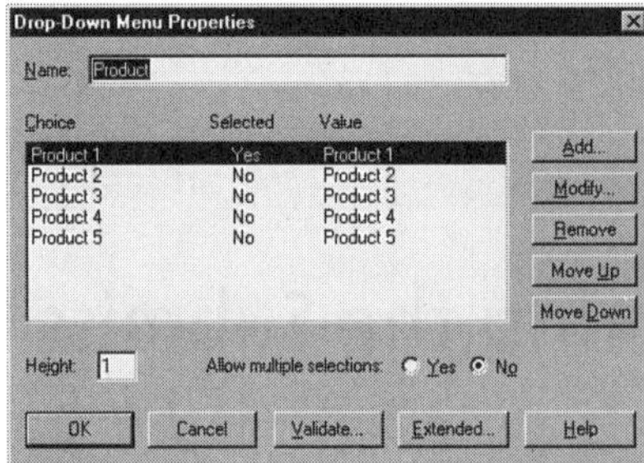

Figure 15.17.
Change the list of products that appear in the drop-down menu in the Drop-Down Menu Properties dialog box.

3. To modify a list item, click the **M**odify button. The Modify Choice dialog box is displayed.
4. In the **C**hoice field, enter a new product. For example, enter `XYZ-5000 P-133 Desktop`.
5. If you want to send a different value to the form handler, select the Specify **V**alue check box, and enter a different value in the field beneath the check

box. If you do not select this option, the value you entered in the Choice field is sent to the form handler.

6. From the Initial State section, choose **S**elected if you want the product to be the default selection in the list or **N**ot selected if you want another item to be selected in the list.
7. Choose OK to exit the Modify Choice dialog box. You return to the Drop-Down Menu Properties dialog box.
8. Continue modifying the drop-down menu list items in this manner. To add more items, click the **A**dd button. The procedure is similar to that described in steps 5–7.
9. In the **H**eight field, enter the number of lines that you want the drop-down menu to display. The default is one line.
10. If you want to allow the user to select more than one choice in the drop-down menu, select **Y**es in the Allow multiple selections area. Otherwise, leave this setting at the default of **N**o.
11. Choose OK to exit the Drop-Down Menu Properties dialog box. You return to the form in the FrontPage Editor. The drop-down menu displays the new list of items.

Now to learn what makes the discussion group tick: Behind each discussion group is a WebBot Discussion Component, which you configure through the Form Properties dialog box. To open the Form Properties dialog box, right-click anywhere in your form and choose Form Properties from the pop-up menu. You should see WebBot Discussion Component listed in the Form **H**andler field of the Form Properties dialog box, as shown in Figure 15.18.

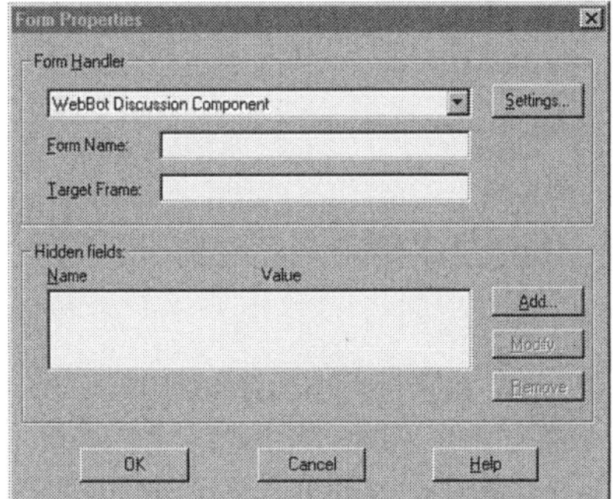

Figure 15.18.
The WebBot Discussion Component is configured through the Form Properties dialog box.

To review or edit the settings of the WebBot Discussion Component, follow these steps:

1. From the Form Properties dialog box, click the **S**ettings button. The Settings for Discussion Form Handler dialog box is displayed, opened to the Discussion tab shown in Figure 15.19.

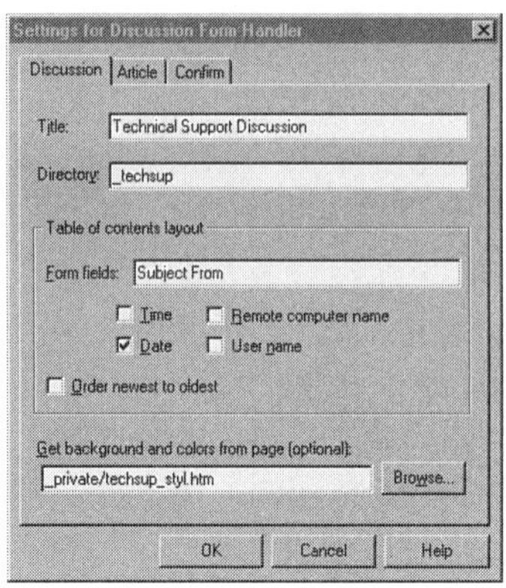

Figure 15.19.
Use the Discussion tab to configure the title and directories for your discussion group.

2. In the T**i**tle field, enter the title for the discussion group. This title is displayed on all articles in the discussion.
3. In the Director**y** field, enter the name of the directory in which the discussion group articles are saved. The directory name should be preceded by an underscore and should contain eight characters or fewer, including the underscore (for example, `_techsup`).
4. Use the Table of contents layout section to define the information that you want to appear in the table of contents page. The following settings apply:

Form fields:	Enter the names of the form fields on the submission form that you want to summarize in the table of contents.
Time:	Select this option if you want the table of contents to display the time that the article was submitted.
Date:	Select this option if you want the table of contents to display the date that the article was submitted.
Remote computer name:	Select this option if you want the table of contents to display the Internet address of the computer that submitted the article.
User **n**ame:	Select this option if you want the table of contents to display the name of the person that submitted the article.
Order newest to oldest:	Select this option if you want the table of contents to display the most recent articles at the top.

5. In the **G**et background and colors from page (optional) field, enter the path to the style sheet that will be used for all the pages in the discussion. You can also use the Bro**w**se button to select a page from your current web.
6. Click the Articles tab in the Settings for Discussion Form Handler dialog box. This tab, shown in Figure 15.20, is used to configure the articles in your discussion.

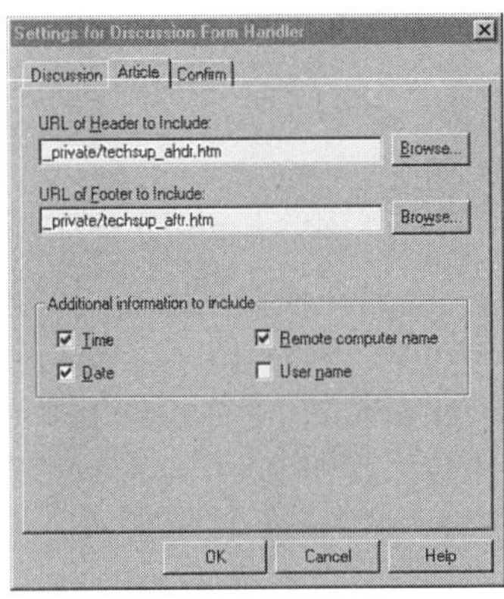

Figure 15.20.
Use the Articles tab to configure the settings for your discussion group articles.

To include these additional items in the Table of Contents, you must also configure the discussion group to include the items in the articles themselves. This is done in step 9, in the Articles tab of the Settings for Discussion Form Handler dialog box.

7. In the URL of **H**eader to Include field, enter the path to the page that contains the header information for the articles in your discussion. You can also use the **B**rowse button to select a page from your current web.
8. In the URL of **F**ooter to Include field, enter the path to the page that contains the footer information for the articles in your discussion. You can also use the Bro**w**se button to select a page from your current web.
9. From the Additional information to include section, choose additional information that you want to include in each article:

Time:	Select this option if you want article to display the time it was submitted.
Date:	Select this option if you want the article to display the date it was submitted.
Remote computer name:	Select this option if you want the article to display the Internet address of the user who submitted the article.
User **n**ame:	Select this option if you want the article to display the name of the person who submitted the article.

10. To configure the confirmation page for the article, click the Confirm tab in the Settings for Discussion Form Handler dialog box (see Figure 15.21).

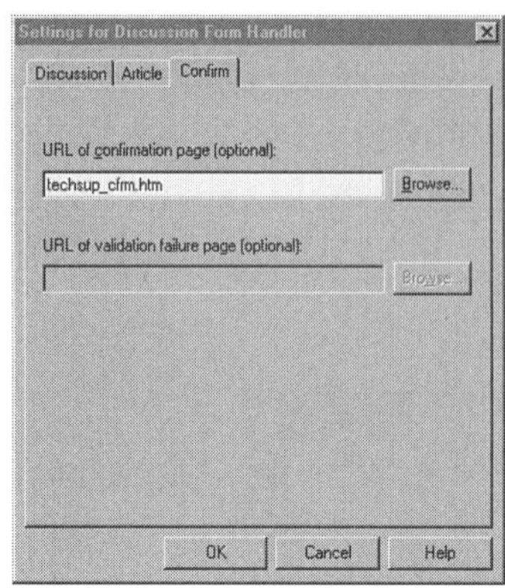

Figure 15.21.
Use the Confirm tab to configure confirmation pages that return to the user after he or she submits the article to your discussion.

Typically, headers and footers for the main pages and articles in your discussion are placed into the `_private` directory in your Web. When the Discussion Web Wizard creates the headers and footers, the filename for the main page header ends in `_head`; the main page footer's filename ends in `_foot`; the article header's filename ends in `_ahdr`; and the article footer's filename ends in `_aftr`.

11. In the URL of **c**onfirmation page (optional): field, enter the path to the page that you want to return to the user after he or she submits articles to the discussion. You can also use the **B**rowse button to locate the page in your current web. By default, this page is placed in the home directory of your web, and the filename ends in `_cfrm`.
12. In the URL of validation failure page (optional): field, enter the path to the page that you want to return to the user if any of the information he or she entered into the form does not meet validation requirements.

NOTE: By default, the Discussion Web Wizard does not validate form fields for you and does not create validation pages. You can validate the information that a user enters in a One-Line Text Box, Scrolling Text Box, Radio Button, or Drop-Down Menu. To validate the information in a form field, double-click the form field you want to validate to open its properties dialog box. Then click the **V**alidate button to open the associated Validation dialog box. Configure the rules that should apply when a user enters information in the form field.

Assume, for example, that you configure the Subject text box in the discussion group's Submission form to verify that a subject has been entered. If the user leaves this field blank, the Discussion WebBot returns the page specified in the URL of validation page field to the user, which informs him or her that a subject must be entered.

For additional information regarding form field validation, see *Laura Lemay's Web Workshop: FrontPage 97* (published by Sams.net).

13. Click OK to apply the new settings to your discussion group. You return to the Form Properties dialog box. Click OK to return to the FrontPage Editor.

Moving Up to a News Server

FrontPage discussions are suitable for personal Web sites and small commercial sites. If you anticipate heavy participation, you might want to consider the addition of a news server on your system. One such server is the Microsoft Internet News Server, which is part of the Microsoft Commercial Internet System. A trial version of this news server is available for download from Microsoft's Web site at `http://www.microsoft.com`. Figure 15.22 displays the home page that is installed to your system after you set up the Microsoft Internet News Server.

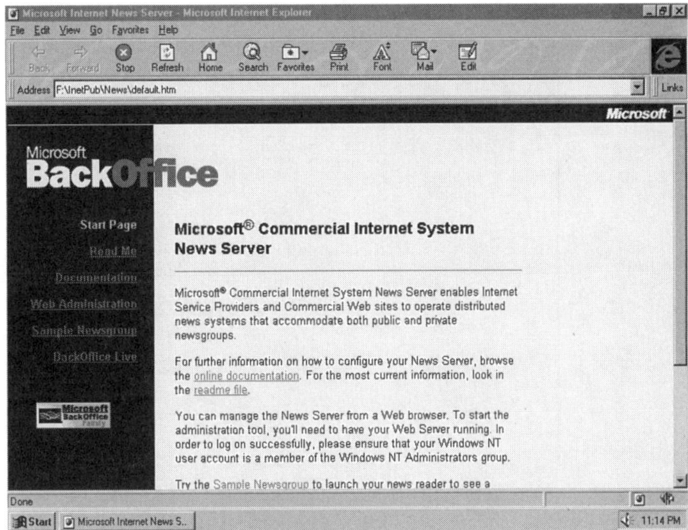

Figure 15.22.
The Microsoft Internet News Server is a commercial-grade news server available as part of the Microsoft Commercial Internet System.

The Microsoft Internet News Server is a commercial-grade NNTP server that allows both public and private newsgroups. It runs on Windows NT Server 4.0 running the Windows NT Service Pack 1 and Internet Information Server 2.0 or higher. It supports SSL communication, secure authentication with encrypted password protection, and logging. Administration can be performed remotely by Web-based administration pages or locally.

Newsgroup articles are read with any NNTP-compatible client, such as the Microsoft Internet Mail and News component furnished with Internet Explorer 3.01 or higher, or the Netscape news reader furnished with Netscape Navigator.

Creating a Link to a Newsgroup

Whether you are creating a link to a newsgroup on the Internet or on your own private news server, the process is relatively the same: You insert text, an image, or a hotspot on your Web page and select it. Then use the Create Hyperlink button in the FrontPage Editor to create the hyperlink, following these steps:

1. From the FrontPage Editor, select the text, image, or hotspot upon which the user will click to navigate to the newsgroup.
2. Choose the Create Hyperlink button on the Standard toolbar. The Create Hyperlink dialog box is displayed.
3. Click the World Wide Web tab, shown in Figure 15.23.

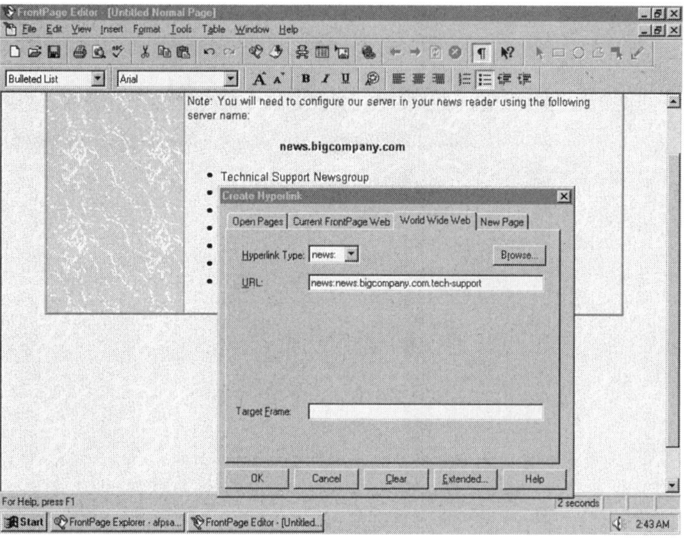

Figure 15.23.
To create a link to a newsgroup on the Internet or on your private news server, use the World Wide Web tab in the Create Hyperlink dialog box.

4. From the **H**yperlink Type field, select `news:`.
5. In URL field, enter the URL of your newsgroup, similar to the following:

```
news:news.bigcompany.com.tech-support
```

6. Choose OK or press Enter. You return to the FrontPage Editor, and the link is complete.

TIP: When you provide a link to a newsgroup on your private server, be sure to inform the users that they must configure your server in their news reader. Provide the appropriate information on the page on which the link is displayed.

Chatting in Real Time

One popular way to interface with people in real time is to get connected through chats. There are several ways that you can interface with people in this manner, some of which you can include right on your Web page. Web page–based chats come in several varieties, and their capabilities vary greatly. They are sometimes written in Java, other times as plug-ins or ActiveX controls. Capabilities and refresh times vary, so you will probably want to shop around on the Internet a bit before you decide which Web-based chat is best for your needs.

You can find lists of chats written in Java or ActiveX at Gamelan. The Java chat page can be found at the following URL:

```
http://www.gamelan.com/pages/Gamelan.net.chat.html
```

Microsoft Chat 2.0 is a chat client that runs as a stand-alone application or as an ActiveX Control. In the stand-alone application, you can participate in a chat in text mode or comic mode. Either application offers good performance and contains several features of interest. Each chat can be monitored by a host, and the chats allow private messaging between participants. You can find more information about this chat client on Microsoft's Web site. The Microsoft Chat 2.0 home page, shown in Figure 15.24, is located at the following URL:

```
http://www.microsoft.com/ie/comichat/default.htm
```

Figure 15.24.
The Microsoft Chat 2.0 home page describes the chat client and provides links for downloading and development information.

Figure 15.25 shows a sample of the ActiveX version of the Microsoft Chat. Insert this control on your Web page using the Insert|Other Components|ActiveX Control command in the FrontPage Editor. After you configure the ActiveX control properties, you use the Insert|Script command to write VBScript to handle the form. A working sample of this chat component, including the VBScript that you need to write, can be found at the following URL:

```
http://www.microsoft.com/ie/comichat/chatsample.htm
```

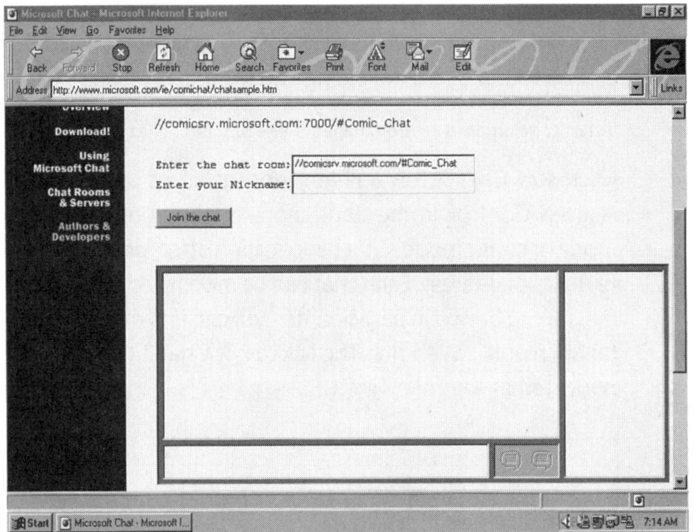

Figure 15.25.
The sample chat page on Microsoft's Web site shows how to include the ActiveX chat control on your Web page.

Many of the chat clients are compatible with Internet Relay Chat (IRC) communications and allow you to create your own private chat rooms. For increased security, consider placing a chat server on your site. The Microsoft Commercial Internet System, which runs under Windows NT Server 4.0 and Internet Information Server 2.0 or higher, includes the Microsoft Internet Chat Server, a commercial-grade chat server that is compatible with Microsoft Internet Chat (MIC) and IRC protocols. Full documentation is installed during the setup process, and the server can be administered locally or remotely. After you install the server on your system, you can use the chat server home page, shown in Figure 15.26, to access product documentation, sample templates, installation verification procedures, and additional information.

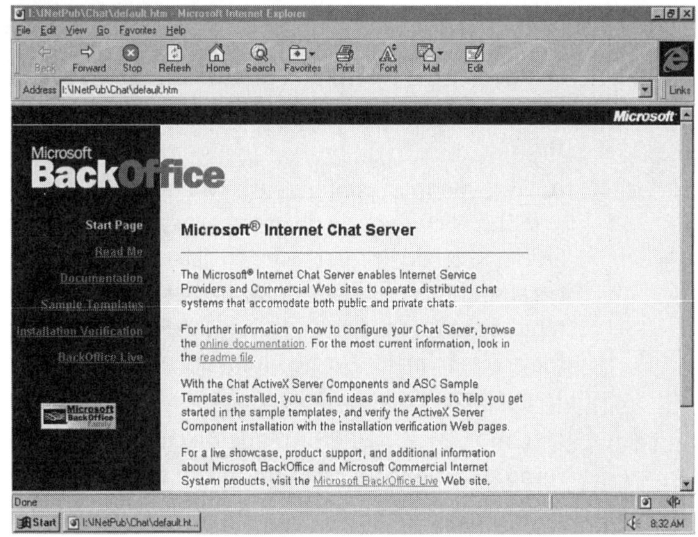

Figure 15.26.
The Microsoft Internet Chat Server includes public and private chats on Internet Information Server 2.0 or higher, running under Windows NT Server 4.0.

Workshop Wrap-Up

The Internet is changing the way we communicate in a big way. Dynamic communication with your friends, peers, and business associates can really make a difference in your Web site. By adding communication through discussion groups, newsgroups, and real-time chatting, you give your site an edge. Using FrontPage, you can create customized discussion groups on topics of your choice. For even greater capability, add private and public newsgroups to your site with a news server. To make your site more exciting, keep in touch with real-time chatting on either Web-based or server-based chats.

Next Steps

In Chapter 16, "Real-Life Examples: Interacting with the Outside World," you'll review an example of how to combine forms and databases into a Web site that updates its content dynamically. Based on links that the user follows and choices entered in forms, pages display different content. You can also refer to the following chapters for related information:

- Chapter 13, "Working with IDC Database Connection," to learn how to use Access databases with IDC files to interact dynamically with your databases
- Chapter 14, "Using Active Server Databases," to learn how to use Microsoft Access with Active Server Pages

Q&A

Q: I'm using a FrontPage discussion group and want to delete some of the messages from the discussions. What is the best way to do this?

A: First, you must configure the web to show documents in hidden directories. This allows you to open the pages in the FrontPage Editor to review the articles. You don't really want to delete the entire article from your web, because this can destroy the links that are generated in the table of contents. Instead, open the article in the FrontPage Editor, and edit the body of the article to read "Deleted from discussion" or something to that effect. Then resave the page to your web.

Q: Can I download FrontPage discussion group articles from my remote server and respond to the articles while offline?

A: You can open the remote web in the FrontPage Explorer and then use the Publish FrontPage Web command to copy the discussion group articles to the web on your local computer. Then, open your browser and go through the discussion group as if you were online. Find the articles you want to respond to, and create the replies through your browser. This generates the responses using the proper threading and also places the responses in the Table of Contents. There is a caveat to this approach, however. If users place additional articles in your online discussion while you are creating your offline responses, you will overwrite them when you publish your responses to your online web. So, be careful with this approach!

SIXTEEN

Interacting with the Outside World

In this chapter, you

- Learn where you can download Microsoft's Active Server Pages from the Web
- Install Microsoft Active Server Pages to your Internet Information Server or Microsoft Personal Web Server
- Examine several pages from the sample Adventure Works site, as well as its associated database

Tasks in this chapter:

- Installing the Active Server Pages Files
- Touring the Adventure Works Shopping Area

Microsoft's Web site contains many examples that you can use to learn more about developing interactive Web pages. Of particular interest are the Active Server Pages samples, which you can download from the Internet Explorer area of Microsoft's Web site. Furnished as part of an upgrade to Internet Information Server 3.0, these Active Server Pages can be installed on Internet Information Server 3.0 or the Microsoft Personal Web Server.

This chapter focuses on some of the pages included with the Active Server Pages files. In particular, the Adventure Works sample site provides many features that will be of interest to those who want to develop online "Shopping Carts" using Active Server Pages technology.

Installing the Active Server Pages Files

It is easy to install the Active Server Pages files and samples on Internet Information Server or the Microsoft Personal Web Server. First, download the Active Server Pages setup file from Microsoft's Web site. You can find these files at the following URL:

```
http://www.microsoft.com/iis/GetIIS/DownloadIIS3/default.htm
```

The Active Server Pages portion of Internet Information Server 3.0 comes in an executable file named `asp.exe`. After you download the file, simply run this executable file to install the Active Server Pages drivers, samples, and tutorials to your Web server. The following items are installed:

- Active Server Pages core files
- ODBC drivers
- Online documentation
- Tutorial
- Adventure Works sample site
- More sample pages

After you install the Active Server Pages, you start them using one of the following procedures:

- To open the Active Server Pages samples from Windows 95 running the Microsoft Personal Web Server, choose Start | Programs | Microsoft Personal Web Server | Active Server Pages Roadmap.
- To open the Active Server Pages samples from Windows NT Server 4.0 running Internet Information Server 3.0, choose Start | Programs | Microsoft Internet Server (Common) | Active Server Pages Roadmap.

When you choose one of these commands, you see the Active Server Pages Roadmap home page, displayed in Figure 16.1. Here, note several areas of interest that will help you learn how to develop Active Server Pages. The navigation bar in the left frame of the frameset takes you to tutorials, scripting guides, and references for Active Server objects, components, and other parameters. The links in the main page take you to VBScript and JScript tutorials and language references, as well as the Adventure Works sample site and additional sample pages.

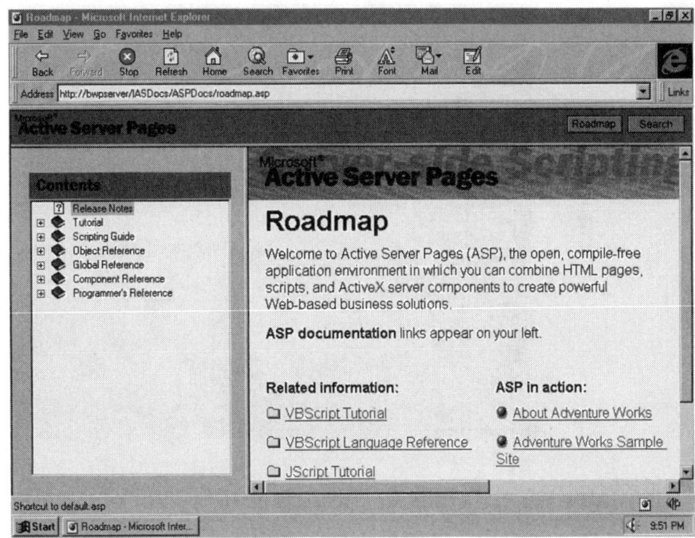

Figure 16.1.
The Active Server Pages Roadmap home page takes you to several areas of interest that can help you learn how to develop Active Server Pages.

The Adventure Works Sample Site

The Adventure Works sample site features several Active Server Pages that display products and allow online shopping through a Shopping Cart program. All pages in this site were developed with Active Server Pages features. You review some of the pages associated with the Shopping Cart in the remainder of this chapter.

The Adventure Works Database

First, begin by reviewing the database that is associated with the Adventure Works site. This database contains tables and queries that work in conjunction with the Active Server Pages in the Web site. The database can be opened in Access 95 or Access 97.

The default installation paths to the Adventure Works database follow:

`\Webshare\ASPSamp\AdvWorks\AdvWorks.mdb` (for Windows 95)
`\InetPub\ASPSamp\AdvWorks\AdvWorks.mdb` (for Windows NT)

Adventure Works Tables

There are eight tables in the Adventure Works database. An example of the first (the Customers table) is shown in Figure 16.2 in Design view. Table 16.1 highlights the database columns in each table.

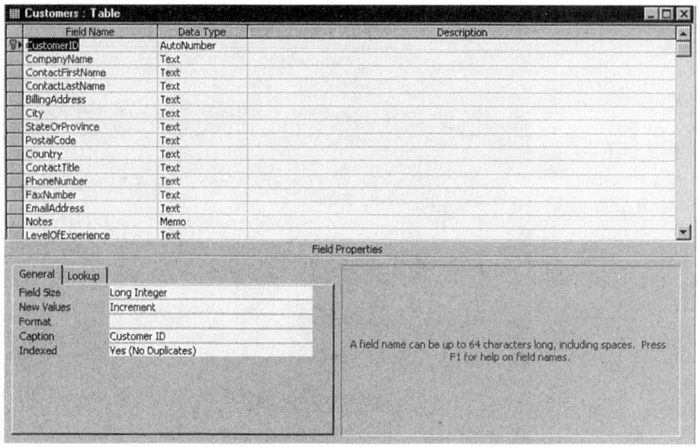

Figure 16.2.
The Adventure Works database contains eight tables, one of which is the Customers table, shown here in Design view.

Table 16.1. Tables in the Adventure Works database.

Table Name	*Description*
Customers	Contains columns for Customer ID, Company Name, Contact First Name, Contact Last Name, Billing Address, City, State/Province, Postal Code, Country, Contact Title, Phone Number, Fax Number, E-Mail Address, Notes, and Level of Experience. Key page associated with this table is the `Customer_Listing.asp` page in the `AdvWorks/Internal` directory of the Adventure Works site.
Employees	Contains columns for Employee ID, First Name, Last Name, Title, Extension, and Work Phone.
Order_Details	Contains columns for Order Detail ID, Order ID, Product ID (a lookup from the Products table), Quantity, Color, Size, Unit Price, and Discount.
Orders	Contains columns for Order ID, Customer ID (a lookup from the Customers table), Employee ID (a lookup from the Employees table), Order Date, PO Number, Ship Contact First Name, Ship Contact Last Name, Ship Name, Ship Address, Ship City, Ship State/Province, Ship Postal Code, Ship Country, Phone Number, Ship Date, Shipping Method (a lookup from the Shipping_Methods table), Freight Charge, and Sales Tax Rate.
Payment_Methods	Contains columns for Payment Method ID, Payment Method, and Credit Card.

Table Name	*Description*
Payments	Contains columns for Payment ID, Order ID, Payment Amount, Payment Date, Credit Card Number, Cardholder Name, Card Expiration Date, Credit Card Authorization Number, and Payment Method ID (a lookup from the Payment_Methods table).
Products	Contains columns for Product ID, Product Code, Product Type, Product Introduction Date, Product Name, Product Description, Product Image URL, Unit Price, and On Sale status.
Shipping_Methods	Contains columns for Shipping Method ID and Shipping Method.

Adventure Works Queries

In addition to the eight tables in the Adventure Works database, there are six queries that retrieve and tabulate sales statistics. Sales are tabulated by product category (camping equipment, climbing equipment, and clothing), and by customer, employee, and product. Figure 16.3 shows the CampingTopSales query in SQL view. The features of each query are listed in Table 16.2.

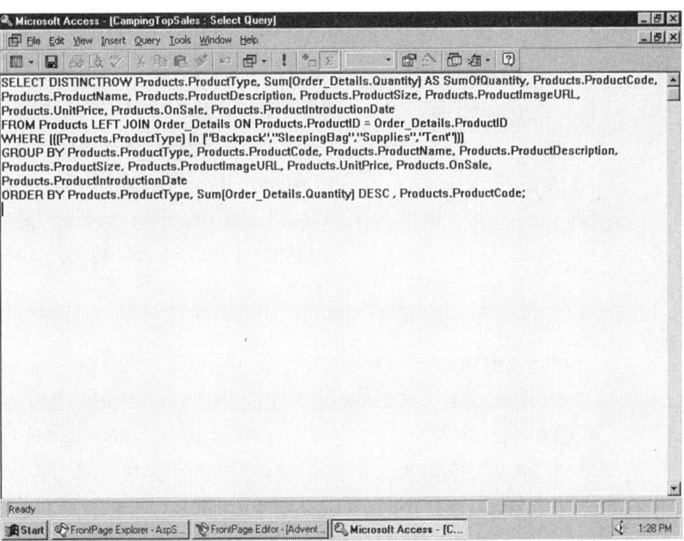

Figure 16.3.
The CampingTopSales query in the Adventure Works database lists the total sales of camping equipment.

Table 16.2. Queries in the Adventure Works database.

Query Name	*Description*
CampingTopSales	Displays the sales of camping supplies (backpacks, sleeping bags, supplies, or tents) from the Products table. Retrieves Product Type, Product Code, Product Name, Product Description, Product Size, Product Image URL, Unit Price, On Sale Status, Product Introduction, and Product Type. From the Order_Details table, it retrieves quantity ordered.
ClimbingTopSales	Displays the sales of climbing products (carabiners, crampons, harnesses, and rock shoes). The fields retrieved by the query are the same as those listed in the CampingTopSales query.
ClothingTopSales	Displays the sales of clothing products (boots, pants, parkas, and shirts) from the Products table. The fields retrieved by the query are the same as those listed in the CampingTopSales query.
SalesByCustomer	Retrieves Company Name, Contact Last Name, Contact First Name, City, and State or Province from the Customers table, and Total Units from the Order_Details table. An expression adds the total amount of sales (Unit Price times Quantity from the Order_Details table).
SalesByEmployee	Retrieves Last Name and First Name from the Employees table and Total Units from the Order_Details table. An expression adds Unit Price times Quantity.
SalesByProduct	Retrieves Product Name from the Products table and Total Units from the Order_Details table. An expression adds Unit Price times Quantity from the Order_Details table.

Connections between the database and the Active Server Pages are managed with the Database Access Component, one of the components furnished with the Active Server Pages installation. You can find further information about this component from the Active Server Pages Roadmap (shown in Figure 16.1). From the Contents frame, expand the Component Reference portion of the tree, and you will see a subtree for the Database Access Component.

Touring the Adventure Works Shopping Area

You are about to embark on a tour of some of the Adventure Works Web pages. In particular, you will step through several pages that display a catalog of products and a very slick online ordering system, developed entirely with Active Server Pages technology.

To begin, proceed as follows:

1. From the Active Server Pages Roadmap page, shown in Figure 16.1, click the Adventure Works Sample Site link in the main frame. You navigate to the Adventure Works Welcome Center page, shown in Figure 16.4. This is the home page for the site.

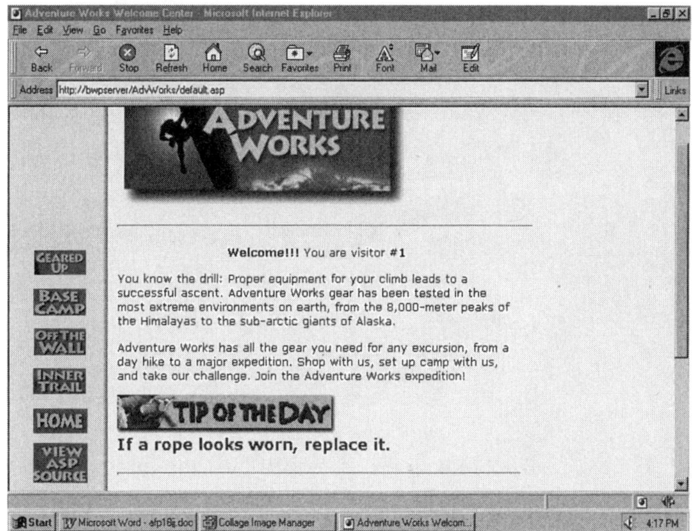

Figure 16.4.
The Adventure Works Welcome Center page is the home page of the Adventure Works sample site.

2. Click the View ASP Source graphic in the left frame. The source code for the page is displayed in another Web page. Black text is standard HTML code, and red text is VBScript associated with the page.
3. Of particular interest on this page are the following features:
   - The first section of the VBScript displayed on this page shows one of two welcome messages, depending on whether the user has previously visited the site. Another script returns the visitor number.

- A Tip of the Day script randomly displays one of ten tips from the `tips.txt` file, which is located in the AdvWorks folder of the Adventure Works sample site.

4. Press the Back button on your browser. You return to the Adventure Works Welcome Center page.
5. Now, click the Geared Up image (the top image in the left-hand portion of the page). You navigate to the Adventure Works Equipment Catalog page shown in Figure 16.5. You can do some online shopping in this section of the Web.

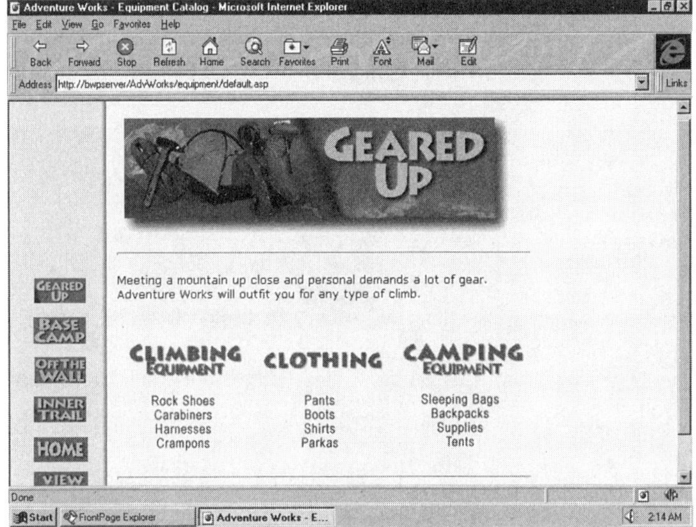

Figure 16.5.
Do some online shopping in the Adventure Works Equipment Catalog.

6. Run your mouse cursor over the three graphics in the main page, which read Climbing Equipment, Clothing, and Camping Equipment. Notice in the status bar that the links take you to the same page but list a different value after the Equipment Type. The link from the Climbing Equipment graphic reads `Shortcut to equip.asp?EquipmentType=Climbing`; the link from Clothing reads `Shortcut to equip.asp?EquipmentType=Clothing`; and the link from Camping Equipment reads `Shortcut to equip.asp?EquipmentType=Camping`.
7. Click the Climbing Equipment link. You navigate to the `equip.asp` page, titled "Adventure Works Catalog—Climbing Equipment," as shown in Figure 16.6. The products shown on the page are those associated with climbing equipment. Now, click the Back button to return to the previous page.

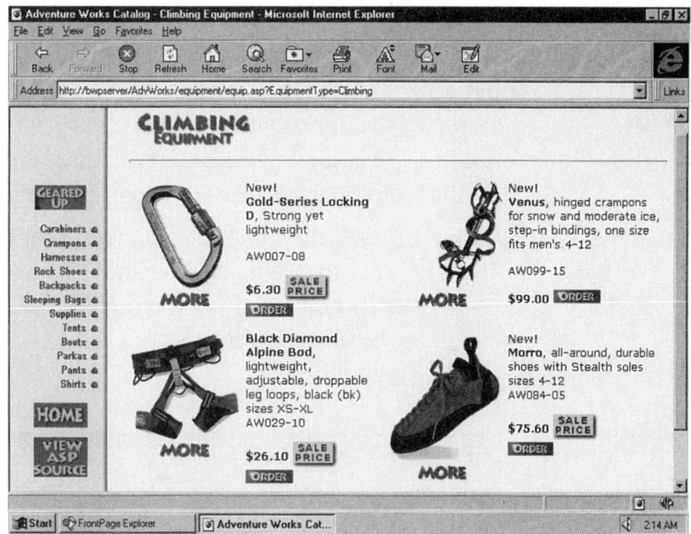

Figure 16.6.
The Adventure Works Catalog—Climbing Equipment page.

8. Click the Clothing link. You again navigate to the `equip.asp` page. However, this time the page is titled "Adventure Works Catalog—Clothing," as shown in Figure 16.7. All the products shown on the page are clothing. Click the Back button to return to the previous page.

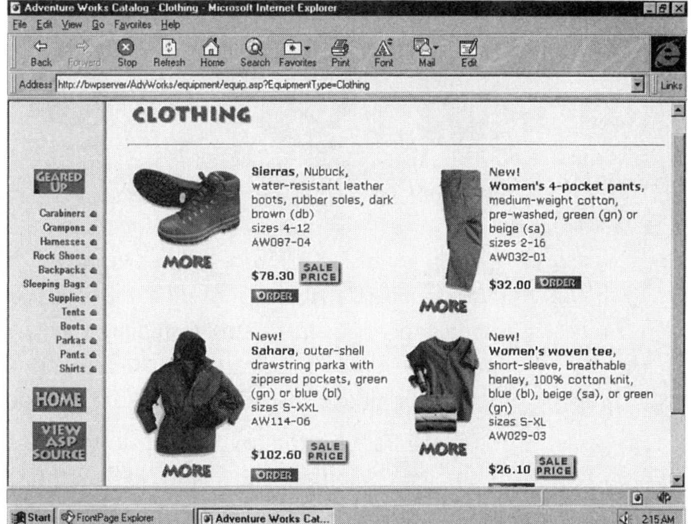

Figure 16.7.
The Adventure Works Catalog—Clothing page.

9. Click the View ASP Source graphic in the left-hand portion of the page. Scroll through the code on the page to view the VBScript associated with this page. There isn't a lot here. The "magic" occurs with the links. The section of each link that follows the question mark (`equip.asp?EquipmentType=Climbing`, for example) contains the instructions for the script on the `equip.asp` page, as you will see in the next steps.
10. Click the Back button to return to the Adventure Works Equipment Catalog. This time, click the Camping Equipment link. You navigate to the `equip.asp` page, which is now titled "Adventure Works Catalog—Camping Equipment" as shown in Figure 16.8. The items on the page are different types of camping equipment.

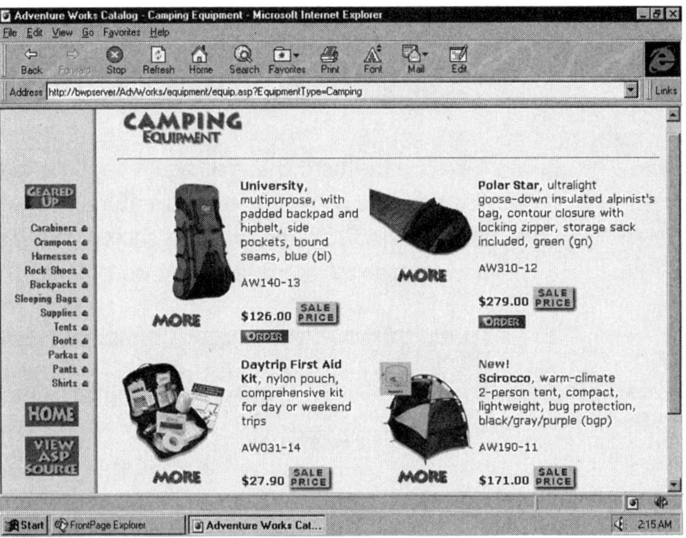

Figure 16.8.
The Adventure Works Catalog—Camping Equipment page.

11. Click the View ASP Source graphic in the left-hand portion of the page. Now, you see a whole lot of VBScript code that is displayed at the top of the page. It defines three cases: Camping, Climbing, and Clothing. Depending on the case (which is defined by the link you followed from the previous page), the title and header graphic of the page changes.
12. Click the Back button to return again to the Adventure Works Catalog—Camping Equipment page. Now, look at the catalog of products that are displayed on the page. Each item in the catalog displays an image, the product name, a description, the product number, and the price. Some of the items are on sale, and others are shown as new items. All this information is also generated by script on the `equip.asp` page. Figure 16.9 shows a small portion of this code.

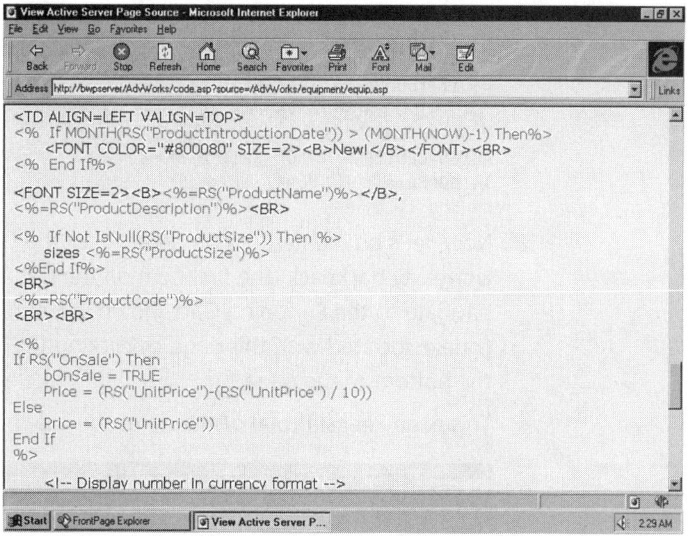

Figure 16.9.
The portion of the code that defines what information displays for each product.

The following lines of code check the Adventure Works database for the product introduction date. If the product has been released within the past month, the word *New* displays in bold purple text:

```
<% If MONTH(RS("ProductIntroductionDate")) > (MONTH(NOW)-1_ Then%>
    <FONT COLOR="#800080" SIZE=2> <B>New!</B></FONT><BR>
<% End If%>
```

The following lines of code check the database for an entry in the `ProductSize` column. If a size is displayed, it is entered on the Equipment Catalog page. Otherwise, the code continues by displaying the product code. The code look like this:

```
<% If Not IsNull(RS("ProductSize")) Then %>
     sizes <%=RS("ProductSize")%>
<%End If%>
<BR>
<%=RS(%"ProductCode")%>
<BR><BR>
```

The following lines of code check the database for an indicator that tells whether the product is on sale. If so, the unit price is decreased by 10%, and an "On Sale" graphic is displayed to draw attention to the sale price. Otherwise, the full price is shown on the page. The code looks like this:

```
<%
If RS("OnSale") Then
     bOnSale = TRUE
     Price = (RS("UnitPrice")-(RS("UnitPrice")/10))
Else
     Price = (RS("UnitPrice"))
EndIf
```

```
%>
<!--Display number in currency format -->
<b><% = FormatCurrency(Price)%></B>
<% If (bOnSale) Then %>
     <IMG SRC="/AdvWorks/multimedia/images/saleTag1.gif" WIDTH="57"
     ➥HEIGHT="32"
ALIGN=CENTER ALT="On Sale"><BR>
<% bOnSale = FALSE%>
<% End If %>
```

13. Now, let's put something on order. Click the Order graphic beneath the University backpack (the first item on the Camping Equipment page). You navigate to the Shopping Cart shown in Figure 16.10. You can view the code associated with this page by clicking the View ASP Source graphic at the bottom of the page.

    This page keeps a total of the items the user has ordered. The Shopping Cart

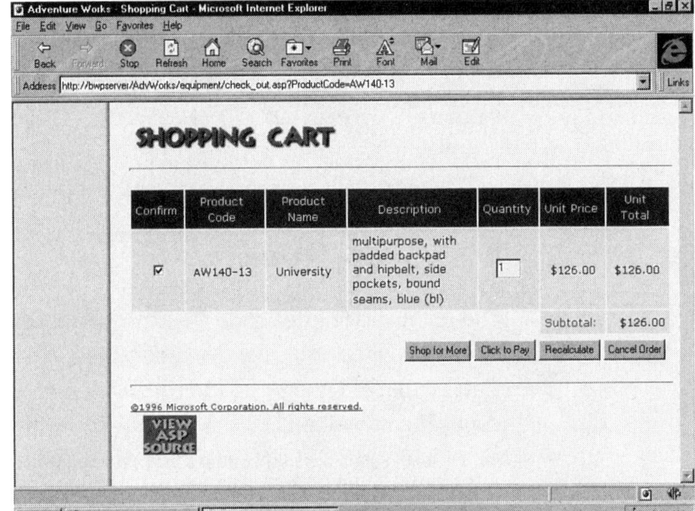

Figure 16.10.
The Shopping Cart keeps track of the items on order.

displays the product code, product name, description, quantity ordered, unit price, and subtotal. Other features on this page are as follows:

- If the user deselects the checkbox in the Confirm column and then presses the Recalculate button, the item is removed from the shopping list.
- If the user changes the quantity in the Quantity column and then presses the Recalculate button, the unit total changes to reflect the number of items ordered multiplied by their unit price. The order subtotal also changes.

- If the user presses the Order More button, he or she is returned to the Adventure Works Catalog.
- If the user presses the Click to Pay button, he or she navigates to the sign-up page to enter customer information.

14. Click the Back button to return to the Shopping Cart; then press the Click to Pay button. The Sign Up page shown in Figure 16.11 is displayed. Here, the user enters his or her personal information.

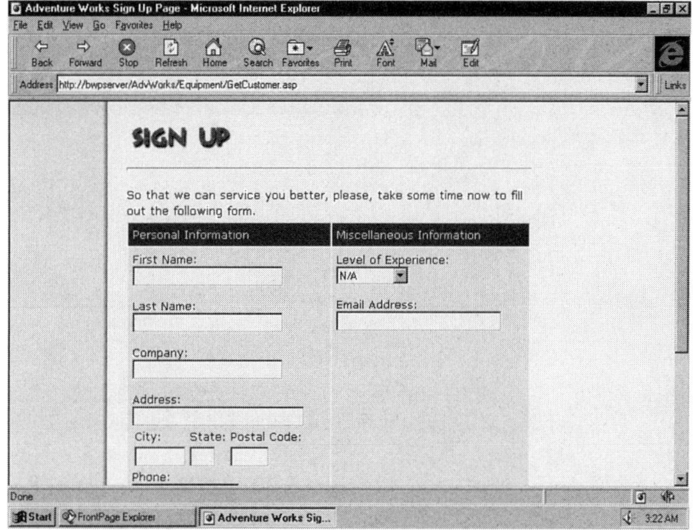

Figure 16.11.
The Sign Up page takes the user's personal information.

15. Click the View ASP Source graphic at the bottom of the page. The script on this page performs validation of the form fields to ensure that each field contains information. When all fields contain information, the user's information is entered into the Customers table in the database. Then a cookie is generated that keeps track of the last time the user placed an order. If the user returns within one year, his or her information is reused. New customers or customers who have not placed an order within the past year must enter their personal information again.
16. Click the Back button to return to the Sign Up page. Enter some information in the field (you can't proceed to the next screen unless all form fields are filled). Then press the Enter Customer Info button. You navigate to the Payment and Shipping page shown in Figures 16.12 and 16.13. Again, validation scripts check to see that each field in the form is filled out. The code also validates that credit card numbers contain at least eight digits.

After the entries are validated, the order is entered into the Adventure Works database. Order details and payment records are generated. The user has one last chance to cancel the order with the Cancel button. Otherwise, he or she selects the Order Now! button, and the Congratulations page shown in Figure 16.14 is returned.

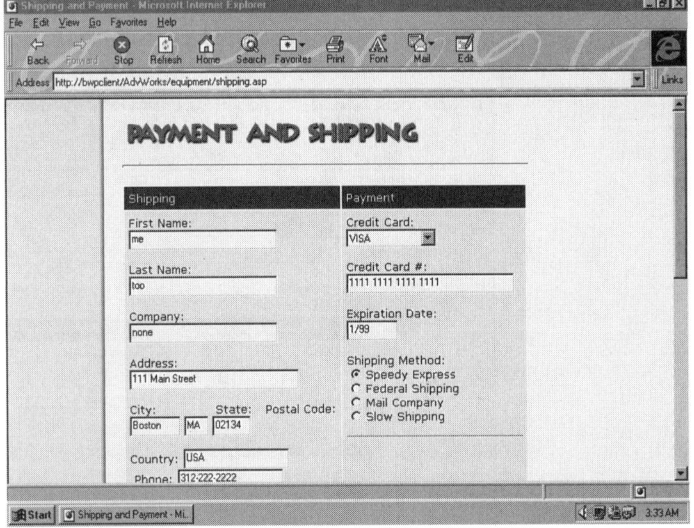

Figure 16.12.
The upper section of the Payment and Shipping page retrieves shipping information and method of payment from the user.

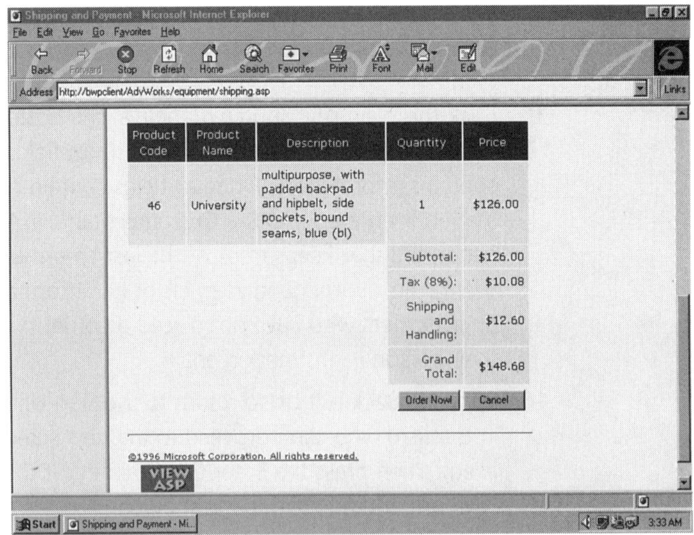

Figure 16.13.
The lower section of the Payment and Shipping page shows the total of the order, including tax and shipping charges.

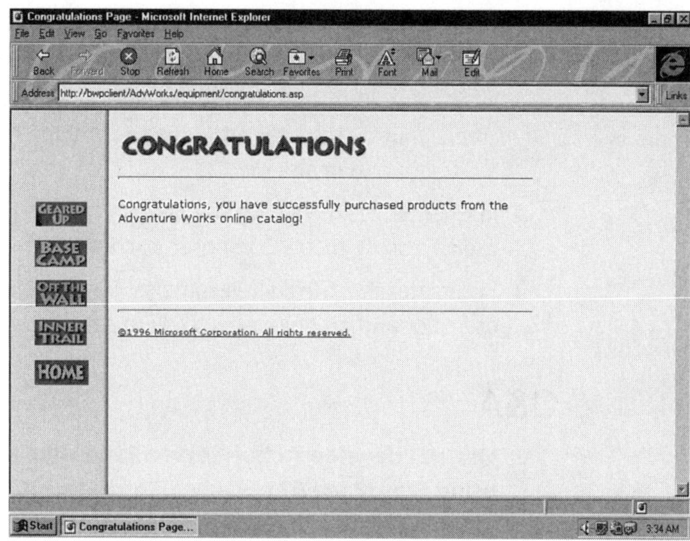

Figure 16.14.
After the user presses the Order Now! button, the Congratulations page displays in his or her browser. The order is complete.

Workshop Wrap-Up

There is much more to explore in the Adventure Works site and in the Active Server Pages Roadmap site. You can learn a great deal by studying the documentation, code, and examples furnished in the Active Server Pages samples. As you can see from the examples shown in this chapter, you can create pages and databases that update dynamically, based on user input and criteria that you program into your pages.

Next Steps

In Part V, "Creating Graphics with Microsoft Image Composer," you learn about how you can use Microsoft Image Composer to create images for your Web. You learn the basics of image creation with more hands-on examples that guide you through the creation of buttons, banners, image maps, montages, and more. Read on to learn about the following topics:

- In Chapter 17, "Microsoft Image Composer Quick Tour," you get a quick overview of the commands and features included in Microsoft Image Composer.
- In Chapter 18, "An Introduction to Graphics on the Web," you learn the basics of image composition and the file formats that are compatible with most browsers.
- In Chapter 19, "Creating Buttons, Icons, and Backgrounds," you learn how to create simple shapes and use symbols to create icons.

- In Chapter 20, "Creating Banners and Text Effects," you learn how to create your own banners or open existing images and add text to them.
- In Chapter 21, "Creating Montages and Image Maps," you learn how to create your own sprites and how to combine them with effects to create montages and image maps.
- In Chapter 22, "Creating Animations," you learn some ways that you can use Microsoft Image Composer to create animated GIFs.
- In Chapter 23, "Real-Life Examples: Setting the Mood," you learn how to use color and graphics effectively to set the mood of your Web site.

Q&A

Q: Can I develop Active Server Pages like those shown in this chapter using FrontPage 97?

A: Yes, you can. You can use ActiveX Controls in conjunction with the Insert|Script command to implement features used in Active Server Pages. It helps to open an Active Server Page in FrontPage 97. This way, you can learn how to construct an Active Server Page. Remember to configure an editor association that opens the FrontPage Editor when you click a file with an `.asp` extension from within the FrontPage Explorer.

Q: Are any other files or features of interest in the Active Server Pages collection?

A: Check out some of the other items in the Component Reference section. From the Active Server Pages Roadmap, expand the Component Reference section of the Contents tree to read about the Browser Capabilities Component and the Content Linking Component. The Browser Capabilities Component furnishes a means to test the user's browser for certain capabilities. From there, you can create code that loads pages that are custom-made for the user's type of browser. The Content Linking Component automatically generates and updates tables of contents and navigation links to previous and subsequent Web pages. In effect, it creates a Web site that you can read like a book!

If VBScript or JavaScript isn't enough for you to learn, you can go far beyond that. Check out the Programmer's Reference section of the documentation to learn how to create your own components for Active Server Pages using C++, Java, or Visual Basic.

PART V

Creating Graphics with Microsoft Image Composer

CHAPTER SEVENTEEN

Microsoft Image Composer Quick Tour

In this chapter, you

- ❑ Learn the basics about MIC
- ❑ Review the function of each of the MIC palettes
- ❑ Overview the menu commands and shortcuts

Tasks in this chapter:

- ❑ Installing Microsoft Image Composer
- ❑ Configuring Your FrontPage Image Editor

Back in the days when I was a budding young artist, I made collages by cutting out many different objects from pages in magazines. Then I smeared glue all around the back of each cutout and pasted each of them on a single piece of cardboard. Eventually, what I ended up with was a bunch of pictures that somewhat resembled a scene, but there were problems. First of all, there was the glue that I got all over my "great" work of art, my hands, my clothes, the rug, the walls, and just about everything else. After being banished to the bathtub, I would come back to the collage and see areas that needed improvement. I'd think, "I should have put that flower over here; I wish that gazebo was bigger; that purple color is way too bright"; and so on. I hoped someday there would be a better way to make collages. With Microsoft Image Composer, there *is* a better way.

What Is Microsoft Image Composer?

With the collage analogy mentioned in the beginning of this chapter, you probably have vague idea of what Microsoft Image Composer (MIC), furnished on the FrontPage 97 CD-ROM as part of the FrontPage 97 Bonus Pack, is all about. Using this image editor, you compose images in much the same way you compose a collage. In MIC, the "collage" is a *composition*. The "cutouts" are known as *sprites*—objects that "float" around on the page. You can rearrange and add effects to these sprites in any way you choose: If you don't like the color of a sprite, you can change it; if you think a sprite needs to be larger or smaller, you can resize it; if a portion of your composition looks better when partially hidden by another object, you can move it forward or backward in the stack; if you want one object to be transparent in areas that partially reveal what's behind, you can manipulate the alpha channel for interesting effects. Your objects remain floating so that you can rearrange them in any way you choose. All this with no glue and no mess!

NOTE: When you save your composition to a file format other than Microsoft Image Composer (MIC) format, the sprites no longer float. If you anticipate the necessity to change your composition later, save your composition in MIC format; then save the file in the format you need for your Web pages (usually GIF or JPG).

Before you begin working with MIC, it might help to familiarize yourself with some of the menu commands and tools that the program offers. First, install the program as outlined in the following task.

Installing Microsoft Image Composer

Microsoft Image Composer is furnished on the FrontPage 97 CD-ROM as part of the FrontPage 97 Bonus Pack. You can install the software from the installation screen that displays when you insert the FrontPage 97 CD-ROM.

Microsoft Image Composer comes with several different options that you can choose to install if you select the Complete/Custom installation during setup. The following options are available:

- Microsoft Image Composer executable files.
- Online Help.
- Impressionist Plug-Ins (a sizable gallery of effects that you can apply to your images).
- Tutorial Samples (some sample files used for the Microsoft Image Composer tutorial).
- Font Samples (additional fonts that you can use in your images).
- Photo Samples (more than 200MB worth of photos and sample sprites). If you do not have the space to install these files, don't worry; Microsoft Image

Composer includes an item in the Help menu that provides previews of all images and sprites and displays the directory on the FrontPage 97 CD-ROM in which they are located.

- Web Art Samples (buttons, icons, background images, banners, and horizontal rules that you can use in your Web pages).

To install Microsoft Image Composer, follow these steps:

1. Insert the FrontPage 97 CD-ROM. Auto-start displays the screen shown in Figure 17.1. (If you do not see this screen, you can run setup if you choose Control Panel | Add Remove Programs.)

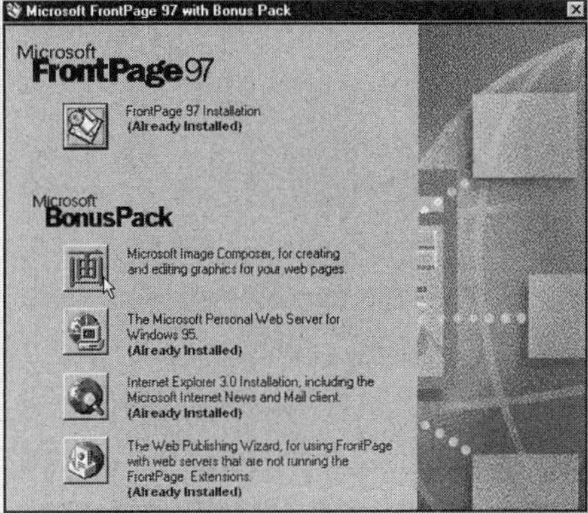

Figure 17.1.
Begin installation of Microsoft Image Composer with the dialog box that displays after you insert the FrontPage 97 CD-ROM.

2. Choose to install Microsoft Image Composer from the auto-start screen. The Microsoft Image Composer Setup dialog box is displayed.
3. Choose **C**ontinue. The Name and Organization Information dialog box is displayed. Enter your name in the **N**ame field and the name of your company in the **O**rganization field. There must be an entry in both fields to continue. If you do not have a company name, enter `None` or something similar.
4. Click OK. The Confirm Name and Organization Information dialog box is displayed. Verify that your information is correct.
5. Click OK. A Microsoft Image Composer Setup dialog box displays your Product ID. Choose OK to continue.
6. Setup searches for installed components and displays a license agreement. To continue with the installation, click I **A**gree.
7. The Microsoft Image Composer Setup dialog box asks what type of installation you want from the screen shown in Figure 17.2. Choose one of the following options:

- Choose **T**ypical Install to install Microsoft Image Composer, On Line Help, Impressionist Plug-Ins, and Tutorial Samples.
- Choose **C**omplete/Custom Install to select any or all of the components from the screen shown in Figure 17.3. To change the folder into which the Photo Samples and Web Art Samples are installed, click the Change **F**older button and enter the new path in the **P**ath field. Then choose OK to return to the Microsoft Image Composer Setup dialog box.
- Choose Comp**a**ct Install to install the minimum files to run Microsoft Image Composer.

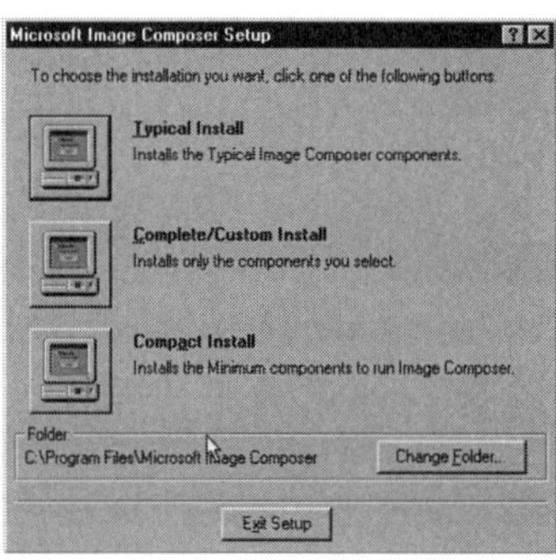

Figure 17.2.
Choose the type of installation you want to perform from the Microsoft Image Composer Setup dialog box.

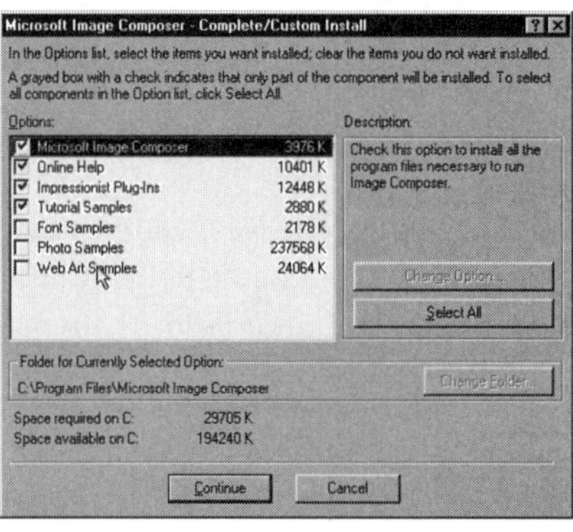

Figure 17.3.
When you choose Complete/Custom install, select any of the Microsoft Image Composer components that you need.

8. To change the folder in which Microsoft Image Composer is installed, click the Change **F**older button. The Change Folder dialog box is displayed. Enter the path in the Path field, and choose OK. You will return to the Microsoft Image Composer Setup dialog box.
9. Choose **C**ontinue. The Choose Program Group dialog box is displayed. Enter the name of the folder in the Program Group field, or accept the default Microsoft Image Composer folder.

10. Click **C**ontinue to proceed. Setup checks for necessary disk space and installs the files. After Setup copies the files, a dialog box informs you that the installation has completed successfully. Choose OK to complete the setup process.
11. Close the Microsoft FrontPage 97 with Bonus Pack screen using the Escape key or by clicking the "X" button in the upper-right corner of the dialog box. Setup is complete.

Configuring Your FrontPage Image Editor

When you work with Microsoft FrontPage, you may sometimes find a need to edit an image while you are working on your Web site. You can configure FrontPage so that when you click an image in your Web site, it opens Microsoft Image Composer and opens the image for editing.

When you install FrontPage 97 and Microsoft Image Composer, many of the file formats you frequently use are configured for you automatically. To verify the configuration, or to add more file formats or editors, configure your FrontPage image editor through the FrontPage Explorer.

To configure Microsoft Image Composer as your image editor, follow these steps:

1. From the FrontPage Explorer, choose **T**ools | **O**ptions. The Options dialog box is displayed.
2. Click the Configure Editors tab, shown in Figure 17.4. Verify that Microsoft Image Composer is configured as your image editor for the following file types (by default): MIC (Microsoft Image Composer format), BMP, DIB, GIF, JPG, TIF, ACC, and TGA.

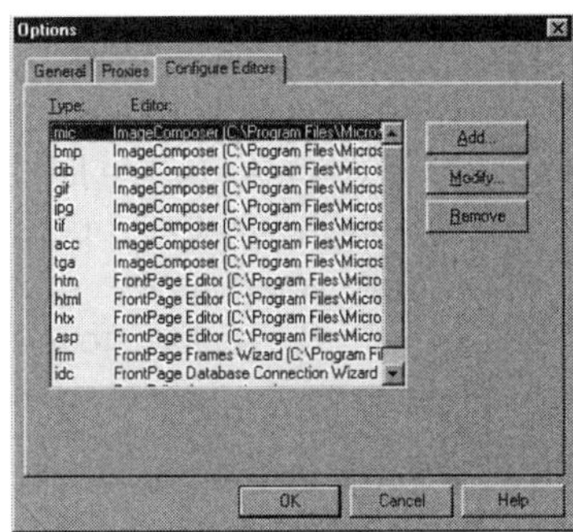

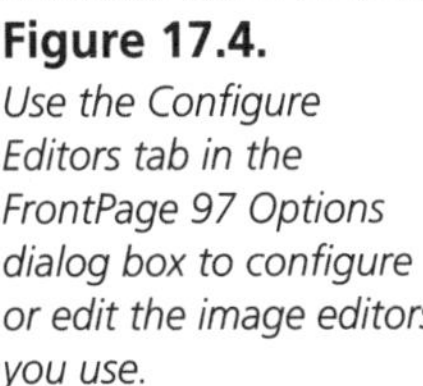

Figure 17.4.
Use the Configure Editors tab in the FrontPage 97 Options dialog box to configure or edit the image editors you use.

3. Associate an image editor with a file extension in the Add Editor Association dialog box. To add a configuration for another file format, click the **A**dd button. The Add Editor Association dialog box shown in Figure 17.5 is displayed.

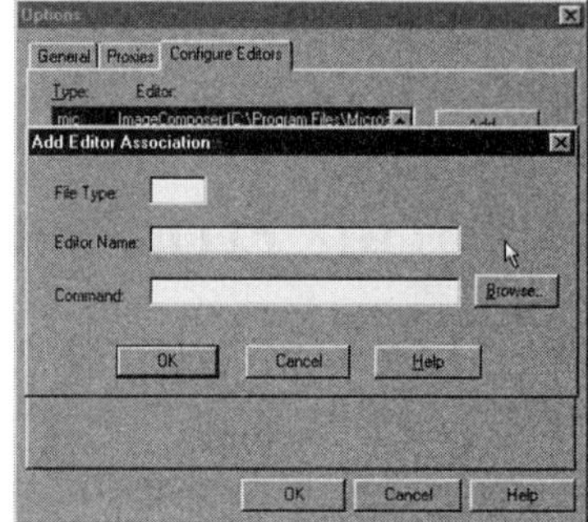

Figure 17.5.
Associate an image editor with a file extension in the Add Editor Association dialog box.

4. Enter the file extension in the File Type field (you do not need to precede the extension with a period). Enter the name of the image editor you want to use in the Editor Name field.
5. In the Command field, enter the path to the executable file for the image editor, or use the **B**rowse button to locate the executable file on your local or network hard drive.
6. Choose OK to return to the Configure Editors tab.
7. Choose OK to exit the Options dialog box and return to the FrontPage Explorer.

The Microsoft Image Composer Workspace

When you initially open Microsoft Image Composer, you will see the screen shown in Figure 17.6. Along the top of the screen is the toolbar, which contains buttons that perform many commonly used commands. The left side of the screen contains the toolbox. Each of the buttons in the toolbox opens a corresponding palette that contains the tools you use while you compose your image. Use the current color swatch, which is displayed beneath the toolbox, to select your current color and create palettes. Finally, the status bar at the bottom of the screen displays messages about the commands you are using.

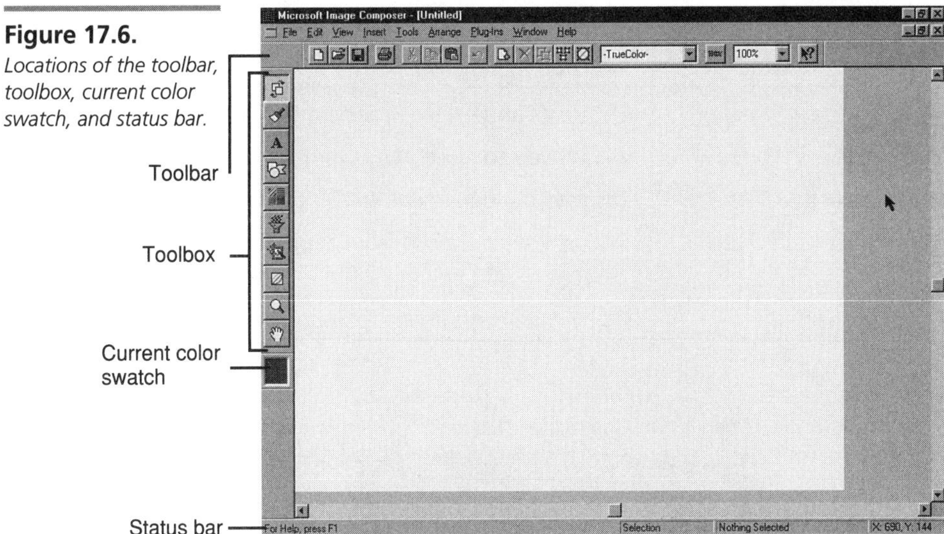

Figure 17.6.
Locations of the toolbar, toolbox, current color swatch, and status bar.

The Standard Toolbar

The Standard toolbar, shown in Figure 17.7, provides buttons that invoke many commonly used commands. From left to right, the toolbar provides access to the following commands and features, as shown in Table 17.1.

Table 17.1. Commands in the Standard toolbar.

Command	*Function*
New	Creates a new composition
Open	Opens an existing image
Save	Saves the current composition
Print	Prints the current composition
Cut	Cuts the selected items into the clipboard
Copy	Copies the selected items into the clipboard
Paste	Pastes the contents of the clipboard into the composition
Insert Image File	Inserts another image into the composition as a sprite
Delete	Deletes the current selection
Duplicate	Duplicates the current selection
Select All	Selects all sprites in the composition

continues

Table 17.1. continued

Command	*Function*
Clear Selection	Deselects all selected sprites in the composition
Color Format	Allows you to select the color format for the composition
Actual Size	Displays the document at 100 percent zoom
Zoom Percent	Allows you to choose from zoom factors ranging from 10 percent to 800 percent
Help	Opens Microsoft Image Composer Help

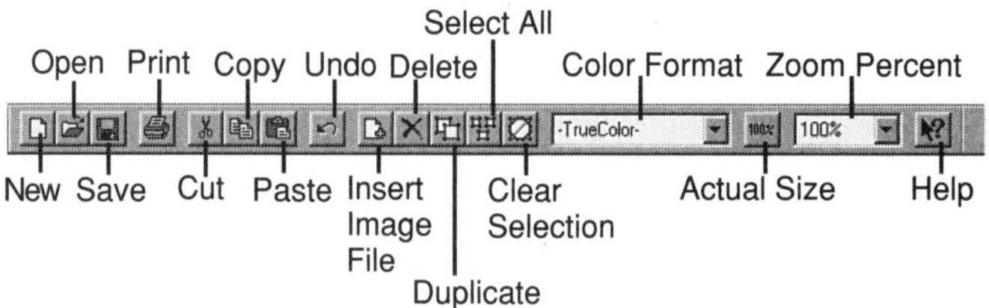

Figure 17.7.
The Standard toolbar provides access to commonly used commands and features.

The Toolbox

The toolbox is the heart of the Microsoft Image Composer application. From here, you can access several different palettes that provide commands and effects that you can apply to the sprites in your composition.

The toolbox is shown in Figure 17.8. In this section, you are introduced to the functions that each palette in the toolbox provides. Only two of the items in the toolbox—Zoom and Pan—do not have palettes. When you choose Zoom from the toolbox, a magnifier is displayed, and you can zoom in and out of your image. When you choose Pan, a grabber is displayed, and you can move the image around in the workspace.

The Arrange Palette

From the Arrange palette, shown in Figure 17.9, you can control the layering and orientation of the sprites in your composition. Many of the commands in the Arrange palette are also found in the Arrange menu, discussed in the section titled "Arrange Menu." Use the Arrange palette to size and scale your sprites, rotate and flip them, send them forward or backward, align a group of selected sprites, and set the home position of sprites.

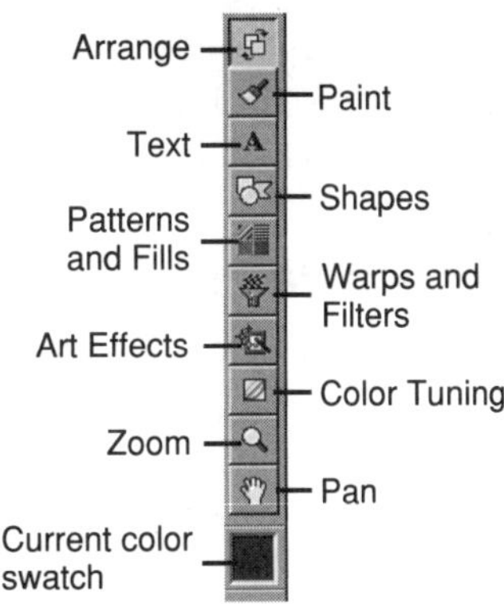

Figure 17.8.
The toolbox provides access to several different palettes that contain the commands and effects you use in your composition.

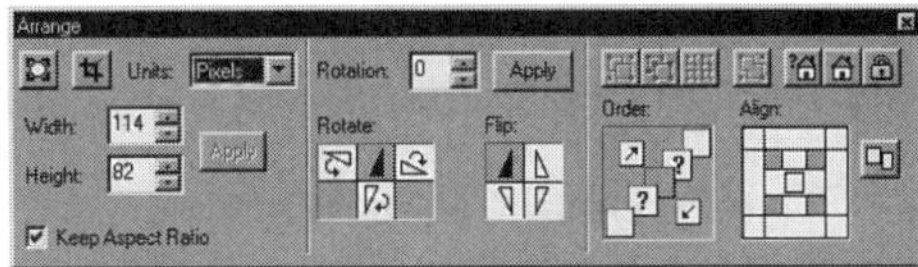

Figure 17.9.
Commands in the Arrange palette control scaling, rotation, grouping, layering, and alignment of sprites.

The Paint Palette

You can find many paintbrushes and tools in the Paint palette, shown in Figure 17.10. If you want more brushes, you can design your own with the Brush Designer, also available in this palette.

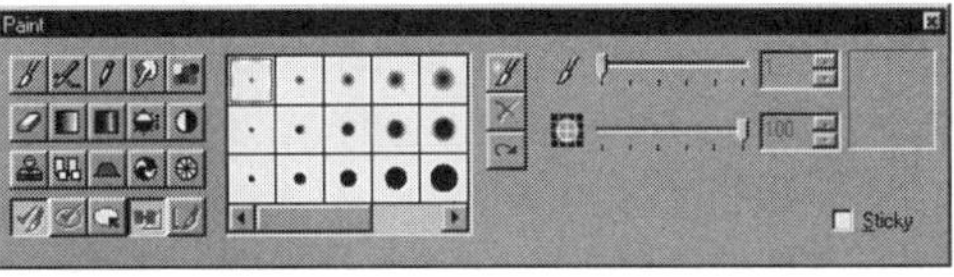

Figure 17.10.
You can select and design paintbrushes with the Paint palette.

You will learn more about effects in **Chapter 21**. The CD-ROM that accompanies this book also provides Web pages that display examples of the effects you can create with Microsoft Image Composer.

The left portion of the palette contains buttons that select the following brushes and effects: Paintbrush, Airbrush, Pencil, Smear, Impression, Erase, Tint, Colorize, Dodge-Burn, Contrast, Rubber Stamp, Transfer, Mesa, Vortex, and Spoke Inversion.

To the right of the brush selection area is the area from which you select brush size and the amount of anti-aliasing that you want the brush to apply when you paint. *Anti-aliasing* creates brush strokes that have a soft edge, thereby blending colors together and reducing the jagged appearance of strokes. The brushes you choose from the top row of the matrix are anti-aliased and have soft edges—for example, an airbrush, which produces very soft strokes. The second row in the matrix produces strokes that are semi–anti-aliased—that is, only the edges of the stroke are anti-aliased. The bottom row of the matrix is used to select brushes that are not anti-aliased. This type of brush produces a stroke with a very hard and jagged edge.

The right half of the Paint palette contains additional tools that you can use when you create your own brushes or edit existing ones. Here you can create your own brushes with the Brush Designer.

The Text Palette

When you want to add text to your composition, use the Text palette, shown in Figure 17.11. From this palette, you select the font and designate its size and transparency.

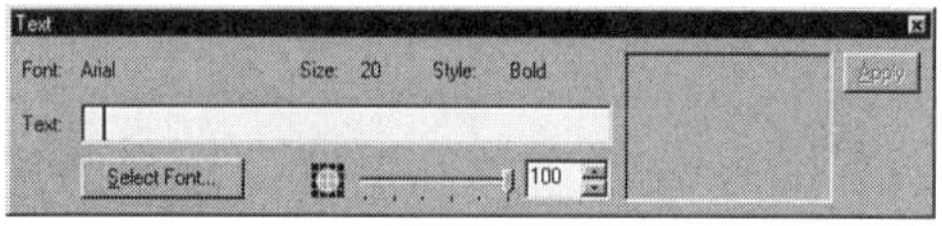

Figure 17.11. *Use the Text palette when you want to add text to your composition.*

You will work with the Text palette in **Chapter 20**.

The Shapes Palette

Use the Shapes palette, shown in Figure 17.12, to draw rectangular, elliptical, or irregularly shaped sprites. You can also use the Shapes palette to cut out areas from other images and create sprites from them. The magic wand tool found in this palette allows you to make a selection based on color.

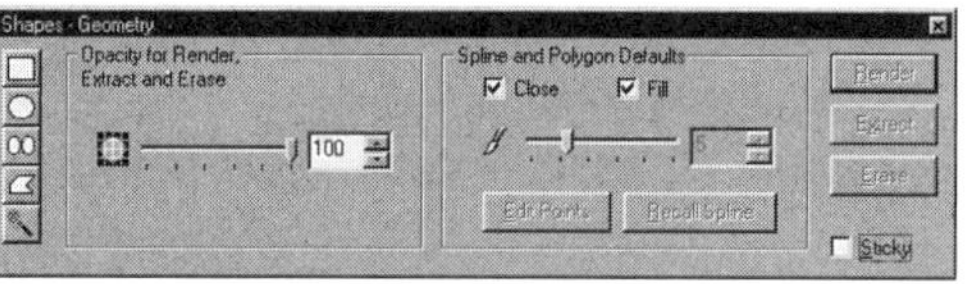

Figure 17.12. *Use the Shapes palette to create new shapes from scratch or to cut out sprites from existing images.*

You will learn more about creating and arranging sprites in **Chapter 21**.

The Patterns and Fills Palette

Figure 17.13 shows the Patterns and Fills palette. Use this palette when you want to fill a selected area with a solid color, pattern, gradient, or other effect.

You will learn to create buttons and backgrounds using the Patterns and Fills palette in **Chapter 19**.

The Warps and Filters Palette

You'll find many interesting effects in the Warps and Filters palette, shown in Figure 17.14. Warps are effects that distort an image in some way, and this palette provides commands that warp images automatically or interactively. Here you can create drop shadows and effects such as embossing. You'll also find blurring filters here.

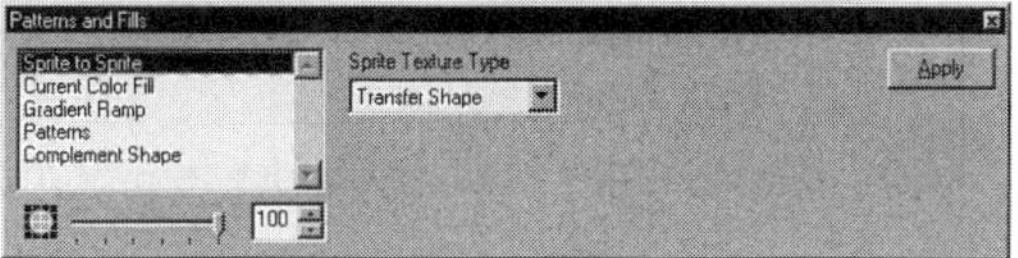

Figure 17.13. *Use the Patterns and Fills palette to fill an area with a color, pattern, gradient, or other effect.*

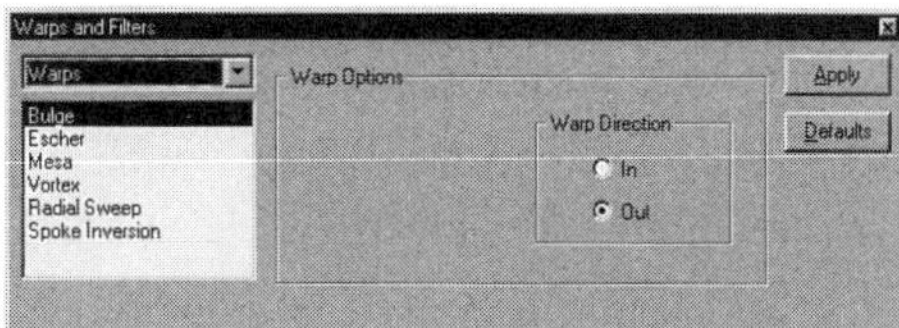

Figure 17.14. *Effects such as warping, drop shadows, embossing, and blurring are found in the Warps and Filters palette.*

See **Chapter 20** to learn how to apply drop shadows to text.

The Art Effects Palette

If it's effects you want, it's effects you'll get. You'll find nearly 50 different effects in the Art Effects palette, shown in Figure 17.15. There are 13 paint effects, 10 sketch effects, 11 graphic effects, 9 exotic effects (my favorites in the group), and 6 utility effects.

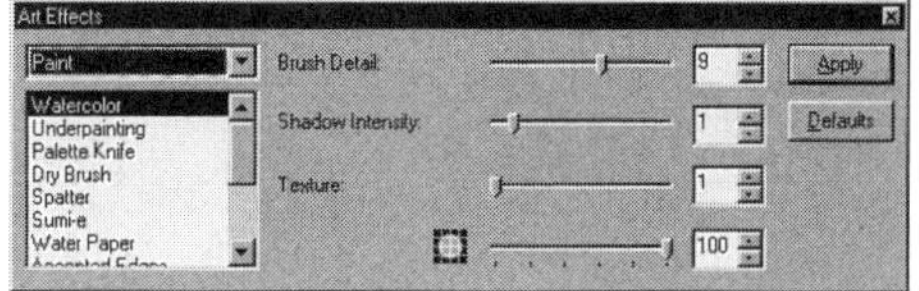

Figure 17.15. *You'll find nearly 50 different effects that you can apply to your sprites in the Art Effects palette.*

I'll show you how to apply some of the effects in the Art Effects palette in **Chapter 21**.

The Color Tuning Palette

The Color Tuning palette, shown in Figure 17.16, provides commands that let you alter the colors in your composition. You can change the color of all channels at once or selectively adjust the red, green, and blue channels in a sprite.

Figure 17.16. *Use the Color Tuning palette to adjust the colors of a sprite.*

The Microsoft Image Composer Menu Commands

The menu commands in Microsoft Image Composer provide a means to create and save images, edit selections, control how you view your composition, and choose additional plug-ins that you can use with your images. In the following seven sections, you'll get an overview of the commands available in each menu and the keyboard shortcuts that invoke the most common commands.

TWAIN is an industry-standard interface for input and output devices and requires special drivers that are usually provided with your scanner.

File Menu

The commands in the File menu allow you to create, open, and save compositions. You can also scan images from within Microsoft Image Composer, provided that you have a scanner that is TWAIN-compliant. The commands and shortcuts in this menu are summarized in Table 17.2.

Table 17.2. File menu commands and shortcuts.

Command	*Shortcut*	*Function*
New	Ctrl+N	Creates a new composition. The Standard toolbar provides a button for this command.
Open	Ctrl+O	Opens an existing composition. The Standard toolbar provides a button for this command.
Close	Ctrl+W	Closes the current composition.
Save	Ctrl+S	Saves the current composition. The Standard toolbar provides a button for this command.
Save **A**s		Saves the current composition under a different filename or graphics format.
Sa**v**e Selection As		Saves the current selection under a different filename or graphics format.
Sav**e** Copy As		Saves a copy of the current composition.
Composi**t**ion Properties		Allows you to view or edit the properties of the current composition.
Scan | **S**elect Scan Source		Allows you to select a TWAIN scanner.
Scan | **A**cquire Scan		Scans an image with the currently selected scanner.
P**r**int Setup		Allows you to change the settings of the printer or printing options.
Print		Prints the current composition. The Standard toolbar provides a button for this command.

Command	Shortcut	Function
Sen**d**		Sends the current composition by e-mail.
E**x**it	Alt+F4	Exits Microsoft Image Composer and prompts you to save any unsaved changes.

Edit Menu

Table 17.3 summarizes the commands and shortcuts that are available in the Edit menu. Use this menu to cut, copy, and paste items into the Windows clipboard, select and duplicate sprites, and make changes to the color or alpha channels in your sprites.

Table 17.3. Edit menu commands and shortcuts.

Command	Shortcut	Function
Undo	Ctrl+Z	Undoes the last operation. The Standard toolbar provides a button for this command.
Cu**t**	Ctrl+X	Cuts the selected sprites into the clipboard. The Standard toolbar provides a button for this command.
Copy	Ctrl+C	Copies the selected sprites into the clipboard. The Standard toolbar provides a button for this command.
Paste	Ctrl+V	Pastes the sprites from the clipboard into the composition. The Standard toolbar provides a button for this command.
Delete	Del	Deletes the selected sprites without placing them into the clipboard. The Standard toolbar provides a button for this command.
Dupl**i**cate	Ctrl+D	Duplicates the selected sprites. The Standard toolbar provides a button for this command.
Select **A**ll	Ctrl+A	Selects all sprites in the composition. The Standard toolbar provides a button for this command.

continues

Table 17.3. continued

Command	*Shortcut*	*Function*
Cl**e**ar Selection	Ctrl+T	Deselects the selected sprites. The Standard toolbar provides a button for this command.
Cop**y** Channel | **R**ed		Copies the red channel into the clipboard.
Cop**y** Channel | **G**reen		Copies the green channel into the clipboard.
Cop**y** Channel | **B**lue		Copies the blue channel into the clipboard.
Cop**y** Channel | **A**lpha		Copies the alpha channel into the clipboard.
Pa**s**te Channel | **R**ed		Pastes the red channel from the image.
Pa**s**te Channel | **G**reen		Pastes the green channel from the image.
Pa**s**te Channel | **B**lue		Pastes the blue channel from the image.
Pa**s**te Channel | **A**lpha		Pastes the alpha channel from the image.
Broadcast Channel | **R**ed		Broadcasts the red channel into all channels.
Broadcast Channel | **G**reen		Broadcasts the green channel into all channels.
Broadcast Channel | **B**lue		Broadcasts the blue channel into all channels.
Broadcast Channel | **A**lpha		Broadcasts the alpha channel into all channels.
P**r**operties	Alt+F4	Shows the properties of the selection and allows you to assign a name.

View Menu

The View menu provides commands that control how you view your composition and which toolbars you can see in the work space. The commands and shortcuts that are available from this menu are summarized in Table 17.4.

Table 17.4. View menu commands and shortcuts.

Command	*Shortcut*	*Function*
Go to **C**omposition Guide		Displays the composition guide in the edit window.
Center on **S**election		Places the current selection in the center of the screen.
Toolbars		Allows you to display or hide the toolbars you select.
Toggle **P**alette View	F2	Shows or hides the tool palette.
Zoom In	Num+	Zooms into the composition by one zoom level.
Zoom **O**ut	Num-	Zooms out from the composition by one zoom level.
Actual Size		Displays the composition in its actual size. The standard toolbar provides a button for this command.

Insert Menu

The Insert menu provides only two commands: The **I**nsert | **F**rom File command allows you to insert another image into your composition as a sprite; and the **I**nsert | From P**h**oto CD command allows you to open an image from a Photo CD-ROM.

Tools Menu

The commands on the Tools menu provide access to the Microsoft Image Composer palettes. All but one of these commands are equivalent to those found in the toolbox, discussed previously in "The Toolbox" section. In addition, the **T**ools | **O**ption command allows you to configure default settings for Microsoft Image Composer. The commands and shortcuts available in the Tools menu are shown in Table 17.5.

Table 17.5. Tools menu commands and shortcuts.

Command	*Shortcut*	*Function*
Arrange	Alt+1	Displays the Arrange toolbox
Paint	Alt+2	Displays the Paint toolbox
Te**x**t	Alt+3	Displays the Text toolbox
Shapes	Alt+4	Displays the Shapes toolbox

continues

Table 17.5. continued

Command	*Shortcut*	*Function*
Patterns and **F**ills	Alt+5	Displays the Patterns and Fills toolbox
Warps and Filters	Alt+6	Displays the Warps and Filters toolbox
A**r**t Effects	Alt+7	Displays the Art Effects toolbox
Color Tuning	Alt+8	Displays the Color Tuning toolbox
Zoom	Alt+9	Zooms into the image by one zoom factor each time the command is chosen
Pa**n**	Alt+0	Allows you to move to a different area in the image by dragging the view
Color Pic**k**er		Displays the color picker
Options		Allows you to define default options for Microsoft Image Composer

Arrange Menu

The commands found in the Arrange menu are summarized in Table 17.6. You can also find these commands in the Arrange palette, discussed in "The Arrange Palette" section and shown in Figure 17.9. The commands in this palette allow you to group, rotate, and arrange the sprites in your composition.

Table 17.6. Arrange menu commands and shortcuts.

Command	*Shortcut*	*Function*
Bring to Fron**t**		Brings the current selection to the front of the stack
Send to Bac**k**		Sends the current selection to the back of the stack
Bring **F**orward		Brings the current selection forward one level in the stack
Send **B**ackward		Sends the current selection back one level in the stack
Lock Position	Ctrl+L	Locks the position of the current selection
Set **H**ome Position	Alt+Home	Sets the home position for the current selection

Command	*Shortcut*	*Function*
Return to **H**ome Position	Ctrl+Home	Returns the selection to its home position
Rotate | **R**ight 90		Rotates the current selection 90 degrees to the right (clockwise)
Rotate | **L**eft 90		Rotates the current selection 90 degrees to the left (counter clockwise)
Rotate | **1**80		Rotates the current selection 180 degrees
Fli**p** | **V**ertical		Flips the current selection vertically
Fli**p** | **H**orizontal		Flips the current selection horizontally
Fli**p** | **B**oth		Flips the current selection both vertically and horizontally
Group	Ctrl+G	Groups all selections into one item
Ungroup	Ctrl+U	Ungroups the current selection into its original components
Explode	Ctrl+E	Returns a flattened selection to its original components
Flatten **S**election	Ctrl+F	Flattens all selections into one item

Plug-Ins Menu

If you have Adobe Photoshop–compatible plug-ins, you may be able to use them with Microsoft Image Composer. Kai's Power Tools is probably one of the most popular plug-ins, and it works well with Microsoft Image Composer. Even if you don't have your own plug-ins, Microsoft Image Composer comes furnished with its own—the Impressionist plug-in. If the filters in the Art Effects palette aren't enough for you, the Impressionist plug-in will give you more than enough to keep you busy for hours. There are dozens and dozens of very interesting effects available with this plug-in.

A screen shot of the Impressionist plug-in dialog box is shown in Figure 17.17. As you select the plug-in effect you want (and there are many), you will see a preview of the effect before you apply it. You'll learn more about this plug-in in Chapter 19.

Figure 17.17.
The Impressionist plug-in, which furnishes dozens of effects, is available through the Plug-Ins menu.

Workshop Wrap-Up

As this brief overview shows, there are many features available in Microsoft Image Composer. As you will learn in Chapters 19–23, there are many ways that you can use Microsoft Image Composer to create outstanding Web graphics. Think of your Web images as collages, and think of the elements of your Web images as cutouts. Piece these elements together to make your banners, buttons, borders, and backgrounds. You'll learn how much fun it is to create art for your Web.

In this chapter, you learned how to install Microsoft Image Composer and how to configure it as your default image editor in FrontPage 97. You also received an overview of the commands, palettes, and effects available. Now that you have a general idea where the commands and effects are found, let's start to apply them to your Web graphics.

Next Steps

In Chapter 18, "An Introduction to Graphics on the Web," you'll learn some general knowledge about creating graphics for Web pages. You'll begin some hands-on projects in Chapter 19, where you will start with the basics. You will learn how to use Microsoft Image Composer to create background images, navigation buttons, and icons for your Web pages. As you progress through the chapters in this part, you will learn how to use some of the effects in your images.

- In Chapter 18, "An Introduction to Graphics on the Web," you'll learn some basic knowledge about Web graphic file formats and palette creation.

- In Chapter 19, "Creating Buttons, Icons, and Backgrounds," you'll start with Web page basics—buttons, icons, and backgrounds for your Web pages.
- In Chapter 20, "Creating Banners and Text Effects," you'll learn how to create your own banners and add text to them.
- In Chapter 21, "Creating Montages and Image Maps," you'll learn how to create your own sprites and combine them with effects to create montages and image maps.
- In Chapter 22, "Creating Animations," you'll learn some ways that you can use Microsoft Image Composer to create animated GIFs.
- In Chapter 23, "Real-Life Examples: Setting the Mood," you'll learn how to use color and graphics effectively to set the mood of your Web site.

Q&A

Q: I opened an image to use for a background for my composition. I put some other sprites on top of it, but when I try to select some of them, I accidentally move the background. Is there any way I can lock the background into place?

A: Yes. Choose Arrange | Lock Position, or use the shortcut Ctrl+L. This will lock the background image or any other selection into place.

Q: I want to use additional plug-ins with Microsoft Image Composer. How do I configure them?

A: Choose Tools | Options, and select the Plug-Ins tab from the Options dialog box. Enter the path to your plug-in directory or use the Browse button to locate the directory on your local or network hard drive. Microsoft Image Composer allows you to specify only one plug-in directory.

CHAPTER EIGHTEEN

An Introduction to Graphics on the Web

Deciding what the look and feel of Web pages should be is probably one of the most challenging aspects of Web page design. Many Webmasters subcontract graphic design of their pages to talented professional graphic artists. For those whose budgets do not permit this additional expense, FrontPage 97 offers a solution: Included in the FrontPage 97 Bonus Pack is Microsoft Image Composer—a very capable graphics program filled with a bountiful supply of effects and tools.

Creating Web Graphics

It is wise to familiarize yourself with some of the basics in Web page graphic design. There are challenges in creating Web page graphics that do not exist in traditional computer graphics design. Most certainly, the Web designer wants graphics that demand attention. However, the smart Web designer considers several factors when creating these graphics. Among these considerations are choosing graphics file formats supported by browsers, using colors that do not dither when pages are viewed in 256-color mode, and the length of time it takes to download a page. This chapter will help you sort through these challenges so that you can tackle your Web page graphics equipped with proper knowledge.

In this chapter, you

- Learn about the graphic file formats that most browsers support
- Add transparency and interlacing to GIF files
- Learn how to compress JPEG images
- Review "safe" browser colors and learn how to choose colors that do not dither in browsers
- Learn ways to reduce the size of your images to reduce download times

Tasks in this chapter:

- Adding Transparency to GIF Files
- Interlacing GIF Files
- Setting JPEG Compression
- Choosing Your Current Color
- Creating Custom Palettes

Web Graphics File Formats

Web browsers support a limited number of graphics file formats. Most can display two formats: GIF and JPEG. Some browsers also can display PNG format, a relatively new graphics format developed in response to a controversy over the GIF file format. Even fewer browsers support the Windows BMP format. The following sections explain more about these formats and when to use them.

You can also create animated GIF files, which are nothing more than a series of image files containing little changes that, when arranged in a sequence, produce an illusion of movement. You'll learn more about animated GIF images in **Chapter 22**.

GIF Format

The GIF file format saves graphics in 256 colors or fewer. GIF images offer several nice features that other Web formats do not currently offer, such as the capability to specify a transparent color or add interlacing, as discussed in the first two tasks in this chapter. GIF files are the format of choice when an image contains large areas of solid color, line art, or cartoons, examples of which are shown in Figure 18.1. To economize on the byte size of a GIF image, you can reduce the number of colors in the palette, as discussed in the "Reducing the Number of Colors" section.

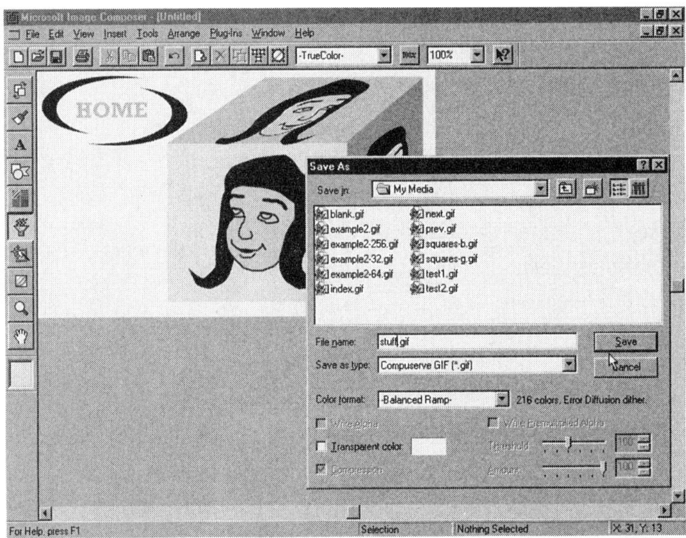

Figure 18.1.
GIF format is best used with line art, cartoon art, and images that have large areas of solid colors.

TASK

Adding Transparency to GIF Files

There are two tips to follow when you develop transparent GIF files (images that contain transparent areas). First, use a composition guide color that does not appear anywhere else in your graphic. This avoids creating "holes" in the GIF file after the transparency is applied.

Second, choose a composition guide color that is the same color as or close to the background color of your Web page. Doing so avoids two problems. If your image contains sprites with anti-aliased (softened) edges, they are harder to detect if your image is created using a background color that is close to that of your Web page. Second, some browsers do not display transparent areas in GIF files and render them opaque. If one of those browsers comes upon a GIF file that contains bright primary colors against a lime green transparent color, the user will see the lime green background.

For example, let's say you are developing a cartoon image that contains red, yellow, green, blue, and white. You want this image to display against a background image that is primarily white but has some light blue patterns in it. The background and the image both contain white (R: 255, G: 255, B: 255). You can specify a composition guide color that is very close to white, such as R: 254, G: 255, B: 255. The visual difference between pure white and the composition guide color is not detectable to the eye; yet, if you choose the composition guide color as the transparent color, the pure white areas in the image are unaffected and appear opaque.

You can choose a transparent color using both Microsoft Image Composer and FrontPage 97. Between the two, Microsoft Image Composer provides better results, as you will see from the following example.

To compare how Microsoft Image Composer and FrontPage 97 add transparency to an image, follow these steps:

1. From Microsoft Image Composer, choose **F**ile | **O**pen (Ctrl+O), or select the Open button on the standard toolbar. The Open dialog box is displayed.

2. Locate `test1.mic` on the CD that accompanies this book and double-click the file to open it. Use this file to experiment with transparent GIF files in Microsoft Image Composer and FrontPage 97.
3. Choose **F**ile | Save **A**s. The Save As dialog box shown in Figure 18.2 is displayed.

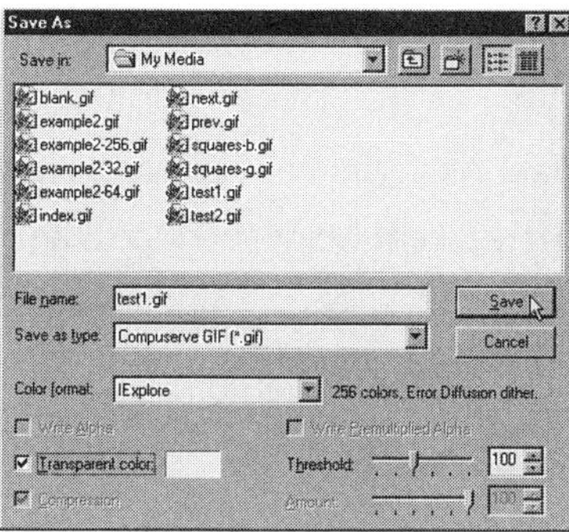

Figure 18.2.
Use the Save As dialog box to add transparency to your GIF image.

4. Use the Save **i**n field to select the drive and directory into which you want to save your image.
5. From the Save as **t**ype field, choose Compuserve GIF (`*.gif`).
6. From the Color **f**ormat field, select the browser-safe palette that you used to develop your image. In this example, choose `Iexplore`.
7. Check the **T**ransparent color check box, and click the color square beside it. The Color Picker is displayed.
8. Click the True Color tab, and select the eyedropper. Then click the white background in the image. Choose OK to return to the Save As dialog box.
9. Use the T**h**reshold slider to adjust the transparency threshold. The default setting is `128`, which will cause some shadowing around the text. Set this value to `100`.

NOTE: I increased the text sprite in this image by stretching it after I created it. This caused the edges of the text to become anti-aliased. I placed additional pixels with subtle color differences around the text sprite to smooth their appearance against the background. Use the threshold slider to eliminate some of the "ghosting" that appears around anti-aliased sprites. All pixels that have a transparency value below the threshold setting are transparent, and all those that have a transparency value above the threshold setting are opaque. Lower settings produce more anti-aliasing, and higher settings produce harder edges.

10. Choose Save. Microsoft Image Composer informs you that it will flatten all the sprites and crop the image to the composition guide. Choose OK to save the file with transparent areas.

Next you will save a version of the file that does not have transparency added. You will use FrontPage 97 to add transparency to this image.

Continue with the image you currently have open in Microsoft Image Composer, and follow these steps:

1. Choose **F**ile | Save **A**s again. The Save As dialog box is displayed.
2. Deselect the Transparent Color check box, and change the filename to `test2.gif`.
3. Choose **S**ave. Microsoft Image Composer informs you that the composition will be flattened and cropped to the composition guide. Choose OK to save the file without transparent areas.

4. Start FrontPage 97 from your Start menu. After the FrontPage Explorer opens, click the Show FrontPage Editor button from the standard toolbar. The FrontPage Editor opens.
5. From the FrontPage Editor, choose the New button to create a new blank page.
6. Choose **F**ile | Page Propert**i**es. The Page Properties dialog box is displayed.
7. Click the Background tab, shown in Figure 18.3. From the Background drop-down menu, choose black for a background color, and click OK to return to the page.

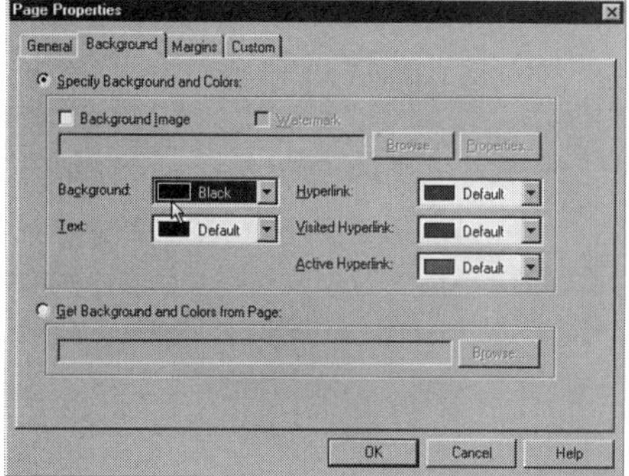

Figure 18.3.
Select a black background color in the FrontPage Editor using the Background tab in the Page Properties dialog box.

NOTE: Normally, you develop your images against a background color that is close to the color you use on your Web page. I selected black here so that you could easily see how each application applies transparency.

8. Choose the Insert Image button from the standard toolbar. The Image dialog box is displayed.
9. Click the Other Location tab.
10. Select the From **F**ile radio button, and click the **B**rowse button. Locate the drive and directory into which you saved your images.
11. Double-click `test1.gif` to insert the image that has transparency into your page. Press Enter to move the insertion point to the next line.
12. Repeat steps 18–20; then double-click `test2.gif` to place it into your page. The image that does not have transparency is displayed in your page.
13. Click the second image; then choose the Make Transparent button from the Image toolbar. Click the white background in the second image to make it transparent.

As you learn to create images throughout Part V, "Creating Graphics with Microsoft Image Composer," you will learn more about saving GIF and JPEG files.

Notice the differences in appearance between the two images in Figure 18.4. Although both images used the same original file in Microsoft Image Composer, the image whose transparency was added in FrontPage 97 does not look quite as good. There is more ghosting around the text, and there are random pixels scattered throughout the image. This is not as evident if the image appears against a light background.

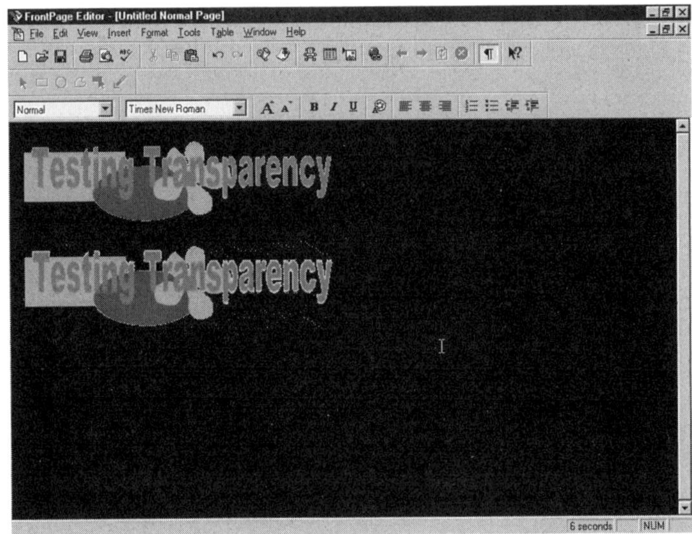

Figure 18.4.
The transparent GIF that you created in Microsoft Image Composer (top) is cleaner than the one you created in FrontPage 97 (bottom).

TASK

Interlacing GIF Files

You can also interlace a GIF file, which means loading the entire image on your page at once but rendering it in progressive steps. During the first pass, an interlaced image appears blocky, but after several additional passes it attains its final appearance. This gives the user an early idea of what the image looks like before the download is complete.

Microsoft Image Composer does not have an option to interlace a GIF file; you can add this feature in FrontPage 97, however. If you intend to use transparency and interlacing on the same image, apply them both in FrontPage.

To add interlacing to a GIF image, follow these steps:

1. Click the second image in your Web page, and press Alt+Enter to open the Image Properties dialog box. Select the General tab, shown in Figure 18.5.
2. Verify that GIF is selected in the Type section.

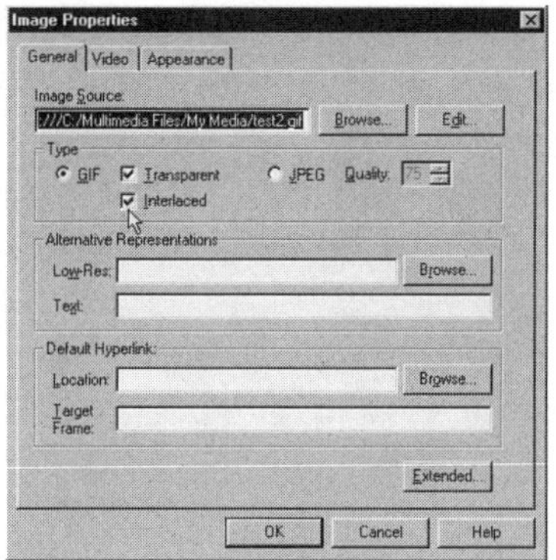

Figure 18.5.
Use the General tab in the FrontPage Editor's Image Properties dialog box to create an interlaced GIF file.

NOTE: If you add interlacing or transparency to a JPEG image, it converts to a GIF file, which usually decreases the number of colors and increases the byte size of the image.

3. Check the **I**nterlaced option to add interlacing to the GIF image.
4. Click OK to return to the FrontPage Editor. When you save your Web page, the image is saved as an interlaced GIF file.

JPEG Format

The JPEG file format works best with photographs, raytraced, or rendered images produced by three-dimensional programs. (See Figure 18.6 for a sample image.) The JPEG format is a true-color file format that uses data compression to reduce the size of an image in kilobytes. When you save your images to JPEG format, you can adjust compression settings to achieve a balance between quality and file size. Lower compression settings produce clearer images but increase the byte size. Higher compression settings reduce the byte size of the image but also reduce the quality of the image and can produce blockiness. In time, you'll learn to anticipate the settings that work best for the content of an image. Generally, compression settings between 10 and 35 work best in Microsoft Image Composer, depending on the composition. Images that consist mostly of photographic quality can use higher compression settings. Images that contain solid areas of color might appear blocky if higher values are used.

The following task shows how to save an image in JPEG format.

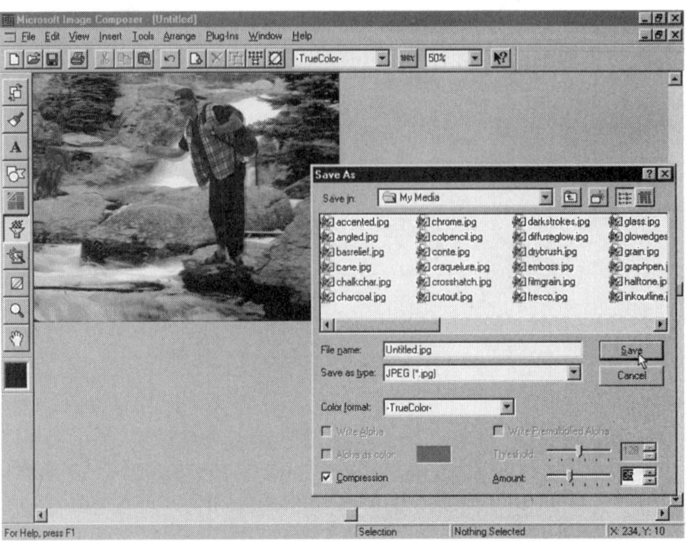

Figure 18.6.
Use JPEG format to save photographs or photorealistic artwork.

TASK

Setting JPEG Compression

When you save your image to JPEG format, Microsoft Image Composer flattens all the sprites and saves only the objects that appear within the composition guide. Set the compression settings in the Save As dialog box.

To save an image to JPEG format, follow these steps:

1. Choose **F**ile | Save **A**s. The Save As dialog box is displayed.
2. Use the Save **i**n drop-down box to locate the drive and directory into which you want to save your graphic.
3. From the Save as **t**ype field, select JPEG (`*.jpg`).
4. Select the **C**ompression check box and set the amount of compression in the **A**mount field, as shown in Figure 18.7. Lower values produce files that are larger in kilobytes but clearer. Higher values produce files that are smaller in kilobytes but reduce the quality of the image.
5. In the File **n**ame field, enter a name for your file.
6. Click **S**ave, or press Enter. The image is saved to the directory you selected.

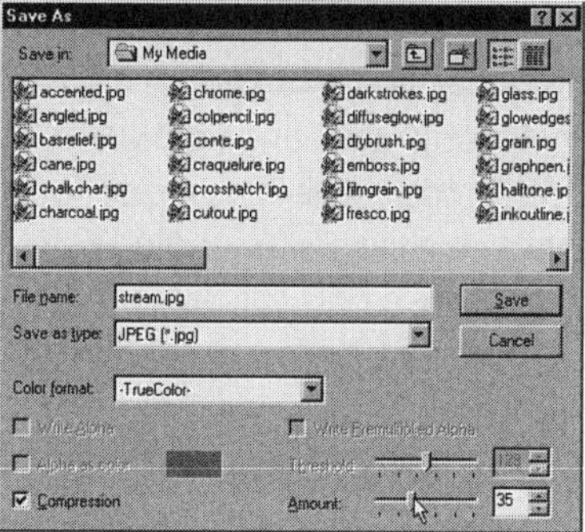

Figure 18.7.
Adjust the Amount slider to set the amount of compression you want to apply to your JPEG image.

PNG Format

In 1994, a controversy arose over the GIF file format due to a patent held by its developer about the compression algorithms used when saving the files. In response to the controversy, the PNG file format was developed by a committee of graphics and multimedia professionals. It offers very good quality and compression, in many ways surpassing those of the JPEG file format. However, at present, few browsers offer built-in support for this file format, although there are plug-ins available that allow a browser to view PNG graphics images.

BMP Format

Some Windows browsers can display BMP images. However, of all the graphics file formats, this file format taxes bandwidth the most because BMP graphics do not use compression to reduce file size. Choose one of the other formats mentioned in lieu of this file format.

Color Concerns

Yet another concern when developing graphics for Web pages is the use of palettes that display colors that do not dither when video display runs in 256-color mode. Remember that though some users browse the Web in high-color (65,536-color) mode or true-color (16 million–color) mode, the majority of users do not. Many users keep their browsers at 640×480 resolution and display 256 colors. When a user browses the Web in 256-color mode, the browser remaps the colors in any image that is displayed on a page to a custom palette. Fortunately, the Windows versions of Netscape Navigator and Internet Explorer contain nearly the same colors in their palettes.

Some users might even choose 16-color video display mode, which will leave your 256-color images looking rather sickly. Though many Web page designers try to consider the lowest common denominator when designing their Web pages, it appears that most choose 256-color mode as the lowest case for color resolution. However, if you want to design graphics that can be viewed in 16-color mode, use the 16 basic colors listed in Table 18.1.

For further information on the significance of the gamma-corrected red/green/blue (RGB) formulas shown in Table 18.1, see the "Browser-Safe Palettes" section.

Table 18.1. The 16 basic colors.

Color	*RGB Formula*	*Gamma-Corrected RGB Formula*
White	`255,255,255`	`255,255,255`
Silver	`192,192,192`	`153,153,153`
Gray	`128,128,128`	`74,74,74`
Black	`0,0,0`	`0,0,0`
Red	`255,0,0`	`255,0,0`
Maroon	`128,0,0`	`74,0,0`
Blue	`0,0,255`	`0,0,255`
Navy	`0,0,128`	`0,0,74`
Lime Green	`0,255,0`	`0,255,0`
Green	`0,128,0`	`0,74,0`
Olive Green	`128,128,0`	`74,74,0`
Yellow	`255,255,0`	`255,255,0`
Fuchsia	`255,0,255`	`255,0,255`
Purple	`128,0,128`	`74,0,74`
Cyan	`0,255,255`	`0,255,255`
Dark Cyan	`0,128,128`	`0,74,74`

Browser-Safe Palettes

There are 216 colors that are common to both the Netscape Navigator and Internet Explorer browser palettes. When you use these 216 colors in your images, you are pretty much guaranteed that the colors will remain pure, without dithering. It is actually quite easy to remember the colors that are safe to use within browsers:

- ❑ Just remember the number 51. When you use graphics software that uses RGB values to designate a color formula, you can use any combination of the numbers 0, 51, 102, 153, 204, and 255 (multiples of 51) to create your red, green, and blue color formula. For example, Red `51`, Green `153`, and Blue `204` create a color that does not dither in a browser.

- When you use software that creates colors based on hexadecimal values, each pair of numbers in the hexadecimal number can contain the values `00`, `33`, `66`, `99`, `CC`, and `FF`. For example, the hexadecimal value of `3399CC` creates the same color as the RGB formula described previously.

These color numbers are "legal" when you enter color values in FrontPage 97; but in Microsoft Image Composer, there is a bit of a catch...

You will sometimes notice that graphics display differently from one monitor to another. Sometimes an image can look perfect on one monitor, but it appears very bright or very dark on another. To compensate for these differences, many graphics software applications allow you to use gamma correction settings that affect the brightness of an image. All monitors display brightness in a nonlinear manner, and the amount of brightness varies from monitor to monitor.

Microsoft Image Composer performs gamma correction when reading and saving files and palettes. This way, images appear the same when viewed on different computer monitors, video monitors, printers, and other output devices. Unfortunately, with Microsoft Image Composer, gamma correction settings affect the RGB values used in the palette. If you enter a formula using the "legal" color values mentioned previously, you get a bit of a surprise when you view them in a browser: After you save your images, place them in your Web pages, and then view them in a browser, you might notice dithering, although you carefully developed your images using colors that should not dither in a browser.

To solve this problem, use one of the browser-safe palettes furnished on the FrontPage 97 with Bonus Pack CD-ROM. Figure 18.8 shows the directory in which the palettes appear. Choose the Custom Palette tab. Then load the Internet Explorer palette or the Netscape palette, as discussed in the "Choosing Your Current Color" section.

What happens if you use the "traditional" RGB values to specify a background color on a Web page in Microsoft FrontPage, and then you need to find that same color in Microsoft Image Composer's browser-safe palette? The key lies in the gamma settings in the Options dialog box.

To view or edit the gamma settings, follow these steps:

1. From Microsoft Image Composer, choose **T**ools | **O**ptions. The Options dialog box is displayed.
2. Select the Gamma tab, shown in Figure 18.9. The default gamma settings are shown in Table 18.2. You can recall these values at any time by clicking the **D**efaults button in the Gamma tab.

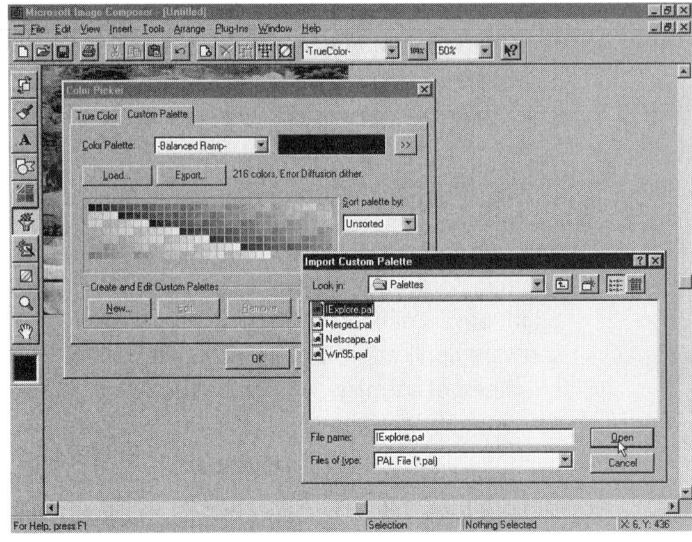

Figure 18.8.
The FrontPage 97 with Bonus Pack CD-ROM furnishes some browser-safe palettes that you can use with your images.

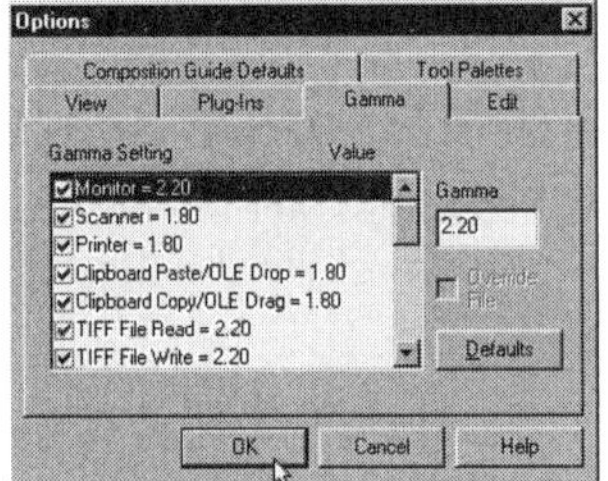

Figure 18.9.
You can adjust the gamma settings for your monitor and for several different file types in the Gamma tab of the Options dialog box.

3. Check the box beside each gamma setting that you want to apply to your images. Change the settings to values that read and write each type of graphics format so that they look suitable on your monitor. Every monitor is different, so you'll need to experiment here. In most cases, the default settings are sufficient. Disabling the gamma settings entirely causes your images and palettes to appear very dark as you work on them in Image Composer.
4. Click OK to save your selections.

Table 18.2. Default gamma correction settings in Microsoft Image Composer.

Device/Image Format	*Setting*
Monitor	2.20
Scanner	1.80
Printer	1.80

Device/Image Format	*Setting*
Clipboard Paste/OLE Drop	1.80
Clipboard Copy/OLE Drag	1.80
TIFF File Read	2.20
TIFF File Write	2.20
GIF File Read	1.80
GIF File Write	1.80
BMP File Read	1.80
BMP File Write	1.80
JPEG File Read	1.80
JPEG File Write	1.80
TGA File Read	2.20
TGA File Write	2.20
Photoshop File Read	1.80
Photoshop File Write	1.80
Palette File Read	1.80
Palette File Write	1.80

When the gamma settings are set to the default values shown in Table 18.2, Microsoft Image Composer adjusts the color values in the browser-safe palette, as shown in Table 18.3. Therefore, if you specify a background color of `51, 153, 204` in FrontPage, the gamma-corrected color in the browser-safe palette in Microsoft Image Composer is `14, 102, 171`.

Table 18.3. The default gamma-corrected browser-safe values.

RGB Value in FrontPage	*Gamma-Corrected Value in Image Composer*
0	0
51	14
102	49
153	102
204	171
255	255

Choosing Your Current Color

Before you create a shape or use a paint tool, you must select a color. When you click the Current Color Swatch beneath the toolbox, the Color Picker is displayed. This dialog box consists of two tabs: the True Color tab and the Custom Palette tab. Generally, you should pick browser-safe colors using the Custom Palette tab, though both methods of color selection are described in the following sections.

Using the True Color Tab

Use the True Color tab in the Color Picker to pick a color from the color matrix in the Color Picker. You can also use the True Color tab to create a color with a RGB color formula.

To choose a color from the True Color tab, follow these steps:

1. Choose **F**ile|**N**ew (Ctrl+N), or select the New button on the toolbar. A new composition is displayed.
2. Click the Current Color Swatch button beneath the toolbox. The Color Picker dialog box is displayed.
3. Click the True Color tab, shown in Figure 18.10. Use this tab to select a color from a color matrix, from an open image, or by entering an RGB or hue, saturation, value (HSV) formula.

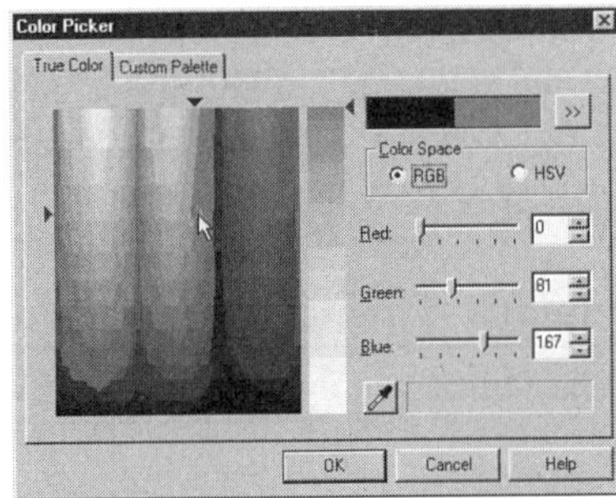

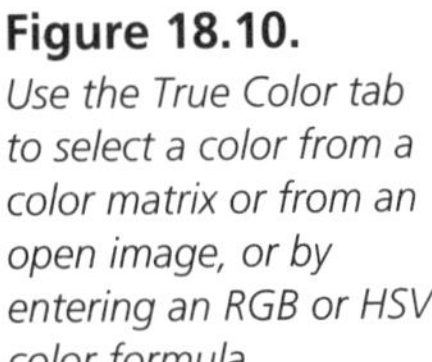

Figure 18.10.
Use the True Color tab to select a color from a color matrix or from an open image, or by entering an RGB or HSV color formula.

4. Select your color using one of the following methods:
   - To select a color from the color matrix, position the circle in the large color matrix over the hue of the color you want to use. Use the vertical bar to the right of the color matrix to add more white or black to the color.
   - To select a color from an open image, click the Eyedropper button in the dialog box. Click the eyedropper on the color you want to select.

- To specify an RGB color formula, select RGB from the Color Space area. Then enter your color formula in the **R**ed, **G**reen, and **B**lue fields.
- To specify an HSV color formula, select HSV from the Color Space area. Enter your formula in the **H**ue, **S**at, and **V**alue fields.

5. Choose OK. The color is displayed in the Current Color Swatch.

Picking a Browser-Safe Color

Use the Custom Palette tab in the Color Picker to choose a color from a browser-safe or custom palette. If you want to use a browser-safe palette, you must load or create a custom palette of your own.

To learn how to create your own custom palettes, see the "Creating Custom Palettes" section.

To load a custom palette and select a color from it, follow these steps:

1. Click the Current Color Swatch button beneath the toolbox. The Color Picker dialog box is displayed.
2. Click the Custom Palette tab, shown in Figure 18.11.

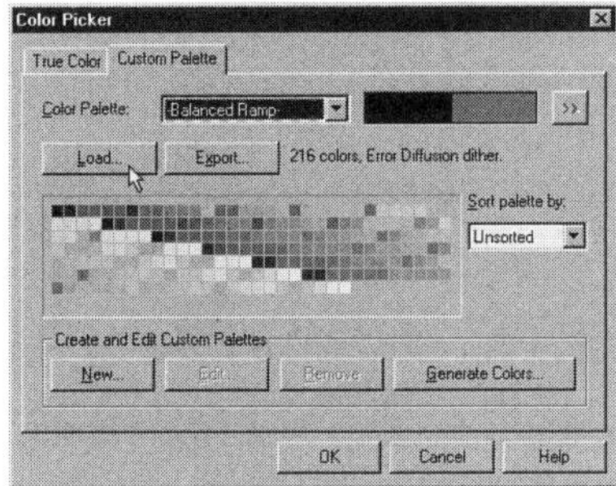

Figure 18.11.
Use the Custom Palette tab to load, edit, or create a custom palette.

3. Click **L**oad. The Import Custom Palette dialog box shown in Figure 18.12 is displayed.
4. Use the Look **i**n drop-down list box to locate the drive and directory in which your custom palette is saved.

NOTE: There are three browser-compatible palettes furnished on your FrontPage 97 with Bonus Pack CD-ROM. You can find these palettes in the `\ImgComp\Mmfiles\Palettes` directory on the FrontPage 97 with Bonus Pack CD: the Internet Explorer palette, `Iexplore.pal`; the Netscape palette, `Netscape.pal`; and a palette that combines both palettes' color values, `merged.pal`.

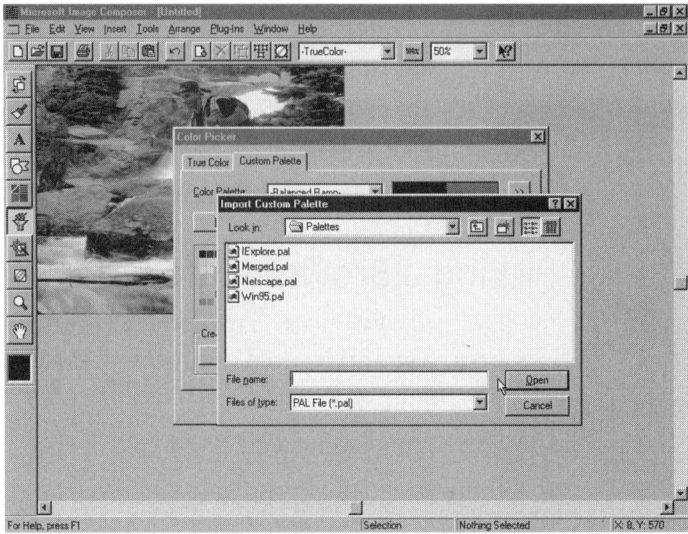

Figure 18.12.
Use the Import Custom Palette dialog box to locate the palette you want to load, edit, or save.

5. Double-click the palette file, which uses a `.pal` extension, to open it. The palette is displayed in the Custom Palette tab.
6. From the colors in the custom palette, click the color that you want to use for your current color.
7. Choose OK. The color is displayed in the Current Color Swatch.

Economizing Your Graphics

The next issue that the Web graphics developer must contend with is how to create graphics that are as "lean and mean" as they can be. Not everyone has a 56K modem or an ISDN connection. Indeed, there are still some who browse the Web using 9600 bps modems. Even with a 14.4 or 28.8 modem, graphics can take some time to load, so you want to economize your graphics as much as you can. There are several ways that you can reduce the amount of bandwidth that your images consume.

Sizing Your Graphics

The first and most logical way to keep the size of an image small is to keep the dimensions of the image small. A 100×100–pixel image consumes roughly 25 percent as much in kilobytes as a 200×200 image. One trick that some Web designers use is to display a smaller image in a larger area on a Web page. For example, the actual size of the image might be 100×100 pixels, but the Web page designer uses HTML commands to stretch the image into a 150×150–pixel square. However, some designers discourage this practice because it taxes the resources of the user's browser. Browsers do not resize an image as well as an image editing program can, so stretching an image to fit a larger area can take away from its appearance. It is best to create your image in the exact size you want to use.

Another alternative is to create a thumbnail version of the actual image to display on a Web page. If the user clicks the thumbnail or a link beside it, he or she then downloads the larger version of the image. This gives the user the opportunity to choose whether to view the image.

To create a thumbnail, a sample of which is shown in Figure 18.13, select all objects in your composition guide. Click the Duplicate button to create a copy, and move the copy to the outside of your composition. With all copied objects selected, choose **A**rrange | Flatten **S**election to flatten all the copied sprites into one object. Drag the lower-right corner of the flattened sprite while holding the Shift key to constrain the aspect ratio. To save the thumbnail as a Web image, choose **F**ile | Sa**v**e Selection As.

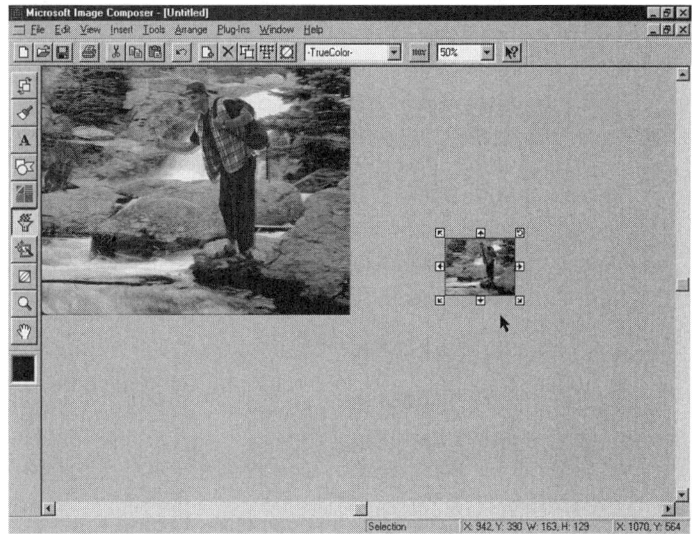

Figure 18.13.
Put a smaller thumbnail version of the image on your Web page, and let the user decide whether to opt to download the larger version of the image.

Trimming Your Images

Another way to economize the size of your image is to crop out any height or width that is not necessary for the image. Often, extra white space can be cropped from an image, leaving enough border around the focal area to frame it, as shown in the right side of Figure 18.14. You can use the Rectangle tool in the Shapes—Geometry palette to crop your image.

There are other ways you can reduce the size of an image. For example, look at your background images. Do you really need a 250×250 pixel image of grid paper? Economize it by cropping the image to contain only one square in the grid. The image tiles as necessary to fill the background.

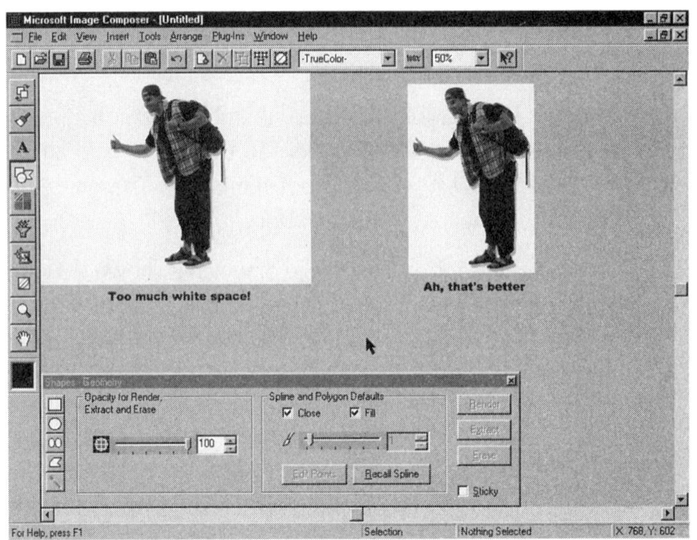

Figure 18.14.
Use as little white space as possible around your image to create a smaller file. You can use the Rectangle tool in the Shapes—Geometry palette to crop your image.

Reducing the Number of Colors

You can reduce the size of a GIF file by reducing the number of colors in its palette. For example, if your GIF file is a line art image or a cartoon that contains only 4 colors, the extra 252 colors in that 256-color palette are not necessary and only add extra weight to that file size. You can reduce the palette so that it contains only the number of colors necessary to display the image correctly.

You can also reduce the number of colors in a 256-color image without too much loss in quality. Depending on the image, you can reduce the palette down to 128 colors, or maybe even 64 colors, without taking away too much from the image. In the Web world, every little bit (and byte) helps.

Creating Custom Palettes

You can generate a custom palette from your image from the Custom Palette tab in the Color Picker. When you generate the colors in the palette, you specify the number of colors that you want to include in the palette. Generally, you want to generate the colors based on those in your current composition. The browser-safe colors you use are automatically included in the palette, because they are included within the image.

You will learn to create more custom palettes in **Chapter 23**.

To generate a custom color that reduces the number of colors in the palette, follow these steps:

1. From Microsoft Image Composer, choose **F**ile | **O**pen (Ctrl+O), or select the Open button on the standard toolbar. The Open dialog box is displayed.

2. Locate `example2.mic` on the CD that accompanies this book and double-click the file to open it. You will use this file to create a custom palette.
3. Click the Current Color Swatch. The Color Picker is displayed.
4. Choose the Custom Palette tab.
5. In the Create and Edit Custom Palettes section, click **N**ew. The New Color Palette dialog box shown in Figure 18.15 is displayed.

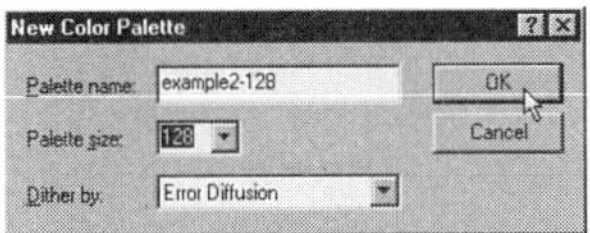

Figure 18.15.
Use the New Color Palette dialog box to assign a name, palette size, and dithering method to your new palette.

6. Enter or choose the following settings for the 128-color palette:

Palette name:	`example2-128`
Palette **s**ize:	`128`
Dither by:	`Error diffusion`

7. Choose OK. You will see 128 empty color squares in the palette area.
8. From the Create and Edit Custom Palettes section, click **G**enerate Colors. The Generate Colors dialog box shown in Figure 18.16 is displayed.

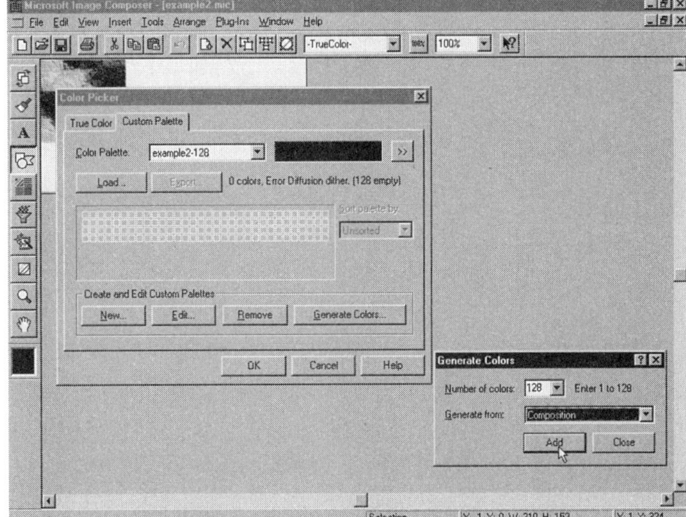

Figure 18.16.
Use the Generate Colors dialog box to add colors from your composition to the palette.

9. Enter or choose the following settings for your palette:

   Number of colors: `128`

   Generate from: `Composition`

10. Click Add. Microsoft Image Composer selects the 128 most-used colors from your image and places them in the palette.
11. Click Close to exit the Generate Colors dialog box.
12. Choose OK. Microsoft Image Composer generates the palette.
13. To apply the palette to your image, select example2-128 from the Color Format drop-down list in the standard toolbar. This gives you a preview of what the file will look like when you save the image using this palette.
14. To save the image using your custom palette, click **F**ile|Save **A**s. The Save As dialog box is displayed.
15. Use the Look **i**n field to select the drive and directory into which you want to save your image.
16. From the Save as **T**ype field, choose Compuserve GIF (`*.gif`).
17. From the Color **f**ormat field, select your custom palette. In this case, choose example2-128, as shown in Figure 18.17.
18. Click Save. The file is saved with 128 custom colors.

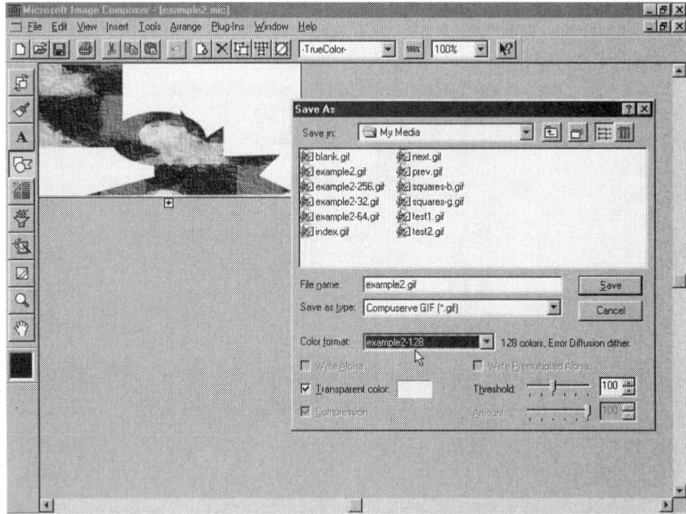

Figure 18.17.
Before you save your image, use the Color format field in the Save As dialog box to apply your palette to the image.

NOTE: Notice how the byte size of the file is reduced as the palette size of this image is reduced:

256 colors: 22,223
128 colors: 19,074
64 colors: 15,462
32 colors: 12,479

Downloading Once, Reusing Many Times

Another way to reduce bandwidth is to reuse graphics wherever you can. This goes beyond using the same buttons, icons, bullets, and horizontal lines in your pages. For example, look at your banners. Often, banner graphics contain repeated elements that give the site a consistent look and feel. For example, one half of a banner might contain a graphic that is common to many pages. The other half contains text that applies to one page. You can split the banner into two files and insert them side by side on your page or within a table. The user downloads the common half only once. When the user navigates to another page that uses the banner, the browser downloads the unique portion and reuses the common half.

Workshop Wrap-Up

The tasks in this chapter represent those that you are sure to use repeatedly. Many before you learned these tips through trial and error. You know ahead of time that you can improve the appearance of an image by choosing browser-safe colors. You can create crisp, clean images and economize on the byte size of the image by setting compression or reducing the number of colors in a palette.

In this chapter, you became more familiar with the graphic file formats used in Web pages. You know when you should save your Image Composer files to GIF and JPEG format. You also learned ways that you can create graphics that do not dither in browsers. Finally, you learned how to eliminate the extra baggage in a file to create the smallest byte size file that you can achieve.

Next Steps

In Chapter 19, "Creating Buttons, Icons, and Backgrounds," you learn how to create basic Web graphics—buttons, bullets, icons, backgrounds, and horizontal lines. You'll learn how to create basic sprites and how to apply simple effects to them.

For more graphics projects, refer to the following chapters:

- In Chapter 20, "Creating Banners and Text Effects," you'll learn how to create your own banners and open existing images and add text to them.
- In Chapter 21, "Montages and Image Maps," you'll learn how to create your own sprites and how to combine them with effects to create montages and image maps.
- In Chapter 22, "Creating Animations," you'll learn some ways that you can use Microsoft Image Composer to create animated GIFs.
- In Chapter 23, "Real-Life Examples: Setting the Mood," you'll learn how to use color and graphics effectively to set the mood of your Web site.

Q&A

Q: I have a hard time getting my JPEG compression settings right the first time. It's also hard sometimes to know how many colors to reduce a GIF palette to. Is there anything that can help?

A: Ulead PhotoImpact GIF/JPEG Smart Saver is a stand-alone or plug-in application that displays two copies of an image side by side so that you can test and compare before and after previews of your image while you adjust settings. It allows you to tell at a glance what the optimum settings are for your image. You can download a 30-day trial version of the stand-alone version of this application from `http://www.ulead.com`. I highly recommend it! One note, though: The application does not read Microsoft Image Composer (`.mic`) file format. You must save your image to a true color file format such as TGA and open that image in the Smart Saver.

Q: What is the difference between the Windows 95 palette and the browser-safe palette?

A: The Windows 95 palette contains 256 colors. It does include many of the colors that are contained in the browser-safe palette. However, it also includes 20 Windows system colors (the "pure" colors shown in Table 18.1 are among them) plus 20 additional colors.

CHAPTER NINETEEN

Creating Buttons, Icons, and Backgrounds

Many Web page designers use the basic B's—bullets, buttons, and backgrounds—to add more color to Web pages. These items can be as plain or as unique as the imagination allows. At times, navigation buttons display common symbols, called *icons*, to direct users to certain features in the web. Whereas some designers prefer to use basic shapes for buttons or bullets, others use small photo clips or create unique symbols of their own. You continue your adventure with Microsoft Image Composer using the geometric drawing tools to create the basic building blocks of Web pages.

Creating Basic Shapes

When you first open Microsoft Image Composer, a blank composition is displayed in your window. If you select one of the tools from the Paint palette and try to draw, however, nothing happens. This is because Microsoft Image Composer works with objects called *sprites*. The sprites float above the composition area, allowing you to add effects or combine them in any way you choose. When you open an existing bitmap, it "floats" above the composition background as a sprite.

In this chapter, you

- ❑ Learn how to create basic shapes
- ❑ Add warps and filters to your sprites
- ❑ Use fonts to create icons
- ❑ Create horizontal rules that break from traditional lines
- ❑ Use the Impressionist plug-in to create a seamless background
- ❑ Change the background color of your composition
- ❑ Save portions of your composition in GIF and JPG.

Tasks in this chapter:

- ❑ Creating Solid Bullets and Buttons
- ❑ Generating a Three-Dimensional Oval or Sphere
- ❑ Making Icons
- ❑ Creating Horizontal Rules
- ❑ Generating a Seamless Background
- ❑ Changing Your Composition Properties
- ❑ Building the Planetary Progression Buttons
- ❑ Saving Selected Sprites in JPG Format
- ❑ Saving Selected Sprites in GIF Format

For your first Microsoft Image Composer project, start by creating some basic shapes. You will learn to create small shapes for bullets and use slightly larger shapes with text for buttons.

Creating Solid Bullets and Buttons

It's easy to create a solid bullet or button. Bullets are typically very small, as they are commonly used next to text. You can make your bullets and buttons any shape or size using the geometric tools in the Tools palette. Each of the objects you create becomes a sprite, or a single floating object. Later, you can group these objects together to make more complex objects, or you can add effects to them.

To create sprites with a solid color, follow these steps:

1. From Microsoft Image Composer, click the New button on the Standard toolbar. A new composition opens.
2. Click the Current Color Swatch to display the Color Picker. Then select the Custom Palette tab.
3. Click Load, and then locate the Internet Explorer palette (`Iexplore.pal`) on your FrontPage 97 with Bonus Pack CD-ROM. You can find it in the `\ImgComp\Mmfiles\Palettes` directory.
4. Select any color from the palette except white.
5. Click the Shapes button in the Toolbox. The Shapes palette shown in Figure 19.1 is displayed, opened to the Shapes—Geometry tab by default.

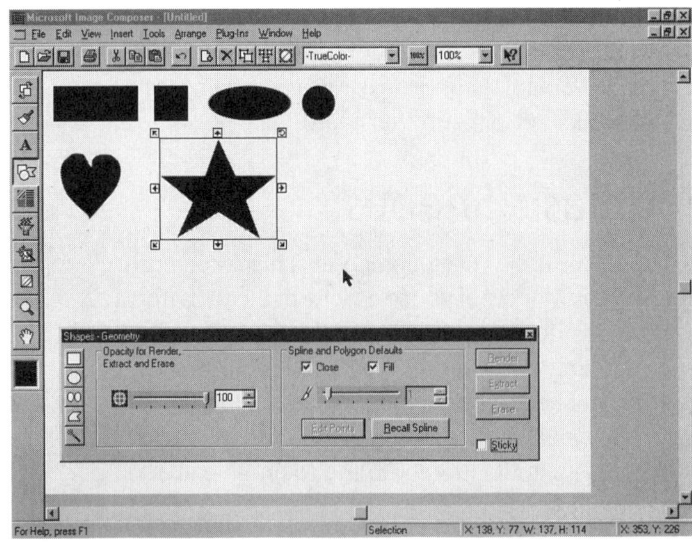

Figure 19.1.
Use the geometric tools in the Shapes—Geometry palette to create rectangles, squares, ovals, circles, spline polygons, and straight-lined polygons.

You also can use the geometric tools to extract, or cut out, portions of a bitmap to create sprites. You will learn more about this in **Chapter 20**.

6. Choose one of the geometric tools in the toolbox to create a shape. Try each of the following examples to create the shapes shown in Figure 19.1:
   - ❑ To create a solid rectangle, click the Rectangle tool. Click anywhere in the composition window to set the upper-left corner of the rectangle, and drag toward the lower-right corner of the rectangle while watching the status bar for the size. Click again when the status bar reads W: 100, H: 40. Release the mouse and click **R**ender to create a 100-pixel wide by 40-pixel high rectangle.
   - ❑ To create a solid square, click the Rectangle tool. Press the Ctrl+Alt keys to constrain the aspect ratio to a square while you draw. Then click to set the upper-left corner, and drag toward the lower-right corner until the status bar reads W: 40, H: 40. Release the mouse and click **R**ender to create a 40-pixel square.

TIP: When you draw an oval or circle, you have to imagine that it is completely enclosed by a bounding box. The upper-left corner of the bounding box corresponds to the left-most and top-most points in the oval. The lower-right corner of the bounding box corresponds to the right-most and bottom-most points in the oval.

   - ❑ To create a solid oval, click the Oval tool. Click anywhere in the composition window to set the upper-left corner of the oval, and drag toward the lower-right corner of the oval while watching the status bar for the size. Click again when the status bar reads W:100, H: 40. Click **R**ender to create an oval that is 100 pixels wide and 40 pixels high.
   - ❑ To create a solid circle, click the Oval tool. Press the Ctrl+Alt keys to constrain the aspect ratio to a circle while you draw. Then click to set the upper-left corner, and drag toward the lower-right corner until the status bar reads W: 40, H: 40. Click **R**ender to create a circle with a 40-pixel diameter.
   - ❑ To create an irregularly shaped spline with curved lines, click the Spline tool. Select Close and Fill, and set the Brush Size to 1. Click to set the first point in the heart (the top center point); then click again to set the second; and so on. Continue setting points in the spline until your heart looks similar to the one shown in Figure 19.1. To edit the points before you render the heart, click **E**dit Points in the Shapes palette. Move the mouse over the outline, and adjust the node points in the spline. Click **R**ender to create the sprite.

NOTE: You cannot edit the points in a sprite after you render it.

- To create an irregularly shaped button with straight lines, click the Polygon tool. Click to set the first point in the star shown in Figure 19.1. Click again to set the second, and so on. Continue setting points in the spline until your shape looks similar to the one shown in Figure 19.1. If you need to adjust the shape of the star, click Edit Points in the Shapes panel, and adjust the points as necessary. Click Render to create the sprite.

Generating a Three-Dimensional Oval or Sphere

If a solid button or bullet doesn't suit your fancy, you can create sprites with a three-dimensional feel. One way to make a circle or oval look more three-dimensional is to first create a gradient, apply the gradient to your circle, and then finish it with a radial sweep warp. Each of these processes is covered in the "Creating a Gradient," "Filling Your Symbols with a Gradient," and "Adding the Radial Sweep Warp" sections.

Creating a Gradient

First you create a gradient that you will use to fill the circle. In this exercise, you make one that diagonally ramps from bright purple at the top to black at the bottom.

To create your own gradient, follow these steps:

1. From the Toolbox, select Patterns and Fills. The Patterns and Fills palette shown in Figure 19.2 is displayed.
2. Select Gradient Ramp from the Patterns and Fills palette.
3. Verify that the Opacity slider at the lower-left side of the palette is set to `100`.
4. In the center of the dialog box, you will see a gradient surrounded by four color squares. You use these squares to create the gradient.
5. Click the upper-left square. The Color Picker dialog box is displayed.
6. Choose the Custom Palette tab and select bright purple (the third color in the third row) from the Internet Explorer palette. Click OK to return to the Patterns and Fills dialog box. The color of the upper-left color square turns bright purple.

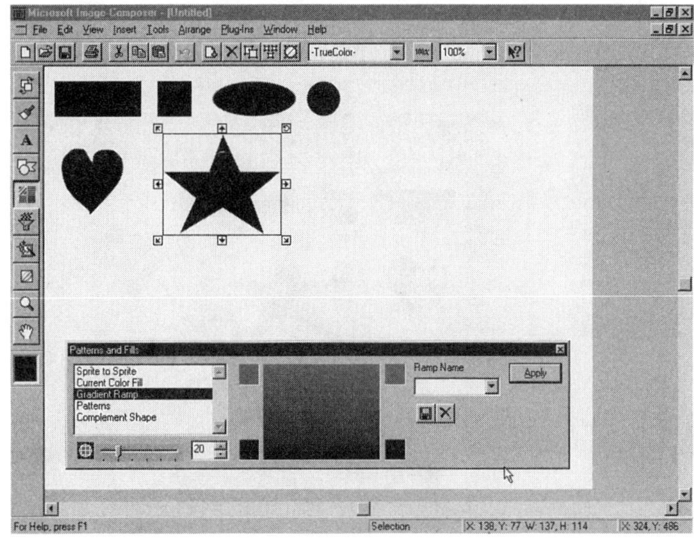

Figure 19.2.
Use the Patterns and Fills palette to combine sprites or fill them with your current color, a gradient ramp, patterns, or complement shapes.

7. Now you can copy the color square you just defined into the upper-right square in the gradient preview. To do this, click and drag the upper-left color square to the upper-right color square and release the mouse. The upper-right color square turns bright purple.
8. Click the lower-left square. The Color Picker dialog box is displayed.
9. Select black from the Internet Explorer palette (the last color). Choose OK to return to the Patterns and Fills palette. The lower-left square turns black.
10. Click and drag the lower-left color square to the lower-right color square. Release the mouse. You now have a gradient that changes from bright purple on the top to black on the bottom.
11. In the Ramp Name field of the Patterns and Fills palette, enter `Purple`.
12. Click the Save Ramp button (the button displaying the disk) to save your new gradient.

Filling Your Symbols with a Gradient

Now you can use the gradient you just made to change the color of your symbols. To fill the symbols with your gradient, follow these steps for each of the symbols in your composition:

1. Click the solid circle and select Duplicate from the Standard toolbar. A copy of the circle is displayed in your composition.
2. With the copy selected, choose Patterns and Fills from the toolbox if it is not still selected. The Patterns and Fills palette is displayed.

3. Select Gradient Ramp and choose Purple from the list of available gradients.
4. Click **A**pply. The circle fills with the purple gradient, as shown in Figure 19.3.

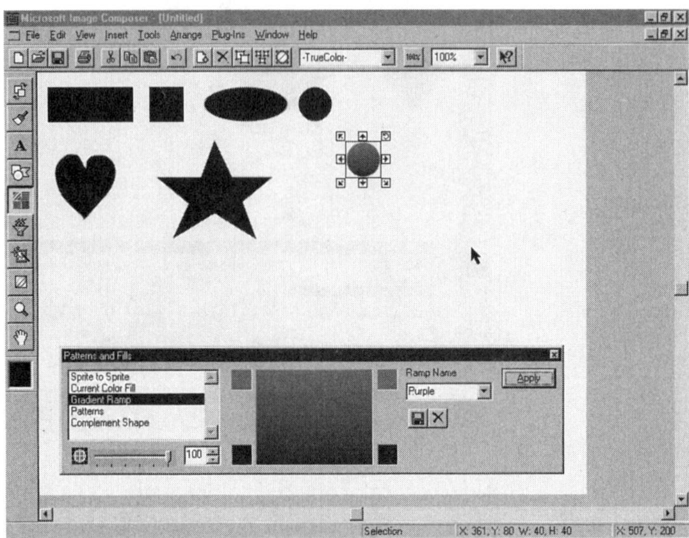

Figure 19.3.
Fill a copy of the solid circle with the purple and black gradient.

Adding the Radial Sweep Warp

Right now, your circle is filled with a gradient that ramps from purple on the top to black on the bottom. Now let's change the appearance of the circle so that black is on the outside, and purple is on the inside. To do this, you must apply a radial sweep warp.

The radial sweep warp works best with linear ramps. If you enter a positive value in the Angle field, the color at the top of the gradient appears on the inside and the color at the bottom of the gradient appears on the outside. If you enter a negative value in the Angle field, the reverse happens: The color at the bottom of the gradient appears on the inside, and the color at the top of the gradient appears on the outside.

To apply the radial sweep warp to your circle, follow these steps:

1. Click the circle that is filled with the gradient ramp.
2. From the toolbox, select Warps and Filters. The Warps and Filters palette is displayed.
3. Select Warps from the drop-down menu. Then select Radial Sweep from the list of warps.
4. In the Angle field, enter `90`.
5. Click **A**pply. The circle now looks like a three-dimensional sphere as shown in Figure 19.4.

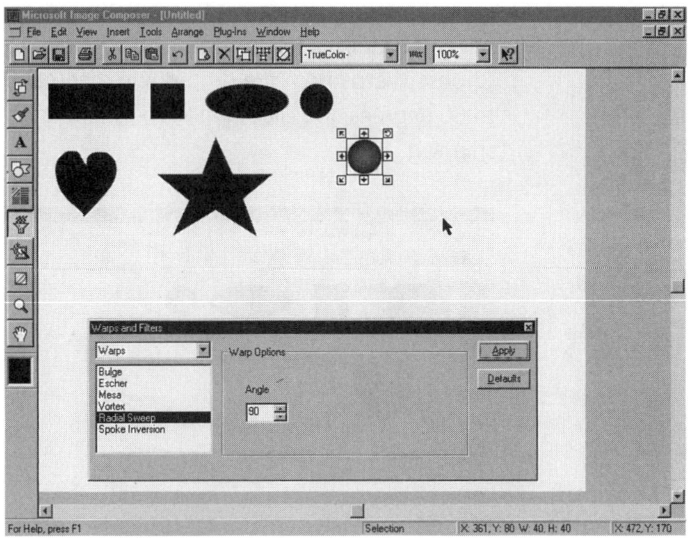

Figure 19.4.
After you apply a radial sweep warp, the circle looks like a sphere.

TIP: If you don't like the way the sphere looks, choose Edit | Undo to return the bullet back to the linear gradient. Then try a new Angle setting. If you reapply a radial sweep warp to a circle that already has the effect, it eventually begins to look like an archery target.

Trying More Warps

Figure 19.5 shows three more sprites on the right side of the composition window that implement some of the additional warps and filters that are available in the Warps and Filters palette. Try some of these examples yourself:

- Click the solid rectangle and press the Duplicate button on the Standard toolbar. Choose Patterns and Fills from the toolbox; then select the Red Blue Green gradient from the Patterns and Fills palette. Choose Warps and Filters from the toolbox. Choose Warps from the drop-down menu and select Vortex. Set the Angle to 45 degrees and click **A**pply. The colors in the gradient now spiral around the center.
- Click the Oval to select it. Choose Patterns and Fills from the toolbox and select the Purple gradient. Then choose Warps and Filters from the toolbox. Choose Warps from the drop-down menu and select Spoke Inversion. Set the Value to `100` and click **A**pply. The gradient radiates from a point in the center of the oval.

- ❑ Click the Star to select it. Choose Patterns and Fills from the toolbox and select the Gold gradient. Then choose Warps and Filters from the toolbox. Choose Warps from the drop-down menu and select Vortex. Set the Angle to 60 degrees and click **A**pply. The shape of the star warps as though it is spinning.

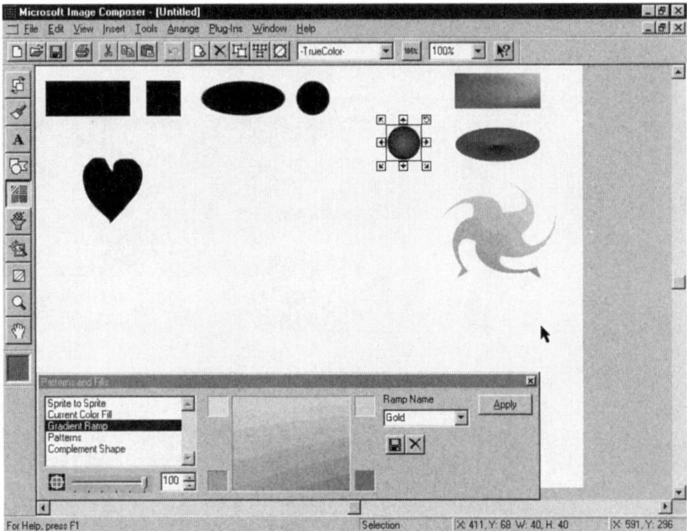

Figure 19.5.
Three additional effects from the Warps and Filters palette are shown at the right of the composition guide.

Making Icons

One of the quickest and easiest ways to create icons is to use the Wingdings font. This font is installed with Windows 95 and Windows NT, and it includes several symbols that you can use to create icons. Table 19.1 lists some of the symbols and the keyboard entry that you use to type the symbol.

Table 19.1. Some handy symbols available with the Wingdings font.

Keyboard Entry	*Wingdings Symbol*
0	Closed File Folder
1	Open File Folder
2	Document with Folded Corner
3	Document
4	Three Documents
5	File Cabinet

Keyboard Entry	*Wingdings Symbol*
) (Shift+0)	Telephone Handset in Circle
! (Shift+1)	Pencil
@ (Shift+2)	Pencil in Hand
$ (Shift+4)	Glasses
& (Shift+7)	Open Book
* (Shift+8)	Envelope
((Shift+9)	Telephone
B	Hand—"OK"
C	Hand—"Thumbs Up"
D	Hand—"Thumbs Down"
E	Hand Pointing Left
F	Hand Pointing Right
G	Hand Pointing Up
H	Hand Pointing Down
J	Smiley Face
K	Face with Straight Mouth
L	Sad Face
,	Closed Mailbox
.	Open Mailbox with Mail
/	Open Mailbox, Empty
:	Computer
<	Floppy Disk

Creating the Symbols for Your Icons

In the following task, you use some of the Wingdings symbols to create circular icons for a Web page. Each icon is placed in a circular sprite, which is outlined with a contrasting color.

To create the icons, follow these steps:

1. Select the Text icon from the Toolbox. The Text palette is displayed.
2. Click **S**elect Font. The Font dialog box is displayed, listing all the fonts available on your system. Scroll down the list to select Wingdings, as shown in Figure 19.6.

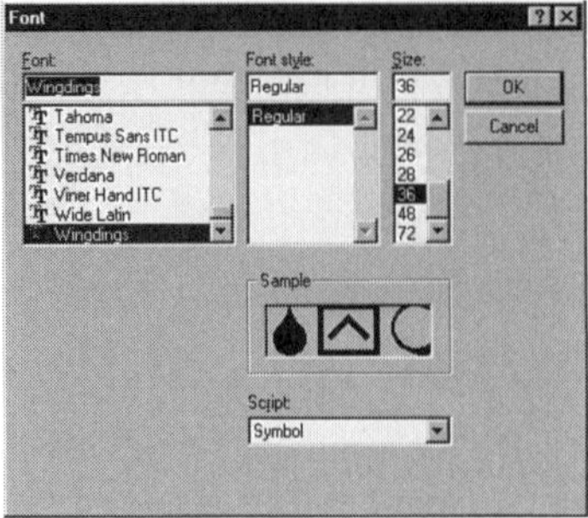

Figure 19.6.
Use the Text palette to select the Wingdings font, which contains symbols that you can use in icons.

3. From the **S**ize list, select 36.
4. Choose OK. You return to the Text palette.
5. Click the Current Color Swatch. The Color Picker is displayed.
6. Click the Custom Palette tab. Select Black (or your color preference) from the custom palette.
7. Choose OK. You return to the Text palette.
8. In the text field, type B (a capital letter *B*). You see a hand symbol instead of the letter.
9. Click **A**pply. The hand symbol is displayed in the document window.
10. Create six more symbols as follows:
    - Press Backspace, type C, and click **A**pply.
    - Press Backspace, type D, and click **A**pply.
    - Press Backspace, type E, and click **A**pply.
    - Press Backspace, type F, and click **A**pply.
    - Press Backspace, type G, and click **A**pply.
    - Press Backspace, type H, and click **A**pply. You should now have seven hand symbols, as shown in Figure 19.7.
11. Click each symbol and arrange them on your document window so that they do not overlap.
12. Click the Current Color Swatch, and choose orange (the 17th color in the third row). Click OK to return to the composition.
13. Select the Shapes palette, and choose the Oval tool. Press the Ctrl+Alt keys while you click and drag to create a circle that has a 50-pixel diameter. The status bar will read W:50, H:50 when the circle is the correct size. Click **R**ender to create the circle.

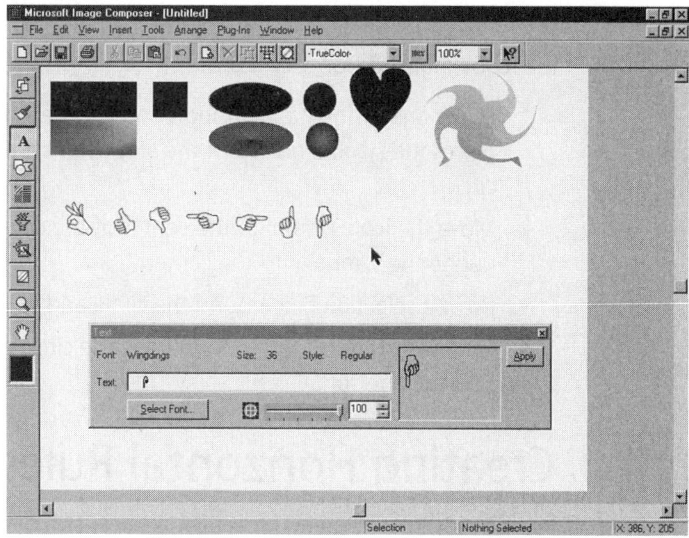

Figure 19.7.
Create seven hand symbols using the Wingdings font.

14. Choose the Warps and Filters palette. From the Warps list, select Outlines, and choose Edge. Set Thickness to `2` and Opacity to `100`. Click the Color square in the Outlines palette and then select the fourth color in the second row (red) for the outline color. Click **A**pply to render the outline.
15. Use the Duplicate button on the Standard toolbar to create six additional copies of the circle. Arrange them in a line, as shown in Figure 19.8.

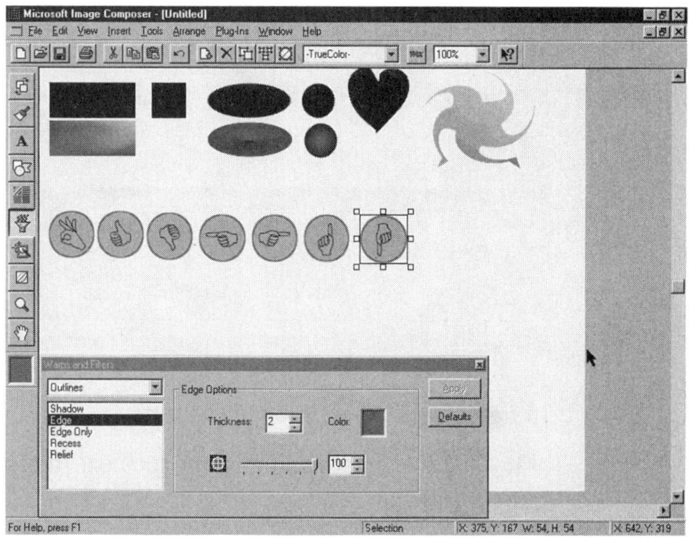

Figure 19.8.
Create seven circles for the icon buttons and arrange them in a line.

Now you will combine the icon symbols with the circles to create your icons. Perform the following steps for each icon:

1. Select one of the hand symbols and choose **A**rrange | Bring to Fron**t**. This places the symbol on top of the stack so that it is displayed in front of the circle.
2. Move the icon symbol to the center of the circle; then use the arrow keys to nudge the symbol into the center.
3. Draw a selection box around the circle and its symbol to select both items.
4. Choose **A**rrange | Flatten **S**election. The circle and the symbol combine to become one sprite.

Creating Horizontal Rules

You already know how to create rectangles, and many horizontal rules you see are made from rectangles. However, horizontal rules don't always have to be rectangular. For example, you can create a wavy line, such as that shown in Figure 19.9.

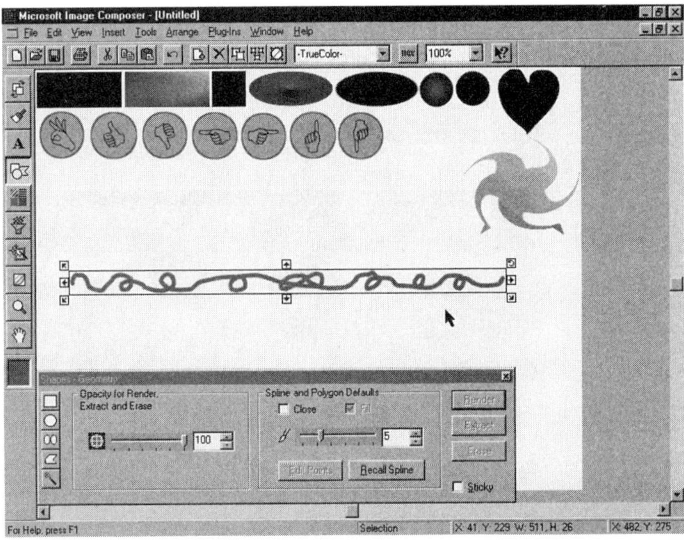

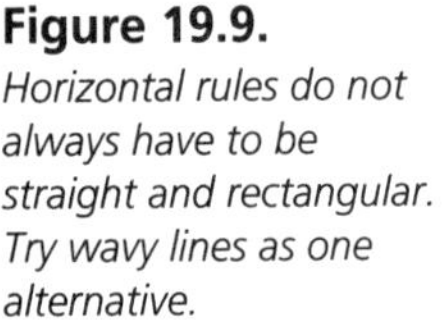

Figure 19.9.
Horizontal rules do not always have to be straight and rectangular. Try wavy lines as one alternative.

To create a wavy line, follow these steps:

1. Click the Shapes button in the toolbox. The Shapes—Geometry palette is displayed.
2. Choose the Spline tool. In the Spline and Polygon defaults section, make sure that Close and Fill are not selected. Set the Spline width to 5.

3. Click the Current Color Swatch and select a color for your spline (you can use any color you like).
4. Click to set the start point in the curved line. Continue clicking at random points to create a curved line.
5. After you click the last point in the line, click **R**ender. The wavy line is displayed in your composition.

TIP: You can reuse your spline to create lines with different widths. Adjust the Width setting in the Shapes palette, and click **R**ecall Spline. The spline is displayed again in your composition. Click Render to create another line using the same spline.

After you render your horizontal line, you can change its color at any time. Select another color, and choose Current Color Fill from the Patterns and Fills palette. Or try some of the other options in the Patterns and Fills palette; for example, fill the line with a gradient or a pattern to add interest. Be daring; fill with a gradient or color and then fill with a pattern after that. You can get some interesting results!

You also can create horizontal rules from photographic images. There is a very good selection of sprites and photographs included on the FrontPage 97 with Bonus Pack CD-ROM. In the following example, you'll use one of those images to create a horizontal line made from billiard balls.

To create the horizontal line, follow these steps:

1. Draw a selection rectangle around all the sprites in your composition and move them out of your composition guide area.
2. Insert your FrontPage 97 with Bonus Pack CD-ROM into your drive. AutoStart might open the FrontPage 97 setup screen. You can press Escape or click the Close button at the upper-right corner of the dialog box to cancel setup.
3. From Microsoft Image Composer, choose **I**nsert | **F**rom File. This keeps your current composition open and inserts the contents of another image into your composition as a sprite.
4. From your CD-ROM drive, locate the `billiard.mic` image in the `ImgComp\Mmfiles\Photos\Metaphor\PhotoDsc` directory. Double-click the file to open it in your composition window.
5. Click the Zoom Percent drop-down menu in the Standard toolbar, and choose 33% to zoom out from your composition.

6. Press the Shift key; then drag the lower-left corner of the billiard image to scale it down to the size of your composition guide, as shown in Figure 19.10.

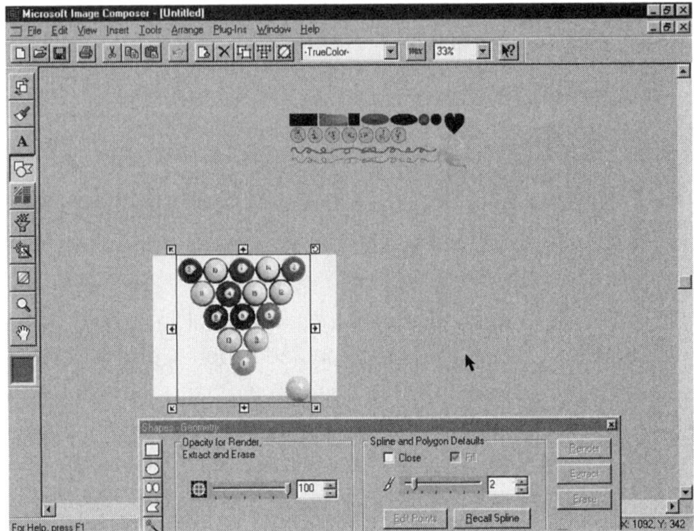

Figure 19.10.
Insert the image `billiard.mic` *from the FrontPage 97 with Bonus Pack CD-ROM. Scale the image to the size of your composition guide.*

You will use the Oval tool to extract each of the billiard balls from this image. You'll use the Ctrl+Alt keys to create circular selections. It will be easier to create your extractions if you zoom in to the image as shown in the figure.

To create each extraction, follow these steps:

1. Choose 300% from the Zoom Percent drop-down menu in the Standard toolbar to zoom in closer to the billiard image.
2. Click the Shapes button in the toolbox. The Shapes—Geometry palette opens.
3. Click to select the billiard image before you select the oval tool. If you create the oval without the original image selected, the oval renders as a solid sprite instead of extracting the area from the billiard image.
4. Click the Oval tool in the Shapes palette.
5. Start your oval in its upper-left corner, at a point slightly below and to the right of an imaginary box that surrounds the first billiard ball. You want the edges of the bounding box to appear just within the boundaries of the billiard ball, as shown in Figure 19.11.

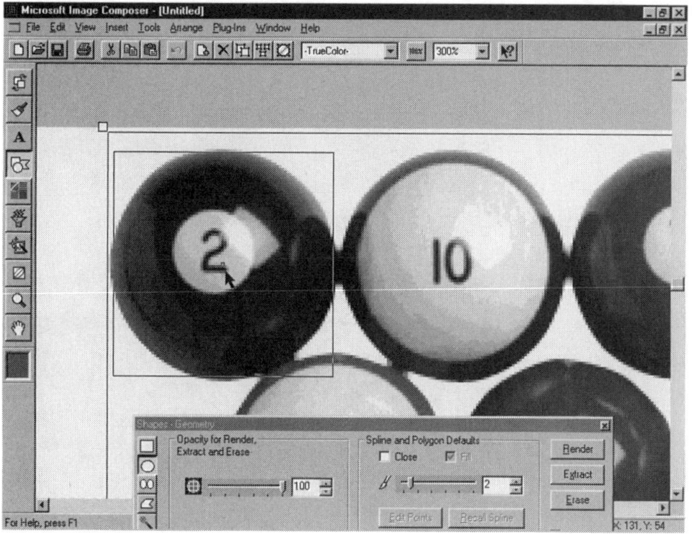

Figure 19.11.
Draw the bounding box for the oval so that its edges appear just within the edges of the billiard ball you want to extract.

TIP: You can adjust the oval before you extract the selection: Move the mouse to the side you want to adjust, and click the small square that is displayed on your oval's bounding box. Then move the adjustment point until it fits just within the billiard ball.

6. When your oval's bounding box is sized correctly, click E**x**tract. Move the copy of the billiard ball away from the original image; then click the original image to reselect it for the next extraction.
7. Continue in this manner until you extract all the billiard balls from the image.
8. After you extract all the billiard balls (there are 16 in all, including the cue ball at the lower-right edge of the image), click the original image and press Delete. This removes the original image from the composition window.
9. Now select each billiard ball and arrange them in a line, as shown in Figure 19.12. You can put them in any order you choose.
10. Click and drag to create a selection box around all the billiard balls to select them.
11. Choose **A**rrange | Flatten **S**election (Ctrl+F). All the billiard balls are flattened to one single object.

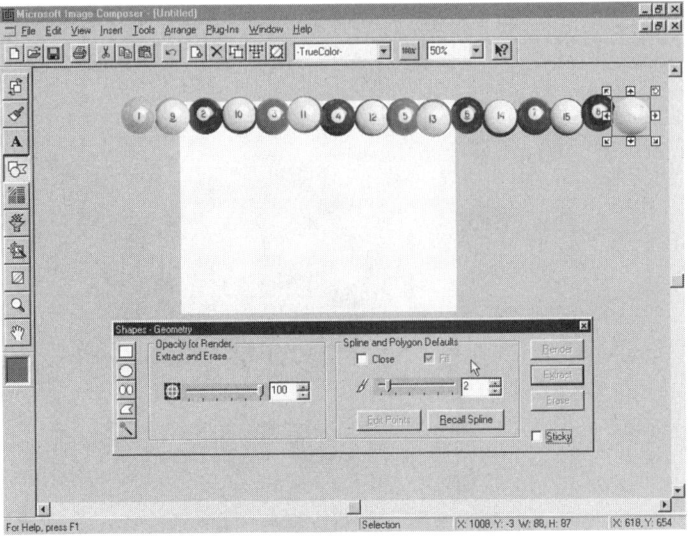

Figure 19.12.
Arrange the billiard ball extractions in a line.

12. Press the Shift key while you drag the lower-right corner of the billiard ball line to resize it. This keeps the proper aspect ratio while you resize the line to a width that is more appropriate for your Web page. A width between 475 and 575 pixels works well. Your horizontal line of billiard balls should look like Figure 19.13 when it is finished.

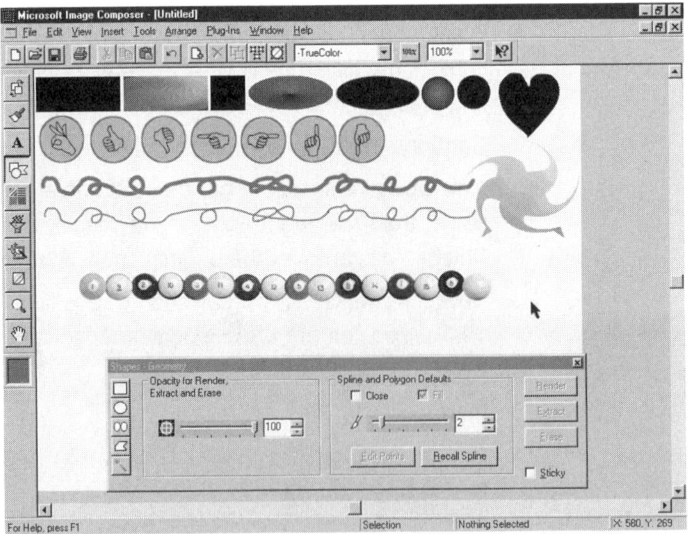

Figure 19.13.
Resize the billiard ball line so that it is a proper width for your Web page.

Generating a Seamless Background

With Microsoft Image Composer, you don't really have a "one-button solution" to create seamless backgrounds. However, there are some features that help you create backgrounds that come close to being seamless. One way is to start with a square that has a solid background color. Then you can use the Impressionist plug-in to add texture to the solid color. This creates some nice effects for backgrounds.

The Impressionist plug-in is quite remarkable. It contains an almost endless supply of effects that you can apply to your compositions. Fortunately, you can run a demo that shows how each choice affects your composition.

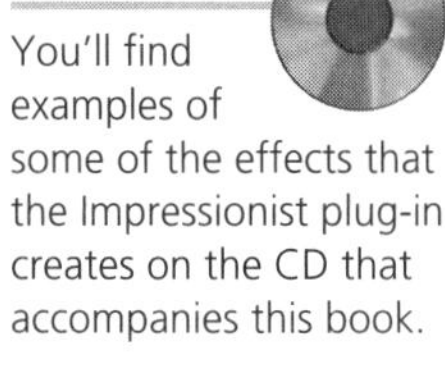

You'll find examples of some of the effects that the Impressionist plug-in creates on the CD that accompanies this book.

To create a background image using the Impressionist plug-in, follow these steps:

1. Click the Current Color Swatch. Choose a light color for your background, and click OK to return to your composition. For this example, I used the ninth color in the first row of the Internet Explorer palette, which is a very light gold color.
2. From the toolbox, click the Shapes button. The Shapes palette is displayed.
3. Choose the Rectangle tool.
4. Press the Ctrl+Alt keys; then click and drag your mouse to create a square that measures 128×128 pixels.
5. Click **R**ender. A solid color square is displayed in your composition window.
6. Choose **P**lug-Ins | Impressionist | Impressionist. The Impressionist dialog box shown in Figure 19.14 is displayed.

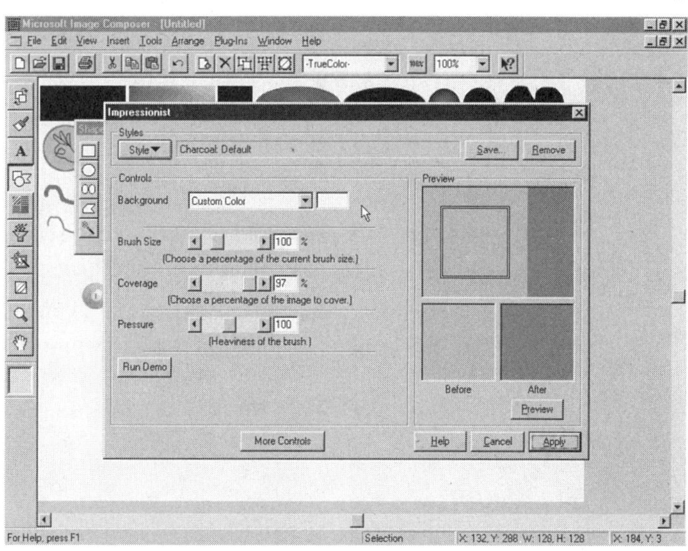

Figure 19.14.

The Impressionist plug-in contains an almost endless supply of effects that you can apply to your sprites.

7. It would take pages to detail all the effects that are available in this filter. Fortunately, there is an easy way to choose one that fits the bill. To preview the effects in the Impressionist plug-in, click the Run Demo button located in the lower-left portion of the dialog box. This goes quite fast on a Pentium computer, but may take some time on a slower processor. When you see an effect you like, press the Esc key to halt the demo. The name of the effect is displayed beneath the Run Demo button. Choose this effect from the Style drop-down menu, and click the **P**review button to make sure it is the right effect. For the example shown in the figure, I used `Conte: Faithful`.
8. To apply the effect to the square, click **A**pply. The square now has a texture and multiple colors.
9. To test how the tiling looks, choose the Rectangle tool again. Draw a square at least twice the size of the original rectangle (in this case, draw a 256×256 pixel square). Click **R**ender to create the square.
10. Select the new large square, and then choose Patterns and Fills from the toolbox. The Patterns and Fills palette is displayed.
11. Select Sprite to Sprite. From the Sprite Texture Type drop-down list, select Tile.
12. Click **A**pply. A Microsoft Image Composer Hint dialog box is displayed, telling you to click a source sprite (you can disable this dialog box by deselecting the Always show this message check box in the lower-left corner). Click OK to close the Hint box; then click your background image. The larger square becomes filled with a tile of the background.
13. Check for obvious seams. You can use the Smudge tool in the Paint palette to smudge some of the obvious seams a bit, as shown in Figure 19.15. (It may be necessary to reduce the Brush Size setting of the Smudge tool down between 3 and 5 to accomplish this.)
14. After you clean the seams, select the Shapes palette again. Click to activate the large rectangle. Then select the Rectangle tool from the Shapes palette again.
15. Press Ctrl+Alt; then drag within the large rectangle to create a square sized the same as the original background image (128×128 in this case).
16. Click E**x**tract. Now you should have a seamless background. To test it again, click the large rectangle and repeat steps 10–13.

Figure 19.15.
Use the Smudge tool from the Paint palette to smooth the obvious seams.

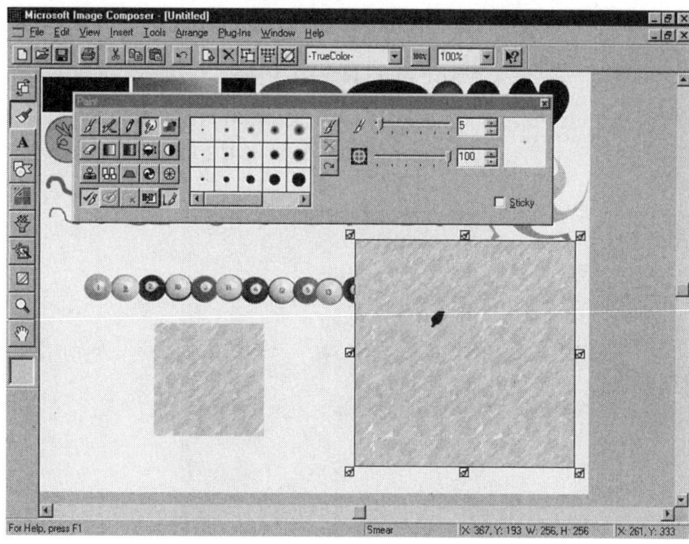

Working on the Planetary Progressions Images

In this chapter and in Chapters 20–23, you will apply some of what you learn in each chapter to create images that work together for a fictitious site that focuses on ecological concerns. The site will use a frameset, and each frame in the frameset will have a different color for a background. One of the frames will be black, one medium blue, and one light blue.

You learn how to size your banners and image maps for frame sets in **Chapter 20**.

In this chapter, you will work on the graphic for the top frame in the frameset, which uses navigation buttons to take the user to the main pages in a section of the Web. The background color for this frame will be a medium blue. To change the color of your composition area, you use the Composition Properties dialog box, described in the following task.

Changing Your Composition Properties

It's always a good idea to develop your graphics using the same background color that your page uses. This way, you can view how the pages will look on your page as you develop them. If you are uncertain of the color that you will use on your pages, you can use a white background if your pages will be light, or a black background if your pages will have a dark color.

To change the background color of your composition, follow these steps:

1. Choose **F**ile | **N**ew (Ctrl+N). A new document is opened.
2. Choose **F**ile | Composi**t**ion Properties. The Composition Properties dialog box shown in Figure 19.16 is displayed.

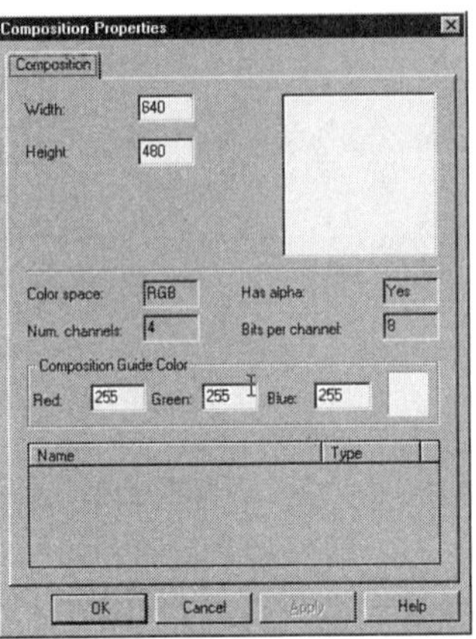

Figure 19.16.
Use the Composition Properties dialog box to adjust the size and background color of your composition guide.

3. To change the size of your composition, enter the width of your composition in the Width field and the height of your composition in the Height field. Unless otherwise noted in the tasks in this chapter, you will create your compositions in a 640×480 composition area, which is the default. If your settings differ, enter 640 in the Width field, and 480 in the Height field.
4. In the Composition Guide Color section, enter the Red/Green/Blue formula that represents the background color of your page. The default composition color is white (Red `255`, Green `255`, Blue `255`). To change the composition guide color to medium blue, enter Red `14`, Green `102`, Blue `255`. As you enter the numbers, the preview square changes.

CAUTION: In Chapter 18, "An Introduction to Graphics on the Web," I stress the importance of using browser-safe colors and to remember the numbers `0`, `51`, `102`, `153`, `204`, and `255`. However, Microsoft Image Composer modifies the palette to compensate for gamma correction. The numbers `14` and `102` in the previous step are gamma-corrected entries for the numbers `51` and `153` when the default gamma correction settings are used in Microsoft Image Composer. For more information, refer to Chapter 18.

5. Choose OK. The composition size and background color changes to medium blue.

Building the Planetary Progression Buttons

Now that you have your composition properties set, you can begin working on the image. First you'll load the Internet Explorer palette from your FrontPage 97 with Bonus Pack CD-ROM. Then you'll create some rectangular buttons. The buttons will be composed of two rectangles, each filled with the same gradient. The gradient on the second rectangle will be flipped horizontally. Then you'll add an accent line and some text.

To load the Internet Explorer palette, follow these steps:

1. Click the Current Color Swatch beneath the toolbox. The Color Picker dialog box is displayed.
2. Click the Custom Palette tab.
3. Click the **L**oad button. The Import Custom Palette dialog box is displayed.
4. From the Look **i**n drop-down menu, locate the drive and directory in which the palette is saved. You'll find the Internet Explorer palette, `Iexplore.pal`, in the `\ImgComp\Mmfiles\Palettes` directory of your FrontPage 97 with Bonus Pack CD-ROM.
5. Double-click the palette file to load it. The palette is displayed in the Color Picker window, as shown in Figure 19.17.

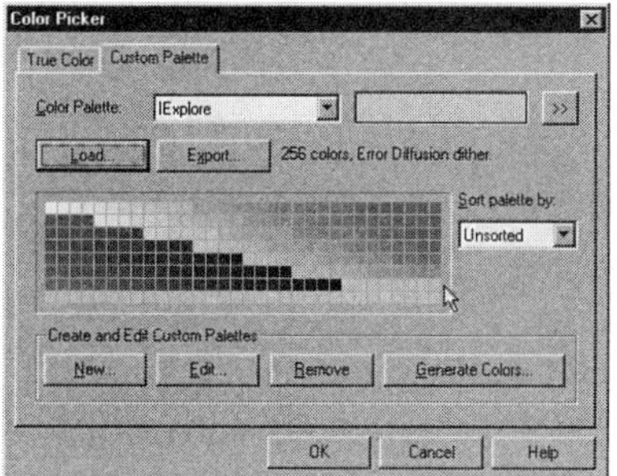

Figure 19.17.
The Internet Explorer palette loads into the Custom Palette tab in the Color Picker.

Next you'll create the first rectangular button. The button measures 60 pixels wide and 35 pixels high. You'll create seven buttons in all, each of which navigate the user to a particular page or feature within a section of the Web site.

To create the first button, follow these steps:

1. Select Black from the Custom Palette tab (the last color in the palette). Choose OK to return to the composition.

2. Choose the Shapes button from the toolbox. The Shapes—Geometry palette is displayed.
3. Click the Rectangle tool. Draw a rectangle that measures 60 pixels wide and 35 pixels high. (The coordinates in the status bar should read W: 60, H: 35.) Click **R**ender to complete the rectangle.
4. Click the Rectangle tool again. Draw a rectangle that measures 56 pixels wide and 31 pixels high. (The coordinates in the status bar should read W: 56, H: 31.) Click **R**ender to complete the second rectangle.
5. From the toolbox, choose Patterns and Fills. The Patterns and Fills palette is displayed. Select Gradient Ramp.
6. You will create a new gradient ramp, using blue and purple. Click the upper-left color square in the gradient. The Color Picker dialog box is displayed. Choose the 13th color in the fifth row of the Internet Explorer palette (dark purple) and click OK. The color is displayed in the Current Color Swatch.
7. Drag the color from the upper-left swatch in the gradient to the lower-left swatch to copy it.
8. Click the upper-right color square in the gradient. The Color Picker dialog box is displayed. Choose the first color in the seventh row (medium blue) and click OK. The color is displayed in the Current Color Swatch.
9. Drag the color from the upper-right swatch in the gradient to the lower-right swatch to copy it. You now have a gradient that ramps horizontally from dark purple to blue, as shown in Figure 19.18.

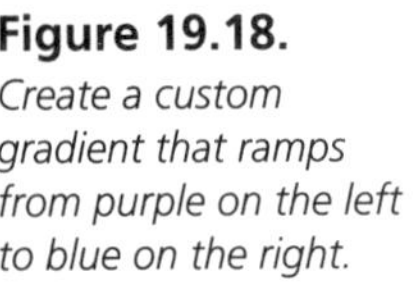

Figure 19.18.
Create a custom gradient that ramps from purple on the left to blue on the right.

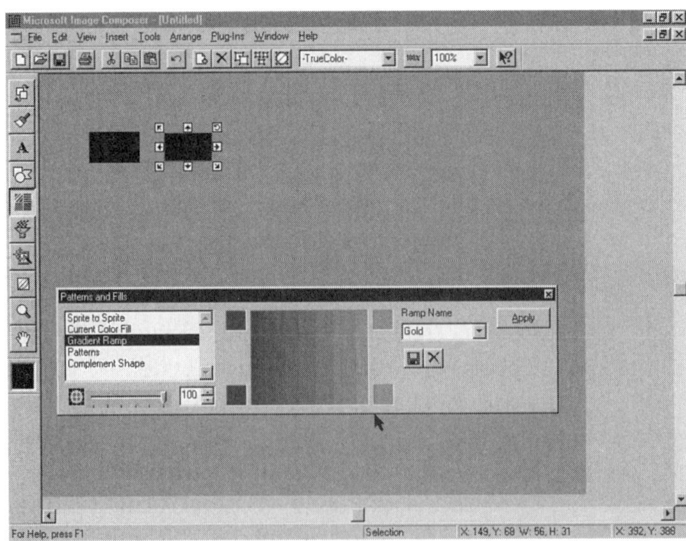

10. Click the first rectangle to select it; then click **A**pply in the Patterns and Fills palette. The rectangle fills with the gradient.
11. Click the second rectangle to select it; then click **A**pply in the Patterns and Fills palette. The second rectangle fills with the gradient.
12. With the second rectangle selected, choose **A**rrange | Fli**p** | **H**orizontal. The second rectangle now ramps from blue to purple.

In the next few steps, you will add a highlight line to the top and right sides of the smaller rectangle. It will help if you zoom in closer to the rectangle before you draw your lines.

To add the highlight, follow these steps:

1. Select the Zoom tool from the toolbox. Click twice to zoom in to the second rectangle, to a zoom factor of 300 percent.
2. Click the Current Color Swatch, and select a light blue (the 23rd color from the left in the fifth row). Then click OK to return to the composition.
3. Click the Shapes palette. The Shapes—Geometry palette is displayed.
4. Select the Polygon tool from the Shapes palette. Choose the following settings:

Opacity:	100
Close:	Unchecked
Fill:	(disabled)
Spline line width:	1
Sticky:	Unchecked

5. Click at the upper-left corner of the second rectangle. Then click the upper-right corner, and finally the lower-right corner.

TIP: Choose **E**dit Points from the Shapes palette to adjust the points in your line if they are crooked. Render the line after you repair your polygon.

6. Click **R**ender. A light blue line is displayed at the top and right edges of the rectangle, as shown in Figure 19.19. (The background in the figure is white to display this more visibly.)
7. Draw a selection box around the second rectangle and the line. Choose **A**rrange | Flatten **S**election to combine the two objects into one object.
8. Move the second rectangle into the first rectangle; then use the arrow keys to nudge the second rectangle into the center of the first. Draw a selection box around the group of sprites that make up the button. Choose **A**rrange | Flatten **S**election to combine the two into one object.

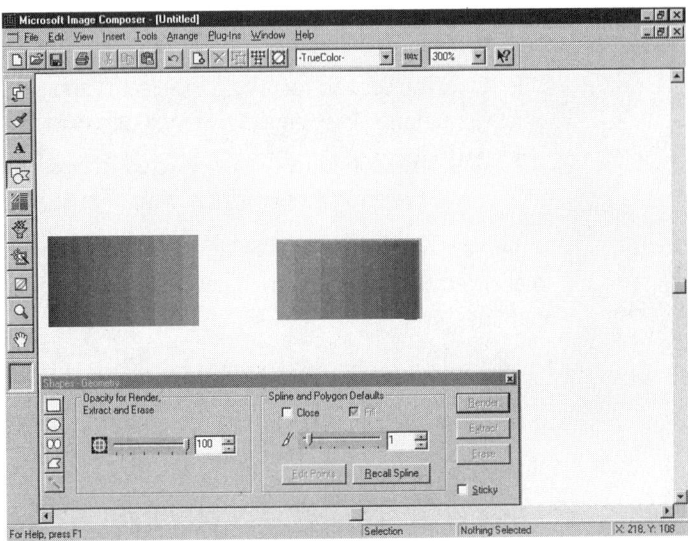

Figure 19.19.
Draw a light blue line along the top and right sides of the smaller rectangle using the Polygon tool in the Shapes palette.

Next you will create six copies of the button and add text to each one. It helps if you align all the buttons before you add your text. This way you can be sure that the text on each button is displayed at the same height.

To create copies of the button and add text, follow these steps:

1. Choose the Actual Size button in the Standard toolbar to return the composition to 100 percent zoom. Press the Home key to return the composition guide to home position.
2. Select the first button and click the Duplicate button on the toolbar six times to create six additional copies.
3. Arrange the seven buttons in a row as closely as you can. Then draw a selection box around the seven buttons. Choose Arrange from the toolbox to open the Arrange palette.
4. Choose Align Tops from the right section of the palette, as shown beneath the mouse cursor in Figure 19.20. If the Microsoft Image Composer hint box is displayed, choose OK; then click any of the buttons to align all buttons at the top.

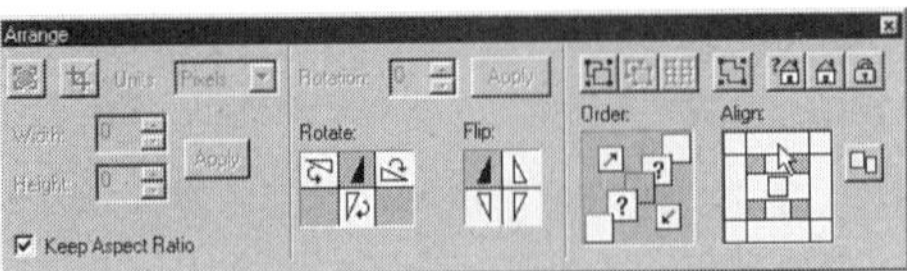

Figure 19.20.
Align the tops of the buttons by choosing Align Tops from the Arrange palette.

5. Click the Current Color Swatch. Select black from the Custom Palette tab (the last color in the palette). Choose OK to return to the composition.
6. Choose the Text tool from the toolbox. The Text palette shown in Figure 19.21 is displayed.
7. Click **S**elect Font and choose Arial Black, 8 point. Click OK to return to the composition.

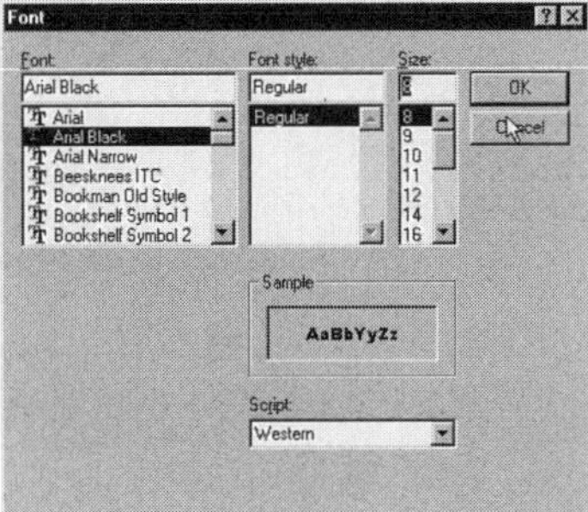

Figure 19.21.
Choose Arial Black, 8 point from the Text palette.

8. Create the following seven text items, clicking **A**pply after each one:

```
Home
Contents
BBS
Chat
Files
Links
Media
```

9. Move one text object into each button, arranging each to the center of the button. Use the arrow keys to nudge each text item into position, making sure that you place each text sprite on the same Y coordinate (shown in the status bar) for each button. This aligns the text to the same height position in each button.
10. After you position each text item, draw a selection box around a button and its corresponding text. Choose **A**rrange | Flatten **S**election to combine them into one object. Repeat this for each button. When you are finished, your buttons should look like Figure 19.22.
11. Choose **File** | **S**ave. The Save As dialog box is displayed.
12. Use the Save **i**n drop-down box to locate the drive and directory into which you want to save your graphic.

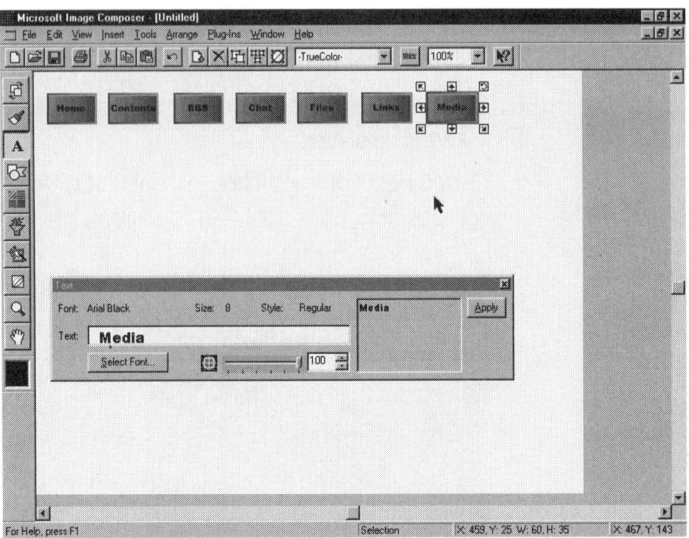

Figure 19.22.
Your buttons are complete, and each has a text label.

13. From the Save as **t**ype field, select Microsoft Image Composer (`*.mic`).
14. In the File **n**ame field, enter `pp-buttons`.
15. Click **S**ave or press Enter. The file is saved to the directory.

Saving Selected Sprites in JPG Format

You can save one or more sprites from your composition as individual files. This way, you can keep all your buttons in one composition in the original Microsoft Image Composer file, and save each button as a GIF or JPEG image to your hard disk.

To save each button as an individual object in JPEG format, follow these steps:

1. Click one of the buttons to select it.
2. Choose **F**ile | Sa**v**e Selection As. The Save Selection As dialog box shown in Figure 19.23 is displayed.

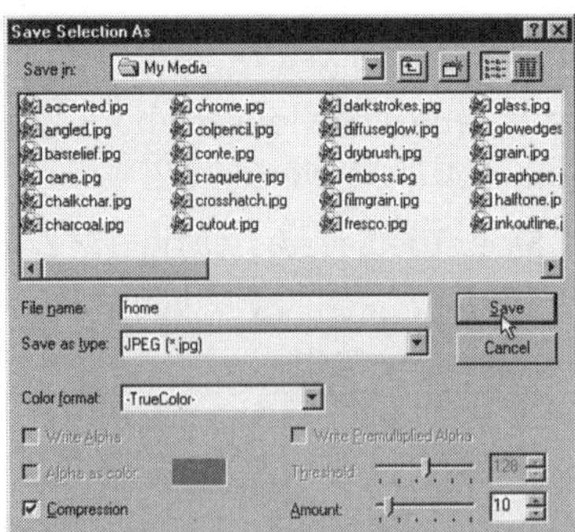

Figure 19.23.
Use the Save Selection As dialog box to save selected sprites from your composition as files. Here, you save them to JPEG format.

3. Use the Save **i**n drop-down box to locate the drive and directory into which you want to save your graphic.
4. From the Save as **t**ype field, select JPEG (`*.jpg`).
5. Select the **C**ompression check box and set the amount of compression in the **A**mount field.
6. In the File **n**ame field, enter a name for your button. For example, enter `Home` for the home button.
7. Click **S**ave or press Enter. The button is saved to the directory.
8. Repeat steps 1 through 7 for each button in your composition.

Saving Selected Sprites in GIF Format

To save each button as an individual object in GIF format, follow these steps:

1. Click one of the buttons to select it.
2. Choose **F**ile | Sa**v**e Selection As. The Save Selection As dialog box is displayed.
3. Use the Save **i**n drop-down box to locate the drive and directory into which you want to save your graphic.
4. From the Save as **t**ype field, select Compuserve GIF (`*.gif`), as shown in Figure 19.24.

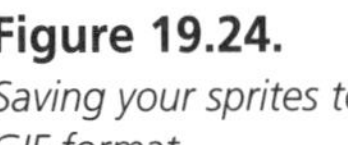

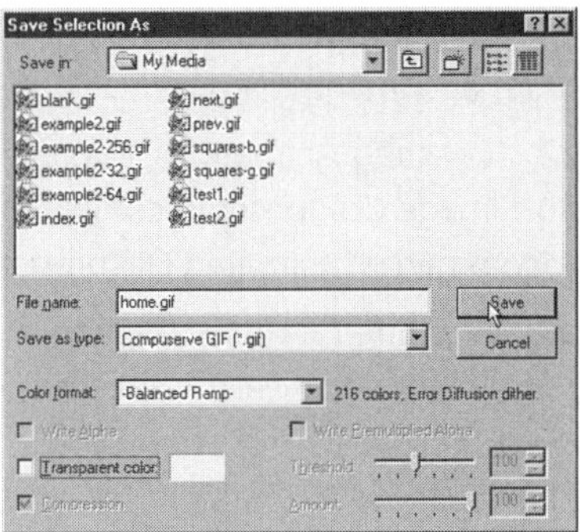

Figure 19.24.
Saving your sprites to GIF format.

5. In the File **n**ame field, enter a name for your button. For example, enter `Home` for the home button.
6. From the Color format field, select the explore browser-safe palette.
7. Click **S**ave, or press Enter. The button is saved to the directory.

Workshop Wrap-Up

The buttons you create do not always have to be rectangles, squares, ovals, and circles. You can combine basic shapes with photographic sprites to create buttons that are more colorful. You can add your text along the sides of a button and use transparency to "float" the button on your page. You can add drop shadows to your buttons with the Outline filter in the Warps and Filters palette. To add more interest to your sprites, use the effects available in the Art Effects palette or the Impressionist plug-in. You'll get some additional ideas in Chapter 23, "Real Life Examples V: Setting the Mood."

Now you know how to create basic shapes in Image Composer. By starting with basic shapes, you can create many different elements for your Web pages. You can combine several different shapes to create buttons, icons, horizontal lines, and backgrounds for your pages. After you create a basic sprite, you can fill with any effects and colors that you choose. You can apply the Impressionist plug-in to a solid-colored sprite to create interesting backgrounds for your pages. The fun is only beginning; there is more to come!

Next Steps

In Chapter 20, you'll look at ways that you can combine sprites with effects to create banners for your Web pages. You'll also learn how to modify existing images to create banners for your site.

- In Chapter 21, "Creating Montages and Image Maps," you'll learn how to create sprites from photographs and how to combine them with effects to create montages and image maps.
- In Chapter 22, "Creating Animations," you'll learn how to create animations using Microsoft Image Composer in combination with several popular shareware or commercial animated GIF programs.
- In Chapter 23, "Real-Life Examples: Setting the Mood," you'll learn how to use color and graphics effectively to set the mood of your Web site.

Q&A

Q: How can I tell if my background is too light or too dark for the text on my pages?

A: The only way you will know for sure is to test the background with some sample text on your pages. The best way to do this is to create a style sheet and include some sample text of different sizes (including sample links) on the page. Use the File | Page Properties command in the FrontPage Editor to assign your background image to the page. Then test several different text and link colors and sizes. If you are unable to find text and link colors that work with your background, you'll need to modify the colors of the background image. It's usually a good practice to stick with background images that are not very "busy" with color, and to use very light or very dark colors.

Q: Can you use animated buttons and icons to link to other pages in your Web?

A: You can use animated GIFs for links much like any other image; but if you place too much animation on a Web page it can be very distracting. However, if you want to create animated buttons, refer to Chapter 22, "Creating Animations." There are some techniques in that chapter that should get you started in creating animation for your Web pages.

CHAPTER

TWENTY

Creating Banners and Text Effects

In this chapter, you

- ❑ Learn how to determine graphics sizes for framesets
- ❑ Create three types of rectangular banners
- ❑ Create an irregularly shaped banner that contains transparent areas
- ❑ Create banners for the Planetary Progressions examples and add text and drop-shadows

Tasks in this chapter:

- ❑ Sizing Graphics for Framesets
- ❑ Creating Rectangular Banners
- ❑ Creating Irregularly Shaped Banners
- ❑ Creating the Planetary Progressions Banners

Banners are typically used to add a graphical header to a Web page. They can also contain links that take you to other areas that relate to the page. You see banners of all types. The most basic banners are lean and mean and simply display the title of the page. Other banners are more colorful and are used primarily to decorate the page. Still others contain transparent areas that allow portions of your page background to show through. Whatever the case, you should try to size your banners so that they load in a reasonable amount of time. You don't want your site visitors to become disinterested in your Web pages because the banners take too long to download.

This chapter shows you some ways that you can create banners and header graphics for your pages. You'll also learn how to size banners and other graphics for your framesets.

Sizing Graphics for Framesets

Banners and graphics are often designed for pages that appear in both full browser windows and framesets. One of the questions that crops up frequently is, "How do you know how to size graphics for framesets?" There are many ways to figure it out, but I'll present just one method here.

You learn about how to economize on the size of your graphics in **Chapter 18**.

One thing you need to consider is how much free area you have available in different browsers. Table 20.1 shows dimensions of the browser windows of three popular browsers as displayed in three resolutions. The measurements were taken with browser toolbars and status bars displayed. As you can see, there are some differences, so plan your graphics around the "worst case."

Table 20.1. Browser areas of three popular browsers.

Browser	*640×480*	*800×600*	*1024×768*
Internet Explorer 3.0	620×316	774×436	1000×574
Netscape Navigator 4.0	636×315	774×426	1000×604
NCSA Mosaic 2.1.1	620×389	774×443	1014×608
"Worst Case"	620×315	774×426	1000×574

The most difficult decision is the resolution for which you want to design your frameset. Chances are your page's user does not view the Web in 1024×768 resolution unless he or she has a larger monitor (or very good eyes to read the small text). It is my opinion that 640×480 resolution is too small to display the main pages in the frameset adequately. If, for example, you have a left navigation frame in your frameset that holds a 150 pixel–wide image map, this leaves you with approximately 450 pixels in width for your main pages. This can sometimes cramp the design of the main page but also causes your main pages to look quite different when viewed in a full browser window at 640×480 resolution. If you design your frameset for 800×600 resolution, you have enough room to design your main pages so that they look pretty much the same when viewed in a full browser window at 640×480 resolution. Then you can suggest that the user view your Web without frames if he or she is viewing the site in 640×480 resolution.

You'll notice that when you open a frameset in the FrontPage Explorer, it opens the Frames Wizard so that you can edit the frameset. Unfortunately, this presents a situation in which you cannot use the **F**ile | Preview in **B**rowser command from the FrontPage Editor to preview a frameset. After I create a frameset in FrontPage, I must open Internet Explorer or Netscape, and enter the URL to the frameset in my Web to preview the page. After the frameset is displayed in the browser, I examine it to make sure that the frames are sized properly—most notably, that there is enough room to display the main page adequately. I adjust the size of the frameset to display the main page in an area that is at least 450 pixels wide (for 640×480 resolution framesets) or 600 pixels wide (for 800×600 resolution framesets). If the frameset needs adjustment, I use the Open With command in the FrontPage Explorer to open the frameset in Notepad or another text editor. After I edit the frameset, I return to the browser and refresh the page for a final check. Here are the steps:

1. Use the Frames wizard in the FrontPage Editor to create your frameset. (This example was created using the Banner with Nested Table of Contents frameset.) The FrontPage Editor saves the frameset to your current web.
2. Open a frame-compatible browser such as Internet Explorer 3.0 (or higher) or Netscape Navigator 2.0 (or higher). Enter the URL for the frameset in your Web. For example:

   `http://servername/webname/framesetname.htm`
3. After the frameset is displayed in the browser, examine the frameset to see if it needs adjustment. For example, the left frame in the frameset shown in Figure 20.1 is a little bit too wide for my liking, so I'll make a change.

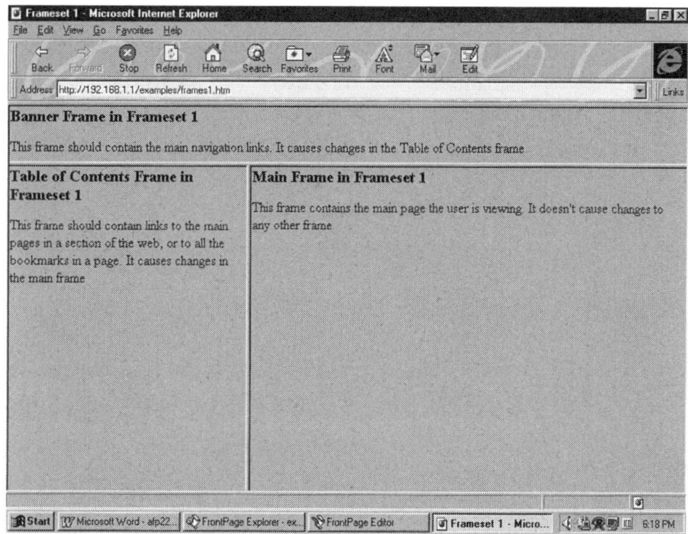

Figure 20.1.
The left frame in the frameset of the Banner with Nested Table of Contents frame is a little bit too wide and could use some adjustment.

4. Return to FrontPage, but go to the FrontPage Explorer instead of the FrontPage Editor. Select the folder in which the frameset is saved.
5. Right-click the frameset file, as shown in Figure 20.2, and choose Open **W**ith from the pop-up menu. The Open With dialog box is displayed.

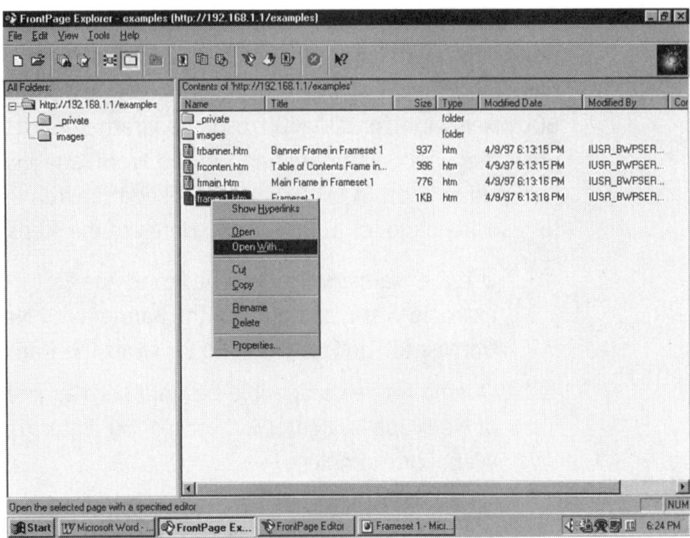

Figure 20.2.
Open the frameset from the FrontPage Explorer to edit the file in Notepad.

6. Choose to open the frameset with your Text Editor. By default, it opens in Notepad.
7. The height of the rows in the frameset are defined with the code `<frameset rows="15%,85%">`. These values are acceptable, so leave them alone. The frameset columns are defined by code that reads as follows:

   ```
   <frameset cols="35%,65%">
       <frame src="frconten.htm" name="contents" marginwidth="1"
       marginheight="1">
       <frame src="frmain.htm" name="main" marginwidth="1"
       marginheight="1">
   ```

   To adjust the width of the left frame, revise the column widths to read:

   ```
   <frameset cols="20%,80%">
   ```

8. From Notepad, choose **F**ile | **S**ave, and exit Notepad. When you return to the FrontPage Explorer, you see the frameset in the Add File to Import List dialog box, and the updated file is automatically imported into your web.
9. Return to your frame-compatible browser, and refresh the page. Now, you see the column widths are changed, as shown in Figure 20.3. You have more room to display the main pages in your web.

Now you see your frameset as it is displayed in the browser, but how do you determine how large to size your graphics? It helps to take a screen capture of the frameset while it is opened in the browser. Before you take your screen shot, consider that the user might have his or her Windows 95 taskbar displayed at the bottom of the page and that the browser might be set to display toolbars and status bars as well. Maximize the browser so that it completely fills your screen at the resolution for which you are designing it. When you capture your screen shot, make sure to save it in an image format that is compatible with Microsoft Image Composer, such as GIF, JPG, TIF, TGA and BMP.

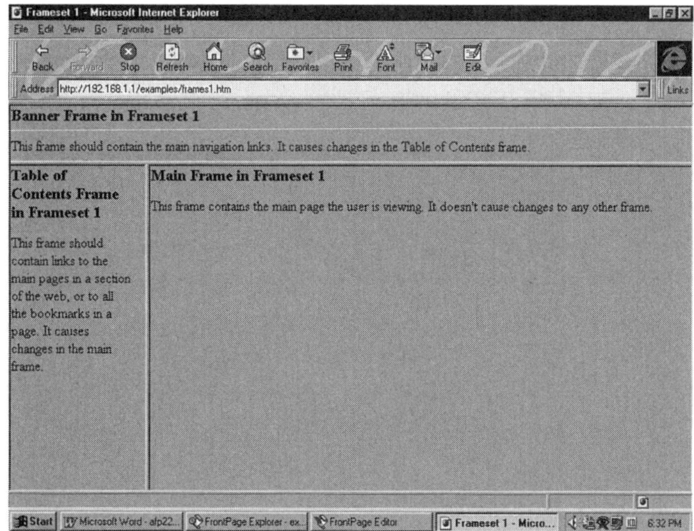

Figure 20.3.
After you edit the file, preview it again in a frame-compatible browser. Now, the left frame is narrower and leaves more room for the main pages in the Web.

TIP: If you don't have a screen capture program, Paint Shop Pro version 4.1.2 includes one among its many features. Paint Shop Pro is available in many retail stores and is an excellent image editing tool in its own right. It would serve you well as a companion program to Microsoft Image Composer. You can download a trial shareware version of Paint Shop Pro from JASC's Web site at the following URL:

`http://www.jasc.com/psp.html`

The next step is to open your screen shot in Microsoft Image Composer. You can use the Rectangle tool in the Shapes: Geometry Palette to help you determine the size of the frames in the frameset. To do so, follow these steps:

1. From Microsoft Image Composer, choose **F**ile | **O**pen (Ctrl+O), or click the Open button on the toolbar. The Open dialog box is displayed.
2. Use the Look in box to locate the drive and directory in which your screen shot is saved. Double-click the file to open it.

3. Choose Shapes from the toolbox. The Shapes: Geometry palette is displayed.
4. Select the Rectangle tool. Click the upper-left corner of one of the frames in your frameset and drag toward the lower-right corner. In Figure 20.4, the Rectangle tool is being used to determine the size of the left frame in the frameset. As you size the rectangle, you see its dimensions in the status bar at the bottom of your screen (for example, W:154, H:366, as shown in the status bar in Figure 20.4). This is the maximum size your image can be for that frame.

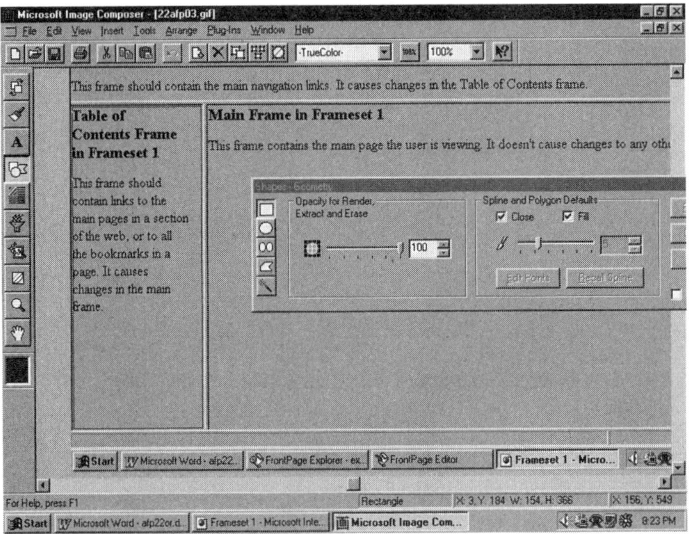

Figure 20.4.
Use the Rectangle tool in Microsoft Image Composer's Shapes: Geometry palette to determine the size of your frame.

NOTE: Don't forget to take into account that scrollbars are added to frames if the page contents do not fit into the frame. Subtract approximately 20–25 pixels from your image dimensions if you anticipate that scrollbars will be present in the left or bottom sides of the frame.

Creating Rectangular Banners

Many ways exist to create banners in Microsoft Image Composer. You can begin with a solid rectangle and use effects to add texture to the solid color. You can fill sprites with gradients or other fills. You can also cut out sprites from other images and arrange them into your composition.

You often see banners that use the same background but contain different text that pertains to the page. The key to creating consistency here is to design the common elements first. Then you create text sprites that use the same font, color, and effects. You can move each text sprite into place before you save the composition into GIF or JPG format.

In the following exercises, you create simple rectangular banners using different effects and tools available with Microsoft Image Composer. First, you create a composition in Microsoft Image Composer and import the Internet Explorer palette by following these steps:

1. From Microsoft Image Composer, choose **F**ile | **N**ew (Ctrl+N), or select the New button on the toolbar. A new composition is displayed in the window.
2. Choose **F**ile | Composi**t**ion Properties. The Composition Properties dialog box is displayed.
3. Enter `525` in the Width field, and `75` in the Height field. Leave the background color set to white (Red: `255`, Green: `255`, Blue: `255`).
4. Click OK to return to the composition. The composition guide resizes to 525x75.
5. Click the Current Color Swatch in the toolbox. The Color Picker is displayed. Click the Custom Palette tab shown in Figure 20.5.

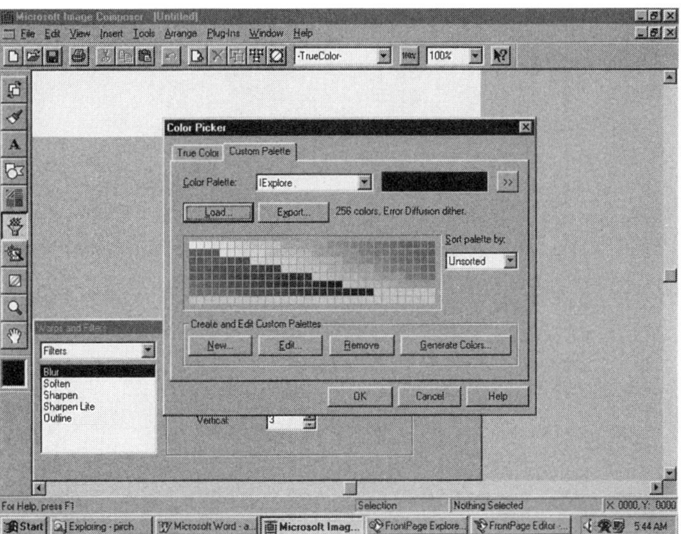

Figure 20.5.
Use the Custom Palette tab to load the Internet Explorer palette.

6. Click **L**oad. Use the Look in box to locate the Internet Explorer palette on your FrontPage 97 with Bonus Pack CD-ROM. You can find the palette in the `ImgComp\Mmfiles\Palettes` directory, under the `Iexplore.pal` filename. Double-click the palette to open it. Choose OK to return to the composition window.

Banner 1: Stone Effect

To create a banner that has a background that looks like stone, follow these steps:

1. Click the Current Color swatch to open the Color Picker. From the Custom Palette tab, select a light color from the Internet Explorer palette. For the example shown in Figure 20.6, I selected light yellow (the third color in the first row). Choose OK to return to the composition.
2. Choose Shapes from the toolbox. The Shapes: Geometry palette is displayed.
3. Choose the Rectangle tool. Draw a rectangle that measures 522 pixels wide and 72 pixels high (W:522, H:72 in the status bar, as shown in Figure 20.6). Click **R**ender to render the rectangle.

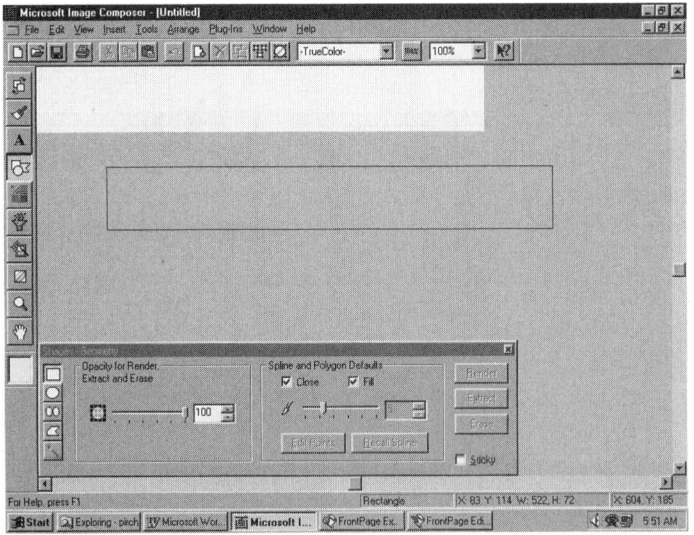

Figure 20.6.
Draw a 522-pixel by 72-pixel rectangle using the Rectangle tool in the Shapes: Geometry palette.

4. Choose Patterns and Fills from the toolbox. The Patterns and Fills palette is displayed.
5. Select Patterns, and then choose Color Noise from the Patterns drop-down menu. Set the Opacity slider to 60. Then click **A**pply. The yellow rectangle fills with random color noise.

6. Choose Warps and Filters from the toolbox. The Warps and Filters palette is displayed.
7. Choose Outlines from the drop-down menu, and then choose Relief from the Outline list. Click **A**pply. The rectangle now has a relief outline, and its size increases to 525×75 pixels.

You learn how to add text to your banners and how to save them to your hard disk in the "Creating the Planetary Progressions Banners" section.

Before you add the text to this banner, move it to the X: 0, Y: 0 position in the composition guide (the status bar reads X:0, Y:0). Then choose **A**rrange | **L**ock Position (Ctrl+L) to lock the rectangle into place. You can now add your text to the banner.

Banner 2: Black with Color Array

To create a banner that has a black background and a multi-colored array, follow these steps:

1. Click the Current Color swatch to open the Color Picker. From the Custom Palette tab, select black (the last color in the Internet Explorer palette). Choose OK to return to the composition.
2. Choose Shapes from the toolbox. The Shapes: Geometry palette is displayed.
3. Set the Opacity slider in the Shapes: Geometry palette to 100.
4. Choose the Rectangle tool. Draw a rectangle that measures 525 pixels wide and 75 pixels high (W:525, H:75 in the status bar). Click **R**ender to render the black rectangle.
5. Choose Patterns and Fills from the toolbox. The Patterns and Fills palette is displayed.
6. Select Patterns, and then choose Color Array from the Patterns drop-down menu. Then click **A**pply. The black rectangle fills with a multicolored array, as shown in Figure 20.7.

TIP: Use the Rectangle tool to extract a single row from the color array to use as a compatible horizontal rule. You can also extract a smaller rectangular area to create compatible buttons.

7. Choose Shapes from the toolbox and select the Rectangle tool from the Shapes: Geometry palette. Using black as your color (it should still be selected), draw a 150×50-pixel rectangle (W:150, H:50 in the status bar). Click **R**ender to create the rectangle.

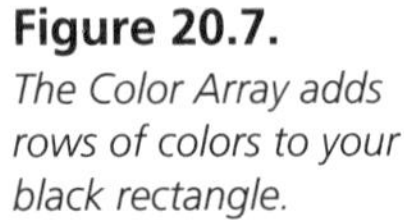

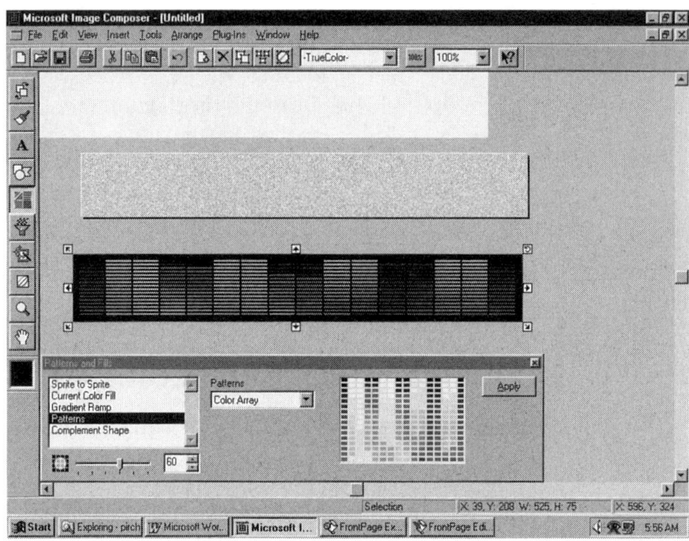

Figure 20.7.
The Color Array adds rows of colors to your black rectangle.

8. Choose Warps and Filters from the toolbox. The Warps and Filters palette is displayed.
9. Choose Outlines, and then choose Edge. Click the Color box in the Warps and Filters palette, and select red (the fourth color in the second row of the Internet Explorer palette). Choose OK to return to the Warps and Filters palette.
10. Set Thickness to 1, and Opacity to 100. Then click **A**pply. The rectangle now has a red outline.
11. Position the small black rectangle at the left or right side of the large rectangle with the color array (your preference). Figure 20.8 shows the smaller rectangle at the right side of the banner. The small rectangle will be used for your banner text.
12. Draw a selection box around the color array rectangle and the smaller rectangle, and choose **A**rrange | **G**roup (Ctrl+G). This groups both items into a single group that you can move together without affecting their relation to each other.

When you position this banner in the composition guide, you can use the X: 0, Y: 0 coordinates in the status bar. Choose **A**rrange | **L**ock Position (Ctrl+L) to lock the background into place so that it does not move when you add your banner text.

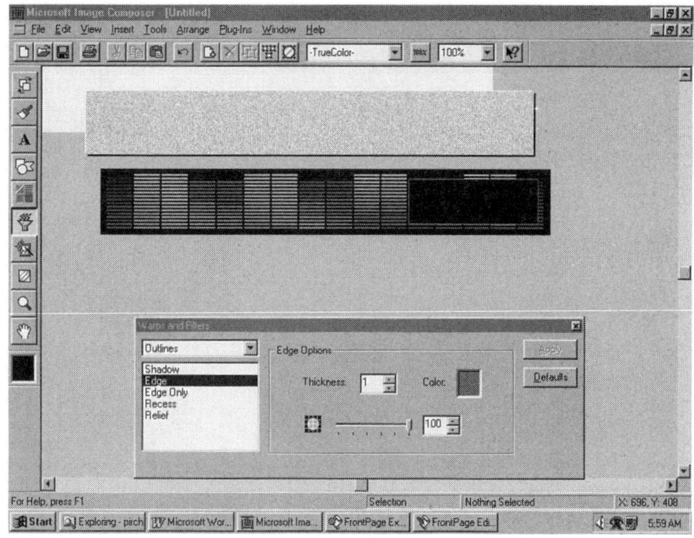

Figure 20.8.
Position the smaller rectangle to the right or left side of the color array banner.

Banner 3: Relief Marble

To create a banner that looks like one piece of marble laid upon another piece of marble, follow these steps:

1. Choose **I**nsert | From **F**ile. The Insert from File dialog box is displayed.
2. Use the Look in box to locate the `marble3.mic` image file from the `ImgComp\Mmfiles\Photos\Backgrnd` directory on your FrontPage 97 with Bonus Pack CD-ROM. Double-click the filename to open it.
3. Choose Shapes from the toolbox. The Shapes: Geometry palette is displayed.
4. Choose the Rectangle tool. Draw a rectangle that measures 522 pixels wide and 72 pixels high (W:522, H:72 in the status bar). Drag from the center of the rectangle to position it over an area in the marble image that you like. Click E**x**tract to extract the rectangle from the larger marble image.
5. Click the original marble image to select it, and press the Delete key to delete it from the composition area. Your extraction remains, as shown in Figure 20.9.
6. Choose Warps and Filters from the toolbox. From the Warps and Filters palette, choose Outlines, and then choose Relief.

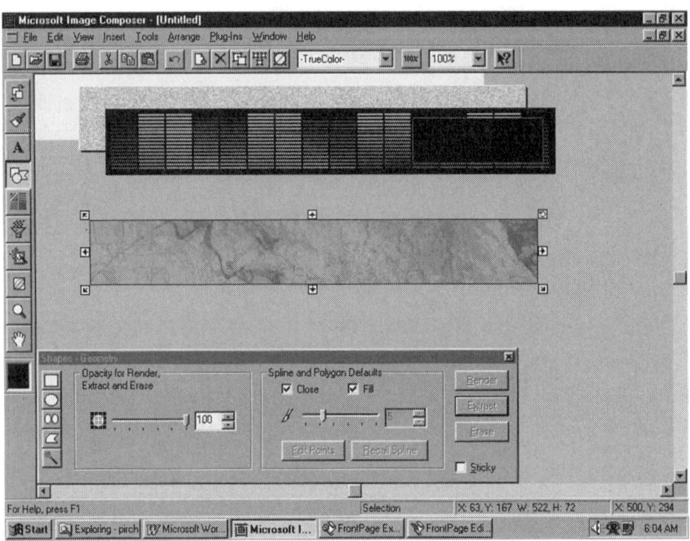

Figure 20.9.
After you extract the smaller area from the marble image, delete the large marble image. Your extraction remains in the composition.

7. Select the 522×72 marble rectangle. Then click **A**pply. The relief effect adds 3 pixels to the width and height of the image, creating a 525×75 banner.
8. Choose the Rectangle tool again. Draw a rectangle that measures 150 pixels wide and 50 pixels high (W:150, H:50 in the status bar). Drag from the center of the rectangle to position it over an area in the marble image that you like. Click E**x**tract to extract the second rectangle from the first one.
9. Select the 150×50 marble rectangle, and drag the right-center adjustment handle until it measures 500 pixels wide and 50 pixels high (W: 500, H: 50 in the status bar). Microsoft Image Composer issues a Large Scale Warning message. Click OK to continue.
10. Choose Warps and Filters from the toolbox. The Warps and Filters palette is displayed.
11. Choose Outlines, and then choose Relief (it should still be selected from the previous steps). Then click **A**pply. The second marble rectangle now appears to be raised over the first marble rectangle.
12. Position the smaller rectangle in the center of the larger marble rectangle, as shown in Figure 20.10.
13. Draw a selection box around both rectangles, and choose **A**rrange | **G**roup (Ctrl+G). This groups both items into a single group that you can move together without affecting their relation to each other.

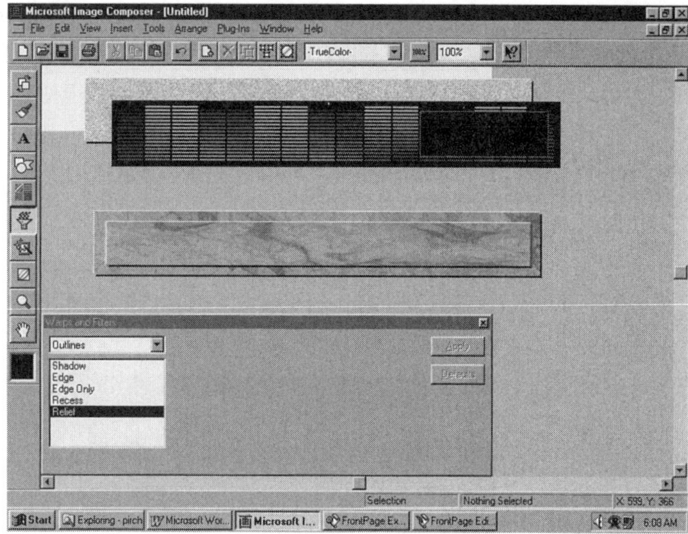

Figure 20.10.
Position the smaller marble rectangle in the center of the larger one.

When you position this banner in the composition guide, you can use the X: 0, Y: 0 coordinates in the status bar. Choose **A**rrange | **L**ock Position (Ctrl+L) to lock the background into place so that it does not move when you add your banner text. A finished version of these three banners is located on the CD that accompanies this book. The filename is `banners.mic`.

Creating Irregularly Shaped Banners

Every graphic that you create is a rectangle or square. However, the content within the graphic area does not always have to be rectangular. You can combine irregular shapes in your banners and save the composition as a transparent GIF file. When you place this GIF file on a colored or patterned background, the background shows through the banner, giving the banner the appearance of being irregularly shaped.

For a complete discussion on adding transparency to your images, refer to "Adding Transparency to GIF Files" in **Chapter 18**.

One way that you can create interesting banners is to extract portions of other images or photographs and arrange them in an interesting manner. You can also use sprites to "cut out" areas in other sprites. You'll learn the latter technique in this task.

1. From Microsoft Image Composer, choose **F**ile | **N**ew (Ctrl+N), or select the New button on the standard toolbar. A new composition window is displayed.
2. Choose **I**nsert | **F**rom File, or click the Insert Image File button on the standard toolbar. The Insert Image File dialog box is displayed.

3. Use the Look in box to locate `bluwater.mic` in the `ImgComp\Mmfiles\Photos\Backgrnd\PhotoDsc` directory on your FrontPage 97 with Bonus Pack CD-ROM. Double-click the filename to open it.
4. Resize the image to 550×120 pixels using the resize handles on the sprite. The status bar should read W: 550, H: 120. Figure 20.11 shows the image resized to the proper size.

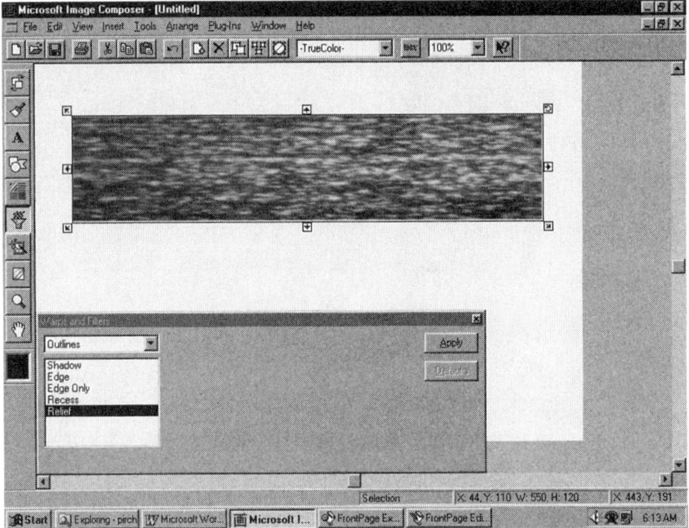

Figure 20.11.
Resize the `bluwater.mic` *image to 550×120 pixels.*

5. Choose **I**nsert | **F**rom File again and insert `starfish.mic` from the `ImgComp\Mmfiles\Photos\Nature\PhotoDsc` directory on your FrontPage 97 with Bonus Pack CD-ROM. Double-click the filename to open it.
6. Resize the starfish to 100×95 pixels, or thereabouts. If you press the Shift key while you drag the lower-right resize handle, the aspect ratio of the image remains the same while you resize it.
7. Choose **I**nsert | **F**rom File again and insert `crab.mic` from the `ImgComp\Mmfiles\Photos\Nature\PhotoDsc` directory on your FrontPage 97 with Bonus Pack CD-ROM. You should already be in the correct directory from the previous selection. Double-click the filename to open it.
8. Resize the crab to 173×114 pixels, or thereabouts. Again, if you press the Shift key while you drag the lower-right resize handle, the aspect ratio remains the same.
9. Position the crab at the left side of the sea image. Choose Patterns and Fills from the toolbox. The Patterns and Fills palette is displayed.

10. Choose Sprite to Sprite. From the Sprite Texture Type drop-down menu, choose Snip. Set the Opacity slider to 100.
11. Click the sea background; then click **A**pply. If the hint dialog box is displayed at this point, click OK. Then click the crab. Move the original crab diagonally toward the upper right, as shown in Figure 20.12, and you will see a cutout in the sea image. This is a transparent area that will allow your background to show through.

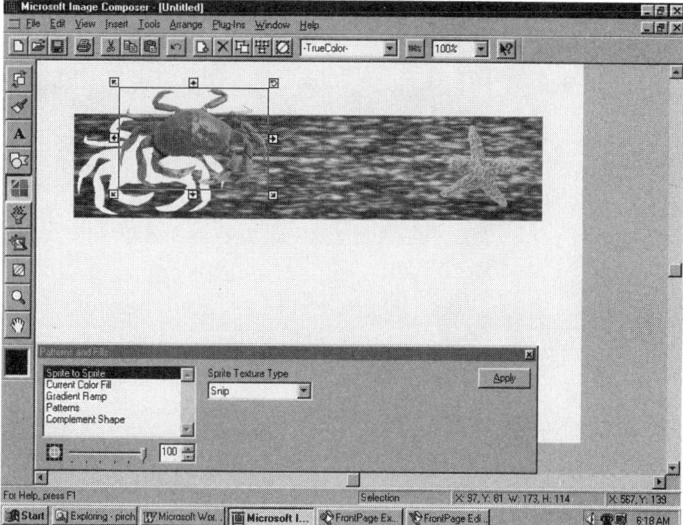

Figure 20.12.
After you apply the Snip effect, move the original crab diagonally toward the upper right of the cutout. The area that was snipped displays your background color through the image.

12. Move the starfish to the right side of the sea background.
13. Click the Current Color Swatch in the toolbox. Choose the Custom Palette tab, and load the Internet Explorer palette (`Iexplore.pal`) from the `ImgComp\Mmfiles\Palettes` on your FrontPage 97 with Bonus Pack CD-ROM. Choose light blue (the 15th color in the third row). Choose OK to return to the composition.
14. Choose the Text tool from the toolbox, and click **S**elect Font. From the Font dialog box, select Times New Roman, Bold Italic, 72 point. Click OK to return to the Text palette.
15. Enter `Seaside Stuff`. Verify that the Opacity slider is set to 100, and click **A**pply. A hint box is displayed, telling you that the text has a large scaling factor. Click OK to continue. The text is displayed on your page as shown in Figure 20.13.

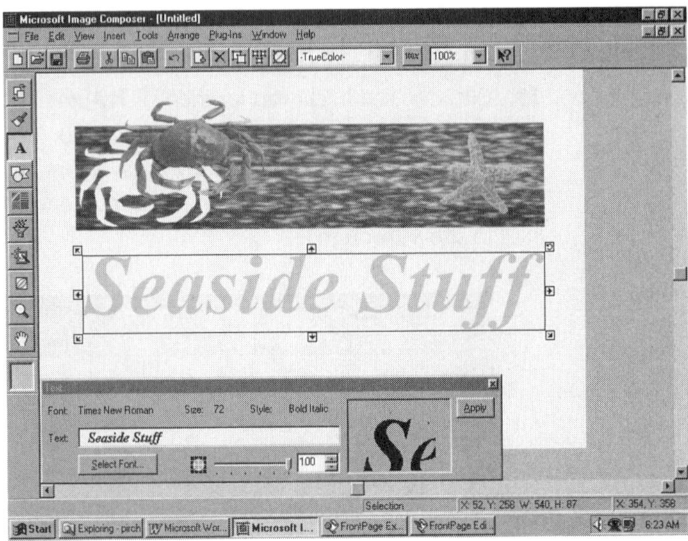

Figure 20.13.
Add light blue text to your composition using the Text tool.

16. Choose Warps and Filters from the toolbox. Select Warp Transforms from the drop-down menu in the Warps and Filters palette, and choose Wave. Click the **D**efaults button to set the effect to its default settings; then click **A**pply. The text warps into a wave.
17. Position the text above the crab and the sea background as shown in Figure 20.14. Then choose **E**dit | Select **A**ll (Ctrl+A) and **A**rrange | **G**roup (Ctrl+G). After you group the sprites, make note of the width and height of the group in the status bar. In the example shown in Figure 20.14, the size is 550 pixels in width and 177 in height; your image might differ.

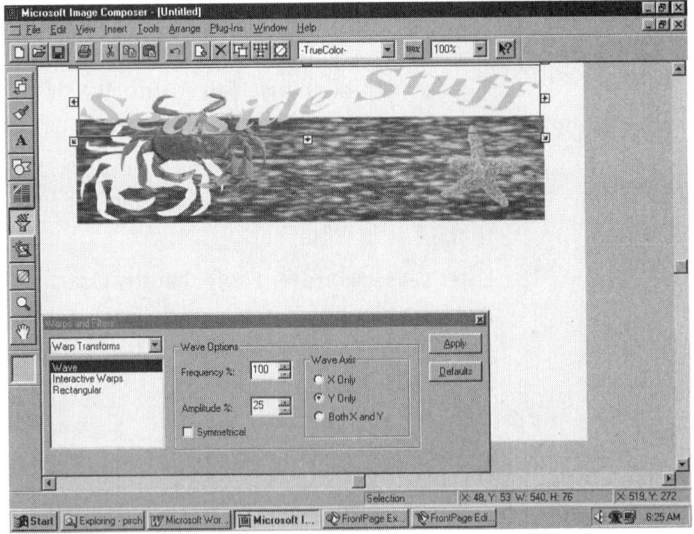

Figure 20.14.
After you group the sprites, make note of the size so you know how large to resize your composition guide.

18. Choose **F**ile | Composi**t**ion Properties. Set the width and height of your composition to the same width and height as the group of sprites. Choose OK to return to the composition.
19. Move the sprite group to the X: 0, Y: 0 coordinate.
20. Choose **F**ile | **S**ave (Ctrl+S), or click the Save button to save your composition as `seaside.mic`.
21. Now you must save your composition as a transparent GIF file so that the white areas will display your page background instead of white. Choose **F**ile | Save **A**s. The Save As dialog box is displayed.
22. From the Save as **t**ype field, choose Compuserve GIF (`*.gif`). From the Color **f**ormat field, choose the Internet Explorer palette (Iexplore).
23. Select the **T**ransparent color check box, and choose white as your transparent color. Then click Save. The image is saved as a transparent GIF file. Figure 20.15 shows the image as it is displayed on a Web page in the FrontPage Editor.

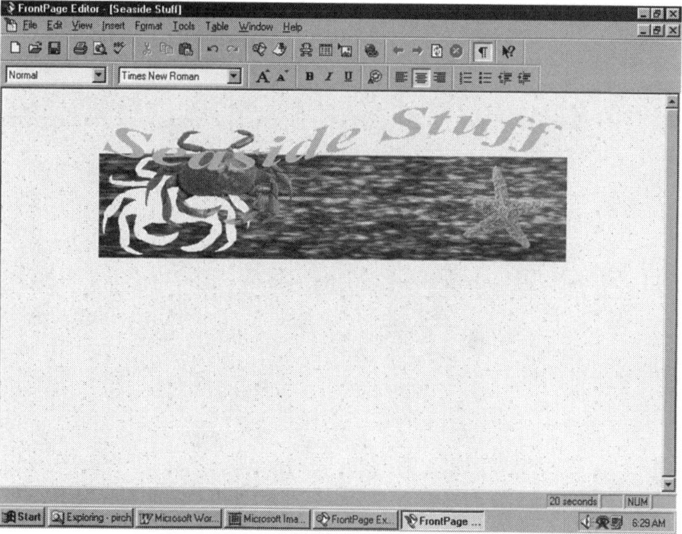

Figure 20.15.
When you place your image on a Web page, the page background shows through the transparent areas.

TASK

Creating the Planetary Progressions Banners

You will create two different types of banners for the Planetary Progressions site: One set of banners is displayed in the top right frame of the frameset and is used to navigate to the primary pages in the section; and the second set is used in the main pages in the Web.

To create the banners for the top right frame, follow these steps:

1. Open `pp-buttons.mic`. You created this graphic in Chapter 19, "Creating Buttons, Icons, and Backgrounds." If you did not complete the task in Chapter 19, you can find the image in the Chapter 19 directory of the CD that accompanies this book.
2. Click the Current Color Swatch. The Color Picker is displayed.
3. Select the Custom Palette tab, and choose the 13th color in the fifth row (dark purple). Click OK to return to the composition. The color is displayed in the Current Color Swatch.
4. Select Shapes from the toolbox. The Shapes: Geometry palette is displayed.
5. Select the Rectangle tool. In the area beneath the buttons, draw a rectangle that measures 520 pixels wide and 2 pixels high. (The status bar will read W: 520, H: 2 when the rectangle is sized correctly.) Click **R**ender to create the line. It is displayed in your composition as shown in Figure 20.16.

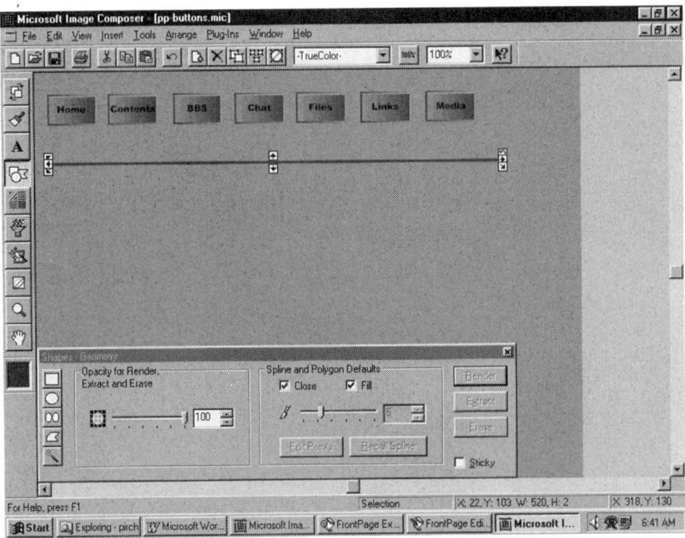

Figure 20.16.
Draw a 520×2-pixel rectangle using the Rectangle tool in the Shapes: Geometry palette.

6. Click the Duplicate button on the standard toolbar twice to make two additional copies of the line.
7. Select all three rectangles by drawing a selection box around them. Choose **A**rrange | Send to **B**ack. This will position the lines behind the buttons when you move the buttons into the composition guide.

8. Move the horizontal lines into the composition guide, and use the arrow keys to nudge them to the following coordinates:

Line 1:	X: 5, Y: 30
Line 2:	X: 5, Y: 50
Line 3:	X: 5, Y: 70

9. Draw a selection box around the three horizontal lines to select them. Choose **A**rrange | Flatten **S**election (Ctrl+F); then choose **A**rrange | **L**ock Position (Ctrl+L) .

Adding a Bitmap

Next you will add a bitmap along the top edge of the graphic. For this area, you will load an image of a planet that looks similar to the Earth. You will cut out a small area of this image and place it along the top edge of the banner.

To cut out a rectangular area from a larger image, follow these steps:

1. Choose **I**nsert | **F**rom File, or select the Insert Image File button on the standard toolbar. The Insert from File dialog box is displayed.

2. Use the Look in drop-down menu to locate the `planet2.tga` image in the Chapter 20 directory on the CD furnished with this book.
3. Double-click `planet2.tga` to open it. The image is displayed in your composition window.
4. Choose Shapes from the toolbox. The Shapes: Geometry palette is displayed.
5. Choose the Rectangle tool, and draw a rectangle that measures 520 pixels wide and 30 pixels high. (The status bar will read W: 520, H: 30.) Drag from the center of the rectangle to position it over an area that looks good for a cutout.
6. After you position the rectangle over the area you want to cut out, click E**x**tract.
7. Select the original `planet2.tga` image, and press Delete.
8. Move the cutout into your composition guide, and use the arrow keys to nudge it into position. (The coordinates in the status bar should read X: 5, Y: 0.)
9. With the cutout selected, choose **A**rrange | **L**ock Position (Ctrl+L). Your image should now look like Figure 20.17.
10. Draw a selection box around the seven buttons. Choose **A**rrange | **G**roup (Ctrl+G), and position them at X: 15, Y: 35.

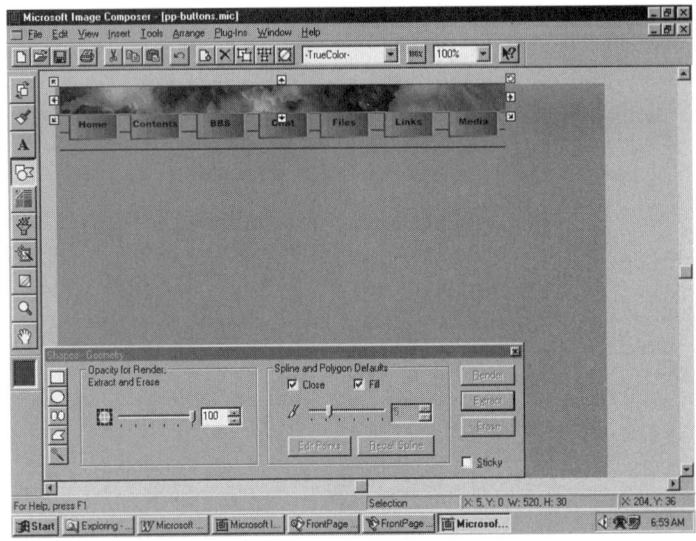

Figure 20.17.
Move the cutout to the upper portion of the banner and lock it into position.

Creating the Banner Text

Now you will create the text that is displayed in each banner. The text will be the same color as the background, and will have a dark black shadow to make it stand out over the planet cutout.

1. Click the Current Color Swatch. The Color Picker dialog box is displayed.
2. Click the Custom Palette tab. Choose medium blue (the first color in the seventh row) and click OK to return to the composition. The color is displayed in the Current Color Swatch.
3. Select the Text tool from the toolbox. The Text palette is displayed.
4. Click **S**elect Font, and choose Arial Black, 24-point. Click OK to return to the composition.
5. Create six text sprites, as shown in the following list. After you enter each item in the text field, click **A**pply to create the text sprite. Position the text in the area next to your composition guide. The text sprites should read as follows:

```
Helping Hands
Earthquake Watch
Endangered Species
Global Warming
Peacemakers
Ecology
```

6. Choose Warps and Filters from the toolbox. The Warps and Filters palette is displayed.
7. From the drop-down list box, choose Outlines. Then choose Shadow from the outline type list. Enter or choose the following settings for your shadow:

Offset X:	2
Offset Y:	2
Opacity:	100%
Color:	Click the color square in the Warps and Filters palette, and select Black from the Custom Palette tab.

8. Select one of the text sprites, and click **A**pply. Repeat this until each text sprite has a black shadow. The completed text sprites should look like Figure 20.18.
9. Choose **F**ile | Composi**t**ion Properties. Resize your composition guide to 530 pixels wide and 75 pixels high.
10. Choose **F**ile | Save **A**s. Save your new composition as `pp-banners.mic`.

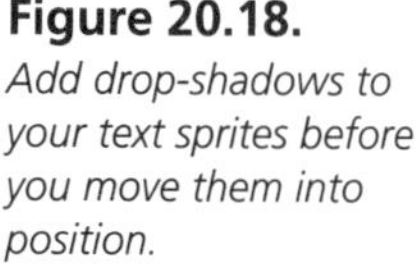

Figure 20.18.
Add drop-shadows to your text sprites before you move them into position.

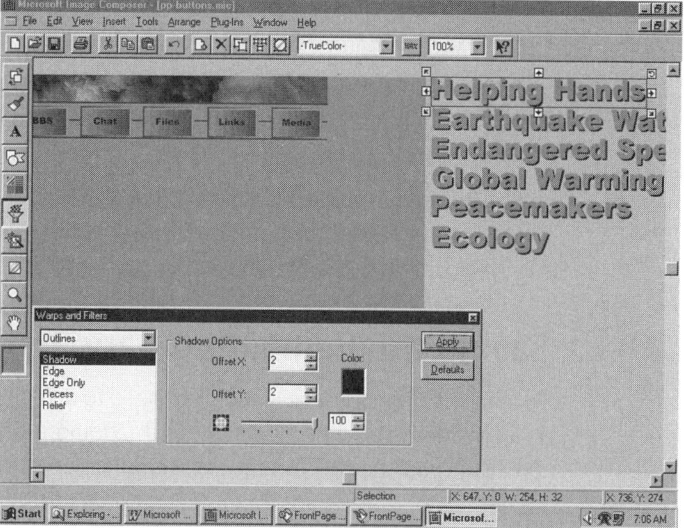

Saving the First Banner

At this point, you can choose to save your banners in either JPG or GIF format. If you choose JPG format, the byte size of the file might be smaller, and the colors in the planet cutout are subtler when the user views your pages in hi-color or true-color format. However, this banner has several areas that are solid in color. These areas sometimes appear blocky after JPG compression, so you want to keep the compression setting on the low side.

The other alternative is to save your banner as a CompuServe GIF image. By choosing this format, you can select a color in your banner to be rendered as transparent, as discussed in the "Creating Irregularly Shaped Banners" section.

For this example, you will save the banners in `.jpg` format. Before you save each image, you will move the correct banner text into place, and then save the image as a `.jpg` file. When you save your composition in any format other than Microsoft Image Composer format, the graphic is cropped to equal the size of the composition guide. Any objects that appear outside the composition guide (such as the extra text sprites) do not appear in the image.

To complete each banner and save it in JPG format, follow these steps:

1. Select the Helping Hands sprite and move it into the composition guide. Use the arrow keys to nudge the sprite until the status bar reads X: 270, Y: 2.
2. Choose **F**ile | Save **A**s. The Save As dialog box is displayed.
3. Use the Save **i**n drop-down menu to locate the directory into which you want to save the images.
4. From the Save as **t**ype drop-down menu, select JPEG (`*.jpg`).
5. In the File **n**ame field, enter **`hhands`**. You do not need to add the extension.
6. Verify that the **C**ompression check box is selected, and enter **`10`** in the **A**mount field. This keeps the solid areas of color relatively clear after the image is compressed.
7. Choose **S**ave. The file is saved to the directory. Microsoft Image Composer warns you that the composition will be flattened and cropped. Choose OK to continue. The file is saved to your hard drive.

Saving the Remaining Banners

For each additional image, you do not need to complete all the steps mentioned in the "Saving the First Banner" section. Each additional image will be saved to the same directory, and the JPG format and compression settings remain the same. Instead, repeat the following steps for each additional text sprite, to create five more banners:

1. Select the text sprite that is currently in the composition guide, and move it to the area beneath the composition guide.
2. Select the text sprite for the banner you want to create, and move it into the composition guide. Position the associated sprite at the following coordinates (one banner at a time):

Earthquake Watch	X: 202, Y: 2
Endangered Species	X: 166, Y: 2

Global Warming	X: 246, Y: 2
Peacemakers	X: 285, Y: 2
Ecology	X: 382, Y: 2

3. Choose **F**ile | Save **A**s. The settings from the previous save will remain. You only need to enter a filename as follows:

Earthquake Watch	Enter `earthquakes`
Endangered Species	Enter `species`
Global Warming	Enter `warming`
Peacemakers	Enter `peacemakers`
Ecology	Enter `ecology`

4. Choose **S**ave. Each image is saved into the same directory as the first banner.

Workshop Wrap-Up

Now that you know how to size graphics for framesets and create banners for your Web pages, you can plan your graphics and Web pages in a more organized manner. Your header graphics can be as basic or as fancy as you choose. Though most banner graphics display page titles, others provide links to other related areas or pages. You can save yourself time while maintaining consistent appearance throughout your Web: Create a background that is common to all the banners in your Web or in a section of your Web, and just change the text for each banner.

You learned a lot of time-saving techniques in this chapter! You learned how to plan your images so that they work whether they are displayed in full browser window or framesets, saving yourself the trouble of duplicating work. You also learned some ways that you can generate colorful banners fairly quickly, using patterns, fills, warps, sprite extractions, and more. You also learned how to create a standard background for your banner and how to save all the text sprites in the same image. When you save your banners to the final Web format, you simply move the text sprite into place and save the file under a new name.

Next Steps

In Chapter 21, "Montages and Image Maps," you will learn how to create montages and image maps for your Webs. You'll also learn about some of the effects that are available in Microsoft Image Composer. For additional information on creating graphics for your Webs, refer to the following chapters:

- In Chapter 17, "Microsoft Image Composer Quick Tour," you get an overview of the commands, palettes, and tools available in Microsoft Image Composer.

- In Chapter 18, "An Introduction to Graphics on the Web," you learn about colors, file formats, and creating browser-safe graphics.
- In Chapter 19, "Creating Buttons, Icons, and Backgrounds," you learn how to create basic shapes and apply effects and text.
- In Chapter 22, "Creating Animations," you learn how to use Microsoft Image Composer and other shareware or retail animated GIF compilers to create animations for your Webs.
- In Chapter 23, "Real-Life Examples: Setting the Mood," you learn how to put it all together to create graphics that really set the mood of a site.

Q&A

Q: Can I create animated banners for my pages?

A: Actually, you can animate just about any image on your Web pages. However, it might not be wise to create animated banners, because they are usually too large in dimension to animate. You'll end up creating a monstrous file that takes a long time to download. Basically, an animation contains multiple images in one file, so you increase the download time for every frame of animation that you add. If you do want to add animation to a banner, consider creating a small image that you can place to one side of the banner, and use the other side of the banner for a static portion (the part of the image that does not animate). For more information about animated GIF files, refer to Chapter 22, "Creating Animations."

Q: I created some Web pages that use some of the images from the Corporate Presence Wizard. I want to create additional banners of my own that look the same. What can I do?

A: Basically, when you have an existing Web image that you want to modify, you must manually edit the pixels in the image to remove the text. This means selecting colors from around the text and drawing over the text areas by hand until the text is completely removed. It's sometimes not easy to edit existing graphics—especially if the text is displayed above photographs.

After you go through the work of editing the text from the image, be sure to save your "plain" version of the banner so that you can create additional banners in the future.

I've included three additional files on the CD (`style1.gif`, `style2.gif`, and `style3.gif`), which are modified versions of the three banners provided with the Corporate Presence Web wizard. Each have been modified so that you can add text to them. Times New Roman and Impact fonts are close to those used in the original banners, and you can use the eyedropper in Microsoft Image Composer's Color Picker to choose the text color used in the banners.

CHAPTER TWENTY-ONE

Creating Montages and Image Maps

Home pages on the Web use many different types of images. Sometimes the home page consists of banners and basic graphics, like those you have been making in Chapter 19, "Creating Buttons, Icons, and Backgrounds," and Chapter 20, "Creating Banners and Text Effects." Other times, significant pages in a site use image maps for navigation. Other sites use more complex images, called *montages*, which are very intricate works of art that really catch the eye. Microsoft Image Composer allows you to create both types of images by combining sprites together using several effects.

In this chapter, you

- Combine sprites to create a montage, using varying transparencies to produce interesting effects
- Experiment with some effects available in Microsoft Image Composer's Paint palette
- Learn how to build your own sprites using basic shapes
- Learn how to plan an image map
- Add effects to all or part of an image
- Learn how to create a sprite by extracting colors from an image using the color lifter
- Edit a sprite to display portions of another sprite from beneath

Tasks in this chapter:

- Creating the Music Page Graphic
- Adding Transparence to Sprites
- Adding the Musical Notes
- Adding Text
- Creating the Planetary Progression Home Page Image Map

Creating the Music Page Graphic

The main focus here is to teach you how to combine images from different sources to create a theme for a Web page. You also learn how to add transparence to the sprites in your images. You can view the subtle differences in colors if you complete the next exercise while viewing your display in high-color (65,536 colors) or true-color (16 million colors) mode. By developing this image in either of these modes, you will see all the subtle differences in color that you can achieve when you work with transparencies and alpha channels. If you do not have a card that displays these higher resolutions, you will see a lot of dithering when you work with this example.

The retail version of FrontPage 97 with Bonus Pack comes with more than 200MB of photos and sample sprites, which are located in the `\ImgComp\Mmfiles` subdirectories on the CD. This task uses some of the images from the sample sprites catalog.

To create the music page graphic, follow these steps:

1. Choose **F**ile | **N**ew (Ctrl+N) or select the New button from the Standard toolbar. A new composition window is displayed.
2. Choose **F**ile | Composi**t**ion Properties. The Composition Properties dialog box, shown in Figure 21.1, is displayed. You want to create a composition that is 600 pixels wide and 315 pixels high. The background will be white, which is the default. Enter the following settings, and then choose OK:

```
Width:      600
Height:     315
```

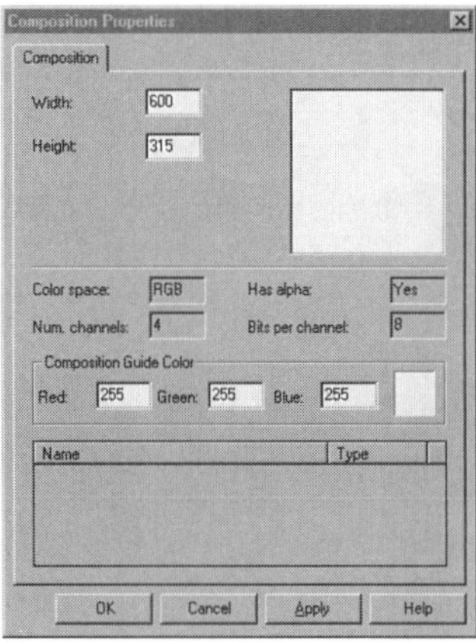

Figure 21.1.
Set the size of your composition in the Composition Properties dialog box.

3. Insert your FrontPage 97 with Bonus Pack CD-ROM into the drive. Then choose **I**nsert | **F**rom File or click the Insert Image from File button on the Standard toolbar. The Insert From File dialog box is displayed.
4. Locate the `\ImgComp\Mmfiles\Photos\Backgrnd\shtmusic.mic` file on the CD. Double-click the filename to open the file.
5. Choose `50%` from the Zoom Percent drop-down list in the Standard toolbar to zoom out by one level. Then press the Home key to position the composition guide and image at the upper-left corner of your window, as shown in Figure 21.2.

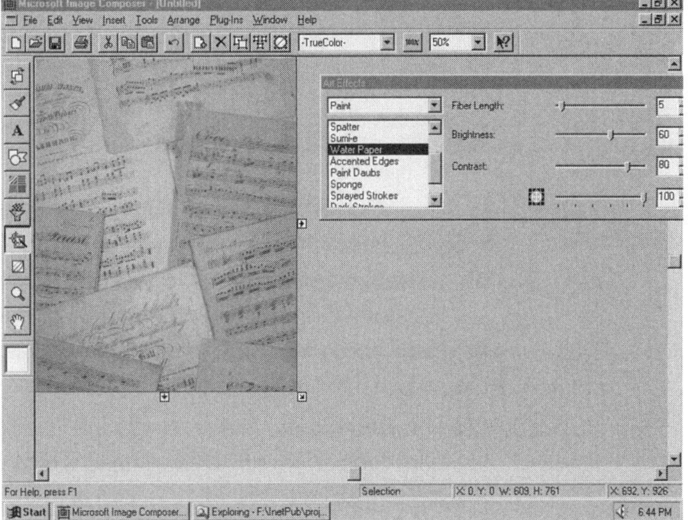

Figure 21.2.
Move the composition guide and the image to the upper-left corner of your window.

6. Click to select the sheet music. Press the Shift key to constrain the aspect ratio of the original image, and drag the lower-right adjustment point to resize the background image until it is slightly wider than 600 pixels (approximately 610 pixels is sufficient).
7. Rather than draw a rectangle inside this large image to extract a portion of it, you can crop this background in a different way. Position the sheet music file so that the area you want to crop is above the composition area. Make sure that the sheet music completely covers the composition area.
8. Choose **F**ile | **S**ave (Ctrl+S) or press the Save button on the Standard toolbar. The Save As dialog box is displayed. From the Save as **t**ype drop-down list, select the Targa (`*.tga`) file format, as shown in Figure 21.3. In the File **n**ame field, enter `music`, and then click **S**ave. Microsoft Image Composer warns you that your composition will be cropped to the composition guide. Choose OK to continue.

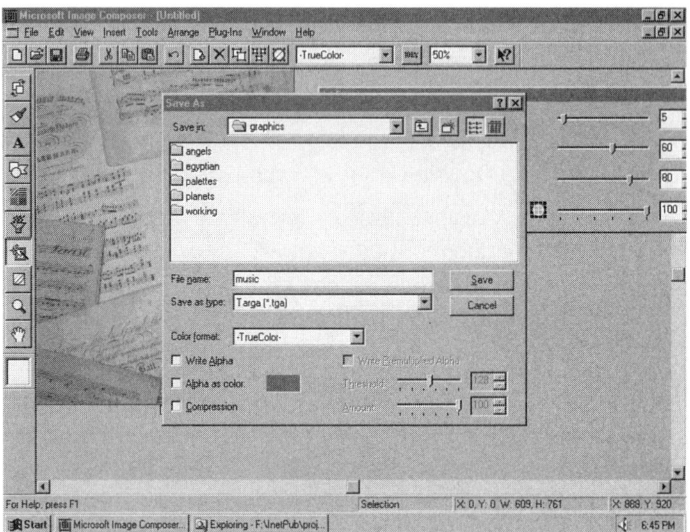

Figure 21.3.
Save your image to Targa file format to crop the background image.

9. Now choose **F**ile | **O**pen, and then choose to open `music.tga`. Microsoft Image Composer tells you that you already have the image open and asks if you want to revert to the last-saved version. Choose OK. The image opens, and you see a cropped version of the sheet music. Next choose **F**ile | Save **A**s; then choose Microsoft Image Composer (`*.mic`) from the Save as **t**ype drop-down list. Click **S**ave to save the file.
10. Click the background image to select it. Then choose Duplicate from the Standard toolbar. A copy of the image is displayed.
11. Choose Patterns and Fills from the toolbar. Select Gradient Ramp, as shown in Figure 21.4, and choose Grayscale Left from the Ramp Name drop-down list.
12. Click **A**pply. The copy fills with the gradient ramp. Drag the bottom resize handle to increase the length of the image by at least 20 pixels. This gives you an area that extends beyond the original image so that you can select it when you add transparency. Move the gradient ramp away from your composition area during the next few steps.
13. Select the sheet music sprite, and click the Warps and Filters button in the toolbox. The Warps and Filters palette is displayed.
14. Choose Warp Transforms from the drop-down menu, and select the Wave transform.
15. Click the **D**efaults button to revert to the default wave settings. Then click **A**pply. The sheet music now looks like a wave, as shown in Figure 21.5.

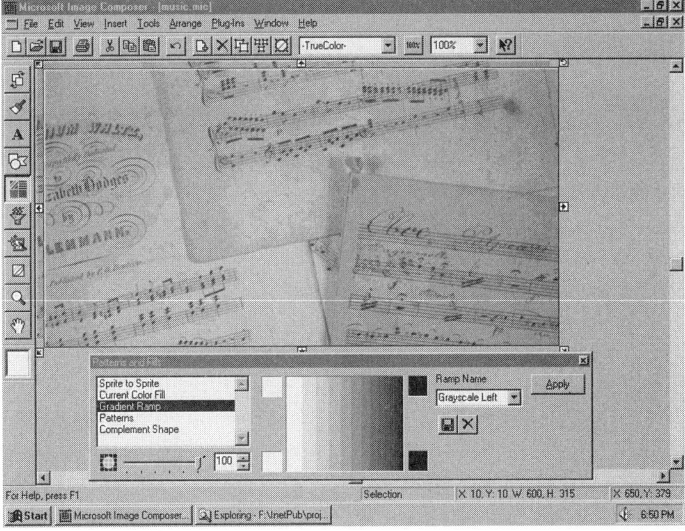

Figure 21.4.
Apply a Grayscale Left gradient to a copy of the background image.

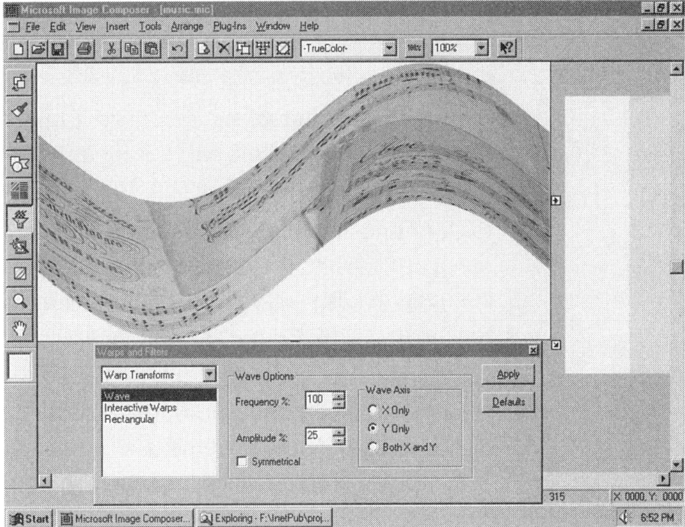

Figure 21.5.
After you apply the warp, the sheet music looks like a wave.

16. Click the Duplicate button on the toolbar. A copy of the sheet music is displayed.
17. With the copy selected, choose **A**rrange | Fli**p** | **H**orizontal. A mirrored image of the sheet music is displayed.
18. You now have some sheet music that is printed backwards. This is primarily used as a filler for the back area. Choose **A**rrange | Send **B**ackward to place the reversed image behind the correct one.

19. Use the arrow keys to nudge the copy until the status bar reads `X: 0, Y: 0`. Your image should now look like Figure 21.6.

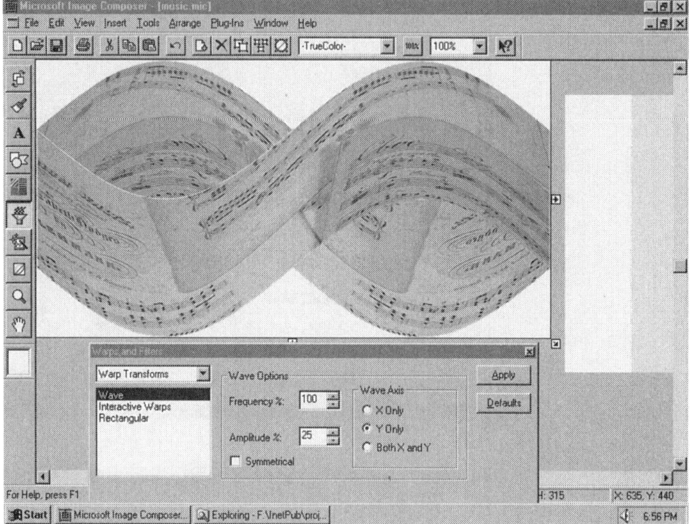

Figure 21.6.
Flip the copy of the sheet music horizontally and place it behind the original.

20. From the Standard toolbar, choose `50%` from the Zoom Percent drop-down box. Draw a selection rectangle around both copies of the sheet music; then choose **A**rrange | Flatten **S**election. The two pieces of sheet music are now one.
21. Click **A**rrange | Send **B**ackward to send the gradient to the back. Move the gradient back into the composition area, and use the nudge keys until the status bar reads `X: 0, Y: 0`. Click the Actual Size button in the Standard toolbar to return the image to actual size. Then press Home to return the composition to Home position if necessary.
22. Choose Patterns and Fills from the toolbox. The Patterns and Fills palette is displayed. Click Sprite to Sprite, and select Transparency Map from the Sprite Texture Type drop-down list, as shown in Figure 21.7.
23. Click the sheet music; then click **A**pply. If the Hint box is displayed, click OK; then click the gradient to apply the transparency map.
24. Select the gradient and delete it from your composition. Now you have a piece of sheet music that is opaque on the left side and gradually fades away toward the right, as shown in Figure 21.8. The pixels that were white in the gradient created solid areas in the sheet music sprite. As the pixels in the gradient got darker, it increased the amount of transparency in the sheet music sprite.

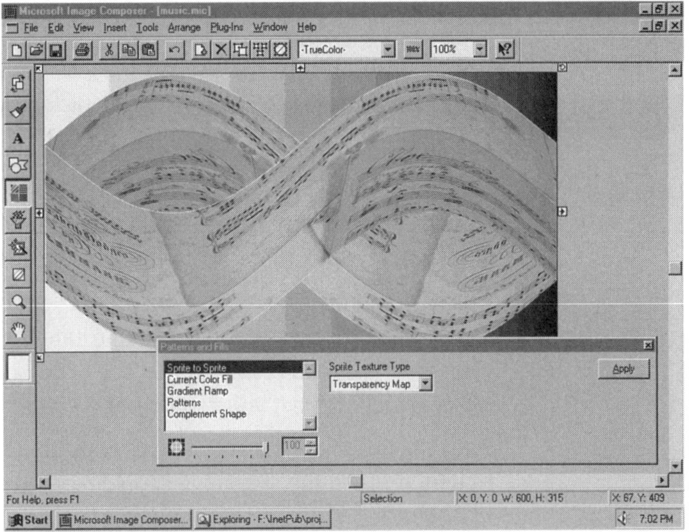

Figure 21.7.
Apply a transparency map to the sheet music using the gradient as the map.

25. Click the Save button on the toolbar to update the image on your hard disk.

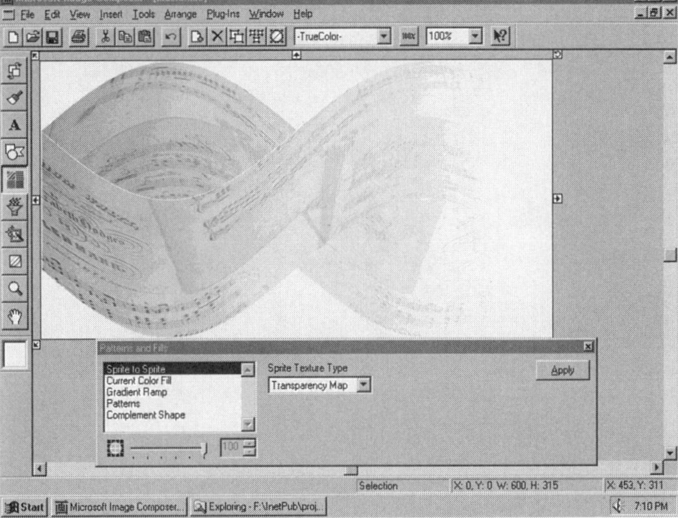

Figure 21.8.
After you apply the transparency map, the image fades away toward the right side.

Adding Transparence to Sprites

In the following steps, you add copies of another sprite from the FrontPage 97 with Bonus Pack CD-ROM. You will add transparence to this image also, to further enhance the appearance of the image.

To proceed with your project, follow these steps:

1. Choose **I**nsert | **F**rom File or press the Insert Image File button on the Standard toolbar. The Insert From File dialog box is displayed.
2. Locate the `\ImgComp\Mmfiles\Photos\Music\guitar2.mic` file on the FrontPage 97 with Bonus Pack CD, and then double-click the filename to open the file.
3. Choose `50%` from the Zoom Percent drop-down list in the Standard toolbar. This gives you a better view of your entire composition.
4. Select the guitar. The upper-right adjustment node enables you to rotate the sprite. Observe the status bar as you rotate the sprite, and stop when the rotation angle reads `135 Deg (135 Deg from base)`. A few degrees higher or lower is acceptable if you can't get it perfect.
5. Press the Shift key; then resize the guitar to a height of 315 pixels (the Height figure in the status bar should read `H: 315`). You may need to return to 100% Zoom Percent to size it exactly.
6. Position the guitar at `X: 0, Y: 0` as displayed in the status bar. Your image should now look like Figure 21.9.

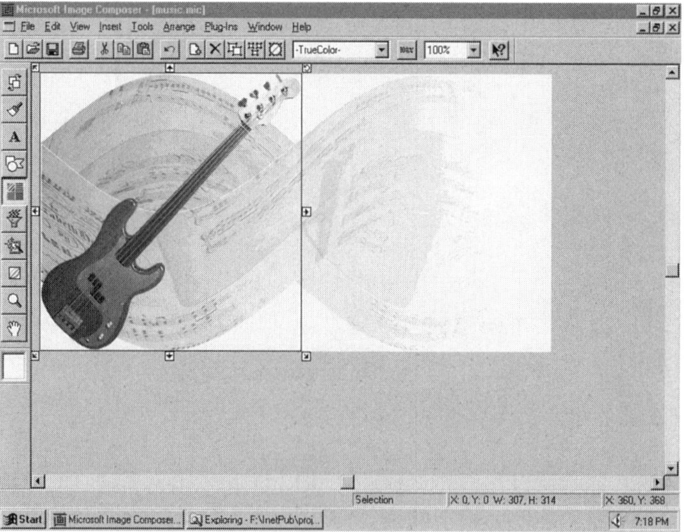

Figure 21.9.
Insert the guitar sprite in your composition, scale it down, and position it at the upper-left corner of your composition.

7. Select the guitar and click the Duplicate button on the toolbar. Move the copy of the guitar to `X: 116, Y: 0`.
8. Click the Duplicate button again. Move the third guitar to `X: 232, Y: 0`.
9. Click the Duplicate button again. Move the fourth guitar to `X: 348, Y: 0`.

10. Click the Duplicate button again. Move the fifth guitar to `X: 464, Y: 0`.
11. Shift-click to select all five guitars. Choose **A**rrange | Flatten **S**election (Ctrl+F). All the guitars become one sprite. Then choose **A**rrange | Send to Bac**k**. Each guitar shows through the sheet music at varying intensities, depending on the transparency of the sheet music. Your image should now look like Figure 21.10.

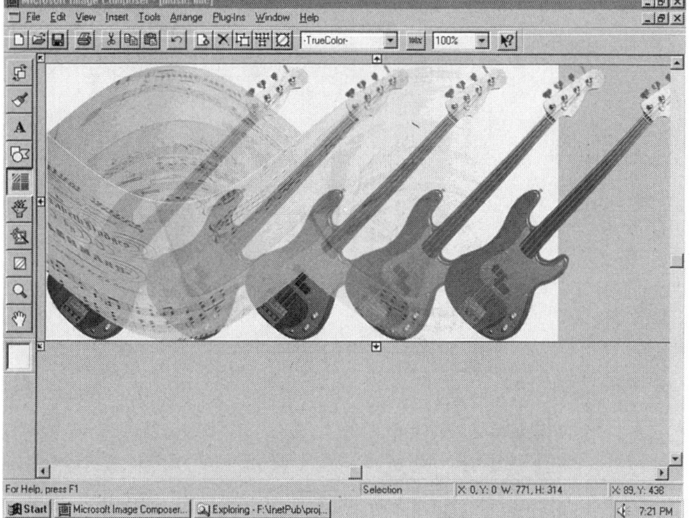

Figure 21.10.
Each of the guitars shows through the sheet music at varying intensities.

12. Choose Shapes from the toolbox. The Shapes palette is displayed.
13. Click the Rectangle. Draw a rectangle that measures 635×315 pixels (`X: 635, Y: 315`), and click Render. The rectangle is displayed in your composition.
14. Click Patterns and Fills from the toolbox. Select Gradient Ramp, and choose the Grayscale Up ramp.
15. With the rectangle selected, click **A**pply. The rectangle becomes filled with the gradient.
16. Move the rectangle to the `X: 0, Y: 0` coordinates. Choose Sprite to Sprite from the Patterns and Fills palette, and select Transparency Map if it is not still selected.
17. Select the guitar group and click **A**pply. If a hint dialog box is displayed, choose OK; then click the lower-right corner of the gradient rectangle.
18. Click the rectangle to select it; then click Delete. Now you can see that the guitars are more opaque near the top and more transparent toward the bottom of the image, as shown in Figure 21.11.

19. Click the Save button on the Standard toolbar to update the image on your disk.

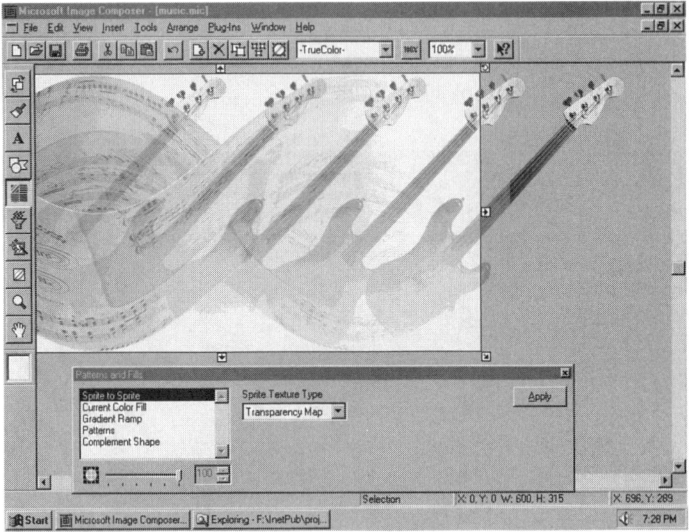

Figure 21.11.
With transparency added, the guitars are more opaque toward the top and more transparent toward the bottom.

NOTE: If you want to experiment with some effects, now is the time to do it. Try the following three examples from the Art Effects palette; they work well with this image. Choose **E**dit | **U**ndo (Ctrl+Z) between each effect to compare the results.

Try Art Effects | Paint | Spatter. Set Spray Radius to 2, Smoothness to 5, and Opacity at 100. Apply the effect to the sheet music.

Try Art Effects | Paint | Watercolor. Set Brush Detail to 14, Shadow Intensity to 1, Texture to 2, and Opacity to 20. Apply the effect to the sheet music.

Try Art Effects | Paint | Sumi-e. Set Stroke Width to 3, Stroke Pressure to 2, Contrast to 5, and Opacity to 40. Apply the effect to the guitars.

Adding the Musical Notes

Now you will add some enhancements to the image: a large staff and some text. Then you'll warp the items using the same warp settings that you applied to the sheet music in the previous task.

1. Click the Current Color Swatch, and select black. Choose OK to return to the composition.
2. Click the Shapes button on the toolbox, and select the Rectangle. Draw a rectangle that measures 600 pixels wide and 5 pixels tall. Click **R**ender to create the rectangle.
3. Click the Duplicate button on the Standard toolbar four times to create four additional copies of the rectangle.
4. Press Home to return the composition to its home position. To build the staff, you're going to offset the rectangular lines for the time being. This way, you won't accidentally select any of the other elements when you apply your warp to the staff. Position the rectangles on your image using the following coordinates:

   Rectangle 1: `X: 70, Y: 0`
   Rectangle 2: `X: 70, Y: 77`
   Rectangle 3: `X: 70, Y: 155`
   Rectangle 4: `X: 70, Y: 232`
   Rectangle 5: `X: 70, Y: 310`

5. Shift-click to select all five staff rectangles and choose **A**rrange | Flatten **S**election (Ctrl+F).
6. Select the Oval tool from the Shapes—Geometry palette. Draw a 75-pixel wide by 58-pixel high rectangle, and click **R**ender. An oval is displayed in your composition.
7. With the oval selected, press the Duplicate button on the Standard toolbar four times. Then move the five notes to the following coordinates, using Figure 21.12 as a guide:

   Note 1: `X: 126, Y: 30`
   Note 2: `X: 126, Y: 208`
   Note 3: `X: 268, Y: 90`
   Note 4: `X: 409, Y: 52`
   Note 5: `X: 532, Y: 132`

8. Choose the Rectangle tool again and draw a rectangle that measures 200 pixels high and 5 pixels wide. Click **R**ender. The rectangle is displayed on your page.
9. Move the rectangle to the right of the first pair of notes, to coordinates `X: 195, Y: 35.`
10. Choose the Rectangle tool again and draw a rectangle that measures 140 pixels high and 5 pixels wide. Click **R**ender.

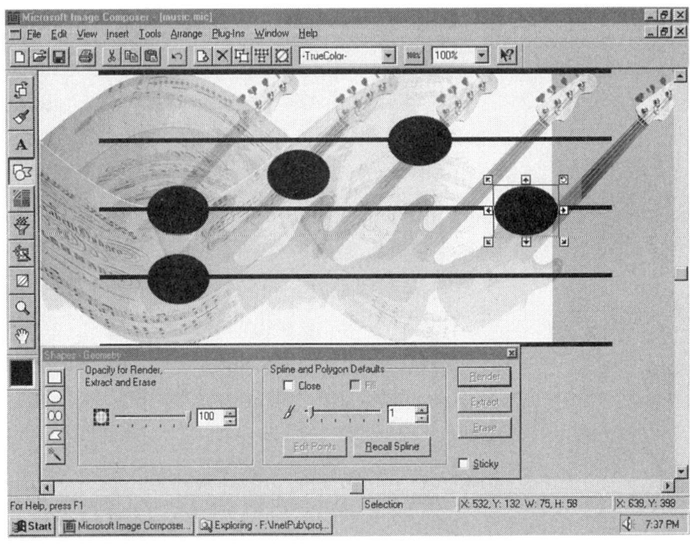

Figure 21.12.
Position the five lines in the staff and the five notes as shown.

11. With your new rectangle selected, click the Duplicate button on the toolbar twice. Position these rectangles at the following coordinates (they will be on the left side of the three remaining notes, as shown in Figure 21.13):

    Stem 1: `X: 269, Y: 117`
    Stem 2: `X: 410, Y: 78`
    Stem 3: `X: 533, Y: 156`

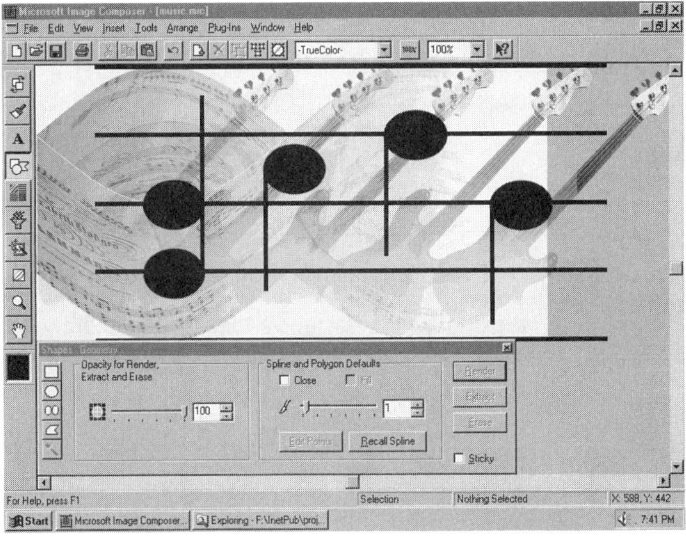

Figure 21.13.
Add stems to the notes like this.

12. Shift-click to select the staff, the five notes, and the four stems. Then choose **A**rrange | Flatten **S**election (Ctrl+F). The selected items become one object.
13. With the staff and notes selected, choose the Warps and Filters palette from the toolbox.
14. Choose Warp Transforms from the drop-down menu, and select the Wave transform.
15. Click the **D**efaults button to revert to the default wave settings in case you have changed them. Then click **A**pply. The staff and text now take on the same wave as the sheet music.
16. Move the staff to the `X: 0, Y: 0` coordinate to align it with the background. Your composition should now look like Figure 21.14.

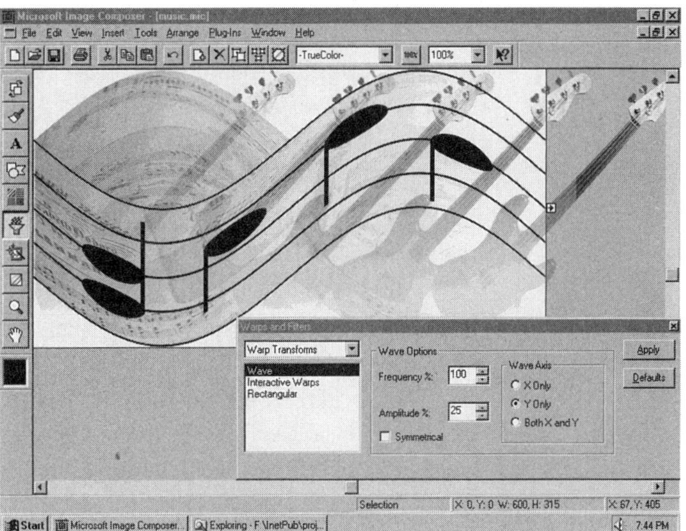

Figure 21.14.
A wave transform is added to the staff and notes.

Adding Text

To finish the image, you'll add some text within the notes. The text will be added in white font. After you enter the text you will rotate the text so that it aligns better with each note; then you'll nudge the text into position.

To add the text to the notes, follow these steps:

1. Choose the Text tool from the toolbox. Click Select Font, and choose Times New Roman, Bold Italic, and 14 point for your font. Click OK to return to the Text palette.
2. Click the Current Color Swatch and choose white for your current color. Click OK to return to the Text palette.

3. Enter `Bands` in the text box and click **A**pply. The text is displayed in the upper-right corner of your composition guide, surrounded by a bounding box. Move it into the top note in the first row. Then drag the rotate point in the upper-right corner of the bounding box downward to rotate the text so that the status bar reads `33 Deg (33 Deg from base)`. Then use the arrow keys to nudge the text to the `X: 64, Y: 204` position.
4. Enter `CDs` in the text box and click **A**pply. Position it in the top note in the first row. Then drag the rotate point in the upper-right corner of the bounding box downward to rotate the text so that the status bar reads `30 Deg (30 Deg from base)`. Then use the arrow keys to nudge the text to the `X: 73, Y: 247` position.
5. Enter `Videos` in the text box and click **A**pply. Position it in the top note in the first row. Then drag the rotate point in the upper-right corner of the bounding box upward to rotate the text so that the status bar reads `-40 Deg (-40 Deg from base)`. Then use the arrow keys to nudge the text to the `X: 210, Y: 169` position.
6. Enter `On TV` in the text box and click **A**pply. Position it in the top note in the first row. Then drag the rotate point in the upper-right corner of the bounding box upward to rotate the text so that the status bar reads `-34 Deg (-34 Deg from base)`. Then use the arrow keys to nudge the text to the `X: 352, Y: 44` position.
7. Enter `Awards` in the text box and click **A**pply. Position it in the top note in the first row. Then drag the rotate point in the upper-right corner of the bounding box downward to rotate the text so that the status bar reads `26 Deg (26 Deg from base)`. Then use the arrow keys to nudge the text to the `X: 467, Y: 75` position. Your composition should now look like Figure 21.15.

8. Click the Save button in the Standard toolbar to update the original version of the file on your hard drive before you save it to JPG format.
9. Choose **F**ile | Save **A**s. The Save As dialog box is displayed.
10. Use the Save **i**n drop-down list to locate the drive and directory to which you want to save the file.
11. From the Save as **t**ype drop-down list, select JPEG (`*.jpg`). The File **n**ame field automatically changes to read `music.jpg`.
12. Verify that the **C**ompression checkbox is checked. Set the **A**mount field to `30`, as shown in Figure 21.16.

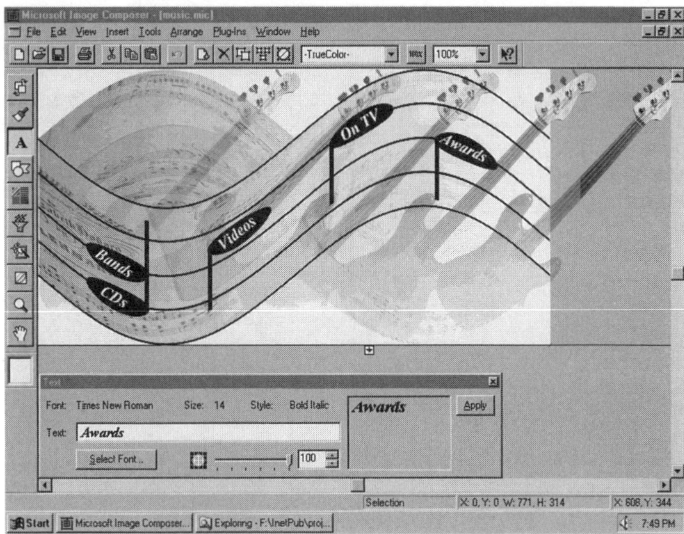

Figure 21.15.
Text is added to the notes.

TIP: The image you created here contains very few areas that have solid colors; the majority of the image is photographic quality. You can generally use a higher compression setting on these types of images without suffering too much deterioration in quality.

Take care not to set your compression settings too high. In most cases, settings between 10 percent and 35 percent work well, depending on the items in the composition. It is very important to save a true-color version of your image in the event that you are not satisfied with the appearance of the image after you compress it. You can reopen the original image (in Microsoft Image Composer format or another true-color format) and compress the original file again.

13. Choose **S**ave. Microsoft Image Composer informs you that your composition will be flattened and cropped to the composition guide. Choose OK to save the image.

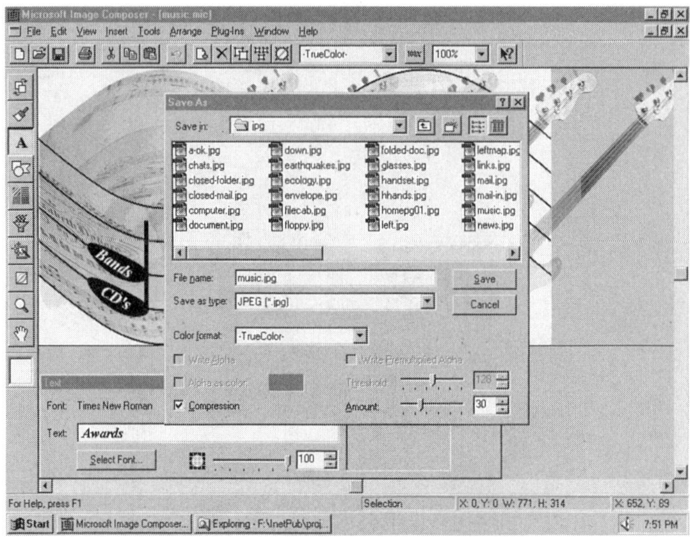

Figure 21.16.

You can usually compress photo-quality images with few solid areas using a higher compression ratio, such as 30, in Microsoft Image Composer.

Creating the Planetary Progression Home Page Image Map

Throughout the chapters in Part V, "Creating Graphics with Microsoft Image Composer," you have been learning to create buttons, banners, and additional items for the fictitious Planetary Progression site to see how graphics can work together to create a mood. Next you will create the graphic displayed on the home page and within the floating frame for the site. This image is displayed on the home page to inform the user about the sections in the web. It is also displayed in the frameset for the site, to navigate the user to the main sections in the web.

To create the home page graphic, follow these steps:

1. Choose **F**ile | **N**ew (Ctrl+N) or select the New button from the Standard toolbar. A new image is displayed.
2. Choose **F**ile | Composi**t**ion Properties. The Composition Properties dialog box is displayed. Create a composition that is 250 pixels wide and 425 pixels high, with a black background. Enter the following properties, as shown in Figure 21.17, and choose OK:

```
Width:      250
Height:     425
Red:        0
Green:      0
Blue:       0
```

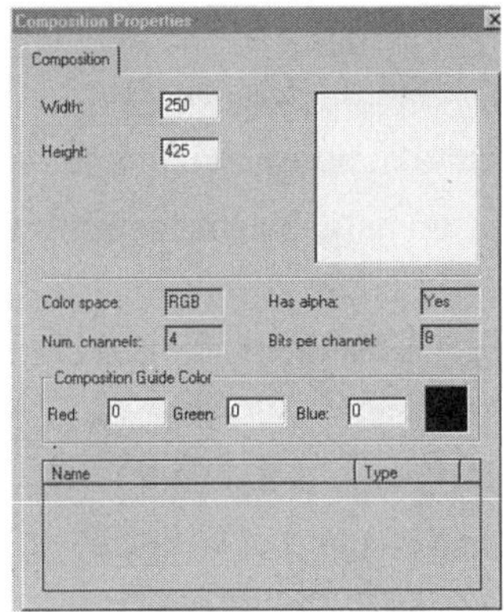

Figure 21.17.
Use the Composition Properties dialog box to create a 250-pixel wide and 425-pixel high composition with a black background.

3. Click the Current Color swatch beneath the toolbox. The Color Picker is displayed.
4. Select the Custom Palette tab. Click **L**oad.
5. Locate `Iexplore.pal` on the FrontPage 97 with Bonus Pack CD, located in the `\ImgComp\Mmfiles\Palettes` folder. The palette loads into Microsoft Image Composer, as shown in Figure 21.18. Leave the **S**ort palette by field at Unsorted.

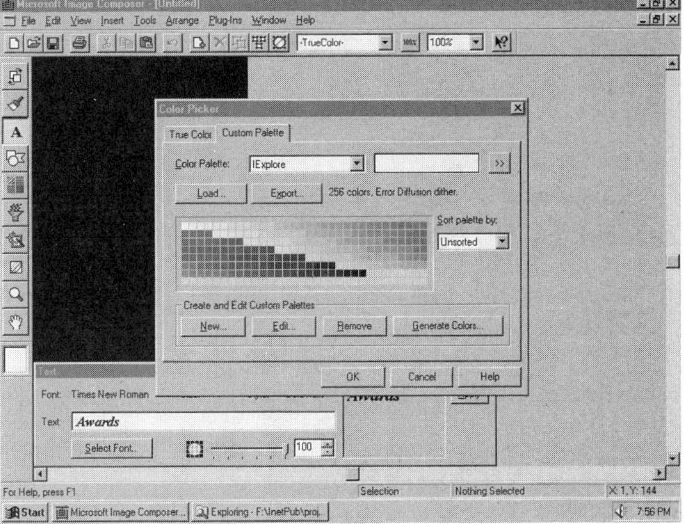

Figure 21.18.
Load the Internet Explorer palette from the FrontPage 97 with Bonus Pack CD-ROM. Leave the palette unsorted.

6. Click OK to return to the composition, and choose **I**nsert | **F**rom File. The Insert From File dialog box is displayed. Locate `Planet2.tga` on the CD that accompanies this book. Double-click the file to open it.

7. If you need to zoom out to see the entire image, choose `50%` from the Zoom Percent drop-down list in the Standard toolbar.
8. Select Shapes from the toolbox. The Shapes palette is displayed.
9. From the Shapes—Geometry palette, select the Oval tool.
10. Press Ctrl+Alt to constrain the oval tool to a square as you draw. Click the upper-left corner of the planet image and drag until you reach near the bottom of the image. Release the mouse.
11. Click E**x**tract to extract a circular area from the image.
12. Select the `planet2.tga` image that you opened, and press Delete. The circular image remains as shown in Figure 21.19.

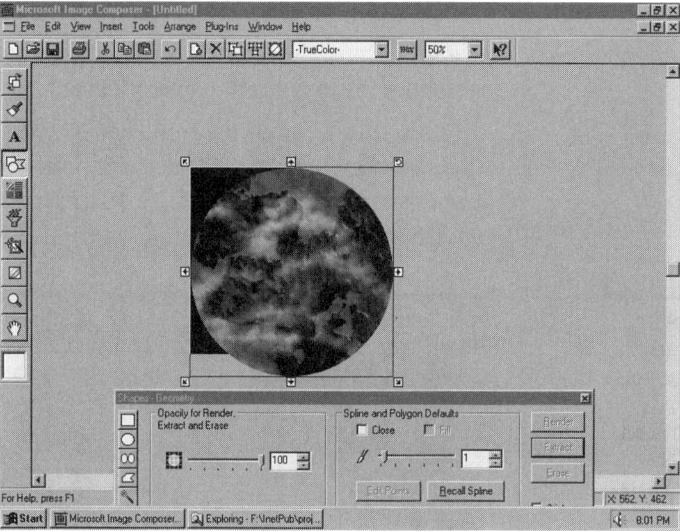

Figure 21.19.
Extract a circle from the original rectangular planet image; then delete the original image from the composition.

13. Choose Warps and Filters from the toolbox. The Warps and Filters palette is displayed.
14. From the drop-down menu, select Warps. Then choose Bulge from the warp list, and choose Out from the Warp Direction field.
15. Click **A**pply. The planet now has a three-dimensional appearance, as shown in Figure 21.20.
16. Zoom back to 100% using the Zoom Actual Size button in the Standard toolbar. Then press Home to return the composition guide to its home position.

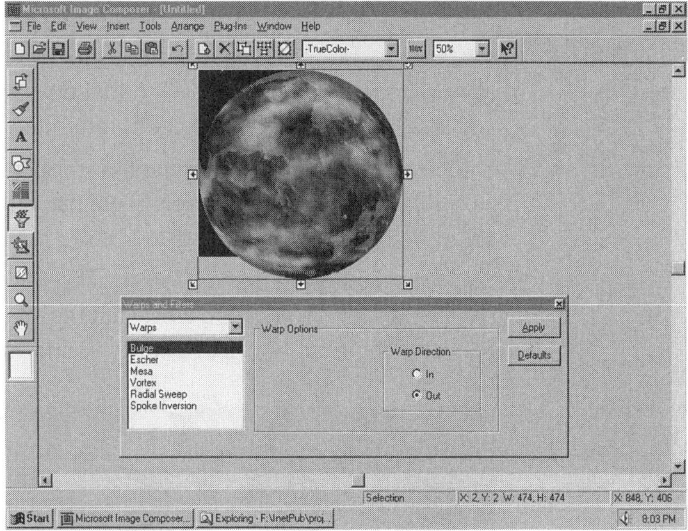

Figure 21.20.
After you apply a bulge warp, the planet looks more three-dimensional.

17. Click to select the planet; then press the Shift key to constrain the aspect ratio of the sprite while you scale it down. Adjust the sprite by moving the lower-right adjustment point until the status bar shows dimensions of `X: 240, Y: 240.`
18. Move the planet image to the approximate center of the composition guide. Use the arrow keys to nudge the planet until the status bar reads `X: 5, Y: 92`.
19. This is a good point at which to save your image so you don't lose the work you've completed thus far. Choose **F**ile | **S**ave (Ctrl+S), or click the Save button on the Standard toolbar. Save the image as `leftmap.mic`.

Your imaginary client wants to give the impression that the fate of the world is in everyone's hands. So, that is the message that you will portray in the main graphic. The CD that accompanies this book has an image of a hand that works perfectly. You'll use the color lifter to extract the hand from the image to make a sprite. This technique works best when an image is surrounded by a solid color.

1. Choose **I**nsert | **F**rom File. The Insert From File dialog box is displayed. Put the CD that accompanies this book into the CD-ROM drive and locate `hand.tga`. Double-click the file to open it. The hand image is displayed in the composition window. Move the image to the right side of the composition window.
2. Choose Shapes from the toolbox. The Shapes—Geometry palette is displayed.
3. Click the Color Lift button (the last button on the left side of the palette). The Shapes—Color Lift palette is displayed.

4. Use the Current Color swatch to select any color but black. This helps you see which pixels the color lifter selects for the extraction. Pick a color that is light or bright, such as yellow, and that does not exist in the image. After you select your color, choose OK to return to the Shapes palette.
5. The default settings in the palette (`Hue: 100`, `Whiteness: 100`, and `Blackness: 40`) work well to select the pixels in the hand. Make sure that the Selection is set to **A**dd, Search Mode is set to **L**ocal, and Feather is `0`.
6. Click anywhere in the hand. Notice that several pixels turn to the color you selected. Continue selecting colors until the hand is completely filled with the color in the current color swatch, as shown in Figure 21.21.

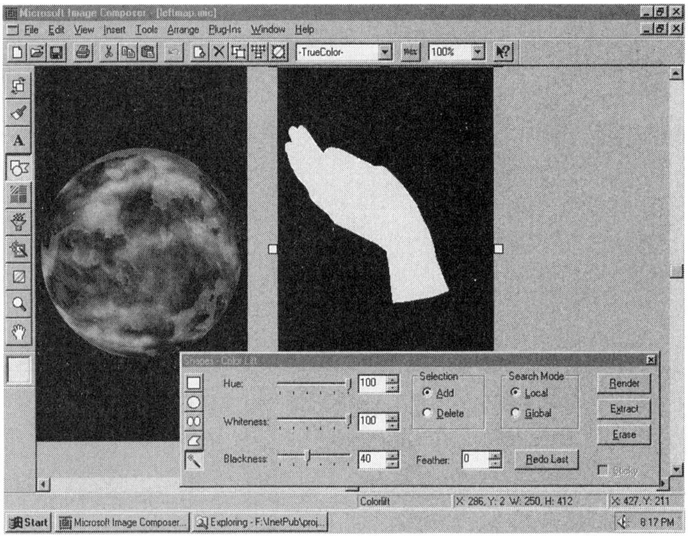

Figure 21.21.
Select the colors in the hand with the color lifter until the hand is filled with the color in the current color swatch.

7. Click E**x**tract. You'll notice that a smaller bounding box is displayed around the hand. Move the selection to the side to make sure that you extracted the hand properly, without holes in the image. If it is acceptable, select the original hand image and press Delete. If it is not acceptable, delete the sprite and try again.
8. Click the hand sprite to select it, and press the Shift key. Using the adjustment point at the lower-right corner, resize the hand sprite until the status bar reads `W: 118, H: 126` (118 pixels wide and 126 pixels high).
9. Move the hand sprite beneath the planet. Use the arrow keys to nudge the hand until the status bar reads `X: 8, Y: 260`.
10. Make sure the hand is still selected, and choose the Duplicate button on the Standard toolbar. A copy of the hand is displayed.

11. Choose **A**rrange | Fli**p** | **H**orizontal. The second hand is now a mirror copy of the first hand.
12. Move the second hand beneath the planet. Use the arrow keys to nudge the position of the second hand until the status bar reads `X: 125, Y:260`.
13. Shift-click to select both hands. Then choose **A**rrange | Send to Bac**k**. The hands appear behind the planet, as shown in Figure 21.22.

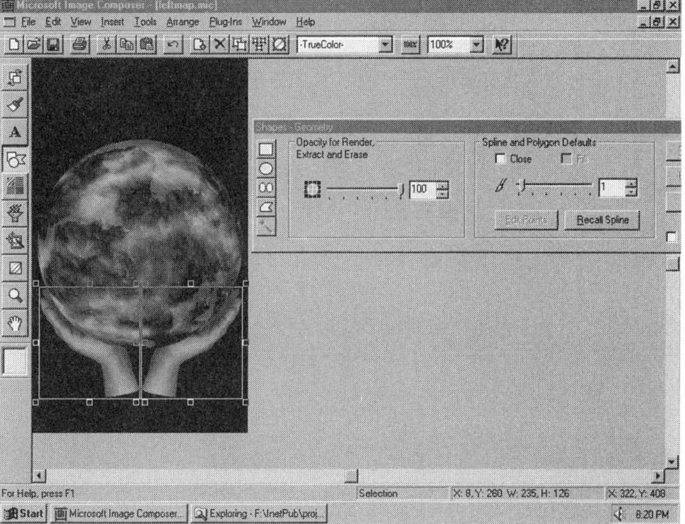

Figure 21.22.
Position the hands partially behind the planet using the Send to Back command.

14. With both hands still in place, Shift-click to add the planet to the selection set. With the planet and both hands selected, choose **A**rrange | **L**ock Position (Ctrl+L). This freezes the position of the sprites so that they don't move while you perform the next steps.
15. Choose Paint from the toolbox to enable the paint tools. Click the planet to select it.
16. Choose the Erase tool (the first tool in the second row). Select the smallest brush size in the first row; this brush produces soft anti-aliased edges.
17. Erase a portion of the planet so that the hands partially wrap in front of it. Use Figure 21.23 as a guide. Zoom in closer to the image if you need to. If you make a mistake, choose **E**dit | **U**ndo (Ctrl+Z) to begin your painting again.
18. When the painting is complete, choose **F**ile | **S**ave (Ctrl+S) or click the Save button on the toolbar to update the file on your hard disk.

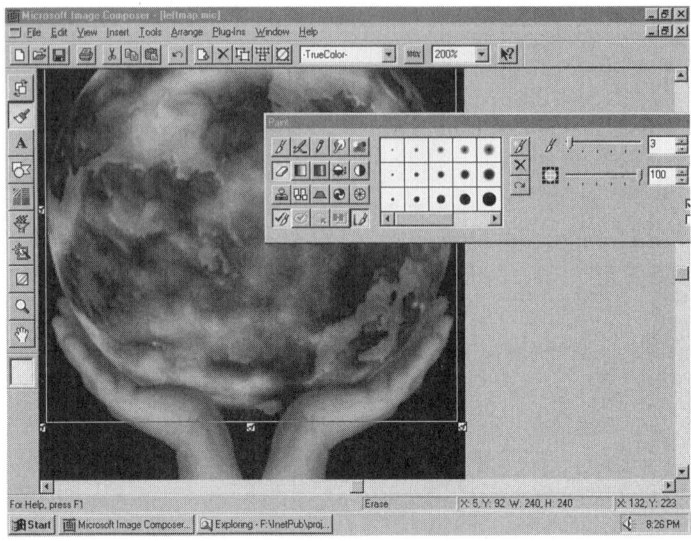

Figure 21.23.
Erase portions of the planet so that the hands wrap around them slightly.

Now you add the name of the site to the image, you add a wave effect to the text, and then you add a bright drop shadow to the text. Follow these steps:

1. Zoom back to 100% using the Actual Size button on the toolbar. Press Home to return the composition guide to the home position.
2. Choose Text from the toolbox. From the Text palette, click **S**elect Font, and choose Arial Black. From the **S**ize field, select 26. Click OK to return to the Text palette.
3. Click the Current Color swatch, and select dark purple (the 13th color in the 5th row of the Custom Palette, as shown in Figure 21.24). Choose OK to return to the Text palette.
4. Enter `Planetary` in the text field and click **A**pply. Move the text to the right side of your composition guide.
5. Enter `Progression` in the text field, and click **A**pply. Move the second line of text beneath the first line.
6. Choose Warps and Filters from the toolbox. The Warps and Filters palette is displayed.
7. Select Warp Transforms from the drop-down list, and then choose Wave.
8. Enter or choose the following settings for your wave:

```
Frequency %:    90
Amplitude %:    20
Symmetrical:    Unchecked
Wave Axis:      Y Only
```

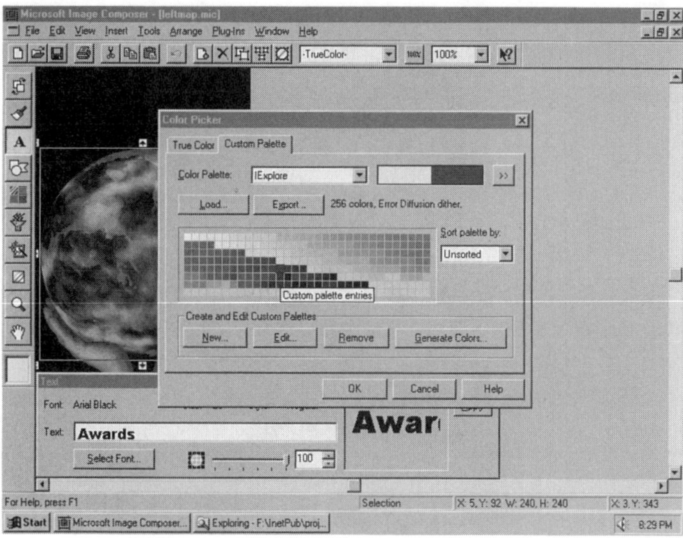

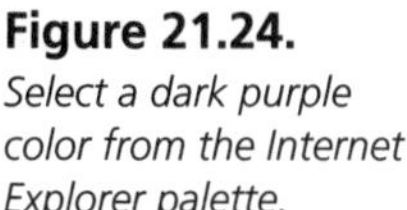

Figure 21.24.
Select a dark purple color from the Internet Explorer palette.

9. Click the first line of text and click **A**pply. Repeat for the second line of text.
10. From the Warps and Filters palette, choose Outlines from the drop-down menu, and select Shadow from the outline type list. Enter or choose the following settings for your outline:

`Offset X:`	1
`Offset Y:`	1
`Opacity:`	100
`Color:`	Click the color swatch and choose bright purple (3rd color in the 3rd row) from the Internet Explorer custom palette.

11. Click the first line of text and click **A**pply. Repeat for the second line of text.
12. Click the `Planetary` text, and position it inside your composition window. Use the nudge keys to move the text until the status bar reads `X: 35, Y: 347`.
13. Click the `Progression` text, and position it inside your composition window. Use the nudge keys to move the text until the status bar reads `X: 19, Y: 366`.
14. Shift-click to select the two lines of text.
15. Choose **A**rrange | **L**ock Position (Ctrl+L). Now the positions of all objects in your composition window are frozen. Your image should now look like Figure 21.25.
16. Choose **F**ile | **S**ave (Ctrl+S), or select the Save button on the Standard toolbar to update the file on your disk.

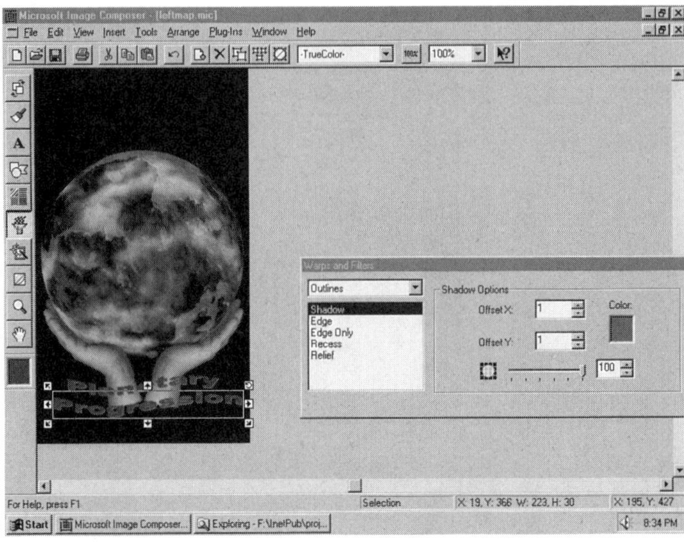

Figure 21.25.
The name of the site is added to the bottom of the image.

The next step is to add the section names to the image. You'll begin by making a long narrow line, using the same dark purple color that you used for the site name. Then you will add the section names in a bright blue color and a dark drop shadow to the names that overlap the planet image.

1. If you still do not have the dark purple color in your current color swatch, click the color swatch and choose the 13th color in the 5th row from the Custom Palette tab in the Color Picker. Choose OK to return to the composition.
2. Click the Shapes button in the toolbox. The Shapes—Geometry palette is displayed.
3. Click the Rectangle tool. Draw a rectangle that measures 233 pixels wide and 2 pixels high. Click **R**ender to complete the rectangle.
4. Press the Duplicate button on the Standard toolbar five times to create five additional copies of the rectangle.
5. Position the six rectangles at the following coordinates:

   Rectangle 1: `X: 8, Y: 30`
   Rectangle 2: `X: 8, Y: 50`
   Rectangle 3: `X: 8, Y: 70`
   Rectangle 4: `X: 8, Y: 90`
   Rectangle 5: `X: 8, Y: 110`
   Rectangle 6: `X: 8, Y: 130`

6. Starting from the outer-right side of your composition, draw a selection rectangle around all six purple lines, and choose **A**rrange | **L**ock Position (Ctrl+L). Your image should now look like Figure 21.26.

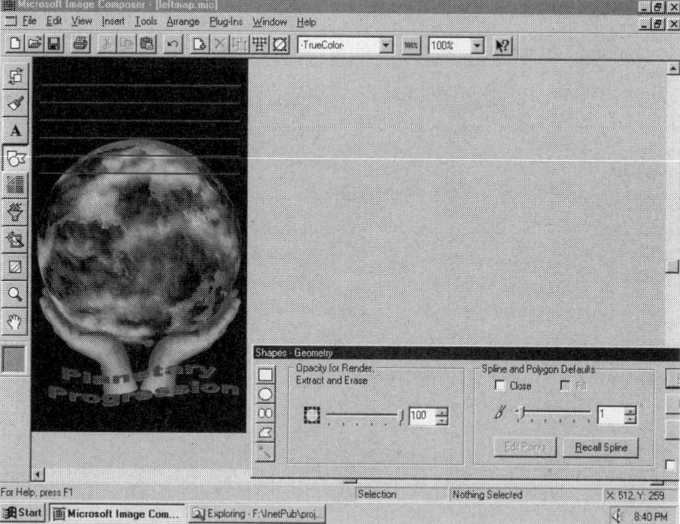

Figure 21.26.
Add lines to the top of the composition.

7. Click the Current Color Swatch, and select medium blue (the first color in the seventh row of the Internet Explorer palette).
8. Select the Text button in the toolbox. The Text palette is displayed.
9. Click **S**elect Font, and choose Arial Black. From the **S**ize field, select 10. Click OK to return to the Text palette.
10. Enter `Helping Hands` in the text field and click **A**pply. Move the text over the first purple line, near the left side of the image. Use the arrow keys to nudge the text until the status bar reads `X: 13, Y: 25`.
11. Enter `Earthquake Watch` in the text field and click **A**pply. Move the text over the second purple line, near the left side of the image. Use the arrow keys to nudge the text until the status bar reads `X: 49, Y: 45`.
12. Enter `Endangered Species` in the text field and click **A**pply. Move the text over the third purple line, near the left side of the image. Use the arrow keys to nudge the text until the status bar reads `X: 87, Y: 65`.
13. Enter `Global Warming` in the text field and click **A**pply. Move the text over the fourth purple line, near the left side of the image. Use the arrow keys to nudge the text until the status bar reads `X: 124, Y: 85`.
14. Enter `Peacemakers` in the text field and click **A**pply. Move the text over the fifth purple line, near the left side of the image. Use the arrow keys to nudge the text until the status bar reads `X: 145, Y: 105`.

15. Enter `Ecology` in the text field and click **A**pply. Move the text over the sixth purple line, near the left side of the image. Use the arrow keys to nudge the text until the status bar reads `X: 185, Y: 125`. Your image should now look like Figure 21.27.

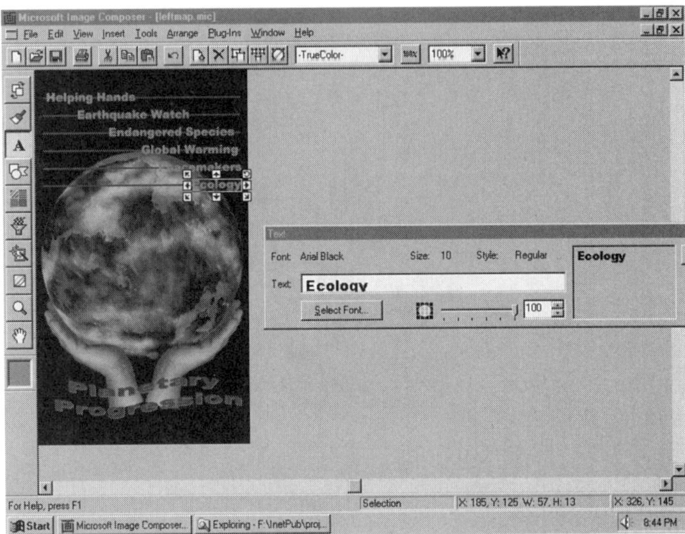

Figure 21.27.
Add section names over the purple lines.

16. The last three lines of text overlap the planet and are a bit difficult to read. You'll add a slight drop shadow to make them stand out a little bit more. From the Warps and Filters palette, choose Outlines from the drop-down menu. Then select Shadow from the outline type list. Enter or choose the following settings for your outline:

`Offset X:`	1
`Offset Y:`	1
`Opacity:`	100
`Color:`	Click the color swatch and choose black (the last color in the palette before the empty squares) from the Internet Explorer custom palette. Choose OK to return to the Warps and Filters palette.

17. Select the Global Warming text and click **A**pply. Repeat for the Peacemakers and the Ecology text.
18. Shift-click to select all six text objects, and choose **A**rrange | **L**ock Position (Ctrl+L).
19. Choose **F**ile | **S**ave (Ctrl+S), or select the Save button on the Standard toolbar to update the file on your disk.

There are a few additional text items to add to the image: First, you will add a "slogan" to the image, and you'll also add the home page URL (even though it is a fictitious one) to the bottom of the page. To add the final items to the image, follow these steps:

1. Select the Text palette from the toolbox. Choose **S**elect Font from the Text palette, and select Times New Roman, Bold Italic, and 20 point for your font. Choose OK to return to the Text palette.
2. Enter `... it's in our hands.` in the Text field.
3. Adjust the Opacity slider to 40.
4. Click the Current Color Swatch, and select white (the first color in the first row) from the Internet Explorer palette. Choose OK to return to the text palette.
5. Click **A**pply. The text is displayed in your composition window. Move it to the center of the planet. The status bar should display the coordinates `X: 23, Y: 203`.
6. Choose the Warps and Filters palette from the toolbox. Then choose Outlines from its drop-down menu, and select Shadow from the outline list. Enter or choose the following settings for your outline:

`Offset X:`	`2`
`Offset Y:`	`2`
`Opacity:`	`100`
`Color:`	Click the color swatch and choose black (the last color in the palette before the empty squares) from the Internet Explorer custom palette.

7. Click the text and click **A**pply. The shadow is displayed behind the text using the same transparency setting as the original text.
8. Click the Current Color Swatch, and select purple (1st color from the 4th row).
9. Choose the Text palette from the toolbox. From the Text palette, click **S**elect Font. Choose Arial, Regular, and 10 point, and click OK.
10. In the Text field, enter the fictitious URL `http://www.sitename.org`. Adjust the Opacity setting to `100`; then click **A**pply. The text is displayed in your composition window.
11. Move the URL beneath the site name, toward the bottom of the composition. Nudge the text until the status bar reads `X: 55, Y: 405`. Your image should now look like Figure 21.28.

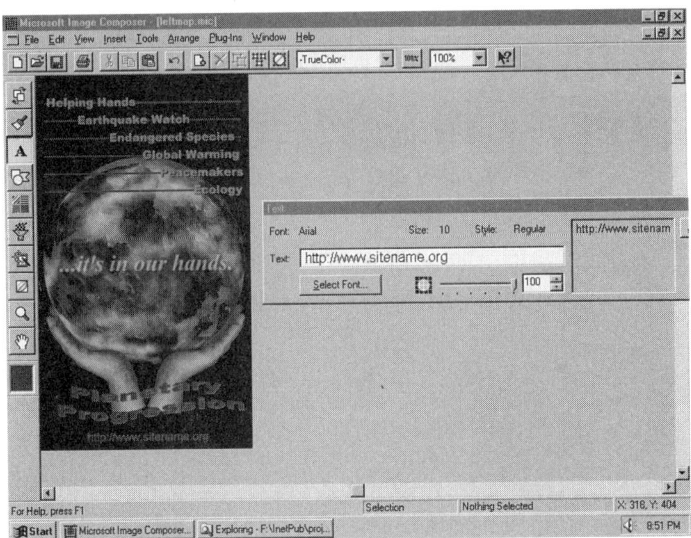

Figure 21.28.
The site URL is placed on the image, and it is ready to save.

12. Before you save the final image to your Web image format, save it in Microsoft Image Composer format for the final time. This way, if you need to go back and make some changes at a later date, you don't have to start all over again. Choose **F**ile | **S**ave (Ctrl+S), or select the Save button on the Standard toolbar to update the file on your disk.
13. Now, select **F**ile | Save **A**s. The Save As dialog box is displayed.
14. Use the Save **i**n drop-down list to locate the drive and directory to which you want to save the file.
15. From the Save as **t**ype drop-down list, select JPEG (`*.jpg`). The File **n**ame field automatically changes to read `leftmap.jpg`.
16. Verify that the **C**ompression check box is selected. Set the **A**mount field to `10`. The compression is set to a low amount to make the text more legible after the file is compressed.

TIP: This image offers challenges in JPG compression settings that the previous task in this chapter did not. This image contains photographic quality and solid areas of color. In addition, there is small text on the image. Solid areas and text can sometimes deteriorate in quality after compression, detracting from the appearance of the image. You generally want to use higher compression settings on images of this type.

17. Choose **S**ave. When Microsoft Image Composer notifies you that the image will be cropped and all sprites flattened, choose OK. The image is saved to your hard disk.

The one thing you have remaining is to make a note of the text colors that you used in your image. This is because you'll want to use the same text colors in your pages, so that everything will blend together nicely. You primarily used dark purple (`Red 51, Green 0, Blue 102`) and blue (`Red 0, Green 102, Blue 255`). You can use these two colors for text and link colors in the FrontPage Editor when you create the style sheet for your Web pages.

Workshop Wrap-Up

The techniques you learned in this chapter provide a basic understanding of how you can combine sprites and effects to build a composition. There are many more such features and effects available, and examples of additional effects are provided on the CD that accompanies this book. Using the techniques you learned in this chapter, you can begin your path of experimentation with an endless supply of tools, combinations, and effects in your images. Indeed, the pleasure of creating artwork lies in the adventures and challenges you face along the way. We each have individual tastes and preferences, and no doubt you'll find some effects that work best for the types of images you want to create. What is most important is that you enjoy your graphic adventures and make them fun!

In this chapter, you learned how to combine sprites and add effects to build a completed composition. Using transparencies, warps, painting effects, text, and other filters, you created a montage and an image map for your Web pages. You also learned some tips on how to decide what compression setting to use in your images.

Next Steps

In Chapter 22, "Creating Animations," you'll learn how to use Microsoft Image Composer to create animation and about several shareware and freeware programs that are available for you to compile your animated GIF files. To learn more about using Microsoft Image Composer, refer to the following chapters:

- In Chapter 19, "Creating Buttons, Icons, and Backgrounds," you learn how to use Microsoft Image Composer to create common and unique buttons.
- In Chapter 20, "Creating Banners and Text Effects," you create your own banners or add text to existing artwork to create banners.
- In Chapter 23, "Real-Life Examples: Setting the Mood," you learn how to use color schemes to create the mood of your Web site.

Q&A

Q: Sometimes I have a sprite that is surrounded by a bounding box, but the effect won't apply to it. What's wrong?

A: There are occasions when it appears as though the image is selected, but it's not active. This usually happens immediately after you render a sprite or when you select a sprite, switch to another application, and return to Image Composer. It appears as though the sprite is selected, but it may need to be reinitialized. Click the sprite again to select it and try your effect again.

Q: I have an image map that uses all photographic images on one side and all text and solid areas on the other. When I set the compression settings, the solid areas look really blocky in the JPEG image. When I save it as a GIF image, the photographic areas don't look good, and the file size in kilobytes is a lot larger. What can I do?

A: If, as you say, one side of your image is all photographic and the other side is all text or solid colors, split the image in two. Save the portion that has the photographic quality work as a `.jpg` image, using a low compression. Then save the side that has solid areas of color and text as a `.gif` image. You can decrease the number of colors in the GIF image to keep the file size small. Make sure that the two individual images, when placed next to one another, are the same size as the original image before you split it up.

C H A P T E R

TWENTY-TWO

Creating Animations

In this chapter, you

- Create three simple animations
- Review several GIF animation utilities
- Learn how to compile animated GIF using three popular shareware or retail GIF animation programs

Tasks in this chapter:

- Creating a Basic Animation
- Creating Fades
- Animating Text
- Compiling Your Animated GIF

Although Microsoft Image Composer is not an animation program, you can use it to create some basic animation files for your web. It takes only a little ingenuity to animate an image. Sometimes, a change in color is all it takes; other times, you can create sprites and locate them in different positions in each frame of the animation. In still other frames you can draw cartoons that change with each frame.

This chapter shows you some ways that you can create animated GIF files without drawing. You'll use three files furnished on the CD that accompanies this book to gain some insight on how to create animations with Microsoft Image Composer.

Creating a Basic Animation

Rather than give complete step-by-step instructions on how to create an animated GIF file, I will briefly outline the steps I used to create the examples on the CD. For the first example, open `beammeup.mic` from the CD that accompanies this book. This is a group of nine different frames.

In brief, you can create a similar animation as follows:

1. Using the Rectangle tool in the Shapes palette, draw a 150-pixel wide by 100-pixel high rectangle (the same size as the animation you want to place on your page). Fill the rectangle with a color that you won't use in the image, such as the navy blue color used in the sample file.
2. Create the spaceship (without the lights). Select all the sprites that make the spaceship, and flatten them into one object.
3. Create a group of six small white circles. Position them evenly so that they span the length of the center of the spaceship.
4. Draw a selection box around the rectangle, the spaceship, and the lights, and choose the Duplicate button on the toolbar. Move the selected items to the right of the first set of sprites. Create a second copy of the items, and position them to the right of the third set of sprites.
5. Choose yellow from your palette, and select Current Color Fill from the Patterns and Fills palette. Apply yellow to the following lights:

First frame:	second and fifth lights
Second frame:	third and sixth lights
Third frame:	first and fourth lights

6. Choose red from your palette, and select Current Color Fill from the Patterns and Fills palette. Apply red to the following lights:

First frame:	third and sixth lights
Second frame:	first and fourth lights
Third frame:	second and fifth lights

7. Select the spaceship and lights in the first frame, and choose **A**rrange | **G**roup (Ctrl+G). Repeat this for the second and third frames. Your composition should now look like Figure 22.1.
8. Select all the sprites in the first row, and choose Duplicate to create a second row of frames. Position the second row of frames beneath the first.

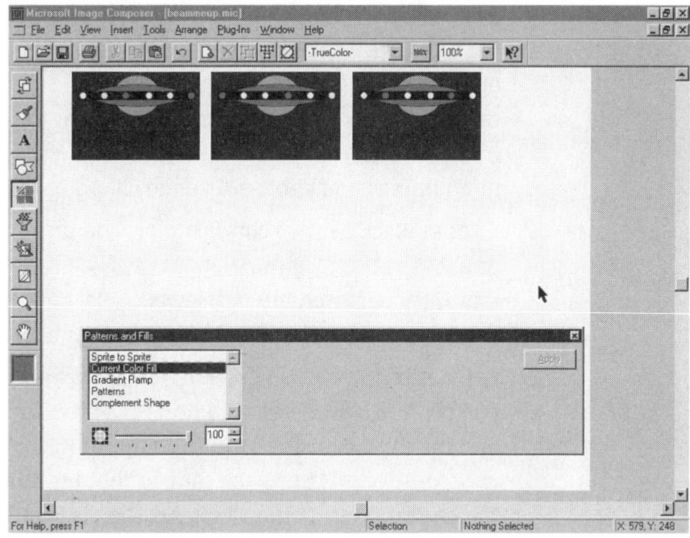

Figure 22.1.
In the first three frames in the animation, the lights cycle.

9. Add a yellow polygon to the first frame in the second row, to represent a large light coming from the bottom. Create a duplicate, and move the copy to the second frame in the second row. Resize the yellow polygon so that it is slightly larger than the first. Duplicate the second polygon and move the copy to the third frame. Resize the third polygon so that it nearly touches the bottom of the rectangle.
10. Click the spaceship in the fourth frame and choose **A**rrange | Bring to Fron**t**. Repeat this for the fifth and sixth frames. Your composition now looks like Figure 22.2.

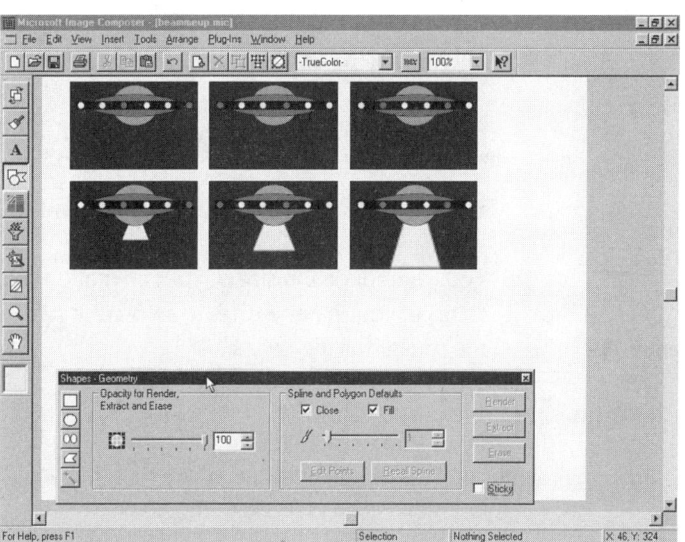

Figure 22.2.
In the second row of frames, a large light appears from beneath the spaceship as the smaller lights continue to cycle.

11. Select all the sprites in the second row and choose Duplicate from the toolbar to create a third row of frames. Delete the yellow polygons from the seventh and eighth frames. Then duplicate the yellow polygon from the ninth frame twice, and position one duplicate at the same relative position in each of the seventh and eighth frames. Click the spaceships in the seventh through ninth frames and choose **A**rrange | Bring to Fron**t**.
12. Choose Black as your current color, and draw a little person with the Polygon tool in the Shapes palette. Use a line width setting of 2, and make sure that Fill and Closed are deselected. Select all the sprites you used to create the person and flatten them into one sprite (**A**rrange | Flatten **S**election).
13. Position one person in each of the seventh through ninth frames. The first person is displayed near the bottom of the light; the second in the middle, and the third near the bottom of the spaceship. Select the spaceship and choose **A**rrange | Bring to Fron**t** so that the spaceship is displayed in front of the person. Your composition now looks like Figure 22.3.

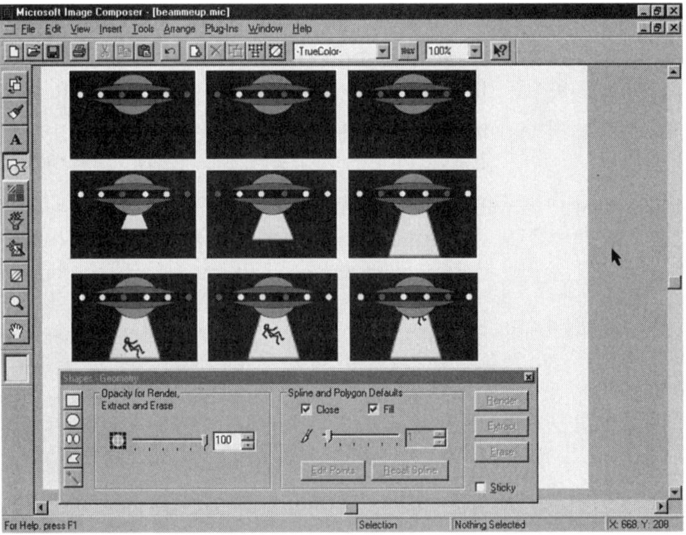

Figure 22.3.
In the third row of frames, a person is beamed aboard the spaceship.

You learn how to create your own custom palettes in **Chapter 18**.

14. You can reduce the size of your animation files if you reduce the number of colors in your palette. Create a 16-color palette, using the composition as the source for the colors.
15. Save the original composition as `beammeup.mic`.

Before you save each frame of your animation as an individual GIF file, flatten the sprites that make up the frame. Make sure that you do not overwrite the original file.

After you flatten the sprites, you cannot unflatten them. You can use the original image to make changes or additions.

Perform the following steps on the `beammeup.mic` file that you now have open in Image Composer:

1. Save a copy of the image under a different filename so that you do not overwrite the original. (For example, save a copy as `beammeup2.mic`.)
2. Draw a selection box around the elements that make up the first frame in the animation. Then, choose **A**rrange | Flatten **S**election (Ctrl+F) to combine the sprites into one element.
3. Repeat step 2 for each additional frame in the animation.
4. Choose **F**ile | **S**ave (Ctrl+S) or click the Save button on the toolbar to update the file on your hard drive.
5. Click the first frame, and choose **F**ile | Sa**v**e Selection As. The Save Selection As dialog box is displayed.
6. Use the Look **i**n field to locate the drive and directory to which you want to save the file. Then enter or choose the following settings:

   File **n**ame: `ship01.gif`
   Save as **t**ype: `Compuserve GIF (*.gif)`
   Color **f**ormat: `beammeup` (the name of the custom palette)

7. Repeat steps 4 and 5 for each additional frame, saving them to sequentially numbered filenames (for example, `ship02`, `ship03`, and so on). You now have frames with which to build an animation.

Creating Fades

Another way that you can create an animation is to make an object fade in or fade out to your web page. For this example, open the `crown1.mic` file, which is furnished on the CD that accompanies this book. In this file, you see seven crowns. Six of the crowns appear on top of gray rectangles that get progressively darker. You will use the rectangles as transparency maps to affect the transparency of each crown. As the gray gets darker, the amount of transparency increases. What you should end up with is a series of images that gets progressively lighter. The project file is shown in Figure 22.4.

Figure 22.4.
Six of the seven crowns in the project image appear on top of gray rectangles. The rectangles will be used as transparency maps.

You can also use a grayscale gradient for a transparency map. This applies transparencies at varying degrees throughout an image. Refer to **Chapter 21** for more information on this technique.

To add the transparency to each image, follow these steps:

1. From the toolbox, choose Patterns and Fills. The Patterns and Fills palette is displayed.
2. From the Patterns and Fills list, select Sprite to Sprite. Then, from the Sprite Texture Type list, click Transparency Map.
3. Click the second crown in the top row (the one in the light gray square). Then click **A**pply. If the Microsoft Image Composer hint box is displayed (it does not appear if you have it disabled), click OK. Then click the light gray rectangle. A new sprite is displayed, which appears lighter than the original.
4. Click the gray rectangle that you used for the transparency map, and press Delete. The partially transparent crown remains.
5. Repeat steps 3 and 4 for each crown, using the rectangle on which it is displayed for its transparency map. After you finish applying all the transparency maps, your image should look like Figure 22.5.
6. Click the Current Color Swatch, and select the Custom Palette tab. Click the Load button, and then locate the `Iexplore.pal` file from the `\ImgComp\Mmfiles\Palettes` directory on your FrontPage 97 with Bonus Pack CD-ROM or your local hard disk. Choose OK to return to the composition.
7. Choose **F**ile | Save **A**s to save your image as `crown2.mic`. From the Save As dialog box, click **S**ave to save the file.
8. Select the lightest crown, and choose **F**ile | Sa**v**e Selection As. The Save Selection As dialog box is displayed.

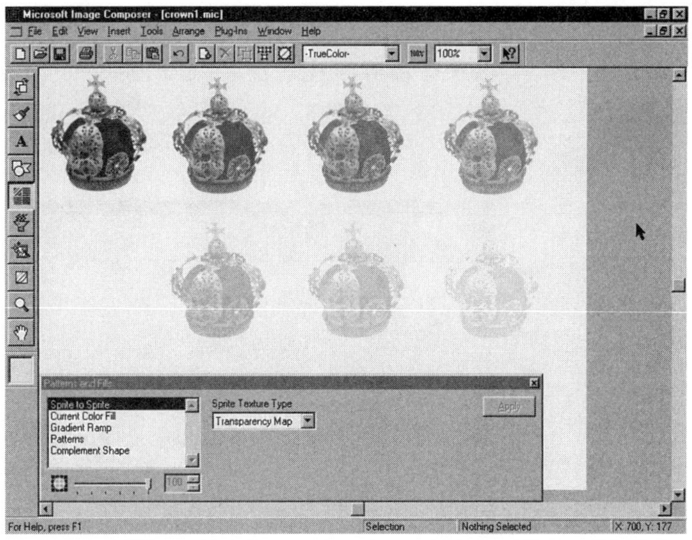

Figure 22.5.
After you apply the transparency maps, the crowns gradually get lighter until they fade away.

9. Use the Look **i**n field to locate the drive and directory to which you want to save the file. Then enter or choose the following settings:

File **n**ame:	`crown01.gif`
Save as **t**ype:	`Compuserve GIF (*.gif)`
Color **f**ormat:	`IExplore` (the name of the custom palette)

10. Repeat steps 8 and 9 for each additional frame. Choose the crown that is progressively darker than the one you previously saved, ending with the crown that is fully opaque. Save them to sequentially numbered filenames (`crown02`, `crown03`, and so on). You now have seven frames with which to build an animation.

Animating Text

You add a marquee to a page using the **I**nsert | Marqu**e**e command in the FrontPage Editor. Java applets can be added to your Web pages with the **I**nsert | **O**ther Components | **J**ava Applet command.

There are many ways that you can animate text. The method that is most economical for bandwidth is to create a marquee (which you can view in Internet Explorer), or to use Java applets or similar custom programs. Sometimes, however, you may choose to create a small animation instead.

The following example uses rectangles filled with the Tile Bottom Left gradient, which is in the Patterns and Fills palette. Each text sprite is placed over a rectangle at varying points so that it "captures" a different range of color from the rectangle. You'll apply the gradient to the text using a Sprite to Sprite fill.

To create text that changes gradient color, follow these steps:

1. Choose **F**ile | **O**pen (Ctrl+O) or click the Open button on the toolbar. Locate the `text.mic` file on the CD that accompanies this book. The image opens in your composition window, as shown in Figure 22.6.

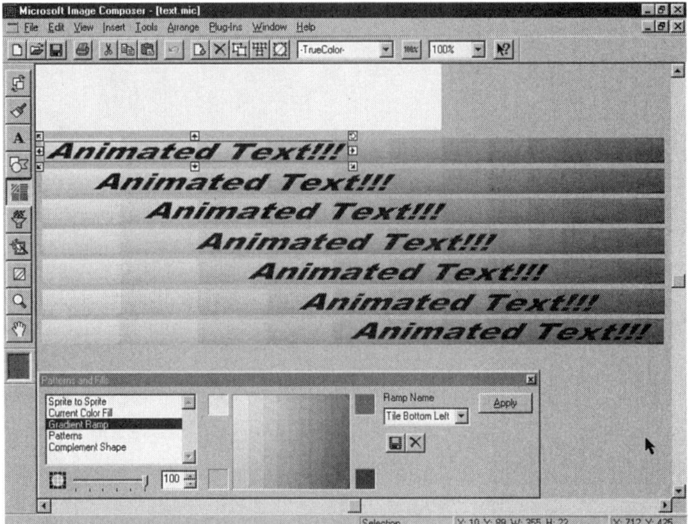

Figure 22.6.
The project image for the animated text consists of gradients and text. You will use the gradients to cycle the colors in the text.

2. Click the first text sprite in the top rectangle to select it.
3. Choose Patterns and Fills from the toolbox, and select Sprite to Sprite. From the Sprite Texture Type list, click Transfer Shape.
4. Click **A**pply. If the Microsoft Image Composer hint box is displayed, choose OK; then click the rectangle on which the text sprite is displayed. It looks as though the sprite has disappeared, but it is still there.
5. Select the rectangle from which you created the transfer shape text, and press Delete.
6. Repeat steps 4 and 5 for each additional text object. After you apply the gradient to each text sprite, each sprite contains different colors, as shown in Figure 22.7.
7. Click the Current Color Swatch, and select the Custom Palette tab. Click the Load button, and locate the `\ImgComp\Mmfiles\Palettes\Iexplore.pal` file from your FrontPage 97 with Bonus Pack CD-ROM or your local hard disk. Choose OK to return to the composition.
8. Select the first text sprite and move it into the white composition guide. Then choose **F**ile | Sa**v**e Selection As. The Save Selection As dialog box is displayed.

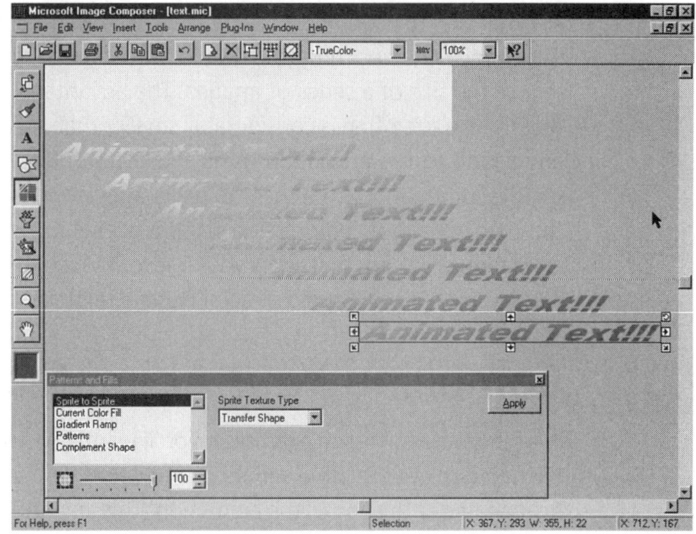

Figure 22.7.
After you apply the Transfer Shape fill, each text sprite contains different colors.

9. Use the Look **i**n field to locate the drive and directory to which you want to save the file. Then enter or choose the following settings:

File **n**ame:	`text01.gif`
Save as **t**ype:	`Compuserve GIF (*.gif)`
Color **f**ormat:	`IExplore` (the name of the custom palette)

10. Repeat steps 8 and 9 for each additional text sprite. Save them to sequentially numbered filenames (`text02`, `text03`, and so on). You now have seven frames with which to build an animation.

Economizing Your Animations

As you get more involved in creating animated GIFs, you will quickly learn that file sizes can get extremely large. This is one of the reasons why most Web developers use them sparingly. However, there are some ways that you can trim the size of your animations.

One obvious way to keep your animation size down is to keep the dimensions small. Most of the animated GIF files you see on the Internet are smaller than 100×100 pixels.

You learn how to reduce the number of colors in a palette in **Chapter 18**.

You might notice that many of the animated GIF files that are available on the Internet use the 16 basic system colors. There is good reason for this: The file sizes get smaller as the number of colors are reduced. You can use Microsoft Image Composer to create any size palette for your images.

It also helps if you turn dithering off when you save your GIF files. This may not be suitable for photographic images, but it is a good alternative for cartoon-type animations in which large areas of solid color are used.

Another way to economize on the file size of animations is to save them as `.avi` files (Video for Windows format). This file format uses different compression schemes to reduce the size of a series of images. The advantage to using the `.avi` file format is that the file size often is considerably smaller than an animated GIF file. You can also add sound to the animation using this format. Because the compression schemes remove information from the original images, however, you can see deterioration in the image quality if compression settings are set too low. Some popular graphics and animation programs that allow you to save in Video for Windows (`.avi`) file format are Autodesk Animator Studio, Fractal Design Painter, and Adobe Premiere.

TASK

Compiling Your Animated GIF

In each of the following examples, you'll learn how to compile a basic animated GIF file that displays the same sequence of images. Some of the images you created will be repeated at the end of the animation. This animation uses the frames created with the `beammeup.mic` image discussed in the "Creating a Basic Animation" section. This animation will sequence `ship01.gif` through `ship09.gif`, followed by `ship06.gif`, `ship05.gif`, and `ship04.gif`. Three popular programs that allow you to assemble animated GIFs are discussed in the "Using Microsoft GIF Animator," "Using GIF Construction Set," and "Using Ulead PhotoImpact GIF Animator" sections.

Using Microsoft GIF Animator

Microsoft GIF Animator is available from the Sitebuilder Network on Microsoft's Web site. When you install this animation program on your system, a command to access the software is added to the Microsoft Image Composer Tools menu. Choose the **T**ools | Microsoft GIF Animator command from Microsoft Image Composer to start the program.

It is easiest to load your series of images in Microsoft GIF Animator in reverse order. In some aspects, this animation utility can be a bit tedious to use, especially if your animation consists of many files. With Microsoft GIF Animator, you cannot load a series of images at once; each image must be loaded one at a time. After that, you assign delays and other settings to each frame.

To compile an animated GIF file using Microsoft GIF Animator, follow these steps:

1. Click the New button on the toolbar, or press Ctrl+N to create a new file.
2. Click the Open button on the toolbar, or press Ctrl+O. The Open dialog box is displayed.
3. Click the last image in your sequence as shown in Figure 22.8 (`ship04.gif`), and click **O**pen to place it in the first frame in the animation.

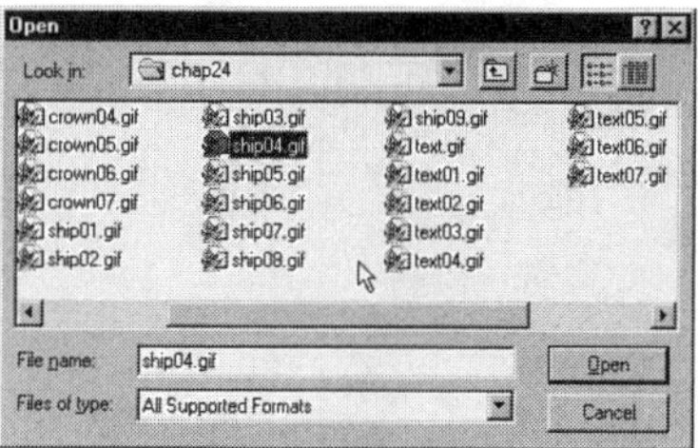

Figure 22.8.
Load the images in reverse order with Microsoft Image Composer.

4. Click the Insert button on the toolbar, or use Ctrl+I. Select the next image in the sequence and click **O**pen. Continue repeating this step until you insert all images in the animation in the following order:

```
ship05.gif
ship06.gif
ship09.gif
ship08.gif
ship07.gif
ship06.gif
ship05.gif
ship04.gif
ship03.gif
ship02.gif
ship01.gif
```

5. To set palette, dithering, and miscellaneous options for the animation, use the Options tab, shown in Figure 22.9. Unless otherwise mentioned, use the default settings. You'll need to change the following:

Import Color Palette	Here, you choose between a Browser Palette or an Optimal Palette. For this animation, select Optimal palette.
Import Dither Method	You can choose among Solid, Pattern, Random, or Diffusion dithering. Because your image contains solid colors, choose Solid.

6. To set looping options for the animation, use the Animation tab shown in Figure 22.10. Check Looping, and check Repeat Forever.

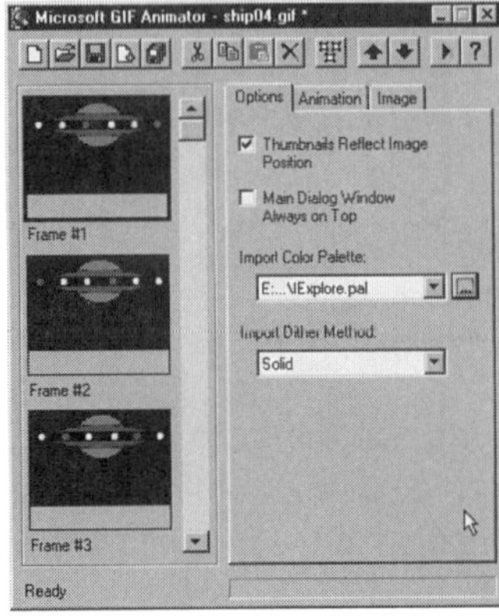

Figure 22.9.
Choose the Optimal Palette and Solid Dither Method from the Options tab.

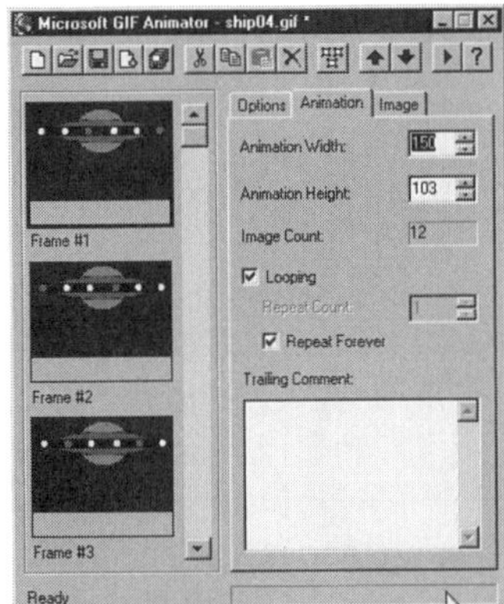

Figure 22.10.
Set the looping for the animation in the Animation tab.

7. To set redraw options for the animation, use the Image tab shown in Figure 22.11. Select the first thumbnail, and check Transparency. Check this to use a transparent color in your animation. Click the color square to select your transparent color from the image, and choose Navy Blue as your transparent color. This color may be difficult to see; it is the last color in the palette, right after the olive green color.
8. Choose the Select All button or press Ctrl+L to select all frames. Enter or choose the following settings from the Image tab:

   Duration (1/100 s): `20`

   Undraw Method: `Restore Background`
9. Click the Preview button in the toolbar, or select Ctrl+R. The Preview dialog box shown in Figure 22.12 displays the animation. Press Esc to stop the preview and return to the main screen.

12. Verify that all your files are listed in the Selected Files list. You should show `ship01.gif` through `ship09.gif`, followed by `ship06.gif`, `ship05.gif`, and `ship04.gif`. Click Next to continue.
13. Click Done. GIF Construction Set remaps the palette to all frames in the image. Next, your images appear in a list that has more control items added (shown in Figure 22.14).

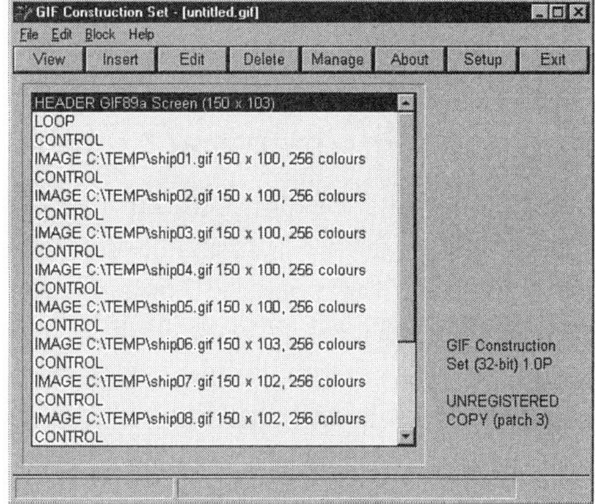

Figure 22.14.
After you load your images, more control blocks are added to the list.

14. To add the transparent color to each frame, double-click the first `CONTROL` line in the construction list. The Edit Control Block dialog box shown in Figure 22.15 is displayed.

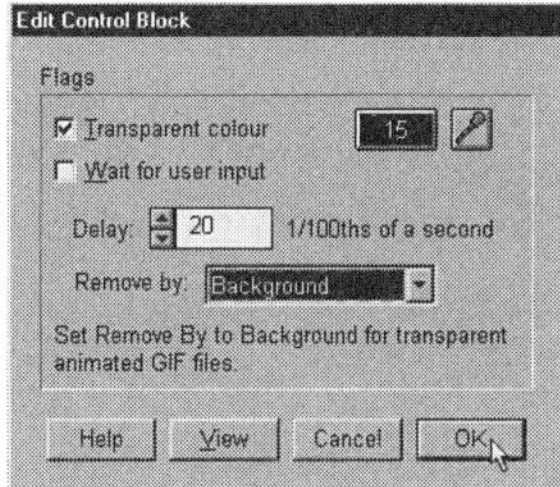

Figure 22.15.
Use the Edit Control Block dialog box to edit each `CONTROL` item in the list to use a transparent color.

15. Click the Transparent colour check box to select it. Choose the eyedropper, and select the navy blue color from the image. You return to the Edit Control Block dialog box.
16. In the Delay field, enter **`20`**.
17. In the Remove by field, choose Background.
18. Choose OK to return to the construction list.
19. Repeat steps 13–16 for each control block in your construction list. There are 12 in all.

20. To preview your animation, click the View button. Press Escape to exit the preview.
21. Choose **F**ile | Save **a**s. The Save As dialog box is displayed.
22. From the Save **i**n field, locate the drive and directory into which you want to save your animation.
23. Enter `beammeup2.gif` in the File name field.
24. From the Save as **t**ype field, select GIF files.
25. Click **S**ave. The animation is saved to the directory.

Using Ulead PhotoImpact GIF Animator

Of the three GIF animation utilities discussed in this chapter, this is probably the easiest to use. Ulead PhotoImpact GIF Animator is part of the Web Extensions that are furnished with Ulead PhotoImpact 3.0.2 or later (a worthy graphics program in its own right). You can also download a trial version of this utility from Ulead's Web site at `http://www.ulead.com`. It contains many features beyond those discussed here, along with an extremely user-friendly interface.

To compile an animated GIF file using Ulead PhotoImpact GIF Animator, follow these steps:

1. Choose **F**ile | **N**ew (Ctrl+N) or click the New button on the toolbar.
2. Choose Layer | Add Images and press the Insert key, or press the Add Images button on the toolbar. The Add Images dialog box is displayed.
3. Use the Look **i**n box to locate the drive and directory in which your images are stored.
4. Click the first image in your sequence, and shift-click to select the last image in the sequence. All the images are highlighted.
5. Click Open. The Build Up Global Palette From Image dialog box shown in Figure 22.16 is displayed.
6. Choose Original palette from the **P**alette drop-down menu, and click Insert. The remaining images are inserted into the animation, using the same palette you chose for the first.
7. Press the Insert key to insert `ship06.gif`. Repeat for `ship05.gif` and `ship04.gif`.
8. In the **D**elay field, enter `20`.
9. Select Transparent **i**ndex and click the color square to select navy blue from the image.

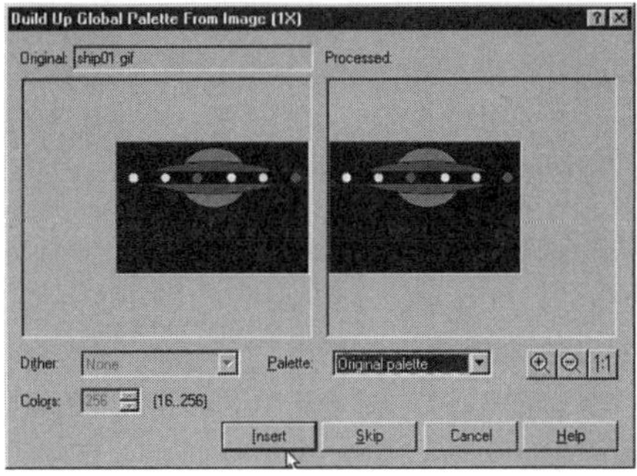

Figure 22.16.
Use the Build Up Global Palette From Image dialog box to select the type of palette you want to use in your animated GIF file.

10. From the How to remove drop-down menu, select To background color. Then click the Global Attribute button to the right of the How to remove drop-down menu. The Global Attribute Change dialog box shown in Figure 22.17 is displayed.

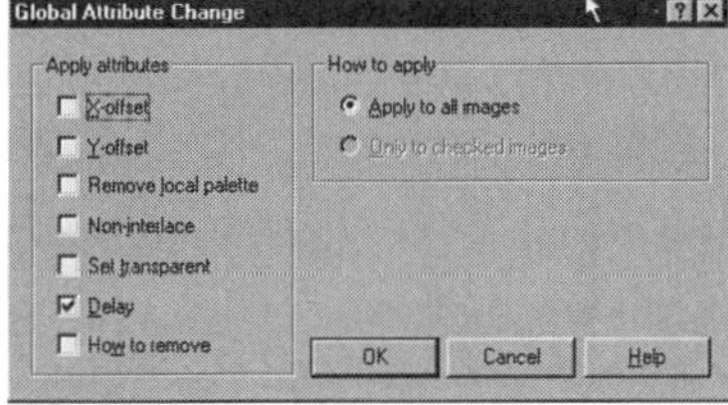

Figure 22.17.
Select Set transparent, Delay, and How to remove in the Global Attribute Change dialog box.

11. Select Set **t**ransparent, **D**elay, and Ho**w** to remove. Verify that **A**pply to all images is selected from the How to apply field.
12. Click OK. You return to the main screen.
13. Click Start Preview. The animation is displayed in the preview window. Click Stop Preview to end the animation preview.
14. Choose **F**ile | Save **A**s. The Save As dialog box is displayed.
15. Use the Save **i**n drop-down menu to choose the drive and directory to which you want to save the file.
16. Enter `beammeup3.gif` in the File name field.
17. In the Save as **t**ype drop-down menu, select GIF files (`*.gif`).
18. Click **S**ave. The animation is saved to your hard drive.

Workshop Wrap-Up

Animating GIF files is only one way you can add animation to your Web pages. Using a little bit of ingenuity, you can create animated GIF files using Microsoft Image Composer. As you can see from some of the simple examples in this chapter, you can create the illusion of movement by changing positions, colors, or transparencies of sprites. You can also increase or decrease sizes of sprites to make them appear as though they are zooming in and out of the screen. After you save each file to your hard disk, you can assemble each individual file into a single animation.

In this chapter, you learned how to create the illusion of animation by changing positions, colors, and transparencies of sprites. The techniques you learned in this chapter can be combined together to create even more interesting animations. You learned how to save each frame in an animation as individually numbered GIF files. You also learned how to combine several images into a single file, using third-party GIF animation programs, how to add delays between frames, and how to apply transparencies to animated GIF files.

Next Steps

In Chapter 23, "Real-Life Examples: Setting the Mood," you will learn how to combine colors effectively to create a mood for your Web site. You can combine colors based on hues, saturation (the purity of the color), or values (how light or dark a color is). By selecting harmonious colors, your Web pages can achieve a sense of balance.

For additional information relating to creating animation for your Webs, see Chapter 4, "Presenting PowerPoint on the Web."

Q&A

Q: I played my animated GIF file back after I put it on my Web page, and my screen seemed to flash in the middle of the animation. It always flashes when it reaches the same point. What did I do wrong?

A: You might not have saved all of your images using the same palette. Palette flash occurs when a frame in an animation uses colors other than those used in other frames. Open the image that flashes, and map it to the same palette that you used for your other frames.

Q: Can you add sound to an animated GIF file?

A: Unfortunately not. If you want to combine sound and animation, you can import your individual GIF files into a program that creates AVI files and combine with sound there. You can also use other Web technologies such as Shockwave or Java to add multimedia content to your web.

Q: Do the delays between every frame in the animation always have to be the same?

A: No, each delay can have a different setting. For example, if you are looping an animation and want the last frame to pause for a while before it loops back again, you can set the delay for that single frame higher.

TWENTY-THREE

Setting the Mood

In this chapter, you

- ❑ Examine several examples on the CD-ROM
- ❑ Create graphics using several different color schemes
- ❑ Use a color wheel to learn how colors relate and blend in harmony with each other

Tasks in this chapter:

- ❑ Designing a Monochromatic Color Scheme
- ❑ Using Colors with Similar Saturation
- ❑ Using Colors with Similar Value

Many times, art and colors are used to set the mood of a site. Sites geared toward children use bright, sunny colors. Pages that focus on mysterious subjects display dark and somber colors. Others use colors within the same range of the color scale, giving a monochromatic appearance.

How can you tell which colors work well together? One way is to use a color wheel that helps you see at a glance how colors blend harmoniously. In this chapter, you'll learn how to use colors together and how to create various color schemes for your pages.

Basics of Color Theory

When you create a color on your computer, you most often define a color formula using a combination of red, green, and blue lights. Each of these primary colors can be blended together from 0 (color completely off) to 255 (color completely on).

Computers work with additive colors; that is, light is added and combined in varying intensities of red, green, and blue to produce a color. The more light you add, the lighter the color gets. When you mix the "primary" additive colors of red, green, and blue light, each at their maximum intensity, you get white. Turning all the lights off gives you black. When you mix two primary colors together at their full intensity, you get what is known as secondary colors. Table 23.1 shows the secondary colors that are produced when you mix the three additive primary colors.

Table 23.1. Secondary colors in the additive color system.

Color 1	*Color 2*	*Secondary Color*
Red	Green	Yellow
Green	Blue	Cyan
Blue	Red	Magenta

An image named `colorwhl.gif`, shown in Figure 23.1, is included on the CD-ROM that accompanies this book. You'll find it easiest if you open the image in Microsoft Image Composer to follow along with some of this basic theory. You can use this color wheel to help visualize how colors work together.

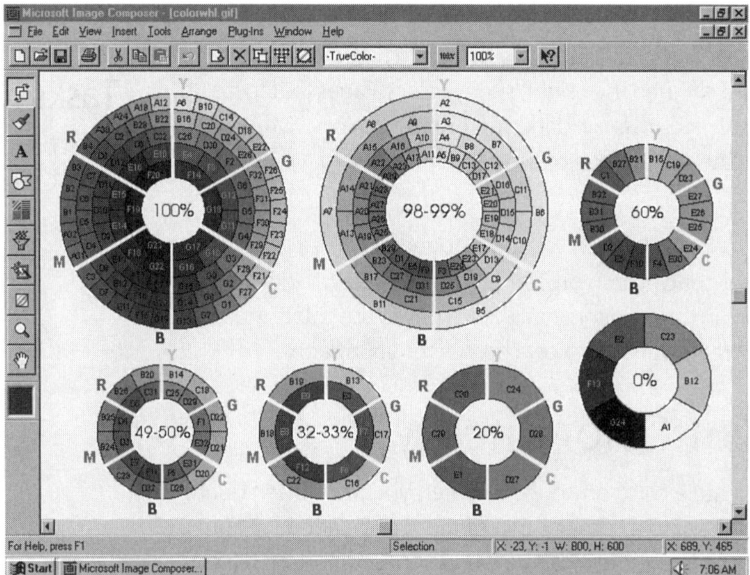

Figure 23.1.
A color wheel can help you visualize how colors work together.

There are several different color wheels on this image, which will be explained throughout this chapter. Notice that each of the color wheels are divided into six segments: Going clockwise from the 12 o'clock position on each wheel, you see sections labeled Y (yellow), G (green), C (cyan), B (blue), M (magenta), and R (red). These are the primary and secondary colors. Notice also how the colors are arranged in each wheel. The colors in the segment starting with yellow ramp clockwise toward green values. Greens ramp toward cyans, cyans toward blues, blues toward magentas, magentas toward reds, and reds back to yellows.

Directly opposite the primary color of red is the secondary color cyan. When colors appear directly opposite of each other, they are said to be *complementary* colors.

Another way to think of a complementary color is the "negative" value of a color. Red and cyan are complements, as are green and magenta, and blue and yellow.

Artists accustomed to working with traditional media find themselves in a quandary when presented with an additive color wheel. Indeed, they find themselves learning a whole new color system. You see, "traditional" art media such as paint, crayons, chalk, and the like use pigments instead of light. Pigments combine in what is known as a *subtractive color method*. Light hits the surface of the red pigment, for example, and it absorbs or subtracts all the colors in the light spectrum *except* red. The red color reflects back so that we can see it.

Whereas the primary colors in the additive color system are red, green, and blue, there is a difference in the subtractive color method: The primary colors are red, *yellow*, and blue. From these three colors, all other colors can be mixed, and white is actually a lack of pigment. When all three primary colors are mixed in this system, you achieve near-black (more of a gray-black) instead of white.

The secondary colors for the subtractive color system are shown in Table 23.2. The cyan and magenta that are part of the additive color wheel are replaced with orange and purple in the subtractive color system. Going clockwise on this color wheel, the colors change from blue to purple, red, orange, yellow, and green. The colors that are directly opposite each other (the complements) are as follows: red to green, yellow to purple, and blue to orange.

Table 23.2. Secondary colors in the subtractive color system.

Color 1	*Color 2*	*Secondary Color*
Red	Yellow	Orange
Yellow	Blue	Green
Blue	Red	Purple

For purposes of this chapter, we will work with the additive color method and learn how to combine colors together using the additive color wheels in Figure 23.1.

Picking Color Schemes

There are some tried-and-true ways to select colors that work well together, and for this you'll get a quick rundown of some basics of color theory. Colors are most often defined using one of two methods for Web graphics development. first, you are probably used to working with colors based on a red, green, and blue color formula. By mixing various amounts of red, green, and blue, you can achieve any one of more than 16 million colors. Second, you can define a color by a hue, saturation, and value formula.

Hue

The *hue* defines the color by a name (red, green, yellow, or purple, for example). In the color wheels, the hue is represented by going around each color wheel in a clockwise or counter-clockwise motion, as shown in Figure 23.2. Beginning at the 12 o'clock position on each wheel, each of the six segments in the wheel move from yellows to greens, cyans, blues, magentas, and reds.

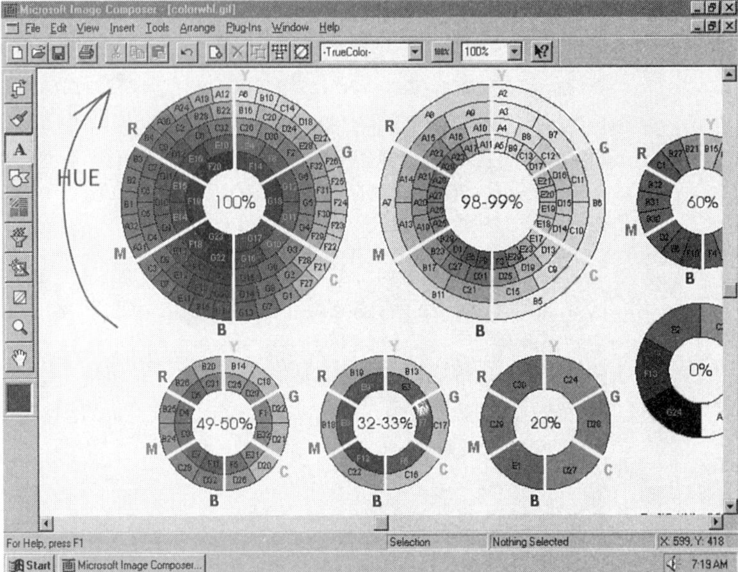

Figure 23.2.
Colors change in hue as you move in a clockwise or counter-clockwise motion around the wheel.

One way to achieve color harmony in your pages is to select colors from the same segment in one or more wheels. To produce pages that are more monochromatic, imagine a straight line from the center of the wheel that passes through each row toward the outside. In Figure 23.3, for example, a straight line passes through the same points in two color wheels. Use the colors that the line intersects. The following task uses colors that give a page a monochromatic appearance.

I've made the job easy for you to relate to how the colors in the wheel relate to the colors in the Internet Explorer palette. You'll notice an alphanumeric designation in each of the colors in the color wheel. The lower-right section of the image contains a key that relates to the Internet Explorer palette when it is loaded in the Custom Palette tab of the Color Picker. If you load the Internet Explorer palette and leave it set to Unsorted in the Sort palette by field, as shown in Figure 23.4, the colors in the key match up perfectly. A code of A24, for example, tells you to select the 24th color in row A (the first row in the palette) .

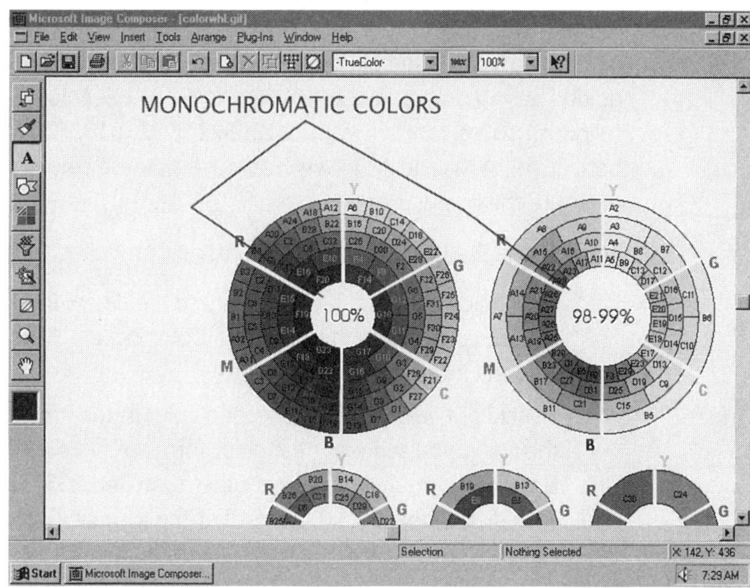

Figure 23.3.
To design a monochromatic page, draw a straight line from the center of one or more wheels, and use the colors that the line intersects.

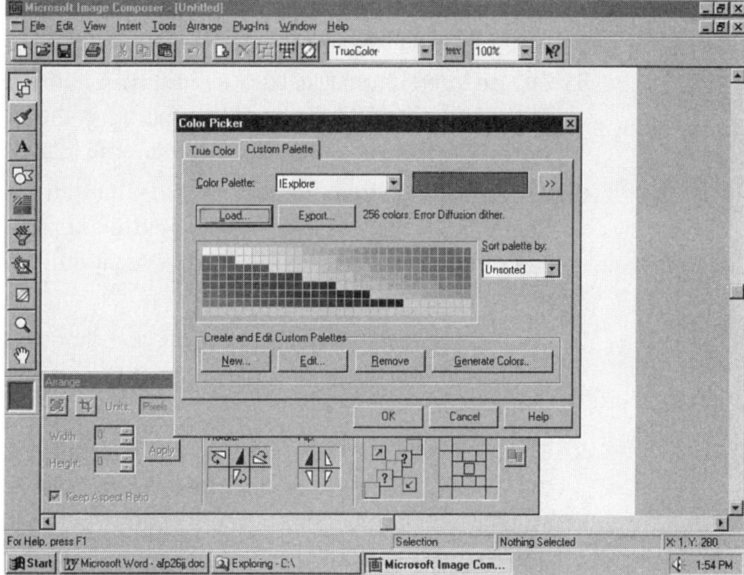

Figure 23.4.
To use the Microsoft Image Composer palette key on the color palette image, use the Unsorted option (default) in the Sort palette by field.

TASK

Designing a Monochromatic Color Scheme

To demonstrate how to select colors for a monochromatic color scheme, complete the following task. These graphics will be simple, as their intent is to help you become familiar with how to use the color wheels in conjunction with the Internet Explorer palette. To select the colors in this image, I "drew" an imaginary line through the golden yellow colors in the 100% and 98–99% color wheels. This gave me the following colors to work with: A12, B22, C32, E10, F20, A8 (though A2 will work better), A9, A10, and A11. We won't use all these colors, but this gives you an idea of where the line was drawn.

To compose the image in Microsoft Image Composer, proceed as follows:

1. From Microsoft Image Composer, create a new image. Double-click the current color swatch to open the Color Picker. Using the Custom Palette tab, load the Internet Explorer palette.
2. Select light yellow A2 (the second color in the first row). If you double-click the color, you see what the color formula is in the Choose Color dialog box. Note this formula in case it is other than Red 255, Green 255, Blue 171 in your dialog box. Click **C**lose to exit the Choose Color dialog box.
3. Choose OK to exit the color picker.
4. Choose **F**ile | Composi**t**ion Properties. Enter `Red 255, Green 255, Blue 171` in the Composition Guide fields. Choose OK to return to Image Composer. The background turns light yellow.
5. Choose **I**nsert | **F**rom File. Locate `goddess.mic` on your FrontPage 97 with Bonus Pack CD-ROM. You can find this file in the `ImgComp\Mmfiles\Photos\Building\PhotoDsc` folder of the CD-ROM.
6. Choose Arrange from the toolbox. From the Arrange palette, shown in Figure 23.5, enter `128` in the Width field, and make sure the Keep Aspect Ratio check box is selected. Then click Apply. The image rescales to 128×415 pixels.
7. Double-click the current color swatch, and choose color C32 (the last color in the third row of the unsorted Internet Explorer palette). Choose OK to return to Image Composer.
8. Choose Warps and Filters from the toolbox. Select Color Enhancement from the Warps and Filters palette drop-down menu, and select Colorize from the list of available color enhancement options. Set Color Opacity to `50`. Apply the filter to the statue.
9. Double-click the current color swatch, and choose color B22 (the 22nd color in the second row of the unsorted Internet Explorer palette). Choose OK to return to Image Composer.
10. Choose Shapes from the toolbox. Select the Oval tool, and draw a 120-pixel wide by 130-pixel high oval. Click **R**ender to render the oval.

As you learned in **Chapter 18**, Microsoft Image Composer alters color values to compensate for gamma correction settings. If your color formulas differ from those shown in this chapter, use the settings from your dialog boxes rather than those shown here.

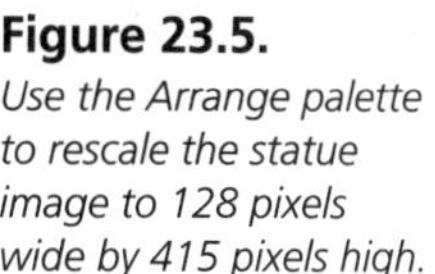

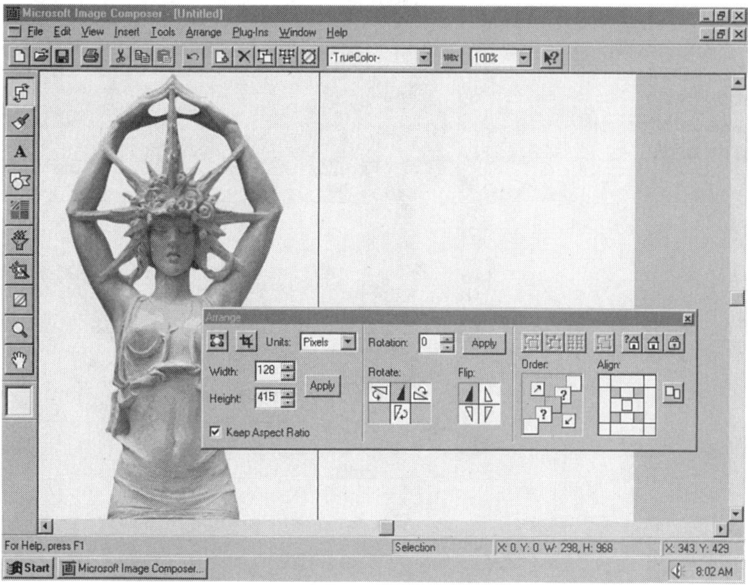

Figure 23.5.
Use the Arrange palette to rescale the statue image to 128 pixels wide by 415 pixels high.

11. Choose the Rectangle tool, and draw a 480-pixel wide by 75-pixel high rectangle. Click **R**ender to render the rectangle.
12. Position the oval at X:6, Y:3, and the rectangle at X:108, Y:30. Select both items and choose **A**rrange | Flatten **S**election (Ctrl+F).
13. Choose Art Effects from the toolbox. From the drop-down menu in the Art Effects palette (shown in Figure 23.6), select Exotic; then choose Craquelure from the list of effects. Select the following settings; then click Apply to apply the effect to the oval and rectangle:

    Crack Spacing: 11
    Crack Depth: 6
    Crack Brightness: 7
    Opacity: 100

14. Move the statue to X:3, Y:6, and choose **A**rrange | Bring **F**orward. Shift-click to select the rectangle/oval group; then choose **A**rrange | **G**roup (Ctrl+G) .

To view the remaining items on the image, open `monochrome.mic` from the CD that accompanies this book. This image is shown in Figure 23.7. In brief, the remaining items in the banner are created as follows:

- ❑ The banner text that reads "Ancient Cultures" was created with two text objects. The back text object is rendered in dark brown color F20 (20th color in the sixth row) and the foreground color is A2 (2nd color in the first row). They are offset slightly so that a small shadow is displayed behind the foreground text. I used the 28-point Viner Hand ITC font.

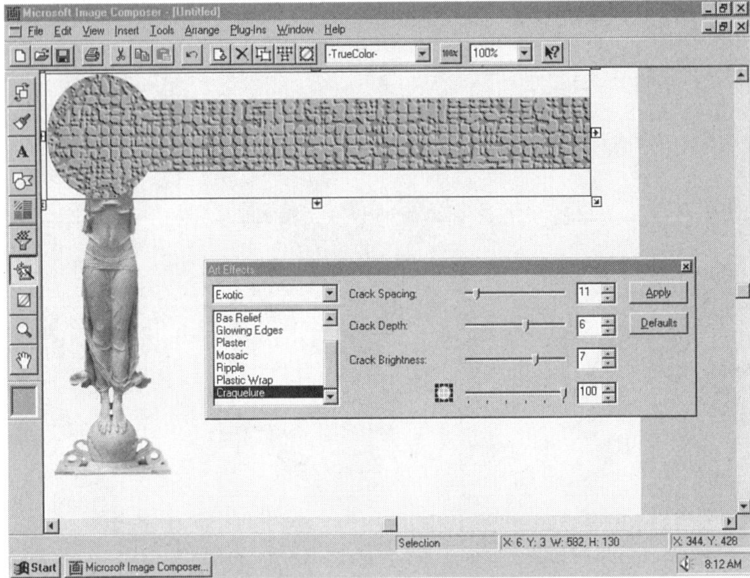

Figure 23.6.
Apply the Craquelure effect from the Art Effects palette to the oval and rectangle.

- The 22×22-pixel circles that accent the first letter of each civilization name are rendered in (from left to right) F20 (20th color in the sixth row), E10 (10th color in the fifth row), C32 (last color in the third row), B22 (22nd color in the second row), and A12 (12th color in the first row).
- The names of the civilizations are rendered in color B22 (22nd color in the second row). In addition, a white capital letter was superimposed over the first letter of each civilization name. I used 16-point Verdana Regular for the font.

When you are finished with your image, save it as `monochrome.mic`.

To complete the monochromatic color scheme, you should also follow through with your page properties. Double-click each of the colors shown in the following list in Microsoft Image Composer to determine their color formulas. Remember that there is a color shift when you see the values in Microsoft Image Composer, so you must translate them to the "real" RGB values in FrontPage, as mentioned in Chapter 18, "An Introduction to Graphics on the Web." In FrontPage, enter the following values in the Background tab of the Page Properties dialog box, as shown in Figure 23.8:

Ba**c**kground:	`A2` (Red 255, Green 255, Blue 204)
Text:	`C32` (Red 153, Green 102, Blue 0)
Hyperlink:	`B22` (Red 204, Green 153, Blue 0)
Visited Hyperlink:	`E10` (Red 102, Green 51, Blue 0)
Active Hyperlink:	`A12` (Red 255, Green 204, Blue 0)

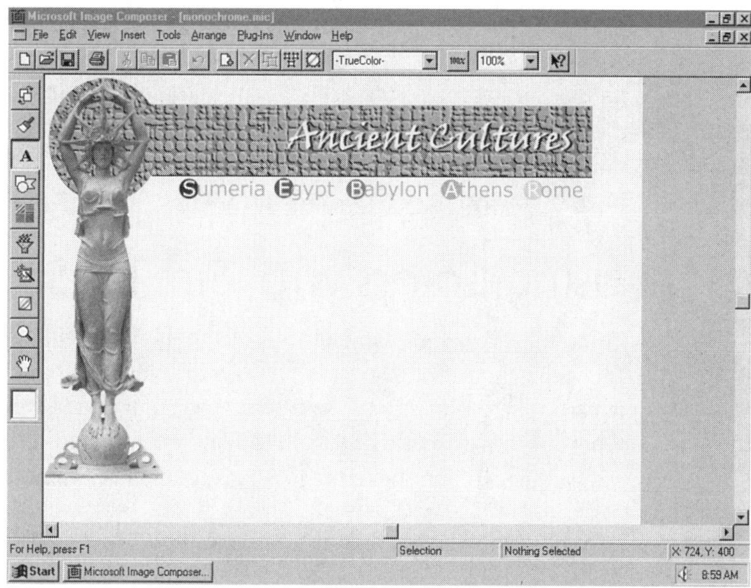

Figure 23.7.
The text and bullets on the image use additional shades from the monochromatic choices.

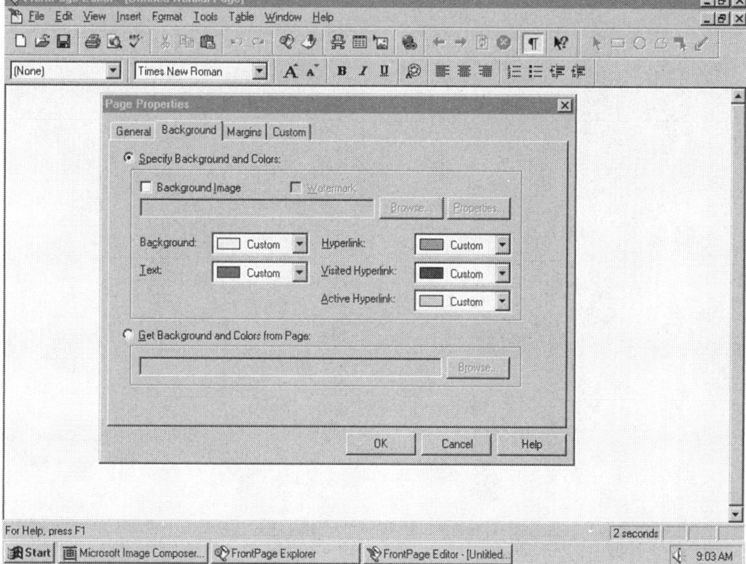

Figure 23.8.
Assign other monochromatic colors to your page background and text colors in the FrontPage Editor.

Saturation

The amount of *saturation* in a color defines its purity. A color that is 100% saturated is its most vivid, whereas a color that approaches 0% saturation gradually becomes more grayed. In the color wheels in the image, the saturation of the colors is represented by the seven different wheels. The color wheel labeled 100% contains the most pure colors in the Internet Explorer palette. Notice as the amount of saturation decreases, the colors become more muted. This is another way you can achieve color harmony using the color wheels: By choosing colors from the same wheel, each of the colors in your pages have a similarity to them. You might find the colors in the 49–50% and 32–33% color wheels to be soothing and relaxing. The following example shows how to modify the previous example using colors with similar saturation values.

Using Colors with Similar Saturation

This example uses the same graphic elements as those discussed in the "Designing a Monochromatic Color Scheme" task, with colors that have similar saturation values. In particular, the image uses colors from the outer ring of the 49–50% saturation color wheel, shown in Figure 23.9. You can find a completed version of this image, named `saturation.mic`, on the CD-ROM that accompanies this book.

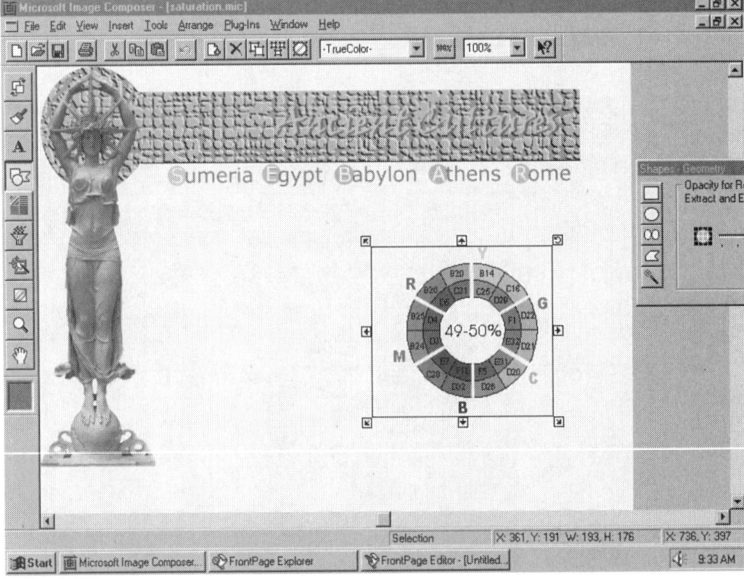

Figure 23.9.
Modify the image using colors from the 49–50% saturation color wheel.

To achieve the same results in your image, you can modify the previous example as follows:

1. Colorize the statue with B20 (the 20th color in the second row of the Internet Explorer palette).
2. The oval and rectangle use D20 (the 20th color in the fourth row of the Internet Explorer palette).

3. The header text uses C31 (the 31st color in the third row) for the shadow and B14 (the 14th color in the second row) for the foreground color text.
4. The bullets use, from left to right, B14 (14th color in the second row), C18 (18th color in the third row), D22 (22nd color in the fourth row), D21 (21st color in the fourth row), and D20 (20th color in the fourth row).
5. The initial caps before each civilization name are white (color A1, the first color in the palette).
6. The main color of the text used for the civilization names is C31 (the 31st color in the third row).
7. For the background of the graphic, use white.
8. To carry a similar color scheme into your page properties in FrontPage, assign the following values in the Background tab of the Page Properties dialog box:

   Ba**c**kground: White, or Red 255, Green 255, Blue 204
   Text: Red 153, Green 102, Blue 51
   Hyperlink: Red 51, Green 153, Blue 153
   Visited Hyperlink: Red 153, Green 51, Blue 153
   Active Hyperlink: Red 102, Green 204, Blue 204

Value

The *value* of a color defines the lightness or darkness of the color. Values closer to 0% are dark or black, whereas values closer to 100% are light or white. Colors that are most pure have a value of 50% and are contained in the outer row of the 100% saturation color wheel. I try to avoid these colors when possible. They are extremely bright and can tire the eyes, especially when used on pure white or pure black backgrounds.

In the color wheels in `colorwhl.gif`, all colors that are in the same row have the same value, with the darker colors toward the center of each wheel. Figure 23.10 shows a segment of one of the color wheels to illustrate this. Shades of gray (which are included in the 0% saturation color wheel in `colorwhl.gif`) always have a hue of 0% and a saturation of 0%. The value varies to achieve the different shades. A nice way to use colors of the same value is to select three to seven adjacent colors in the same row of a color wheel. This type of color scheme is known as an *analogous scheme*, because all of the colors contain similar hues as well as a common value.

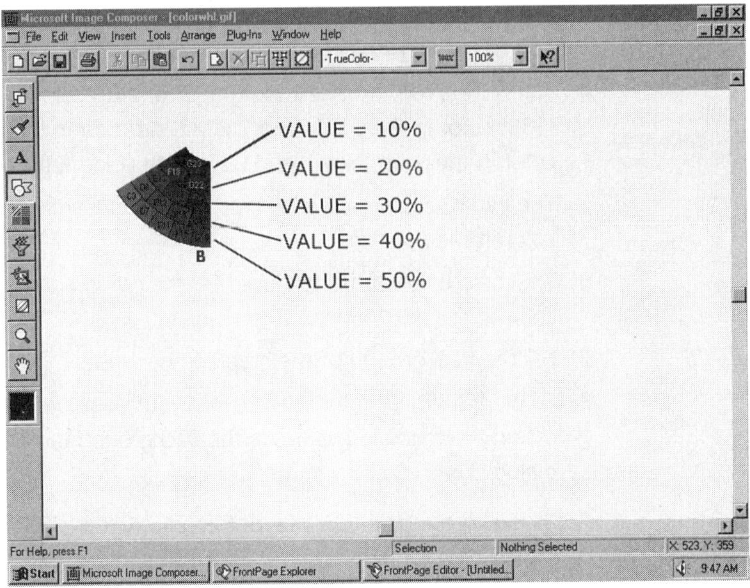

Figure 23.10.
All colors included in the same row of a color wheel have the same value, as this segment shows.

Using Colors with Similar Value

The following analogous colors will work well with the default page properties in FrontPage, but in particular they are striking against a black background because darker colors are used here. A completed version of this image, named `value.mic`, can be found on the CD that accompanies this book. To modify the colors of the previous example using an analogous color scheme, select the following colors:

1. Colorize the statue with D9 (the 9th color in the fourth row of the Internet Explorer palette).
2. The oval and rectangle use F17 (the 17th color in the sixth row of the Internet Explorer palette).
3. The header text uses D11 (the 11th color in the fourth row) for the foreground color text and Black (the last color in the palette) for the shadow.
4. The five bullets before the civilization names use the following colors (from left to right):

First Bullet:	E13—13th color in the fifth row
Second Bullet:	D9—9th color in the fourth row
Third Bullet:	D10—10th color in the fourth row
Fourth Bullet:	D11—11th color in the fourth row
Fifth Bullet:	D12—12th color in the fourth row

5. The section names use the same color as the banner (the 17th color in the sixth row). The initial cap for the section names is white.
6. For the background of the graphic, use black or white. If you use these colors on a white background, the default page properties will work well in FrontPage. If you use them on a white background, you'll want to lighten your text color and tone down the link colors a bit in FrontPage.

Workshop Wrap-Up

There you have it—a handy little tool that helps you select colors that work together. Eventually, as you develop more images, you won't need the color palette at all because it will come as second nature to you. However, for those who are new to graphics development, working with a palette really helps you see how colors work together. By combining colors that have similar hues, saturations, or values, you create harmony in your images. Follow the colors through in your text and link colors, and all blends together to create the mood of your site.

Next Steps

It is hoped that the information provided in these chapters give you some familiarity with the tools and techniques that you have available with Microsoft Image Composer. For further discussion on creating graphics for your Web sites, I highly recommend *Laura Lemay's Web Workshop: Advanced Graphics and Web Page Design* by Jon M. Duff, James L. Mohler, and Laura Lemay (Sams.net). Another good reference book that contains many color examples in full color is *Laura Lemay's Guide to Sizzling Web Site Design* by Molly E. Holzschlag (Sams.net; 1-57521-221-8). Although these books don't focus on Microsoft Image Composer, they offer some great theory and ideas for creating images for your Web pages.

Q&A

Q: Are there any other ways that I can select colors that work together?

A: If working with the color palettes doesn't suit your fancy, there is another way you can find colors that work well together: You can sort the Microsoft Internet Explorer palette in several different ways. From the Sort palette by drop-down menu in the Custom Palette tab of the color picker, you can sort the palette by Hue, Saturation, Value, Red, Green, or Blue. However, the color relationships are not quite as obvious as when you see them arranged in a circle.

Q: Do I always have to follow these rules when I create images for the Web?

A: No, not really—the ideas I've offered in this chapter serve as a guide to helping you select colors that relate to each other in different ways. Every artist uses different techniques, and this is only one approach. You always have the freedom to develop your graphics in any way you choose!

PART

VI Appendixes

APPENDIX

A Online Resources

In this appendix:

- Active Server Pages
- Cascading Style Sheets
- HTML Layout Control
- Internet Database Connector Files
- Internet Information Server
- Microsoft Image Composer
- Microsoft Office/Related Applications

The resources that appear in this appendix are Web pages and sites that provide further information on the topics mentioned in this book. Included in the list are URLs for several articles in the Microsoft Knowledge Base.

Active Server Pages

Here are some Web sites and pages that display technical information, tips and tricks, frequently asked questions, and download areas for Active Server Pages:

- Active Server Pages—Download: The download area for Microsoft Active Server Pages:

  `http://www.microsoft.com/msdownload/iis_asp.htm`

- Questions about installation and setup of Active Server Pages:

  `http://www.microsoft.com/support/activeserver/content/faq/setup/default.htm`

- Active Server Pages Frequently Asked Questions: Contains questions about active database objects (ADO) in Active Server Pages:

  `http://www.microsoft.com/support/activeserver/content/faq/data/default.htm`

- Active Server Pages Frequently Asked Questions: A general FAQ page in Word for Windows format that you can download or view online:

  `http://www.microsoft.com/syspro/technet/boes/bo/iiserver/prodfact/aspfaq.doc`

- Active Server Pages—Technical Support: Access to technical support files and services relating to Active Server Pages:

  `http://www.microsoft.com/support/activeserver/`

Knowledge Base Articles about Active Server Pages can be found on Microsoft's Web site. The following section provides a list of some Knowledge Base articles that pertain to using Access 97, FrontPage 97, and Internet Information Server with Active Server Pages.

General Help

- How to Create a Simple Query in an ActiveX Layout (Q158737):

  `http://www.microsoft.com/kb/articles/q158/7/37.htm`

- HOWTO: Creating a Dynamically Growing Form Using ASP (Q163499):

  `http://www.microsoft.com/kb/articles/q163/4/99.htm`

- HOWTO: Disabling Cookies Sent by Active Server Pages (Q163010):

  `http://www.microsoft.com/kb/articles/q163/0/10.htm`

- How to Modify `.alx` File Objects from Active Server Pages (Q157748):

  `http://www.microsoft.com/kb/articles/q157/7/48.htm`

- How to Stop Users from Displaying a Frame Outside Its Frameset (Q159977):

  `http://www.microsoft.com/kb/articles/q159/9/77.htm`

- How to Use `Response.Redirect` in a Server Script (Q159402):

  `http://www.microsoft.com/kb/articles/q159/4/02.htm`

Using Access 97 with Active Server Pages

- INF: Check NT Permissions when Using IDC/ASP Files with Access (Q161333):

  `http://www.microsoft.com/kb/articles/q161/3/33.htm`

- INF: How to Use ASP Files to Query a Secure MS Access Database (Q163159):

  `http://www.microsoft.com/kb/articles/q163/1/59.htm`

- INF: How to Verify that ASP Is Working on Your Web Server (Q162976):

  `http://www.microsoft.com/kb/articles/q162/9/76.htm`

- PRA: ASP Query Cannot Be Used with the LIKE Predicate (Q162977):

  `http://www.microsoft.com/kb/articles/q162/9/77.htm`

- PRB: Constant for Output to Method Incorrect in Help (Q163510):

  `http://www.microsoft.com/kb/articles/q163/5/10.htm`

- PRB: "Data Source Name Not Found" Err Msg Opening Web Page (Q159682):

  `http://www.microsoft.com/kb/articles/q159/6/82.htm`

- PRB: Export to ASP or IDC Ignores Filter/`OrderBy` Properties (Q162981):

  `http://www.microsoft.com/kb/articles/q162/9/81.htm`

- PRB: Format Properties Ignored when Exporting Queries to ASP (Q163014):

  `http://www.microsoft.com/kb/articles/q163/0/14.htm`

- PRB: Form Control Format Property Ignored when Exported to ASP (Q163034):

  `http://www.microsoft.com/kb/articles/q163/0/34.htm`

- PRB: Unable to Access Script in ALX from Script in HTML (Q163397):

  `http://www.microsoft.com/kb/articles/q163/3/97.htm`

Using Active Data Objects

- `ADO.Connection` Updated to `ADODB.Connection` (Q162840):

  `http://www.microsoft.com/kb/articles/q162/8/40.htm`

Using VBScript with Active Server Pages

- DOC: Values for Scripting Object Constants Defined (Q163009):

  `http://www.microsoft.com/kb/articles/q163/0/09.htm`

- FIX: INVALID APPLICATION NAME Error in Active Server Pages (Q163501):

  `http://www.microsoft.com/kb/articles/q163/5/01.htm`

Using FrontPage 97 with Active Server Pages

- Using FrontPage 97 to Edit, Manage Active Server Pages (Q161779):

  `http://www.microsoft.com/kb/articles/q161/7/79.htm`

Cascading Style Sheets

The following list contains links to information about several browsers that support cascading style sheets. Follow the link to obtain additional information about each browser:

- Adobe FrameMaker "HoTaMaLe":

  `http://www.adobe.com/prodindex/framemaker/exportpi.html`
- Amaya (W3C's browser and authoring tool):

  `http://www.w3.org/pub/WWW/Amaya/`
- Arena (W3C's browser):

  `http://www.w3.org/pub/WWW/Arena/`
- DeltaPoint Quick Site 2.0:

  `http://www.deltapoint.com/qsdeved/index.htm`
- Emacs-w3 (Gnuscape Navigator):

  `http://www.cs.indiana.edu/elisp/w3/docs.html`
- Lexicon:

  `http://www.cs.ucl.ac.uk/staff/b.rosenberg/lex/index.html`
- Netscape Navigator 4.0 (Netscape Communicator), in Beta at time of publication:

  `http://home.netscape.com/`

The following Web pages offer a good amount of information about the tags used in cascading style sheets, as well as those supported by Windows and Macintosh versions of Internet Explorer 3.0:

- CSS1 Support in Microsoft Internet Explorer 3.0: This page describes how Microsoft Internet Explorer 3.0 for Windows supports cascading style sheets:

  `http://www.shadow.net/~braden/nostyle/ie3.html`
- CSS1 Support in MSIE 3.0 for Macintosh: This page describes how Microsoft Internet Explorer 3.0 for Macintosh supports cascading style sheets:

  `http://www.cwru.edu/lit/homes/eam3/css1/msie-css1.html`
- Introduction to Cascading Style Sheets: The Web Design Group's introduction to cascading style sheets contains a tutorial, structure and rules, descriptions of properties, linking style sheets to HTML, references, and many tips and tricks. Be sure to read the page about style sheet dependence and things you should avoid when using cascading style sheets. You can find them all at the following address:

  `http://www.htmlhelp.com/reference/css/`
- Microsoft Site Builder Workshop: A User's Guide to Style Sheets: Microsoft's Style Sheets Guide includes an introduction to cascading style sheets, ways to add them to your Web pages, a style reference guide, tips and tricks, and sample pages:

  `http://www.windows.com/workshop/author/css.htm`

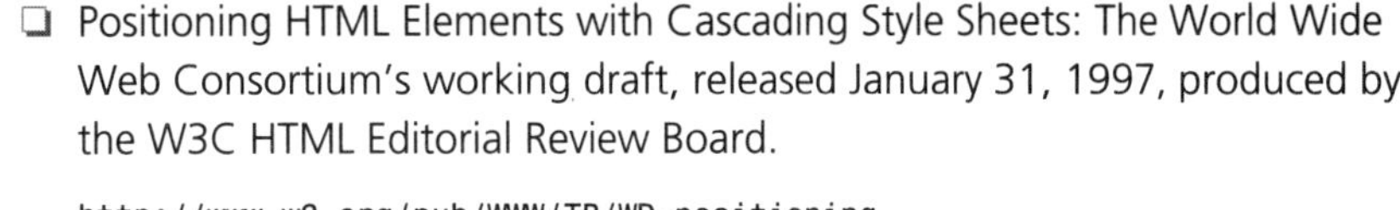

- Positioning HTML Elements with Cascading Style Sheets: The World Wide Web Consortium's working draft, released January 31, 1997, produced by the W3C HTML Editorial Review Board.

  `http://www.w3.org/pub/WWW/TR/WD-positioning`

- Web Style Sheets: The World Wide Web Consortium's page of links to anything and everything you need to know about cascading style sheets and how to use them on your site. You can find this page at the following address:

  `http://www.w3.org/pub/WWW/Style/`

The following Knowledge Base article pertains to special considerations that apply when using FrontPage 97 to develop pages that use cascading style sheets:

- FrontPage 97 May Remove CSS ID, Class, Style Attributes (Q162234):

  `http://www.microsoft.com/kb/articles/q162/2/34.htm`

HTML Layout Control

The following pages provide links to information about the HTML Layout Control and where you can download the control.

- Using the HTML Layout Control: Contains examples of pages that were created using the HTML Layout Control. Examples include Winston's Playhouse, Mr. ActiveX Eggplant Head, an online version of Minesweeper, Solitaire, and the Volcano Coffee Company sample pages. Internet Explorer 3.0 and HTML Layout Control are required to view the samples:

  `http://www.microsoft.com/ie/most/howto/layout.htm`

- The Microsoft HTML Layout Control: Technical information about designing pages with the HTML Layout Control, how the HTML Layout Control works, and compatibility and future support:

  `http://www.microsoft.com/workshop/author/layout/alayout.htm`

- Microsoft HTML Layout Control Download Area: Download area for the Microsoft HTML Layout Control:

  `http://www.microsoft.com/ie/download/layout.htm`

Internet Database Connector Files

Microsoft's Web site offers several Knowledge Base articles about Internet Database Connector (IDC) files. The list that follows includes pages that discuss using IDC files with Access 97, Internet Information Server, and FrontPage 97.

Using Access 97 with Internet Database Connector (IDC) Files

- INF: Check NT Permissions When Using IDC/ASP Files with Access (Q161333):

  `http://www.microsoft.com/kb/articles/q161/3/33.htm`
- INF: How to Use IDC Files to Query a Secure MS Access Database (Q161172):

  `http://www.microsoft.com/kb/articles/q161/1/72.htm`
- PRA: IDC Parameter Queries Cannot Use LIKE and Wildcards (Q163893):

  `http://www.microsoft.com/kb/articles/q163/8/93.htm`
- PRB: "Data Source Name Not Found" Err Msg Opening Web Page (Q159682):

  `http://www.microsoft.com/kb/articles/q159/6/82.htm`
- PRB: Error "HTTP/1.0 403 Access Forbidden" Browsing IDC Page (Q160754):

  `http://www.microsoft.com/kb/articles/q160/7/54.htm`
- PRB: Export to ASP or IDC Ignores Filter/`OrderBy` Properties (Q162981):

  `http://www.microsoft.com/kb/articles/q162/9/81.htm`
- PRB: IDC Files Display Hyperlinks as Text in Web Browser (Q163654):

  `http://www.microsoft.com/kb/articles/q163/6/54.htm`
- PRB: IDC Using Parameter Query May Return "Too Few Parameters" (Q162980):

  `http://www.microsoft.com/kb/articles/q162/9/80.htm`
- PRB: ODBC Error Using IDC Files to Query SQL Server Tables (Q161015):

  `http://www.microsoft.com/kb/articles/q161/0/15.htm`
- PRB: Queries Exported to HTX/IDC Appear with Different Format (Q163181):

  `http://www.microsoft.com/kb/articles/q163/1/81.htm`

Using FrontPage 97 with Internet Database Connector Files

- Drop-Down Populated by IDC Query Shows Code Instead of Data (Q159437):

  `http://www.microsoft.com/kb/articles/q159/4/37.htm`
- IDC Wizard Deletes SQL Query Without Trailing Carriage Return (Q163588):

  `http://www.microsoft.com/kb/articles/q163/5/88.htm`

- Internet Database Connector Wizard Runs on Non-IDC Server (Q160810):

  `http://www.microsoft.com/kb/articles/q160/8/10.htm`

- Personal Web Server Doesn't Support Multiple Queries in IDC Files (Q160809):

  `http://www.microsoft.com/kb/articles/q160/8/09.htm`

- Strings with Spaces Fail as Default Values in IDC (Q159442):

  `http://www.microsoft.com/kb/articles/q159/4/42.htm`

- Syntax Error if Query Contains Parameter Values (Q159435):

  `http://www.microsoft.com/kb/articles/q159/4/35.htm`

Using Internet Information Server with Internet Database Connector Files

- How to Dynamically Populate a Select Control with IDC (Q156757):

  `http://www.microsoft.com/kb/articles/q156/7/57.htm`

- How to Use the IIS HTTP Environment Variable (Q155706):

  `http://www.microsoft.com/kb/articles/q155/7/06.htm`

- IDC Queries to Access Fail from IIS 2.0 (Q155255):

  `http://www.microsoft.com/kb/articles/q155/2/55.htm`

- IDC Queries to Access Fail from IIS 2.0 or MSPWS 1.0 Servers (Q162245):

  `http://www.microsoft.com/kb/articles/q162/2/45.htm`

- Using the IDC "%z" Parameter (Q156756):

  `http://www.microsoft.com/kb/articles/q156/7/56.htm`

Internet Information Server

The following Web pages provide information about Internet Information Server 2.0, as well as downloads to upgrade to Internet Information Server 3.0.

- Download IIS 3.0: Download page for Microsoft Internet Information Server 3.0. Requires Windows NT Server 4.0 running Internet Information Server 2.0. You can download Active Server Pages, Microsoft Index Server 1.1, Microsoft NetShow, FrontPage 97 Server Extensions, and Crystal Reports for Internet Information Server. Its address follows:

  `http://www.microsoft.com/iis/getiis/downloadiis3/default6.htm`

- Internet Information Server 3.0 Home Page: Pages that help you learn, evaluate, and download Internet Information Server 3.0. An IIS Showcase also appears in this section of Microsoft's Web site. Its address follows:

  `http://www.microsoft.com/iis/default.asp`

- Microsoft Internet Information Server Home Page: The home page for Microsoft Internet Information Server on Microsoft's site provides links to a product overview, evaluation tools, a list of partners and products, the Internet Resource Center, product support and Knowledge Base articles, and news and events. Its address follows:

  `http://www.microsoft.com/InfoServ/`

- Windows NT Server Support Site: The Windows NT Server support site area of Microsoft's Web site includes links to authorized support centers, file patches, hardware compatibility lists, and troubleshooting guides. Its address follows:

  `http://www.microsoft.com/ntserversupport/`

The Knowledge Base articles in the following sections include information about using Internet Information Server with Access 97 and FrontPage 97.

Using Access 97 with Internet Information Server

- General Error=51 Connecting to an Access Datasource (Q156526):

  `http://www.microsoft.com/kb/articles/q156/5/26.htm`

Using FrontPage 97 with Internet Information Server

- FrontPage Configuration Settings for Windows NT Servers (Q162145):

  `http://www.microsoft.com/kb/articles/q162/1/45.htm`

- FrontPage Explorer Does Not Prompt for Login on IIS Web (Q153629):

  `http://www.microsoft.com/kb/articles/q153/6/29.htm`

- FrontPage Explorer Doesn't Accept Blank Password (Q163587):

  `http://www.microsoft.com/kb/articles/q163/5/87.htm`

- FrontPage Requires Allow Anonymous or No NTLM on IIS 1.0 (Q158820):

  `http://www.microsoft.com/kb/articles/q158/8/20.htm`

- FrontPage Server Extensions Leak Memory on IIS Server (Q162233):

  `http://www.microsoft.com/kb/articles/q162/2/33.htm`

- Large Files Corrupted When Uploaded to IIS Over SSL (Q158912):

  `http://www.microsoft.com/kb/articles/q158/9/12.htm`

- MS Internet Information Server Not in Server Type List (Q152389):

  `http://www.microsoft.com/kb/articles/q152/3/89.htm`
- Registration WebBot not Supported on IIS Web Server (Q155770):

  `http://www.microsoft.com/kb/articles/q155/7/70.htm`
- Runtime Web Bot Fails on IIS 2.0 with Multiple Home Directories (Q155281):

  `http://www.microsoft.com/kb/articles/q155/2/81.htm`
- Unable to Complete Transaction on Server with NTLM (Q160618):

  `http://www.microsoft.com/kb/articles/q160/6/18.htm`
- Unable to Save to IIS Server if Permissions Incorrect (Q163584):

  `http://www.microsoft.com/kb/articles/q163/5/84.htm`

Microsoft Image Composer

For additional information and examples from Microsoft Image Composer, check out the following links:

- GIF Animator for Windows 95 (Download Page): Download the U.S. English version of Microsoft GIF Animator on this page:

  `http://www.microsoft.com/imagecomposer/gifanimator/samples.htm`
- Microsoft Image Composer Gallery: Links to a Sample Showcase, free sprites (most of which are available on the FrontPage 97 with Bonus Pack CD-ROM), a Web Art page, a GIF Animator Sample page, third-party images, and information on Image Composer design contests. Its address follows:

  `http://www.microsoft.com/imagecomposer/gallery/gallery.htm`
- Microsoft Image Composer Home Page: An area of the Microsoft Web site that is devoted to the use of Microsoft Image Composer. Areas to learn and use Microsoft Image Composer, Microsoft GIF Animator, a gallery of samples, and a download area are included at this address:

  `http://www.microsoft.com/imagecomposer/default.htm`
- Using Image Composer FAQ: Microsoft Image Composer FAQ from Microsoft's Web Site, found at the following address:

  `http://www.microsoft.com/imagecomposer/usingic/icfaq.htm`
- Using Image Composer: Tips and Tricks: A Tips and Tricks area on Microsoft's Image Composer Web site. Contains many tips on using the many features and effects available in Microsoft Image Composer. Its address follows:

  `http://www.microsoft.com/imagecomposer/usingic/ictips.htm`

The following Knowledge Base article pertains to Microsoft Image Composer:

- Inserted TIFF Files Appear as Broken Images (Q160232):

  `http://www.microsoft.com/kb/articles/q160/2/32.htm`

Microsoft Office/Related Applications

The following Knowledge Base articles are located on Microsoft's Web site.

Access 97

The following Knowledge Base articles on Microsoft's Web site focus on using Access 97 with Web documents and Web servers. They also provide additional information on Web-related procedures found in Access 97.

General Help

- INF: New Features in Microsoft Access 97 (Q160874):

  `http://www.microsoft.com/kb/articles/q160/8/74.htm`

Using Access 97 with Web Formats—General

- PRB: Lookup Fields Ignored when Exporting to Internet Formats (Q162908):

  `http://www.microsoft.com/kb/articles/q162/9/08.htm`

Using Access 97 with Web Servers

- INF: Files for Testing System DSN Available on MSL (Q163603):

  `http://www.microsoft.com/kb/articles/q163/6/03.htm`

- INF: Permissions Necessary to View HTML, IDC, and ASP Files (Q162975):

  `http://www.microsoft.com/kb/articles/q162/9/75.htm`

Working with Hyperlinks

- INF: How to Edit Data in a Hyperlink Field in a Table (Q159327):

  `http://www.microsoft.com/kb/articles/q159/3/27.htm`

- INF: Hyperlink Starts New Access or Internet Explorer Instance (Q159368):

  `http://www.microsoft.com/kb/articles/q159/3/68.htm`

- PRA: Hyperlink Base Property Not Displayed in Properties View (Q162747):

  `http://www.microsoft.com/kb/articles/q162/7/47.htm`

- PRB: ASP Files Display Hyperlinks as Text in Web Browser (Q163706):

  `http://www.microsoft.com/kb/articles/q163/7/06.htm`

Working with the Publish to Web Wizard

- INF: Server and Browser Requirements for Publish to Web Wizard (Q159325):

  `http://www.microsoft.com/kb/articles/q159/3/25.htm`

- PRB: Publish to the Web Wizard Does Not Allow Custom File Name (Q163443):

  `http://www.microsoft.com/kb/articles/q163/4/43.htm`

Working with Queries

- PRB: Action Queries Cannot Be Exported to HTML, IDC, or ASP (Q163443):

  `http://www.microsoft.com/kb/articles/q163/4/43.htm`

Excel 97

The following Knowledge Base articles on Microsoft's Web site focus on using Excel 97 in conjunction with Internet-related documents. Topics include general help, using the Excel 97 Wizards that relate to Internet development, using Excel 97 with FrontPage 97, and working with hyperlinks and queries.

General Help

- Article List: Microsoft Excel 97 Components (Q162319):

  `http://www.microsoft.com/kb/articles/q162/3/19.htm`

Using the Internet Assistant Wizard

- XL97: How to Use the Internet Assistant Wizard (Q158079):

  `http://www.microsoft.com/kb/articles/q158/0/79.htm`

Using the Web Form Wizard

- XL97: Defined Name is Used by Form Created in Web Form Wizard (Q161899):

  `http://www.microsoft.com/kb/articles/q161/8/99.htm`

- XL97: Error when You Display Form Created by Web Form Wizard (Q161795):

  `http://www.microsoft.com/kb/articles/q161/7/95.htm`

- XL97: Errors in Web Form Wizard Saving Form to FrontPage (Q161898):

  `http://www.microsoft.com/kb/articles/q161/8/98.htm`

- XL97: Macro Created in Form by Web Form Wizard (Q161902):

  `http://www.microsoft.com/kb/articles/q161/9/02.htm`

Using Excel 97 with FrontPage 97

- XL97: Cannot Use Form on FrontPage Personal Web Server (Q162024):

  `http://www.microsoft.com/kb/articles/q162/0/24.htm`

- XL97: Errors in Web Form Wizard Saving Form to FrontPage (Q161898):

  `http://www.microsoft.com/kb/articles/q161/8/98.htm`

Working with Hyperlinks

- XL97: "Create Hyperlink Here" Does Not Work in Unsaved File (Q156883):

  `http://www.microsoft.com/kb/articles/q156/8/83.htm`

- XL97: Double-Clicking Hyperlink May Activate Edit Mode (Q154901):

  `http://www.microsoft.com/kb/articles/q154/9/01.htm`

- XL97: Error Creating Hyperlink with Chart Sheet in Workbook (Q159668):

  `http://www.microsoft.com/kb/articles/q159/6/68.htm`

- XL97: Error Updating Link to Web Document (Q155128):

  `http://www.microsoft.com/kb/articles/q155/1/28.htm`

- XL97: Error Using "Mailto:" with `FollowHyperlink` Method (Q161324):

  `http://www.microsoft.com/kb/articles/q161/3/24.htm`

- XL97: Invalid Site Error Using Relative Hyperlink Path (Q156893):

  `http://www.microsoft.com/kb/articles/q156/8/93.htm`

- XL97: No Menu Choice to Select All Hyperlinks (Q156353):

  `http://www.microsoft.com/kb/articles/q156/3/53.htm`

- XL97: Worksheet Events Don't Occur After Clicking Link (Q162051):

  `http://www.microsoft.com/kb/articles/q162/0/51.htm`

Working with Queries

- XL97: Cannot Use Edit Query Button on Sheet with Web Query (Q158247):

  `http://www.microsoft.com/kb/articles/q158/2/47.htm`

- XL97: How to Create Web Query (`.iqy`) Files (Q157482):

  `http://www.microsoft.com/kb/articles/q157/4/82.htm`

- XL97: How to Programmatically Perform a Web Query (Q162080):

  `http://www.microsoft.com/kb/articles/q162/0/80.htm`
- XL97: How to Specify Dynamic Web Query Parameters (Q162051):

  `http://www.microsoft.com/kb/articles/q162/0/51.htm`
- XL97: Web Query File is Case-Sensitive (Q162025):

  `http://www.microsoft.com/kb/articles/q162/0/25.htm`

FrontPage 97

The following Knowledge Base articles on Microsoft's Web site focus on FrontPage 97. Topics include creating hyperlinks, general help, using FrontPage with Office 97 applications, and using FrontPage with Web servers.

Creating Links

- Can't Resolve FTP or Gopher Links or Links Generate Errors (Q151557):

  `http://www.microsoft.com/kb/articles/q151/5/57.htm`

General Help

- FrontPage Editor Deletes Unknown Attributes in HTML (Q161420):

  `http://www.microsoft.com/kb/articles/q161/4/20.htm`
- FrontPage: Error "Unable to open…" and "404 Not Found" (Q143089):

  `http://www.microsoft.com/kb/articles/q143/0/89.htm`
- How to Make a Web Page that Displays Data from a Database (Q161155):

  `http://www.microsoft.com/kb/articles/q161/1/55.htm`
- How to Publish a FrontPage Web to the Internet (Q161414):

  `http://www.microsoft.com/kb/articles/q161/4/14.htm`
- New Features in FrontPage 97 (Q161415):

  `http://www.microsoft.com/kb/articles/q161/4/15.htm`
- Permission Settings Changed After Reinstalling Extensions (Q161847):

  `http://www.microsoft.com/kb/articles/q161/8/47.htm`
- Permissions Not Retained when Web Is Renamed (Q161964):

  `http://www.microsoft.com/kb/articles/q161/9/64.htm`

Using FrontPage 97 with Microsoft Office

- Can't Use Proofing Tools (Spelling Checker) or Text Converters (Q160226):

  `http://www.microsoft.com/kb/articles/q160/2/26.htm`

- Differences Between Word and FrontPage for Web Authoring (Q163300):

  `http://www.microsoft.com/kb/articles/q163/3/00.htm`
- General File Transfer Error–3 Installing FrontPage 97 (Q163665):

  `http://www.microsoft.com/kb/articles/q163/6/65.htm`
- How FrontPage 97 Handles Document Conversion to HTML (Q160833):

  `http://www.microsoft.com/kb/articles/q160/8/33.htm`
- Imported Word Data Does Not Retain Bullets (Q160224):

  `http://www.microsoft.com/kb/articles/q160/2/24.htm`

Using FrontPage 97 with Microsoft Personal Web Server

- Memory Leak in FrontPage Extensions on MS Personal Web Server (Q160225):

  `http://www.microsoft.com/kb/articles/q160/2/25.htm`
- Switching from FrontPage Personal Web Server to Microsoft Personal Web Server (Q161418):

  `http://www.microsoft.com/kb/articles/q161/4/18.htm`
- Why Are There Two Versions of the Personal Web Server? (Q161150):

  `http://www.microsoft.com/kb/articles/q161/1/50.htm`

Using FrontPage 97 with Web Servers—General

- Don't Need Web Server to Use FrontPage 97 (Q161154):

  `http://www.microsoft.com/kb/articles/q161/1/54.htm`
- FrontPage: Basic Troubleshooting Utilities (Q143093):

  `http://www.microsoft.com/kb/articles/q143/0/93.htm`
- FrontPage Installs Extensions on Port 443 (Q161423):

  `http://www.microsoft.com/kb/articles/q161/4/23.htm`
- How to Assign IP Restrictions in FrontPage (Q156981):

  `http://www.microsoft.com/kb/articles/q156/9/81.htm`
- Minimum NTFS File Permissions Required by FrontPage 97 (Q162144):

  `http://www.microsoft.com/kb/articles/q162/1/44.htm`
- WebBot Browse-Time Components Don't Function on Disk-Based Web (Q160227):

  `http://www.microsoft.com/kb/articles/q160/2/27.htm`
- Web Servers Supported by FrontPage 97 (Q161158):

  `http://www.microsoft.com/kb/articles/q161/1/58.htm`

- When to Use the FrontPage Personal Web Server Versus Microsoft Personal Web Server (Q161417):

  `http://www.microsoft.com/kb/articles/q161/4/17.htm`

Office 97

- OFF97: Memory Problems when Hyperlinking Between Programs (Q157763):

  `http://www.microsoft.com/kb/articles/q157/7/63.htm`

PowerPoint 97

- PowerPoint 97: Opening from and Saving to an FTP Site (Q159317):

  `http://www.microsoft.com/kb/articles/q159/3/17.htm`
- PPT97: Sample Code to Open a Web Site in Internet Explorer (Q161720):

  `http://www.microsoft.com/kb/articles/q161/7/20.htm`
- What Is the Publish to ASF Add-In for PowerPoint 97? (Q160848):

  `http://www.microsoft.com/kb/articles/q160/8/48.htm`

Word 97

- What's New in Word 97 (Q157478):

  `http://www.microsoft.com/kb/articles/q157/4/78.htm`
- Word 97 Can't Open HTML Document with Nested Tables (Q157774):

  `http://www.microsoft.com/kb/articles/q157/7/74.htm`
- Word 97: General Information About Web Page Authoring (Q159948):

  `http://www.microsoft.com/kb/articles/q159/9/48.htm`

APPENDIX

B Additional Books

In this appendix:

- Other Books in the Laura Lemay's Web Workshop Series
- Microsoft Access 97
- Microsoft ActiveX/Active Server Pages
- Microsoft FrontPage 97
- Microsoft Internet Information Server
- Microsoft Office 97
- Microsoft Windows NT 4.0
- Microsoft Products—Other
- Web Publishing—General

The list of books in this appendix offer additional information about the topics discussed in this book. All of the books mentioned herein are published by Sams.net or Sams Publishing. The URL that follows each title presents a description of the contents of the publication, as well as a link to order the book on line directly from the publisher.

Other Books in the Laura Lemay's Web Workshop Series

If you like this book, be sure to check out the other books in the Laura Lemay's Web Workshop series. Each book follows the same format used here and focuses on specific topics using a friendly hands-on approach.

The middle of each of the following URLs contains a lowercase `hg`. This should not be confused with a lowercase `hq`.

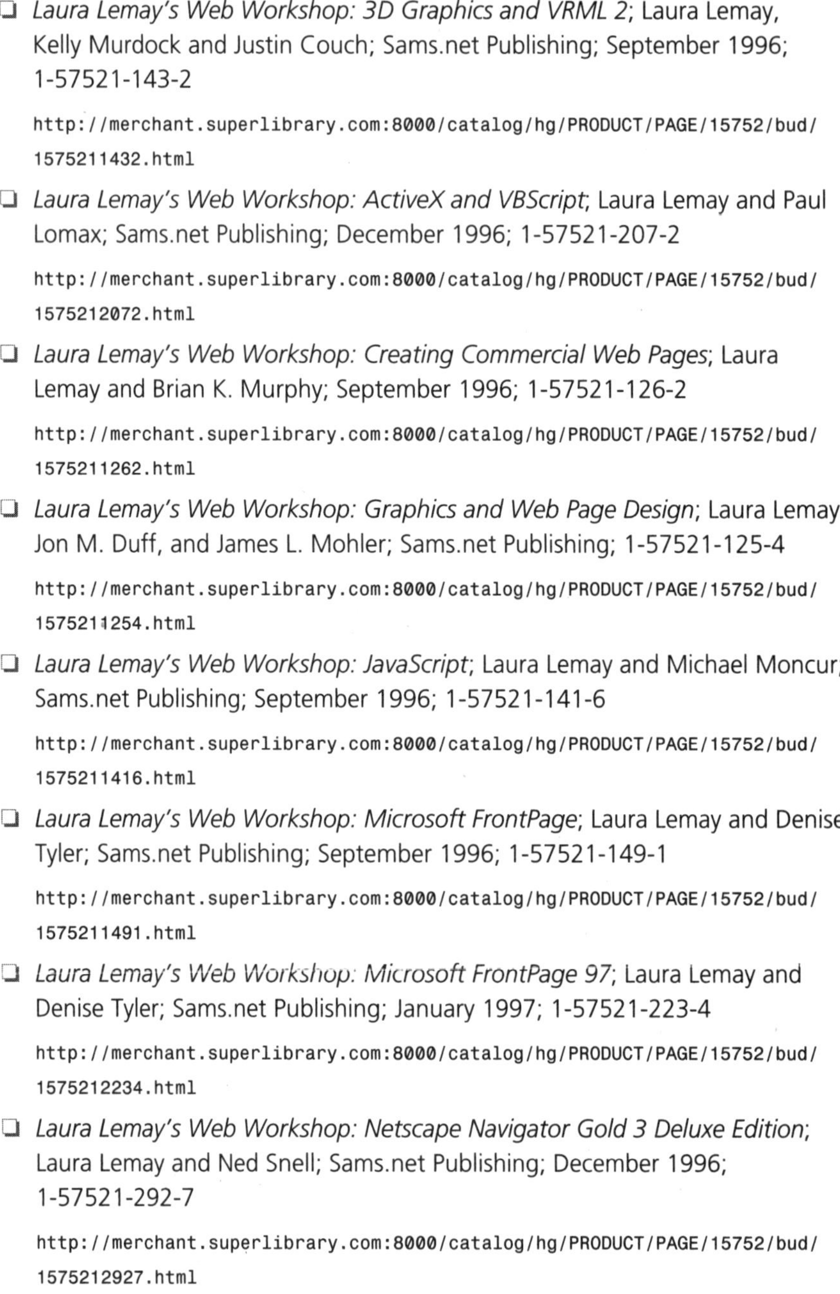

- *Laura Lemay's Web Workshop: 3D Graphics and VRML 2*; Laura Lemay, Kelly Murdock and Justin Couch; Sams.net Publishing; September 1996; 1-57521-143-2

  `http://merchant.superlibrary.com:8000/catalog/hg/PRODUCT/PAGE/15752/bud/1575211432.html`

- *Laura Lemay's Web Workshop: ActiveX and VBScript*; Laura Lemay and Paul Lomax; Sams.net Publishing; December 1996; 1-57521-207-2

  `http://merchant.superlibrary.com:8000/catalog/hg/PRODUCT/PAGE/15752/bud/1575212072.html`

- *Laura Lemay's Web Workshop: Creating Commercial Web Pages*; Laura Lemay and Brian K. Murphy; September 1996; 1-57521-126-2

  `http://merchant.superlibrary.com:8000/catalog/hg/PRODUCT/PAGE/15752/bud/1575211262.html`

- *Laura Lemay's Web Workshop: Graphics and Web Page Design*; Laura Lemay, Jon M. Duff, and James L. Mohler; Sams.net Publishing; 1-57521-125-4

  `http://merchant.superlibrary.com:8000/catalog/hg/PRODUCT/PAGE/15752/bud/1575211254.html`

- *Laura Lemay's Web Workshop: JavaScript*; Laura Lemay and Michael Moncur; Sams.net Publishing; September 1996; 1-57521-141-6

  `http://merchant.superlibrary.com:8000/catalog/hg/PRODUCT/PAGE/15752/bud/1575211416.html`

- *Laura Lemay's Web Workshop: Microsoft FrontPage*; Laura Lemay and Denise Tyler; Sams.net Publishing; September 1996; 1-57521-149-1

  `http://merchant.superlibrary.com:8000/catalog/hg/PRODUCT/PAGE/15752/bud/1575211491.html`

- *Laura Lemay's Web Workshop: Microsoft FrontPage 97*; Laura Lemay and Denise Tyler; Sams.net Publishing; January 1997; 1-57521-223-4

  `http://merchant.superlibrary.com:8000/catalog/hg/PRODUCT/PAGE/15752/bud/1575212234.html`

- *Laura Lemay's Web Workshop: Netscape Navigator Gold 3 Deluxe Edition*; Laura Lemay and Ned Snell; Sams.net Publishing; December 1996; 1-57521-292-7

  `http://merchant.superlibrary.com:8000/catalog/hg/PRODUCT/PAGE/15752/bud/1575212927.html`

Microsoft Access 97

For additional information on designing and implementing databases using Microsoft Access 97, refer to the following titles:

- *Access 97 Unleashed*, Second Edition; Dwayne Gifford, et al.; Sams Publishing; December 1996; 0-67230-983-1

  `http://merchant.superlibrary.com:8000/catalog/hg/PRODUCT/PAGE/06723/bud/0672309831.html`

- *Alison Balter's Mastering Access 97 Development*, Second Edition; Alison Balter; Sams Premier; January 1997; 0-67230-999-8

  `http://merchant.superlibrary.com:8000/catalog/hg/PRODUCT/PAGE/06723/bud/0672309998.html`

- *Teach Yourself Access 97 in 14 Days*, Fourth Edition; Paul Cassel; Sams Publishing; December 1996; 0-67230-969-6

  `http://merchant.superlibrary.com:8000/catalog/hg/PRODUCT/PAGE/06723/bud/0672309696.html`

Microsoft ActiveX/Active Server Pages

ActiveX controls are an integral part of Active Server Pages, which can be used to deploy Access 95 database integration on the Web. For information on using ActiveX controls, refer to the following publication. (Another publication on ActiveX controls is listed in the "Other Books in the Laura Lemay's Web Workshop Series" section.)

- *ActiveX Programming Unleashed*, Second Edition; Weiying Chen, et al.; Sams.net Publishing; December 1996; 1-57521-154-8

  `http://merchant.superlibrary.com:8000/catalog/hg/PRODUCT/PAGE/15752/bud/1575211548.html`

Microsoft FrontPage 97

In addition to the two FrontPage titles mentioned in the "Other Books in the Laura Lemay's Web Workshop Series" section, the following two books offer additional information about creating Web pages with Microsoft FrontPage 97:

- *Microsoft FrontPage 97 Unleashed*, Second Edition; William R. Stanek; Sams.net Publishing; December 1996; 1-57521-226-9

  `http://merchant.superlibrary.com:8000/catalog/hg/PRODUCT/PAGE/15752/bud/1575212269.html`

- *Teach Yourself Microsoft FrontPage 97 in a Week*; Donald Doherty; Sams.net Publishing; January 1997; 1-57521-225-0

  `http://merchant.superlibrary.com:8000/catalog/hg/PRODUCT/PAGE/15752/bud/1575212250.html`

Microsoft Internet Information Server

For further information about developing Internet and intranet Web sites using Microsoft Internet Information Server, refer to the following three titles. (The first title focuses on a new add-on for Internet Information Server 3.0.)

- *Designing and Implementing Microsoft Index Server*; Mark Swank and Drew Kittel; Sams.net Publishing; December 1996; 1-57521-212-9

  `http://merchant.superlibrary.com:8000/catalog/hg/PRODUCT/PAGE/15752/bud/1575212129.html`

- *Designing and Implementing Microsoft Internet Information Server 2*; Arthur Knowles and Sanjaya Hettihewa; Sams.net Publishing; July 1996; 1-57521-168-8

  `http://merchant.superlibrary.com:8000/catalog/hg/PRODUCT/PAGE/15752/bud/1575211688.html`

- *Microsoft Internet Information Server 2 Unleashed*; Arthur Knowles; Sams.net Publishing; September 1996; 1-57521-109-2

  `http://merchant.superlibrary.com:8000/catalog/hg/PRODUCT/PAGE/15752/bud/1575211092.html`

Microsoft Office 97

Office 97 can be used very effectively in conjunction with FrontPage 97 in an intranet environment and offers many ways to assist in Web page development. The following three books offer additional information and how-to instructions on using Office 97:

- *Microsoft Office 97 Unleashed*, Second Edition; Paul McFredries, et al.; Sams Publishing; December 1996; 0-67231-010-4

  `http://merchant.superlibrary.com:8000/catalog/hg/PRODUCT/PAGE/06723/bud/0672310104.html`

- *Teach Yourself Microsoft Office 97 in 24 Hours*, Second Edition; Greg Perry; Sams Publishing; December 1996; 0-67231-009-0

  `http://merchant.superlibrary.com:8000/catalog/hg/PRODUCT/PAGE/06723/bud/0672310090.html`

- *Teach Yourself Web Publishing for Office 97 in a Week*; Michael A. Larson; Sams.net Publishing; February 1997; 1-57521-232-3

  `http://merchant.superlibrary.com:8000/catalog/hg/PRODUCT/PAGE/15752/bud/1575212323.html`

Microsoft Windows NT 4.0

For those who are unfamiliar with the Windows NT Workstation or Windows NT Server operating systems, several books focus on these operating systems. If you are interested in using Microsoft Internet Information Server in conjunction with FrontPage, the titles that discuss Windows NT Server 4.0 will be a valuable addition to your library. They include the following:

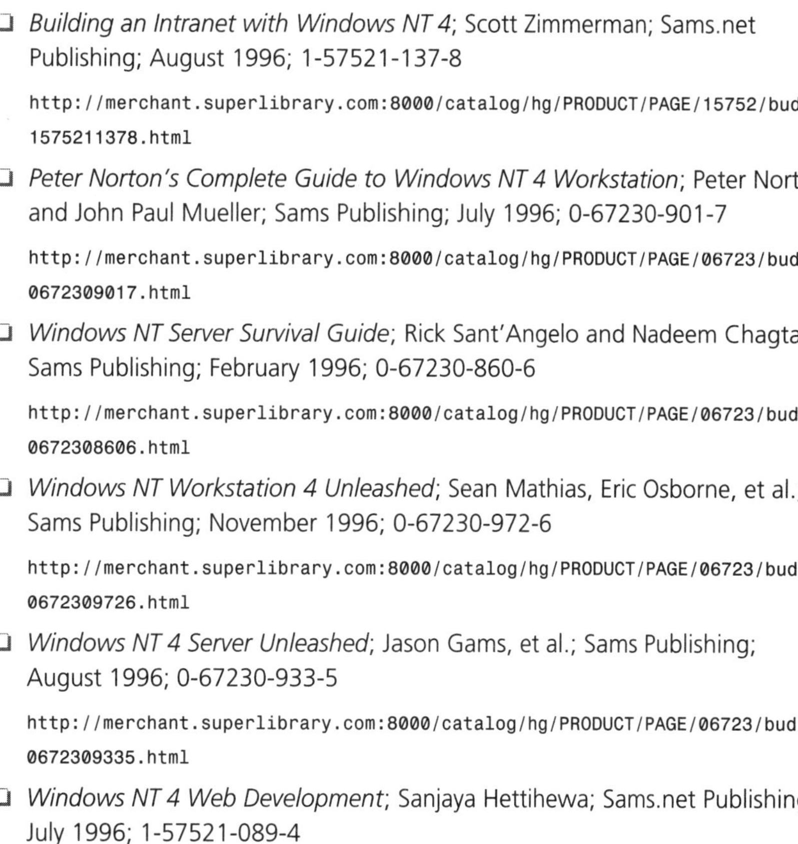

- *Building an Intranet with Windows NT 4*; Scott Zimmerman; Sams.net Publishing; August 1996; 1-57521-137-8

  `http://merchant.superlibrary.com:8000/catalog/hg/PRODUCT/PAGE/15752/bud/1575211378.html`

- *Peter Norton's Complete Guide to Windows NT 4 Workstation*; Peter Norton and John Paul Mueller; Sams Publishing; July 1996; 0-67230-901-7

  `http://merchant.superlibrary.com:8000/catalog/hg/PRODUCT/PAGE/06723/bud/0672309017.html`

- *Windows NT Server Survival Guide*; Rick Sant'Angelo and Nadeem Chagtai; Sams Publishing; February 1996; 0-67230-860-6

  `http://merchant.superlibrary.com:8000/catalog/hg/PRODUCT/PAGE/06723/bud/0672308606.html`

- *Windows NT Workstation 4 Unleashed*; Sean Mathias, Eric Osborne, et al.; Sams Publishing; November 1996; 0-67230-972-6

  `http://merchant.superlibrary.com:8000/catalog/hg/PRODUCT/PAGE/06723/bud/0672309726.html`

- *Windows NT 4 Server Unleashed*; Jason Gams, et al.; Sams Publishing; August 1996; 0-67230-933-5

  `http://merchant.superlibrary.com:8000/catalog/hg/PRODUCT/PAGE/06723/bud/0672309335.html`

- *Windows NT 4 Web Development*; Sanjaya Hettihewa; Sams.net Publishing; July 1996; 1-57521-089-4

  `http://merchant.superlibrary.com:8000/catalog/hg/PRODUCT/PAGE/15752/bud/1575210894.html`

Microsoft Products—Other

The following books focus on other Microsoft products that are designed for Internet or intranet applications:

- *Microsoft BackOffice 2 Unleashed*, Second Edition; Joe Greene, et al.; Sams Publishing; November 1996; 0-67230-816-9

  `http://merchant.superlibrary.com:8000/catalog/hg/PRODUCT/PAGE/06723/bud/0672308169.html`

- *Microsoft Internet Explorer 3 Unleashed*; Glenn Fincher, Joe Kraynak, et al.; Sams.net Publishing; September 1996; 1-57521-155-6

  `http://merchant.superlibrary.com:8000/catalog/hg/PRODUCT/PAGE/15752/bud/1575211556.html`

Web Publishing—General

The books listed here cover topics of a general nature, most of them focusing on Internet or intranet development:

- *Building an Intranet*; Tim Evans; Sams.net Publishing; May 1996; 1-57521-071-1

  `http://merchant.superlibrary.com:8000/catalog/hg/PRODUCT/PAGE/15752/bud/1575210711.html`

- *Client/Server Unleashed*; Neil Jenkins, et al.; Sams Publishing; August 1996; 0-67230-726-X

  `http://merchant.superlibrary.com:8000/catalog/hg/PRODUCT/PAGE/06723/bud/067230726X.html`

- *Creating Commercial Web Sites*; Kim and Brad Hampton; Sams.net Publishing; October 1996; 1-57521-169-6

  `http://merchant.superlibrary.com:8000/catalog/hg/PRODUCT/PAGE/15752/bud/1575211696.html`

- *Developing Intranet Applications with Java*; Jerry Ablan; Sams.net Publishing; September 1996; 1-57521-166-1

  `http://merchant.superlibrary.com:8000/catalog/hg/PRODUCT/PAGE/15752/bud/1575211661.html`

- *Internet 1997 Unleashed*, Second Edition; Jill Ellsworth, Billy Barron, et al.; Sams.net Publishing; December 1996; 1-57521-185-8

  `http://merchant.superlibrary.com:8000/catalog/hg/PRODUCT/PAGE/15752/bud/1575211858.html`

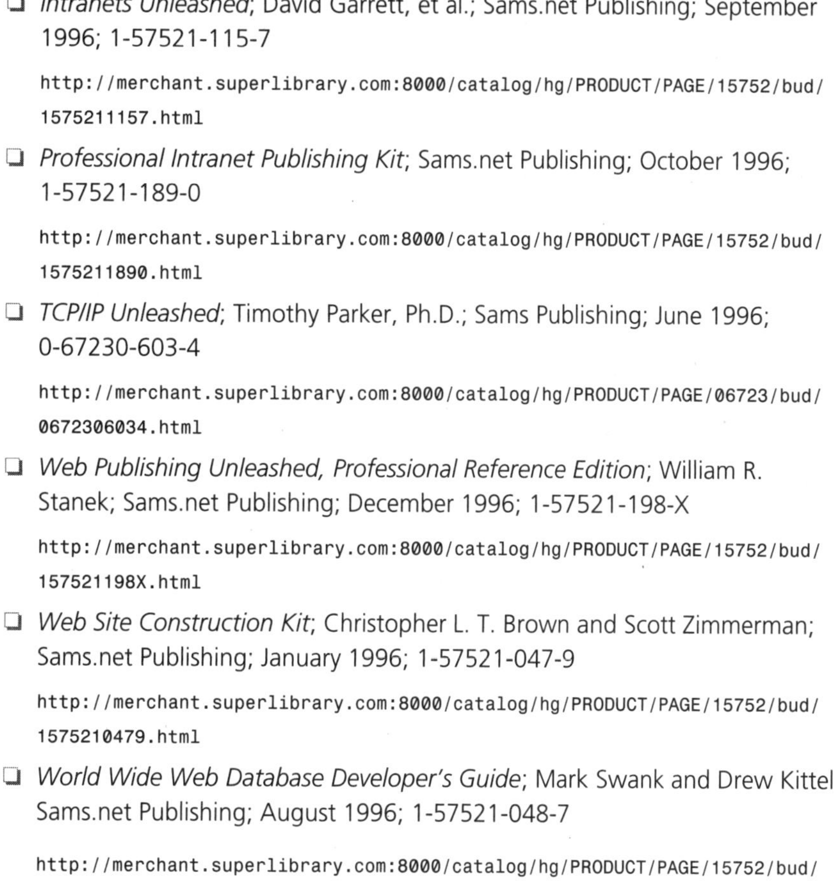

- *Intranets Unleashed*; David Garrett, et al.; Sams.net Publishing; September 1996; 1-57521-115-7

  `http://merchant.superlibrary.com:8000/catalog/hg/PRODUCT/PAGE/15752/bud/1575211157.html`

- *Professional Intranet Publishing Kit*; Sams.net Publishing; October 1996; 1-57521-189-0

  `http://merchant.superlibrary.com:8000/catalog/hg/PRODUCT/PAGE/15752/bud/1575211890.html`

- *TCP/IP Unleashed*; Timothy Parker, Ph.D.; Sams Publishing; June 1996; 0-67230-603-4

  `http://merchant.superlibrary.com:8000/catalog/hg/PRODUCT/PAGE/06723/bud/0672306034.html`

- *Web Publishing Unleashed, Professional Reference Edition*; William R. Stanek; Sams.net Publishing; December 1996; 1-57521-198-X

  `http://merchant.superlibrary.com:8000/catalog/hg/PRODUCT/PAGE/15752/bud/157521198X.html`

- *Web Site Construction Kit*; Christopher L. T. Brown and Scott Zimmerman; Sams.net Publishing; January 1996; 1-57521-047-9

  `http://merchant.superlibrary.com:8000/catalog/hg/PRODUCT/PAGE/15752/bud/1575210479.html`

- *World Wide Web Database Developer's Guide*; Mark Swank and Drew Kittel; Sams.net Publishing; August 1996; 1-57521-048-7

  `http://merchant.superlibrary.com:8000/catalog/hg/PRODUCT/PAGE/15752/bud/1575210487.html`

APPENDIX C

What's on the CD-ROM

Types of software on the CD-ROM:

- Graphics Utilities and Plug-Ins
- Java, Java Applets, and Java Scripts
- Microsoft Products and Utilities
- Miscellaneous

Graphics Utilities and Plug-Ins

Paint Shop Pro from JASC Inc.

SnagIt32 from TechSmith Corp.

ACDsee from ACD Sytems LTD.

Map This

Java, Java Applets, and Java Scripts

Sample Java Applets from the Web

Sample Java Scripts from the Web

Microsoft Products and Utilities

Microsoft Visual J++ 1.1 Trial Edition (see the End-User License Agreement at the back of this book)

Microsoft Visual Basic Control Creation Edition (see the End-User License Agreement at the back of this book)

Internet Explorer 3.02

Internet Assistant for Microsoft Access for Windows 95

Internet Assistant for Microsoft Excel for Windows 95

Internet Assistant for Microsoft PowerPoint for Windows 95

Internet Assistant for Microsoft Word for Windows 95

Microsoft ActiveX Control Pad (includes HTML Layout Control)

Microsoft Excel Viewer for Windows 95

Animation Player for Windows 95

Microsoft PowerPoint Viewer for Windows 95

Microsoft Word Viewer for Windows 95

Miscellaneous

Adobe Acrobat Reader

WinZip 6.2 from NicoMak Computing

WS-FTP Client Software

WWW Gif Animator 1.1 from Irmgard Wasinger and Ramin Nourbakhch

INDEX

Symbols

A

B

G

H

I

J–K

Q–R

S

T

U

V

W–Z

Technical Support:

If you need assistance with the information in this book or with a CD/Disk accompanying the book, please access the Knowledge Base on our Web site at **http://www.superlibrary.com/general/support**. Our most Frequently Asked Questions are answered there. If you do not find the answer to your questions on our Web site, you may contact Macmillan Technical Support **(317) 581-3833** or e-mail us at **support@mcp.com**.

Laura Lemay's Web Workshop: NetObjects Fusion 2

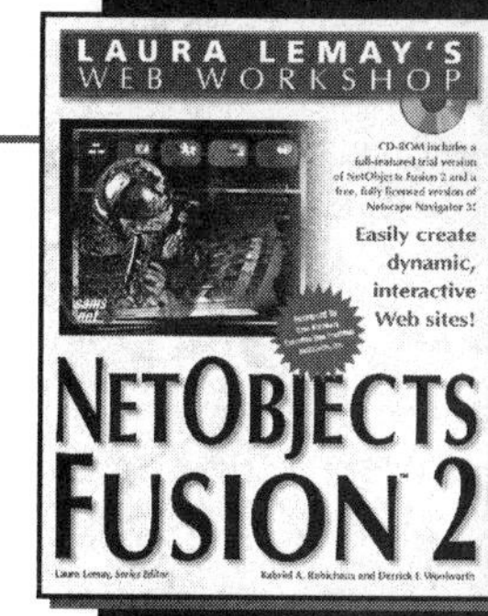

—Kabriel Robichaux and Derrick Woolworth

NetObjects Fusion has been recognized as one of the best, most advanced Web site authoring tools on the market. With this straightforward, hands-on guide, you learn how to use it effectively to create high-impact Web pages and applications—with ease. This book is written in the same style as Laura Lemay's best-selling *Teach Yourself Web Publishing* books. The CD-ROM is designed to be an interactive workshop. It includes a special demonstration version of NetObjects Fusion and an electronic version of Laura Lemay's *Teach Yourself Web Publishing with HTML 3.2 in 14 Days, Professional Reference Edition,* along with some of the best Web publishing tools and materials.

Price: $39.99 USA/$56.95 CDN *Casual–Accomplished*
ISBN: 1-57521-278-1 *550 pages*

Laura Lemay's Web Workshop: Designing with Style Sheets, Tables, and Frames

—Molly Holzschlag

Web page designers have long complained that HTML is too primitive a language to allow them the same control over the layout and design of their Web pages that they're used to in a desktop publishing environment. *Laura Lemay's Web Workshop: Designing with Stylesheets, Tables, and Frames* gives intermediate to experienced Web authors a practical, example-rich guide to controlling the appearance and layout of Web pages. The book provides a clear, hands-on guide to designing and creating sophisticated Web page layout with stylesheets, tables, and frames. The CD-ROM includes a hand-picked selection of the best Web publishing tools and utilities, including custom-designed stylesheets and page layout templates.

Price: $39.99 USA/$56.95 CDN *Casual–Accomplished*
ISBN: 1-57521-249-8 *500 pages*

Laura Lemay's Web Workshop: Microsoft FrontPage 97

—Laura Lemay and Denise Tyler

The latest release of Microsoft's FrontPage not only integrates completely with the Microsoft Office suite of products, but it also enables a Web author to develop and manage an entire Web site. You can easily add Excel spreadsheets and Word documents to a Web page or site. The previous version of FrontPage allowed only single-page development and didn't work with Office. This book shows you how to exploit these new features on your Web or intranet site, and teaches you basic design principles, link creation, and HTML editing. The CD-ROM contains the entire book in HTML format, templates, graphics, borders, scripts, and some of the best Web publishing tools available.

Price: $39.99 USA/$56.95 CDN *Casual–Accomplished*
ISBN: 1-57521-223-4 *650 pages*

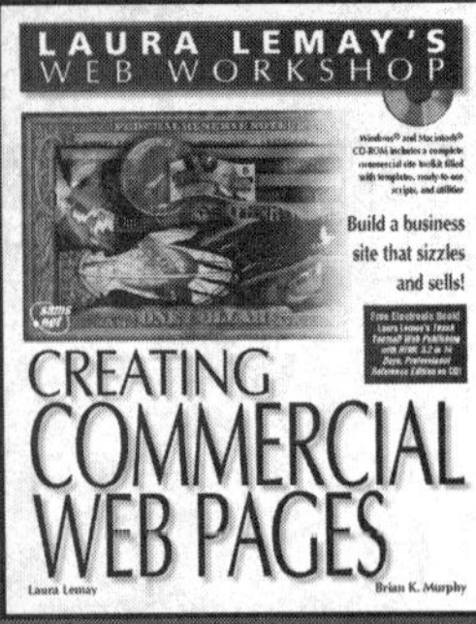

Laura Lemay's Web Workshop: Creating Commercial Web Pages

—Laura Lemay and Brian K. Murphy

Filled with sample Web pages, this book shows you how to create commercial-grade Web pages using HTML, CGI, and Java. In the classic clear style of Laura Lemay, author of the best-selling *Teach Yourself Java*, you learn not only how to create the page, but also how to apply proven principles of design that will make your Web page a marketing tool. The CD-ROM includes all the templates in the book, plus HTML editors, graphics software, CGI forms, and more.

Price: $39.99 USA/$56.95 CDN *Accomplished*
ISBN: 1-57521-126-2 *528 pages*

Laura Lemay's Web Workshop: 3D Graphics and VRML 2

—Laura Lemay, Kelly Murdock, and Justin Couch

This is the easiest way for you to learn how to add three-dimensional virtual worlds to Web pages. The book describes the new VRML 2.0 specification, explores the wide array of existing VRML sites on the Web, and steps you through the process of creating your own 3D Web environments. The CD-ROM contains the book in HTML format, a hand-picked selection of the best VRML and 3D graphics tools, plus a collection of ready-to-use virtual worlds.

Price: $39.99 USA/$56.95 CDN *Casual–Accomplished*
ISBN: 1-57521-143-2 *400 pages*

Laura Lemay's Web Workshop: Graphics and Web Page Design

—Laura Lemay, Jon M. Duff, and James L. Mohler

With the number of Web pages increasing daily, only the well-designed will stand out and grab the attention of those browsing the Web. This book illustrates, in classic Laura Lemay style, how to design attractive Web pages that will be visited over and over again. The CD-ROM contains HTML editors, graphics software, and royalty-free graphics and sound files.

Price: $55.00 USA/$77.95 CDN *Accomplished*
ISBN: 1-57521-125-4 *500 pages*

Add to Your Sams.net Library Today with the Best Books for Internet Technologies

ISBN	Quantity	Description of Item	Unit Cost	Total Cost
1-57521-278-1		Laura Lemay's Web Workshop: NetObjects Fusion 2	$39.99	
1-57521-249-8		Laura Lemay's Web Workshop: Designing with Stylesheets, Tables, and Frames	$39.99	
1-57521-223-4		Laura Lemay's Web Workshop: Microsoft FrontPage 97	$39.99	
1-57521-126-2		Laura Lemay's Web Workshop: Creating Commercial Web Pages	$39.99	
1-57521-143-2		Laura Lemay's Web Workshop: 3D Graphics and VRML 2	$39.99	
1-57521-125-4		Laura Lemay's Web Workshop: Graphics and Web Page Design	$55.00	
1-57521-305-2		Teach Yourself Web Publishing with HTML in 14 Days, Second Professional Reference Edition	$59.99	
		Shipping and Handling: See information below.		
		TOTAL		

Shipping and Handling: $4.00 for the first book, and $1.75 for each additional book. If you need to have it immediately, we can ship the order to you in 24 hours for an additional charge of approximately $18.00, and you will receive your item overnight or in two days. Overseas shipping and handling adds $2.00. Prices subject to change. Call between 9:00 a.m. and 5:00 p.m. EST for availability and pricing information on latest editions.

201 W. 103rd Street, Indianapolis, Indiana 46290

1-800-428-5331 — Orders 1-800-835-3202 — Fax 1-800-858-7674 — Customer Service

CD-ROM

Installing the CD-ROM

Windows 95/NT 4

1. Insert the CD-ROM into your CD-ROM drive.
2. From the Windows desktop, double-click the My Computer icon.
3. Double-click the icon representing your CD-ROM drive.
4. Double-click the Setup.exe icon to run the installation program.
5. Installation creates a program group with the title of the book as the group name. This group will contain icons to browse the CD-ROM.

NOTE: If Windows 95 or NT 4.0 is installed on your computer and you have the AutoPlay feature enabled, the Setup.exe program starts automatically when you insert the disc into your CD-ROM drive.

The following are the minimum system requirements for the Visual Basic Control Creation Edition and the Visual J++ 1.1 Trial Edition:

- Personal computer with a 486 or higher processor
- Microsoft Windows 95 or Windows NT Workstation 4.0 or later
- 8 MB of memory (12 recommended) if running Windows NT Workstation
- CD-ROM drive
- VGA or higher resolution monitor (SVGA recommended)

Si vous avez acquis votre produit Microsoft au CANADA, la garantie limitée suivante vous concerne :

GARANTIE LIMITEE

GARANTIE LIMITEE — Sauf pour celles du REDISTRIBUTABLES, qui sont fournies "comme telles", sans aucune garantie quelle qu'elle soit, Microsoft garantit que (a) la performance du LOGICIEL sera substantiellement en conformité avec le(s) manuel(s) de produits qui accompagne(nt) le LOGICIEL pour une période de quatre-vingt-dix (90) jours à compter de la date de réception ; et (b) tout matériel fourni par Microsoft accompagnant le LOGICIEL sera exempt de défaut de matière première ou de vice de fabrication dans des conditions normales d'utilisation et d'entretien pour une période d'un an à compter de la date de réception. Toute garantie implicite concernant le LOGICIEL et le matériel est limitée à quatre-vingt-dix (90) jours et un (1) an, respectivement.

RECOURS DU CLIENT — La seule obligation de Microsoft et votre recours exclusif seront, au choix de Microsoft, soit (a) le remboursement du prix payé ou (b) la réparation ou le remplacement du LOGICIEL ou du matériel qui n'est pas conforme à la Garantie Limitée de Microsoft et qui est retourné à Microsoft avec une copie de votre reçu. Cette Garantie Limitée est nulle si le défaut du LOGICIEL ou du matériel est causé par un accident, un traitement abusif ou une mauvaise application. Tout LOGICIEL de remplacement sera garanti pour le reste de la période de garantie initiale ou pour trente (30) jours, selon laquelle de ces deux périodes est la plus longue.

AUCUNE AUTRE GARANTIE — MICROSOFT DESAVOUE TOUTE AUTRE GARANTIE, EXPRESSE OU IMPLICITE, Y COMPRIS MAIS NE SE LIMITANT PAS AUX GARANTIES IMPLICITES DU CARACTERE ADEQUAT POUR LA COMMERCIALISATION OU UN USAGE PARTICULIER EN CE QUI CONCERNE LE LOGICIEL, LE(S) MANUEL(S) DE PRODUITS, LA DOCUMENTATION ECRITE ET TOUT MATERIEL QUI L'ACCOMPAGNENT. CETTE GARANTIE LIMITEE VOUS ACCORDE DES DROITS JURIDIQUES SPECIFIQUES.

PAS D'OBLIGATION POUR LES DOMMAGES INDIRECTS — MICROSOFT OU SES FOURNISSEURS N'AURONT D'OBLIGATION EN AUCUNE CIRCONSTANCE POUR TOUT AUTRE DOMMAGE QUEL QU'IL SOIT (Y COMPRIS, SANS LIMITATION, LES DOMMAGES ENTRAINES PAR LA PERTE DE BENEFICES, L'INTERRUPTION DES AFFAIRES, LA PERTE D'INFORMATION COMMERCIALE OU TOUTE AUTRE PERTE PECUNIAIRE) DECOULANT DE L'UTILISATION OU DE L'IMPOSSIBILITE D'UTILISATION DE CE PRODUIT MICROSOFT, ET CE, MEME SI MICROSOFT A ETE AVISE DE LA POSSIBILITE DE TELS DOMMAGES. EN TOUT CAS, LA SEULE OBLIGATION DE MICROSOFT EN VERTU DE TOUTE DISPOSITION DE CETTE CONVENTION SE LIMITERA AU MONTANT EN FAIT PAYE PAR VOUS POUR LE LOGICIEL.

La présente Convention est régie par les lois de la province d'Ontario, Canada. Chacune des parties à la présente reconnaît irrévocablement la compétence des tribunaux de la province d'Ontario et consent à instituer tout litige qui pourrait découler de la présente auprès des tribunaux situés dans le district judiciaire de York, province d'Ontario.

Au cas où vous auriez des questions concernant cette licence ou que vous désiriez vous mettre en rapport avec Microsoft pour quelque raison que ce soit, veuillez contacter la succursale Microsoft desservant votre pays, dont l'adresse est fournie dans ce produit, ou écrire à : Microsoft Sales Information Center, One Microsoft Way, Redmond, Washington 98052-6399.

If this product was acquired outside the United States, then local law may apply.

Should you have any questions concerning this EULA, or if you desire to contact Microsoft for any reason, please contact the Microsoft subsidiary serving your country, or write: Microsoft Sales Information Center/One Microsoft Way/Redmond, WA 98052-6399.

If you have a specific question regarding the licensing of redistributables, you may call the Microsoft Technical Sales Information Team at (800) 426-9400 (United States only) or send inquiries by fax to Microsoft Visual C++ Licensing Administrator, (206) 936-7329 (United States only).

LIMITED WARRANTY

LIMITED WARRANTY. **Except with respect to the REDISTRIBUTABLES, which are provided "as is," without warranty of any kind,** Microsoft warrants that (a) the SOFTWARE PRODUCT will perform substantially in accordance with the accompanying written materials for a period of ninety (90) days from the date of receipt, and (b) any hardware accompanying the SOFTWARE PRODUCT will be free from defects in materials and workmanship under normal use and service for a period of one (1) year from the date of receipt. Some states and jurisdictions do not allow limitations on duration of an implied warranty, so the above limitation may not apply to you. To the extent allowed by applicable law, implied warranties on the SOFTWARE PRODUCT and hardware, if any, are limited to ninety (90) days and one year, respectively.

CUSTOMER REMEDIES. Microsoft's and its suppliers' entire liability and your exclusive remedy shall be, at Microsoft's option, either (a) return of the price paid, or (b) repair or replacement of the SOFTWARE PRODUCT or hardware that does not meet Microsoft's Limited Warranty and that is returned to Microsoft with a copy of your receipt. This Limited Warranty is void if failure of the SOFTWARE PRODUCT or hardware has resulted from accident, abuse, or misapplication. Any replacement SOFTWARE PRODUCT or hardware will be warranted for the remainder of the original warranty period or thirty (30) days, whichever is longer. **Outside the United States, neither these remedies nor any product support services offered by Microsoft are available without proof of purchase from an authorized international source.**

NO OTHER WARRANTIES. To the maximum extent permitted by applicable law, Microsoft and its suppliers disclaim all other warranties, either express or implied, including, but not limited to, implied warranties of merchantability AND fitness for a particular purpose, with regard to the SOFTWARE PRODUCT, and any accompanying hardware. This limited warranty gives you specific legal rights. You may have others, which vary from state/jurisdiction to state/jurisdiction.

NO LIABILITY FOR CONSEQUENTIAL DAMAGES. To the maximum extent permitted by applicable law, in no event shall Microsoft or its suppliers be liable for any special, incidental, indirect, or consequential damages whatsoever (including, without limitation, damages for loss of business profits, business interruption, loss of business information, or any other pecuniary loss) arising out of the use of or inability to use thE software product, even if Microsoft has been advised of the possibility of such damages. Because some states and jurisdictions do not allow the exclusion or limitation of liability for consequential or incidental damages, the above limitation may not apply to you.

h. **Termination.** Without prejudice to any other rights, Microsoft may terminate this EULA if you fail to comply with the terms and conditions of this EULA. In such event, you must destroy all copies of the SOFTWARE PRODUCT and all of its component parts.

3. COPYRIGHT. All title and copyrights in and to the SOFTWARE PRODUCT (including but not limited to any images, photographs, animations, video, audio, music, text, and "applets" incorporated into the SOFTWARE PRODUCT), the accompanying printed materials, and any copies of the SOFTWARE PRODUCT are owned by Microsoft or its suppliers. The SOFTWARE PRODUCT is protected by copyright laws and international treaty provisions. Therefore, you must treat the SOFTWARE PRODUCT like any other copyrighted material except that you may install the SOFTWARE PRODUCT on a single computer provided you keep the original solely for backup or archival purposes. You may not copy the printed materials accompanying the SOFTWARE PRODUCT.
4. U.S. GOVERNMENT RESTRICTED RIGHTS. The SOFTWARE PRODUCT and documentation are provided with RESTRICTED RIGHTS. Use, duplication, or disclosure by the Government is subject to restrictions as set forth in subparagraph (c)(1)(ii) of the Rights in Technical Data and Computer Software clause at DFARS 252.227-7013 or subparagraphs (c)(1) and (2) of the Commercial Computer Software—Restricted Rights at 48 CFR 52.227-19, as applicable. Manufacturer is Microsoft Corporation/One Microsoft Way/Redmond, WA 98052-6399.
5. EXPORT RESTRICTIONS. You agree that neither you nor your customers intend to or will, directly or indirectly, export or transmit (i) the SOFTWARE or related documentation and technical data or (ii) your software product as described in Section 1(f) of this EULA (or any part thereof), or process, or service that is the direct product of the SOFTWARE, to any country to which such export or transmission is restricted by any applicable U.S. regulation or statute, without the prior written consent, if required, of the Bureau of Export Administration of the U.S. Department of Commerce, or such other governmental entity as may have jurisdiction over such export or transmission.
6. NOTE ON JAVA SUPPORT. THE SOFTWARE PRODUCT CONTAINS SUPPORT FOR PROGRAMS WRITTEN IN JAVA. JAVA TECHNOLOGY IS NOT FAULT TOLERANT AND IS NOT DESIGNED, MANUFACTURED, OR INTENDED FOR USE OR RESALE AS ONLINE CONTROL EQUIPMENT IN HAZARDOUS ENVIRONMENTS REQUIRING FAIL-SAFE PERFORMANCE, SUCH AS IN THE OPERATION OF NUCLEAR FACILITIES, AIRCRAFT NAVIGATION OR COMMUNICATIONS SYSTEMS, AIR TRAFFIC CONTROL, DIRECT LIFE SUPPORT MACHINES, OR WEAPONS SYSTEMS, IN WHICH THE FAILURE OF JAVA TECHNOLOGY COULD LEAD DIRECTLY TO DEATH, PERSONAL INJURY, OR SEVERE PHYSICAL OR ENVIRONMENTAL DAMAGE.

MISCELLANEOUS

If you acquired this product in the United States, this EULA is governed by the laws of the State of Washington.

If you acquired this product in Canada, this EULA is governed by the laws of the Province of Ontario, Canada. Each of the parties hereto irrevocably attorns to the jurisdiction of the courts of the Province of Ontario and further agrees to commence any litigation which may arise hereunder in the courts located in the Judicial District of York, Province of Ontario.

lawsuits, including attorney's fees, that arise or result from the use or distribution of the End-User Application; and (vi) not permit further distribution of the REDISTRIBUTABLES by the user of the End-User Application.

2. DESCRIPTION OF OTHER RIGHTS AND LIMITATIONS.

   a. **Academic Edition Software.** If the SOFTWARE PRODUCT is identified as "Academic Edition" or "AE," you must be a "Qualified Educational User" to use the SOFTWARE PRODUCT. To determine whether you are a Qualified Educational User, please contact the Microsoft Sales Information Center/One Microsoft Way/Redmond, WA 98052-6399 or the Microsoft subsidiary serving your country.

      If you are a Qualified Educational User, you may either (i) exercise the rights granted in Section (1), OR (ii) if you intend to use the SOFTWARE PRODUCT solely for instructional purposes in connection with a class or other educational program, you may install a single copy of the SOFTWARE on a single computer for access and use by an unlimited number of student end users at your educational institution, provided that all such end users comply with all other terms of this EULA.

   b. **Not for Resale Software.** If the SOFTWARE PRODUCT is labeled "Not for Resale" or "NFR," then, notwithstanding other sections of this EULA, you may not resell, or otherwise transfer for value, the SOFTWARE PRODUCT.

   c. **Limitations on Reverse Engineering, Decompilation, and Disassembly.** You may not reverse engineer, decompile, or disassemble the SOFTWARE PRODUCT, except and only to the extent that such activity is expressly permitted by applicable law notwithstanding this limitation.

   d. **Separation of Components.** The SOFTWARE PRODUCT is licensed as a single product. Its component parts may not be separated for use on more than one computer.

   e. **Rental.** You may not rent, lease, or lend the SOFTWARE PRODUCT.

   f. **Support Services.** Microsoft may provide you with support services related to the SOFTWARE PRODUCT ("Support Services"). Use of Support Services is governed by the Microsoft policies and programs described in the user manual, in "online" documentation, and/or in other Microsoft-provided materials. Any supplemental software code provided to you as part of the Support Services shall be considered part of the SOFTWARE PRODUCT and subject to the terms and conditions of this EULA. With respect to technical information you provide to Microsoft as part of the Support Services, Microsoft may use such information for its business purposes, including for product support and development. Microsoft will not utilize such technical information in a form that personally identifies you.

   g. **Software Transfer.** You may permanently transfer all of your rights under this EULA, provided you retain no copies, you transfer all of the SOFTWARE PRODUCT (including all component parts, the media and printed materials, any upgrades, this EULA, and, if applicable, the Certificate of Authenticity), **and** the recipient agrees to the terms of this EULA. If the SOFTWARE PRODUCT is an upgrade, any transfer must include all prior versions of the SOFTWARE PRODUCT.

e. **Redistributable Files.** *Provided* that you comply with Section 1(f), in addition to the rights granted in Section 1(a), Microsoft grants to you a nonexclusive, royalty-free right to reproduce and distribute the object code version of the following portions of the SOFTWARE PRODUCT (collectively, the "REDISTRIBUTABLES"): (i) SAMPLE CODE (including any modifications you make); and (ii) the Java Support for Internet Explorer files: msjava.inf, jautoexp.dat, javaDbg.txt, javaEE.dll, javasntx.dll, setdebug.exe, regsvr32.exe, jit.dll, javaprxy.dll, jdbgmgr.exe, msjava.dll, msawt.dll, vmhelper.dll, javart.dll, jview.exe, mfc40.dll, msvcrt40.dll, classr.exe, classd.exe, javasup.vxd.

f. **Redistribution Requirements.** If you redistribute the REDISTRIBUTABLES, you agree to: (i) distribute the REDISTRIBUTABLES in object code only in conjunction with and as a part of a software application product developed by you that adds significant and primary functionality to the REDISTRIBUTABLES ("Licensed Product"); (ii) distribute **all** of the REDISTRIBUTABLES if you choose to distribute any one or more of them in your Licensed Product; (iii) not use Microsoft's name, logo, or trademarks to market your Licensed Product; (iv) include a valid copyright notice on your Licensed Product; (v) indemnify, hold harmless, and defend Microsoft from and against any claims or lawsuits, including attorney's fees, that arise or result from the use or distribution of your Licensed Product; (v) not permit further distribution of the REDISTRIBUTABLES by your end user.

   The following **exceptions** apply to Subsection (f)(v), above:

   (A) You may permit further redistribution of the REDISTRIBUTABLES by your distributors to your end-user customers if your distributors only distribute the REDISTRIBUTABLES in conjunction with, and as part of, your Licensed Product and you and your distributors comply with all other terms of this EULA;

   (B) *Provided that* your end user complies with all other terms of this EULA, you may permit your end users to reproduce and distribute the object code version of the files listed below, designed to be redistributed as a Component Object Model (COM) object, for use in development of another application ("COM Files"), only in conjunction with and as a part of an application and/or Web page that adds significant and primary functionality to the COM Files. **COM Files:** Msvcrt.dll, Olepro32.dll, Mfc42.dll, and Msvcirt.dll;

   (C) You may permit your end users to reproduce and distribute the object code version of the REDISTRIBUTABLES for use in development of an application created by your end user ("End-User Application"), *provided that* your end user agrees to: (i) distribute the REDISTRIBUTABLES in object code only in conjunction with and as a part of a software application product developed by them that adds significant and primary functionality to the REDISTRIBUTABLES ("End-User Application"); (ii) distribute **all** of the REDISTRIBUTABLES if they choose to distribute any one or more of them in an End-User Application; (iii) not use Microsoft's name, logo, or trademarks to market the End-User Application; (iv) include a valid copyright notice on the End-User Application; (v) indemnify, hold harmless, and defend Microsoft from and against any claims or

END-USER LICENSE AGREEMENT FOR MICROSOFT SOFTWARE

MICROSOFT VISUAL J++ VERSION 1.1, TRIAL USE EDITION

IMPORTANT—READ CAREFULLY: This Microsoft End-User License Agreement (''EULA'') is a legal agreement between you (either an individual or a single entity) and Microsoft Corporation for the Microsoft software product identified above, which includes computer software and may include associated media, printed materials, and ''online'' or electronic documentation (''SOFTWARE PRODUCT''). By installing, copying, or otherwise using the SOFTWARE PRODUCT, you agree to be bound by the terms of this EULA. If you do not agree to the terms of this EULA, do not install, copy, or use the SOFTWARE PRODUCT.

SOFTWARE PRODUCT LICENSE

The SOFTWARE PRODUCT is protected by copyright laws and international copyright treaties, as well as other intellectual property laws and treaties. The SOFTWARE PRODUCT is licensed, not sold.

1. GRANT OF LICENSE. This EULA grants you the following rights:

   a. **Software Product.** Microsoft grants to you, as an individual, a personal, nonexclusive license to make and use copies of the SOFTWARE for the sole purposes of designing, developing, and testing your software product(s). Except as provided in Section 2(a), you may install copies of the SOFTWARE PRODUCT on an unlimited number of computers provided that you are the only individual using the SOFTWARE PRODUCT. If you are an entity, Microsoft grants to you the right to designate one individual within your organization to have the right to use the SOFTWARE PRODUCT in the manner provided above.

   b. **Electronic Documents.** Solely with respect to electronic documents included with the SOFTWARE PRODUCT, you may make an unlimited number of copies (either in hardcopy or electronic form), provided that such copies shall be used only for internal purposes and are not republished or distributed to any third party.

   c. **Storage/Network Use.** You may also store or install a copy of the SOFTWARE PRODUCT on a storage device, such as a network server, used only to install or run the SOFTWARE PRODUCT on your other computers over an internal network; however, you must acquire and dedicate a license for each separate computer on which the SOFTWARE PRODUCT is installed or run from the storage device. A license for the SOFTWARE PRODUCT may not be shared or used concurrently on different computers.

   d. **Sample Code.** In addition to the rights granted in Section 1(a), Microsoft grants to you the right to use and modify the source code version of those portions of the SOFTWARE PRODUCT that are identified as sample code in the documentation ("SAMPLE CODE"), for the sole purposes of designing, developing, and testing your software product(s), *provided* that you comply with Section 1(f), below.

service that is the direct product of the SOFTWARE, to any country to which such export or transmission is restricted by any applicable U.S. regulation or statute, without the prior written consent, if required, of the Bureau of Export Administration of the U.S. Department of Commerce, or such other governmental entity as may have jurisdiction over such export or transmission.

MISCELLANEOUS

If you acquired this product in the United States, this EULA is governed by the laws of the State of Washington.

If you acquired this product in Canada, this EULA is governed by the laws of the Province of Ontario, Canada. Each of the parties hereto irrevocably attorns to the jurisdiction of the courts of the Province of Ontario and further agrees to commence any litigation which may arise hereunder in the courts located in the Judicial District of York, Province of Ontario.

If this product was acquired outside the United States, then local law may apply.

Should you have any questions concerning this EULA, or if you desire to contact Microsoft for any reason, please contact the Microsoft subsidiary serving your country, or write: Microsoft Sales Information Center/One Microsoft Way/Redmond, WA 98052-6399.

LIMITED WARRANTY

NO WARRANTIES. Microsoft expressly disclaims any warranty for the SOFTWARE PRODUCT. The SOFTWARE PRODUCT and any related documentation is provided "as is" without warranty of any kind, either express or implied, including, without limitation, the implied warranties or merchantability, fitness for a particular purpose, or noninfringement. The entire risk arising out of use or performance of the SOFTWARE PRODUCT remains with you.

NO LIABILITY FOR DAMAGES. In no event shall Microsoft or its suppliers be liable for any damages whatsoever (including, without limitation, damages for loss of business profits, business interruption, loss of business information, or any other pecuniary loss) arising out of the use of or inability to use this Microsoft product, even if Microsoft has been advised of the possibility of such damages. Because some states/jurisdictions do not allow the exclusion or limitation of liability for consequential or incidental damages, the above limitation may not apply to you.

f. **Software Transfer.** You may permanently transfer all of your rights under this EULA, provided you retain no copies, you transfer all of the SOFTWARE PRODUCT (including all component parts, the media and printed materials, any upgrades, this EULA, and, if applicable, the Certificate of Authenticity), **and** the recipient agrees to the terms of this EULA. If the SOFTWARE PRODUCT is an upgrade, any transfer must include all prior versions of the SOFTWARE PRODUCT.

g. **Termination.** Without prejudice to any other rights, Microsoft may terminate this EULA if you fail to comply with the terms and conditions of this EULA. In such event, you must destroy all copies of the SOFTWARE PRODUCT and all of its component parts.

3. UPGRADES. If the SOFTWARE PRODUCT is labeled as an upgrade, you must be properly licensed to use a product identified by Microsoft as being eligible for the upgrade in order to use the SOFTWARE PRODUCT. A SOFTWARE PRODUCT labeled as an upgrade replaces and/or supplements the product that formed the basis for your eligibility for the upgrade. You may use the resulting upgraded product only in accordance with the terms of this EULA. If the SOFTWARE PRODUCT is an upgrade of a component of a package of software programs that you licensed as a single product, the SOFTWARE PRODUCT may be used and transferred only as part of that single product package and may not be separated for use on more than one computer.

4. COPYRIGHT. All title and copyrights in and to the SOFTWARE PRODUCT (including but not limited to any images, photographs, animations, video, audio, music, text, and "applets" incorporated into the SOFTWARE PRODUCT), the accompanying printed materials, and any copies of the SOFTWARE PRODUCT are owned by Microsoft or its suppliers. The SOFTWARE PRODUCT is protected by copyright laws and international treaty provisions. Therefore, you must treat the SOFTWARE PRODUCT like any other copyrighted material except that you may install the SOFTWARE PRODUCT on a single computer provided you keep the original solely for backup or archival purposes. You may not copy the printed materials accompanying the SOFTWARE PRODUCT.

5. DUAL-MEDIA SOFTWARE. You may receive the SOFTWARE PRODUCT in more than one medium. Regardless of the type or size of medium you receive, you may use only one medium that is appropriate for your single computer. You may not use or install the other medium on another computer. You may not loan, rent, lease, or otherwise transfer the other medium to another user, except as part of the permanent transfer (as provided above) of the SOFTWARE PRODUCT.

6. U.S. GOVERNMENT RESTRICTED RIGHTS. The SOFTWARE PRODUCT and documentation are provided with RESTRICTED RIGHTS. Use, duplication, or disclosure by the Government is subject to restrictions as set forth in subparagraph (c)(1)(ii) of the Rights in Technical Data and Computer Software clause at DFARS 252.227-7013 or subparagraphs (c)(1) and (2) of the Commercial Computer Software—Restricted Rights at 48 CFR 52.227-19, as applicable. Manufacturer is Microsoft Corporation/One Microsoft Way/Redmond, WA 98052-6399.

7. EXPORT RESTRICTIONS. You agree that neither you nor your customers intend to or will, directly or indirectly, export or transmit (i) the SOFTWARE or related documentation and technical data or (ii) your software product as described in Section 1(b) of this License (or any part thereof), or process, or

(iii) **Redistribution Requirements.** If you redistribute the SAMPLE CODE or REDISTRIBUTABLE SOFTWARE (collectively, "REDISTRIBUTABLES"), you agree to: (A) distribute the REDISTRIBUTABLES in object code only in conjunction with and as a part of a software application product developed by you that adds significant and primary functionality to the SOFTWARE and that is developed to operate on the Windows or Windows NT environment ("Application"); (B) not use Microsoft's name, logo, or trademarks to market your software application product; (C) include a valid copyright notice on your software product; (D) indemnify, hold harmless, and defend Microsoft from and against any claims or lawsuits, including attorney's fees, that arise or result from the use or distribution of your software application product; (E) not permit further distribution of the REDISTRIBUTABLES by your end user. The following **exceptions** apply to subsection (iii)(E), above: (1) you may permit further redistribution of the REDISTRIBUTABLES by your distributors to your end-user customers if your distributors only distribute the REDISTRIBUTABLES in conjunction with, and as part of, your Application and you and your distributors comply with all other terms of this EULA; and (2) you may permit your end users to reproduce and distribute the object code version of the files designated by ".ocx" file extensions ("Controls") only in conjunction with and as a part of an Application and/or Web page that adds significant and primary functionality to the Controls, and such end user complies with all other terms of this EULA.

2. DESCRIPTION OF OTHER RIGHTS AND LIMITATIONS.

   a. **Not for Resale Software.** If the SOFTWARE PRODUCT is labeled "Not for Resale" or "NFR," then, notwithstanding other sections of this EULA, you may not resell, or otherwise transfer for value, the SOFTWARE PRODUCT.

   b. **Limitations on Reverse Engineering, Decompilation, and Disassembly.** You may not reverse engineer, decompile, or disassemble the SOFTWARE PRODUCT, except and only to the extent that such activity is expressly permitted by applicable law notwithstanding this limitation.

   c. **Separation of Components.** The SOFTWARE PRODUCT is licensed as a single product. Its component parts may not be separated for use by more than one user.

   d. **Rental.** You may not rent, lease, or lend the SOFTWARE PRODUCT.

   e. **Support Services.** Microsoft may provide you with support services related to the SOFTWARE PRODUCT ("Support Services"). Use of Support Services is governed by the Microsoft policies and programs described in the user manual, in "online" documentation, and/or in other Microsoft-provided materials. Any supplemental software code provided to you as part of the Support Services shall be considered part of the SOFTWARE PRODUCT and subject to the terms and conditions of this EULA. With respect to technical information you provide to Microsoft as part of the Support Services, Microsoft may use such information for its business purposes, including for product support and development. Microsoft will not utilize such technical information in a form that personally identifies you.

END-USER LICENSE AGREEMENT FOR MICROSOFT SOFTWARE

Microsoft Visual Basic, Control Creation Edition

IMPORTANT—READ CAREFULLY: This Microsoft End-User License Agreement ("EULA") is a legal agreement between you (either an individual or a single entity) and Microsoft Corporation for the Microsoft software product identified above, which includescomputer software and may include associated media, printed materials, and "online" or electronic documentation ("SOFTWARE PRODUCT"). By installing, copying, or otherwise using the SOFTWARE PRODUCT, you agree to be bound by the terms of this EULA. If you do not agree to the terms of this EULA, do not install or use the SOFTWARE PRODUCT; you may, however, return it to your place of purchase for a full refund.

SOFTWARE PRODUCT LICENSE

The SOFTWARE PRODUCT is protected by copyright laws and international copyright treaties, as well as other intellectual property laws and treaties. The SOFTWARE PRODUCT is licensed, not sold.

1. GRANT OF LICENSE. This EULA grants you the following rights:

   a. **Software Product.** Microsoft grants to you as an individual, a personal, nonexclusive license to make and use copies of the SOFTWARE for the sole purposes of designing, developing, and testing your software product(s) that are designed to operate in conjunction with any Microsoft operating system product. You may install copies of the SOFTWARE on an unlimited number of computers provided that you are the only individual using the SOFTWARE. If you are an entity, Microsoft grants you the right to designate one individual within your organization to have the right to use the SOFTWARE in the manner provided above.

   b. **Electronic Documents.** Solely with respect to electronic documents included with the SOFTWARE, you may make an unlimited number of copies (either in hardcopy or electronic form), provided that such copies shall be used only for internal purposes and are not republished or distributed to any third party.

   c. **Redistributable Components.**

      (i) Sample Code. In addition to the rights granted in Section 1, Microsoft grants you the right to use and modify the source code version of those portions of the SOFTWARE designated as "Sample Code" ("SAMPLE CODE") for the sole purposes of designing, developing, and testing your software product(s), and to reproduce and distribute the SAMPLE CODE, along with any modifications thereof, only in object code form provided that you comply with Section d(iii), below.

      (ii) Redistributable Components. In addition to the rights granted in Section 1, Microsoft grants you a nonexclusive royalty-free right to reproduce and distribute the object code version of any portion of the SOFTWARE listed in the SOFTWARE file REDIST.TXT ("REDISTRIBUTABLE SOFTWARE"), provided you comply with Section d(iii), below.